C000186970

THE OLYMPIC GAMES
in Transition

Jeffrey O. Segrave, PhD
Donald Chu, PhD
Skidmore College

Editors

Human Kinetics Books
Champaign, Illinois

Library of Congress Cataloging-in-Publication Data

The Olympic games in transition.

Includes bibliographies.
1. Olympic games—History. I. Segrave, Jeffrey.
II. Chu, Donald.
GV721.5.O419 1988   796.4'8   87-3902
ISBN 0-87322-111-7

Senior Editor: Gwen Steigelman, PhD
Developmental Editor: Laura E. Larson
Production Director: Ernie Noa
Projects Manager: Lezli Harris
Copy Editors: Ann Bruehler and Laura E. Larson
Assistant Editor: Julie Anderson
Proofreader: Linda Purcell
Typesetter: Yvonne Winsor
Cover and Text Design: Keith Blomberg
Illustrations By: Keith Blomberg
Text Layout: The Admakers
Printed By: Versa Press, Inc. and R & R Bindery Service, Inc.

ISBN: 0-87322-111-7

Printed in the United States of America

10 9 8 7 6 5 4 3 2 1

Human Kinetics Books
A Division of Human Kinetics Publishers, Inc.
Box 5076, Champaign, IL 61820

1-800-DIAL-HKP
1-800-334-3665 (in Illinois)

Contents

Acknowledgments   vi

Preface   vii

Section 1   The Ancient Games   **1**

Chapter 1   Olympia I   7
Pindar

Chapter 2   The Ancient Olympics: Sport, Spectacle, and Ritual   11
Noel Robertson

Chapter 3   Professionalism in Archaic and Classical Greek Athletics   27
David C. Young

Chapter 4   The Ecumenical Olympics: The Games in the Roman Era   37
Thomas F. Scanlon

Section 2   Modern Revival   **65**

Chapter 5   Toward Modern Revival of the Olympic Games: The Various "Pseudo-Olympics" of the 19th Century   71
Gerald Redmond

Chapter 6   The Genesis of the Modern Olympic Games   89
John A. Lucas

Chapter 7   Why I Revived the Olympic Games   101
Pierre de Coubertin

Section 3   The Modern Olympic Movement   **107**

Chapter 8   An Organizational Analysis of the International Olympic Committee   113
March L. Krotee

Chapter 9   Toward a Definition of Olympism   149
             Jeffrey O. Segrave
Chapter 10   The Olympic Celebration of the Arts   163
             Susan J. Bandy

Section 4   The Games Themselves   171

Chapter 11   The Olympic Games of 1896   179
             Pierre de Coubertin
Chapter 12   The Games That Almost Weren't   191
             Al J. Stump
Chapter 13   The Nazi Olympics   201
             Allen Guttmann
Chapter 14   Diplomatic Fun and the Games: A Commentary   221
             on the United States Boycott of the 1980 Summer
             Olympics
             James A.R. Nafziger
Chapter 15   The Background, Nature, and Implications of the   237
             Organization of the "Capitalist Olympics"
             Howard L. Nixon II

Section 5   Individuals and Events   253

Chapter 16   A Matter of Time: The U.S.A.—U.S.S.R. Basket-   257
             ball Game at the 1972 Munich Olympics
             Glenn Begly
Chapter 17   A Reminder of What We Can Be   267
             E.M. Swift
Chapter 18   Double Visions: Olympic Games and American   279
             Culture
             John J. MacAloon

Section 6   Issues and Problems   295

Chapter 19   Amateurism: The Myth and the Reality   303
             Andrew Strenk
Chapter 20   Politics and Nationalism in the Olympic Games   329
             Jean M. Leiper
Chapter 21   Capitalism, Commercialism, and the Olympics   345
             Richard Gruneau and Hart Cantelon
Chapter 22   Tryphosa, Melpomene, Nadia, and Joan: The   365
             IOC and Women's Sport
             Betty Spears
Chapter 23   Steroids   375
             Majorie Shuer

Section 7   The Future of the Games   387

Chapter 24   Should the Olympic Games Be Abolished?   393
             David A. Rose
Chapter 25   The Olympic Games: Mirror of the World   407
             Richard Espy

Chapter 26   The Olympic Games: Past, Present, and Future   419
             Sir Roger Bannister
Chapter 27   A Decalogue of Olympic Games Reform   427
             John A. Lucas
Chapter 28   The Modern Olympics: A Sociopsychological   433
             Interpretation
             Allen Guttmann

Acknowledgments

As in any venture of this kind, a large debt of thanks is owed to numerous people. First, I would like to express my appreciation to Skidmore College and the Department of Physical Education and Dance, which have supported all my endeavors so willingly and so wholeheartedly. I would also like to thank Nancy Homiak, our tireless secretary, who has now seen three edited volumes come to fruition. The fact that they are all in print at all is in no small measure due to her efforts. I also owe a special gratitude to numerous colleagues—but particularly Drs. Tim Brown, Tom Scanlon, and Dave Rose, whose support, advice, and editorial assistance have been invaluable.

But by far my greatest debt of thanks goes to my coeditor, Don Chu, without whose insight, assistance, and friendship I would have achieved far less than I have, including this endeavor. Establishing a working, scholarly relationship with anyone is hard enough, but for it to be a colleague in the same department, and a longtime friend, is rare indeed. I have been most fortunate.

Jeffrey O. Segrave

Preface

To the typical college student today, whose memory probably reaches back no further than the 1972 Munich and Sapporo Games, the story of the Olympics must seem little more than the story of one controversy on top of another—a sort of ongoing international soap opera featuring diplomatic bickering and political sabotage. In many ways this would not be an inaccurate picture. For the last 15 years or so, the Olympic Movement has provided the backdrop to a continuous stream of high level political disputes and debates. The last truly international Olympic celebration in which all eligible nations participated was held in 1972 in Munich, and even these games were interrupted by the now infamous machinations of an extremist political group. The African boycott of the 1976 Montreal Games, the U.S.-led boycott of the 1980 Moscow Games, and the Soviet-led boycott of the 1984 the Los Angeles Games have all served to mar successive Olympiads and keep the Olympic soap opera in the headlines, even during non-Olympic years. Add to these problems the numerous other afflictions that have besieged the Olympic Movement in recent years—ranging from the economic trials of the Los Angeles and Montreal Games to the athletic tribulations of Olympic eligibility—and it would indeed be difficult not to view the Olympics as a sort of "femme fatale" luring individuals and nations into compromising and dangerous situations.

As if all this were not enough, the years since the Los Angeles Games have already been filled with stories similar to those that put recent Olympics in the forefront of controversy in the first place. No sooner had the summer games been awarded to Seoul than concern was voiced because South Korea had no formal diplomatic relations with as many as 44 Olympic nations, including the entire socialist bloc. That situation, as Johnson (1984) recently pointed out, "doesn't exactly augur well for a tranquil

Olympics'' (p. 77). Spending an estimated $3 billion to host the games coupled with the failure of the organizing committee to raise a projected $1 billion for the sale of television rights has renewed doubts about the economic wisdom of Olympic stewardship. But perhaps the greatest threat to the welfare of the Seoul games is the current political tension caused by North Korea's demand to be allowed to participate in hosting the games. Although whispers of boycott have been rumored, nothing has yet to materialize. However, the 1988 Olympics are hardly home free as the debacle surrounding the 1986 British Commonwealth Games has strikingly shown. A total of 31 out of 58 members of the Federation chose to boycott the "Friendly Games" to protest British Prime Minister Margaret Thatcher's adamant stand against full economic sanctions against South Africa. Should boycott strike the Seoul Olympics we might see yet another version of the Goodwill Games.

Although the Olympic movement has not always been submerged in political turmoil, the current malaise does raise several important questions: How and why has all this come about? What is so different about the Olympics that they, rather than numerous other international sporting spectacles, should be submitted to a constant barrage of political, economic, and athletic ills? Will these problems ever come to an end? Or will the Games come to an end first? These and many other questions like them are the subject matter of this book.

We have chosen to entitle this book *The Olympic Games in Transition* because it traces the games from their genesis in classical Greek times right up to the present day. During more than 1,000 years of history, the Games have been subjected to numerous changes. The current era of boycott diplomacy suggests that we are today in the throes of yet another transition—one from which the Games may not emerge intact. This volume then, like its predecessor, *Olympism* (Segrave & Chu, 1981), comprises a compilation of essays that seek to critically examine the entire panoply of the Olympic Movement—its philosophy, its personalities, its issues and problems, its past, and its future. The text is cross-disciplinary in nature and boasts a wide array of scholars whose expertise is drawn from a variety of disciplines including classical studies, anthropology, English, sociology, law, and physical education. The book includes essays by ex-Olympic athletes, top-level sport administrators, reporters, and freelance writers. Many of the essays are original contributions, whereas others have been reprinted from a variety of sources. Several have been reprinted from *Olympism* (Segrave & Chu, 1981) and have been revised and updated by their authors.

The Olympic Games in Transition is presented as an appropriate text for undergraduate and graduate students. The book adheres to a chronological treatment of the development of the games and is divided into easily identifiable and distinct sections. The text represents no particular ideology and is not aligned to any one school of thought. We have, in fact, tried to include as many differing points of view and disciplinary approaches as possible. We have also included "Suggestion for Further

Reading" sections to aid in class discussions, to provide additional information and alternative views, and to assist in the preparation of essays and term papers.

None of this is to say, of course, that our efforts are devoid of shortcomings. We recognize from the start that through the process of selection alone, we inevitably limit the scope of the volume. But we attempt to present a balanced, reflective, and stimulating discussion on the past, present, and future of the Olympic Games, for they are indeed a remarkable institution and a compelling subject for study. They are resilient and profound, a window into the soul of the very world in which we live. Our hope is that this collection of essays will not only introduce students to the subtleties and complexities of the games but that it will also excite them to further inquiries that go beyond the mundane and superficial, and (dare we say it) the purely athletic.

Jeffrey O. Segrave
Donald Chu

References

Johnson, W.O. (1984). A rich harvest from a sea of troubles. *Sports Illustrated*, **61**, 60-84.

Segrave, J.O., & Chu, D. (Eds.). (1981). *Olympism*. Champaign, IL: Human Kinetics.

The Ancient Games

The precise origin of the ancient Olympic Games is not known. What is known is that the name Corebus of Elis is the first to appear in the official Olympic register, a chronological list of Olympic victors initially compiled by the Elian, Hippias. Corebus's victory in the footrace in the Games of 776 B.C. marks the first historical record of the Games at Olympia, and the Olympiad celebrated in that year was considered the first. What is also known is that religious, cultural, and athletic festivals were held at Olympia long before the 8th century B.C. But the marriage of sacred and secular activities in the worship of Olympian Zeus transformed Olympia into the focal point of the Greek world and the Olympic Games into the most spectacular sporting festival of antiquity.

Although Greek athletics attained their most memorable expression in the Olympic Games, sporting contests had gained a prominent place in the cultural life of the Greeks before 776 B.C. Sporting contests of these times are depicted in Homer's epic poems, the *Iliad* and the *Odyssey*. Written during the 8th century B.C., they endowed the Greeks with a rich cultural heritage that included a love of athletics. An elaborate description of the funeral games held to honor the fallen warrior, Patroclus, is contained in the 23rd Fable of the *Iliad* and provides one of the first literary accounts of athletics. Homer describes a whole program of activities that were to form the center of the Panhellenic festivals. The athletic events were organized and administered by the heroic archetype, Achilles, and included chariot racing, boxing, wrestling, the footrace, armed fighting,

1

a throwing contest similar to the shot put, archery, and spear throwing. A similar account is contained in the *Odyssey*, as Odysseus, returning to Greece, reaches the land of the Phaeacians and is entertained by King Alcinous with sporting activities that included running, jumping, wrestling, boxing, the pentathlon, and the discus.

Homer's descriptions indicate that athletics during the epic period emerged as both a part of everyday life and in association with the exploits of a warrior elite. But the traditions and lore contained in the *Iliad* and *Odyssey* also gave expression to a cultural ideal and the two principal aspects that composed it; namely, the ideal of physicality and the ideal of intellectuality. The ideal of physicality, embodied in Achilles, the man of vigor and action, and the ideal of intellectuality, personified in Odysseus, the man of wisdom and contemplation, coalesced to provide the foundations for the athletic ideal of ancient Hellenism. This ideal aimed at the harmonious and enduring balanced development of individual qualities in a vigorous physical medium. As Bloch (1976) notes, the ideal was "a profoundly original conception and a philosophy of life" (p. 55). That special blend of moral, physical, and intellectual excellence that typified Homer's cultural heroes was called *arete* and its pursuit became the hallmark of classical Greek culture. The ideal stressed the love of perfection and beauty—beauty of both body and mind. "It can hardly be denied" writes Smiley (1980), "that this interest in physical training was responsible for their prodigious mental attainments and intellectual achievements" (p. 177).

When the secular tradition of Homeric athletics merged with the sacred traditions of Olympia, the Olympic festival became the point of reference for the Greek world. Which of the two influences was most profound in the genesis of Greek athletics remains a matter of conjecture, but religious ceremonies and games were held at Olympia before the first official Olympiad. The oldest sanctuary at Olympia belonged to the chthonic earth goddess, Ge, whose altar has been dated earlier than the 13th century B.C. Although athletic games were not included in the cult of Ge, footraces and chariot races were subsequently held as part of the ritual ceremonies in honor of the goddess, Hera, and the agrarian god, Pelops. These fertility games were gradually assimilated into the cult of the ascendant deity, Zeus, and the Olympic Games became deeply symbolic and religious. As the German historian, Deubner (1936) described,

> The Olympic Games were sacred games, staged in a sacred place and at a sacred festival; they were a religious act in honor of the deity. Those who took part did so in order to serve the god and the prizes which they won came from the god. For when the wreath woven from the branch of sacred olive was placed on the victor's head it transmitted to him the life-giving properties with which that tree was charged. The Olympic Games had their roots in religion. (p. 5)

For more than a thousand years athletic festivals remained a significant feature of Greek cultural life. Local festivals included the Delian festival, the Panathenean Games, and the Antioch games; national, Panhellenic games included the Olympic, Pythian, Isthmian, and Nemean games. The most prestigious were the Olympic games.

Firsthand accounts of the early Olympic games have yet to be discovered, and the exact beginnings of the games remain lost in myth and legend. The poet Pindar, however, writing in the 5th century B.C., ascribes the origins of the games to Heracles, who "founded the Olympiad out of the spoils of his warfare" (*Olympia*, II). According to the 9th century B.C. historian Pansanias, Oxylus, King of Elis, held the games, but they were discontinued until the time of King Iphitus, who renewed them on a grander scale. Pansanias also recorded that the sacred Olympic truce was revived by Iphitus in consultation with Lycurgus of Sparta and Cleosthenes of Pisa in order to precipitate the cessation of hostilities. Despite obtuse origins, by the 4th century B.C. Olympia had evolved into a religious, athletic, intellectual, and artistic center of incredible popularity.

The festival served as a podium for some of the great intellectuals of the day including Lysias, who spoke from the temple of Zeus; Gorgius, who entertained the Greeks with his new Sicilian oratory; Herodotus, who read passages of his history of the Persian Wars; and Anaxagoras, who demonstrated his powers of prophecy. The philosophers Plato, Aristotle, Socrates, and Isocrates, the orator Demosthenes, and the historian Thucydides also visited Olympia. All forms of classical Greek art were exhibited at Olympia, including the Hermes of Praxiteles, the Nike of Paeonius, and Pheidias' gold and ivory statue of the enthroned Zeus. Greek sculpture also found beauty in athletics. Although Pausanias lists 192 statues in the sacred grove commemorating athletes of outstanding ability, the most widely acclaimed sculptures remain Myron's discus thrower, Polyclitus's Spear Bearer, and Lysippus's wrestler. As Smiley (1980) has noted, "it would be impossible to conceive of Greek sculpture, without Greek athletics" (p. 188). Athletics not only contributed to the art of sculpture, but they also gave inspiration to poets, the greatest of whom was the lyricist, Pindar. His 44 Olympian odes sang the praises of Olympic victors and caused the Roman poet Horace to declare that one of the odes of Pindar was worth more than a thousand statues.

Despite the remarkable fame of Olympia, the truly refined athletic interest declined from the end of the 5th century B.C., at first slowly. Accomplishment in philosophy, rhetorics, and prose replaced athleticism and undermined the whole person concept glorified in the Greek ideal. The physical decline of the sanctuary was accompanied by a waning adherence to Zeus worship and the growing secularization of the games. As Drees (1968) notes, "the spontaneous unity of cult and contest developed into two separate spheres: the sacred and the profane" (p. 158).

Civil war and Macedonian conquest further compromised the integrity of Olympia. By 146 B.C. Rome became the cultural heir to Greece. The intellectual and spiritual disposition of the Romans was more practical and utilitarian than the Greeks, and in Rome itself, athletics developed into sometimes beastly and exhibitionist spectacles. Under Roman influence, the cult of the Emperor was incorporated into the sanctuary, and the games became more international in character. However, they retained considerable popularity, surviving until 393 or 394 A.D. when they were finally abolished by the Christian Emperor, Theodosius I. During the period of their existence, which encompassed a whole millennium, the Olympic Games underwent numerous transitions as they emerged from the dawn of prehistory into the light of classical Greece, and on into the era of Roman influence. The four readings in this section cover the entire sweep of the epoch of the ancient Olympic Games.

The section opens with one of Pindar's odes, namely *Olympia I*. Composed in honor of Hieron, ruler of Syracuse, for his first victory in the horse race in 476 B.C., Lucian declared it to be "just about the most beautiful of all his poems" (Gallus, 7). Aside from the splender of the proem, Pindar's use of the story of Pelops, whose chariot-race was a prototype of the ancient games, is particularly interesting.

In the second chapter, Noel Robertson describes the main athletic events in the program of the ancient Olympics, noting the popularity of the chariot races and the symbolic primacy of the footraces. Robertson also discusses the Olympic rituals and presents a description of the sanctuary itself.

David Young concentrates on one aspect of the ancient games, the concept of amateurism. In this essay, Young explodes the myth of the amateur Greek athlete, ascribing its exaltation to the adherents of a 19th-century conception of sport. He includes the founding fathers of the modern games, who sought to perpetuate their own ideals in which participation in sport was confined to a social elite.

Finally, Thomas Scanlon analyzes the games of the Roman era. Scanlon rejects the traditional view that the games entered a period of degeneration and degradation under Roman domination (e.g., Palaeologos, 1976). Instead, he presents a revisionist interpretation, arguing that the games experienced a necessary metamorphosis that endowed them with an international flavor while maintaining their Hellenic essence. Consequently, rather than accounting for their demise as a result of corruption, debauchery, and professionalism (e.g., Henry, 1976), Scanlon posits that the real threats were in fact adverse ideologies, natural disasters, barbarian invasion, a faltering Greek economy, and an increasingly unstable government in Rome.

References

Bloch, R. (1976). Sports in the ancient world. *Diogenes*, **94**, 53-77.

Deubner, L. (1936). *Kult und spiel in alten Olympia* [Worship and play in old Olympia]. Leipzig: Hoffman.

Drees, L. (1968). *Olympia: Gods, artists, and athletes*. New York: Frederick A. Praeger.

Henry, B. (1976). *An approved history of the Olympic games*. New York: G.P. Putnam's Sons.

Palaeologos, C. (1976). The ancient Olympic games. In Lord Killanin & J. Rodda (Eds.), *The Olympic Games* (pp. 24-26). New York: MacMillan.

Smiley, C.N. (1980, November 10). Olympia and Greek athletes. *Art and Archaeology*, pp. 177-189.

Suggested Reading

Bloch, R. (1968). The origins of the Olympic Games. *Scientific American*, **219**, 79-86.

Casson, L. (1984). The first Olympics: Competing "for the greater glory of Zeus." *Smithsonian*, **15**, 64-80.

Finley, M.I., & Pleket, H.W. (1976). *The Olympic Games: The first thousand years*. New York: Viking Press.

Gardiner, E.N. (1930). *Athletics of the ancient world*. London: Oxford University Press.

Harris, H.A. (1964). *Greek athletes and athletics*. London: Hutchinson.

Harris, H.A. (1973). *Sport in Greece and Rome*. Ithaca, NY: Cornell University Press.

Schoebel, H. (1966). *The ancient Olympic Games*. Princeton, NJ: D. Van Nostrand.

Young, D.C. (1984). *The Olympic myth of Greek amateur athletics*. Chicago: Ares.

1
Olympia I

Pindar

Best of all things is water; but gold, like a gleaming fire,
by night outshines all pride of wealth beside.
But, my heart, would you chant the glory of games,
look no further than the sun
by day for any star shining brighter through the deserted air,
nor shall we sing games greater than the Olympian.
From there the manifold song is spread
by the skill of poets, to celebrate
the son of Kronos, visiting
the magnificent hearth of Hieron,

who handles the scepter of dooms in Sicily, rich in flocks,
reaping the crested heads of every excellence.
He takes his pleasure also
in the splendor of music, such
as we men play at the friendly table. Then take the Dorian
  lyre from its peg,
if any grace of Pisa or Pherenikos
has enthralled your mind to sweetest tasks
when by Alpheos' waters he sped
his bulk, with the lash laid never on,
and brought to the arms of victory his lord,

Originally published in *Odes of Pindar* (2nd ed., pp. 1-4) translated by Richmond Lattimore,
1976, University of Chicago Press. Reprinted by permission.

king of Syracuse, delighting in horses; and his fame shines
in a land of good men where Lydian Pelops went to dwell,
Pelops, whom he who clips the earth in his great strength,
Poseidon, loved, when Klotho lifted him out
of the clean cauldron, his shoulder gleaming ivory.
Great marvels in truth are these, but tales
told and overlaid with elaboration of lies
deceive men's thought, against the true account.

Grace, who brings to fulfillment all things for men's delight,
bestowing favor, many a time makes
things incredible seem true.
Days to come are the wisest witnesses.
It is better for a man to speak well of the gods; there will be
   less blame.
Son of Tantalos, against the ancients I will say
that when your father summoned the gods
to that stateliest feast at beloved Sipylos,
and gave them to eat and received in turn,
then he of the shining trident caught you up,

his heart to desire broken, and with his horses and car of gold
carried you up to the house of Zeus and his wide honor,
where Ganymede at a later time
came for the same desire in Zeus.
But when you were gone, and men from your mother looked
   long, nor brought you back,
some one of the spiteful neighbors whispered,
how they took you and with a knife
minced your limbs into bubbling water,
and over the table divided and ate
   flesh of your body, even to the last morsel.

I cannot say that any god could gorge thus; I recoil.
Many a time disaster has come to the speakers of evil.
If they who watch over Olympos have honored
any man, that man was Tantalos; but he was not
able to swallow his great fortune, and for his high stomach
drew a surpassing doom when our father
hung the weight of the stone above him,
He waits ever the stroke at his head and is divided from joy.

That life is too much for his strength; he is buckled fast
   in torment,
agony fourth among three others, because he stole
and gave to his own fellowship
that ambrosia and nectar
wherewith the gods made him immortal. If any man thinks
   to elude

God, he is wrong. Therefore, the immortals sent his son
back to the fleeting destiny of man's race.
And when at the time of life's blossoming
the first beard came to darken his cheeks,
he thought next upon marriage, to win

Hippodameia, the glorious daughter of a king in Pisa.
He walked alone in the darkness by the gray sea,
invoking the lord of the heavy trident,
and he appeared clear at his feet.
He spoke: "Look you, Poseidon, if you have had any joy of
     my love
and the Kyprian's sweet gifts, block the brazen spear
of Oinomaos, carry me on the fleeter chariot
to Elis, and bring me to victory.
Thirteen suitors he has killed now, and ever
puts off the marriage of his daughter.

"The great adventure never accepts a man without strength:
but if we are destined to die, why should one sit
to no purpose in darkness and mull a nameless old age
without any part of glory his own? So my way
lies this hazard; yours to make good the end."
He spoke, with words not wide of the mark.
The god, increasing his fame, gave him
a golden chariot and horses never weary, with wings.

Overcoming strong Oinomaos, he took the maiden and
     brought her to bed.
She bore him six sons, lords of the people, blazing in valor.
Now he lies at the Alpheos
crossing, and shares prime offerings.
His tomb is thronged about at the altar where many strangers
     pass; but the glory
of Pelops flashes afar from Olympia
in the courses where speed is matched with speed
and a man's force harsh at the height.
And the winner the rest of his lifetime
keeps happiness beside him sweeter than honey

as far as the games go; but the day-by-day excellence
is best that can come to any man. Be it my work to crown,
in the rider's rhythm and song
of Aiolis, that king. I believe
there is no man of our time greater both ways, for wisdom in
     beautiful things and power's weight
we shall ever glorify by skill in the folds of song.
Some god, in charge of your thoughts,
takes care of you, Hieron.

May he not leave you soon.
So shall I hope to find once more

even a sweeter word's way to sing and help the chariot
    fleeting,
coming again to the sunny hill of Kronos. For me
the Muse in her might is forging yet the strongest arrow.
One man is excellent one way, one in another; the highest
fulfills itself in kings. Oh, look no further.
Let it be yours to walk in this time on the heights.
Let it be mine each time to stand beside you
in victory, for my skill at the forefront of the Hellenes.

2

The Ancient Olympics: Sport, Spectacle, and Ritual

Noel Robertson

The setting of Olympia in a broad fertile river valley, at the confluence of the Alpheius and Cladeus Rivers, is not at all typical of the bare rocky landscape of Greece. The geographical situation of Olympia near the west coast of the Balkan Peninsula is also surprising: Olympia is remote from the harbours and trade routes of the busy east coast facing the Aegean; remote, too, from the great centers of political power and cultural predominance such as Chalcis, Athens, Corinth, and Argos; and remote even from other festival sites such as Delphi, Nemea, and the Isthmus. The sanctuary of Olympia was, to begin with, nothing more than a sacred grove at the foot of the hill of Cronus, without any monumental buildings. In its earliest days it must have looked much the same as it does

Originally published in *Classical News and Views* (now *Classical Views*), 1976, **20**, 73-85. Reprinted by permission.

now, with pine trees growing over the ruins and olive groves nearby; the ancient trees, however, were planes and wild olives.

The Horse Races

It was horse breeding, a ruinous but obsessive luxury in early Greece, that made the fortune of Olympia. Elis, the region of Greece in which Olympia lies, was isolated and backward but also peaceful and richly endowed with fertile farmland and lush pasturage. In the earliest tradition, which goes back well before 776, Elis was already famous for horse breeding and chariot racing. According to Homer, Elis is the home of Nestor, the greatest horseman and charioteer among all the heroes of the Trojan War. Odysseus, too, while dwelling in the island of Ithaca off the west coast, pastures large herds of horses in Elis. Chariot racing was the passion of the rough chieftains who ruled Greece in prehistoric days (say 1,000 to 700 B.C.) and who saw their style of life reflected in Homer's epic poems about a legendary past.

Among the oldest figured scenes on Greek vases is the legendary chariot race that was held, along with other sporting contests, at the funeral of Patroclus, friend of Achilles. Some vases, including the superlative François Vase, also show the prize for which the charioteers are contending—a bronze tripod cauldron of the type used for boiling meat in the great feasts that belong to the heroic way of life. Nestor says that as a youth in Elis he won such cauldrons in chariot races—evidently referring to a legendary prototype of the Olympic Games. The prize also had ritual significance, for during the worship that accompanied the Olympic Games the flesh of a sacrificial victim was boiled in a bronze cauldron. The cauldron became a very common symbol of victory; the Panhellenic alliance that defeated the Persian invaders in 480 to 479 B.C. set up a monumental cauldron 30 feet high at the shrine of Delphi to commemorate the victory. The cauldron has long vanished, but the column of three entwined serpents that helped support it still stands in the hippodrome of Constantinople, where the monument was taken in after days.

The premier event at Olympia was a race of four-horse chariots; the greatest magnates and dynasts of the Greek world entered teams and charioteers. A Greek charioteer, standing astride a two-wheel bronze frame drawn by four galloping horses, must have felt like a human cannon ball. Indeed, it might be held that since the end of Greek chariot racing every other sport has been tame by comparison. The hippodrome was not an oval track but simply a straight stretch of ground about 600 yards long by 200 yards wide. The chariots raced up and down this stretch of ground around a turning post at either end; between the turning posts there was no barrier to separate the lanes, and head-on collisions were not unknown. In this respect a Roman circus, with a *spina* running down the middle, was safer than a Greek hippodrome. And the Romans raced only 12 chariots at a time, whereas a field of 40 or 50 often started in Greek races. The spectacle of 200 horses pulling 50 chariots in this restricted space, and all converging on the turning post at once, defies imagination.

Early Greek nobles drove chariots, but when the invention of the bit made riding possible, they furnished cavalry and took to racing astride (though still without saddle or stirrups, which were much later developments); horse races were held at Olympia from the mid-600s onward. Another innovation in the program lasted only briefly; this was mule-cart racing, introduced in 500 and dropped again in 444. Fine mules were prized, especially at Elis, where special mares were mated with donkeys in a husbandry practice that is reflected in the myth of Hippodameia's abduction by Pelops. But the event was too unexciting to capture interest.

Nothing whatever remains of the hippodrome, for it was swept away by the River Alpheius, which changed course in the Middle Ages and for a time ran further north than its present channel.

The Footraces

Although the equestrian races brought the greatest excitement and renown, the central part of the program, charged with ritual significance, was the footraces. The shortest race came first, and the list of victors in this race goes all the way back to 776 B.C. and continues to the end of the Olympic Games. This list came to be used as the linchpin of Greek chronology, the only common denominator in a country where every city-state counted years by a different series of magistrates. The footraces took place in the stadium adjoining the sanctuary on the east. In later days the sanctuary was filled with buildings and statues, and from the fourth century onward the stadium was clearly marked off from the sanctuary. Yet the sanctuary had once been no more than a sacred grove (as its Greek name *Altis* indicates), where Zeus was worshipped under the open sky; and the footraces originally ended inside the grove near the great altar of Zeus.

The Events

The stadium at Olympia is simply an earth track about 200 yards long by about 30 yards wide, enclosed by low banks of earth where the spectators sat. The shortest race known to the Greeks was run from one end of the stadium to the other. The next was twice the length of the stadium; the runners racing down one side of the track and back up the other executed a *double flute*, the popular name of the race. At other festivals the next event was a race of intermediate length, but besides the two short races Olympia had only a single "long" race, probably 20 lengths of the stadium and so a little over 2 miles.

This is a much simpler program than we find at any modern track meet. The Greeks ran no race as short as our 100-yard dash and none as long as the marathon, which has figured in modern Olympic Games ever since the first celebration of 1896. A distance of 26 miles over a variable course makes this the most arduous of all athletic events, and indeed the marathon was introduced in the first Olympics at Athens as an endurance test recalling the feat of the Athenian runner Philippides, who ran messages for his countrymen during their struggle with the Persian invaders at Marathon. In his last effort (according to later and more embroidered accounts) he brought the news of victory from Marathon to Athens and fell dead as he gasped out the words, "We have conquered." The modern marathon has not yet taken any lives, at least in Olympic competition, but it is a punishing ordeal that often taxes runners to the point of collapse and prostration. Long-distance running had no place at Olympia or at any other festival, and a modern writer commends the Greeks for observing, here as elsewhere, the principle of "nothing in excess." The reason for the omission, however, was simply lack of time or lack of interest. In the ancient world professional long-distance runners, such as Philippides, very commonly performed military and diplomatic errands, and men trained for such tasks achieved feats that (if at all true) are well beyond the reach of modern athletes. Our sources generally leave it doubtful whether sport or duty prompted these feats.

Racing over hurdles was unknown in Greece. But an interesting variation was the race in armor (or at least in token pieces of armor: helmet, greaves, and shield) over two lengths of the stadium. This event was introduced at Olympia fairly late, in 520 B.C., no doubt in consequence of the training that had come to be required for Greek heavy infantry. The Athenian soldiers at Marathon reputedly charged the enemy at the run while wearing full armor; only intensive training could enable them to put forth such effort and to keep formation at the same time. Greek soldiers drilled on the same grounds (the gymnasium) where athletes practiced, and so their training led naturally to competitions at Olympia and elsewhere.

At Olympia and in most other festivals the race in armor was not of much account. It was otherwise at the Freedom Festival, which in later days commemorated the Persian defeat on the battlefield of Plataea in 479 B.C. Here the runners wore full armour and even carried a particularly large and cumbersome shield; and the course was equivalent to 15 lengths of the stadium (something under 2 miles), stretching from the victory trophy on the battlefield to the altar of Zeus of the Free outside the town gates of Plataea. The winner was proclaimed "Finest of the Greeks," and we are even assured by a late authority that death was the penalty for a winner who competed a second time and lost.

The runners in armor wore bronze helmet and greaves and nothing else. Greek athletes, whether in track and field or in the combative sports, exercised and competed naked, to the scandal of other ancient peoples, including the Romans. Modern scholars may be right in ascribing a ritual purpose to the nakedness of young men competing at a festival. The Greeks, however, took a common-sense view of the matter, recalling that loincloths had been the rule in early days until a fateful race in which the leader's drawers came undone and tripped him up, causing him to lose the race (in one version, even inflicting fatal injury); the judges humanely decreed that runners should thereafter compete naked.

At most Greek festivals events were held separately for three age classes: men, youths, and boys. But Olympia always remained attached to an Archaic system that recognized two classes only: "boys" between the ages of 17 and 20 and men above this age. Many of the men's events were also held for boys, though we do not know whether the boys' competition followed the men's in each event or was reserved for another day in the festival program.

Women were strictly debarred from attending the Olympic Games; any woman found in the vicinity could expect to be flung from a neighboring cliff. The only woman to defy the ban and survive was a widow who came to Olympia in disguise to train her son for competition after her husband's death. She was discovered during the Games when she vaulted a fence to congratulate her victorious son, but the circumstances were redeeming and she was pardoned. The women, however, had a festival of their own at Olympia, held at a different time of year. They ran races in honour of Hera, the consort of Zeus, but in contrast to male runners, the girls are always shown very modestly attired, even for the sprint. The philosopher Plato, an early spokesman for the equality of women, lays it down in his visionary writings that women, too, shall exercise and compete naked, but he admits to anticipating that public opinion will be outraged.

The Stadium

The stadium at Olympia in which the footraces and some other events were held reemerged in the late 1950s from the deep alluvial mud accumulated during the Middle Ages, thanks to the efforts of German archaeologists who used bulldozers as well as shovels. The track has a layer of thin sand over a base of hard clay; the sand could be raked smooth before each event. Along the sides and ends of the track is a continuous stone channel with basins at intervals, which were evidently used not for drainage but for drinking water during the contests. All around the track, at both ends as at both sides, are low sloping earth banks where spectators stood or sat. There are no seats at all, except on the judges' stand at the south side of the stadium. Opposite the judges' stand on the north side is an altar that marks the place reserved for the priestess of Demeter (a sole exception to the ban against women).

The earth banks of the Olympic stadium are strangely austere. Almost all other stadiums we know of (and they are found up and down the Greek world in every little town) have stone seats, and Olympia could easily have acquired this amenity: Wealthy benefactors were always at hand, eager to be known for such works. But here, too, the authorities at Olympia preferred an archaic simplicity.

A starting sill of stone, with two parallel grooves for the runners' feet, runs across either end of the stadium. The sill is divided into blocks about 4 feet long—each evidently serving as a station for a runner (or for two runners?), because the seam between adjacent blocks is punctuated by a square hole for the wooden post of a starting gate. The post hole at the middle of the sill is larger than the others and doubtless held the turning post for the longer races, when the starting gates would be dismantled.

At another stadium, used for the Isthmian Games, the starting gates can be reconstructed with some confidence from the traces left on the stone pavement behind the starting sill. A horizontal arm is pivoted on a vertical post, and the arm can be dropped like a railway signal when a cord supporting the arm is released by the starter, who stands in a pit behind the runners. The cords held by the starter ran across the pavement through a series of grooves that radiated from the starter's pit to the starting posts.

Placing the cords underfoot does not seem very satisfactory, and another solution was to run them along a track in an architrave *above* the starting line; the cords could be gathered together at the middle of the starting line and passed to a starter nearby. But no trace of either arrangement remains at Olympia, and we do not know how the starting gates were opened.

In any case the runner stands on his mark behind the starting line, his toes planted in the parallel grooves 7 inches apart; the rear edge of each groove is vertical to give him purchase, and the forward edge is chamfered so that he will not stub his toe in lunging forward. He leans forward over the gate with both arms stretched out in front of him, waiting for the gate to drop. A runner in heavy armor, who carries a shield in his left hand, adopts the same pose with only the right arm extended. Although this posture does not make for such a fast start as our own crouch-and-spring, a modern authority has nonetheless expressed a preference for the Greek starting gate over a starting gun as the best means of preventing false starts.

In the longer races runners ran up and down the track around the turning post at either end. It was surely an exciting moment when a field of, say, 20 runners approached the turning post; unfortunately, we do not know what tactics were permitted in maneuvering for position. Modern runners would find such a sudden turn intolerable. The Olympic stadium at Athens, built by a wealthy patron for the first modern Olympiad of 1896, closely follows the plan of the ancient stadium that lay on the same site, except for the design of the track. Most of the ancient track in the center of the stadium was left unused, and the periphery was enlarged, encroaching on the seating space, so as to form the existing track. Even so, the hairpin turn at the end is much too tight from a modern point of view, and the stadium has long been disused for serious athletics.

At Olympia the stadium in its final form, laid out in the 300s B.C., was separated from the sanctuary to the west by an earth embankment that accommodated spectators. Athletes and officials entered the stadium from the sanctuary, emerging out of a vaulted passage as in modern stadiums. Earlier stadiums extended into the sanctuary area. The next earlier, dating from the 400s, lay about 100 yards further west, and the earliest of all lay still further west; how much further remains uncertain, but in the original form of the stadium the west end must have nearly reached the altar of Zeus in the middle of the sanctuary.

The Pentathlon

The pentathlon was a set of five events (the meaning of the Greek word), in which a single winner was declared. The five events, often shown on Greek vases, were jumping, discus throwing, javelin throwing, the foot race (a single length of the stadium), and wrestling. The three field events—the jump, discus, and javelin—existed only as part of the pentathlon. So a man might be the best jumper in Greece, but he would never win a victory in competition unless he could also throw, run, and even wrestle to a high standard. The reason for the comparative neglect of these special skills was doubtless that field events are not so exciting to watch. As in modern times the spectators were at least as important as the athletes.

On the other hand, the variety of events comprised in the pentathlon favored the all-round athlete and so the ordinary man. A first-class wrestler would be too beefy to race, and a first-class runner would be too slight to wrestle. Every Greek boy could go in for the pentathlon in his local gymnasium, and the vase paintings suggest that pentathlon training was extremely common, perhaps almost universal. The present Olympic program has no close counterpart to the pentathlon: Reviving the pentathlon might do something to boost athletics in modern schools.

The Jump

The jump was a running jump performed in the stadium; the jumper was often seen running past the turning post, swinging weights in either hand as he went. The ground in the stadium was, of course, broken up for the jump, and the tradition at Olympia was that each athlete should do his own breaking up. The jump was accompanied by flute music, which must have helped to time the rather complex movements of running, swinging the weights, and finally jumping.

The jumper would run up to the takeoff point, swinging the weights back and forth at arm's length. We often see athletes practicing arm movements alone, and sometimes the coach pointing out a flaw. When the jumper took off, he swung his arms (still holding the weights) and his legs forward. As he was about to land, he swung his arms backward, just like a modern jumper.

This at least is how I understand the Greek jump, but the matter is embroiled in controversy. The trouble starts with what looks like a splendid piece of evidence. As a rule the Greeks kept no record of times and distances for athletic events, because what excited them was the momentary competition, not the long-term record. But a record for the jump is in fact reported: 55 feet! The modern record for the running long jump, after many years of progressively heightened performance, is about 29 feet. In the middle of the 19th century, when some English jumpers experimented with weights, distances up to 30 feet were claimed. Such early records are always suspect, and in any case even 30 feet is a long way short of 55 feet. So we can say without fear of contradiction that it is humanly impossible to cover 55 feet in a single jump.

The prevailing solution is to understand the Greek event not as a single jump, but as a hop, step, and jump. The modern Olympic record for this event is about 56 feet, and that might seem to clinch the matter. But we ought to be aware that the modern event is in fact inspired by this interpretation of the Greek jump, for it was originally introduced in the present Olympic program as the supposed equivalent. In fact, none of the ancient descriptions or illustrations give the slightest warrant for postulating a hop and a step as well as a jump. And the weights would be nothing but an impediment to a multiple jump. (Some scholars will argue that the weights, though unserviceable, were nonetheless retained out of blind conservatism; but this notion is excluded by the vase paintings, which prove that swinging the weights effectively was a very important element of the jump.)

The Greek jump, then, was a single jump, and we are left with the seeming record of 55 feet. A minority of scholars, whose learning deserves to be commemorated, have suggested that a different, smaller foot was used to measure jumps. The only support for such an idea is a passage of a Greek comic writer, who represents Socrates (in the character of a mad scientist) as measuring a flea's jump in flea's feet. When a flea lands on Socrates's head, he wants to measure the jump as a scientific experiment. So he takes the flea and imprints its feet in hot wax, then uses the wax shoes thus formed to measure out the jump. Scholars of a literal turn of mind accordingly believe that jumps were regularly measured in miniature feet. But perhaps the comic writer's fantasy suggests rather that in real-life, jumpers, when practicing, would use a sandal to take a rough measurement of their jumps. If so, a jumper's foot would be the same as anyone else's.

My own inclination is to dismiss the record of 55 feet as a burlesque invention. It comes in an epigram on a famous athlete, Phaÿllus of Croton, who is said to have jumped "five feet over fifty" and to have thrown the discus "five feet under a hundred." If 55 feet is a very long jump, 95 feet is a very short discus throw, for modern throwers can manage over 200 feet. Phaÿllus was renowned (as we know on other grounds) for his speed and nimbleness but may have been a duffer when it came to throwing the discus. On this view the two records ascribed to him are respectively a comic exaggeration and a comic underestimate: He could jump nearly as far as he could throw the discus.

A good many jumping weights have been recovered at Olympia and elsewhere. Some of these were made to be dedicated in token of victory, but even the utilitarian examples vary a good deal in size, shape, and weight; it is clear that these weights were also used as dumbbells for general exercising.

The Discus Throw

The jump was followed by the discus throw. The thrower takes his stand holding the discus in the left hand then swings the discus in the left hand from behind up to head level in front of him. At the end of the swing he grasps the discus in the right hand, and his left foot is forward. He now swings the discus back in the right hand, and at the end of this swing his right foot is forward, ready to act as a pivot during the final forward swing, when the thrower turns through a slight arc to give his cast an extra snap. Greek art preferred to render (as in Myron's *Discobolus*) the end of the backward swing, as the athlete is poised for the effort of throwing. At the moment of throwing the discus, the athlete would be off balance and therefore unsuitable for sculpture.

Discus throwers often appear in vase-paintings, and the variety of poses depicted in these scenes enables us to reconstruct the sequence given above. The movement differs from modern discus throwing, in which the athlete turns a full circle, sometimes two full circles, before releasing the discus. A modern thrower can do this because he has a 45° sector in which to pitch the discus. After spinning around through one or two full circles, an athlete hardly knows which way he is throwing, and it is common for modern discus throwers to commit a foul. An ancient discus thrower, competing in a narrow stadium, could not allow himself such latitude without inflicting casualties among the spectators.

How far could a Greek athlete throw the discus? We do not know, because Phaÿllus's record, as we saw, is illusory. We cannot even be sure how much a competitive discus weighed at Olympia or at other festivals, for the surviving examples vary widely. In the modern Olympics the statutory weight is 4-1/2 pounds, which was arrived at as the mean weight of a number of ancient examples.

The Javelin Throw

The third event of the pentathlon was javelin throwing. The athlete's javelin was made of elderwood, lighter than the dogwood javelin used in war; but both sorts were thrown with the aid of a leather thong. Athletes are often seen tightening the thong by holding the javelin steady against the ground; the thong was wound around the javelin near its midpoint and looped round the forefinger or the first two fingers. The javelin thrower then set off at a run and threw his missile down the length of the stadium. The thong would help in two ways. Because it increased the leverage of the throw, the javelin would go farther, and because it imparted a twirl to the shaft, the javelin would fly straighter and pitch on its tip.

Scoring the Pentathlon

So much for the three field events, which came first, to be followed by running and wrestling. Scholars have often debated how the pentathlon was scored. Modern analogies give no help, though two events in the present Olympic program have been inspired by the ancient pentathlon.

The modern pentathlon does not resemble its ancient namesake at all, for it consists of five oddly assorted events that are meant to simulate the skills needed by a soldier carrying a message through hostile territory in wartime. Much closer is the modern decathlon or set of ten events in track and field. There is no wrestling, and the shot put and racing over hurdles are included along with variations of the Greek events. Performance is measured by a points system, and points are awarded on a scale determined by previous Olympic records. Thus it is possible for an athlete to win the decathlon without winning a single event within the decathlon. One of the most exciting contests in the modern decathlon was played out in 1960 between the American Rafer Johnson and a rival (and friend) from Formosa; the Formosan placed first in 7 out of 10 events, and yet Johnson still won the Gold Medal on points.

All this is very far from Greek practice. Because the Greeks cared for nothing but victory, they never gave points or medals even for second place. In the pentathlon the winner was the man who defeated all adversaries. The result was probably obtained as follows: If a man won each of the first three events, he was a clear winner and the last two events were dropped; a three-event winner enjoyed special distinction. But if the first three events produced two or three winners, they went to the foot race; if only two previous winners were competing, this event might give a clear winner with three victories. But if not, then the two or three contenders squared off for wrestling; if three remained, lots were drawn and one contender gained the advantage of a bye while his rivals fought the first match.

The Heavy Events

We have yet to consider what the Greeks called "heavy" events. These were boxing, wrestling, and the pankration, a kind of fierce injurious combat like judo. The wrestling in question here was a separate event, much more serious than the pentathlon wrestling in which runners, jumpers, and throwers were engaged.

Boxing came first. There were no rounds, and the match continued until one party held up his hand to acknowledge defeat. Boys as well as men boxed at Olympia, and both wore leather thongs around hands and forearms. In early days, as witnessed by vase paintings, a single thong perhaps 15 feet long was wrapped around each hand; the aim was to keep the fingers together, to protect the knuckles and perhaps to stiffen the wrists. Later the wrapping became much more elaborate. The best evidence comes from the famous bronze statue of a seated boxer in the Terme Museum. On his forearm at the upper end of the wrapping is a sheepskin pad (like a tennis player's) for wiping off the sweat and blood. Around his knuckles, over the thongs, are wound three broad, thick leather bands. Scholars looking at the bronze statue have taken away different impressions of the hardness or softness of these three bands. At the least they must have stung, for their nickname was "the ants." But whereas Roman boxing gloves were loaded with jagged hunks of metal, the Greeks never allowed such barbarous devices.

Vase paintings show some very convincing blows dealt in boxing matches. Hitting with the open hand was also permissible and effective. Greek boxers wore ear guards in training but not in competition, and cauliflower ears were the boxer's hallmark then as now. The punching bag used in training was filled with seeds, flour, or sand according to the boxer's confidence and ability. Flute players sometimes accompanied boxing practice; perhaps they encouraged fancy footwork. Boxing matches might last a long time, and evasive tactics could win the day. We hear of Greek boxers dancing away from opponents like the younger Mohammed Ali and even of one whose opponent grew so exhausted, or so vexed, that he fell down dead.

In wrestling, the next event, three falls brought defeat. Any part of the body touching the ground, even a knee, counted as a fall. So it was important to get a good hold at the start. Wrestling holds are often illustrated in Greek art, sometimes in the person of Heracles or Theseus, the great "culture heroes" who were said to have wrestled certain primitive enemies. We see the body hold, applied from the front or even better from behind; the heave, where the waist is clasped from above; and the flying mare.

The most exciting and punishing of the "heavy" events was the all-in, no-holds-barred pankration, which admitted such judo-type blows as the elbow in the face and the knee in the groin. Eye gouging and biting were, however, disallowed. As in boxing the struggle went on until one party raised his arm. Pankratiasts were at least as burly as boxers and wrestlers and even likelier to bear the marks of their profession, like the well-worn veterans seen in Greek art.

The Program and the Ritual

We have now covered all the events of the Olympic program. The victor in each event received such magic emblems of victory as a fillet of wool and a palm branch. But the special insignia of Olympia was a crown of wild olive leaves. In early days Greek festivals gave quite substantial prizes—cauldrons, clothing, armour, olive oil, and the like. The practice arose at Olympia, however, of conferring a token prize only, the olive crown, and this practice was afterward imitated by some other leading festivals, which adopted distinctive crowns of laurel, parsley, or pine.

Nonetheless, Greek athletes were well subsidized by their fellow citizens, and victors at Olympia or at other national festivals were extravagantly honored at home; a life endowment of meals and lodging in the town hall was a very usual reward. We would be wrong to regard Greek athletics of any period as exemplifying the amateur spirit.

The Olympic Games, and later a growing number of other festivals, returned every 4 years. The pattern of five intersecting rings inscribed on an altar at Delphi stands for the 4-year cycle and of course provides the modern Olympic logo. Each ring is a solar year, and there are five instead of four because the Greeks reckoned inclusively. The 4-year cycle belongs to an ancient method of periodically adjusting the solar and lunar calendars. It also gave each individual a chance to compete during his 4 years of eligibility as a boy (age 17 to 20) and again during his prime as a man.

The Olympic Games belonged to the worship of Zeus, and the most ancient and holy instrument of his worship was the great ash altar in the center of the sacred grove. As described by a late Greek writer, it consisted of a steep mound 22 feet high, formed entirely of charred bones and ashes, the debris of perhaps 10 centuries of animal sacrifice, which was compacted and cemented with water—more precisely, with the holy water of the Alpheius River. Athletes and other worshippers could mount the broad platform near the base, but only priests and diviners ascended the mound itself, on steps imprinted in the side, to offer sacrifice at the top. The animal victim offered to Zeus was a fine unblemished bull, and among the sculptures recovered at Olympia is a life-size marble exemplar of the sacrificial bull, dedicated by a priestess of Demeter, who assisted at the sacrifice as also at the Games themselves.

Another very early landmark in the sanctuary was a shrine of the hero Pelops, lying just west of the ash altar. As a legendary hero (or "saint," as we might say), Pelops shared the honors of the Olympic Games with the high god Zeus. From the usual Greek view the Games were celebrated in his memory, just as in epic poetry and in the early days of Greece games were celebrated at the funeral of a chieftain.

The sacrifice to Pelops was a contrast in every way to the sacrifice to Zeus, and the two events formed the ritual focus of the Olympic Games. The Olympic festival ran for 5 days during the summer month that corresponds roughly to August. Greek months followed (or were ideally meant to follow) the phases of the moon, and the full moon of August came on the second night of the festival. That night saw the sacrifice to Pelops. The victim was a black ram, slaughtered in a pit (in contrast to the high altar of Zeus); the animal was dismembered, and the flesh placed in a tripod cauldron. On the next day (the third day, and the midpoint of the festival) there followed the sacrifice to Zeus. The winner in the foot race ignited the fire on the altar of Zeus, and the fire was then used to heat the cauldron and boil the flesh of the ram.

The great temple of Zeus, built in the 5th century B.C., is decorated with tripods at the gable ends of the roof, symbolizing this sacrificial procedure. The sculptured group in the gable at the east (the front of the temple) showed the legendary first chariot race at Olympia that Pelops won. Pelops himself is really nothing but the mythical reflection of the ritual. His name means "Dark One," and the most famous of his myths told how Tantalus, Pelop's wicked father, killed and dismembered the boy, boiled the remains in a cauldron, and served the dish (unidentified) to the gods. The only deity who partook, unwittingly, was Demeter, and this detail explains why the priestess of Demeter was so prominent in Olympic ritual.

The full significance of the ritual and the Games is matter for speculation. We might think of a kind of initiation rite, in which the Games themselves were a test and an ordeal prescribed for young men during a period of seclusion from their community. The priestess of Demeter, as the sole woman attending the festival, would then represent the domestic milieu that the young men have now left behind. Pelops and the black ram are their boyhood identity or perhaps rather the transitional state just before they enter manhood.

At any rate, the athletic contests were grouped round the ritual just described. The foot races took place on the third day of the festival and the horse races on the second, as did also the pentathlon; the heavy events came on the fourth day.

The Sanctuary and Its History

The earliest building erected in the sacred grove was the temple of Hera, the goddess who presided at the women's games held at another time of year. It may seem surprising that Hera received a temple of Olympia long before Zeus, but a Greek temple is essentially a house for the comfort of the deity concerned; a house was needed for Hera and the women she represented because they belonged to the domestic sphere, whereas Zeus was well content to be worshipped out-of-doors.

Ranged along the north edge of the sanctuary, just outside the sacred grove, are the "treasuries" or lodges built by those states—mostly belonging to the western part of the Greek world—that in early days regularly sent delegates and competitors to Olympia and so needed space for gear and dedications. In front of the treasury stood a series of 13 bronze statues of Zeus, all paid for out of fines that were imposed for misconduct during competition.

Through the course of centuries all kinds of articles and monuments were dedicated at Olympia by individuals and cities to record victories at the games or, just as often, to commemorate victories on the battlefield.

The excavation of Olympia has yielded the bronze helmet that the Athenian general Miltiades dedicated after his epochal victory over Persia. Another utilitarian object of dedication is the bronze head of a 5th-century battering ram. Only a few of these victories were gained over foreign enemies. Neighboring Greek states were very commonly at odds with each other, and a splendid statue of the winged lady Victory, ranking as almost the finest extant piece of 5th-century marble sculpture in the round, was set up at Olympia by a Greek state that scored a victory over a hated neighbor in the late 400s.

We often read in modern textbooks that a general peace descended over Greece during the Olympic festival. This is misguided. Wars continued as usual between the city-states of Greece, and only athletes and delegates en route to the games could claim immunity while traversing hostile territory. It is in fact very doubtful whether even this limited provision had much effect.

At first the sanctuary had a rustic air, but from the 400s onward a great many buildings, religious and secular, were erected at Olympia. The most magnificent was the temple of Zeus, one of the largest temples in Greece, which after about 460 dominated the sanctuary.

The temple housed the great statue of Zeus, nearly 40 feet high, wrought of gold and ivory by the Athenian sculptor Pheidias. One of the first buildings to be excavated at Olympia was a Christian church dating from the twilight years of the ancient world. When the German archaeologists explored it more fully during the 1950s, the original fabric of the church proved to be the workshop in which Pheidias created his statue. The workshop is a full-scale replica of the inner chamber of the temple of Zeus, constructed so that Pheidias could fashion his statue in much the same setting it was to occupy. The debris buried outside the walls of the workshop-church included terra-cotta molds used to cast the gold drapery of the statue and (surpassing all expectation) the broken base of a 5th-century drinking cup inscribed ''property of Pheidias.''

West of the sanctuary, beside the River Cladeus, were the athletic buildings, which came into use during the month preceding each Olympic festival, when intending competitors were required to lodge and train at Olympia itself. Chief among the athletic installations was the gymnasium, an open area as long as the stadium, where athletes could practice running, jumping, throwing, and also boxing, which needed a good deal of open ground for evasive action. Next to the gymnasium on the south was the palaestra, another athletic building standard throughout the Greek world, used for wrestling and the pankration. The bathing facilities, which drew on the water of the Cladeus, were placed nearby.

The excavators of Olympia have been able to trace nearly all the buildings and monuments existing around 160 A.D., when the venerable site was visited by a Greek antiquarian and traveller, who described what he found there. These were the last great days of Roman power and opulence, which Edward Gibbon described as the happiest in human history.

Within 100 years ancient society came close to collapsing under a wave of barbarian attacks and internal disorders, and though much was saved by great effort or sheer luck, Olympia did not survive the crisis.

3
Professionalism in Archaic and Classical Greek Athletics

David C. Young

The popular picture of ancient Greek amateurism is quite fictitious. I refer to the usual image of the highly trained and idealistic athlete who competed for a mere olive crown and some glory. This myth was founded—against all other evidence—on a misleading passage in Herodotus and a tongue-in-cheek joke in Lucian. It was conceived by partisans of the 19th-century Anglo-American amateur movement. They wished to legitimize with an ancient precedent their own athletic system, which sought to restrict participation to a wealthy, leisured class. The myth of the ancient amateur was then promoted by the founders and officials of the modern Olympic Games, the brilliant problem-child of 19th-century amateurism.

Originally published in *Ancient World*, 1983, **7**, 45-51. Reprinted by permission.

No ancient Olympic athlete would be eligible for the modern games. All had competed for financial gain, merely one criterion by which modern athletes are classified "professional." "Amateur" is, in fact, one thing for which the Greeks did not even have a word. When E.N. Gardiner (1910) argues that *idiotes* is the ancient Greek for "amateur" he is wrong (p. 130). *Idiotes* means "untrained" or "noncompetitor," surely not what we mean by "amateur athlete." And *idiotes athletes*, a "noncompetitor athlete," would be a contradiction in Greek terms; for the word *athletes* literally means "competitor for a prize."

Gardiner, who gave us our traditional picture, claimed that all Greek professionalism was a later corruption of an earlier amateur system. But he was the spokesman for a contemporary cause. Like other educated Englishmen of his day, by "amateur" he meant "well-born," "aristocrat." By "professional" he meant "working class." Nowadays we define these terms very differently. The distinction now regularly turns on the making of money through sports. Yet in an otherwise excellent article, H.W. Pleket (1976) abandons the current definitions and reverts to the 19th-century point of view, where the terms divide according to social rank.

Although noting that all Greek athletes of all periods accepted whatever financial rewards they could win—often large indeed—Pleket will not grant that all were professionals. True professionalism, he argues, is a full-time way of life in which a man's income, his livelihood, comes from his athletic successes. This "full" professionalism, Pleket says, did not exist before classical times; well into the later 5th century, all athletes were landed aristocrats. They were already wealthy. They had no occupation and no need to earn a living. They did not need the large amounts of money that they won in athletics. Therefore they were not "professionals." Pleket reserves that term for the "lower class" athletes of "later times." His argument is an obvious attempt to preserve some kind of amateurism for archaic Greece. But even his timetable is open to serious question. I here examine some of the evidence that bears on these several matters; my conclusions will differ sharply both from the popular, romanticized view and from Pleket's more subtle thesis.

In Homer, men occasionally join in athletic games and exercises for which there is no material reward. But we know what lavish prizes Achilles sets for each event in Patroclus's funeral games. They may be unusually large, for it is an extraordinary occasion. But there were other games with other prizes. In *Iliad* 9 Agamemnon says that his race horses have already won him a fortune: "A man who possessed as much as these horses have won in prizes would be far from poor; he would be rich in precious gold."

Horse racing is still the sport of kings and of the wealthy. But running is not. In *Iliad* 22 Achilles pursues Hector

> very swiftly; for they were not competing for a sacrificial animal nor an ox-hide—things that are prizes in foot-races. At stake in the race

was Hector's life. As race-horses quickly round the turns, and a large
prize is set, such as a tripod or a woman, when a man has died; that
is how Achilles and Hector whirled three times round Priam's city
on swift feet.

Prizes for runners were clearly smaller, but—as clearly—common enough
in Homer's own day. For most archaic Greeks a victim or an ox hide was
something of real value.

It is probable that the very early Olympics, like the earliest Pythian
Games, offered valuable prizes. And Hesiod speaks of the athlete who
proudly brings his prize home to his parents. He knew well. Hesiod won
a tripod himself in a poetry event. No wealthy aristocrat, his father had
fled his native land in poverty. Lesky sees Hesiod as a "peasant." If athletic games were purely aristocratic, then the sons of Amphidamas allowed
people such as Hesiod to compete in poetry but barred them from the
athletic events proper. That policy makes little sense.

In the numerous games besides the "Big Four" crown festivals there
were prizes of value. Pindar says so. Even the minor awards should not
be belittled. The warm winter coat given victors at Pellene was worth
many days pay to a humble man in ancient times. Bronze objects,
presumably tripods, were the prizes in Tegea and in the Theban Iolaeia,
silver cups at Marathon and Sicyon—prizes worth real money. Such
games were frequent, numerous, and apparently open to all free-born
Greeks. It is difficult to imagine that talented but low-born athletes passed
up these prizes in deference to the wealthy.

We cannot place a value on the tripods and silver bowls. We do not
know their weight nor their equivalent in wages or buying power. But
a much neglected inscription (IG^2 II 2311) permits us to make a rough
guess about Panathenaic prizes in the classical period, Plato's Athens:
apparently 100 amphoras of olive oil for the stade (200-m dash) victor,
80 amphoras for the winning pancratiast, and 60 for each winner in the
other events. The boys' prizes were half as much, and the youths' slightly
more than the boys'.

Olive oil prices vary greatly with the year, the place, and the purpose;
but for my calculations I use the *cheapest* figure attested for the classical
period, 12 drachmas an amphora—much cheaper by far than the majority
of recorded prices. The prize for the stade race, then, was equivalent to
at least 1,200 drachmas (100 × 12). If we take the *highest* possible wage
for the period of the inscription, 1.417 drachmas a day, we find that the
stade prize equals a *minimum* of 847 days wages for a skilled worker of
that time. If the worker, such as a carpenter, were fully employed year
round, it would take him almost 3 years of work to earn as much as the
successful sprinter won in about 25 seconds on the track.

For a modern equivalent, I calculate the stade prize as equal to *at least*
$67,800 U.S. 1980. That would be a decent purse even in modern golf
or tennis. And the Panathenaic prize was tax free. When I mention such

figures, $67,000 for a brief performance in the stadium, colleagues actually scream at me: "You're wrong. Impossible. No way. Don't say that. Don't say even a tenth of that. You're a kook." But I have rechecked my figures many times. They are, if anything, too conservative.

The only attempt to translate the Panathenaic prizes into meaningful modern figures appears in Stephen Miller's new book of ancient sources, *Arete* (1979, pp. 45f). Miller's figures are much smaller than mine, only a seventh as large ($9,600 for the stade victory). But Miller himself confesses that the amounts in his translation are far too small, based on the notion that a skilled worker in America right now makes $8.00 a day (p. iii). No one makes so little; the legal minimum wage is 3 times that much. Certainly no carpenter nowadays receives $8 a day. In my own city they in fact are paid $101 a day, more than $12 per hour. So I founded my calculations on $80 a day, $10 an hour, for our modern carpenter—a realistic amount. And I stick by my dollar equivalents for the ancient Panathenaic prizes. The men's stade victor won the equivalent in wages of $67,800 or more. His counterpart in the boys' race won the equivalent of about $34,000 U.S. 1980.

It is, of course, perilous and in some ways pointless to compare classical drachmas with 1980 dollars because the working conditions, daily needs, and standards of living are very different (things that tend to make ancient prizes worth more, not less). And I know my figures offend. But I have a point to make and, like Hesiod, if you do not like my one *logos* I just offer another. This one has no reference at all to modern values. I cleave safely to a classical Athenian context. What could the winning sprinter buy with his 1,200 drachmas in Plato's Athens? The answers are enlightening if not surprising. He could buy six or seven medium-priced slaves, people; or a nice house or two in town; or several houses in the country. The amount $67,000 begins to seem a not wholly unreasonable figure for comparison.

This is the classical period, although archaic Panathenaic prizes seem to have been the same. In Hellenistic times even minor games offered prizes bigger than this and sometimes gave large guarantees. The archaic period itself deserves a look.

We already know of silver bowls and bronze tripods at such places as Eleusis and Tegea. True, in the restructured Olympics the officials gave a crown of olives, nothing more. That did not stop the winning athletes' own home cities from rewarding them lavishly. Solon, we hear, *"reduced"* to 500 drachmas the award that the Athenian treasury would pay an Athenian Olympic victor. We also hear that he valued a sheep at 1 drachma and valued a bushel of grain the same. In classical times a workman needed to labor almost 8 1/2 days (8.47) to earn the price of a sheep. It could hardly have been significantly less in Solon's time. A sheep is a sheep, Solonian or Platonic. Thus 500 Solonian drachmas equal 4,235 days wages at this time, or more than *14 years wages*, at 300 working days per year. For my $10 an hour modern carpenter that comes to $338,800, tax free (4,235 × $80). I do not dare tell colleagues this figure. If it seems an outrageous error, you may seek to hire my Berkeley friend's $8 a day carpenter and reduce the amount to a paltry $33,880. But I suggest that you look in the 1895 Sears catalogue, not the current one, to see what it will buy.

Or, if you will, I shall sketch you another *logos*—one with no reference outside of Solon's time. If one Solonian drachma equaled, as Plutarch says, one Solonian bushel, then a single Olympic victory was worth 500 bushels. The very same amount as an annual yield from a landowner's estate placed that owner in the very richest of Solon's four classes, the *pentacosiomedimnoi*. These were the wealthiest citizens, whose rich-get-richer and poor-get-poorer policies caused the crisis that Solon sought to resolve. The sum of $338,000, as equivalent annual income for our own wealthy elite, does not sound so unreasonable howsoever much we wish Solon would not give it to an athlete for a few seconds sprint along the Alpheus.

Solon—or his successor—"reduced" the Isthmian victory award to 100 drachmas, $67,760 in my figures, and winners of the other "nonmoney" games got their pay-off, too. In the mid-5th century, at least, Athens rewarded the victors in any of these games with free meals at public expense for life, a pension that no modern professional athlete enjoyed until a few years ago. The athletic pensions of the Roman Empire are magnificent and notorious.

The sources which record Solon's Olympic prize are late and often untrustworthy. I would not trust them if there were no corroborating evidence from the 6th century itself. Apparently Athens was not alone in giving cash rewards. Sybaris, we read, offered athletes large cash prizes, no doubt befitting its proverbial wealth. More importantly, we now have the 6th-century inscription of an athlete from Sybaris. He states that he made a valuable dedication to Athena, probably the institution of a shrine, with a tithe from his Olympic prize. That cannot be a 10th of an olive crown.

Most telling of all is the comment of the poet Xenophanes in that same 6th century. Like Socrates much later, Xenophanes is indignant that Olympic victors receive free public board and seats of honor. But that is not all. The athlete gets beside all that, Xenophanes complains, a "payment which will be a treasure to him": δῶρον, ὅ οἱ χειμήλιον εἴη. In Homer *keimelion*, "treasure," refers to the valuable possessions, such as objects of gold, that belong to the wealthy or to the gifts exchanged by well-heeled *xenoi*. Thus Xenophanes's *doron* certainly means *doron*—a substantial payment perhaps like the 500 drachmas of Solon's Athens.

The poet's objection may be directed at the policy of a specific city but more probably aims at that of many cities. And the world to which Xenophanes mainly refers—with large cash prizes and public athletic pensions—is surely the one in which he spent most of his long life, namely, the Greek colonies of Magna Graecia and Sicily in the last half of the 6th century. Strong circumstantial evidence suggests that the western colonies, throughout Xenophanes's life, recruited athletes and paid them well. I cannot here speak of all the colonies; I focus on a single Greek *polis* in southern Italy, Croton. Croton's case probably presents an extreme example of a more general policy.

Our Olympic records are nearly complete for only one event, the premier footrace, the stade. For more than a century, from 588 to 484 B.C., Croton's sprinters dominated the stade, winning almost as often as the runners from all other cities combined, 12 of the 27 times the race was contested. In this same period Sparta won the stade only twice (7%) and Athens—all of Peisistratid Athens and more—not even once (0%). Yet Croton won 44% of the time: 588, 584, 576, 564, 560, 548, 508, 504, 496, 492, 488, and 484. In one stade race the first seven places fell to Croton. The lacuna in stade victories, 544 to 512, is well filled by wrestling, where Milo of Croton won at least six Olympic victories from 540 to 516. In fact Croton won more than a fifth (23 of 109) of all Olympic victories known to us from the period 588 to 484. Yet after 480 Croton apparently never won the Olympic stade again nor any other event at any of the "Big Four" festivals. There is not one Crotoniate among the known Olympic victories of the next 800 or so years, which number more than 700: 23 of 109, then, suddenly, 0 of more than 700.

How could the dominating power of Greek athletics sink to absolutely nothing in one Olympiad? How could a single colony enter at one Olympiad the seven fastest men in the archaic Greek world? One possible solution is obvious: Croton could have recruited athletes from other cities and paid them; then some sudden change cut off the funds. Other evidence supports this hypothesis. After Croton destroyed Sybaris in 510, the Pythagoreans who controlled Croton expanded her prestige and power. Coinage reveals that Croton enjoyed political dominion over its neighboring cities from 510 to 480. But about 480 some of these other cities began to mint their own independent coins. This independence suggests that Croton's political and economic domination was collapsing. Because 480 is the precise date when Croton's athletic empire collapsed, as well, we may connect the two—and infer some political change or economic necessity that terminated the fabled athletic program. We can actually watch Croton's athletic empire fall by noting the career of her champion sprinter, Astylos.

Astylos won both the Olympic stade and the diaulos in 488 and again in 484, competing for Croton in both Olympiads. He won the same two races again in 480—but not for Croton. That time he ran for Syracuse. Pausanias says that he switched cities to please the Syracusan tyrant, who probably purchased Astylos' services with a large *doron*. We know no other reason why Astylos should have suddenly turned Syracusan; we do know that Croton may have found it difficult to pay him his stipend.

Pleket roundly asserts that Astylos was a wealthy aristrocat. He was no piker, that is certain. For his epinician he employed Simonides, for his statue, Pythagoras of Samos. But we know absolutely nothing of his birth nor of his life before he ran for Croton. Perhaps a landed Crotoniate noble would abandon his own country to please Syracuse; but it seems unlikely. Pleket accords Astylos a noble birth simply because he spent money. But his money may have come more from the stadium than from his father's fields.

Modern scholars and the Pauly-Wissowa graciously but gratuitously grant noble birth to other specific archaic athletes, such as Milo of Croton and Theogenes of Thasos. But their evidence is downright ridiculous. We know nothing of Milo's nor of Theogenes' birth; and that is the case with almost all archaic athletes in the gymnastic events. A few, we know with certainty, *were* aristocrats. But it is only a modern hope—nay, a policy—that all were. While we elevate the unknown birth of an Astylos or a Milo, we suppress the ancient reports of early athletes with lowly occupations. One cannot avoid the first victor, Koroibos "the cook," so Pleket makes that a priestly title, not an occupation. But he ignores Polymnestor "the goatherd" and Amesinas "the cowherd"—both early Olympic victors (596 and 460 B.C.) but scarcely mentioned in modern books. Aristotle preserves a much earlier epigram in which an Olympic victor says he once sold fish.

Because some retired athletes played a role in politics, modern scholars claim that they belonged to prominent families, for we assume that wealth and high birth were prerequisite to a political career. But these men may have received their civic importance *because* of their athletic prominence and wealth. We blindly assume the reverse, that they became athletes because they were prominent and wealthy. Our sources say that the famous boxer, Glaukos of Carystus, ended his life embroiled in lethal Sicilian politics as Gelon's governor of Camarina. But our sources also say that Glaukos began his 6th century athletic career as a mere farmboy from Euboea. How could a mere farmboy finance the trip to Olympia? Anything near to one Panathenaic prize in a boy's event would be enough to launch a talented boy toward the top.

In a speech of Isocrates, Alcibiades's son explains that his father entered the Olympic chariot race rather than one of the athletic events proper, *gymnastika*, because "he knew that some of the athletes were of low birth, came from small towns, and were poorly educated." Nothing here, *pace* Pleket, suggests a recent development. There is no word for "nowadays," no οἱ νῦν ἀθληταί, no mention of bygone days when the stade competitors were all aristocrats. (Athletes came from small towns from the start.) The contrast that Alcibiades drew between the classes depended on the difference between equestrian and athletic events, not old times and new. The equestrian events were always the domain of the wealthy elite. Pleket has shown no new onset of professionalism—no matter how it be defined.

I can no more than mention here some other features of early Greek sport that strongly suggest professionalism. The employment of professional coaches, some themselves former athletes, goes back to the mid-6th century. Further, as H. Harris (1964) noted in the case of Democedes, there seems a thin line between Croton's renowned medical school and a coaching staff (pp. 145f). Then there are the extraordinarily long careers, a decade or two, enjoyed by many ancient athletes, such as Milo, Astylos of Syracuse and Croton, and Ergoteles of Knossos and Himera. I must forgo the details here. But I note that few, if any, real parallels occur among modern amateur athletes, certainly not among our Olympic sprinters, who must soon abandon their rigorous training for more gainful careers.

Several late archaic athletes from distant islands clearly spent most of their time touring the mainland in the manner of a modern professional golfer. A carefully staggered sequence offered them at least one of the "Big Four" crown games every year and scores of minor festivals which paid rewards directly. The early 5th-century boxer and pancratiast, Theogenes of Thasos, claimed 1,300 athletic victories in a 22-year career. We disbelieve him merely because we cannot imagine an aristocrat spending every week of 6 months each year, for the prime of his life, in an athletic road show that toured the small towns of Greece—just for the joy of hitting and being hit. The record remains a possibility.

I would not argue that ancient athletics were just the same as modern professional sports. Many, perhaps most, ancient athletes were wealthy and well born. That I do not deny. But the evidence suggests that some were professional in any sense of the word and that, from the 6th century at least, large amounts of money could be made. If some athletes did support themselves with their winnings, no penalty was applied. I can find no evidence that the concept of amateurism was even known to the Greeks, and therefore I close with some topical comments.

In each Olympic year there will be a clamor because some countries support their athletes more than others. "Pure" amateurism will be extolled and decried once more. We can at least absolve the Greeks of any blame for our own problem and deal with it as we may. The presence of professional athletes at the early, most idealized ancient Olympics suggests that we ourselves overrate the importance of money. After the 1979 World Series, Willy Stargell remarked that the Series money was unimportant; he would have played for free. He loved the game and just wanted this chance to play his best against the best. Athletics, especially in the Olympic events, is the only honest specialty demanding talent and training where we color the participants with corruption if they profit from it. No one denies a painter, musician, doctor, or professor the right to make a living through his or her art. Whether Greek athletes did or did not accept money had nothing to do with their integrity of character. A few prominent Greeks such as Socrates objected to the money heaped upon athletes but never questioned their right to accept it. Yet Socrates did condemn another group for taking money, professors. How many of us would be here today if teaching for pay were thought unethical or illegal?

One notable element of athletic competition is that, on the stadium field, there is no class distinction. Ancient athletics in theory, and I think to a degree in reality, were open to all Greeks. The noble and the not noble would have competed nude on the same ground for the same prize; but at the finish line there was a difference. Both kinds of athletes shared at least one motivation, for it was common to almost all Greeks: a love of competition and a desire to be first, to rise above ordinary human limitations and achieve what other men cannot. In Pindar the key word is literally *to be distinguished*, κρίνεσθαι, separated out from the mass of other men. In that word, I suspect, lies the principal force behind Greek athletics, not in money.

References

Gardiner, E.N. (1910). *Greek athletic sports and festivals*. London: Macmillan.

Harris, H.A. (1964). *Greek athletes and athletics*. London: Hutchinson.

Miller, S. (1979). *Arete*. Chicago: Ares.

Pleket, H.W. (1976). Games, prizes, athletes and ideology. *Arena*, 1, 49-89.

Young, D.C. (1984). *The Olympic myth of Greek amateur athletics*. Chicago: Ares.

Note

1. The brief text appearing here is, with negligible exceptions, that which I read at the 1979 meeting of the American Philological Association in Boston. I have not sought to alter its oral nature; for that would belie the reality and liveliness of the pleasant occasion for which it was composed. Nor have I attempted to detail and discuss my sources; to do so requires a whole book. Those who wish to find out more about the subject and to see the evidence on which my heterodox views rest are directed to that book (see Young, 1984). There I also elaborate how the 19th-century amateur movement distorted our view of ancient sport.

4
The Ecumenical Olympics: The Games in the Roman Era

Thomas F. Scanlon

Standard modern histories of the Olympics during the Roman Era charac-
terize the period as one of "the monopoly of professionals," "the general
degradation of athletics," the exploitation by the "clever politics of Roman
expansion," and the victimization by "the all-conquering power of Christianity" (Gardiner, 1973, pp. 165, 166, 174; cp. Brein, 1978, p. 88; Herrmann, 1972, p. 185; Juethner & Brein, 1965, p. 135). The Roman Era is,
according to these versions, a period when Greeks were forced to under-
go the indignities of Roman affronts to Hellenic ideals in order to enjoy
the financial security of the *pax Romana*. In short, the era was a period
"between farce and restoration," as the title of one treatment summarizes
the condition (Ebert *et al.*, 1980, pp. 109-114). These historical overviews
accurately present the facts of the years from 146 B.C. to A.D. 394 when
Olympia was part of the Roman province of Greece, but the interpretation of Olympian development as a gradual decline or distancing
from high classical ideals to profit-minded professionalism is essentially

erroneous. David Young has very convincingly exposed the unhistorical view that an ideal period of amateurism preceded the late Classical and Hellenistic "decline" of professionalism (Young, 1984). The professional Greek athletes of Roman times were carrying on fundamentally the same, if somewhat better organized, traditions of competing for money or for valuable prizes. The following essay seeks to give a more balanced and accurate view of Olympia's fate as neither "farce" nor "restoration," but as a transformation from a center of Hellenic culture to one of "ecumenical," or international culture. The farce of Roman indignities was occasional and short-lived; the restoration of the Olympics as they had been in Classical and pre-Classical Greece never occurred. Rather, the Games underwent a gradual and permanent metamorphosis that scrupulously preserved most ancient religious and athletic traditions of the festival in its physical appearances. At the same time, the character of the celebration was altered by incorporating the Cult of the Emperor into the sanctuary and by playing host to a more cosmopolitan pool of competitors. The metamorphosis was necessary and encountered remarkably little resistance from Elean organizers. It is a mistake to think of the resulting "ecumenical Olympics" as a somehow debased or inferior version of the earlier festival. They were, rather, a surprisingly vigorous, new creation with some international flavoring, but they had a strong Hellenic essence that survived centuries of radical political, economic, and religious changes in the Mediterranean world of Rome.

In the analysis that follows I have divided the Olympics in the Roman Era into four somewhat arbitrary but usefully distinguishable periods:

1. the Late Republic, 146 to 40 B.C., from the period when Rome annexed Greece as a province to the rise of the first emperor, Augustus
2. the Julio-Claudian Era, 36 B.C. to A.D. 67, encompassing the reigns of Augustus through Nero
3. the middle Imperial Period, A.D. 69 to 177, including Vespasian to Marcus Aurelius and the Olympic renaissance of the second century
4. the late Imperial Period, A.D. 181 to 383, from the emperors Commodus to Theodosius I, when the games showed great resilience against the political and financial deterioration of the Empire

A survey of the significant political and cultural events of each period with reference to Olympia will be followed by a closer look at the Games themselves and the ethnic origins of known Olympic victors for that period.

The Late Republic, 146 to 40 B.C.

Rome had aided Greece in the Second Macedonian War (200 to 197 B.C.) against Philip V of Macedon, who was finally defeated by Titus Quictius

Flamininus at Kynoskephalai in 197 B.C. At the Isthmian Games of 198 B.C., Flamininus made a dramatic declaration of the freedom of the Greeks. After some initial resistance to Roman supremacy, Elis, the patron city of the Olympics, was forced to join the Achaian league, which became an instrument of Roman hegemony in Greece. During the Third Macedonian War (169 to 168 B.C.), the Achaians fully supported the Roman general Quintus Marcius Philippus (Dittenberger & Purgold, 1966, hereafter cited as *I.01.*, 318; Polybius, 28.13) and erected an equestrian statue in his honor at Olympia. After the defeat of King Perseus of Macedon at Pydna in 168, the Roman commander Lucius Aemilius Paulus visited Olympia, was deeply moved by Phidias' monumental statue of Zeus, and offered homage to the god (Livy, 28.5). The statue and the cult of the supreme Olympian continued to transfix visiting Romans for centuries to come.

The Achaian league's open defiance of Rome in 146 B.C. precipitated the repressive campaign of the Roman general Mummius, culminating in his capture and sack of Corinth in 146 B.C. The Achaian league was dissolved, and Greece, retaining the vestiges of independence, became a Roman province. Thus Rome enacted her usual policy of political division of a country into smaller units that retained local government and customs but were ultimately accountable to the central authority of Rome. Although Mummius's soldiers were guilty of pillaging in Greece, the commander himself acted with restraint and respect, eventually "repairing the site in Isthmia and adorning the temples in Delphi and Olympia" (Polybius, 39.6.1). Mummius was in fact the first Roman on record to set up a dedication at a Greek sanctuary: "He dedicated a bronze Zeus at Olympia from the spoils of Achaia" (Pausanias, 5.24.4). The Roman's legacy lived on, as we discover from the inscription on a monument one century later in honor of Mummius and the ten legates who administered Greece under him (*I.01.*, 278, 281, 319). The commander was popular at Olympia and the Eleans were grateful for his respect. The historian Polybius may have even intervened on Olympia's behalf because Elis also set up a statue of Polybius at Olympia (Polybius, 39.5.1-6; *I.01.*, 302.)

The greatest indignity perpetrated by the Romans against Olympia in this period, and the only occasion in history when the sanctuary was plundered by a Roman, occurred in 86 B.C. when Sulla took statues and other treasures from Olympia and other major Greek sanctuaries to pay for a successful campaign against Mithridates VI. The Roman commander assumed a dictatorship at Rome in 80 B.C., and, to celebrate the event, transferred the entire Olympic festival to Rome except for the boys' stade (200 meter) footrace (Appian, *Bellum Civile (Civil War)*, 1.99; *id.*, *Bellum Mithridaticum (Mithridatic War)*, 54; Gardiner, 1973, pp. 152-153; Juethner & Brein, 1965, p. 135; Plutarch, *Sulla*, 12; Sextus Julius Africanus, *Olympionikai (Olympic Victors)*, 175). "His excuse," Appian (*Bellum Civile*, 1.99) tells us, "was that the masses needed a breathing spell and revitalization after their toils." Insult was added to injury in what seems to have been the only attempt in history to reestablish or at least to rival the games with those in another city (Matthews, 1979). Sulla's animosity toward Olympic officials may have been exacerbated because they had previously dedicated an honorary statue to Sulla's Roman arch-foe, Marius (*I.01.*, 326). The transfer, however, had no lasting effect because Sulla died before the next Olympiad and the games returned home to stay.

Too much weight, however, should not be put on the effects of the Sullan Olympics. Overall détente between Rome and Olympia was good in this period, as evidenced by the numerous honorary statues to Roman officials at Olympia in the late second to first centuries B.C. (Gardiner, 1973, p. 153). Noteworthy among these were statues to Q. Fufius Calenus (*I.01.*, 330), Caesar's legate in central Greece, and possibly even to Caesar himself (*I.01.*, 365). These statues were conspicuously placed alongside the Sacred Way running south of the Altis (Olympic sanctuary). The "decline of competition" after Sulla that Gardiner (1973, p. 153) alleges is simply not accurate. The relatively complete record of ten athletic and five hippic victors for the 72 B.C. Games shows that, among athletic victors, four were from Asia Minor, one from Egypt, three from mainland Greece beyond the Olympic region of Elis, and two from Elis. All known hippic victors were local Eleans in the five Olympiads before Sulla's Games. Gardiner's claim (1973, p. 154) that "corruption reappears" after Sulla is equally misleading because the instance of bribery in 68 B.C. (Pausanias, 5.21.9) was an isolated case, and it was properly punished by officials.

It is clear that Olympia and Greece in general were suffering financially in the late Republic due to civil wars and petty boundary disputes in the new Roman province, for example, the disputes documented on Olympic inscriptions (*I.01.*, 47, 48, 52). The dearth of athletic victor statues from this period can also be explained by financial circumstances (*I.01.*, 211-213). Economics also certainly limited the Olympic hippic events almost exclusively to the noble Eleans who were renowned for their horse-breeding in the area. Numerous inscriptions document Olympic victories in horse or chariot races during this period (*I.01.*, 191-218), and the victors are all Eleans. In fact, the last *non*-Elean hippic victor was a Trojan man, Akestorides, who won in 212 B.C. (*I.01.*, 184 = Moretti, 1957, no .590). If we exclude the victories by Roman emperors or noblemen in the centuries to follow, not until about A.D. 193 (*I.01.*, 329 = Moretti, 1957, no. 895) do we meet another non-Elean among known victors in horse events. Lack of serious competition for the Eleans in the Roman period may also be explained by the fact that the Roman circuses occupied the attention of profit-minded horse breeders and offered a market that was absent in Hellenistic Greece or earlier.

The Romans could offer no rival, however, to the purely athletic contests of Greek festivals. If gladiatorial games were popular throughout the Roman world, they were still no substitute for the beautiful, graceful, and skilled contests of the Greeks. The Roman people themselves clearly admired Greek athletics from the frequent exhibits of athletes, sometimes even together with gladiatorial and musical contests, sponsored by Romans during the Republic (Meier, 1894). The first appearance of Greek athletics in Rome was in 186 B.C. at games sponsored by M. Fulvius Nobilior (Livy, 39.22.2). M. Aemilius Scaurus held games with athletes in Rome in 58 B.C., as did Pompey in 55 B.C., M. Curio in 53 B.C., and Julius Caesar in 46 B.C.

It is not surprising that when an earthquake struck Olympia in about 40 B.C. and caused the roof of the Temple of Zeus to collapse, a prominent Roman, Marcus Agrippa, friend of Octavian (later the Emperor Augustus), assisted in the restoration of the sanctuary (*I.01.* no. 913, and pp. 696 ff.). Nor is it surprising that when the Olympics were in serious financial difficulty in 12 B.C. they were subsidized by a large donation from King Herod I of Judaea, who saw the festival as "the only remnant of ancient Greece" (Josephus, *Bellum Judaicum,* 1.427; Laemmer, 1974, p. 111).

From Table 1 we can see that in the late Republic the majority of known Olympic victors (39 = 58%) came from the Peloponnese, followed by those from Asia Minor (14) and the northern and central Greek mainland or islands (7). By city, Elis contributed by far the majority of known victors (24), although 18 of those were hippic victors, followed by Sicyon and Alexandria with four each. Sicyon's success is understandable since the city was relatively close to Olympia, but Alexandria's number of victories is less obviously explainable. Egyptian Alexandria had been a center of Hellenism since its founding by Alexander in the fourth century, and prior to 144 B.C. had to its credit a total of six known Olympic victors, all between 296 and 212 B.C. (Moretti, 1957, nos. 512, 539, 555, 569, 575, and 586). In view of Alexandria's status as an educational and cultural center, it is surprising that it was not more successful at the Olympics during the late Republican period. At least three victors in this period came from the far reaches of the Mediterranean world not yet incorporated as Roman provinces: one from Philadelphia (Lydia), another from Seleukia on the Tigris (Mesopotamia), and a third from Cyrene (North Africa). These areas all sooner or later became Roman provinces, but their presence on the lists in this period is a great testimony to the extent to which Greek culture had spread ahead of Roman imperialism. This period also witnesses the last three victors from the province of Macedonia; Macedonia proper had previously given at least nine victors to the Olympics between 408 and 264 B.C. (Moretti, 1957, nos. 349, 434, 439, 445, 463, 527, 533, 549, and 552). The series of Macedonian Wars with Rome had not only reduced that province's political power, but caused her to lose her place of honor at Olympia.

All of the known hippic victories in this period are the 18 by Elis, which suggests that the patron city of the Games held the great advantage of not having to transport horses during this economically depressed period. It may have been a matter of Olympic pride that the Eleans may have decided to continue the hippic events despite the lack of serious competition from other states lest the prestigious noble contests lapse from the program, as did happen later on two separate occasions.

Table 1   Regions and Cities of Olympic Victors in the Late Roman Republic, 144 to 40 B.C. (Roman province in parentheses)

A. Asia Minor (and islands)
   Adramyttium, 1 victor (Asia)
   ''Asia,'' 1 (Asia)
   Hypaia, Lydia, 1 (Asia)
   Kos, 2 (Asia)
   Kyzikos, 1 (Asia)
   Miletos, 2 (Asia)
   Nikaia 2 (Bithynia)[a]
   Philadelphia, Lydia, 1 (Asia)
   Seleukia on Tigris, 1
      (Mesopotamia)[b]
   Tralles, 1 (Asia)

   Total, 14

C. Peloponnese (all Achaia)
   Akriai, Lakonia, 2
   Argos, 2
   Elis, 24
   Kyparissa, Lakonia, 2
   Messenia, 2
   Sikyon, 4
   Sparta, 2
   Tritea, Arkadia 1

   Total, 39

D. Egypt/N. Africa (all Aigyptos)
   Alexandria, 4
   Kyrene, 1[c]

   Total, 5

E. Italy/Sicily
   Tauromenion, 1 (Sikilia)
   Thurii, 1 (Italia)

   Total, 2

Note. This and other tables are based on Moretti (1957).
[a]Not a province until 75-4 B.C.
[b]Not a province until A.D. 197-9
[c]Not a province until 75 B.C.

The Julio-Claudian Era,
36 B.C. to A.D. 67

If the last century of the Roman Republic was the nadir of the ancient
Olympics, the establishment of the new political order of the Roman Empire under Augustus was the fortuitous gift of a second life, which maintained the Games for another four centuries. The boon of Augustus's
political and cultural enlightenment to Olympia and Greek athletics in
general is well known. The victory of the emperor-to-be, Octavian, over
Anthony at Aktion (Latinized spelling: Actium) in northwestern Greece
in 31 B.C. secured for him supreme power in Rome. The Aktian Games
were established by Augustus in 28/27 B.C. as a quadrennial celebration
of his success, and the festival was included in the sacred Circuit (*periodos*)
of traditional Greek festivals—the Olympia, Nemea, Isthmia, and Pythia.
Circuit victors (*periodonikeis*) proudly listed the Aktia in their honorary
inscriptions, often higher than the Isthmia or Nemea (Moretti, 1953, nos.
58, 62, 67, 68, 69, 70, 71, 75, 77, 78, 79, 80, 81, 82, 84, 85, 87, 88, 90).
Romans even began to reckon years in Aktiads, that is, four-year periods
analogous to Olympiads and counted from 28/27 B.C. (Reisch, 1893, cols.
1213-1214).

The establishment of Olympic "spinoffs" or "isolympian games" was itself no innovation. Such games had been popular especially in Asia Minor
since Hellenistic times, and they show, in their imitation, the sincerest
form of flattery for the mother festival at Olympia. So Augustus and later
Roman emperors themselves imitated the practice with their own isolympian festivals. An *Augustalia* was held in Rome and Naples (A.D. 2) to
honor Augustus (Wissowa, 1893, cols. 2361-62; Habel, 1931, col. 630).[1]
The *Kaisareia*, or "Emperor's Games," were eventually held in seven
cities, *Aktias* in local versions were held in nine cities, and *Rhomaias*, or
"Roman Games," were held in 16 cities according to Moretti's index
(1953). The Roman Senate in A.D. 28 added the quadrennial "Games for
the Health of the Emperor" (*Ludi pro salute Caesaris*), and Nero contributed his own *Neroneia* in A.D. 60 with a special place on the program
for musical events, the favorite contests of the ruler.

Augustus had no special love for the Greeks, the former allies of his
enemy Anthony, but his admiration for "classical" Greece and his desire
to revive religiosity and cults throughout the empire were part of his larger
plan to conquer by assimilation of cultures, or by what may be called *syncretism*. Syncretism is the attempt to combine or reconcile differing beliefs and is usually applied to the natural amalgamation of religious or
philosophical beliefs that try to accommodate one another. But the term
is particularly apt for the historical process whereby the religious beliefs
and cultural (including athletic) customs of Greece and Rome were
accommodated to one another during the early Roman empire. As it became less possible to retain a pure ethnic identity in the Mediterranean
basin, and as Rome, unified by a single leader, assumed more financial
and military power, both Greece and Rome took on a more international

or ecumenical character. Imperial Rome incorporated individual Greek (and other) states by granting citizenship to powerful and sympathetic civic leaders, by granting a degree of autonomy to cities that were held ultimately accountable to Rome, and by fostering the identification of Greek and Roman religions, a phenomenon particularly evident at Olympia.

The centerpiece of Greco-Roman religious syncretism at Olympia was the *Metroön* or "Temple of the Mother Goddess," a Hellenistic structure just east of Hera's temple and just north of the Altar of Zeus in the oldest part of the sanctuary. Shortly prior to Octavian's assumption of the semi-divine title "Augustus" in 27 B.C., the Achaian League set up in his honor a two-and-a-half times life size, gold and silver alloy statue of the Roman leader in the center of the Metroön (*I.01.*, 367). The statue portrays Augustus in the image of Zeus with all of his attributes—scepter and lightning bolts in hand. The political implications of the monument are clear: The Greeks accepted the divinity of the emperor even before Octavian himself would acknowledge it, and the Greeks assumed the politico-religious leader into their pantheon to recognize his ultimate power in the very image of a "Zeusified" Augustus. The iconography is a marvellous gesture of Olympia's and Greece's final willingness, if not their enthusiasm, to accept the Roman overlordship which had been present for more than a century. The presence of the Imperial Cult in the sanctuary is all the more remarkable when one recalls that no other "foreign" gods were admitted there before or after this time. Statues of other emperors, Claudius, Domitian, Titus, and their wives were later placed in the temple, and statues of still others were placed elsewhere in the Olympic Altis (Pausanias, 5.20.9). Above the architrave of the Temple of the Cult of the Emperor was emblazoned an inscription that advertised the role of the emperor in this new period of ecumenism: "Augustus, Son of God and Savior of Greece and the Whole Inhabited World" (*I.01.*, 366).

Another sign of Olympic revival and a renewed sense of pride was the appearance of inscribed lists of Olympic cult officials kept in the sanctuary that dated from 36 B.C. to A.D. 265 (*I.01.*, 135-234, nos. 58-141). Most of the offices were indeed much older and their names give us a fascinating glimpse of the sophisticated religious hierarchy that was honored by the monuments of the Roman Imperial period:

- "ministers of god" (*theokoloi*)
- "festival heralds" (*spondophoroi*)
- "seers" (*manteis*)
- "sacred key keepers" (*kleidoukhoi*)
- "flautist" (*auletes*)
- "guide" (*exegetes*)
- "priest of daily sacrifices" (*kathemerothytes*)
- "secretary" (*grammateus*)
- "wine pourer" (*oinokhoös*)
- "libation priest" (*epispondorkhestes*)
- "wood cutter" (*xyleus*)

- "house-master" (*steganomos*)
- "cook" (*mageiros*)

This list is in the order in which they were recorded, with the most important first, in inscriptions from Augustus onward with some minor changes. Some of their ranks are augmented in the second century, presumably to deal with increased tourism. The "guide," for instance, would have shown visitors like Pausanias around the site and explained the mythical traditions and the "seers" would have helped to interpret private sacrifices (*I.01.*, 139).

Attention was also given to improving athletic facilities and to increasing imperial visibility in the contests during the early Empire. The ceremonial entrance tunnel into the stadium from the sanctuary may have been constructed in the late Hellenistic or early Imperial times (Herrmann, 1972, p. 259, note 703). The stadium in its "fourth" stage was renovated during Augustus's reign when the south wall was raised to provide more room for spectators and the "judges' box" area was refurbished (Herrmann, 1972, p. 184).

Augustus himself never competed in or even attended any Olympics, but members of the imperial family are recorded as victors in chariot races. Tiberius, soon to be adopted as Augustus's son and later made emperor, won in the four-horse chariot race in about 20 to 4 B.C. (*I.01.*, no. 218 = Moretti, 1957, no. 738), and Germanicus, adopted son of Tiberius, won in the same event in A.D. 17 (Sextus Julius Africanus). Tiberius seems to have had less interest or need to be interested in the Olympics during his reign (A.D. 14 to 37) than did Augustus. Perhaps his own previous participation and the firm establishment of the Imperial Cult under Augustus provided enough stability in Rome-Olympia relations that no intervention or improvements were needed.[2] But with Caligula (A.D. 37 to 41), his mad, autocratic successor, there occurs another incident of the sort perpetrated by Sulla in which the Roman leader attempts to steal the Olympic thunder, this time literally. Caligula ordered the colossal statue of Zeus of Pheidias to be brought to Rome, where he intended to replace its head with his own. This seems to have been one of the emperor's many attempts to style himself as a Hellenistic monarch. Legend has it that the transport ship was struck by lightning on its way to Greece and that when workers attempted to dismantle the statue at Olympia the monument laughed and shook the scaffolding, which sent the workers into a panic (Dio Cassius, 59.28.3-4; Josephus, *Antiquitates Judaicae* (*Jewish Antiquities*), 19.8-10; Suetonius, *Caligula*, 57.1). More likely, such wondrous excuses were invented to dissuade the emperor from a task that the Eleans strongly opposed and that would have invited revolt. In any case, Caligula's attempt at usurpation of Olympian tradition failed even worse than Sulla's, and the episode serves to illustrate the durability of the sanctuary even in the face of imperial threats.

Little of note happened regarding relations between Rome and Olympia under Claudius (A.D. 41 to 54), perhaps out of benign neglect, again as with Tiberius, but relations under his successor, Nero (A.D. 54 to 68), were notorious. Among Nero's passions were horse racing and music, and he indulged in both of these in his tour of Greek festivals in A.D. 67. Three honorary inscriptions at Olympia (*I.01.*, 370, 373, 374) attest to Nero's special interest in the sanctuary, but the erasure of his name out of *damnatio memoriae* on another (287) reminds us of his unpopularity among officials there, at least after his visit. Nero felt drawn to Greece because his talents were not appreciated by Romans: "The Greeks alone are worthy of my genius; they really listen to music" (Suetonius, *Nero,* 22.3). The emperor arranged for all of the Circuit Games to be held in one extraordinary year, A.D. 67, so that he might compete, win at each one, and become a *periodonikes.* The Olympics were thus postponed from A.D. 65 (Africanus; Eusebius, *Chronicles,* II.273 Aucheri; Pausanias, 10.36.4; Philostratus, *Life of Apollonius of Tyana,* 5.7; Suetonius, *Nero,* 23.1). The Eleans hurriedly built a villa for Nero in the southeast corner of the Altis, adjoining the southwest corner of the stadium. A monumental gateway was built to enter the sanctuary near the villa. Nero entered and was of course victorious in the contests of heralds, foals, and regular four-horse chariots, all normal parts of the program. But he also ordered the inclusion of musical contests in lyre and tragedy to display his talents in those areas, as well as the exceptional ten-horse chariot. Of the latter event, Suetonius (*Nero,* 24.2) reports, "He lost his balance, fell from the chariot, and had to be put back in; but though he was not able to go on, and quit before running the course, he was nevertheless crowned victor." On account of this, Dio Cassius relates (63.14), he gave to the Hellanodikai, the judges, an award of 250,000 drachmas that the Emperor Galba, Nero's successor, later ordered them to pay back.

But Nero's must hypocritical and transparent attempt to use games for political purposes was his speech at the Panhellenic site of Isthmia on the eve of his departure back to Rome, when he presented the entire province of Achaia with its freedom (Suetonius, *Nero,* 24.2). The gesture was an obvious imitation of Flamininus' real donation of freedom to Greece in 197 B.C., which also took place in the stadium at Isthmia. If the Greeks cheered Nero's proclamation of freedom in A.D. 67, it was probably not because they believed it would truly come to pass, but because by their cheers they could let the emperor know that they sincerely desired their freedom. Nero is said to have returned from Greece with a total of 1808 crowns from his victories (Dio Cassius, 63.20)—and the number is credible. Likewise, the pomp and splendor of his triumphal return to Rome wearing the Olympic and Pythian crowns was a parody of the return of an athlete and a military hero all in one (Suetonius, *Nero,* 25.1-2). Nero's achievement was, of course, one of illusion built upon illusion which vanished quickly after his death a year later. Not only did he fail to foster the new spirit of the ecumenical Games revived under Augustus, but he even brought upon himself the enmity of the Olympic officials who declared these games invalid, an "Anolympiad." Nero had supposedly also ordered the destruction or removal of all victor statues in the Altis, but it was probably never carried out because many survived until Pausanias' time. A few statues were, however, taken from Olympia back to Rome by Nero (Pausanias, 5.15.8, 5.26.3).

Table 2 Regions and Cities of Olympic Victors in the Julio-Claudian Era, 36 B.C. to A.D. 67 (Roman province in parentheses)

A. Asia Minor
   Aigai, Kilikia, 1 (Syria)
   Aiolia, 1 (Asia)
   Alexandria Troas, 1 (Asia)
   Antioch, Syria, 5 (Syria)
   Ephesos, 3 (Asia)
   Halikarnassos, 1 (Asia)
   Karia, 1 (Asia)
   Laertes, Kylikia, 1 (Syria)
   Laodikaia, Phrygia, 2 (Asia)
   Magnesia on Maiander, 4 (Asia)
   Miletos, 8 (Asia)
   Olympos, Bithynia, 1 (Bithynia)
   Perge, Pamphylia, 1 (Gallatia)
   Pergamon, 2 (Asia)
   Philadelphia, 4 (1 in Asia,
      3 in Lydia-Pamphylia)
   Seleukia, Pieria, 1 (Syria)
   Sidon, 2 (Syria)
   Stratonikaia, Karia, 2 (Asia)
   Tiatira, Lydia, 1 (Asia)
   Tyana, Kappadokia*,1
   Total, 42

B. North and Central Greece
   Antikyra, Phokis, 1 (Achaia)
   Nikopolis, 1 (Epiros)
   Total, 2

C. Peloponnese (all Achaia)
   Aigion, 3
   Argos, 1
   Elis, 6
   Epidauros, 1
   Patrai, 1
   Zakynthos, 1
   Total, 13

D. Egypt
   Alexandria, 1 (Aegyptus)

(Cont.)

E. Italy
   Rome, 10
   Thurii, 1
   Total, 11
F. Crete
   Kidonia, 1

ᵃNot a province until A.D. 17

The regional origins of known Olympic victors from 36 B.C. to A.D. 67, the Julio-Claudian era of the early empire, shows that the Peloponnese with 13 victors has fallen to a distant second to Asia Minor with 42 (Table 2). North and Central Greece has also declined to a miserable two native victors after having boasted 41 in the Hellenistic period, and dropped to seven in the late Republican periods (see Appendix). Egypt can show only one known Olympic victor from this period. Italy has a respectable eleven victors, but ten of these are from Rome, including the "fixed" six victories of Nero, and two others by members of the imperial family. So the only truly healthy display of Olympic talent at this time comes from Asia, and we must ask why this is so in the face of declining success from every other sector of the Greco-Roman world.

The reasons for Asia's success and other regions' decline are to be sought in the traditional reasons of economics and politics. The impoverished cities of the Greek mainland had little to offer the Roman imperial economy except the excellent ports of Patrai, refounded by Augustus, and Corinth, refounded by Julius Caesar. But even these were more international centers of mercantile exchange than centers of the old Hellenic spirit (Gardiner, 1973, p. 158). The problem for mainland Greece was not, as Gardiner argues (p. 168), that the Olympics became more commercialized under the Romans, who saw the games as "the greatest market" (*maximus mercatus*, Cicero, *Tusculan Disputations*, 5.3). The problem was that Greece was not commercialized enough nor unified enough in the Classical and Hellenistic periods to support the luxury of elaborate training schools with surplus capital. In fact, Cicero's allusion to the Olympics as *maximus mercatus* is actually a quote from the 6th century B.C. Greek philosopher-statesman Pythagoras, who compares life to "that market place which was considered in renown to be of the greatest pomp of the games of all Greece; for just as in that place some seek the glory and fame of the crown by exercise of their bodies, others are led by the search for eating and drinking and by profit" (Cicero *loc. cit.*). Similarly, Livy compares Corinth as the administrative site of the contemporary Isthmian Games to a *mercatus* (Livy, 33.32.3). Livy and Cicero are probably both translating an original Greek description of and pun on the name of the "athletic festival" (*agones*) as "market place" (*agora*), and so the designation of games as *mercatus* is more accurately a Roman translation of a Greek characterization of the games as a commercialized center at least since Archaic times.

So, the explanation for the decline in the athletic market in Greece and its success in Asia can be seen in a shift of capital by Rome and elsewhere to the large, wealthy, and resource-rich cities from Byzantium to Alexandria. The single most successful city in number of Olympic victors in this period (if we discount Rome, whose numbers are padded by "imperial" victories) is Miletos with eight *Olympionikai*. Prior to Rome's annexation of Greece as a province in the second century B.C., Miletos had produced only six known Olympic victors in some 600 years since the founding of the Games, that is, one in the Archaic period (596 B.C.), one in the Classical period (472 B.C.), and four others with a total of six victories in the early Hellenistic period (388, 324, 320, 316, 308, and 296 B.C.). A century and a half elapsed before Miletos's next victory at the start of the Roman period (144 B.C.), and not until the early Empire, from 24 B.C. until A.D. 45 to be precise, did the city gain an impressive line of eight victories (see Moretti, 1957, for sources). This time lapse was no doubt due to the prosperity of the city under Augustus's reign when capital became free enough to spend on gymnasia and talented youths were encouraged to represent the city in the great festivals. We know of one such boxer, Nikophon, an Olympic victor in 8 B.C.(?) (Moretti, 1957, no. 735; *Palatine Anthology*, 6.256) who probably came from a wealthy, noble family and later became chief priest of the local Cult of the Emperor. Regarding political patronage of the city, we know, for example, that Augustus twice assumed the titular office of Asymnetie of Miletos (17/16 and 7/6 B.C.), as did Tiberius (8/9 B.C.). The "Friends of Augustus" (*Philosebastoi*) at Miletos even built a temple to the Emperor Caligula for the province of Asia as a whole (Cook, Adcock, & Charlesworth, 1952, pp. 497, 563). The case of this one Asian city may illustrate how others managed to maintain a successful athletic program in the atmosphere of imperial patronage and commercial prosperity.

Less easily explained perhaps is the dirth of Olympic victors from Egypt and Alexandria during the early Empire when the area prospered financially (Table 2). Even in the Hellenistic period relatively few victors were from an area that was a booming center of Greek culture and the arts (see Appendix). Perhaps athletics had not yet become popular in that city known more as an intellectual refuge since the fourth century. Perhaps internal, racial unrest between Greeks and Jews in the early empire interfered with gymnasium enrollments because Roman administrators would have discouraged youth organizations of Greeks who might band together for political reasons against Jews or even Romans. The fact that the Emperor Claudius had to issue a special decree of Alexandrian citizenship to all who had become *epheboi*, that is, members of the youths' athletic training schools, suggests that this group had previously been disenfranchised and possibly discouraged from active participation in athletics. Whatever the reason for the absence of Egyptian victors in the early Empire, we will see that this group makes a respectable showing in the late first to third centuries. Two noteworthy developments in the Olympic program occur in this period concerning the heavy events and the hippic contests. After A.D. 37, no one was allowed to enter both boxing and the pankration and thus win the title "Successor of Heracles" as others had done previously (Dio Cassius, 79.10; Gardiner, 1973, p. 166; Pausanias, 5.21.10). Whether this was due to violation of the old Hellenic ideal of "nothing in excess," as Gardiner suggests, or whether officials simply wished to avoid too many "sweeps" by specialized heavy athletes in these events is uncertain. At least two contemporary athletes testify to the fact that *sophrosyne*, the traditional ideal of restraint or moderation, was still alive, namely the boxer Melanchomas (Dio Chrysostom, *Orations*, 29-30) and a pankratiast Tiberius Claudius Rufus (*I.01.*, 54), but this is not to suggest that that ideal had ever died, nor that they were less frequently observed in the Roman period.

Regarding the hippic events of this period, we learn from Africanus in the entry for the 199th Olympiad (A.D. 17) that "the horse races which had been withdrawn for some time were restored and [Germanikos] son of the Emperor Tiberios won in the four-horse chariot."[3] Similarly under the 222nd Olympiad (A.D. 109) Africanus mentions that "the hippic events were revived." The reasons for the hiatus on these two occasions can only be surmised, but it may be that financial hardship in Elis and the rising popularity of the Roman circuses were contributing factors. No substantial building or renovation was undertaken at Olympia after the reign of Augustus (ending in A.D. 14) and before that of Hadrian (beginning in A.D. 117).

The Middle Imperial Period, A.D. 69 to 177

From the example of the Julio-Claudian emperors, the prosperity or neglect of the "ecumenical Olympics" clearly was directly related to the degree of enthusiasm that each emperor felt towards the Games. After Nero's farcical Olympics, the Games fell into a temporary decline or at least kept a "low profile" until the great Olympic revival under Hadrian (A.D. 117 to 138) and his successors. The Flavian Emperor Vespasian (A.D. 69 to 79) is better known for his benefaction of the Colosseum, technically the "Flavian Amphitheater," but some inscriptions at Olympia do mention him in unclear contexts (*I.01.*, 350, 376). Titus (A.D. 79 to 81) and Domitian (A.D. 81 to 96) were honored with statues in the Cult of the Emperor's Temple, but their presence or influence at Olympia is otherwise unrecorded (*I.01.*, 377 mentions Domitian in an unclear context). Nerva's (A.D. 96-98) and Trajan's (A.D. 98 to 117) connections with Olympia were not particularly close, to judge from inscriptions (*I.01.*, nos. 437, 378) and other evidence, although the revival of the hippic events in A.D. 109 in Trajan's time marks the beginning of what becomes a full-scale Olympic Renaissance under Hadrian.

Olympia had never lost its attraction for men of learning, but their enthusiasm for Classical Greek and Olympian culture seems to have re-kindled in the late first and through the second centuries A.D. For in-stance, the philosophizing mystic, Apollonius of Tyana, took refuge from Nero at Olympia, where he preached from the steps of the Temple of Zeus on wisdom, manliness, and moderation (Gardiner, 1973, p. 168; Flavius Philostratus, *Life of Apollonius of Tyana*, 4.31). The Temple and its magnificent colossal, chryselephantine cult statue of Zeus by Pheidias, one of the Seven Wonders of the ancient world, became a kind of trendy forum and a focus for intellectuals of the day during this classicizing era. Quintilian in his *Institutio Oratia* (*Education of the Orator*, 12.10.9), pub-lished circa A.D. 95, mused that the "beauty [of Pheidias' Zeus] added something to the received religion; to such an extent did the majesty of the work rise to the level of the god." Similarly, Dio Chrysostom's great "Olympic Speech," *Olympiakos Logos*, published in A.D. 97, praised Zeus in our almost monotheistic, Christian picture of the "peaceful and mild . . . giver of life, . . . Father of all, Protector and Savior of men" (*Oratovio* 12.74). The Stoic philosopher Epiktetos (A.D. 55 to 135) warned his disciples that it would be "a misfortune if one dies without having seen the Zeus of Pheidias" (*Dissertatio* 1.6.23). These outpourings of praise for a statue from intellectuals of various persuasions and of Greek, Roman, and Asian origin show not mere iconolatry or art appreciation, but an almost spiritual, aesthetic bond among "idea men" of the middle Im-perial period who could find great solace in the old cult of classical Olym-pianism. The fact that both the religious and the athletic traditions of old Panhellenism could find new cultural life in an ecumenical world insured the survival of the Olympics so long as the "paganism" of Rome flourished.

The strongest imperial endorsement of this "Olympic Renaissance" came under Hadrian (A.D. 117 to 138), the great philhellene, and his Antonine successors. Hadrian admitted Greeks to full citizenship of Rome and propagated Greek ideals and values. He showed personal devotion to the cult of Zeus by completing the construction of the Temple of Olym-pian Zeus in Athens, which had been incomplete for over 600 years. Hadrian even accepted the title, "Olympian" (*Olympios* for himself in A.D. 128; and in the East he was worshipped as "Zeus Panhellenios") (Laemmer, 1967, p. 11). Hadrian's coins carried the image of the Zeus of Pheidias on them in a wonderfully effective propagandistic strategy promoting almost complete syncretism of Greek and Roman ideals of leadership.

An inscription (*I.01.*, 57, A.D. 128) which details numerous honors given to the "most divine" emperor in thanks for his manifold grants of as-sistance to Greek cities, temples, festivals, and games shows that Hadri-an's propaganda and his real benefactions to Greece were effective and were happily received by the Achaian League. It is a testimony to the continued political sensitivity of the Achaian League that they also set up honorific statues at Olympia to individual family members of Hadrian's successor, Antoninus Pius, namely, one to his wife Faustina (*I.01.*, 613), one to his adopted son, L. Aelius Aurelius Commodus (*I.01.*, 618), and one to his daughter Faustina (*I.01.*, 382), later the wife of the Emperor Marcus Aurelius (*I.01.*, 614).

The most significant alteration to the athletic facilities at Olympia during Hadrian's reign was the enlargement of the stadium in phase V with a higher south wall, and an enlarged judges' box (Herrmann, 1972, p. 190). This was the last significant stadium alteration since Augustus and indicates the revived interest in Greek athletics under Hadrian. Visitors and cult facilities were also improved during the second century. The Leonidaion, a kind of summer palace or hostel for VIPs, was renovated. The Prytaneion, a council house, and the Theokoleon, a priest's house, were then modernized. What were perhaps the first Roman hot baths at Olympia, the Kladeos Thermai, were built west of the Altis in the early second century A.D. Hot baths were also built opposite the gymnasium and north of the sanctuary at that time (Herrmann, 1972, pp. 189-190).

The greatest display of munificence toward tourists and perhaps the most controversial structure of this period was the so-called Nymphaeum of Herodes Atticus, a monumental fountain built by the Athenian millionaire, sophist, and cultural philanthrope (Graindor, 1930). The fountain, which was properly called the Nymphaeum of Regilla (Herodes' wife, *I.01.*, 610), was the crowning glory of a water channel built by Herodes circa A.D. 160. A good, permanent water source undoubtedly was needed for the great number of tourists. But more probably the appearance and location of the private citizen's monument to himself caused scandal among the conservative Olympic officials than the fact that the amenity was even offered to alleviate the traditionally hot and dusty site. The Nymphaeum, situated in the oldest part of the sanctuary on the east side of the Temple of Hera, was a curved exedra shape on which statues of the Emperors Hadrian, Antoninus Pius, and Marcus Aurelius, as well as Attica personified and Herodes' entire family, were placed. That Pausanias passed by the monument in silence despite his otherwise thorough tour of the site in A.D. 174 may have indicated that the structure was controversial and the author thus avoided taking sides. Lucian's *On the Death of Peregrinus* 19 (late 2nd century) indicates that a conservative Elean element objected to the introduction of such conveniences: The Cynic Peregrinus is nearly stoned by the people when he objects to the fountain as an effeminate innovation (Gardiner, 1973, pp. 168, 173; Herrmann, 1972, pp. 191-192). Yet hot baths were added in less ostentatious locations in this period without any adverse comments.

The truth behind the Nymphaeum controversy, Lucian's joke, and Pausanias' silence is difficult to uncover, however, because Herodes himself was doubtless in favor with the conservative Eleans. His wife, Regilla, held the most sacred Olympic position open to a woman, that of the priestess of Demeter Chamyne. Pausanias (6.21.1-2) tells us that "Herodes Atticus has dedicated statues of Demeter and Kore in Pentetic marble in place of the ancient ones."

One of the greatest testimonies to the Olympic fascination of both tourists and men of letters in the second century is the simple fact that Pausanias devoted nearly a full two of his ten books in the *Guide to Greece* to Olympia (i.e., Books V and VI: Peter Levi's Penguin edition [1971] is highly recommended). Fortunately, Pausanias' visit to Olympia occurred in A.D. 174 at a period when the Hadrianic-Antonine Renaissance had taken place. Pausanias describes the site toward the end of its 1,000-year history, but before its 3rd-century decline. The amount of space devoted to Olympia may be a greater indication of the keen interest of Pausanias's wealthy Roman and Asian audience than his own personal tastes, although both are present in the *Guide*. Thus the tourist and the man of letters are synthesized in a work epitomizing the ecumenical interests of the second-century citizen in the site.

One indication that the emperors supported athletics in the middle Imperial period is the foundation of games by or in honor of the ruling Caesar. The Capitolia, which was established by Domitian in A.D. 86, became one of the sacred Circuit Games with the Olympics, and, at least in its early years, included a footrace for girls (Dio Cassius, 67.8.1; Suetonius, *Domitian*, 4.4).[4] Hadrian's tremendous popularity in Greece and Asia is attested to by the proliferation of games in his honor, at least twelve in various cities (Moretti, 1953, index): Alexandria, Ankyra, Antiochia, Anazarbos, Athens, Ephesos, Gaza, Hadrianeia, Herakleia, Kyzikos, Smyrna, and Tarsos.

By this time popular tastes for athletic events were also changing in Greece and the East. That musical and poetry contests are listed ahead of athletic contests by A.D. 127 on some victor lists, whereas athletic contests had come first in the Augustan period and earlier, indicates an increasing popularity in non-athletic entertainment and skills (Bilinski, 1979, pp. 111-112). The Olympics resisted the trends and never admitted musical or poetry contests, but certain singers were honored for their "Olympic hymns," which may have accompanied the opening procession, the central sacrifice to Zeus, or the prize ceremony (Bilinski, 1979, p. 113; *I.01.*, no. 482, A.D. 233; *I.01.*, no. 547, 2nd century A.D.). The contests for heralds and trumpeters with which the Olympics opened were not classified as musical contests because the volume and not the beauty of voices or tone counted most in these events (Pausanias, 6.14.10). Flute playing as an accompaniment for events like discus- and javelin-throwing and jumping was customary, but the musicians held purely honorary positions at the Olympics.

There is also an indication that within athletic contests themselves, popular taste was shifting from the more traditionally prestigious track and field events to the more violent and showy "heavy" events in boxing, wrestling, and the all-out, karate-style pankration. In an inscription recording the prizes for the local games at Aphrodisias during Imperial times, heavy events get much bigger prizes than footraces and pentathlon, whereas a fourth century B.C. prize list from the Panathenaic games in Athens gives more money to the stade race winner than to any other athletic victor (Ebert, 1966, 383 ff.; Ebert et al., 1980, p. 112).

Public and imperial subsidies to successful athletes, not surprisingly, continued into late Imperial times. Subsidies in some form had been given to victors in the Circuit games since Archaic Greek times in order to encourage participation in the Olympics and other crown games without value prizes. Dio Chrysostom (*De gloria* [*On Glory*] 66.11), circa late first, early second century A.D.) mentions that victorious athletes were paid five talents in his day. The Emperor Carinus (A.D. 283-4, *Historia Augusta: Carinus*, 19.2) gave gold, silver, and silken garments as gifts to athletes during his reign.

Table 3   Regions and Cities of Olympic Victors in the Middle Imperial Period, A.D. 69 to 177. (Roman province in parentheses)

A. Asia Minor
   Adana, 2 (Kilikia)
   Aigai, Aiolis, 1 (Asia)
   Antioch, 1 (Syria)
   Apamea, 2 (Bithynia)
   Chios, 2 (Asia)
   Ephesos, 8 (Asia)
   Iasos, 1 (Asia)
   Kappadokia, 1 (Galatia)
   Keramos, Karia, 1 (Asia)
   Kyme, Aiolis, 1 (Asia)
   Laodikaia, Lykaonia, 1 (Galatia)
   Magnesia on Maiander, 1 (Asia)
   Magnesia at Siphylos, 2 (Asia)
   Miletos, 2 (Asia)
   Pergamon, 1 (Asia)
   Philadelphia, Lydia, 1 (Asia)
   Rhodes, 2 (Asia)
   Sardis, 3 (Asia)
   Seleukia, 1 (Syria)
   Side, 2 (Lykia-Pamphylia)
   Smyrna, 2 (Asia)
   Tarsos, 2 (Kilikia)
   Tenos, 1 (Asia)
   Tralles, 1 (Asia)
   Xanthos, 3 (Lykia-Pamphylia)
   Total, 45

B. North and Central Greece
   (all Achaia)
   Aigina, 2
   Athens, 1
   Elatara, Phokis, 1
   Total, 4
C. Peloponnese (Achaia)
   Elis, 1
   Sikyon, 6
   Sparta, 1
   Total, 8
D. Egypt (Aegyptos)
   Alexandria, 16
   Arisonoite, 2
   Total, 18
E. Italy (Italia)
   Rome, 1

The regional origins of Olympic victors in this period (Table 3) generally maintained the trends seen in the early Empire. Asia Minor continued to contribute the majority of victors (45 of 74 total known). The Peloponnese declined further from 13 victors in the early Empire to eight in the middle period. Italy declined surprisingly further from eleven to one, indicating, perhaps, a disinclination for noble Romans to be involved in Greek athletics even though philhellenic interest as benefactors and tourists was obviously high. But the most radical shift came in victors from Egypt and North Africa, who tallied only one victor in the previous period, but had 18 (16 of which were Alexandrian) in the middle Empire. Alexandria may have finally adopted Hellenism wholeheartedly and overcome internal problems of finances and race relations from previous periods. The acceptance of athletics indicates the adoption of Greek culture at a popular level in Egypt, a change that had been centuries in coming but one that was to endure into the late Empire. With the syncretism of Egypt, the ecumenical Olympics were now more truly international than ever.

Ephesos, which had previously had only three victors in the Classical period (Moretti, 1957, nos. 414, 431, 438 = 368, 356, and 352 B.C.) and three in the early Empire, now boasted eight Olympic victors at a time when the city prospered. Sikyon, which had no known victors in the early Empire when it ceased to sponsor the Isthmian games, was again visible with six Olympic victories (all by Aelius Granianos), the strongest showing in the Peloponnese (Moretti, 1957, nos. 848, 850-852, 856, 858 = A.D. 133[?], 137[?], 141[?], and 145[?]).

Only two hippic victors are recorded for this period, a Roman in the four-horse chariot (*I.01.*, no. 236; Moretti, 1957, no. 866 = A.D. 153[?]). Africanus reports that the hippic events were only revived in A.D. 109 after an indefinite moratorium at Olympia, but does not name any hippic victors in that Olympiad. The last previous known hippic victories were those of Nero in A.D. 67. These sources seem to indicate a decline both in finances and in the quality of competition at Olympia in the period between Nero and Trajan, followed by the Hadrianic renaissance. The hippic events, however, even with their revival, may still lack a good international field of competitors which, apart from Romans, seems to have been absent throughout the Roman era.

The Late Imperial Period, A.D. 181 to 393

After the final burst of Olympic splendor under the Antonines, the Games, like the Roman Empire itself, underwent a slow process of disintegration and ultimately death. The late second and third centuries showed inferior architecture, no major improvements, and, to judge from coin finds, a decrease in visitors and deflated currency (Herrmann, 1972, p. 193). Africanus' list of Olympic victors ends in A.D. 217, and thereafter we find numerous Olympiads for which we know of no individual victors (Rutgers, 1862). Indeed, we can only assume that the Olympics did take place without exception every four years from A.D. 217 to their demise in the late fourth century.

The Games were probably flourishing under imperial patronage into the first half of the 3rd century A.D. because we find honorary inscriptions for a dedication to Julia Domna, wife of the Emperor Septimius Severus (A.D. 193 to 211; *I.01.*, no. 387), and for one to the Emperor Caracalla (*I.01.*, no. 386 dated to A.D. 211 to 215). But no later emperors are mentioned in the monuments at the site. Certain emperors who showed an interest in Greek athletics may have supported the Olympics. Severus Alexander (A.D. 222-235) even participated in wrestling (*Historia Augusta, Severus Alexander,* 27); and the Emperor Carinus (A.D. 283 to 284) gave gifts to athletes in the games that he sponsored (*Historia Augusta, Carinus,* 19.2). Gordian III (A.D. 238 to 244) had games in his honor in at least two Greek cities, Athens and Aphrodisios (Moretti, 1953, pp. 203, 267).

Olympia also continued in its tradition as a center of the arts. Aurelios Apollonios, an orator from Antioch, was honored by the Olympic Council in Olympiad 225 (= A.D. 221 to 224) with a statue (Bilinski, 1979, p. 112). And Sperkhios of Pisa in A.D. 233 was honored as "blameless on account of his song" written for some sacred ceremony at the Games (*I.01.*, no. 482). But the greatest testimony to the cultural syncretism of this ecumenical age is the history written by A. Asinius Quadratus, whose complete history of Rome was entitled, *The Thousand Years* (*Khilieteris*), covering the period 776 B.C. to A.D. 223 and erroneously forcing the foundation of Rome to coincide with that of the Olympic Games. The Eleans honored him with a statue for "honoring Olympia in word and deed" (*I.01.*, 356). Here we find that the Olympic reality is validated and acknowledged by making the site a kind of twin sister to Rome. According to Quadratus, at least both great historical movements shared an antiquity, a tradition, and a greatness that survived a millennium. The spirit of the ecumenical Games is thereby celebrated jointly with Rome's in this work written toward the end of the period of Olympic greatness.

That the lists of Olympic cult officials end in A.D. 265 (*I.01.*, pp. 138-142) is no accident because the East German Heruli invaded Greece in A.D. 267 and attacked Athens, Corinth, Argos, and Sparta. Olympian authorities built a great wall around the Temple of Zeus and the Council House (Bouleterion) from the materials of other buildings in the Altis. The idea was to guard the core of the sacred sanctuary and the great statue of Zeus (Herrmann, p. 192). The invaders probably never reached Olympia, but the siege preparation scarred the site permanently. The Herulian invasion did not destroy Olympia, but it did mark the beginning of the end.

Around A.D. 300 an earthquake damaged the Temple of Hera and the palaistra. It may have also damaged the roof of the Temple of Zeus, which was repaired in A.D. 303 during the reign of Diocletian (Mallwitz, 1972, pp. 113-114). Olympia showed the will to survive despite even natural disaster and the weakening financial state of Greece in this period.

One hundred years passed before the death blow came to the festival, which had strained under but survived all previous external threats. We are told by an eleventh century historian, Georgios Kedrenos (*Historia Comparativa* (*Comparative History*), 322B and 348A) of the last Oympiad (293rd), which occurred under Theodosius I in 393 or 394 before his edict against pagan festivals. Kedrenos reports that the Zeus of Pheidias was moved to Constantinople where it was kept in the palace of the patrician Lausos and was eventually lost in a fire. But the source may well be in error (Herrmann, 1972, p. 196). The Edict of Theodosius II on November 13, 426 ordered the destruction of all pagan temples. A late source records the burning down of the temple of Zeus at that time (Scholiast to Lucian's *Rhetorical Precepts* 6 [221 Jacobitz]). Archaeology shows rather that another earthquake brought down the temple and traces of burning are absent. The cult statue was probably dismantled by opponents of paganism. In A.D. 395, two years after Theodosius I's Edict, the Goths under Alaric invaded as far as the Peloponnese, although Olympia was probably passed by. Pheidias's Zeus statue probably suffered from both Christians and barbarian invaders and was not to have survived, at the latest, the 426 Edict. During the first half of the 5th century, a Christian church was built on the site of Pheidias's Olympic workshop. Thus the Olympic religion and the ecumenical festival were literally and figuratively subsumed by new, more dogmatic or more barbaric forces in Greece.

One fallacy regarding the late Olympics that has been perpetuated in the handbooks is that the Games in late antiquity "were rather victims, like most things in history, of an inner decline and the external effect of force" (Herrmann, 1972, p. 194). The real threats to the Olympics in the Roman era were external—adverse ideologies, natural disasters, barbarian invasions, a failing economy on the Greek mainland, and the eclipse of the stabilizing central authority of secular Rome. Even if Quadratus' chronology regarding the simultaneous founding of Rome and the Olympics is false, the roughly simultaneous fall of pagan Rome and the Olympics is not coincidental. The evidence for internal decline of the Games is slim. Philostratus' *Gymnastics* (A.D. 215 to 225) is the last literary assessment of Greek athletics, and it contrasts the ideals of the old system of training in Archaic and Mythical Greece with the inferior contemporary practices. But Philostratus is preoccupied with his own ideological preconceptions, which leave him in error and out of step with his times on many issues (Poliakoff, 1982, pp. 143-147). To assume decline in the quality or ideals of the Olympics because of a lack of monuments associated with them is equally dangerous. The fact that the last recognized victor statue was erected in A.D. 261 (*I.01.*, no. 243), and the latest cult records date to A.D. 265 (*I.01.*, 138) only suggests that capital was lacking to erect such monuments. Similarly, the last known horse races were in the mid-3rd century (*I.01.*, no. 239 and *Inscriptiones Graecae* II-III² .3767 = Moretti, 1953, p. 89; 1957 no. 932), but the events may merely lack documentation from this period, or they, too, may have again suffered a moratorium for financial reasons.

Table 4   Regions and Cities of Olympic Victors in the Late Imperial Period, A.D. 181 to 277 and 369 (excluding the Olympic years 265 and 273 for which no victors are known)

A. Asia Minor
   Armenia, 1 (Kappadokia)
   Bithynia, 3 (Bithynia-Pontos)
   Daldis, 1 (Asia)
   Ephesos, 6 (Asia)
   Kyzikos, 2 (Asia)
   Magnesia on Maiander, 1 (Asia)
   Miletos, 1 (Asia)
   Nysa, Karia, 1 (Asia)
   Philadelphia, 2 (one in Asia,
      one in Lydia)
   Phoinikia, 2 (Syria)
   Rhodes, 1 (Asia)
   Salamina, 3 (Kypros)

(Cont.)

Sinope, 4 (Bithynia-Pontos)
Smyrna, 2 (Asia)
Tiatira, Lydia, 1 (Asia)

Total, 31

B. North and Central Greece
Athens, 2 (Achaia)

C. Peloponnese (Achaia)
Sparta, 2
Korinth, 1

Total, 3

D. Egypt/N. Africa
Alexandria, 11 (Aegyptos)
Antinoe, 1 (Aegyptos)
"Egypt" (Aegyptos)
Hermopolis, 1 (Aegyptos)
Kyrene, 1 (Kyrene)
Naukratis, 1 (Aegyptos)
Oxyrhynchos, 1 (Aegyptos)

Total, 17

E. Crete
Gortyn, 1 (Krete-Kyrene)

A greater testimony to the continued popularity and prestige of the ecumenical games to the end is the international pool of known victors. The last known Olympic victor was Varazdates, a Persian Arsacid from Armenia who won in boxing in A.D. 385 (Moretti, 1957, no. 944). The last previous known hippic victors were from Rhodes and Athens. By region, Asia still supplied the majority of victors in the late Empire as it had in the middle Empire (Table 4). Egypt still provided the second greatest number, a testimony to the continued presence of financial capital in Egypt and Asia in the later Empire. By city, Alexandria still had the most victors (11) and Ephesos still the second most (six). North and Central Greece, with two, and the Peloponnese with three known victors were at their nadir, again probably for economic reasons. The total absence of victors from Italy is puzzling, but shows a lack of interest perhaps due to domestic problems present since the late first century.

Conclusion

The syncretism between Rome and Olympia is a particularly clear example of how Rome slowly "fine-tuned" her responses to foreign cultures incorporated into the Empire. Alternations between abuse and neglect by the central government were finally tempered into standard policy. Augustus knew the value of adaptation and quickly established the presence of the Cult of the Emperor next to that of Zeus at Olympia. The extremes of Caligula and Nero were typical of all else in their reigns, but the more usual benign support of the Olympic cult and festival is exemplified by Hadrian and the Antonines. Rome never truly dominated Olympia, but rather joined it to control political allegiance, just as Olympia welcomed Roman rulers in order to finance the Games. Mainland Greece was never ousted from the competition; it simply could not compete with Asia and Egypt in wealth and leisure to devote to training. Neither the quality of athletic performance nor the standards of Olympic ideals were compromised in this Roman era, so far as our limited sources reveal. Rather the Olympics maintained the excellence of those of Classical Greece, and added to it the more international dimension of ecumenism, which is the prime inheritance of our modern Olympics.

Notes

1. The full epithet of the Augustalia at Naples was "Italica Romaia Sebasta Isolympica," or "the Italian and Roman Games of Augustus based on the Olympic Program." They were quinquennial, reckoned by an era of "Italids," had a mandatory, thirty-day training period, boys' (17-20 years old) and mens' classes of competitors, and an athletic and equestrian program identical to that of Olympia. All of this we are fortunate to learn from the lengthy inscription (*I.01.*, no. 56) of the first century A.D. (cf. Gardiner, p. 159).

2. Two (*I.01.*, nos. 369, 371) and possibly three (including 370) inscriptions honor Tiberius as patron and benefactor of the city of Elis and presumably its sponsorship of the Olympics, but nothing else is known of the nature of his subsidy to the Games.

3. Against Africanus' mention of the long discontinuation of horse races prior to A.D. 17, evidence shows eight inscriptions recording hippic victors at Olympia between 60 B.C. and A.D. 1 (Moretti, 1957, nos. 705, 707, 711, 714, 720, 740, 741, and 750). We might better place this hiatus between circa A.D. 17 and A.D. 53, for which period no hippic victories are recorded in the sources. Africanus may have incorrectly listed the hiatus under Germanikos' victory; the author's reliability in this entry has already been questioned by the omission of Germanikos' name from the text as we have it (Gelzer, 1880, Part 1, p. 169).

4. Female competitions were in vogue in Greek games of the Imperial period. One inscription honors a benefactor of games at Isthmia, Lucius Castricius Regulus, who "introduced [poetry contests in honor of] the divine Julia Augusta, and [a contest (*certamen*)] for

girls" at the Tiberea Kaisareia Sebasteia early in A.D. 23(?) (cf. Kent, 1966, pp. 70, 73, no. 153). Another inscription (A.D. 47) commemorates the victories of three daughters of Hermesianax of Tralles in the stade races at the Pythian, Isthmian and Nemean panhellenic games, as well as victories in local games in various events. A third inscription from the Imperial period records races for daughters of magistrates in the Sebasta Festival at Naples (*Inscriptiones Graecae*, XIV.691). Whether liberalized rules allowing girls to compete in Greek contests were influenced by the practices of female gladiators at Rome (Juvenal, *Satire*, 6.246-267), or, as is more likely, that both phenomena were simply manifestations of a larger and wealthier leisure class in Greece, Rome, and elsewhere during the Empire, is difficult to determine.

References

Bilinski, B. (1979). Il fisico e l'intelletto: Equilibrio o supremazia nell'epoca ellenistica e greco-romana. [The Physical and the Intellectual: Balance or Supremacy in the Hellenistic and Greco-Roman Eras]. In Agoni Gínnici, *Componenti artistiche ed intellectuali nell'antica Agonistica Greca* (pp. 87-114). Wroclaw, Warsaw, Krakow, and Gdansk: Zaklad Narodowy Imienia Ossolinskich Wydawnictwo Polskiej Akademii Nauk.

Brein, F. (1978). Die Leibesuebungen in alten Griechenland. [Athletics in Ancient Greece]. In H. Ueberhorst (Ed.), *Geschichte der Leibesuebungen* (Vol. 2, pp. 88-89). Berlin, Munich, and Frankfurt: Bartels and Wernitz.

Cook, S.A., Adcock, F.E., & Charlesworth, M.P. (Eds.). (1952). *The Cambridge Ancient History. Vol. X: The Augustan Empire, 44 B.C.-A.D. 70*. Cambridge, England: Cambridge University Press.

Dittenberger, W., & Purgold, K. (Eds.). (1966). Die Inschriften von Olympia. *Olympia*. Amsterdam: Hakkert. (Reprinted from Curtius, E., & Adler, F., 1896, Die Inschriften von Olympia, *Olympia* (Vol. 5), Berlin: Ashwer & Springer). Here abbreviated as *I.01* followed by the inscription number, unless otherwise indicated.

Ebert, J., et al. (1980). *Olympia von den Anfängen bis zu Coubertin* [Olympia from the Beginnings to Coubertin]. Leipzig: Koehler and Amelang.

All citations of ancient authors are the standard ones found in any edition of that author's text in the original Greek or Latin. Numbers indicate book (if any), chapter, and paragraph or verse of standard editions. Readers may most easily consult the Loeb Classical Library for English translations and *The Oxford Classical Dictionary* (1972) (2nd ed.) for information about ancient authors.

Ebert, J. (1966). Zu griechischen agonistischen Inschriften [On the Greek Agonistic Inscriptions]. *Wissenschaftliche Zeitschrift der Universität Halle, Geistliche-sprachwissenschaftliche Reihe*, **15**, 375-387.

Gardiner, E.N. (1973). *Olympia: Its history and remains.* Washington, DC: McGrath. (Reprint of Oxford: Clarendon, 1925)

Gelzer, H. (1880, 1885). *Sextus Julius Africanus und die byzantanische Chronographie* [Sextus Julius Africanus and Byzantine chronographie]. Leipzig: [no publisher given].

Graindor, P. (1930). *Hérode Atticus et sa famille* [Herodes Atticus and His Family]. Cairo: Faculté des Lettres, Université Egyptienne.

Habel, E. (1931). "Ludi Publici," *Realencyclopaedie der klassischen altertumswissenschaft* (Supplement Vol. 5, cols. 608-630).

Herrmann, H.-V. (1972). *Olympia: Heiligtum und Wettkampfstätte* [Olympia: Shrine and Competition sites]. Munich: Hirmer.

Juethner, J., & Brein, F. (1965). Die Leibesübungen der Römer. [The Athletics of the Romans]. In *Die athletischen Leibesübungen der Griechen. Band I. Geschichte der Leibesübungen* (pp. 131-143). Vienna: H. Boehlaus.

Kent, J. (1966). *Corinth* (Vol. 8, pp. 70-73). Princeton, NJ: Princeton University Press.

Läemmer, M. (1967). *Olympien und Hadrianeen im antiken Ephesos* [The Olympian and Hadrian Games in Ancient Ephesos]. Cologne: Deutsche Sporthochschule Köln.

Läemmer, M. (1974). Die Kaiserspiele von Caesarea im Dienst der Politik des Königs Herodes [The Emperor's Games of Caesarea in Service of the Politics of King Herod]. *Koelner Beitraege zur Sportwissenschaft*, **3**, 95-163.

Mallwitz, A. (1972). *Olympia und seine Bauten* [Olympia and its Buildings]. Athens: Kasas.

Matthews, V.J. (1979). Sulla and the games of the 175th Olympiad (80 B.C.). *Stadion*, **5**, 239-247.

Meier, P.J. (1894). Agon im Rom. In Pauly-Wissowa's, *Realencyclopaedie der klassischen Altertumswissenschaft* (Vol. 1, part 1, columns 866-867). Stuttgart: Olms.

Moretti, L. (1957). *Olympionikai* [Olympic Victors]. Rome: Accademia Nazionale dei Lincei.

Moretti, L. (1953). *Iscrizioni Agonistiche Greche* [Greek Agonistic Inscriptions]. Rome: Signorelli.

Poliakoff, M. (1982). *Studies in the Terminology of the Greek Combat Sports.* Koenigstein/Ts.: Hain.

Reisch, E. (1893). Agones. In Pauly-Wissowa's *Realencyclopaedie der klassischen Altertumswissenschaft* (Vol. 1, part 1, cols. 836-866), Stuttgart: Olms.

Rutgers, I. (Ed.). (1862). *Olympionicarum fasti* or *List of Victors at the Olympian Games*. Chicago: Ares (1980 reprint).

Wissowa, G. (1893). "Augustalia," *Realencyclopaedie der klassischen Altertumswissenschaft* (Vol. 2, part 1, cols. 2361-2362).

Young, D.C. (1984). *The Olympic Myth of Greek Amateur Athletics*. Chicago: Ares.

Appendix: Regional Origins of Olympic Victors From 776 B.C. to A.D. 277[1]

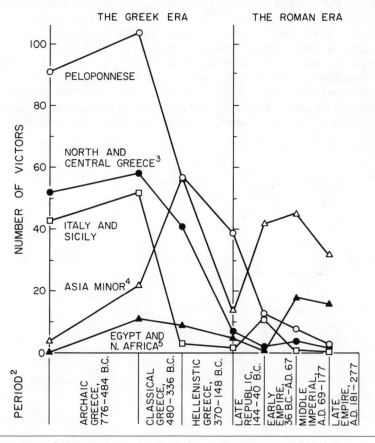

[1]All numbers of victors, determination of regions or native cities of victors, and estimates of the dates of victories are based on Moretti (1957).

(Cont.)

[2]The following concordance of Moretti's (1957) numbers with dates has been followed in the compilation of this graph:

Moretti numbers 1 to 195 = 776 to 484 B.C. (Archaic Greece)
Moretti numbers 196 to 461 = 480 to 336 B.C. (Classical Greece)
Moretti numbers 462 to 639 = 332 to 148 B.C. (Hellenistic Greece)
Moretti numbers 640 to 718 = 144 to 40 B.C. (Late Republican Rome)
Moretti numbers 719 to 795 = 36 B.C. to A.D. 67 (Early Imperial Rome)
Moretti numbers 796 to 882 = A.D. 69 to 177 (Middle Imperial Rome)
Moretti numbers 883 to 942 = A.D. 181 to 277 (Late Imperial Rome)

[3]"North and Central Greece" includes Makedonia, Epiros, and the cities of Akhaia north of Korinth, namely Antikyra, Aigina, Athens, Delphi, Elataia, and Megara.
[4]"Asia Minor" includes the Rome provinces of Asia, Bithynia, Gallatia, Kappadokia, Kilikia, Kypros, Lydia, Lykia, Mesopotamia, Pamphylia, Pontos, and Syria.
[5]"Egypt and North Africa" includes Aigyptos and Kyrene. Krete, which was included in the province of Kyrene in the Roman era, has not been included in the statistics in the Appendix nor in Tables 1 to 4 due to the small number of its Olympic victors and the difficulty of assigning it to any one of the geographical regions as defined here. We should in any case note that Krete had two known Olympic victors in the Archaic Period (Moretti, 1957, nos. 158 and 181), five in the Classical period (Moretti, 1957, nos. 274, 296, 367b, 390, 398), one in the Julio-Claudian Era (Moretti, 1957, no. 752), and one in the late Empire (Moretti, 1957, no. 906). Its reputation as a haven for pirates in the Hellenistic period and later may in part account for the dirth of known victors from that time on.

Modern Revival

The celebration of the first modern Olympic Games appropriately took place in Athens, Greece, in 1896. The resurrection of the Olympic Games may be attributed to the remarkable initiative of one man, Pierre Fredy, Baron de Coubertin (1863 to 1937). As MacAloon (1981) notes, ''No modern institution so important as the Olympics owes its existence so fully to the actions of a single person'' (p. xii). As a result of Coubertin's ceaseless efforts, the ancient Olympics were revived in modern garb. Though the ancient Games survived more than 1,000 years (776 B.C. to 393/4 A.D.), their modern counterparts have, to date, yet to survive 100 years.

The driving force that moved Coubertin to reestablish the Olympic Games was the result of numerous influences. His personal philosophy was derived from a mixture of ancient Greek, medieval, and English teachings. His inspiration was drawn from the revelations he experienced when visiting educational institutions in Great Britain and the United States during the 1880s and 1890s. Coubertin's conviction was engendered by an overwhelming devotion to sport and physical education as representing something other than a perfunctory and transient expression of the human circumstance. His rationale was drawn from a patriotism that had been nurtured out of the humiliation and turmoil that France and the Third Republic had suffered as a result of the 1870-1871 Franco Prussian

War. But above all, Coubertin idealized the concept of the Greek scholar-athlete resurrected in the late 19th century in the form of the English sporting gentlemen. To Coubertin, the athletic Englishman was the personification of the Aristotelian virtue of *eutrapelia*, an individual of vitality and versatility in both body and mind, and endowed with a sense of proportion. The education and disposition of the English sporting gentlemen represented a code that Coubertin became convinced should be granted universal appellation and recognized as a viable force in the creation of international goodwill and magnanimity (Lucas, 1976).

Yet, notwithstanding Coubertin's obsession with the British Empire, many other factors predisposed the late 19th century to be receptive to the reestablishment of the Olympic Games. The reverence for ancient Greek traditions and thought, revitalized during the era of Humanism and the Renaissance, expressed itself anew in the writings of several 18th- and 19th-century philosophers including Lessing, Fichte, Schiller, Goethe, Kant, Hegel, Humboldt, and Herder in Germany; Benedetto Croce and Giovanni Gentile in Italy; and the active school of Oxford idealists including T.H. Green, Bernard Bosanquet, F.H. Bradley, and Lord Haldane in England. These writers collectively inspired the optimistic and idealistic inclinations of the time. Their romantic reaffirmation of the worth and beauty of the human spirit owed much to classical Greek heritage. Like the ancient Greeks, these romantics conceived of human progress in terms of men of commanding physical and intellectual endowments, who through love of letters, art, science, and administration strenuously endeavored to cultivate the soul and the collective human community.

The Greek Eight-Year War of Independence (1821 to 1829), culminating in the 1838 liberation of Greece from under Turkish domination, also rejuvenated romantic enthusiasm for Greek history and culture. Eulogized and popularized by the English poet, Lord Byron, the final resurgence of Greek independence endeared the Greeks to the free societies of the Western world. The war also aroused every impulse behind the romantic, idealistic mood of the time. It was similar to the Crusades in its heroism and in its struggle between the Cross and the Crescent. In nearly every country, including the United States, funds were raised to help the Greeks in their Homeric struggle. "We are all Greeks," cried Shelley, and Philhellenism created a new current of opinion, a great flow of sympathy in favor of nationalism and liberalism.

The reawakening of interest in Greek culture was also stimulated by the publication in 1767 of Johann Joachim Winckelmann's *History of Antique Art*, which expressed the nobility and simplicity of Greek art, and which, more importantly, aroused considerable interest in exhuming the ancient stadium at Olympia. The project of unearthing Olympia was initiated by the French Morea expedition of 1829, which partially excavated the temple of Zeus. But the man who really brought Olympia and the idea of reviving the Olympic Games to life was Ernst Curtius, the leader of the German excavations at Olympia that began in 1875. Within 6 years,

Curtius excavated the entire altis and unearthed priceless individual discoveries such as the Hermes of Praxiteles and the Nike of Paionius. The results of Curtius's excavations, published in various scientific works between 1890-1897, spread rapidly throughout the Western world. The impact was not lost on Coubertin (1908), who later wrote,

> Germany had excavated the ruins of ancient Olympia; why then should France not restore the old splendors? From here it was not too far to a less splendid, but fertile and practical idea to renew the Games, especially as it seemed that international sport should play a new role in the world. (p. 9)

A necessary prelude to the reestablishment of the modern Olympic Games was the late 19th-century growth of sport and physical education. Germinating in England, the cult of athletics had begun to take firm hold in the United States and in various European and colonial countries, most notably Germany, Sweden, Holland, and Australia. By the mid-19th century, systems of gymnastics and physical education had emerged in Europe in response to demands for nationalistic revitalization and patriotic enculturation. The systems pioneered by Jahn in Germany, Per Hendrick and Hjalmer Ling in Sweden, Nachtegall in Denmark, and Froebel and Jacques-Dalcroze in Switzerland had transposed themselves in varying degrees to the United States, Britain, and France. The rapid growth of collegiate and community sport clubs further attested to the vitality of sport in the industrialized and urbanized societies of the Western world. In the United States, the decades of the 1870s and 1880s witnessed the establishment and organization of numerous sport associations, leagues, and clubs.

The late 19th century also marked the beginning of significant international sporting competition. Following the America's Cup competition of 1851, numerous international sport exchanges took place between the United States, Great Britain, and the rest of Europe in track and field, rowing, cycling, cricket, shooting, baseball, yachting, soccer, golf, and tennis. In 1879 Bryce reported in the *North American Review* that "as a means of bringing the family of nations into more friendly relations international athletic contests have within a few years proved to be very effective" (quoted in Betts, 1974, p. 194).

The development of national and international sport during the 19th century provided the historical circumstances favorable to the establishment of a single international multisport festival built around the British tradition. That tradition had given form and substance to much of the sporting ethos. However, the Philhellenic movement in 18th- and 19th-century Europe, defined and nurtured predominantly by the German cultural temperament and intellectual leadership, predisposed the world toward framing this festival within the Olympic mold. Consequently, although Coubertin may be credited with successfully uniting these two strains within the framework of the modern Olympic Games, others before him had either set up, attempted to set up, or called for Olympic Games in one form or another.

These various pseudo-Olympics are the subject of the first reading in this section. In this essay, Gerald Redmond chronicles the Olympic Games of the 19th century, arguing that they, rather than the ancient games, may in fact be appropriately considered the legitimate forebears of the modern games. Among the numerous pseudo-Olympics to which Redmond alludes are the remarkably resilient Olympic games of Robert Dover, which were instituted at the turn of the 16th century, and which, despite several suspensions, are still celebrated to this day on Dover's Hill, in the parish of Western Subedge, in Gloucestershire, England.

John Lucas, on the other hand, focuses specifically on the immediate history of Coubertin's creation, the modern international Olympic movement. Particular attention is paid to Coubertin, his philosophy, and the influences that most profoundly affected him, notably the pedagogy of Dr. Thomas Arnold.

In the final reading Coubertin himself answers why he revived the Olympic games. Published in 1908 on the eve of the London Olympics, no doubt in large measure as an entreaty to the English, this article typifies the romantic rhetoric of Coubertin. It also contains many of the themes that run throughout his published work, including his reverence for the ancient Olympics and his devotion to an Anglo-Saxon conception of sport with its attendant elitism and moralism.

References

Betts, J.R. (1976). *America's sporting heritage: 1850-1950*. Reading, MA: Addison-Wesley.

Coubertin, P. de (1908). *Une campaign de vingt-et-un-ans* [A 21-year-old campaign]. Paris: Librarie de L'Education Physique.

Lucas, J.A. (1976). The influence of Anglo-American sport on Pierre de Coubertin—Modern Olympic games founder. In P. Graham & H. Ueberhorst (Eds.), *The modern Olympics* (pp. 17-26). Cornwall, NY: Leisure Press.

MacAloon, J.J. (1981). *This great symbol: Pierre de Coubertin and the origins of the Modern Olympic Games*. Chicago: University of Chicago Press.

Suggested Reading

Coubertin, P. de (1979). *Olympic memoires*. Lausanne: International Olympic Committee.

Killanin, Lord, & Rodda, J. (Eds.). (1976). *The Olympic Games*. New York: MacMillan.

Kortzfleisch, S. von (1970). Religious Olympism. *Social Research*, **37**, 231-236.

Leiper, J.M. (1976). *The International Olympic Committee: The pursuit of Olympism, 1874-1970*. Unpublished doctoral dissertation, University of Alberta, Edmonton.

Lowe, B., Kanin, D., & Strenk, A. (Eds.). (1978). *Sport and international relations*. Champaign, IL: Stipes.

Nafziger, J.A.R. (1971). The regulation of transnational sports competition: Down from Mount Olympus. *Vanderbilt Journal of Transnational Law*, **5**, 180-212.

Sloane, W.M. (1912). The Olympic idea—Its origin, foundation, and progress. *Century Magazine*, **84**, 408-414.

5

Toward Modern Revival of the Olympic Games: The Various "Pseudo-Olympics" of the 19th-Century

Gerald Redmond

Baron de Coubertin was *not* the first or the only person in the 19th century who either attempted a revival of the Olympic Games of Ancient Greece or promoted a modern multisport festival described as "*Olympic* Games." Recent literature on the history of sport reveals that many such revivals or festivals occurred long before the first of his modern Olympic Games at Athens in 1896, and in several countries. None of them survived intact to the 20th century, however, and the Baron's enterprise in this respect was the most successful and long lasting. Yet these other previous pseudo-Olympics—to coin an umbrella term for convenience of general reference—albeit temporary, were important in their own right and deserve the significant place that is now beginning to be found for them in Olympic and sport history. In particular, these games were important precursors to Coubertin's persistent initiative; and actually, the Baron himself was aware of some of these antecedents to his own accomplishment, a fact not generally appreciated. In addition, recent research is questioning the overdrawn link between the ancient Greek Games of Olympia and Coubertin's modern counterpart, and suggests that these pseudo-Olympics had far more in common with the Olympic Games of today, and were therefore more influential than realized.

The Cotswold Games

The first non-Coubertin meeting with an Olympic label that has received the most attention from modern sport chroniclers is that associated with English gentleman Robert Dover (1582?-1652). Whether Dover was the *founder* of his "*Olimpick*" or Cotswold Games (Burns, 1981, p. 11), or whether he actually *revived* "an obsolete English rural sports meeting dating back to the 16th century" (Arlott, 1975, p. 185) is not certain. Dover was a Catholic lawyer, an extroverted anti-Puritan sportsman, whose annual Games became popular with all classes: "Gentleman, Yeoman and Labourer alike enjoyed themselves in good order" (p. 185). Exactly how they enjoyed themselves is also a matter of some conjecture, but over the years among the varied amusements included were events such as horse racing, coursing, running, jumping and leaping, throwing the sledgehammer, "spurning and pitching the bar," wrestling, quarter-staff fencing, backswords, and dancing and feasting. These Games ceased with Dover's death, but were reinstated after the Restoration in what has been described as "the second phase" from *circa* 1660 to 1852. A "third phase" is now in process with a revival dating from celebrations during the 1951 Festival of Britain (Burns, 1981; see also Bendikson, 1932).

Mandell, in his book, *The First Modern Olympics* (1976), provides a brief account of how the word *Olympia* passed into medieval Latin literature and how the adjective *Olympian* was later used by Shakespeare in 1592 (in *Henry VI*, and in *Troilus and Cressida*) and by Milton in 1667 (in *Paradise Lost*). He also cites subsequent use of the word *Olympique* by Flaubert, Gide, Voltaire, and others in France. With regard to the "Olimpick" appendage to Dover's Cotswold Games, Mandell also quotes from *Annalia Dubrensia*, an anthology of poems dedicated to Dover and his Games published in 1636. Part of one poem by Michael Drayton runs as follows:

As those brave Grecians in their happy dayes,
On Mount Olympus to their Hercules
Ordain'd their games Olimpik, and so nam'd
Of that great Mountaine; for those pastimes fam'd:
Where then their able Youth, Lept, Wrestled, Ran,
Threw the arm'd Dart; and honour'd was the Man
That was the Victor; in the cirkute there
The nimble Rider, and the skil'd Chariotere
Strove for the Garland; In those noble Times
There to their Harpes the Poets sang their Rimes;
That whilst Greece flourish't, and was onely then
Nurse of all Arts, and of all famous men:
Numbering their years, still their accounts they made,
Either from this or that Olympiade,
So Dover, frome these Games, by thee begun,
Wee'l reckon Ours, as time away doth run.

The final poem in the book is by Dover himself.

I cannot tell what Plannet rul'd, when I
First undertooke this Mirth, this jollitie;
Nor can I give account to you at all,
How this conceit into my braine did fall,
Or how I durst assemble, call together
Such multitudes of people as come hither.
Whilst Greece frequented active Sport and Playes,
From other men they bore away the Prayse;
Their common-Wealths did flourish; and their Men
Unmatch'd were for worth and Honour then;
But when they once those pastimes did forsake,
And unto drinking did themselves betake,
So base they grew, that at this present day
They are not men, but moving lumps of Clay . . .
                                        (Mandell, 1976, pp. 26-31)

In his book, *Sport and Society: Elizabeth to Anne (1969)*, Brailsford states that hunting, gaming, and chess playing were added to Dover's Games "to attract the gentry . . . and there was even a Homeric harpist to give the games an Olympic flavour" (pp. 102-103).

Despite these many Olympic allusions, most investigators agree that the Cotswold Games really represented the most successful composite revival of English popular festivals. Other revivals of traditional country sports probably existed in the 17th century, some of them called "Olympics" (Mandell, 1976, pp. 31-32); it has been suggested that this resulted in "often giving them a sophistication that they had never before possessed, a grace and finesse unknown to them in their bucolic days" (Brailsford, 1969, pp. 51-52). The comparisons with the ancient Olympic Games, in fact, were often literary devices of the time to associate Englishmen with much admired ancient Greece—Mandell refers to "devices to link Englishmen with the revered Greeks" (Mandell, 1976, p. 31)—or to praise the works of certain authors. Joachim Ruhl, author of the most comprehensive study on the Cotswold Games to date, shares this view (Ruhl, 1975). In a letter of clarification to this writer, Ruhl has stated, "Dover's Games were *no* 'Olympic' Games, but Games to show the Puritans that sports were good for merriment and the defence of the nation. . . . There was *no* connection between Robert Dover's and the Modern Olympic Games" (Ruhl, 1980). Burns' view of the "Olimpik" allusions in *Annalia Dubrensia* is that "allowing for poetic exaggerations, the effect was to raise the tone of the Games," and that "there may have been even more of an Olympic ideal underlying the Games as they developed" because of Dover's sentiments as "a loyal Royalist" against the growing force of Puritanism with the opposition to various sports in England during the 17th century (Burns, 1981, pp. 19-20).

However, the Cotswold Games are not the focus here and are only of peripheral concern with regard to the pseudo-Olympics of the 19th century. But they are pertinent in one important respect. Recently Ruhl (1985) reiterated that while it was not Dover's intention to revive the Olympic Games, nevertheless, "The *Annalia Dubrensia* with all its allusions to the panhellenic festivals, however, must be regarded as unique and as one of the earliest sources keeping alive the memory of the Olympic Games in very critical times" (p. 201). In fact, they are the most prominent example of the fact that long before 1896 or even the beginning of the 19th century, the adjective "Olympic" (whether deliberate or deserved or not) was becoming the most prized description for an athletic festival, embarking on its way to represent the modern epitome of athletic excellence as well of ancient deeds. Another early English example of this trend is contained in a letter dated April 30, 1679 from Colonel Edward Cooke in London to the Duke of Ormond, Viceroy of Ireland, in Dublin, in which he presumes "to give your Grace an account of Hampton Court Olympic, where the King honoured the pastimes with his presence, and thousands followed his example, so that the breadth of the paddock course was fair to be divided with stakes and ropes" (Robbins, 1908, p. 147).

To follow this trend in the 18th century, a selection of Olympic allusions could include the revival at Worlitz in Germany, in 1779 and the idea, formulated in 1790, of a revival of "Olympic Games" in Paris (later described by Coubertin and Jusserand):

> To the military exercises were added under the Directoire, which prided itself on its Hellenism, a number of public games, revived from the Greeks, races, athletic meetings, chariot races, held in the Champ de Mars. Voltaire without leaving his native land could have thought himself transported to the Olympic Games. (Messinesi, 1973, p. 52)

MacAloon, in his book, *This Great Symbol: Pierre de Coubertin and the Origins of the Modern Olympic Games* (1981), also refers to these Champ de Mars Olympics and makes mention of the fact that in 1793 Guts Muths had included a section on the Olympic Games in his book, *Gymnastik für Jugend*. By the time of the second edition in 1804 "he [Muths] was flirting with the idea of a revival" (MacAloon, 1981, pp. 138, 146-147); so was another individual in Sweden around this time, where "the idea of reviving the Olympic Games . . . was expressed as early as 1800 by the Rev. Count Fr. Bogilsaus von Schwerin in Sala" (Svahn, 1980).

19th-Century Pseudo-Olympics

In the 19th century, we have a continuation of Olympic allusions, analogies, and ideas for revival and also some actual determined and persuasive attempts, sometimes involving a series over many years, in several countries, and all prior to 1894. Some of these pre-Coubertin revivals of the Olympic Games have been neglected by historians, while others have been elaborated upon in detail. This difference is understandable, for some games are more significant than others, particularly with respect to their impact in terms of recognition (by Coubertin himself, as well as by the world at large), emulation, or longevity. Taken in total, however, they suggest an inexorable modern movement toward the eventual establishment of an international Olympic revival, that is, the achievement that became Coubertin's monument.

How many people are aware, for example, that what MacAloon (1981) has described as *"the first true prototype of the modern Games"* (p. 147, italics added) emerged in Sweden under the initiative of Professor Gustav Johann Schartau of the University of Lund, 29 years before Coubertin was born? In July, 1834, Schartau organized pan-Scandinavian Games, called "Olympic Games" in the press of the time, at Ramlösa near Helsinborg, with competitions in wrestling, jumping, climbing, and running events. The second "Scandinavian Olympic Games" were held there again in August, 1836, with similar events. A composition and recitation contest was held for "the best treatise on the ancient Olympic Games, compared to the medieval tournaments, together with the usefulness of the revival of competitive contests in our time," with a prize of "a wreath of oak and laurel leaves" (Svahn, 1980, p. 36). However, these Games were not held again—such revivals apparently were *not* deemed useful at that time—one suggested reason being "the competition with horseracing, embellished by royalty and gold-laced hussar uniforms, was too keen" (MacAloon, 1981, p. 147, p. 269; Svahn, 1980, p. 36).

Elsewhere in Europe during the 1830s, in the Grand Duchy of Poznan, a traveling group of professional athletes performed a show entitled "Greek Competition," which was partly modeled on the ancient Greek and Roman Games (Liponski, 1983). Such an endeavor may be termed circus or show business rather than sport (although much of sport is admittedly theater, of course), but again the Greek connection for these popular entertainments is interesting. Another similar example, this time in the New World, was the show at Franconi's Hippodrome in New York City, U.S.A. in 1853, which staged reenactments of a medieval tournament, a stag hunt, a steeplechase, and the Greek Olympic Games. This show was a large affair for more than 5 months, with a troupe of 150 performers and 100 animals, attended by 10,000 spectators (*New York Times*, March 25—September 2, 1853, *passim*).

Montreal Olympic Games

In British North America, 11 years before Franconi's "Principal *artistes*" were playing their indoor Olympian roles, an outdoor "Olympic Club" was formed in Montreal for "foot running" and other summer sports. This club was probably the first such club to include the adjective "Olympic" in its title, a practice that others have adopted since. (A notable American example is the Olympic Club of San Francisco, formed in 1860.) This Montreal club organized a 2-day festival held on August 28 and 29, 1844, which was described as the "Montreal Olympic Games." These Games included as many as 29 events, and were given the unprecedented patronage and support of the Governor-General Sir Charles Metcalf, and the City Corporation. Wise and Fisher, in their book, *Canada's Sporting Heroes* (1974), were certainly not reticent in their evaluations of the significance of these Montreal Olympic Games of 1844.

> Neither in Britain nor in the United States had anything quite like these Games yet been held. Toronto, a few years earlier, had held a number of field days; so had some American cities. *But in their size, organization, variety, and social and cultural diversity, Montreal's Olympics were unique; on the basis of them Montreal has a strong claim to be considered one of the birthplaces of modern organized sport.* (p. 13, emphasis added)

When the French language press in Quebec referred to "*Les Jeux Olympiques à Montreal*" in 1976, at the time the modern Games of the XXIst Olympiad were being celebrated in that city, one wonders how many of them were aware that their predecessors were using the same phrase 132 years earlier. However, the Montreal Olympic Games of 1844 remain a singular 19th-century event, not celebrated again either in annual form or as part of a series. But if we return to rural England 5 years later, in 1849, we find a more enduring and deliberate revival of the Olympic Games that endured for more than 40 years. Furthermore, a definite connection existed through them with Coubertin and the modern Olympic Games.

Much Wenlock Olympic Games

Dr. W.P. Brookes staged his annual "Olympic Games" in a valley near the village of Much Wenlock in Shropshire, where he had also founded the Much Wenlock Olympian Society. These Games included direct and obvious Olympic ceremony, pageantry, and symbolism. They included uniformed heralds, marching band, banners of local athletic associations, and hymn-singing children casting flower petals, as well as a processional route from two local inns to the "Olympian Fields" where banners with Greek inscriptions were raised and champions were crowned with laurel by women. The participants planted trees that had been "solemnly baptized with champagne" and dedicated to the Greek ministers in London and to the Greek Royal Family. In return, the King in Athens sent a large silver urn for the victor in the pentathlon. Other events included cricket (which was included in the program for the 1896 Olympic Games in Athens but then cancelled because no one entered), jumping, running, tilting at a ring from horseback, and "prizes for literary competitions and other artistic works" (Mandell, 1976, p. 32).

MacAloon (1981) informs us that Coubertin became aware of these "Olympic Games of Much Wenlock" in 1889.

> Coubertin's circular notice of the upcoming Paris Congress on Physical Training had been inserted in a number of English newspapers, and in response came a pamphlet from Dr. W.P. Brookes, a surgeon and magistrate, and founder and *archon* of the Wenlock "Olympic festival." Brookes offered Coubertin his fondest encouragements for the exposition Congress and invited the baron to visit Wenlock at his earliest convenience. Coubertin responded and in October 1890, journeyed to Shropshire to see its 40-year-old "Olympic Games." (p. 147)

Coubertin was "utterly bemused and delighted by what he saw" (MacAloon, 1981, p. 147), and subsequently provided the most detailed descriptions of the Much Wenlock Olympic Games (Coubertin, 1890, 1897). In his recent and perspicacious analysis of Coubertin as founder of the modern Olympic Games, David Young agrees that he was "entranced" by the Much Wenlock experience, and states, "Thus it seems that even the name of his Olympic Games, like their philosophy, came more from England than from Greece," and adds in a footnote, "Coubertin never set foot in Greece until he went to Athens to negotiate arrangements for the Greeks' 1896 Olympics; his knowledge of ancient Greek history, culture, and literature was superficial, at best" (Young, 1984, p. 59).

Greek Olympic Games

Mention has been made of Brookes's tenuous but valued connections with Greece; and in 1897 Coubertin referred to Brookes's unsuccessful earlier efforts to export his Olympic festival idea to Athens itself, suggesting that the proposal was declined by the Greek Government because Coubertin's own Paris Congress (1894) "had not met to recognize and revive the Olympian Games on a permanent and broader scale" (Coubertin, 1909, p. 65). MacAloon rightly suspects that "the real reason why this proposal was likely refused was that the Greeks already had their own 'Olympic Games' " (MacAloon, 1981, p. 150). In his 1909 book: *Une Campagne de Vingt-et-un Ans*, Coubertin later referred to Brookes's sense of internationalism, stating, "At the time of King Otho and Queen Amalia he had sent to Athens a fine cup destined to be offered to the winners of the footraces decorated with the name 'Olympics' which took place on the occasion of some national anniversary I don't any longer remember" (Coubertin, 1909, p. 53). MacAloon calls this a "frank misrepresentation," for "Coubertin was only too aware of the history of the pre-1896 Greek Olympics," induced by the fact that by this time Coubertin had his own personal axe to grind in his dealings with the Greeks who were striving to have Athens as a permanent home for the revived Olympic Games (MacAloon, 1981, pp. 150-151).

What were these rival pre-1896 Greek Olympics, known to the baron, to which Brookes had donated a trophy and received one in return? They were "Olympic Games," founded by a rich grain dealer named Evangelios Zappas, and celebrated in 1859, 1870, 1875, and 1888 or 1889 (confusion exists over the year of the last festival) at Athens.

The 1859 Games were held in a flat city square, Place Louis, not far from Omonoia, because no stadium was available. Among the events included were sprint and distance races appropriately called *diaulos* and *dolichos*, jumps, discus and javelin throws, rope climbing, and wrestling. Competitors took an oath that they would not cheat or foul their opponents. Olive wreaths, money, and other prizes were distributed by the King before an enthusiastic but disorderly crowd that had to be vigorously controlled by police and soldiers. In his 1973 history of the modern Olympic Games, Messinesi describes these Games as "the first Olympic Games of the modern era" (p. 53).

Young is of the opinion that "the 1870 Athens Olympics was the most modern and sophisticated that the world had seen at that time," with events that were common to the ancient Greeks as well as to more modern ones and gymnastic contests. They were celebrated on the site of the ancient Panathenaic stadium, enjoyed by 30,000 spectators, and widely praised. The 1875 Games were a less successful affair, with a much smaller crowd of spectators, and among them was a critical and biased eyewitness named John Mahaffy, whom Young credits with having "founded the academic myth of ancient Greek amateurism, on which other amateur partisans relied" (Young, 1984, pp. 30-56). Mahaffy's satirical account appeared in the *Macmillan's Magazine* of 1875 (Mahaffy, 1876).

Like MacAloon, Young also suspects Coubertin's alleged amnesia and indifference to these four 19th-century Athens Olympic Games, accusing him of intentionally wrapping them in darkness. He believes, too, that these are "the pre-Coubertin modern Olympic Games which have had the most historical impact on our own world" (Young, 1984, p. 28). For somewhat different reasons and with less elaboration, his view is shared by Messinesi (1973).

> Whereas they had next to no, or entirely no, effect on the success of the 1896 Athens Olympic I Games, it is interesting to note that the regulations elaborated for them, as also the program of events, were somewhat similar to those adopted thirty-seven years later for the modern Olympic Games, and must have had a paramount influence on the first and subsequent Olympic Games. (p. 53)

To Messinesi, in fact, these pre-1896 Games in Athens were "the most note-worthy revival in the form of 'Olympic Games,'" even while he admits that "from 1850 onward athletic games were being organized in many countries of Europe and the United States" (pp. 52-53).

British Olympic Athletic Festivals

Although none of the researchers so far has mentioned them, another series of four "Olympic festivals" in "mid-Victorian England" took place between the first (1859) and second (1870) Olympic Games in Athens, which Rees (1977) has brought to our attention. He tells us that the Olympic athletic festivals held in Britain between 1862 and 1867 were the "most important and the most well-documented." This statement suggests that similar festivals were held in other years, and that these festivals "upheld and encouraged the ideals of true amateurism from the beginning" (p. 21). The 1862 Olympic festival was held at the Mount Vernon Parade Ground in Liverpool on June 14, 1862, before an estimated crowd of between 7,000 and 10,000 people, "including the elite of the neighborhood" (p. 22). Two "muscular Christians" who were very actively involved with the planning and organization were philanthropist Charles Pierre Melly, president of the Liverpool Athletic Club, and John Mulley, honorary secretary of the Club. After a Grand Procession of competitors led by a military band, a program of 22 events was featured. Apart from running, walking, jumping, throwing, and wrestling events, contests in broadsword, sabre, and bayonet, as well as in boxing, gymnastics, Indian club, and dumbbell exercises were held. More than 200 athletes competed for gold, silver, or bronze medals, and the champion's Gold Medal was presented by His Worship the Mayor to "the most successful competitor of the day" (p. 22). Yet another interesting feature of this festival was the establishment of a prize essay competition in which the winner was awarded a gold medal and for which more than 50 entries were submitted to the Olympic Committee. The topic chosen for the essayists was *Mens Sana in Corpore Sano* (i.e., "A sound mind in a sound body").

The Olympic festival of 1863 was reported as even more successful, attracting a crowd estimated at between 12,000 and 15,000 spectators

(3,000 of them seated). The program now included a swimming race from New Brighton to the Prince's Pier. Although the competitors at the previous festival were mainly from the Liverpool area, because "its fame soon spread," more than half of the entries in 1863 were "from other parts of the country" (Rees, 1977, p. 22). Unfortunately, because the Mount Vernon Parade Ground was no longer available in 1864, having been sold as building lots, the Liverpool Athletic Club selected the less exclusive Zoological Gardens as the site for its third festival, a choice that was not popular and was criticized in the press. The presence of betting men in the grounds, being allowed "to carry on their nefarious craft," was particularly abhorred by some (p. 23). No festival was held in 1865, possibly because Charles Melley and John Mulley were more preoccupied with the new Liverpool Gymnasium that opened that year. Subsequent Olympic festivals were organized by the Athletic Society of Great Britain. The first Olympic festival sponsored by the Society was actually held in Llandudno, North Wales, in 1866, but the following year it returned to Liverpool, where the last and greatest of these mid-Victorian Olympic festivals was held at the new venue of Sheil Park. The program of events had been so greatly increased that the festival of 1867 extended over 3 days. A huge crowd was in attendance throughout, and it was reported that "the crush was so great that on the final day the barriers broke and the crowd surged into the enclosure in front of the stands, to the great annoyance of the ladies" (p. 23). In fact, Rees hypothesizes that these Olympic festivals came to an end because "the respectable classes withdrew their support" (p. 23).

These urban Liverpool Olympics, together with the rural Much Wenlock variety, reflected in part the English victorian fascination with the world of ancient Greece; the paramount position of Classics in the Public Schools' curriculum was one obvious indication. Other manifestations were also apparent. Several studies have analyzed this relationship between an ancient and modern civilization and culture (particularly as the Victorians have been comprehensively placed under the microscope in recent years), but Richard Jenkyns in his *The Victorians and Ancient Greece* (1980) establishes it fully in a scholarly way, and includes a section on athletics (pp. 210-226). These two worlds, centuries apart, invited analogies that 19th-century English gentlemen were quick to make. Indeed, such comparisons were not only fostered, but Greek history could even be reinterpreted in a Victorian mold. In fact, it has been cogently argued that this interpretation occurred in the process that led to Coubertin's eventual founding of the modern Olympic Games (Young, 1981).

Scottish Highland Games

Yet another significant athletic influence came from 19th-century Britain, originating not in England, but across the northern border in Scotland, again with some Classical analogies being drawn. At those "Olympic

Games" in British North America in 1844, members of the Montreal Olympic Club won most of the track and field events, although they were hard pressed by Scottish competitors from the 93rd Highlanders regiment. Track and field events have always been the core of any Olympic program, and no race did more to spread track and field events throughout the world in the form of an organized sport competition or festival than did the Scots with their Highland Games. This traditional Scottish custom became common and popular in Australia, Britain, Canada, New Zealand, South Africa, and the United States—sometimes before reported crowds of between 20,000 or 30,000 people—long before the first modern Olympic Games of 1896 (or even some earlier pseudo-Olympics). One is not referring here to four occasions in one city, such as in Athens or Liverpool, but literally *hundreds* of such Highland Games in many cities, towns, and villages around the world (see, for example: Berthoff, 1953; Cox, 1969; Diem, 1960; Donaldson, 1966; Lindsay, 1969; Webster, 1973).

E. Norman Gardiner—before dealing with the ancient Olympic festival in his epic work, *Athletics of the Ancient World* (1930)—wrote about Homeric sports and stated that "The nearest parallel to them is to be found in the sports of the Highland Clans, but it is possible that, if we knew more, other parallels might be found whenever a similar state of society has existed" (p. 27). In the modern world, many parallels have inevitably been drawn between the Olympic Games and the Highland Games. But Scots have not always found them to be flattering. As early as 1901, in his classic book, *Men of Muscle and the Highland Games of Scotland*, Donaldson wrote favorably of the ancient Greek Olympic Games, and yet was quite adamant that

> No part of the great competition had the remotest similitude to Scottish Highland Games, which, although on a much smaller scale than the meetings among the Greeks, are more romantic and pleasing to the Scotsman in all climes than a dozen Olympic Games, even if they were instituted by Hercules in honour of Jupiter. (pp. 1-2)

Much more recently, in a 1976 history of the Olympic Games, another Scot stated that the development of sport in the mid-19th century English public schools and the Highland Games boom of the same period "had a more direct influence than did that of the ancient Games upon the program of the 1896 Games" (Killanin & Rodda, 1976, p. 90). He went on further to state,

> Immigrant Scots carried to the United States an intact athletics culture, and the first New World highland games were held in Boston in 1853. Thus, when Coubertin visited the United States forty years later, he unwittingly came face to face with a Celtic culture. The final Olympic track-and-field program directly reflected Coubertin's experience in England and the United States. (p. 90)

Although one can agree with the last sentence, the second one is fanciful, and the first one is inaccurate. The Boston Caledonian Games of 1853 were *not* the first in the New World, for Highland Games were celebrated in British North America in Glengarry (1819), Prince Edward Island (1838), Lancaster (1840), Toronto (1847) and Sydney, N.S. (1848) before this date (Redmond, 1982, pp. 160-166). It is difficult to imagine that Coubertin, visiting the "melting pot" of the United States—where for example, we are told that in 1890 "the Scottish nationality ranks among the smallest" in the population of New York City (Wilson, 1890, p. 513)—came "face to face with a Celtic culture," unless of course he attended one of the many Caledonian Games meetings there, but this is not indicated. A more credible analysis was offered earlier by John Rafferty in his book review of *The Caledonian Games in Nineteenth-Century America* (Redmond, 1971):

> Some might think it significant that when the modern Olympic Games were established in Athens in 1896 competitors from the United States won the long jump, the hop, step and jump, the shot-put, the pole vault and the high jump, indeed all the Caledonian Games events except the hammer throw. The reason for that omission was that there was no hammer throw in the first Olympic Games. It was introduced in 1900 and the States won it then. (p. 2)

Most people would agree that the Olympic Games and the Scottish Highland Games have diverged significantly in this century. The Olympic Games have become a gargantuan enterprise, beset with many complex problems and cries for reform, whereas the Highland Games festival has retained much more of its traditional character despite encountering some modern problems as well. In a letter to the *Canadian Magazine* of January 3, 1976, a reader praised the Highland Games, this Scottish "World festival," and decried the "huge debt" and fanfare surrounding the Montreal Olympic Games of 1976 (p. 27). Although comparisons may well be odious at times, given the spectacular international success of Scottish Highland Games in both the 19th and 20th centuries and their internationally acknowledged role in the spread of track and field events, the many attempts to incorporate them into Olympic history are understandable. Young (1984) is the most recent Olympic author to state that Scotland's importance has been neglected and welcome the fact that the Highland Games "are beginning to receive proper historical recognition" (pp. 16-17). In that respect we can all enjoy Ann Donaldson's recent book on the Scottish Highland Games in the United States (Donaldson, 1986).

The Anglo-Saxon Olympiad

Also in Britain, and again before the Baron's Olympic Games were underway, an Englishman named J. Astley Cooper endeavored to promote an "Anglo-Saxon Olympiad." This he advocated first in an article in the *Greater Britain* magazine, followed by a letter to *The Times* newspaper

(October 30, 1891) and pursued further in articles entitled "An Anglo-Saxon Olympiad" and "The Pan-Brittanic Gathering" in the *Nineteenth Century* magazine (September, 1892; July 1893). While Cooper pontificated in this fashion, the Olympic Club of San Francisco theatrically celebrated an elaborate "Revival of the Ancient Greco-Roman Games" in April, 1893. Coubertin himself visited the Olympic Club on his Californian tour in the fall of that year (Young, 1984, p. 181). But Cooper had a problem in deciding who belonged to the Anglo-Saxon race, although he was firm in his intention that only "the flower of the Race" would compete (Mandell, 1976, pp. 32-33). His rather convoluted proposals for a unifying scheme involving three sections—industrial, intellectual, and athletic—among English-speaking nations, including the United States, stimulated debate and interest, but floundered in the wake of Coubertin's progress toward his more dramatic and international festival (Redmond, 1978, p. 5). For a personal postmortem on Cooper's unrealized projects, see his article entitled "The Olympic Games: What Has Been Done and What Remains to be Done" (1908), published in *Nineteenth Century*, in which he described the Athens Games of 1896 as "a hybrid, babel gathering" (p. 1011).

From Cooper's unrealized proposal stemmed an "Inter-Empire Sports Meeting" in 1911, several track and field contests between British Empire and United States teams immediately following the Olympic Games of 1920, 1924, and 1928, and eventually the first British Empire Games at Hamilton, Canada, in 1930 (Agbogun, 1970). Thirteen of these Games featuring the nations of the British Commonwealth have been celebrated to date.

Conclusion

Clearly, from Olympic literature as well as from more general histories of sport (a few of which have been indicated here), the modern Olympic Games are exactly that—*modern*. Yet too often a tendency has been to compare them only, and usually unfavorably, with the ancient Greek Games at Olympia. Although "a historical continuity between ancient and modern Olympism is an established fact," as Roditchenko (1976) stated, "Certain scholars tend to hyperbolize the importance of ancient social patterns of Olympism for the modern society" (p. 3). Despite the tendency to leap backwards from 1896 to ancient Greece, recently completed and ongoing research into the various "Olympic Games" of the 19th century strongly suggests that when Coubertin's Olympics emerged they had far more in common with these pseudo-Olympics of the 19th century than they ever did with the Games held at Olympia some 2,000 years earlier. In his keynote address at the 1984 Olympic Scientific Congress, Mandell suggested that it was perhaps time to "dismiss the connection" between the modern and ancient Olympic Games (Mandell, 1984).

Coubertin's knowledge of certain pseudo-Olympics and proposals for revival and their influence upon him are coming to light. The great stress that had been laid upon the undoubted influence of English public schools' athleticism upon Coubertin—*Tom Brown's Schooldays* and all that—has unfortunately overwhelmed some other influences of the times in this new world born of the Industrial Revolution.

One is reminded of that great Christian, William Blake (1757-1827), who saw and worried about this unprecedented world of factories coming, and asked in the Preface to *Milton* (Lister, 1968):

> And was Jerusalem builded here
> Among these dark satanic mills?
> (p. 105)

We can ask in similar fashion, "And was Olympia recreated here?" The honest answer must be "no." Coubertin deserves the accolades for his determined accomplishment in an imperfect world; however, as Sir Roger Bannister (1980) emphasized by quoting another famous poet, Robert Browning: "A man's reach must exceed his grasp or what's a heaven for." As we have seen, many others before Coubertin were also reaching for an Olympic ideal, with varying amounts of success. They deserve the place that is now beginning to be found for them in the history of the revival of the modern Olympic Games; their recognition is a significant prologue to Coubertin's monumental achievement.

References

Agbogun, J.B. (1970). *A history of the British Commonwealth Games, 1930-1966.* Unpublished master's thesis, University of Alberta, Edmonton.

Arlott, J. (Ed.). (1975). *The Oxford companion to sports & games.* London: Oxford University Press.

Bannister, R. (1980, February). *The Olympic Games: Past, present and future.* Address given at the Olympic Symposium at Skidmore College, Saratoga Springs, NY.

Bendikson, L. (1932). Forgotten Olympics of King James's reign: How Captain Dover encouraged English sports. *Game and Gossip, 10*(5), 7-8, 54.

Berthoff, R.T. (1953). *British immigrants in industrial America.* Cambridge: Harvard University Press.

Brailsford, D. (1969). *Sport and society: Elizabeth to Anne.* Cambridge: Harvard University Press.

Burns, F. (1981). *Heigh for Cotswold! A history of Robert Dover's Olympick Games.* Chipping Camden: Robert Dover's Games Society.

Canadian Magazine. (1976, January 3). Letter to the editor, p. 27.

Cooper, J.A. (1892, September). An Anglo-Saxon Olympiad. *The Nineteenth Century,* p. 32.

Cooper, J.A. (1893, July). The pan-Britannic gathering. *The Nineteenth Century*, p. 24.

Cooper, J.A. (1908, June). The Olympic Games: What has been done and what remains to be done. *The Nineteenth Century*, p. 63.

Coubertin, P. de (1909). *Le Batailles de l'education physique: Une campagne de vingt-et-uns ans (1887-1908)*. Paris: Librairie de L'Education Physique.

Cox, A.E. (1969). *A history of sports in Canada, 1868-1900*. Unpublished doctoral dissertation, University of Alberta, Edmonton.

Diem, C. (1960). *Welt Geschichte des Sports und der Leiberserziehung* [World history of sports and physical education]. Stuttgart: J.G. Cotta'sche Buch.

Donaldson, A. (1986). *The Scottish Highland Games in the United States*. Gretna, LA: Pelican.

Donaldson, G. (1901). *Men of muscle and the highland games of Scotland, with brief biographies of the leading athletes of the last fifty years, with portraits*. Glasgow: Carter and Pratt.

Donaldson, G. (1966). *The Scots overseas*. London: Robert Hale.

Gardiner, E.N. (1930). *Athletics of the ancient world*. Oxford: Clarendon Press.

Jenkyns, R. (1980). *The Victorians and ancient Greece*. Cambridge, MA: Harvard University Press.

Killanin, Lord, & Rodda, J. (Eds.). (1976). *The Olympic Games: 80 years of people, events and records*. Don Mills, Ontario: Collier MacMillan Canada.

Lindsay, P.L. (1969). *A history of sport in Canada, 1807-1867*. Unpublished doctoral dissertation, University of Alberta, Edmonton.

Lister, R. (1968). *William Blake*. London: G. Bell.

MacAloon, J.J. (1981). *This great symbol: Pierre de Coubertin and the origins of the modern Olympic Games*. Chicago: University of Chicago Press.

Mahaffy, J.P. (1876). The Olympic Games at Athens in 1875. *Macmillan's Magazine*, **32**, 325-327.

Mandell, R.D. (1976). *The first modern Olympics*. Berkeley: University of California Press.

Mandell, R. (1984, July). *The Olympic Games: Past, present, and future*. Paper presented at the Olympic Scientific Congress, Eugene, OR.

Messinesi, X.L. (1973). *A branch of wild olive: The Olympic Movement and the ancient and modern Olympic Games*. New York: Exposition Press.

New York Times. (March 25, 1853 to September 2, 1853.)

Rafferty, J. (December 18, 1971). Review of *The Caledonian games in nineteenth-century America*. *The Scotsman*, p. 2.

Redmond, G. (1971). *The Caledonian games in nineteenth-century America*. Rutherford, NJ: Fairleigh Dickinson University Press.

Redmond, G. (1978). A brief history of the Commonwealth Games. In G. Redmond (Ed.), *Edmonton '78: The official pictorial record of the XI Commonwealth Games* (pp. 5-26). Edmonton, Alberta: Executive Sport Publications.

Redmond, G. (1982). *The sporting Scots of Nineteenth-Century Canada.* London and Toronto: Associated University Presses.

Rees, R. (1977, January). The Olympic festivals of mid-Victorian England. *Olympic Review*, pp. 21-23.

Robbins, A.F. (1908, August 22). Olympic Games in England. *Notes and Queries*, p. 147.

Roditchenko, V.S. (1976, July). *A political-philosophical analysis of Olympism.* Paper presented at the International Congress of Physical Activity Sciences, Quebec City.

Ruhl, J.K. (1975). *Die "Olympischen Spiele" Robert Dover* [Robert Dover, The "Olympic Games"]. Heidelberg: Carl Winter Universitätsverlag.

Ruhl, J.K. (1985). The "Olympic Games" of Robert Dover, 1612-1984. In N. Müller & J.K. Ruhl (Eds.), *Olympic Scientific Congress 1984 official report: Sport history* (pp. 192-203). Nierderhausen: Schors-Verlag.

Svahn, A. (1980). "Olympic Games" in Sweden 1834. *ICSPE Review*, **3**, 35-36.

Webster, D. (1973). *Scottish highland games.* Edinburgh: Reprographia.

Wilson, J.L. (1890, June 28; July 5). The foreign element in New York City: The Scotch. *Harper's Weekly*, pp. 513-516, 522.

Wise, S.F., & Fisher, D. (1974). *Canada's sporting heroes: Their lives and times.* Don Mills Ontario: General Publishing.

Young, D.C. (1984). *The Olympic myth of Greek amateur athletics.* Chicago: Ares Publishers.

Zeigler, E.F. (Ed.). (1979). *History of physical education and sport.* Englewood-Cliffs, NJ: Prentice-Hall.

Appendix

A Chronology of "Pseudo-Olympics" Before 1896 (Allusions, Analogies, Proposals, and Revivals)

1612?	Robert Dover's Cotswold "Olympick Games," lasted intermittently until 1852 (a "third phase," from 1951, now in process). Also reported that, "elsewhere in England in the 17th Century there were athletic festivals called "Olympics."

(Cont.)

1679   "Hampton Court Olympics," England.

1819   (to date). St. Fillans, Scotland. "Highland Games" of Gaelic origin, revived, then spread by Scottish emigration. Very popular in the 19th Century—and still celebrated today—in Australia, Britain, Canada, New Zealand, South Africa, and the United States. Often compared to the Olympics.

1830s   "Greek Competitions" in the Grand Duchy of Poznan.

1834   "Olympic Games" in Ramlösa (Sweden).

1836   Second "Olympic Games" in Ramlösa (Sweden).

1844   Montreal "Olympic Games," in British North America (later Canada).

1849   (And then "for more than forty years")—Dr. W.P. Brookes' Olympic Games near the village of Much Wenlock in Shropshire (England).

1853   Franconi's Hippodrome in New York City (U.S.A.) featured "many of the most attractive games of ancient Greece and Rome."

1859   First Zappeion featuring Olympic Games at Athens (Greece), by Evangelios Zappas.

1862   First Olympic festival in Liverpool (England) organized by Liverpool Athletic Club.

1863   Second Olympic festival in Liverpool, organized by Liverpool Athletic Club.

1864   Third Olympic festival in Liverpool, organized by Liverpool Athletic Club.

1866   First Olympic festival in Llandudno (Wales), organized by Athletic Society of Great Britain.

1867   Second Olympic festival in Liverpool, organized by Athletic Society of Great Britain.

1870   Second Olympic Games at Athens (Zappas had died in 1865).

1870s   "Olympic Games" in Wrzesnia (Poland).

1875   Third Olympic Games at Athens.

1888   Fourth Olympic Games at Athens.

1892   J. Astley Cooper, of England, main proponent of an "Anglo-Saxon Olympiad" or "Pan-Britannic Gathering." Unsuccessful, but believed by many to be origin of present Commonwealth Games, first celebrated as the "British Empire Games" in Canada, 1930, and still in progress.

1893   "Revival of the Ancient Greco-Roman Games" by the Olympic Club of San Francisco (U.S.A.).

6

The Genesis of the Modern Olympic Games

John A. Lucas

The modern Olympic Games are among the fastest growing and most important social phenomenon of our times. Aside from religion, world sport represents the most comprehensive organization in social spheres. The Olympic Movement has become a part of modern civilization. Over 100 nations of the world regularly participate in these quadrennial games.

Portrait of the Baron

Pierre Fredy, Baron of Coubertin, promoter and organizer of the modern Olympic Games, was born in Paris, January 1, 1863 and died in Geneva on September 2, 1937 at the age of 74 years. In male descent, one can

Originally published in *A History of Sport and Physical Education to 1900* (pp. 331-340), edited by Earle F. Zeigler, 1973, Champaign, IL: Stipes; and also appearing in *Olympism* (pp. 22-32) edited by Jeffrey Segrave and Donald Chu, 1981, Champaign, IL: Human Kinetics. Reprinted by permission.

trace his genealogy back five centuries to the Roman Fredi family and to a later French aristocracy in the region of Havre (Diem, 1952, p. 44). His French ancestors were consistently people of wealth and accomplishment. Only 7 years of age at the outbreak of the Franco-Prussi Prussian War [sic], the young Coubertin was reared in a household that felt they and the nation had been humiliated by Prussia's ludicrously easy victory over an effeminate, nonsporting, excessively intellectual French population; "it was a decadence which existed only within themselves" (Coubertin, 1918/1966, p. 47).

The brilliantly educated Coubertin became convinced that the classic French pedagogy of his day did not fit modern conditions. The aristocratic and impressionable youth first came in contact with a phase of English society in 1875 at the age of 12. He had read a French translation of Thomas Hughes's English classic, *Tom Brown's School Days at Rugby*. The distorted image of vigorous English youths, future leaders of the pervasive and powerful British Empire, disporting endlessly on the verdant English athletic fields was to profoundly influence the young baron throughout his long life. He made a dozen trips to England between 1883 and 1887 in order to acquaint himself more intimately with the British sporting philosophy of the famed English public schools and with "a desire to attach my name to a great pedagogical reform" (Coubertin, 1908, p. 2).

The Influence
of Dr. Thomas Arnold

The figure of Dr. Thomas Arnold, headmaster of the Rugby school from 1828 to 1842, is one of the most important and least understood personalities in the evolution of the modern Olympic Games. Dr. Arnold was the single most important influence on the life and thought of Pierre de Coubertin. The Baron's philosophical approach to the many facets of his life combined the "wholeness" of the Grecian spirit of antiquity with the extreme 19th-century moralism of Thomas Arnold. Coubertin's concept of Grecian thought, exemplified in the trinity of "character, intellect, and body," was inextricably fused with the image of disciplined austerity and sportsmanship of the English Rugby School. The anglophilic Coubertin was convinced that the vigor, wealth, and power of Great Britain were due primarily to its unique system of public education.

The Reverend Thomas Arnold, D.D., was the greatest, if not the first of the great headmasters. Arnold entrusted the government of the school to the senior boys and the senior boys added a fourth item to Arnold's trio of ideals ("first, religious and moral principle; secondly, gentlemanly conduct; thirdly, intellectual ability," and in that order of importance), placing it perhaps first on the list—namely, athletic proficiency secured through compulsory organized games.

Baron Pierre de Coubertin was convinced that the sports-centered English public school system of the late 19th century was the rock upon which the vast and majestic British Empire rested. In the recondite scholarship of Dr. Arnold and in the ensuing trend toward manly sport at Rugby and in England, Coubertin saw a catharsis, not only for the English but for Frenchmen and eventually all mankind. The genius of Arnold had sown the seed. The genius of Coubertin responded. The latter's life-long devotion to the Hellenic trinity of body, mind, and spirit, coupled with a compelling faith in the character-building qualities of English sport education, formed the rationale for his dream of universal amateur athletics. The guiding principle of this Olympic Movement, called "Olympism," was viewed by its creator as a pervasive religion, a cult of beauty, and an instrument for world peace. The singular dedication of the idealistic Frenchman and those of his associates resulted in one of the most comprehensive organizations in social spheres—the international Olympic Movement. Had Thomas Arnold lived to see the first modern Olympic Games in 1896, he would have, I think, beamed his approval.

The Formative Years of the International Olympic Movement

International competitive sport was not widespread prior to 1890, this despite the rapidly increasing national interests in sport and physical education. The first international congress for the promotion of physical education was held in Paris, June 8 to 15, 1889, in connection with the Universal Exposition. Its organizer and general-secretary was Pierre de Coubertin, and the presiding officer was Jules Simon, President of France. In the fall of that same year the famous Boston "Physical Training Conference" drew 34 speakers from America and the Continent. Among the 16 medical doctors, one general, one earl, two barons, one doctor of law, and one doctor of philosophy, was the youthful Baron de Coubertin. He spoke eloquently of the magnanimity of Thomas Arnold, "the greatest of modern teachers." He emphasized that from a moral and social point of view, no system stands higher than that of English athletic sports, and it should be carefully studied by nations of the Western world.

The French Third Republic had been struggling valiantly for stability as well as change since the disastrous days of 1870 to 1871. The revival of French athletics and the introduction of primitive physical education in the school system began modestly in the late 1880s. The precocious Pierre de Coubertin, despite his noble birth, was an ardent supporter of the French republican government and in turn received strong support for school and club athletics throughout France. From M. Coubertin's busy pen came directions, game manuals, "pleadings, monitions, and trumpet-call." In a short few years, French physical education and sports had begun to flourish. Ellery H. Clark (1896), Athens Olympic champion, was "astonished" to find athletic and rowing clubs springing up in abundance. "Passing through Paris on our way home, we noticed advertised in one of the sporting papers five or six different, athletic meetings on one day alone" (p. 21). It was a fitting tribute to a small tireless group of French educators and friends of Baron Coubertin. France, "the alluvium of ages and peoples, the fertile seedplot of generous ideas," had at last emerged as a nation where physical education and athletics began to take their proper place. However, Coubertin realized that to give them a really national popularity and high degree of skill, a thoroughly international outlook was needed. It was to this end that the next years 1892 to 1896 were devoted.

The Critical Years

The Baron de Coubertin was reaching the zenith of his energy, ambition, and vision. He knew exactly what he wanted. Not yet 30 years old, he realized that some form of internationalization was needed to "purify" sport, not only in France, but throughout the world. Ancient Greek history had occupied his study and thought for some years. He had often dreamed of Olympia with its symbolic harmony of body and mind.

French sporting dignitaries arrived at the old Sorbonne on November 25, 1892. Ostensibly, the meeting was held to celebrate the remarkable progress of the French athletic club system. In reality, Coubertin saw beyond this and planned secretly to make the Sorbonne the cradle for his "baby," the reestablishment of the ancient Olympic Games on an international basis. In his *Memoires Olympiques* (1931) the Baron frankly admitted, "Le bébé avait été substitué" (p. 8). Impressive speeches by George Bourdan and Jules Jusserand were delivered. Pierre de Coubertin completed the historic cycle with "Les exercises physiques dans le monde moderne." He had calculated the termination of his expose with a dramatic resolution proclaiming the rebirth of the Olympic Games. The dramatic conclusion of Coubertin's speech was met with great applause and an abysmal lack of understanding. His plan was merely a symbolic narrative, beautiful and idealistic, but no more. "There was a total lack of comprehension," sighed the young Baron. He retreated as gracefully as possible. The public was unprepared. Coubertin, writing to his American friend Bill Henry (1948) many years later, scoffed at the idea that "Olympism" was "in the air" during the period of the 1890s. "It was born artificially," he wrote (p. 22). Coubertin had conceded haste and during the winter of 1892 to 1893 "we had to pitch our tune in a lower key." He devoted the next 3 years to travel, speech-making, and a study of his grandiose plan. His second trip to America in the fall of 1893 took him to the universities of California, Stanford, Tulane, and Princeton.

On November 27, 1893, at the University Club in New York City, persons "judged the most qualified to assist in our enterprise" were invited. Representatives of Harvard, Yale, Princeton, and Columbia were present. Coubertin attempted to convince them that the idea of an Olympian games was not a dream. However, he was disillusioned because the "secret war between the universities and the A.A.U." convinced him that the conception of an international Olympic sporting festival was still foreign to American ideas.

The Great Camouflage of 1894—
The Congress at the Sorbonne

The unifying ability of Pierre de Coubertin had been sorely missed in France during his 4 months' absence. The amateur athletic clubs were in turmoil. Coubertin's impressive January, 1894 circulars, sent to all European sporting clubs and calling for a world congress of sportsmen, had received "a very irregular and scattered response." The inimitable Coubertin realized the status of his pet project was precarious. He reacted in characteristic fashion and worked very hard toward the successful realization of the June congress. The main concern of the Paris meeting was ostensibly the problem of amateur athletics. Members of the aristocracy and even royalty accompanied sporting leaders to the second Sorbonne meeting. Seventy-nine delegates, representing world sporting societies and academic institutions, sat through the 8-day conference (Lucas, 1962, pp. 99, 176-178).

The congress proved to be a more brilliant affair than anyone had anticipated. The week was enlivened by receptions, banquets, athletic exhibitions in the Bois du Bologne, and "felicitous speech making" (Shaw, 1894, p. 645). The *New York Times* said there were 3,000 people present. Some of France's most brilliant men of letters delivered speeches "enflamed in idealism." The magnificence of the Sorbonne, recently adorned with the artistry of the brilliant Puvis de Chavannes, visibly moved the audience. It was as the Baron de Coubertin had hoped and planned. The final portion of the opening day program was the singing of the "Hymne à Apollon," recently discovered among the excavations at Delphi. This fragment of Greek music had been deciphered and transposed by Professor Reinach and sung by a Mme. Remacle. A choral group accompanying the soloist was under the direction of the famous composer-conductor Gabriel Faure. It was impressive; the audience had been "softened" and the stage was set.

The International Athletic Congress had split into two committees: one to discuss the perplexing problem of amateurism and professionalism (a serious matter even in the 19th century!), the other to consider the revival of the Olympic Games. Elaborate resolutions regarding amateurism plus a proposal that "international sport competition should be held every fourth year on the lines of the Greek Games" were forwarded. Coubertin had done his work well and in a spirit of "antique eurythmie," all motions were carried unanimously. Coubertin's "baby," the renaissance of the Olympic Games, had indeed become a near reality.

The Genesis of the Modern Games

The 10th proposal on the agenda of the congress, the idea of an international Olympic committee, was accepted without serious opposition. Twelve members, selected by Coubertin, won unanimous approval. Demetrius Bikeles, probably the best known man of letters in Greece, was chosen president of the "Comité," while Coubertin was pleased with his election to secretary-general as it was "the mainspring in the administration of the C.I.O."

The fundamental basis of the IOC, that of absolute independence for each member, was laid that day and has not changed to the present day. It was essential that this first group of 15 men value internationalism above nationalism. Members of the 1894 Committee (and all subsequent members) were not representatives of their respective countries to the IOC. Rather, they were members of the IOC to the nations of the world. A country does not elect members to the Committee. The Committee chooses members from the country. "It took orders from no one," affirmed the Baron. No person or faction, thinking differently from the main body, was capable of gaining admittance. "The very fact that this Committee is self-recruiting makes it immune to all political interference, and it is not swayed by intense nationalism" (Coubertin, 1925/1951, p. 15).

Coubertin was fully aware that his system of a self-perpetuating committee would be criticized. To him, public interference with Olympic sports organizations was fatal. He felt that the best way to serve democracy did not always consist in a wholesale surrender to the electoral system; had the IOC been chosen on the same principles as other governing bodies, it would have disappeared or been subject to endless and debilitating bickering.

There seemed practical reasons for Coubertin's method of recruiting IOC members. Financially independent and without known political connections, their viewpoint was capable of greater internationalism. They could be counted on to support whatever was for the interest of the Olympic Movement, even against their own country. In summary, their first allegiance was to a principle and an idea—The Olympic Idea.

The choice of Athens for the new world Games was, in a sense, unfortunate. Greece was in political and military turmoil, and utterly bankrupt. Coubertin traveled to Athens in the fall of 1894 and in his movements about the city was convinced that the people zealously desired the Games. Crown Prince Konstantine, handsome and vigorous, took full command of the Games Committee. Merchants, Greek aristocrats, and colonists from Marseilles, Alexandria, and London responded enthusiastically and $100,000 was raised. An additional $390,000 was donated by the Alexandrian merchant, George Averoff. The ancient stadium was rebuilt in native white marble, and the city felt the approach of the great event. Every house was decorated with flowers and flags. A triumphal arch was erected on the theatre square, myriads of lanterns lined and spanned the streets, bearing the letters "O.A." ("Olympiakoi Agones"—Olympic Games). It was a glorious fortnight.

The first Olympic Games began on Sunday, April 5, 1896. That year by chance, the Orthodox Easter and the Catholic Easter coincided. More important to the success of the Games, it was the 75th anniversary of the Greek War of Independence (1821 to 1829). The 33-year-old Baron saw a life-dream fulfilled. The years ahead were filled with crisis and a halting progress. On this day, however, he was radiant with joy.

The Conception of Modern International Olympism

The Olymic Idea was and is a grand attempt to fuse academic training with moral and physical education. The catalyst would be sport. It always remained the "raison d'être" of Pierre de Coubertin's elaborate plan of educational reform. He coined the word "Olympism" to refer to his interpretation of the amateur code. There are three main characteristics of Olympism. All honestly interpreted views of the purposes of the Olympic Movement may be subsumed under "religion first, then peace, and finally beauty." The whole movement embraces sport under the influence of religion, literature, art, and an "international education on the broadest physical and mental lines" (Cook, 1906, p. 11).

The Religion of Olympism

Olympism as conceived by Coubertin stands on the premise that no philosophy and no religion preaches loftier sentiments than those included in "pure" amateur athletic competition and the amateur code. The origin of Olympism lies in the love of athletic training and competition displayed by the pre-Hellenistic Greeks. From earliest times, athletic games had been associated with religious festivals. The intimacy of sport and religion in these antique games gave them a wonderful vitality. Coubertin attempted to reincarnate wholly this verve and reverence, despite the passage of 15 centuries.

The Peace of Olympism

The hope for world peace through international Olympic competition is an essential element of Olympism. Coubertin was often known to display feelings and actions not unlike the romanticism of an earlier period.

His classical bent toward thought, harmony, and beauty may have found expression in his unbounded enthusiasm for a better mankind. He was convinced that "the Olympic Games will be a potent, if indirect factor in securing universal peace" (Coubertin, 1896, p. 39).

The Beauty of Olympism

Coubertin had hoped to develop interest in the Fine Arts at the Olympic Games. Artistic beauty was epitomized in the essential beauty of man's body, mind, and spirit. Pierre de Coubertin looked upon the Olympic athlete with a heroic outlook. The Greeks could not think any physical form beautiful unless it was healthy. This Greek cult of beauty was essentially that taken by Coubertin. "Without athletics, Greek art and the Greek conception of beauty would have been inconceivable" (Hyde, 1921, p. 57). The Greek Olympics included manliness, rhythm, art, beauty, and balance. The French Baron hoped these things would be included in the modern Games.

The Olympic Idea and the Olympic Ideal

Olympism remains a central expression of a Greek idea that the body of man has a glory as well as his intellect and spirit. It encompasses an understanding that the body and mind should alike be disciplined. It is by the harmonious discipline of body that men may be led to understand, as Socrates said, his chief and proper concern: knowledge of himself and of the right way to live. All of us who love beauty, peace, athletics, who have done no "impiety or sacrilege," who believe in fair play, are advocates of Olympism, and "are Greeks in the highest sense" (Horton, 1896, p. 266).

The Age of Progress

The years 1883 to 1896 represent a segment of history encompassing the greatest material gain and social progress in modern Western civilization. The revival of the Olympic Games during this period represents a logical manifestation of this growing trend of optimism. Had Baron de Coubertin never been born, some other form of universal athletic competition would probably have emerged into the 20th century. The unique form of internationalism that did arise is, however, indisputably his. He attempted to fuse elements of Hellenism and idealized English sportsmanship into youth's need and desire for organized athletics. His conception was preeminently humanistic and no single institution has succeeded more than the Olympic Movement in bringing into physical contiquity the youth of the world. The Olympic Games were born in a quite marvelous era, the last decades of the 19th century. No other portion of this 100-year period could have produced them.

The Humanism
of Pierre de Coubertin

The Athenian ideal of citizen was artist, athlete, soldier, statesman, and philosopher, all in one. All his life, Pierre de Coubertin attempted to strive toward this ideal, not only for himself, but for the youth of mankind. He worshiped the greatness and eloquence of the ancient Greeks. The second ideal upon which his philosophy was based included the conception of English sportsmanship. In his own time, the close of the 19th century was characterized by Anglo-Saxon union and supremacy. He was convinced that the society of the English public school, epitomized by the Rubgy School of Dr. Thomas Arnold, had been the precursor of Britain's world supremacy. Thus, Coubertin's mind dwelt both in the distant past and the present. To him, the two greatest forces for good were "Hellenic completeness" and the ideals in English sport. From the beginning, they served as motive and philosophy for the revival and continuation of the Olympic Games. He vainly fought for the elimination of brutality, overspecialization, and desire for material gain. His idealism has, however, greatly helped the Games from being dominated by these evils.

Coubertin was schooled in an atmosphere of patriotism, "Christian ethics without Christian religion," and abiding love of the literature and thought of antiquity. They were the ideals that infused certain French humanistic thinkers of the times. Pierre de Coubertin was an admirer and pupil of the serene classical spirit which had been reawakened among certain scholars of the Third Republic. This "spirit" was composed of a moral wholeness, combining energy, order, and beauty. The philosophy of Pierre de Coubertin took on certain aspects of Humanism and Hellenism, both possessing a common motif. They both realize the possibility of the good life upon this earth, the noble and creative potentialities of man as an active citizen of a democratic state. They represent cultures based upon the ideals of the classical Greeks and have the highest regard for athletic vigor, grace, cultivation of art and science, and devotion to the ethics of civic and social organizations. They delight in man as man and in man's body as well as in his mind. Consciously or unconsciously, Coubertin attempted to rekindle, if not recreate, the original spirit of antiquity, one that had been imperfectly revived in the 15th century. He seemed bent on the task of reviving or bringing to light those arts and sciences so essential to human dignity and human progress. The tendency toward classical humanism pervaded much of the thought and action of Pierre de Coubertin. The nature of the Olympic Movement could not have escaped being influenced by it.

Coubertin and the Olympic Movement

Each of us has tendencies toward eclecticism in his choice of beliefs or "schools" of thought. So it was with Coubertin. There are elements of idealism, romanticism, rationalism, and naturalism in the vast writings of Pierre de Coubertin. He probably would have preferred to be called a humanist teacher. Professor Louis Meylan (1944) said that "The integral humanism of Pierre de Coubertin was his strongest characteristic" (p. 49). Coubertin was a dreamer, an irascible temperamentalist, an inexhaustible workman, and one who sometimes displayed grandiose conduct and dictatorial mannerisms. He was above all, very human. His humanistic spirit, with its highest concept of man, continually searched for the means to enable all individuals to realize their noble potentialities in a good life upon this earth. The element of humanism is inescapable in the philosophy of Olympism.

The simultaneous emergence of Baron de Coubertin and certain national and international manifestations described in this chapter resulted in the rebirth of the Olympic Games. The peculiar circumstances of late 19th-century Europe made it possible for Coubertin and his associates, through herculean effort, to bring about a dramatic change in international amateur athletics. The Olympic Games occurred as a result of the work of this man and certain pertinent conjectures present during the period 1883 to 1896.

Sir Charles Oman once said that the historian must submit the results of his research with a frank acknowledgment that his work bears the impress of his personality and inevitably of his moral judgment of men and things. This last summing-up has been one of optimism and promise, as indeed has been the current of the entire chapter. If nations are to live together, people must live together. "National integrity is personal integrity writ large," views Erwin D. Canham (1959), editor of the *Christian Science Monitor* (p. 183). The Olympic Games are capable of great good to the individual participants. Better individuals contribute to better nations. The sovereign states are a little more able to do business with one another. The philosophy of Olympism may blend with a larger character of ideals that serves as a standard of conduct, beckoning and drawing man upward. In this disturbed and irresolute world we can observe a certain regularity; "a law of oscillation," says Charles Beard (1932):

> Rise is followed by fall, and fall by rise; it is a mistake to think that the human race is always deteriorating. There has been, through the series of oscillations, a gradual ascent. The world has not degenerated. The modern age is not inferior to classical antiquity; the races of the earth form now a sort of "mundane republic." (p. 49)

References

Beard, C.A. (1932). Introduction. In J.B. Bury (Ed.), *The idea of progress— An inquiry into its origin and growth*. New York: Macmillan.

Canham, E.D. (1959). *Man's great future*. New York: Longman's Green.

Clark, E.H. (1896). The Olympic Games and their influence upon physical education. *American Physical Education Review, 1*, 11-21.

Cook, T.A. (1906, November). On Coubertin and the Olympics. *Bailey's Magazine of Sports and Pastimes*, p.11.

Coubertin, P. de. (1896). The Olympic Games of 1896. *The Century Magazine, 53*, 39-53.

Coubertin, P. de. (1908). *Une campagne de vingt-et-un ans, 1887-1908*. Paris: Librairie de l'Education Physique.

Coubertin, P. de. (1931). *Memories olympiques*. Lausanne: Bureau international de Pedagogie sportive.

Coubertin, P. de. (1951, January). Olympism and the IOC. *Bulletin du C.I.O.*, pp. 15-16. [Address at the Olympic Congress, Prague, May 29, 1925].

Coubertin, P. de. (1966). What can we now ask of sport? *The Olympic idea—Discourses and essays*. [Address given to the Greek Liberal Club of Lausanne, 24 February, 1918]. Cologne: Carl Diem Institute.

Diem, C. (1952, January). Pierre de Coubertin's ancestry. *Bulletin du C.I.O.*, p. 14.

Henry, B. (1948). *An approved history of the Olympic Games*. New York: G.P. Putnam's Sons.

Horton, G. (1896). Revival of Olympian Games. *North American Review, 162*, 266.

Hyde, W.W. (1921). *Olympic victor monuments and Greek athletic art*. Washington, D.C.: Carnegie Institution of Washington.

Lucas, J.A. (1962). *Baron Pierre de Coubertin and the formative years of the modern international Olympic Movement, 1883-1896*. Unpublished doctoral dissertation, University of Maryland, College Park.

Meylan, L. (1944). Le pedagogue et l'humaniste. *Jubile Olympique*. Lausanne: Librairie Payot.

Shaw, A. (1894). The re-establishment of the Olympic Games. *The Review of Reviews, 10*, 643.

7
Why I Revived
the Olympic Games

Pierre de Coubertin

If in reviving the Olympic Games I had merely sought to restore one of
the noblest and most interesting of ancient institutions, I do not think
I should have needed excuse, for such an ambition would certainly have
been both comprehensible and legitimate. It might, however, have been
reasonably characterized as a fanciful and superfluous undertaking. There
is so much necessary work to be done to supply the myriad needs of our
day that we ought not to waste ourselves in unnecessary efforts. I have
in mind a saying of the great Dr. Arnold about the cultivation of some
rare plants. "How interesting," he said, "to give oneself up to this if
only one's life could be twice as long as it really is!" But the Olympic
Games are in no way comparable to the cultivation of rare plants. It is
my profound conviction that they are one of the cornerstones of progress
and health for the youth of our day. Let it be understood that if among
the readers of this article there are any who despise athletic sports, and
see in them nothing but expensive and puerile amusements, I do not
address myself to them, for we have no common ground of argument.
But I do not expect to encounter such a point of view, which would be
quite out of date. Certainly there have been abuses, particularly in England
and the United States, and it is always right to combat abuses; but this

Originally published in *Fortnightly Review*, **90** (July 1908), 110-115.

does not affect the value of the fundamental principle underlying the practice of athletic sorts—that there is nothing else upon which young men can employ their strength in their hours of recreation and liberty with such advantage both moral and physical. It is not at the moment when the whole civilized world, from Petersburg to Madrid and from Tokyo to Punta Arenas, is adopting Anglo-Saxon ideas on this point that Anglo-Saxons themselves are likely to renounce them.

Well, then, the athletic life of modern youth demands the revival of the Olympic Games; and in that conviction I called for their revival, thinking not merely of France or England, Greece or Italy, but of humanity in general. But, I may be asked, what difference do you make between the Olympic Games and what are nowadays called world championships? Were the games of antiquity anything else than our competitions for world championships, on their own lines, and taking into account the then meaning of the word "world"? I do not deny that, and I agree that world championships do form part of the Olympic Games: Nevertheless the Olympic Games are "something else" as well, and it is just this "something else" that matters, as it is not to be found in any other variety of athletic competition.

There are two ways of regarding athletic sport: first, the individual point of view, which is, let me hasten to say, the best and the most desirable. On the day when a nation exists in which each young man possesses sufficient taste for physical exercises to make him practice them regularly, either alone or with his comrades, seeking in wholesome sports an admirable means to perfect his health and increase his strength, then on that day humanity—or a section of it, at least—will have realized perfection. But we are not there yet, and hence we are constrained to regard athletic sport from a second and quite different point of view—that of organized competition. Athletics for the sake of winning something: This is at once the potent incentive and the dangerous canker with which we have to reckon. Potent incentive, we cannot deny: the most potent of all, in fact. Human society is worked by the principle of competition; it has always been so, and is so more than ever. Competition is becoming more and more intense, bringing in its train greater and greater dangers of corruption. Unbridled competition entails grave risks to the spirit of fair play, occasions the commission of blameworthy acts, and engenders a lamentable atmosphere of jealousy, envy, vanity, and mistrust. This may be seen in all branches of activity, and athletic life cannot escape from it. Certainly athletic organizations, societies, and federations lead no placid and peaceful existence; they are torn by violent quarrels, and too often seek to injure one another to steal away each other's champions. This state of things will continue, being indeed, almost inevitable. I am forced to acknowledge that the individual practice of athletic sports, regularly and perseveringly undertaken for the sake of health, beauty, and harmony, is a chimera. A few individuals may be capable of this, but the rank and file never will be.

We must therefore, fall back upon the system of organized competition, and allow it to dominate athletic sport. But we can give it a counterpoise, a regulator, as did those ancient Greeks who, we find, had to grapple with most of the problems that perplex us; and their regulator was Olympia. At Olympia vulgar competition was transformed, and in a sense sanctified, by contact with national sentiment superbly excited.

Overexcited, I might even say: for it was excess that in the end ruined and corrupted ancient athleticism. But the end came very slowly. For centuries athleticism, its home in Olympia, remained pure and magnificent. There states and cities met in the persons of their young men, who, imbued with a sense of the moral grandeur of the Games, went to them in a spirit of almost religious reverence. Around them were assembled men of letters and of the arts, ready to celebrate the victories of their energy and muscle; and these incomparable spectacles were also the delight of the populace. No doubt low ambitions and mean passions were present; there is no human assembly without them, no human institution that they do not infest. But despite them the whole result was something grandiose and strong, which dominated Hellenic civilization, influencing happily and gloriously the youth of the country, and through them the entire nation.

Such were the Olympic Games of ancient times; such ought to be those of our own day. I perceived clearly the danger of athleticism in an atmosphere of advertisement and bluff, such as our modern atmosphere is apt to be in a society where effort is generally applied to the quest for material gain, where consequently athletic sports are likely to be commercially exploited by the organizers of public exhibitions. I saw the necessity for reestablishing the Olympic Games as a supreme consecration of the cult of athletics practiced in the purest spirit of true sport, proudly, joyfully, and loyally. But to reach a realization of the idea many stages had to be traveled, and naturally this took time. First of all, the new Games must be exclusively modern in form; to revive chariot races, for instance, would only have been to institute a hippodrome devoid of interest for the mass of young men, and to make mere actors of the participants; while, as modern sports are very numerous, an overloaded program would result. Secondly, the new Games must be international; that is to say, the competitors must be the best representatives of civilized nations. In ancient time, they were already international in the sense that there was as much difference between the citizens of the various cities of Greece, Italy, and Egypt as there could be now between an Englishman, a Spaniard, and an Italian. Those cities readily went to war with one another, and even in times of peace their rivalries were acute. But in our days, despite the rapidity and number of means of transport, it is not easy to bring together periodically representatives of all countries, because of the difficulties they encounter in leaving their daily occupations, and in finding, either wholly or in part, the necessary contingent expenses.

It was done, however, in 1896, 1900, and 1904, not to speak of the Athenian series of games inaugurated in 1906. We may therefore consider that one stage has been accomplished, and that the Olympic Games of London are going to consummate definitive success. Our English friends have brought a truly admirable zeal and intelligence to the preparation of the Fourth Olympiad. Lord Desborough has been a matchless president; and how can I say enough of the moving and working spirit of the organization, the Rev. R.S. deCourcy Laffan, who gives us a spectacle of antique virtue revived in devoting to the cause of athletic sport a mind of the highest culture, accustomed to interest itself in the great concerns of morals and philosophy? Surely, when during 12 years they have been celebrated with an ever increasing brilliancy of success, the Olympic Games will have given proof of sufficient vitality to assure their future, and we shall no longer need to fear any break in the continuity of our revived Olympiads.

Will the achievement then have reached the culminating point for which I have been aiming? Far from it; and I do not even hesitate to say that in my eyes only the pedestal of the structure is complete. Anyone who studies the ancient Games will perceive that their deep significance was due to two principal elements: beauty and reverence. If the modern Games are to exercise the influence I desire for them they must in their turn show beauty and inspire reverence—a beauty and a reverence infinitely surpassing anything hitherto realized in the most important athletic contests of our day. The grandeur and dignity of processions and attitudes, the impressive splendor of ceremonies, the concurrence of all the arts, popular emotion and generous sentiment, must all in some sort collaborate together. This cannot be achieved by a single Olympiad, nor even by three or four; it will need at least a quarter of a century. But, then, when one aspires to create or recreate institutions of this magnitude the first condition is not to be in a hurry.

Here again, moreover, we must be resolutely modern. Let us have no clumsy and tactless restitutions. But it is possible to draw inspiration from the past without copying it. To take one example from many: At Olympia the competitors—and it was certainly not one of the least impressive episodes of the Games—assembled before the statue of Jupiter and took solemn oath that they would compete fairly and loyally, swearing also that they were without reproach and worthy to meet their adversaries. Jupiter is no more, and we have lost faith in statues. But I imagine the athletes of the future taking oath before the Games each upon the flag of his own country, and in presence of the flags of other lands affirming solemnly that they have always been loyal and honorable in sport, and that it is in a spirit of loyalty and honor they approach the Olympic contests. Would not this provide a scene of dignified beauty fit to inspire actors and spectators alike with the most noble and generous emotions? And similarly, if for vulgar choruses and bands performing selections from operettas we were to substitute an interpretation by great massed choirs of masterpieces by a Handel or a Gluck, should we not be confirming in the completest manner the marriage of Arts and Sports—that is to say, of muscular strength and creative imagination, those two poles of human life?

In this order of ideals all is yet to be done; but much is prepared in the path of progress. The International Olympic Committee, in summoning in 1906 a conference that met at the Comedie Francaise in Paris, and discussed the best means for henceforward drawing together Sports, Arts, and Letters, gave the signal for a movement of high importance in this line. Henceforth the scattered efforts of artists can be directed toward a definite aim. Sculptors and musicians have already grasped the possibility of seeking new inspiration in athleticism. At this moment all Brussels is admiring the splendid group, "Lutteurs à Cheval," from the chisel of the great Belgian sculptor, Jacques de Lalaing; Paris has been hearing with emotion Augusta Holmes's fine oratorio, entitled "Ludus pro Patria"; and the ears of Athenians still ring with the harmonies of the "Olympic Hymn" composed by the Greek musician Samara. Architects have meanwhile, although it is true but timidly, attempted to evolve plans for gymnasiums modeled on antique ideals. When he died, Bartholdi, the celebrated sculptor, left the International Olympic Committee the designs for a "Monument des Sports," which should be one of the finest works of art that the world has seen. On another side, dramatic art is by degrees accustoming itself once more to the open air, and in many different countries performances recalling the theater of antiquity take place. Finally, in Switzerland the well-known musician Jaques-Dalcroze is striving with admirable zeal to reform choreographic art, degraded as it has been by the vulgarity and stupidity of our modern dances.

Thus on all sides individual efforts are ready to converge toward an ideal of general harmony. The arts are drawing together; sound, line, color, and form seem to be preparing to associate once more in movement, which is living beauty, and thus to constitute the spectacular element of the modern Olympiad. With their aid may be framed a worthy setting for the Games—a setting in which shall move athletes well prepared to assist in the great festival, and conscious of the special glory it confers upon them. It is now the rule that no one can take part in the Olympic Games save as a representative of his own country. This is a first step, for previously the nationality of competitors had not always been taken into account, but merely their technical qualities. A fundamental article of the general regulations drawn up in 1894 reserves the right of the organizing committees to reject any candidate whose character or previous record of conduct might reflect injuriously upon the dignity of the institution. We must establish the tradition that each competitor shall in his bearing and conduct as a man of honor and a gentleman endeavor to prove in what respect he holds the Games and what an honor he feels it to participate in them. Then we should revive, as I have said, the ceremony of the oath; and we should seek the means to conclude the Olympiad with a distribution of prizes commensurate with the dignity of the occasion. At present this prize giving takes place in a wretchedly undignified fashion. The victors, hastily clothed, listen to some dull little speech, and then carry their prizes off under their arm in the midst of the rough cheers of their comrades. The question of costume is a somewhat delicate one. Modern dress, for men at least, is not a thing of beauty. But the costume of his sport is to the athlete what his uniform is to the soldier, and it is in that garb he ought to appear at the final ceremony. The procession of victors—ridiculous in the clothes of town life—would at once gain charm if fencers carried their weapons and tennis players their racquets, if cyclists led their machines and polo-players held their sticks, all wearing the costumes of their respective sports.

Such is my view of the development that ought to take place in the institution of the modern Olympic Games. I myself am determined to work for this, and I feel assured of the concurrence of all my loyal collaborators, among whom I count—and in the first rank—Father Time himself, for without him in such undertakings nothing lasting can be achieved. Lasting the work must be, to exercise over the sports of the future that necessary and beneficent influence for which I look—an influence that shall make them the means of bringing to perfection the strong and hopeful youth of our white race, thus again helping toward the perfection of all human society.

The Modern Olympic Movement

The modern international Olympic Movement came into being on June 23, 1894, at the International Congress of Paris. A total of 79 delegates representing 49 sports associations from 12 countries unanimously voted for the restoration of the Olympic games and for the creation of a permanent and stable International Olympic Committee (IOC). The principles and details of the Olympic Movement, including the structure and organization of the games, had been meticulously prepared by Coubertin. "They followed me almost with debate," he later declared, "I had successively voted the fundamental principles previously resolved in my mind" (Coubertin, 1931, p. 19). Executive authority for the reestablishment of the games was vested in the hands of a 15-member committee, and to this day the IOC has remained the wellspring of the Olympic Movement.

In addition to the IOC, the Olympic Movement comprises the International Sports Federations (IF) and the National Olympic Committees (NOC). The IFs are primarily responsible for the management, administration, and promotion of the sports on the Olympic program. The IOC also recognizes several IFs whose sports have yet to be included in the Olympic games. The NOCs represent the IOC and are delegated by it to promote the Olympic Movement in their respective territories. They are also responsible for safeguarding the IOC's rules and regulations. Every nation must have an NOC to be eligible for Olympic participation.

Although both the IFs and the NOCs have been brought into closer cooperation with the IOC, primarily as a result of Lord Killanin's more recent efforts to democratize the Olympic Movement (Miller, 1979), the IOC itself still retains ultimate power and authority. As Monique Berlioux, long-serving Director of the IOC, states, "The IOC has unquestionable powers as guide, guardian, and arbiter. It is the supreme body in the Olympic Movement, the rock, the foundation stone" (1976, p. 12). In order to keep the games independent of government interference and to protect them from partisan interests, the 15 original IOC members were handpicked by Coubertin himself. In effect, the IOC appointed itself and assumed its own authority. The principles of self-election and self-perpetuation have remained to the present day. Although the process may be viewed as "undemocratic" (Killanin, 1983, p. 13), it has clearly had some important practical benefits. "I am convinced" writes MacAloon (1981), "that if IOC members had been more 'constitutionally' elected . . . certainly the 1896 games and most likely the whole series of modern Olympics as we know them would never have taken place" (p. 181).

The IOC meets in full session only once a year, or twice in an Olympic year, and much of the ongoing work is carried out in subcommittee or by the various Commissions that study and advise on such issues as finance, television, and eligibility. A Commission for the International Olympic Academy (IOA) also exists. The idea of an IOA grew from Coubertin's call for an "Olympic Study Center," which "would more than anything else support progress" of the Olympic Movement, "and preserve it from ideological deviation" (Coubertin, 1931, p. 181). Although the IOC agreed to the foundation of an IOA as early as 1949, the first session was not held until 1961 in ancient Olympia, where the Academy is now housed in a $2 million facility. The IOA is controlled and financed by the Hellenic Olympic Committee, and it functions as a forum for the exchange of ideas on various Olympic issues.

The IOC's most important functions are to select the host cities for the games and ensure that Olympic rules are followed, to recognize and support the IF's and NOC's rights, to negotiate television rights, and to elect new IOC members (Killanin, 1983). Since 1955, incoming members of the IOC have had to take an oath, which includes the clause:

> I bind myself to promote the Olympic Movement to the best of my ability and to guard and preserve its fundamental principles as conceived by the Baron Pierre de Coubertin, keeping myself as a member free from all political, sectarian and commercial influence. (quoted in Berlioux, 1976, p. 12)

The fundamental principles of the Olympic Movement are listed in the annually published *Olympic Charter*, as are the aims, which are

- to promote the development of those physical and moral qualities which are the basis of sport,
- to educate young people through sport in a spirit of better understanding between each other and of friendship, thereby helping to build a better and more peaceful world,
- to spread the Olympic principles throughout the world, thereby creating international goodwill,
- to bring together the athletes of the world in the great four-yearly sport festival, the Olympic Games. (*IOC*, 1984, p. 6)

As the aims suggest, the Olympic movement is more than a bureaucratic structure. It possesses both a practical and doctrinal manifestation. The practical manifestation is the Olympics themselves, the winter and summer games that are held every 4 years and that are still, as Coubertin designed, "ambulatory" in nature. The doctrinal manifestation of the Olympic movement is expressed in a philosophy of life and sport, which Coubertin himself called Olympism.

At the core of Olympism was Coubertin's fundamental belief in the symbiotic development of intellectual, moral, and physical attributes. He embraced the derivative of the basic classical ideal of *mens sane in corpore sano* (a healthy mind in a healthy body). As Lucas (1981) states, it was "a grand attempt to fuse academic training with moral and physical education" (p. 28). Coubertin himself defined Olympism as a "school of nobility and of moral purity as well as of endurance and physical energy—but only if . . . honesty and sportsmanlike unselfishness are as highly developed as the strength of the muscles" (1931, p. 208). Sport was regarded as a central dynamic in the human experience, and Coubertin generated an ideology that linked sport and the Olympic Games to an universal appeal for peace through international understanding, and promoted mutual international respect for cultural and national differences. In 1894 he declared,

Healthy democracy, wise and peaceful internationalism, will penetrate the new stadium and preserve within it the cult of disinterestedness and honor which will enable athletics to help in the tasks of moral education and social peace as well as of muscular development. That is why every four years the revived Olympic Games must give the youth of all the world a chance of happy and brotherly encounter which will gradually efface the peoples' ignorance of things which concern them all, an ignorance which feeds hatred, accumulates misunderstandings, and hurtles events along a barbarous path toward a merciless conflict. (Coubertin, 1894/1967, p. 10)

Coubertin's emphasis on the social, educational, and moral possibilities in sport, rather than the professional motif in particular, caused him to place much faith in the "pure amateur spirit" of Olympism. These same principles also account for Olympism's stance against commercial, political, racial, national, and sectarian exploitation and discrimination.

"The Olympic Games are not only to enhance muscular strength," he delcared in 1912, "they are intellectual and artistic" (p. 84). The aesthetic component of Coubertin's ideology manifested itself in his continuous adherence to the idea of an Olympic arts competition. In 1906 he convened a Consultive Conference on Art, Letters, and Sport to study ways in which art and literature could be incorporated into the Olympic Movement. As a result the first "pentathlon of the Muses" was staged at the 1912 Stockholm Games.

Although the Olympic Movement has grown considerably over the last 90 years, it has displayed an uncommon consistency in both structure and ideology, and it still bears the indelible stamp of its creator, Pierre de Coubertin. The growth of the games has been spectacular. From relatively meager beginnings they have emerged as the most impressive sporting event of the late 20th century, surpassing even the Super Bowl, the World Series, and World Cup Soccer in their appeal and power. The growth of the Olympic bureaucratic structure has been equally spectacular, and the IOC is now firmly ensconced at the core of an interlocking network of regional, national, and international sport bodies that govern amateur sport around the globe. The Olympic philosophy, Coubertin's Olympism, has increasingly become the subject of analysis and debate. It has been glorified and vilified. Yet the philosophy still serves as the life blood that nourishes the entire Olympic movement. It has also served, as we shall see later, to create numerous problems for the Olympic Movement.

The essays in this section discuss the various manifestations of the Olympic Movement: its structure, philosophy, and the fine arts festival. The story of the games themselves is the subject of the next section. In the first essay, March Krotee presents a critical analysis of the IOC, arguing that despite its commitment to idealistic and egalitarian principles, the IOC's organization and structure tend toward a rigid oligarchy in which power is vested in the hands of a few, as a result of which change becomes problematic. In the second reading, Jeffrey Segrave presents a definition of modern Olympism. Describing Olympism as a set of goals or aspirations that provides the blueprint for the conduct of the games, Segrave argues specifically that Olympism stands for education, international understanding, equal opportunity, fair and equal competition, cultural expression, the independence of sport, and excellence. The cultural component of Olympism, the fine arts festival, is the subject of the final essay in this section. In it, Susan Bandy concludes that although arts competitions have been a feature of the Olympic Movement since 1912, the truly refined relationship that characterized the practice of sport and art during the classic Greek era has yet to be attained in modern times.

References

Berlioux, M. (1976). The history of the International Olympic Committee. In Lord Killanin & J. Rodda (Eds.), *The Olympic Games* (pp. 12-23). New York: Macmillan.

Coubertin, P. de. (1912). All games, all nations. *Olympic Review*, pp. 82-86.

Coubertin, P. de. (1931). *Memoires Olympiques*. Lausanne: Bureau international de pedagogie sportive.

Coubertin, P. de. (1967). Athletics in the modern world and the Olympic Games. In C. Diem (Ed.), *The Olympic idea: Discources and essays*. Stuttgart: Hoffman. (Original work published 1894)

Killanin, Lord. (1983). *My Olympic years*. New York: William Morrow.

Lucas, J.A. (1981). The genesis of the Modern Olympic Games. In J. Segrave & D. Chu (Eds.), *Olympism* (pp. 22-32). Champaign, IL: Human Kinetics.

MacAloon, J.J. (1981). *This great symbol: Pierre de Coubertin and the origins of the modern Olympic Games*. Chicago: University of Chicago Press.

Miller, G. (1979). *Behind the Olympic rings*. Lynn, MA: H.O. Zimmon.

International Olympic Committee. (1984). *Olympic charter*. Lausanne: Comité International Olympique.

Suggested Reading

Leigh, M. (1974). Pierre de Coubertin: A man of his time. *Quest, 22*, 19-24.

Lucas, J.A. (1963). *Baron de Coubertin and the formative years of the Modern Olympic Movement*. Unpublished doctoral dissertation, University of Maryland, College Park.

MacAloon, J.J. (1980). *This great symbol: Pierre de Coubertin and the origin of the Modern Olympic Games*. Chicago: University of Chicago Press.

Mandell, R.D. (1976). *The first Modern Olympics*. Berkeley, CA: University of California Press.

Redmond, G. (1971). *The Caledonian games in nineteenth-century America*. Rutherford, NJ: Fairleigh Dickinson University Press.

Weber, E. (1970). Pierre de Coubertin and the introduction of organized sport in France. *Journal of Contemporary History, 5*, 3-26.

8

An Organizational Analysis of the International Olympic Committee

March L. Krotee

Modern sport and the Olympic Games in particular have developed into one of the most ubiquitous, unique, and pervasive dimensions of our society. The origins of the modern Olympic Games have been vigorously chronicled by historians (Gardiner, 1910, 1925; Kieran & Daley, 1961; Killanin & Rodda, 1976; Lucas, 1962; Weyland, 1952). Few social scientists, however, have attempted to study systematically and offer sociological, psychosocial, or sociophilosophical interpretations of the issues, problems, trends, and future of this omnipresent sporting force (Bannister, 1980; Guttmann, 1978; Krotee, 1979a; Lenk, 1976, 1979; Lüschen, 1979).

From the earliest representation of the ancient Olympic Games as a symbolically sacred athletic offering to reigning deities to the most recent geopolitical representation (as portrayed by the boycott of the 1980 and 1984 Games in Moscow and Los Angeles), the Olympic Games have offered an on-going and seemingly untapped source for sociological study. During the apparent rise and demise of the Olympic Games what seems

This chapter is based on the article "A Sociological Perspective of the Olympic Games" by M.L. Krotee that originally appeared in J. Segrave and D. Chu (Eds.) *Olympism* (pp. 207-226), Champaign, IL: Human Kinetics.

to be evident is the number of sociological factors that lend themselves to social scientific scrutiny. These include secular movements, religious factors, nationalistic and cultural milieu, equal competitive opportunities, economic influences, amateurism or specialization issues, social mobility, organization, ideology, rationalization, quantification and records, and political involvement (Krotee, 1979b, 1981; Lowe, Kanin, & Strenk, 1978; Viken, Krotee, & Stone, 1979; Ueberhorst, 1976).

One such line of social scientific endeavor is examining and relating the organization and structure of the critical appendage of the Olympic Games—the International Olympic Committee (IOC)—with existing sociological theory. It is the intent of this work to describe and examine the development of the institutional organization of the IOC and relate its formulization to Michels's Theory of Organizational Structure in an attempt to elucidate some of the problems and issues concerning the study of this sociological reference group.

The Rebirth of the Olympic Games

The rebirth of the Olympic Games was heavily nurtured by and committed to the lofty ideals of equality, peace, and goodwill of their creator, Baron Pierre Fredy de Coubertin. Coubertin stated that if the German Reich had excavated the ruins of ancient Olympia through an 1875 pact with the Greek government, why then should France not restore the old splendor? From here it was not too far to a less splendid but fertile and practical idea to renew the Games, especially because it seemed that international sport should play a new role in the world (Coubertin, 1896, 1908). As Coubertin idealistically, humanistically, nationalistically, and optimistically envisaged, youth, education, and athletics were intricately bound; international rivalry in sports would promote international amity in broader fields, and all humankind would benefit.

Thus, the inherent struggle over the Olympic ideal reappeared at the Grand Hall of the Sorbonne in Paris at the International Athletic Congress on June 16, 1894. Also resurfacing was the activating force that resulted in the renascence of the Olympic Games. The Congress was to have served as a forum to discuss the growing conflicts and turmoil within the world's amateur sporting organizations. Dialogue concerning rules, regulations, and the amateurism/professionalism dilemma was to have dominated the 10-item agenda. What emerged, however, was the decision to establish a 14-member International Olympic Committee and to revive the ancient Olympic Games and conduct them in Athens in 1896. Coubertin stated:

> The re-establishment of the Olympic Games based upon the conditions conforming to the needs of modern life would serve to bring

together every four years representatives of all nations, and it is permissible to suppose that these peaceful and courteous contests would supply the best of internationalism. (cited in Leonard & Affleck, 1947)

The response to Coubertin's appeal was described by Professor William Milligan Sloane of Princeton University, one of the original members of the hand-chosen IOC. The Belgians were hostile, the Britons were lukewarm, the uninvited Germans represented by Baron von Reiffenstein took no notice whatsoever, and the French vowed not to send a team if the Germans were invited. Even the Greek government was financially skeptical of becoming the recipients of the dream that had been born and had flourished in ancient Olympia.

Nevertheless, on the 75th anniversary of Greece's declaration of independence from Turkey, on a rainy Monday morning on March 25, 1986 (Wednesday, April 6 on the new Georgian calendar not yet adopted by Greece) in the lavishly remodeled stadium of Herodis, King George I of Greece formally opened the first modern Olympic Games. The ancient Greek Olympic Games that had been halted by the Roman Emperor Theodosius I had been revived after a lapse of 14 centuries by an idealistic, patriotic, and nationalistic Frenchman who believed in sport for all (except women) and who seemed to bury his egalitarian passions in a quadrennial festival for the elite athlete. Thus, the modern Olympic Games emerged as the ideal mixture of physical prowess, moral attitude, religion, beauty, and peace for the betterment of humankind—a 19th-century dream seemingly already in conflict with the emerging transnational and dilemmatic 20th century.

A Sociological View of the International Olympic Committee

An analysis of the IOC may also serve as an introspective testament to the patriotic intensity and tenacious psychosocial profile of its creator and mentor from the year of the first modern Olympic Games until 1925—Baron Pierre de Coubertin. Although he was always the champion of individual freedom, human rights, democracy, moral humility, and integrity, Coubertin, on June 13, 1894, at the International Athletic Congress in Paris, personally hand-selected 14 men to serve as the foundation for the reconstruction of the modern Olympic Movement as he believed it should be constructed. Coubertin preached that:

> the foundation of real human morality lies in mutual respect—and to respect one another it is necessary to know one another. . . . Let us export oarsmen, runners, fencers; there is the free trade of the future—and on the day when it shall take place among the customs

of Europe the cause of peace will have received a new and powerful support. (United States Olympic Committee, 1979b)

The Baron was, of course, elected Secretary General of the newly anointed "Comité." Thus, Olympism sought to contribute all that sport could to the social, educational, moral, and aesthetic integrity of the quality of life of the individual.

The original members of the IOC charged to carry out Coubertin's will included Demetrios Vikélas, President of the Committee (Greece), Ernest Callot (France), General Alexander D. von Boutowski (Russia), Colonel Gustav Balck (Sweden), Professor William Milligan Sloane (United States and Princeton University), Dr. and Conseiller Jiri Guth-Jarkowski (Bohemia, at this time part of the Danube-Monarchy), Fr. Ference Kemeny (Hungary), Lord Amphtill and Charles Herbert (Great Britain), Dr. J.B. Zubiaur (Argentina), Leonard C. Cuff (New Zealand), Count Lucchesi Palli and Earl Andria Garafa (Italy), and Count Maxime de Bousies (Belgium). Even though the official interlocking rings of the Olympic flag, flown initially in Antwerp in 1920, symbolize the union of the five continents, the original IOC membership was dominated by the selection of representatives of the European sporting nations and, for the most part, special acquaintances of the Baron. This slight flaw in democratic procedure made little difference in the internal mechanism of the Committee because Coubertin reigned over the International Olympic Committee; was sole director of the Games' form and character; and developed the Olympic Charter, Olympic Protocol, and the athlete's oath as well as the format for the opening and closing ceremonies. He personally assumed all administrative and financial duties. Even today, few major alterations from his legacy have emerged from this self-elected, self-anointed, and self-perpetuated entity where members are not delegates from countries but delegates to countries.

For the social scientist, the organization and structure of the IOC are worth sociological description and inspection. The Committee seems to be a formal, rationally organized bureaucratic social structure as described by Weber. This includes possessing well-defined goals, interests, purposes, and clear patterns of activity and maintaining acceptable modes of regulations and control which functionally relate to the purpose of the organization (Cassenelli, 1953; Melser, 1971; Merton, 1957; Parsons, 1951). Careful scrutiny of the IOC, however, reveals that the Committee patterns itself after Michels's (1959) Theory of Organizational Structure. Michels (1876-1936) was a German-Italian sociologist who studied cooperative societies, social movements, and various internal structures of Western European political groups. From his observations, he found that these groups, despite their commitment to the ideal of equality, failed to maintain these ideals in their own structures and instead developed rigid and rather permanent oligarchies. He thus formulated the "iron law of oligarchy." Michels believed that certain fundamental sociological laws prohibited the attainment of social equality no matter what economic or political system prevailed. He believed that the power of the organization was in its political makeup and influence of its members.

Thus, in examining the organization, structure, and membership of the IOC, one needs only to examine its mailing address—Chateau de Vidy, 1007 Lausanne, Switzerland, an 18th-century mansion overlooking Lake Geneva—to detect a slight air of elitism. Further study of the past and present Committee membership (see Appendix A) reveals such personages as the Marquess of Exeter, Cheik Gabriel Gemayel, Prince Regnant Francois Joseph II of Liechtenstein, Prince Faisal Abdul Aziz, and the Raja Bahlendra Singh as well as assorted dukes, counts, barons, and generals. This selected royal roll does little but confirm the spirit of democratic elitism. Like the initial Committee membership selected by Coubertin, today's IOC, as well as its past presidents, seems to be dominated by the elite upper class and, for the most part, European patrimony (see Figure 1 and Table 1).

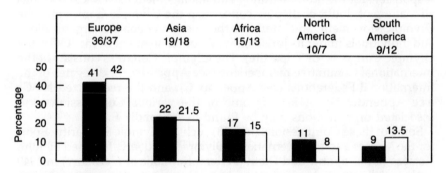

Figure 1   The membership of the IOC by continent. Total members = 89 in 1980, 88 in 1984; ■ = 1980, □ = 1984. Adapted from Krotee, 1980.

Table 1   The Presidents of the International Olympic Committee, 1894-1987

First	Demetrias Vikélas	Greece	1894-1896
Second	Baron Pierre de Coubertin	France	1896-1925
Third	Count Henry de Baillet-Latour	Belgium	1925-1942
Acting president	J. Sigfrid Edström	Sweden	1942-1946
Fourth	J. Sigfrid Edström	Sweden	1946-1952
Fifth	Avery Brundage	United States	1952-1972
Sixth	Lord Michael Killanin	Ireland	1972-1980
Seventh	Juan Antonio Samaranch	Spain	1980-present

The membership of the Committee is self-recruited and is restricted to those who speak French or English and are citizens of and reside in a country that possesses a recognized National Olympic Committee (NOC). Technically, only one member from any country should be on the Committee, including countries where the Games have been hosted, except for the largest and most active countries in the Olympic Movement. The members are representatives of the IOC in their countries and not their countries' delegates; they may not accept from governments any instructions that would interfere with the independence of their vote. Membership ceases if a member resigns, becomes inactive, reaches the age of 72 if elected after 1965, changes nationality, or is deemed unworthy by the Committee.

The IOC consists of a president, who is elected by secret ballot for an 8-year term; three vice-presidents, who serve 4-year terms; and an executive board of the four officers and five additional members (see Appendix B). This body ensures that the rules are observed, is directly responsible for the administration and management of finances, decides all matters of doubt or dispute concerning the Olympic Games and the Olympic Movement, and interprets the rules and penalizes organizations and individuals under its jurisdiction. Another segment of the IOC is the Olympic Congress (or Tripartite). The Olympic Congress consists of the International Committee membership (see Appendix A), delegates of the International Federations (see Appendix C), and the recognized NOCs (see Appendix D). A list of some of the various Commissions and associated organizations may be found in Appendix E.

Some of these Commissions ($n = 18$) such as Olympic Solidarity, Sport for the Masses and the International Olympic Academy, founded by John Ketséas (Greece) and Carl Diem (Federal Republic of Germany) in 1949 and officially opened in consort with the German Archaeological Society handing over to the Greek government its excavations of ancient Olympia in June 1961, focus on the educational processes that promote, protect and reinforce the philosophy, ideals and spirit of Olympism.

These Commissions serve as focal points and outreach mechanisms to establish a myriad of local, regional, continental and global dialogues between the primary players of the Olympic Movement. These include sport participants, coaches, educators, and administrators, among others. Their meetings serve as forums to address salient Olympic-related topics ranging from sport medicine (Niger) to sport administration (Kenya) and from swimming (Luxemborg) to boxing (Penang). Olympic Solidarity, headquartered in Lausanne, Switzerland, also has played an active role in the elite North-South International Sports Dialogue, conducted every 2 years in Dubrovnik, Yugoslavia. The Commissions have and will continue to play a significant role in supporting the organizational structure and conduct of the Olympic Movement.

The juridical objectives and powers of the IOC remain today much as they have in the past. As described by the Olympic Charter that was adopted in Montevideo, Uruguay, April, 1979, the IOC is a nonprofit body, corporate by the international law, and has juridical status and perpetual succession. Its aims are to (a) encourage the organization and development of sport and sport competition; (b) inspire and lead sport within the Olympic ideal, thereby promoting and strengthening friendship between the sportsmen of all countries; (c) ensure the regular celebration of the Games; and (d) make the Olympic Games ever more worthy of their glorious history and of the high ideal that inspired their revival (Comité Internationale Olympique, 1979).

The International Olympic Committee is financed by the cities entrusted with organizing the Games as well as by monies accrued from the Games. Its jurisdiction includes such areas as entry, eligibility, program, participation of women, events, equipment, art exhibits, traveling expenses, housing, technical aspects, prizes, media, choice of site, time and duration, and music—in short, all aspects of the Games. In the final analysis, the IOC currently consisting of 89 members (see Appendix A), has supreme authority on all questions concerning the Olympic Games and the Olympic Movement. The Amateur Sports Act of 1978 (Federal Law 95-606), enacted by President Carter on November 8, 1978, further designates the United States Olympic Committee (USOC) as the central coordinating agency in the United States for all sports in Olympic programs (United States Olympic Committee, 1979a). A summary of the Amateur Sports Act can be found in Appendix F. The various interrelationships of the IOC, International Federations, and the USOC can be found in Appendices G and H.

Michels's Theory Applied

The structure, organization, function, and moralistic doctrine of the IOC provide the democratic and idealistic egalitarian conceptual framework to which Michels's theory may be applied. Michels's theory is that oligarchy or a form of organization in which the power is vested in a few arises in even the most idealistic of all organizations. He believed that ideals and ideology serve only as rationalizations to preserve a position of power within a social organization. Michels studied the interaction between the nature of the social organization and the individuals involved, particularly the size, complexity, or organizational function and the coordination of group activities. Also of significance were the psychosocial tendencies of the organization's leaders and followers, which he felt were critical to the formation of an oligarchic structure. The interaction of the above factors is expressed in Figure 2.

As shown previously, the fundamental range of Michels's theory as applied to an examination of the IOC seems to result in a semblance of "goodness of fit." The IOC and its associated affiliations comprise a large number of groups and individuals representing omnifarious forms of technosport (see Appendices C and D). The complexity of the coordinated

functioning and interrelationships of these multidimensional organizations with the IOC represents a herculean charge (Nafziger, 1971). These
technical and administrative features of the structure of the IOC serve
to operate against democratic determination and thus reflect Michels's
model of causal relationships contributing to the development of an oligarchical structure.

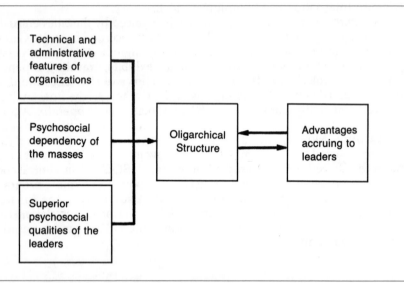

Figure 2   Causal relationships among variables contributing to the development
of an oligarchical structure. Adapted from Smesler, 1971.

The psychosocial dependency of the public on the continuation and
conduct of the Olympic Games has been evident since 1894, when Baron
de Coubertin and Crown Prince Constantine financially revived the seemingly fiscally doomed inaugural Games destined for Athens. The Games
have since mushroomed into a multimillion dollar business venture administered by the IOC which delegates various aspects of its role through
a labyrinth of appointed committee substructures. Thus, Michels pur-
ported that the mechanical and technical possibility of direct governing
of the Olympic Games by the public is impractical. This is due to a myriad
of reasons, such as the voluntary and transnational nature of the organization and the need for constant communication and coordination. These
factors negate the equal involvement of all members even within the IOC
itself. As a result, the technical specialization of what Michels refers to
as expert leadership is requisite. Such are the origins of centralized power
and the formulization of oligarchy, where all related variables (as in Figure
2) seem to slide in one focal direction. It reflects an organization that gives

birth to the dominion of the elected over the electors, of the mandatories over the mandators, and of the delegates over the delegators. It reflects an organization where countertendency does not thrive and a dependency of the masses is created due to the enormous amount of effort, time, and monies required to ensure a successful Olympic outcome.

To ensure this success and perpetuate itself, an organization with the magnitude of the IOC needs the direction and guidance of superior leadership. The psychosocial attributes of superior and domineering leadership that has been reflected throughout the history of the IOC are also an integral component of Michels's causal conceptual framework. Michels mentioned leaders with strength of conviction, pride, force of ideas, moral correctness, and extreme dedication, and certainly these attributes have been more than characterized by the past and present leadership of the Committee (see Table 1 and Appendices A and B). These attributes seem to expand as do the self-adulation and the notion of indispensability of the leaders as their years in office unobtrusively accumulate. The leaders of the IOC remain securely placed and psychologically gratified; they possess information, cultural accessories, and wealth—all of which fit snugly into Michels's conceptual framework. Michels's theory also suggests that a minority of leadership gives orders to the majority, that the minority of leaders are the primary source of political action, that individuals in these positions of power may pursue their own interests at the exploitation of others, and that those leaders tend to consolidate their positions over long periods of time.

Michels's theory also allows for further and future attempts by the Committee to maintain credibility, to ensure that the organization still identifies itself with democracy and the Olympic ideal, and to represent the good of all. The IOC's establishment of a network of external commissions and committees to investigate itself and to make recommendations to itself indicates such attempts. One recently formed committee is concerned with discrimination against female participation in the Games, despite the Olympic ideal reflected in Rule 3 of the Olympic Rules that purports to develop both boys and girls, men and women through competitive sport and physical training. (It should be noted that the 1984 Games included a record 62 events for women, including 13 new events.) Table 2 illustrates the historic flow of male and female Olympic participation patterns reflecting the continued discrimination against female athletes by the IOC and its complex web of substructures. The IOC has also established committees to consider enlarging and equalizing the Committee, to investigate discriminatory practices against developing and socialist countries, and to ensure more input and establish closer relations with International Federations and the NOCs.

Recent steps such as appointing Committee delegates who are younger and less socially conspicuous and who possess sporting ties and encouraging referendums from various substructures (see Appendices C, D, and E) also fit into Michels's schema.

Table 2 Historical Chart of the Modern Olympic Games[a]

Olympic Site—Dates of Competition	No. of Nations	No. of Events	No. of Women's Events	Men's Sports	Women's Sports	Men Athletes	Women Athletes	Total Athletes	Women Athletes %	Women Events %
I. Athens, Greece—April 6-15, 1896	13	42	—	10	—	311	—	311	0	0
II. Paris, France—May 14-Oct. 28, 1900	22	60	2	16	2	1,066	11	1,077	1	.03
III. St. Louis—July 1-Oct. 29, 1904	12	67	1	14	1	517	8	625	1.5	.014
IV. London—Aug. 27-Oct. 29, 1908	22	104	3	21	2	1,998	36	2,034	1.8	2.9
V. Stockholm, Sweden—May 5-July 22, 1912	28	106	6	13	2	2,447	57	2,504	2	5.6
VI. Berlin, Germany—not celebrated, World War I, 1916										
VII. Antwerp, Belgium—April 20-Sept. 9, 1920	29	154	7	21	3	2,543	64	2,607	2.6	4.6
VIII. Paris, France—May 3-July 27, 1924	44	137	10	17	3	2,956	136	3,092	4.6	8
IX. Amsterdam, Holland—July 28-Aug. 12, 1928	46	120	14	14	4	2,724	290	3,014	9.5	11.6
X. Los Angeles—July 31-Aug. 14, 1932	38	124	14	14	3	1,281	127	1,408	10	11.2
XI. Berlin, Germany-Aug. 1-16, 1936	49	142	14	19	4	3,736	328	4,064	8	10
XII. Tokyo and Helsinki—not celebrated, World War II, 1940										
XIII. London, England—not celebrated, World War II, 1944										
XIV. London, England—July 29-Aug. 14, 1948	59	138	19	17	5	3,714	385	4,099	7.7	13.7
XV. Helsinki, Finland—July 19-Aug. 3, 1952	69	149	24	17	5	4,407	518	4,925	8.8	16
XVI. Melbourne, Australia—Nov. 22-Dec. 8, 1956	67	145	25	17	5	2,971	371	3,342	11.5	17
*Stockholm—June 10-17, 1956	29	3	—	—	—	145	13	158	0	0
XVII. Rome—Aug. 25-Sept. 11, 1960	84	150	30	18	5	4,736	610	5,346	11.4	20
XVIII. Tokyo—Oct. 10-24, 1964	94	162	33	20	6	4,854	732	5,586	12.4	20
XIX. Mexico City—Oct. 12-27, 1968	112	172	39	19	6	4,750	781	5,531	14	22.6
XX. Munich—Aug. 26-Sept. 11, 1972	123	196	42	21	7	7,019	1,125	8,144	13.8	21.4
XXI. Montreal, Canada—July 17-Aug. 1, 1976	88	199	49	21	10	4,915	1,274	6,189	20.6	24.6
XXII. Moscow—July 19-Aug. 3, 1980	79	200	50	21	11	4,625	1,247	5,872	22.9	25
XXIII. Los Angeles—July 28-Aug. 12, 1984	140	223	62	21	13	6,459	1,619	7,078	22.9	27.8

Olympic Winter Games

I. Chamonix, France—Jan. 25-Feb. 5, 1924	16	13	2	5	1	281	13	294	4	14.3
II. St. Moritz, Switzerland—Feb. 11-19, 1928	25	13	2	5	1	366	27	363	7.4	15.4
III. Lake Placid—Feb. 4-13, 1932	17	14	2	5	1	277	30	307	10	13.3
IV. Garmisch-Partenkirchen, Germany—Feb. 6-16, 1936	28	17	3	5	2	680	76	756	10.	16.7
V. St. Moritz—Jan. 30-Feb. 9, 1948	28	24	6	6	2	636	77	713	10.8	25
VI. Oslo, Norway—Feb. 14-25, 1952	30	22	6	5	2	624	108	732	15	27
VII. Cortina, Italy—Jan. 26-Feb. 5, 1956	32	24	7	5	2	687	132	819	16	28
VIII. Squaw Valley, CA—Feb. 18-28, 1960	30	27	11	5	3	502	146	648	22	39.7
IX. Innsbruck, Austria—Jan. 29-Feb. 9, 1964	36	34	13	7	4	758	175	933	18	37
X. Grenoble, France—Feb. 6-18, 1968	37	35	13	7	4	1,063	230	1,293	19	37
XI. Sapporo, Japan—Feb. 2-13, 1972	35	35	13	7	4	927	218	1,128	19	37
XII. Innsbruck, Austria—Feb. 4-15, 1976	37	37	14	7	4	1,013	218	1,261	17.3	38
XIII. Lake Placid—Feb. 13-24, 1980	38	39	14	7	4	1,012	271	1,283	21	35
XIV. Sarajevo, Yugoslavia—Feb. 7-19, 1984	49	40	15	7	4	1,127	283	1,490	19	37.5

Upcoming Games

XXIV. Games of the Olympiad, Seoul, Korea—Sept. 17-Oct. 2, 1988
XV. Olympic Winter Games, Calgary, Alberta, Canada—Feb. 13-28, 1988

[a]Courtesy of the USOC.
[b]Equestrian events only because of immigration laws for permitting horses to enter Australia.

The Future of the Olympic Games

As events surrounding the boycotted 1980 and 1984 Olympic Games continue to unfold and more problems and questions confront the IOC, only time will tell if its present oligarchic power structure, which may have been needed to reinstate the Olympic Games in the earlier years of the Olympic Movement, can withstand the pressures of true democratic spirit. It remains to be seen if, as Michels's theory suggests, an organization that compromises and enters into promiscuous relationships with other elements in society sacrifices its political virginity, which may have disastrous and enduring consequences. In this instance, the consequences are the life of the Olympic Games and the Olympic Movement itself. Unless the Olympic forum is radically shaken, such as opening up of the Games to "professionals," it appears that the IOC will not lose its grip on the Olympic olive branch, or indeed, the Olympic forum will not be altered to allow for harmonious direction of wills toward identical objectives and practical aims. When such change is lacking, an organization no longer contributes to society and eventually becomes ineffective and dissolves. It appears that the Moscow and Los Angeles Games may have provided such a turning point in history. Ultimately, however, the effects of the seemingly reciprocal boycotts of the 1980 and 1984 Games and their surrounding associated controversies remain to be determined as the Games of the XXIVth Olympiad move to Seoul.

Acknowledgments

The author wishes to acknowledge and thank the International Olympic Committee; Dr. Otto Szymiczek, Dean of the International Olympic Academy; the United States Olympic Committee; and C. Robert Paul, Jr., of Olympic House for their assistance in preparation of this manuscript.

References

Bannister, R. (1980, February). *The Olympic Games: Past, present, and future*. Paper presented at the Olympic Symposium at Skidmore College, Saratoga Springs, NY.

Beck, R.H. (1974). The Greek tradition and today's physical education. In C.A. Bucher (Ed.), *Dimensions of physical education*. St. Louis, MO: C.V. Mosby.

Cassenelli, C.W. (1953). The law of oligarchy. *The American Political Science Review*, **47**, 773-784.

Comité International Olympique. (1979). *Olympic charter 1979*. Lausanne: Comité International Olympique.

Coubertin, P. de. (1896). The Olympic Games of 1896. *The Century Magazine*, **53**, 39-53.

Coubertin, P. de. (1908). *Une campagne de vingt-et-un ans 1887-1908*. Paris: Librarie de L'Education Physique.

Gardiner, E.N. (1910). *Greek athletic sports and festivals*. London: McMillan.

Gardiner, E.N. (1925). *Olympia: Its history and remains*. Oxford: Clarendon Press.

Guttmann, A. (1978). *From ritual to record*. New York: Columbia University Press.

Kieran, J., & Daley, A. (1961). *The story of the Olympics*. Philadelphia: J.B. Lippincott.

Killanin, L.M., & Rodda, J. (Eds.). (1976). *The Olympic Games: 80 Years of people, events, and records*. Don Mills, Ontario: Collier MacMillan Canada.

Krotee, M.L. (Ed.). (1979a). *The dimensions of sport sociology*. West Point, NY: Leisure Press.

Krotee, M.L. (1979b). The rise and demise of sport: A reflection of Uruguayan society. *The Annals of the American Academy of Political and Social Science*, **445**, 151-154.

Krotee, M.L. (1980, April). *Sport sociology: Issues and problems of the Olympic Games*. Paper presented at the American Alliance of Health, Physical Education, Recreation and Dance Conference. Detroit, MI.

Krotee, M.L. (1981). Sociological perspectives of the Olympic Games. In J. Segrave & D. Chu (Eds.), *Olympism* (pp. 207-226). Champaign, IL: Human Kinetics.

Lenk, H. (1976). Toward a social philosophy of the Olympics: Values, aims and reality of the modern Olympic Movement. In P.J. Graham & H. Ueberhorst (Eds.), *The modern Olympics* (pp. 109-169). West Point, NY: Leisure Press.

Lenk, H. (1979). *Social philosophy of athletics*. Champaign, IL: Stipes.

Leonard, F.E., & Affleck, G.B. (1957). *A guide to the history of physical education*. Philadelphia: Lea & Febiger.

Lowe, B., Kanin, D.B., & Strenk, A. (1978). *Sport and international relations*. Champaign, IL: Stipes.

Lucas, J. (1962). *Baron Pierre de Coubertin and the formative years of the modern international Olympic Movement*. Unpublished doctoral dissertation, University of Maryland, College Park.

Lüschen, G. (1979). The organization and policies of National Olympic Committees—A pilot project. In M.L. Krotee (Ed.), *The dimensions of sport sociology* (pp. 238-250). West Point, NY: Leisure Press.

Merton, R.K. (1968). *Social theory and social structure*. New York: Free Press.

Michels, R. (1959). *Political parties, 1911* (E. Paul & C. Paul, Trans.). Dover: [n.p.].

Nafziger, J.A.R. (1971). The regulation of transnational sports competition: Down from Mount Olympus. *Vanderbilt Journal of Transnational Law*, **5**, 180-212.

Parsons, T. (1951). *The social system*. New York: Free Press.

Smelser, N.J. (1971). *Sociological theory: A contemporary view*. New York: General Learning Press.

Ueberhorst, H. (1976). Return to Olympia and the rebirth of the Games. In P.J. Graham & H. Ueberhorst (Eds.), *The modern Olympics* (pp. 13-26). West Point, NY: Leisure Press.

United States Olympic Committee. (1979a). *Constitution and by-laws*. Colorado Springs, CO: United States Olympic Committee.

United States Olympic Committee (1979b). *The Olympic Games*. Colorado Springs, CO: United States Olympic Committee.

United States Olympic Committee. (1983). *The Olympic Games*. Colorado Springs, CO: United States Olympic Committee.

United States Olympic Committee. (1985). *An Olympic primer*. Colorado Springs, CO: United States Olympic Committee.

Viken, J.P., Krotee, M.L., & Stone, G.P. (1979). Popular culture and the erosion of class distinctions in the mass sport of drag racing. In M.L. Krotee (Ed.), *The dimensions of sport sociology* (pp. 127-140). West Point, NY: Leisure Press.

Weyland, A.M. (1952). *The Olympic pageant*. New York: Macmillan.

Appendix A

List of Past and Present Members of the IOC Since Its Foundation

	Election	Name	Country	Cessation of Functions
1	1894	*Baron Pierre de Coubertin*	France	*1925*
2	1894	*Ernest Callot*	France	1913
3	1894	*Dimetrius Vikélas*	Greece	1897
4	1894	*General de Boutowski*	Russia	1900
5	1894	*General Victor Balck*	Sweden	1921
6	1894	*Professor William M. Sloane*	United States	1925
7	1894	*Conseiller Jiri Guth-Jarkovsky*	Bohemia	1943
8	1894	*Fr. Franz Kemény*	Hungary	1907

(Cont.)

Election	Name	Country	Cessation of Functions
9 1894	Lord Ampthill	Great Britain	1898
10 1894	Charles Herbert	Great Britain	1906
11 1894	Dr. José Benjamin Zubiaur	Argentina	1907
12 1894	Leonard A. Cuff	New Zealand	1905
13 1894	Comte Lucchesi Palli	Italy	1895
14 1894	Comte Maxime de Bousies	Belgium	1901
15 1894	Duc d'Andria Carafa	Italy	1898
16 1895	Dr. Wilhelm Gebhardt	Germany	1909
17 1897	Rév. R.S. de Courcy Laffan	Great Britain	1927
18 1897	Comte Alexandre Mercati	Greece	1925
19 1897	Comte Brunetta d'Usseaux	Italy	1919
20 1898	Baron F.W. de Tuyll de Serooskerken	Netherlands	1924
21 1899	Comte de Talleyrand Périgord	Germany	1903
22 1899	Colonel Holbeck	Denmark	1906
23 1899	Prince Georges Bibesco	Rumania	1901
24 1899	Baron Godefroy de Blonay	Switzerland	1937
25 1900	Théodore Stanton	United States	1904
26 1900	Gaspar Witney	United States	1905
27 1900	H. Hébrard de Villeneuve	France	1911
28 1900	Prince Serge Beliosselsky de Beliozersk	Russia	1908
29 1900	Comte de Ribaupierre	Russia	1910
30 1900	Comte Clarence de Rosen	Sweden	1948
31 1901	Prince Edouard de Salm Horstmar	Germany	1905
32 1901	Commandant Reyntiens	Belgium	1903
33 1901	Colonel Sir Howard Vincent	Great Britain	1907
34 1901	Miguel de Beistegui	Mexico	1931
35 1902	Comte de Mejorada del Campo, Marquis de Villamejor	Spain	1921
36 1903	Comte César de Wartensleben	Germany	1913
37 1903	Comte Henri de Baillet-Latour	Belgium	1942
38 1903	James Hyde	United States	1908
39 1903	Carlos F. de Candamo	Peru	1922
40 1904	Comte Albert Bertier de Sauvigny	France	1920
41 1905	General comte von der Assebourg	Germany	1909
42 1905	Richard Coombes	Australia	1932

(Cont.)

Election	Name	Country	Cessation of Functions
43 1905	Prince Alexandre de Solms Braunfels	Austria	1909
44 1905	Capitaine Heinrik Angell	Norway	1907
45 1906	E.N. Tzokow	Bulgaria	1912
46 1906	Capitaine Grut	Denmark	1912
47 1906	Lord Desborough of Taplow	Great Britain	1909
48 1906	Duc de Lancastre	Portugal	1912
49 1907	Manuel Quintana	Argentina	1910
50 1907	Comte Geza Andrassy	Hungary	1938
51 1907	Thomas Heftye	Norway	1908
52 1908	Allison Armour	United States	1919
53 1908	Baron R. de Willebrand	Finland	1920
54 1908	Prince Scipion Borghese	Italy	1909
55 1908	Comte Albert Gautier Vignal	Monaco	1940
56 1908	Colonel Johan T. Sverre	Norway	1927
57 1908	Georges A. Plagino	Rumania	1949
58 1908	Prince Simon Troubetzkoi	Russia	1910
59 1908	Selim Sirry Bey	Turkey	1930
60 1909	Baron de Wenningen	Germany	1914
61 1909	Sir Theodore Cook	Great Britain	1915
62 1909	Senator Jules de Muzsa	Hungary	1946
63 1909	Conseiller Attilio Brunialti	Italy	1913
64 1909	Professor Jigoro Kano	Japan	1938
65 1910	Comte A.F. Sierstorpft	Germany	1919
66 1910	Angelo C. Bolanaki	Egypt (Greece from 1933)	1963
67 1910	Maurice Pescatore	Luxembourg	1929
68 1910	Prince Léon Ouroussoff	Russia	1933
69 1911	Prince Othon de Windischgraetz	Austria	1919
70 1911	Sir John Hanbury Williams	Canada	1921
71 1911	Evert Jansen Wendell	United States	1921
72 1911	Abel Ballif	France	1913
73 1912	Comte Rodolphe de Colloredo Mansfeld	Austria	1919
74 1912	Professor O.N. Garcia	Chile	1919
75 1912	Comte de Penha Gardia	Portugal	1940
76 1912	General S.W. Djoukitch	Serbia	1949
77 1913	Comte Armin Muskau	Germany	1919
78 1913	Raul de Rio Branco	Brazil	1938
79 1913	Dimitrius Stancioff	Bulgaria	1929

(Cont.)

Election	Name	Country	Cessation of Functions
80 1913	*Sydney Farrar*	South Africa	1919
81 1913	*Colonel Hansen*	Denmark	1922
82 1913	*Albert Glandaz*	France	1944
83 1913	*Duke of Somerset*	Great Britain	1920
84 1913	*General Carlo Montu*	Italy	1939
85 1913	*Georges Duperron*	Russia	1915
86 1914	*Marquis Melchior de Polignac*	France	1950
87 1918	*P.J. de Matheu*	Central America	1941
88 1919	*Baron de Laveleye*	Belgium	1939
89 1920	*Carlos-Silva Vildosola*	Chile	1922
90 1920	*Dorn y de Alsua*	Ecuador	1929
91 1920	*Judge Bartow Weeks*	United States	1921
92 1920	*Ernst Krogius*	Finland	1948
93 1920	*Comte Clary*	France	1933
94 1920	*Brigadier gen. R.J. Kentish*	Great Britain	1933
95 1920	*Sir Dorabji J. Tata*	India	1930
96 1920	*Marquis Guglielmi*	Italy	1930
97 1920	*Arthur Marryatt*	New Zealand	1925
98 1920	*Henry Nourse*	South Africa	1943
99 1920	*Professor Dr Franjo Bucar*	Yugoslavia	1947
100 1920	*J. Sigfrid Edström*	Sweden	1952
101 1921	*J.G. Merrick*	Canada	1946
102 1921	*H. Echevarrieta*	Spain	1923
103 1921	*Nizzam Eddin Khof*	Persia	1923
104 1921	*Dr. F. Ghigliani*	Uruguay	1937
105 1922	*T. de Alvear*	Argentina	1932
106 1922	*Dr. C.T. Wang*	China	1957
107 1922	*Ivar Nyholm*	Denmark	1931
108 1922	*Baron de Güell*	Spain	1954
109 1922	*William May Garland*	United States	1948
110 1922	*General Ch. H. Sherrill*	United States	1936
111 1922	*The Earl Cadogan*	Great Britain	1929
112 1922	*J.J. Keane*	Ireland	1951
113 1922	*Prince Casimir Lubomirski*	Poland	1930
114 1923	*Ricardo C. Aldao*	Argentina	1949
115 1923	*Arnaldo Guinle*	Brazil	1961
116 1923	*Dr. Ferreira Santos*	Brazil	1962
117 1923	*J. Matte Gormaz*	Chile	1928
118 1923	*Porfirio Franca*	Cuba	1938
119 1923	*Marquis de Guadelupe*	Mexico	1924

(Cont.)

	Election	Name	Country	Cessation of Functions
120	1923	*Alfredo Benavides*	Peru	1957
121	1924	*Secrét. d'Etat Theodore Lewald*	Germany	1938
122	1924	*Dr. Oskar Ruperti*	Germany	1929
123	1924	*James Taylor*	Australia	1944
124	1924	*Dr. Martin Haudek*	Austria	1928
125	1924	*Duc d'Albe*	Spain	1927
126	1924	*Colonel P.W. Scharroo*	Netherlands	1957
127	1924	*Dr. S. Kishi*	Japan	1933
128	1924	*Jorge Gomez de Parada*	Mexico	1927
129	1924	*Prince Samad Khan*	Persia	1927
130	1925	*David Kinley*	United States	1927
131	1925	*Baron A. Schimmelpenninck van der Óye*	Netherlands	1943
132	1925	*Comte Alberto Bonacossa*	Italy	1953
133	1925	*J.P. Firth*	New Zealand	1927
134	1926	*Duc Adolphe-Frédéric de Mecklenburg-Schwerin*	Germany	1956
135	1926	*Georges Averoff*	Greece	1930
136	1926	*J. Dikmanis*	Latvia	1947
137	1927	*Marquis de Pons*	Spain	1930
138	1927	*Hon. Ernest Lee Jahncke*	United States	1936
139	1927	*Lord Rochdale*	Great Britain	1933
140	1927	*Dr. M. Saenz*	Mexico	1932
141	1927	*Sir Thomas Fearnley*	Norway	1950
142	1928	*Dr. Theodore Schmidt*	Austria	1939
143	1928	*Sir George McLaren Brown*	Canada	1940
144	1928	*Dr. F. Akel*	Estonia	1932
145	1928	*Lord Freyberg*	New Zealand	1930
146	1928	*Ignace Matuszewski*	Poland	1939
147	1929	*Dr. Karl Ritter von Halt*	Germany	1964
148	1929	*Stephan G. Tchaprachikov*	Bulgaria	1944
149	1929	*Don Alfredo Ewing*	Chile	1933
150	1929	*Lord Aberdare*	Great Britain	1957
151	1930	*N. Politis*	Greece	1933
152	1930	*Augusto Turati*	Italy	1931
153	1930	*Kremalettin Sami Pacha*	Turkey	1933
154	1931	*Comte de Vallellano*	Spain	1952
155	1931	*C.J. Wray*	New Zealand	1934
156	1931	*Général Dr. Rouppert*	Poland	1946
157	1932	*Horacio Bustos Moron, Jr.*	Argentina	1952

(Cont.)

Election		Name	Country	Cessation of Functions
158	1932	*Prince Axel de Danemark*	Denmark	1958
159	1932	*G.C. Sondhi*	India	1966
160	1932	*Comte Paolo Thaon di Revel*	Italy	1964
161	1933	*Sir Harold Luxton*	Australia	1951
162	1933	*The Marquess of Exeter*	Great Britain	1981
163	1933	*Sir Noël Curtis Bennett*	Great Britain	1950
164	1933	*Dr. Jotaro Sugimoura*	Japan	1936
165	1933	*Rechid Saffet Atabinen*	Turkey	1952
166	1934	*François Piétri*	France	1966
167	1934	The Lord Porritt, G.C.M.G.	New Zealand	1967
168	1934	*S.E. Mohammed Taher*	Egypt	1968
169	1934	*Comte Michimasa Soyeshima*	Japan	1948
170	1934	*Ing. Segura Marte R. Gomez*	Mexico	1973
171	1936	*Avery Brundage*	United States	1972
172	1936	Prince régnant François-Joseph	Liechtenstein	1980
173	1936	*Joakim Puhk*	Estonia	1942
174	1936	*Prince Iesato Tokugawa*	Japan	1939
175	1936	*Hon. Jorge B. Vargas*	Philippines	1980
176	1937	*Frederic-René Coudert*	United States	1948
177	1937	*Général Henri Guisan*	Switzerland	1939
178	1937	*Joaquin Serratosa Cibils*	Uruguay	1958
179	1938	*Général Walther von Reichenau*	Germany	1942
180	1938	*Dr. Miguel A. Moenck*	Cuba	1969
181	1938	*Antonio Prado, Jr.*	Brazil	1955
182	1938	Johan Wilhelm Rangell	Finland	1967
183	1939	*Baron de Trannoy*	Belgium	1957
184	1939	Dr. H.H. Kung	China	1955
185	1939	*Général Giorgio Vaccaro*	Italy	1949
186	1939	*Dr. M. Nagai*	Japan	1950
187	1939	*Dr. Sh. Takaishi*	Japan	1967
188	1939	*A.V. Lindbergh*	South Africa	1939
189	1939	Nicholas de Horthy, Jr.	Hungary	1948
190	1946	*Hugh Richard Weir*	Australia	1975
191	1946	*R.W. Seeldrayers*	Belgium	1955
192	1946	Jean-Claude Patterson	Canada	1954
193	1946	*Dr. Joseph Gruss*	Czechoslovakia	1965
194	1946	*Armand Massard*	France	1970
195	1946	*Major-général C.F. Pahud de Mortanges*	Netherlands	1964

(Cont.)

Election	Name	Country	Cessation of Functions
196 1946	*Benedikt G. Waage*	Iceland	1966
197 1946	S.A.R. le grand duc Jean de Luxembourg	Luxembourg	
198 1946	*Dr. José Pontes*	Portugal	1956
199 1946	J. Dowsett	South Africa	1951
200 1946	*Reginald Honey*	South Africa	1982
201 1946	*Albert Mayer*	Switzerland	1969
202 1946	*Jean Ketséas*	Greece	1965
203 1947	*Dr. Manfred M. Ritter von Markhof*	Austria	1969
204 1947	*Sidney Dawes*	Canada	1967
205 1947	Shou-Yi-Tung	China	1958
206 1947	*Raja Bhalendra Singh*	India	
207 1948	*Bo Ekelund*	Sweden	1965
208 1948	*Dr. Georges Loth*	Poland	1961
209 1948	*Stanko Bloudek*	Yugoslavia	1959
210 1948	*Dr. Ferenc Mezö*	Hungary	1961
211 1948	Enrique O. Barbosa Baeza	Chile	1952
212 1948	*John Jewett Garland*	United States	1969
213 1948	*Erik von Frenckell*	Finland	1976
214 1948	Général Miguel Ydigoras Fuentes	Guatemala	1952
215 1948	*Olaf Christian Ditlev-Simonsen, Jr.*	Norway	1967
216 1949	Prince Rainier III	Monaco	1950
217 1949	Ahmed E.H. Jaffer	Pakistan	1956
218 1950	*Ryotaro Azuma*	Japan	1969
219 1950	*James Brooks B. Parker*	United States	1951
220 1950	*Prince Pierre de Monaco*	Monaco	1964
221 1951	Lord Luke of Pavenham	Great Britain	
222 1951	Comte Jean de Beaumont	France	
223 1951	Dr. Giorgio de Stefani	Italy	
224 1951	Constantin Andrianov	U.S.S.R.	
225 1951	Lewis Luxton	Australia	1974
226 1952	General Vladimir Stoytchev	Bulgaria	
227 1952	Lord Killanin	Ireland	1980
228 1952	Cheik Gabriel Gemayel	Lebanon	
229 1952	*Général José de J. Clark*	Mexico	1971
230 1952	*Aleksei Romanov*	U.S.S.R.	1979
231 1952	*Enrique Alberdi*	Argentina	1959

(Cont.)

Election	Name	Country	Cessation of Functions
232 1952	Julio Gerlein Comelin	Colombia	
233 1952	Pedro Ibarra Mac-Mahon, baron de Güell	Spain	
234 1952	Douglas F. Roby	United States	
235 1952	Dr. Augustin Sosa	Panama	1967
236 1952	*Général Gustaf Dyrssen*	Sweden	1970
237 1952	*Dr. Julio Bustamante B.*	Venezuela	1968
238 1955	Dr. Alejandro Rivera Bascur	Chile	
239 1955	Suat Erler	Turkey	
240 1955	*Ki Poong Lee*	Korea	1960
241 1955	Prince Gholam Reza Pahlavi	Iran	1980
242 1955	Alexandru Siperco	Rumania	
243 1956	Willi Daume	Germany	
244 1957	Saul Christovão Ferreira Pires	Portugal	1962
245 1958	S.A.R. le prince Albert de Liège	Belgium	1964
246 1958	Eduardo Dibos	Peru	1982
247 1959	Syed Wajid Ali	Pakistan	
248 1959	*Ivar Emil Vind*	Denmark	1977
249 1960	Reginald Stanley Alexander	Kenya	
250 1960	Boris Bakrac	Yugoslavia	
251 1960	*Mario L. Negri*	Argentina	1977
252 1960	Ahmed Eldemerdash Touny	Egypt Arab Rep.	
253 1961	Wlodzimierz Reczek	Poland	
254 1961	Hadj Mohammed Benjelloun	Morocco	
255 1963	Sir Adetokunbo Ademola	Nigeria	
256 1963	Général Raul Pereira de Castro	Portugal	
257 1963	João Havelange	Brazil	
258 1963	Marc Hodler	Switzerland	
259 1963	*Alfredo Inciarte*	Uruguay	1975
260 1963	S.M. le roi des Hellénes	Greece	1974
261 1964	*Arpad Csanadi*	Hungary	1983
262 1964	Prince Alexandre de Mérode	Belgium	
263 1964	Major Sylvio de Magalhães Padilha	Brazil	
264 1964	*Me. Giulio Onesti*	Italy	1981
265 1964	Jonkheer Herman A. van Karnebeek	Netherlands	1977
266 1964	*Sang Beck Lee*	Korea	1966
267 1965	*Amadou Barry*	Senegal	1969

(Cont.)

	Election	Name	Country	Cessation of Functions
268	1965	Gunnar Ericsson	Sweden	
269	1965	Frantisek Kroutil	Czechoslovakia	1981
270	1965	*Vice-admiral Pyrros Lappas*	Greece	1980
271	1965	Mohamed Mzali	Tunisia	
272	1966	*Dr. h.c. Georg von Opel*	Germany	1971
273	1966	Juan Antonio Samaranch	Spain	
274	1966	*Dr. h.c. Heinz Schöbel*	German Dem. Rep.	1980
275	1966	Jan Staubo	Norway	
276	1966	S.A.R. le prince Georges William de Hanovre (ès qualité)	International Olympic Academy	1971
277	1967	*Koy Young Chang*	Korea	1977
278	1967	Paavo Honkajuuri	Finland	1981
279	1967	Tsuneyoshi Takeda	Japan	1981
280	1967	James Worrall	Canada	
281	1968	Agustin Carlos Arroyo Yerovi	Ecuador	
282	1968	José Beracasa A.	Venezuela	1981
283	1968	Dr. Abdel Mohamed Halim	Sudan	1982
284	1968	H.H. sultan Hamengku Buwono IX	Indonesia	1976
285	1968	*René Rakotobe*	Madagascar	1971
286	1969	C. Lance S. Cross	New Zealand	
287	1969	Raymond Gafner	Switzerland	
288	1969	Louis Guirandou-N'Diaye	Ivory Coast	
289	1969	Masaji Kiyokawa	Japan	
290	1969	Virgilio de León	Panama	
291	1969	*Dr. Rudolf Nemetschke*	Austria	1976
292	1970	Maurice Herzog	France	
293	1970	Henry Hsu	Taiwan	
294	1970	General Sven Thofelt	Sweden	1976
295	1971	General Prabhas Charusathiara	Thailand	1974
296	1971	Vitaly Smirnov	U.S.S.R.	
297	1971	Ydnekatchew Tessema	Ethiopia	
298	1972	Berthold Beitz	Germany	
299	1972	Pedro Ramirez Vazquez	Mexico	
300	1973	Tony Bridge	Jamaica	
301	1973	Manuel Gonzalez Guerra	Cuba	
302	1973	Ashwini Kumar	India	
303	1973	Kéba M'Baye	Senegal	
304	1974	Air chief marshal Dawee Chullasapya	Thailand	

(Cont.)

Election	Name	Country	Cessation of Functions
305 1974	Dr. Eduardo Hay	Mexico	
306 1974	*David H. McKenzie*	Australia	1981
307 1974	Julian K. Roosevelt	United States	
308 1974	Mohammed Zerguini	Algeria	
309 1975	*Me. Epaminondas Petralias*	Greece	1977
310 1976	Matts Carlgren	Sweden	
311 1976	Dr Kevin O'Flanagan	Ireland	
312 1976	Peter Tallberg	Finland	
313 1976	José D. Vallarino Veracierto	Uruguay	
314 1977	Bashir Mohamed Attarabulsi	Libya	
315 1977	Richard Kevan Gosper	Australia	
316 1977	Major General Niels Holst-Sørensen	Denmark	
317 1977	Lamine Keita	Mali	
318 1977	Cornelis (Kees) Kerdel	Netherlands	
319 1977	*Taik Soo Kim*	Korea	1983
320 1977	Shagdarjav Magvan	Mongolia	
321 1977	Roberto Guillermo Peper	Argentina	
322 1977	German Rieckehoff	Puerto Rico	
323 1977	Phillipp von Schoeller	Austria	
324 1977	Lieutenant-Général Dadong Suprayogi	Indonesia	
325 1978	René Essomba	Cameroon	
326 1978	Hon. Datuk Seri Hamzah Bin Haji Abu Samah	Malaysia	
327 1978	Yu Sun Kim	D.P.R. Korea	
328 1978	*Nikolaos Nissiotis*	Greece	
329 1978	Richard W. Pound	Canada	
330 1981	Vladimir Cernusak	Czechoslovakia	
331 1981	Nikos Filaretos	Greece	
332 1981	Mrs. Pirjo Haggman	Finland	
333 1981	Zhenliang He	People's Republic of China	
334 1981	Gunther Heinze	German Dem. Rep.	
335 1981	Mrs. Flor Isava Fonseca	Venezuela	
336 1981	Sheikh Fahid Al-Ahmad Al-Sabah	Kuwait	
337 1982	Franco Carraro	Italy	
338 1982	Philip Walter Coles	Australia	
339 1982	Iyan Dibos	Peru	

(Cont.)

Election	Name	Country	Cessation of Functions
340 1982	Mrs. Mary Alison Glen-Haig	Great Britain	
341 1982	Chiharu Igaya	Japan	
342 1983	H.R.H. Prince Faisal Abdul Aziz	Saudi Arabia	
343 1983	General Zein El Abdin M.A.A. Gadir	Sudan	
344 1983	Anani Matthia	Togo	
345 1983	Roque Napoleón Muñoz Peña	Dominican Republic	
346 1983	Pat Schmitt	Hungary	
347 1985	Major General Robert H. Helmick	United States	
348 1985	Henry E. Olufemi Adefope	Nigeria	
349 1985	Francisco J. Elizalde	Philippines	
350 1985	Carlos Ferrer	Spain	
351 1985	S.A.S. le Prince Héréditaire Albert de Monaco	Monaco	

Note. Deceased members' names are italicized.
Courtesy of the IOC.

Appendix B

International Olympic Committee Executive Board

President/Président
S.E.M. Juan Antonio Samaranch (1980) • (Spain)

Vice-Presidents/Vice-Présidents
S.E.M. Louis Guirandou-N'Diaye (1980) • (Ivory Coast)
1er vice-président
M. Alexandru Siperco (1982) • (Roumania)
2e vice-président
M. Ashwini Kumar (1983) • (India)
3e vice-président

(Cont.)

Membres/Members
M. Virgilio de Leon (1980) • (Panama)
Le prince Alexandre de Mérode (1982) • (Belgium)
M. Julian K. Roosevelt (1982) • (United States)
M. Richard W. Pound (1983) • (Canada)
Major Sylvio de Magalhães Padilha (1983) • (Brazil)

Directeur/Director
Mme. Monique Berlioux

Directeur Sportif/Sports Director
M. Walther Tröger

Directeur de la Solidarité Olympique/Director of Olympic Solidarity
M. Ansolmo Lopez

Courtesy of the IOC.

Appendix C

International Sports Federations Recognized by the IOC Along With United States Member of the International Federation

International Federation for Olympic Sports	United States Member
IAAF—International Amateur Athletic Federation (Track and Field) (1912) (168)	Athletics Congress of the USA (TAC)
FITA—International Archery Federation (1931) (60)	National Archery Association (NAA)
FIBA—International Amateur Basketball Federation (1932) (151)	Amateur Basketball Association of the U.S.A. (ABAUSA)
FIBT—International Bobsleigh and Tobogganing Federation (1923) (23)	U.S.A. National Bobsled Federation, Inc. (NATBOB)

(Cont.)

International Federation for Olympic Sports	United States Member
AIBA—International Amateur Boxing Association (1946) (125)	U.S.A. Amateur Boxing Federation, Inc. (USAABF)
FIC—International Canoe Federation (1924) (39)	American Canoe Association (ACA)
FIAC—International Amateur Cyclists Federation (1900) (129)	U.S. Cycling Federation (USCF)
FIE—International Fencing Federation (1913) (68)	U.S. Fencing Association (USFA)
FIFA—International Association Football Federation (soccer) (1904) (150)	U.S. Soccer Federation (USSF)
FEI—International Equestrian Federation (1921) (69)	American Horse Shows Association (AHSA)
FIG—International Gymnastics Federation (1881) (78)	U.S. Gymnastics Federation (USGF)
IHF—International Handball Federation (1946) (80)	U.S. Team Handball Federation (USTHF)
FIH—International Hockey Federation (field hockey) (1924) (85)	Field Hockey Association of America (men's) (FHAA) U.S. Field Hockey Association (women's) USFHA
IIHF—International Ice Hockey Federation (1908) (31)	Amateur Hockey Association of the U.S. (AHAUS)
IJF—International Judo Federation (1951) (104)	U.S. Judo, Inc. (USJ)
FIL—International Luge Federation (1957) (26)	U.S. Luge Association, Inc. (USLA)
IUPMB—International Union for Modern Pentathlon and Biathlon (1948) (54)	U.S. Modern Pentathlon Association (USMPA) U.S. Biathlon Association (USBA)
FISA—International Federation of Rowing Societies (1892) (55)	U.S. Rowing Association (USRA)

(Cont.)

International Federation for Olympic Sports	United States Member
UIT—International Shooting Union (1907) (90)	National Rifle Association of America (NRAA)
ISU—International Skating Union (1892) (32)	U.S. Figure Skating Association (USFSA) U.S. International Speed Skating Association (USISA)
FIS—International Ski Federation (1924) (51)	U.S. Ski Association—Competitive Division (USSA)
FINA—International Amateur Swimming Federation (1908) (97)	U.S. Diving, Inc. (USD) U.S. Swimming, Inc. (USS) U.S. Synchronized Swimming, Inc. (USS) U.S. Water Polo, Inc. (USWP)

Courtesy of the USOC.

Appendix D

National Olympic Committees (Recognized by the International Olympic Committee as of September, 1985)

AFG	Afghanistan	BER	Bermuda
ALB	Albania	BHU	Bhutan
ALG	Algeria	BOL	Bolivia
AND	Andorra	BOT	Botswana
ANG	Angola	BRA	Brazil
ANT	Antiqua	IVB	British Virgin Islands
AHO	Antilles Netherlands	BRU	Brunei
EGY	Arab Republic of Egypt	BUL	Bulgaria
ARG	Argentina	BIR	Burma
AUS	Australia	CMR	Cameroun
AUT	Austria	CAN	Canada
BAH	Bahamas	CAY	Cayman Islands
BRN	Bahrain	CAF	Central Africa
BAN	Bangladesh	CHA	Chad
BAR	Barbados	CHI	Chile
BEL	Belgium	TPE	Chinese Taipei
BIZ	Belize	COL	Colombia
BEN	Benin	CGO	People's Rep. of Congo

(Cont.)

CRC	Costa Rica	KEN	Kenya
CUB	Cuba	KUW	Kuwait
CYP	Cyprus	LAO	Laos
TCH	Czechoslovakia	LIB	Lebanon
PRK	Democratic Peoples Republic of Korea	LES	Lesotho
		LBR	Liberia
GDR	Democratic Republic of Germany	LBA	Libya
		LIE	Liechtenstein
YMD	Democratic Republic of Yemen	LUX	Luxembourg
		MAD	Madagascar
DEN	Denmark	MAL	Malaysia
DOM	Dominican Republic	MAW	Malawi
DJI	Djibouti	MLI	Mali
ECU	Ecuador	MLT	Malta
ESA	El Salvador	MAR	Morocco
GEQ	Equatorial Guinea	MRI	Mauritius
ETH	Ethiopia	MTN	Mauritania
FU	Fiji Islands	MEX	Mexico
FIN	Finland	MON	Monaco
FRA	France	MGL	Mongolia
GAB	Gabon	MOZ	Mozambique
GAM	Gambia	NEP	Nepal
FRG	German Federal Republic	NZL	New Zealand
GHA	Ghana	NCA	Nicaragua
GBR	Great Britain	NIG	Niger
GRE	Greece	NGR	Nigeria
GRN	Grenada	NOR	Norway
GUA	Guatemala	OMA	Oman
GUI	Guinea	PAK	Pakistan
GUY	Guyana	PAN	Panama
HAI	Haiti	NGU	Papua New Guinea
HOL	Holland (The Netherlands)	PAR	Paraguay
HON	Honduras	CHN	Peoples Republic of China
HKG	Hong Kong	PER	Peru
HUN	Hungary	PHI	Philippines
ISL	Iceland	POL	Poland
IND	India	POR	Portugal
INA	Indonesia	PUR	Puerto Rico
IRN	Iran	QAT	Qatar
IRQ	Iraq	ROM	Roumania
IRL	Ireland	RWA	Rwanda
ISR	Israel	SMR	San Marino
ITA	Italy	SAU	Saudi Arabia
CIV	Ivory Coast	SEN	Senegal
JAM	Jamaica	SEY	Seychelles
JPN	Japan	SLE	Sierra Leone
JOR	Jordan	SIN	Singapore

(Cont.)

SOL	Solomon Islands	TUR	Turkey
SOM	Somalia	UGA	Uganda
KOR	South Korea	UAE	United Arab Emirates
ESP	Spain	USA	United States of America
SUD	Sudan	URS	U.S.S.R.
SRI	Sri Lanka	VOL	Burkina-Faso
SUI	Switzerland	URU	Uruguay
SUR	Surinam	VEN	Venezuela
SWI	Swaziland	VIE	Vietnam
SWE	Sweden	ISV	U.S. Virgin Islands
SYR	Syria	SAM	Western Samoa
TAN	Tanzania	YAR	Yemen Arab Republic
THA	Thailand	YUG	Yugoslavia
TOG	Togo	ZAI	Zaire
TGA	Tonga	ZAM	Zambia
TRI	Trinidad and Tobago	ZIM	Zimbabwe
TUN	Tunisia		

Courtesy of the USOC.

Appendix E

Commissions of the IOC

Commission Pour L'Académie Internationale Olympique/ Commission for the International Olympic Academy
Président/*Chairman:* M. Mohamed Mzali.

Vice-Président/*Vice-Chairman:* M. Nikolaos Nissiotis.

Membres/*Members:* Mme. Flor Isava Fonseca, M. Roberto G. Peper, M. Wlodzimierz Reczek, M. Giorgio de Stefani, M. Ahmed D. Touny, M. Mohamed Zerguini, Mme. Monique Berlioux (esq.)[b]

Représentants des/*Representatives of:* F.I./*IFs*—M. Francesco Gnecchi-Ruscone, C.N.O./*NOCs*—M. Marian Renke.

Commission D'Admission/Eligibility Commission
Président/*Chairman:* M. Willi Daume.

Vice-Président/*Vice-Chairman:* M. Alexandru Siperco.

Membres/*Members:* M. Franco Carraro, M. Gunnar Ericsson, M. Raymond Gafner, Général Niels Holst-Sorensen, M. Ydnekatchew Tessema, M. Peter Tallberg (esq.), M. Walther Tröger (esq.).

Commission Des Athlètes/Athletes Commission
Président/*Chairman:* M. Peter Tallberg.

Vice-Président/*Vice-Chairman:* Mme. Pirjo Haggman.

Membres/*Members:* M. Thomas Bach (FRG), M. Sebastian Coe (GBR), M. Ivar Formo (NOR), M. Kipjoge Keino (KEN), M. Bojan Krizaj (YUG), M. Edwin Moses (USA), Mme. Svetla Otzetova Guenova (BUL), M. Vladislav Tretyak (URS), M. Walther Tröger (esq.).

Commission Culturelle/Cultural Commission
Président/*Chairman:* M. Pedro Ramirez Vazquez.
Vice-Président/*Vice-Chairman:* M. Boris Bakrac.
Membres/*Members:* M. Matts Carlgren, M. Philipp Schoeller, M. José D. Vallarino Veracierto, Mme. Monique Berlioux (esq.).

Commission Des Finances/Finance Commission
Président/*Chairman:* Comte de Beaumont.
Vice-Président/*Vice-Chairman:* Lord Luke.
Membres/*Members:* M. Syed Wajid Ali, M. Berthold Beitz, Me. Marc Hodler, Mme. Monique Berlioux (esq.).

Commission Juridique/Juridical Commission
Président/*Chairman:* M. Kébe Mbaye.
Vice-Président/*Vice-Chairman:* M. Marc Hodler.
Membres/*Members:* Dr. Agustin C. Arroyo, M. Raymond Gafner, Datuk Seri Hamzah Bin Haji Abu Samah, M. James Worrall, M. François Carrard (esq.). M. Georges Straschnov (esq.).

Commission Medicale/Médical Commission
Président/*Chairman:* Prince Alexandre de Mérode.
Vice-Président/*Vice Chairman:* Dr. Eduardo Hay.
Secrétaire/*Secretary:* Pr. Albert Dirix.
Membres/*Members:* Pr. René Essomba, Dr. Kevin O'Flanagan, Mme. Mary Alison Glen Haig, Mme. Monique Berlioux (esq.).
[Fr.]/[Eng.] Un représentant de chaque comité d'organisation des Jeux/*A representative of each organizing committee for the Games:*
Représentants des/*Representatives of:* F.I./*IFs*—Dr. Hans Howald, Dr. Wolf Montag.
[Fr.]/[Eng.] La commission comprend également trois sous-commissions/*The commission also includes three sub-commissions:*
Antidopage et biochimie/*Antidoping and biochemistry:* Pr. Arnold Beckett, Dr. Claus Clausnitzer, Pr. Manfred Doenike, Dr. Robert Dugal, Pr. Vitaly Semenov.
Biomécanique et physiologie/*Biomechanics and physiology:* Pr. Wolfgang Baumann, Pr. Robert Gregor, Pr. Paavo Komi, Pr. Heinz Liesen, Pr. Vladimir Zatsiorsky.
Médecine du sport et orthopédie/*Sports medicine and orthopaedics:* Pr. Iba Diop Mar, Pr. Yoshio Kuroda, Pr. Ludwig Prokop, M. Miroslav Slavik.

Commission Du Mouvement Olympique/
Commission for the Olympic Movement

Président/*Chairman:* S.E. M. Juan Antonio Samaranch.

Membres/*Members:* [Fr.]/[Eng.] Membres de la Commission exécutive du C.I.O. et président de la Commission des athlétes/*Members of the IOC Executive Board and President of the Athletes Commission.*

[Fr.]/[Eng.] 9 représentants des Fédérations Internationales/9 *representatives of the International Federations.*

[Fr.]/[Eng.] 9 représentants des Comités Nationaux Olympiques/9 *representatives of the National Olympic Committees.*

Mme. Monique Berlioux (esq.).

Commission Conjointe Des Moyens D'Information/
Joint Mass Media Commission

Bureau/*Board:*

Président/*Chairman:* S.E. M. Juan Antonio Samaranch.

Membres/*Members:* M. C. Lance S. Cross, M. Masaji Kiyokawa, M. Ashwini Kumar, Mme. Monique Berlioux (esq.).

Membres/*Members:*

[Fr.]/[Eng.] Les membres des commissions de presse, de radio et de télévision/*Members of the press, radio and television commissions.*

Commission De Presse/Press Commission

Président/*Chairman:* M. Masaji Kiyokawa.

Membres/*Members:* M. Bashir Attarabulsi, M. Roy A. Bridge, M. Julian K. Roosevelt, M. Ydnekatchew Tessema, Mme. Monique Berlioux (esq.).

Un représentant de/*A representative of:*
— [Fr.]/[Eng.] chaque comité d'organisation des Jeux/*each organizing committee for the Games.*
— [Fr.]/[Eng.] chacune des cinq agences internationales/*The five international agencies:* A.F.P., A.P., Reuters, Tass, U.P.I.

Représentants/*Representatives:*
— [Fr.]/[Eng.] de la presse écrite/*Of the written press:* M. Massimo Della Pergola, M. John Rodda, M. Andres Mercé Varela.
— [Fr.]/[Eng.] des photographes/*Of the photographers:* M. Albert G. Riethausen.
— [Fr.]/[Eng.] des F.I./*of the IFs:* M. Borislav Stankovic, M. Walter Wasservogel.
— [Fr.]/[Eng.] des C.N.O./*Of the NOCs:* M. Hassine Hamouda, M. Tsuyoshi Miyakawa.

Commission De Radio/Radio Commission

Président/*Chairman:* M. Ashwini Kumar.

Membres/*Members:* M. Phillip W. Coles, M. Günther Heinze, M. Cornelis Kerdel, M. German Rieckehoff, Mme. Monique Berlioux (esq.).

[Fr.]/[Eng.] Représentants de la radiodiffusion/*Representatives of radio broadcasting:* Mme. Nina Balasova, M. Eric Walter.

Commission De Télévision/Television Commission

Président/*Chairman:* M.C. Lance S. Cross.

Membres/*Members:* M. Ivan Dibos, Sheikh Fahid Al-Ahmad Al-Sabah, M. Jan Staubo, Mme. Monique Berlioux (esq.).

Représentants des/*Representatives of:*
— [Fr.]/[Eng.] Comités d'organisation (été/hiver)/*Organizing Committees (summer/winter).*
— [Fr.]/[Eng.] Radiodiffuseurs/*Broadcasters:* M. Marcel Deschamps, M. Jarle Hoysaeter, M. Henrikas Juskhevitshus.
— [Fr.]/[Eng.] Agences télévisées/*Television agencies:* M. Neil Mallard.
— [Fr.]/[Eng.] Radiodiffuseurs hôtes/*Host Broadcasters:* M. Georges Croses, M.S. Marjanovic.
— [Fr.]/[Eng.] F.I./*IFs:* M. Gian Franco Kasper.
— [Fr.]/[Eng.] C.N.O./*NOCs:* M. Nelson Paillou, M. Ivan Slavkov.

Commission Des Nouvelles Sources De Financement/
Commission of New Sources of Financing

Président/*Chairman:* S.E. M. Louis Guirandou-N'Diaye.

Membres/*Members:* M. Reginald Alexander, M. Berthold Beitz, M. Maurice Herzog, M. Henry Hsu, Mme. Monique Berlioux (esq.), colonel Don Miller (esq.), M. Dick Palmer (esq.), M. Adrian Vanden Eede (esq.).

Commission Pour Le Programme/
Commission for the Programme

Président/*Chairman:* M. Vitaly Smirnov.

Vice-Président/*Vice-Chairman:* M. Franco Carraro.

Membres/*Members:* M. Matts Carlgren, M. Vladimir Cernusak, M. Suat Erler, M. Nikos Filaretos, M. Cornelis Kerdel, M. Peter Tallberg (esq.), M. Walther Tröger (esq.).

Représentants des/*Representatives of:* F.I./*IFs:* M. Olaf Poulsen, M. Max Rinkenburger, C.N.O./*NOCs:* Mme. Nadia Lekarska.

Commission De Révision De La Charte/
Commission of Revision of the Charter

Président/*Chairman:* Me. James Worrall.

Membres/*Members:* M. Raymond Gafner, M. Kéba Mbaye, M. Alexandru Siperco, M. François Carrard (esq.), M. Georges Straschnov (esq.).

Commission Pour La Solidarité/
Olympic Solidarity Commission

Président/*Chairman:* S.E. M. Juan Antonio Samaranch.

Vice-Président/*Vice-Chairman:* M. Mario Vazquez Raña.

Membres/*Members:* M. Constantin Andrianov, Air chief marshal Dawee

Chullasapya, M. Kevan Gosper, M. Zhenliang He, M. Lamine Keita, M. Anselmo Lopez (esq.).

[Fr.]/[Eng.] 5 vice-présidents de l'A.C.N.O./*5 Vice-Chairmen of the ANOC.*

[Fr.]/[Eng.] Secrétaire général de l'A.C.N.O./*Secretary General of the ANOC.*

[Fr.]/[Eng.] Trésorier de l'A.C.N.O./*Treasurer of the ANOC.*

[Fr.]/[Eng.] Représentants des/*Representatives of:* F.I./*IFs:* M. Horst Schreiber, M. Klaus Kotter.

Groupe De Travail «Sport De Masse»/
Working Group "Masses Sport"

Président/*Chairman:* M. Antonin Himl.

Conseil De L'Ordre Olympique/
Council of the Olympic Order

Président/*Chairman:* S.E. M. Juan Antonio Samaranch.

Membres/*Members:* les trois vice-présidents du C.I.O./*the three IOC Vice-Presidents,* le Directeur du C.I.O./*the IOC Director* (esq.).

Note. (esq.) = és qualités/*ex-officio.*
Courtesy of the IOC.

Appendix F

The Amateur Sports Act of 1978 (Federal Law 95-606)

In the closing hours of the 95th Session of Congress, the Amateur Sports Act of 1978 was enacted and later signed by President Jimmy Carter on Nov. 8, 1978. The Act was designed to promote and coordinate amateur athletic activities in the United States, to recognize certain rights for U.S. athletes, to provide for the resolution of disputes involving national sports organizations and/or athletes, as well as to designate the United States Olympic Committee as the central coordinating agency for all sports on the programs for the Olympic and Pan American Games.

In conjunction with its role as a coordinating body, the Olympic Committee has other responsibilities in improving amateur athletic opportunities. According to a report of the Senate Committee on Commerce, Science and Transportation, the USOC "should look at the overall spectrum of amateur athletic activity and, where inadequacies exist, either encourage amateur sports organizations to provide programs or institute its own programs."

In order to prevent deceptive practices involving the use of the Olympic trademark or trade name, the Act clarifies the section of the USOC

Charter which provides for trademark protection and updates that section to make it current with the 1946 Trademark Act. The penalty for illegal use of the Olympic name or mark has been changed in order to make offenders subject to civil rather than criminal action.

The Act further recognizes that part of the USOC Constitution dealing with athletes' rights and freedom to participate in competitions open to all classes of athletes.

One of the outstanding features of the Act is the provision for the recognition of national governing bodies for sports on the programs for the Olympic and Pan American Games. For recognition, amateur sports organizations must apply to the USOC and meet certain criteria designed to ensure that the most capable and representative organization be designated. All amateur sports governing bodies must agree to binding arbitration in disputes involving its recognition as a national sports governing body or involving the opportunity of an amateur athlete to participate in open competition.

One of the most important criteria for the national sports governing bodies is that of autonomy. In other words, it must determine for itself the programs best suited for its sport. A similar autonomy requirement was written into the USOC Constitution in 1977.

Both the USOC Constitution and the ACT mandate that all national sports governing bodies maintain membership open to all organizations conducting national programs which are capable of developing athletes for international competitions. It is provided that these national organizations be accorded reasonable representation on the governing councils of the national governing bodies.

Giving approval or the sanctioning of international amateur athletic competition is an important *right* of the national governing body. Every person or organization seeking to hold or sponsor amateur athletic competition between athletes representing the U.S. and those representing a foreign country must obtain the approval or sanction of the appropriate national governing body.

There have been many disputes in the last 50 years involving many of the nation's most influential national sports organizations. However, prior to the enactment of Federal Law 95-606 a new spirit prevailed and a great majority of these national organizations agreed to "pull together" to enhance the overall amateur sports program in the United States.

Furthermore, all national organizations have been encouraged to seek membership in, and participate in, the activities of the national sports governing body, thus ensuring a strong "vertical organization of organizations with similar goals" for a unified effort.

The Act further backstops the USOC Constitution in requiring that on all governance councils, including the USOC, "recent or active" athletes must be accorded at least 20 percent of the membership on the councils.

In the resolution of disputes involving national organizations or national organizations and athletes, the Act provides for arbitration before a board of arbitrators appointed by the American Arbitration Association. The

USOC Constitution provided parallel provisions in 1977, and in 1978 and 1979 strengthened provisions concerning the challenge process involving a national sports governing body and an organization seeking to replace it.

Appendix G

The Relationships of Organizations Concerned With the Olympic Games

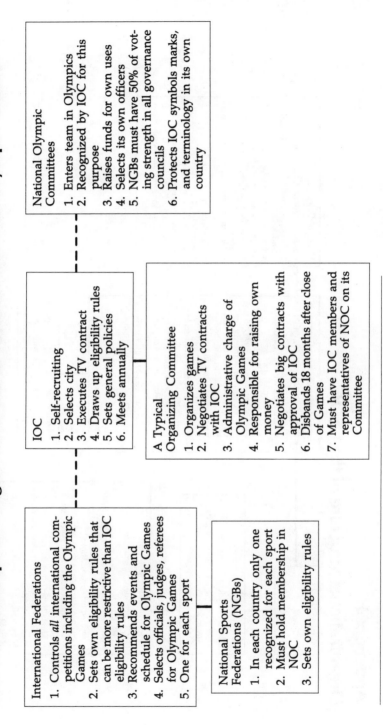

International Federations

1. Controls *all* international competitions including the Olympic Games
2. Sets own eligibility rules that can be more restrictive than IOC eligibility rules
3. Recommends events and schedule for Olympic Games
4. Selects officials, judges, referees for Olympic Games
5. One for each sport

National Sports Federations (NGBs)

1. In each country only one recognized for each sport
2. Must hold membership in NOC
3. Sets own eligibility rules

IOC

1. Self-recruiting
2. Selects city
3. Executes TV contract
4. Draws up eligibility rules
5. Sets general policies
6. Meets annually

A Typical Organizing Committee

1. Organizes games
2. Negotiates TV contracts with IOC
3. Administrative charge of Olympic Games
4. Responsible for raising own money
5. Negotiates big contracts with approval of IOC
6. Disbands 18 months after close of Games
7. Must have IOC members and representatives of NOC on its Committee

National Olympic Committees

1. Enters team in Olympics
2. Recognized by IOC for this purpose
3. Raises funds for own uses
4. Selects its own officers
5. NGBs must have 50% of voting strength in all governance councils
6. Protects IOC symbols marks, and terminology in its own country

Courtesy of the USOC.

Appendix H
Organizational Structure of the USOC

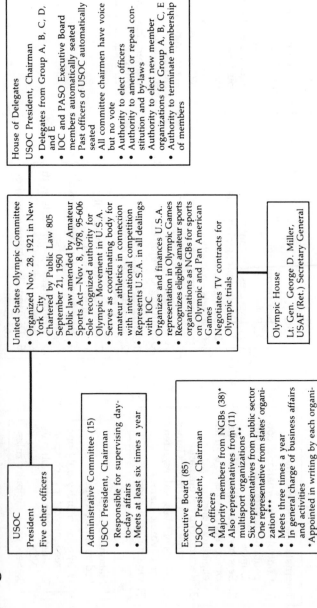

United States Olympic Committee
- Organized Nov. 28, 1921 in New York City
- Chartered by Public Law 805 September 21, 1950
- Public law amended by Amateur Sports Act—Nov. 8, 1978, 95-606
- Sole recognized authority for Olympic Movement in U.S.A.
- Serves as coordinating body for amateur athletics in connection with international competition
- Represents U.S.A. in all dealings with IOC
- Organizes and finances U.S.A. representation in Olympic Games
- Recognizes eligible amateur sports organizations as NGBs for sports on Olympic and Pan American Games
- Negotiates TV contracts for Olympic trials

House of Delegates
USOC President, Chairman
- Delegates from Group A, B, C, D, and E
- IOC and PASO Executive Board members automatically seated
- Past officers of USOC automatically seated
- All committee chairmen have voice but no vote
- Authority to elect officers
- Authority to amend or repeal constitution and by-laws
- Authority to elect new member organizations for Group A, B, C, E
- Authority to terminate membership of members

USOC
President
Five other officers

Administrative Committee (15)
USOC President, Chairman
- Responsible for supervising day-to-day affairs
- Meets at least six times a year

Executive Board (85)
USOC President, Chairman
- All officers
- Majority members from NGBs (38)*
- Also representatives from (11) multisport organizations**
- Six representatives from public sector
- One representative from states' organization***
- Meets three times a year
- In general charge of business affairs and activities

*Appointed in writing by each organization
**Elected by House of Delegates
***Elected by state organization

Olympic House
Lt. Gen. George D. Miller, USAF (Ret.) Secretary General

Courtesy of the USOC.

9

Toward a Definition of Olympism

Jeffrey O. Segrave

The Olympic Games are the most powerful expression of international sport. That they are ultimately only an expression of a deeply profound belief in the educational value of sport is perhaps less well known. But for Pierre de Coubertin, the founder of the modern Olympic Movement, the games represented the institutionalization of an ideal that extolled sport as a moral and social endeavor. Coubertin's vision was derived from a synthesis of ideas that he drew from both a classical Greek and a 19th-century English public school conception of sport. Although he initially enlisted these ideas in support of a social reform platform directed against his native France, he ultimately internationalized his thinking to generate a philosophy that placed sport at the center of a universal campaign for peace and international understanding. He called his philosophy of social reform Olympism.

The Background to Olympism

Like many of his contemporaries, Coubertin responded to the beleaguered circumstance of France after the Franco-Prussian War by committing his efforts to national revival. Coubertin in particular turned toward youth: "I shall burnish a flabby and cramped youth, its body and its character, by sport, its risks and even its excesses" (quoted in Eyquem, 1976, p. 138). During the course of this self-appointed task, Coubertin digested the didactic view of English character-building sport that he first encountered in Hippolyte Taine's *Notes sur l'Angleterre* [Notes on England] (1872) and that he later observed in the legacy of Thomas Arnold at Rugby School. The incorporation of games and athletics in the English school curriculum deeply impressed Coubertin. The vigor and confidence that he saw in the English nation devolved, in his mind, from the integration of classical learning, sport, and spiritual values that formed the core of the English educational system. But above all, "the role played there by sport," he wrote, is "what appears to be most worthy of notice"; its role "is at once physical, moral, and social" (Coubertin, 1887, p. 642). To Coubertin, sport became a catalyst that would, he wrote, "reestablish in our younger generations, the equilibrium between body and mind so long ruptured . . . and produce the spirit and leadership, good sense, and character" (1888, pp. 248-249). Consequently, in Coubertin's idealized vision ethical conduct, moral integrity, and strength of character became the products of an Arnoldian education and the basis for his educational view of sport, *la pédagogie sportive* as Coubertin called it. This view would not only serve to nourish his resolve to introduce organized sport to France (see Weber, 1970), but it would also serve to sustain his notion of Olympism (see Lucas, 1976).

The integration of mind, body, and spirit was also the basis of a classical Greek conception of life, and the connection was never lost on Coubertin. "After all" he declared in 1894, "there are not two parts to a man, body and soul; there are three, body, mind, and character. Character is not formed by the mind, but primarily by the body. The men of antiquity knew this, and we are painfully relearning it" (1967b, p. 7). As much as he idealized the legacy of Arnold (see MacAloon, 1981, pp. 43-88), so he also romanticized and exaggerated the Greek outlook on sport (see Natan, 1958, pp. 51-53). To Coubertin, Olympia, the ancient capital of sport, became "the cradle of a view of life strictly Hellenic in form," and "a powerful symbol of this marvellous tripod which supported Hellenic civilization, constituted by sport, art, and good citizenship" (1967a, p. 107). The practice of Greek sport in the service of noble goals, namely the worship of Olympian Zeus and the moral and political unity of the Greek world, inspired Coubertin. To both English and Greek athletics, he ascribed the highest values of ethical behavior: "Like the athletics of antiquity, modern athletics is . . . an impassioned soaring which is capable of going from play to heroism" (1967a, pp. 118-119). Coubertin's admiration for Greek athletics led him easily to conceive of a modern version of the ancient games at Olympia as the symbol of his own allegiance to educational sport, with its attendant moralism and emphasis on human dignity and responsibility.

A Definition of Olympism

Both the English and Greek models of sport profoundly affected Coubertin, their philosophical underpinnings providing the basis for his doctrine of Olympism. When the distinctly Christian ethic was stripped away from the English conception, and the cult of Hellenism was divorced from the Greek formulation, Coubertin was left with a view of sport as a broadly-based humanitarian endeavor dedicated to the pursuit of ethical conduct and international harmony. This view was highly altruistic and optimistic, as the IOC's proposed definition of Olympism reflects.

Olympism is an overall philosophy of life, exalting and combining in a balanced whole the qualities of body, will, and mind. Olympism sets out to create a way of life based on the joy of effort, the educational values of good example and a respect for universal fundamental ethical principles.

It has, as a goal, to place sport at the service of the harmonious development of humankind, with the object of creating a peaceful society concerned with the preservation of human dignity. (*Toward a Definition of Olympism in Canada, 1985*)

Olympism's emphasis on the explicit pursuit of social values distinguishes the Olympic movement and the Olympic Games from all other international sport institutions. No other international sport event was specifically designed to serve as a vehicle for social improvement or to contribute to "the general welfare and betterment of humanity" (Coubertin, 1967b, p. 39). No other international sport event has sought to spread its ideals to every corner of the globe. These features of Olympism have also served to enhance the enormous appeal and popularity of the Olympic Games themselves.

The Aspirations of Olympism[1]

Despite the ubiquitousness of the term Olympism, and the rhetorical uses to which it has been put, a clear, precise, and simple definition that goes beyond generality has yet to be formulated (Lenk, 1976; Segrave & Chu, 1981). As Wandzilak (1980) has noted, "The abstractness of the concept of Olympism limits the degree to which this term can be understood" (p. 37). However, Olympism may be conceived as a set of specific goals or aspirations that provides the blueprint for the conduct of the Olympic Games in particular, and for the conduct of sport in general.

For Education

"That which is most important in the lives of modern people (is) education" declared Coubertin in 1890 (*Toward a Definition of Olympism in Canada, 1985*). Reacting to what he saw as the evils of a 19th-century industrial civilization, with its concomitant tendencies toward materialism and commercialism, Coubertin championed the cause of character-building sport. In particular, he advocated amateur sport as being the most viable vehicle for inculcating youth with appropriate moral values. "Sport is a physical discipline," he argued, "sustained by an enthusiastic addiction to unnecessary effort. Daring for the sake of daring, and without real necessity—it is in this way that our body rises above its animal nature" (1922, p. 64). This discipline, according to Coubertin, was sport's "nobility, and even its poetry . . . its essence, its object, and the secret of its moral worth" (p. 64). By endorsing a view of sport based on "perfect disinterestedness and the sentiment of honor" (1896, p. 55), Coubertin felt that the experience of competition would have a beneficial educational impact on the athlete. It would enhance the development of desirable physical, mental, social, and moral qualities and would provide the opportunity for growth and, above all, self-understanding.

Consequently, while Coubertin committed his life to the reetablishment of the Olympic Games, he forever drafted sport into the larger service of social change and social education. For Coubertin the Games remained only the "pedagogical manifestation" of a much more deep-seated belief in the liberating values of amateur sport. As one of his primary biographers has noted, "It is ironic today to realize that Coubertin was not primarily concerned with furthering the Olympic Games. His objective was to use the Games as a platform to popularize the educational role of sport—the moral as well as the physical development of the athlete" (Eyquem, 1976, p. 139). Even Coubertin himself declared that he restored the games "to enoble and strengthen sport, in order to assure their independence and duration and thus to set them better to fill the educational role which devolves upon them in the modern world" (quoted in Eyquem, 1976, p. 139).

The goal of education is manifested in numerous Olympic traditions. One example is the expectation, still implicit in the rules governing eligibility, that both training and competition be undertaken as a preparation for a subsequent career. Another is in the Olympic creed: "The most important thing in the Olympic Games is not to win but to take part, just as the most important thing in life is not the triumph but the struggle. The essential thing is not to have conquered but to have fought well." The educational aspirations of Olympism are also transmitted through the Olympic scientific congresses, the Olympic Solidarity Commission, and in particular the International Olympic Academy, which seeks to illustrate "the ideals of modern athletes, the pure conscience and honest values on which they are based and their achievements in our time, so that today's youth may profit from them in the future" (Pouret, 1971,

p. 11). Not the least of Olympism's educational aspiration is the expectation that the athlete embody the high ethical values, which Coubertin himself ascribed to amateur sport, of chivalry, honesty, and sportsmanship.

For International Understanding

The use of the Olympic Games in the service of peace and international understanding was also a derivative of Coubertin's belief in *la pédagogie sportive*. Adopting an essentially rationalistic perspective, the issues of war and peace were for Coubertin largely a matter of education, of knowledge and ignorance. "Wars break out because nations misunderstand each other," he wrote in 1896.

> We shall not have peace until the prejudices which now separate the different races shall have been outlived. To attain this end, what better means than to bring the youth of all countries periodically together for amicable trials of muscular strength and agility? (p. 55)

Consequently, the Olympics were to serve as a sort of "Esperanto of the races," as Giraudoux (1928) put it, and the positive moral values that accrued from sport were to serve as the foundation for peace: "Peace could only be a product of a better world. A better world only a product of better individuals. Better individuals could only be developed in fierce athletic competition" (Coubertin, quoted in Henry, 1948, p. 12).

The issues of patriotism and nationalism were also a question of education for Coubertin. As he wrote, "To ask the peoples of the world to love one another is merely a form of childishness. To ask them to respect one another is not in the least utopian, but in order to respect one another it is first necessary to know one another" (1967a, p. 118). The Olympic Games would provide the opportunity for athletes, officials, and spectators to meet in an atmosphere of friendliness and mutual conciliation. Cultivation of physical and athletic prowess itself was to engender patriotism, a love of one's country, and a desire to serve it, rather than nationalism, a hatred of other countries. Although, as MacAloon (1981) has argued, the history of the games has tended to model the problems of patriotism and nationalism rather than their resolution, Coubertin forever hoped that the games would ultimately foster patriotism without nationalism. The distinction was important to Coubertin, and it became one of the fundamental ideological features of Olympism.

This special blend of patriotism, peace, and international understanding coalesced in Coubertin's belief in what he termed "internationalism," which he wrote "should be the state of mind of those who love their country above all, who seek to draw to it the friendship of foreigners by professing for the countries of those foreigners an intelligent and enlightened sympathy" (1898, p. 434). As a central expression of internationalism, the games were to provide a forum where cultural differences could be celebrated and where individuals could learn to recognize and respect national diversity. In the process, people could cultivate generosity, tolerance, and what Coubertin (1915) called *le respect mutuel* (mutual respect). In this way the games would, he hoped, "be a potent, if indirect factor in securing universal peace" (Coubertin, 1896, p. 55).

This aspiration is perhaps best expressed in Fundamental Principle 3 of the *Olympic Charter* (1985), which states, "No discrimination in them (the Olympic Games) is allowed against any country or person on grounds of race, religion or politics" (p. 6). The hope of promoting peace is also realized in the composition of the International Olympic Committee and in numerous Olympic traditions, including the opening and closing ceremonies and the Olympic village. The aspiration for peace is represented symbolically in the Olympic flag, the Olympic flame, and the flight of doves. Not the least of Olympism's hopes is that athletes will act in the spirit of magnanimity and mutual respect.

For Equal Opportunity

Despite the elitism of the Olympic Games, where entrance and performance are typically reaffirmations of excellence, Coubertin's ideology was toward a more egalitarian aspiration. Emerging from his vision for educational reform in France was a passionate desire to provide the underprivileged with a genuine access to culture. To the youth of France he wrote,

> I shall enlarge its vision and its hearing by showing it with wide horizons, heavenly, planetary, historical, horizons of universal history which, in engendering mutual respect, will bring about a ferment of international peace. All this is to be for everyone, with no discrimination on account of birth, caste, wealth, situation or occupation. (quoted in Eyquem, 1976, p. 138)

Sport was a part of this vision, and in the end when Coubertin enlarged his horizons beyond France, it became a critical component of Olympism. Olympic sport was to become for Coubertin "the dowry of all races" (1959, p. 226).

Consequently, Coubertin established the Olympic Games "to exalt the individual athlete, whose very existence is necessary for the involvement of the community in athletic sports, and whose achievements provide an example to be emulated" (quoted in Eyquem, 1976, p. 139). Both the Games themselves and individual Olympic athletes were to function as ideal educational models. Their purpose was to popularize sport, extend its benefits to all, and create what Coubertin called "a democracy of youth" (*Toward a Definition of Olympism in Canada*, 1985). In Coubertin's eyes, the opportunities for all became inseparable from the opportunities for the gifted.

In order that 100 indulge in physical culture, 50 must practice a sport.
In order that 50 practice a sport, 20 must specialize. In order that 20
specialize, 5 must be capable of outstanding performances. It's impossible to break the circle. One thing follows another. (Comte-
Offenbach, 1983)

As a role model for mass participation in sport, the Olympic Games
have successfully fulfilled their function. Moreover, the Olympic movement lends its support to numerous other regional events such as the
Pan-American Games, all of which promote the development of sport.
The use of athletic facilities specifically built for Olympic competition also
contributes to public sport. In addition, the IOC through Olympic solidarity and the National Olympic Committee (NOC) programs like the
Canadian Olympic Academy's Junior Olympic and the United States
Olympic Committee's (USOC) Educational Council encourage participation in numerous other ways. In 1984, the IOC specifically created a working group to study "Mass Sport."

For Fair and Equal Competition

Of the many features of Olympism, none was more critical than Coubertin's emphasis on fair play. From the very beginning, he advocated sport
as a moral and social endeavor. As a result he rejected the professional
ethic on the grounds that "Men give up their whole existence to one particular sport, grow rich by practicing it, and thus deprive it of all nobility,
and destroy the just equilibrum of man by making the muscles preponderate over the mind" (Coubertin, 1896, p. 55). Instead, he canvased for
an ideal whereby "honesty and sportsmanlike unselfishness are as highly
developed as the strength of the muscles" (1931, p. 208). Coubertin always
recognized that sport could serve two masters:

Athleticism can put into play the most noble as well as the most vile
passions; it can develop disinterestedness and the sentiment of honor
as well as the love of gain; it can be chivalrous or corrupt, virile or
festival; finally, it can be used to consolidate peace or to prepare for
war. (1931, pp. 22-23)

Coubertin sided with the positive view. Sport was to be an honorable
and heroic affair characterized by "the spirit of chivalry" (1931, p. 23)
and the joy of effort. In the U.S., Sloane (1912) endorsed Coubertin's
vision, arguing that Olympism stood "to purify sport, abolish selfish and
underhand methods in the struggle for athletic supremacy, secure fair
play for all, even the weakest, and, as far as possible, make the contest
and not the victory the joy of the young" (p. 411).

According to Coubertin, the benefits of sport are most readily available when equal and worthy competition is available—when the contestants are evenly matched and when the prize is neither gratuitous nor

unobtainable. As Coubertin wrote, "the important thing in life is not the triumph but the struggle. The essential thing is not to have conquered but to have fought well. To spread these percepts is to build up a stronger and more valiant and, above all, more scrupulous and more generous humanity" (quoted in Henry, 1948, p. 1).

The Olympic oath, which is taken by one athlete on behalf of all, aspires to fair play and states, "In the name of all competitors I promise that we shall take part in these Olympic Games, respecting and abiding by the rules which govern them, in the true spirit of sportsmanship, for the glory of sport and the honor of our teams" (*Olympic Charter*, 1985, p. 62). The goal of fair play is also implicit in the IOC's rules on doping, which prohibit the use of certain drugs as inimical to the spirit of fair and equal competition (see Dardik, 1980). The aspiration of equal competition is also expressed in the establishment of weight categories, rules concerning equipment and implements, and to a certain extent in the IOC's growing concern over the use of children in Olympic-level competition. In recent years, the IOC has also sought to address the issue of inequality of competition, whereby the bulk of medals are garnered by athletes from the developed countries, through the redistributive provisions of the International Solidarity Commission.

For Cultural Expression

To Coubertin, Olympism was the embodiment of a view of life that celebrated the inner harmony of mind, body, and spirit. Olympism was the restatement of an ancient Greek perspective, most cogently expressed in the concept of *Kalos Kagathia*—a concept that denoted the successful integration of moral, artistic, intellectual, and physical creativity. Coubertin argued that writers and artists gathered together not by mere chance at Olympia, and he sought to infuse his modern Olympics with the same balance, the same "eurythmy" as he called it—the marriage of "Muscle and Mind" (Coubertin, 1931). "The Olympic Games are not only to enhance muscular strength," he declared, "they are intellectual and artistic" (quoted in Lenk, 1976, p. 122). Consequently, Coubertin endowed Olympism with a rediscovered Platonic humanism in which the body and mind were to provide reciprocal inspiration. Olympism was to be a cultural movement as well as an educational one.

Although clearly less publicized than the sport program, the Olympic Movement to this day seeks to enrich sport by encouraging the visual, performing, and creative arts. Fundamental Principle 39 in the *Olympic Charter* (1985) specifically instructs each organizing committee to arrange "exhibitions and demonstrations of the host country's art (architecture, literature, music, painting, sculpture, photography, and sport philately)" (p. 22). Moreover, several other international sporting events, such as the 1978 Commonwealth and 1983 World University Games in Edmonton, have included art performances and exhibitions. This goal is expressed in the inclusion of aesthetically appealing sports in the Olympic program, including ice dancing, synchronized swimming, and rhythmic gymnastics.

For the Independence of Sport

Subscribing to the views of his mentor in France, Frederic Le Play, Coubertin argued that the solution to the problems he identified lay in social and cultural reform, not politics. In his early years he declared,

> It is only too evident that no governmental contrivance will alone give the country what it lacks, stability and inner peace. Nothing can make up for the deficiency of true and conscientious social reform . . . it must be accomplished in ideas and customs before being realized in institutions. (quoted in MacAloon, 1981, p. 88)

These sentiments paved the way for Coubertin's separation of sport and politics. Consequently, buttressed by his commitment to internationalism and the universal ideals of peace and brotherhood, Coubertin strove to isolate Olympism from political interference and sectarian interests. Numerous other IOC presidents defended the idea of separating sport and politics. Most notably, Avery Brundage later declared of the Olympic movement: "We are a sports group, organized and pledged to promote clean competition and sportsmanship. When we let politics, racial questions or social disputes creep into our actions we're in for trouble" (quoted in Smith, 1980, p. 16).

Coubertin himself institutionalized this aspiration in the very charter of the IOC. To this day, it has operated on the basis of self-perpetuation. "As the best means of safeguarding liberty and serving democracy" he said, "it is not always best to abandon ourselves to the popular will. Rather we must maintain, in the midst of the vast electoral ocean, strong islands that will ensure independence and stability" (quoted in Henry, 1948, p. 12). The principle of "reverse deputation" also embodies Coubertin's hope for the apolitical sanctity of the Olympic Movement. The IOC membership should be loyal to the causes of Olympism first and foremost. As a result, IOC members are considered ambassadors of the ideals of Olympism to their respective countries, not delegates of their nations to the IOC. Despite protestations by the IOC and like the issues of patriotism and nationalism, the Olympic Games mirror the problem rather than the resolution of the "sport and politics do not mix" formulation.

For Excellence

As the word itself suggests, Olympism connotes excellence. And indeed to Coubertin himself, Olympism represented the pursuit of the very best: "Effort is the greatest joy. Success is not a goal, but a means to aiming higher still" (quoted in Eyquem, 1976, p. 143). This creed applied not only to athletics; it applied with equal vigor to activities of the mind and spirit. The Olympic Movement, Coubertin hoped, would glorify all three.

To celebrate physical excellence, Coubertin created the Games themselves as the apotheosis of his grand ideal. To celebrate intellectual excellence, he labored until his "pentathlon of the Muses" became a part of the Olympic festival in 1912. To celebrate spiritual excellence, he forever campaigned for the moral and social benefits to be accrued from devotion to sport—for "the nobility of conviction, the cult of unselfishness and honesty, the chivalrous spirit and manly energy" (Coubertin, 1931, p. 22) that characterizes amateur sport. Instead of the classic dictum *mens sana in corpore sano*, he substituted *mens fervida in corpore lacertoso* (an impassioned mind in a vigorous body). Excellence, for Coubertin, ultimately resided in the pursuit of sport in the name of progress and social and cultural unity. As Lucas (1980) put it:

> His faith in the usefulness of amateur athletic training and competition was based on the ancient Athenian assumption that man's mind, body, and spirit, were somehow interdependent. It was his hope that modern societies might, in his lifetime, emulate the best the Greeks had to offer. He called this "best" by the name Olympism. (p. 78)

The spirit of excellence that pervades the entire Olympic movement is best captured in the Olympic motto "Citius, Altius, Fortius" ("Faster, Higher, Stronger"). The spirit is perhaps more completely captured in Lenk's (1984) proposal that the motto be supplemented with *pulchrius* and *humanitas*, thereby adding the aesthetic and humanitarian dimensions that are so critical within the Olympic Movement. Excellence is symbolized by the podium and the medal ceremonial, and, as a standard, is applied to all aspects of the Olympic project—from facility design to officiating.

Conclusion

That the Olympic Games may have failed to live up to the aspirations of Olympism is less to indict Olympism itself than to indict the practice of sport as it has developed during the 20th century. But the discontinuities and inconsistencies in Coubertin's thought cannot be denied. As Lucas (1976) has shown, Coubertin never fully resolved the contradictions inherent in promulgating a lifetime, sport-for-all sport philosophy while at the same time patronizing a specially privileged elite of achievement and performance. Similarly, although Coubertin consistently advocated the political purity of Olympism, he forever proselytized the democratic character of the Olympic Movement, willingly manipulating political forces to further his aims. Likewise, although he promoted sport in the name of patriotism, he failed to recognize that for too many, patriotism invariably connoted a feeling of hatred for other cultures.

These unresolved conflicts were bequeathed to Olympism. They were also bequeathed to the Olympic Games, which as MacAloon (1981) has argued, have emerged as the dramatic representation of two competing world views—"that men are what the social and cultural structures they inhabit make of them; that men are what they become when for a time, they suspend those structures" (p. 6). But at its best, Olympism presents a noble and honorable vision of sport dedicated to ideals of universal worth. As in ancient times, Olympism is the manifestation of a fundamental dialectic between body and soul, existence and essence, individual and group, and competition and cooperation. By seeking to assuage conflict and enhance harmony, Olympism places sport in the service of an enlightened humanity. As the current IOC President, Juan Antonio Samaranch, has put it,

> Olympism surpasses sports. It is inseparable from education in its widest and most complete sense. It combines physical activity, art and the spirit and tends toward the formation of the complete man. Thus it concerns all, whatever our age, our sex or our performances. It is an "assembler," a unique factor of reconciliation and comprehension among men. (*Toward a Definition of Olympism in Canada*, 1985)

This ability to bring people together in the end is the essence of Olympism, and the source of its power and appeal.

Note

1. The framework for this section, and to some extent this entire essay, is adapted from *Toward a Definition of Olympism in Canada*, a Discussion Document prepared for the 1985 Olympic Academy of Canada, University of British Columbia, June 23-24, 1985. I am particularly indebted to Bruce Kidd at the University of Toronto for supplying me with this information.

References

Comte-Offenbach, P. (1983, May 11-14). *Olympism, the Olympic Games, the problems.* Paper presented at the FSGT International Conference, Paris.

Coubertin, P. de. (1887). L'Education anglaise [English education]. *La Reforme Sociale, 13,* 632-652.

Coubertin, P. de. (1888). Le Remede au surmenage et la transformation des lycees de Paris [The cure for strain and the transformation of the secondary schools of Paris]. *La reforme sociale, 16,* 241-249.

Coubertin, P. de. (1896). The Olympic Games of 1896. *Century Magazine*, **53**, 39-55.

Coubertin, P. de. (1898). Does cosmopolitan life lead to international friendliness? *American Monthly Review of Reviews*, **17**, 429-434.

Coubertin, P. de. (1915). *Le respect mutuel* [Mutual respect]. Paris: Alean.

Coubertin, P. de. (1922). *Pedagogie sportive* [Sport pedagogy]. Paris: Cres.

Coubertin, P. de. (1931). *Memoires Olympiques* [Olympic memoires]. Lausanne: Bureau international de pedagogie sportive.

Coubertin, P. de. (1959). *Olympische Erinnerungen* [Olympic Memoires]. Frankfurt: Limpert Verlag.

Coubertin, P. de. (1967a). Olympia 1929. In C. Diem (Ed.), *The Olympic idea: Discourses and essays* (pp. 107-119). Stuttgart: Hofmann.

Coubertin, P. de. (1967b). Speech by Baron de Coubertin at the Paris Congress, 1894. In C. Diem (Ed.), *The Olympic idea: Discourses and essays* (pp. 6-7). Stuttgart: Hofmann.

Dardik, I. (1980). Olympism and the use of drugs in athletics. *Proceedings of the National Olympic Academy—IV* (Vol. 1). Bloomington: Indiana University.

Eyquem, M.T. (1976). The founder of the modern Games. In Lord Killanin & J. Rodda (Eds.), *The Olympic Games* (pp. 138-143). New York: MacMillan.

Giraudoux, J. (1928). *Maximes sur le sport* [Maxims on sport]. Paris: Grasset.

Henry, B. (1948). *An approved history of the Olympic Games*. New York: G.P. Putnam's Sons.

Toward a definition of Olympism in Canada. (1985, June 23-24). A discussion document for the 1985 Olympic Academy of Canada, University of British Columbia.

Lenk, H. (1976). Toward a social philosophy of the Olympics: Values, aims, reality of the modern Olympic Movement. In P. Graham & H. Ueberhorst (Eds.), *The modern Olympics* (pp. 107-167). Cornwall, NY: Leisure Press.

Lenk, H. (1984). The essence of Olympic man. *International Journal of Physical Education*, **21**, 9-14.

Lucas, J.A. (1976). The influence of Anglo-American sport on Pierre de Coubertin—Modern Games founder. In P. Graham & H. Ueberhorst (Eds.), *The modern Olympics* (pp. 17-26). Cornwall, NY: Leisure Press.

Lucas, J.A. (1980). *The modern Olympic Games*. New York: A.S. Barnes.

MacAloon, J.J. (1981). *This great symbol: Pierre de Coubertin and the origins of the modern Olympic Games*. Chicago: University of Chicago Press.

Natan, A. (1958). *Sport and society*. London: Bowes and Bowes.

Olympic Charter. (1985). Lausanne: Comite International Olympique.

Pouret, H. (1971). The Olympic philosophy. In *Report of the XI Session of the International Olympic Academy*. Athens: Hellenic Olympic Committee.

Segrave, J., & Chu, D. (Eds.). (1981). *Olympism*. Champaign, IL: Human Kinetics.

Sloane, W.M. (1912). The Olympic Idea—Its origin, foundation and progress. *Century Magazine*, **84**, 408-414.

Smith, R. (1980, January 4). Boycott the Moscow Olympic. *New York Times*, p. 16.

Taine, H. (1872). *Notes sur l'Angleterre* [Notes on England]. Paris: Hachette.

Wandzilak, T. (1980). The Olympic Academics concept. *Journal of Physical Education and Recreation*, **51**, 37, 73.

Weber, E. (1970). Pierre de Coubertin and the introduction of organized sport in France. *Journal of Contemporary History*, **5**, 3-26.

10
The Olympic Celebration of the Arts

Susan J. Bandy

With the establishment of the modern Olympic Games in 1896 Pierre de Coubertin, French educational reformer and founder of the Games, sought to establish fine arts competitions to be held in conjunction with the Games. Coubertin's devotion to including the fine arts as part of the Games stems from the influence of ancient Greek philosophy upon Coubertin's philosophy of life, education, and sport and from his attempt to fashion the modern Olympics on the ideals of the ancient Olympic festival.

The Ancient Greek Ideal

Unlike other cultures that had preceded it, the Greeks argued for the importance of the human being in the world. Humanity was seen as the principal source of all truth and the principal object of all truth (see Osterhoudt, 1982, p. 10). The importance placed upon the human being resulted in a philosophy and cultural ideal that influenced all aspects of Greek life.

The basis of this philosophy is first evidenced in the writings of Homer and was described as *kalogathia* (*kalos* meaning "beautiful," and *agathos*, "good," "noble," and "learned"). As the Greek culture progressed toward its Golden Age in the 5th and 4th centuries B.C., the ideals of *arete*, the striving for excellence, and *aidos*, "honor," "respect," and "modesty," further refined the Greek philosophy and established ideals that governed human action.

To achieve these ideals, education was devoted to the full and harmonious development of all dimensions of the human being—intellectual, moral, and physical. As a result, education consisted of gymnastics, which trained the body, and music, which trained the mind. Gymnastics developed physical vigor and strength, and music provided the refining influence with the development of the intellect. Gymnastics and music were not separated; together they comprised all of Greek education.

By virtue of this philosophy and education, which cultivated and preserved the ideal's embodied in this philosophy, sport was given a prominent place in the Greek culture. Sport was viewed, together with religion, art, and politics, as manifestations of the harmoniously educated man, *kaloskathos*. The panhellenic festivals served as arenas for the expression not only of physical excellence but of intellectual and moral excellence as well. In addition, the cultural ideals of *arete* and *aidos* embodied in this philosophy affected the conduct of these festivals and resulted in the inclusion of all aspects of human expression.[1]

The athletic festivals were held as part of the religious ceremonies in honor of the gods. Athletes offered their skill and physical prowess to the gods, striving for excellence with honor, dignity, and modesty and striving always to be first and to inspire others. In addition to the athletes, others sought to display their excellence in contests in music, poetry, and recitation. The athletic victor and his victories were later captured and immortalized in the sculpture, vase paintings, and poetry of such well-known artists as Polycleitus and Phidias, Exekias and Euphronius, and Pindar and Euripedes, respectively.

With this unified view of humanity, the ancient Greeks established the union of all aspects of human expression and thereby granted sport a place among the other forms of artistic expression. Neither prior to nor since the Golden Age of Greece has a culture or a civilization considered sport as an art form.[2] Pierre de Coubertin's goal, however, was to create a similar union of sport and the arts with the inclusion of fine arts competitions in the modern Olympic Games.

Coubertin and the Fine Arts Competition

Coubertin, a French artistocrat, received a classical education and, as a young man, became enamored with Greek philosophy and the Greek ideal of the triumvirate of mind, body, and spirit. He was further influenced in his early years by France's defeat in the Franco-Prussian War of 1870 and his exposure to the English public schools. Unlike the *lycées* of France, the curriculum of the English public schools included a physical education and competitive sports program.

As a result of these influences, Coubertin sought to revitalize his country by introducing the youth of France to fitness, competition, and a spirit of fair play through competitive sport and games. To accomplish this goal, Coubertin formed the League of Physical Education and campaigned for the introduction of physical training into the *lycées*.

After devising a system for the salvation of France, Coubertin became obsessed with his Olympic dream and thereafter devoted his life to the revitalization of the Olympic games. In 1896 his dreams were realized with the first of the modern Olympic Games. Not long after the Games were established Coubertin attempted, through the introduction of the fine arts competitions as a part of the Games, to further model the games on the ideals and events of ancient panhellenic festivals. Coubertin (1970) hoped to ennoble sport through the arts (pour en beneficier et les sports ennoblir) (p. 17) and capture and give enduring "life" to the grace, beauty, and dignity of the human struggle in sport. In turn, sport, with a beauty of its own, could provide the focus and stimulation for composers, poets, painters, sculptors, and writers. Coubertin further maintained that art is the harmonizing force for sport, "a force promoting harmony by reconciling opposites; it must spiritualize and ennoble the clash of muscular strength by relating it to a high vision of humanity" (1970, p. 17).

To accomplish this goal, Coubertin organized a conference of representatives of art, literature, and sport in May, 1906, in Paris, to examine to what extent and how the arts could be integrated into the modern Olympic Games. He invited these representatives to "come study to what extent and in what way art and literature could be included in the celebration of the Modern Olympiads and be associated with the practice of sport in general so as not only to benefit from it but at the same time ennoble it" (1979, p. 50). He wrote that the union of sport and the arts could "constitute the spectacular element of the Modern Olympiad." With the aid of the arts, sport could provide a setting "which shall move athletes well prepared to assist in the great festival, and conscious of the special glory it confers upon them" (Coubertin, 1908, p. 114).

Coubertin's proposal for inclusion of competition in the arts was favorably received. At the conference he proposed the creation of contests in architecture, sculpture, painting, music, and literature, with prizes to be awarded every 4 years for unpublished works directly inspired by sport. The proposal included the following program:

Architecture: Conditions and characteristics of the modern gymnasium. Open-air clubs and athletic centres, swimming pools, rifle ranges, riding schools, yacht clubs, fencing schools, architectural materials, motifs, costs and quotations.

Dramatic art: Open-air performances. Main principles: sport on the stage.

Choreography: Processions, parades, grouped and coordinated movements, rhythmic dances.

Decoration: Stands and premises, flagpoles, shields, garlands, hangings, spotlights, night festivals, torchlight sports.

Literature: Literary contests, conditions governing these contests, the emotional side of sport, source of inspiration for the man of letters.

Music: Open-air orchestras and choirs, repertoire, rhythms, fanfares, conditions governing an Olympic music contest.

Painting: Individual figures and groups. Possibilities and conditions governing an Olympic painting contest, help given to the artist by photography.

Sculpture: Athletic attitudes and movements in relation to art. Interpretation of effort, objects given as prizes, statuettes and medals. (Pouret, 1976, pp. 160-161)

With the acceptance of this proposal, the International Olympic Committee (IOC) formulated the rules for the competitions in art. Accordingly, works had to be created by living artists within the given Olympiad ("Olympic Art Competitions," 1948, p. 50), be published, be interpretative or expressive of sport ("Art as related to sport," 1932, p. 64), and be approved by the Olympic Committee of their nation (Mechlin, 1932, p. 137). The IOC further delegated the responsibility of the competition to the host cities. The acceptance of the proposal and Coubertin's continued support for the inclusion of the competitions in the arts resulted in their inclusion of the "Pentathlon of the Muses" in the 1912 Games in Stockholm and their continued inclusion through the XIV Olympiad of 1948.[3]

The quality and success of these competitions varied, and their success varied from one Olympiad to another. In 1949, the IOC changed the nature of the "Pentathlon of the Muses" from one of competition to one of exhibition. However, in 1951 the competitions were again abolished. The 1952 games did not include the competitions, and in 1954, the fine arts competitions were again abolished. The decision to abolish these competitions has been attributed to the IOC's question concerning the professional status of the artists.[4] The decision can also be attributed to the difficulty of constituting juries, recruiting orchestras, transporting works of art, and a lack of interest in the arts competition by the general public (Pouret, 1970, p. 66), and to the lack of concern on the part of the IOC (Finley & Pleket, 1976, p. 78). However, these competitions never received widespread recognition or support, nor were they favorably received by professional critics. Criticism centered largely around the quality of the works, the lack of interest in the competitions, and the lack of competent judges (Pouret, 1976, p. 162). Competitive art within the framework of the Olympics declined almost from its beginning, as evidenced from Coubertin's remarks in 1920.

I have not spoken of the art contests. They are not yet equal to it, although far in advance of 1912. The writers seem to be intimidated by subjects on sports; musicians have nothing to do with them; architects walk around their Palace of Sports, of which they are seeking the eternal silhouette, a monument already out of use before having existed. As for the sculptors, a rather humorous incident happened regarding them. Having no knowledge of technique, the jury put aside the reproduction of bodily movements in all their exactness and perfection, because such movements were not considered sufficiently "artistic." Let us hope that the contests of the Eighth Olympiad will be the final dedication of the value of inspiration offered by the Games, and will tempt young talents to combine artistic taste with physical hardihood. (Coubertin, 1920)

As a result of such concerns, the fine arts competitions were replaced after the 1948 Games by cultural festivals, gymnastic and dance demonstrations, art exhibitions, theater performances, and the like. After the 1968 Games in Mexico City, the IOC amended the rules and regulations to recommend that cultural exhibitions be limited to national rather than international perspectives.

Although much effort has been devoted to the "Olympic Celebration of the Arts," as evidenced by the recent 10-week program held in conjunction with the 1984 Games in Los Angeles and previous programs in Rome (1960), Tokyo (1964), Mexico City (1968), Montreal (1972), and Moscow (1980), these celebrations have failed to achieve the union of sport and art desired by Coubertin. In some ways, the exclusion of the arts competitions in 1948, the limiting nature of the rule changes regarding the arts exhibitions in 1969, and the ongoing lack of public interest in the arts competitions and exhibitions have prevented the union of sport and the arts that was recognized in ancient Greece and desired by Coubertin for the modern Olympic Games. If we briefly reexamine the ancient Greek circumstances in which the union of sport and the arts was nourished and flourished, other conclusions of a more general and perhaps instructive nature can be drawn.

Conclusions

The place of sport in ancient Greece, the realization of its expressive and human dimensions, and the consequent union of sport and the arts were made possible by the prominence given to the human being in Greek philosophy. Its place was also due to the Greeks' desire to develop all dimensions of the human being. As a result, sport and other forms of art were viewed as manifestations of the harmoniously educated man. This view provided sport with an intimate connection with the arts. Although sport began as a means of preparation for welfare during the time of Homer, it rather quickly came to be intrinsically regarded during the Golden Age as an end in and of itself, apart from its instrumental value.

Although Coubertin was greatly influenced by this philosophy and the ideals that it embodied, he used sport initially to promote French nationalism and then, through the modern Olympic Games, to promote international peace, goodwill, and friendship through athletic competition.

The union of sport and the arts in the modern world, which Coubertin desired, has been further precluded by a view of the human being that is very much different from the unified and holistic view of the ancient Greeks. A dualistic-tending view, one that regards the mind and body as separate and virtually unrelated aspects of the human being, has tended to dominate modern perceptions of the human being. As a result, sport has come to be regarded as an activity of the body and athletic achievement almost exclusively as an indication of physical strength and prowess. Although sport continues to inspire artists and serve as the subject for many artistic creations as it did in the ancient Greek culture, our instrumental regard for the Olympic Games and fragmented view of the human being tend to separate sport from the arts in the modern world. This view makes the union of sport and the fine arts unlikely.

Notes

1. Scholarship devoted to the ancient Greek view and practice of sport suggests that the ideal was only partly realized (Osterhoudt, 1982, p. 13), perhaps never existed (Czula, 1975, p. 12), or was only realized during a short period of the 5th century, under the purifying influence of the enthusiasm brought about by the war with Persia (Gardiner, 1910, p. 2). Nonetheless, this view and ideal prompted Coubertin to recreate the Olympic Games and fashion the Games around it.

2. A similar view of sport appeared in the Renaissance , during which time the insights of the ancient Greeks were rekindled.

3. For further reading pertaining to these competitions see the following: "Art as Related to Sport, a Competition and Exhibition" (1932, p. 64); Fuoss (1952, pp. 12-13, 24-25); Lenk (1980, pp. 107-167); Mechlin (1932, pp. 136-150); "Olympic Art Competitions" (1948, p. 50); Pouret (1976, pp. 160-161).

4. According to one argument, artists should not have been allowed to compete in these competitions because they were not amateurs. For further reading refer to "Art and Amateurism," 1970, p. 11.

References

Art as related to sport, a competition and exhibition. (1932, January). *American Magazine of Art*, p. 64.

Coubertin, P. de. (1908, July). Why I revived the Olympic Games. *Fortnightly Review*, pp. 110-115.

Coubertin, P. de. (1920). The seventh Olympic Games. *Report of the American Olympic Committee*. Greenwich, CT: Conde Nast.

Coubertin, P. de. (1970). Art and amateurism. In C. Diem (Ed.), *The Olympic idea: Discourses and essays* (pp. 11-18). Stuttgart: Verlag Karl Hofman.

Coubertin, P. de. (1979). *Olympic memoirs*. Lausanne: International Olympic Committee.

Czula, R. (1975). Pierre de Coubertin and modern Olympism. *Quest*, **24**, 10-18.

Finley, M.I., & Pleket, H.W. (1976). *The Olympic Games: The first thousand years*. New York: The Viking Press.

Fuoss, D.E. (1952). Problems connected with the Olympic Games. *The Amateur Athlete*, **22**, 12-13, 25, 30.

Gardiner, E. (1910). *Greek athletic sports and festivals*. London: MacMillan.

Lenk, H. (1976). Toward a social philosophy of the Olympics: Values, aims, reality of the modern Olympic Movement. In P.J. Graham & H. Ueberhorst (Eds.), *The Modern Olympics* (pp. 107-167). Cornwall, NY: Leisure Press.

Mechlin, L. (1932). The Olympic art exhibition. *The American Magazine of Art*, **25**, 136-150.

Olympic art competitions. (1943, September). *Connoisseur*, pp. 50-51.

Osterhoudt, R.G. (1982). *Sport: A humanistic overview*. Tempe: Arizona State University.

Pouret, H. (1970). The contemporary Olympic Games and the arts. *Report of the Ninth Session of the International Olympic Academy at Olympia*. Athens: International Olympic Committee.

Pouret, H. (1976). Art and the Olympics. In Lord Killanin & J. Rodda (Eds.), *The Olympic Games* (pp. 160-164). New York: Macmillan.

The Olympic art exhibition. (1932). *The American Magazine of Art*, **30**, 136-150.

The Games Themselves

With the exception of the years 1916 and 1940 and 1944, when the games were suspended during World Wars I and II respectively, and 1906, when the so-called Interium games were held in Athens, the modern Olympics have been celebrated every 4 years since their inception. The inaugural games of the modern era were opened by King Constantine on April 5, 1896, in Athens, Greece. Three hundred and eleven athletes from 13 countries assembled before an audience of approximately 80,000, which as Richardson (1896) aptly noted at the time, "was enough to stir that deep feeling caused by the presence of a multitude, the feeling which made Xerses weep at the Hellespont" (p. 274). On the other hand, 8,250 accredited media representatives reported the exploits of 7,800 athletes from 140 nations to an estimated worldwide television audience in excess of 2 billion during the 23rd Olympic Games held in Los Angeles in 1984. As MacAloon (1981) noted, "In scarcely 80 years, the Olympic Games have grown from a fin-de-siècle curiosity of regional interest to an international cultural performance of global proportion" (p. ix; see also Table 1).

Table 1 The Cycle of the Modern Olympic Games

Olympiad	Date	City	Winter Olympic Games
I	1896	Athens	
II	1900	Paris	
III	1904	St. Louis	
IV	1908	London	
V	1912	Stockholm	
VI	1916	Not celebrated	
VII	1920	Antwerp	
VIII	1924	Paris	Chamonix, France
IX	1928	Amsterdam	St. Moritz
X	1932	Los Angeles	Lake Placid
XI	1936	Berlin	Garmich-Partenkirchen
XII	1940	Not celebrated	
XIII	1944	Not celebrated	
XIV	1948	London	St. Moritz
XV	1952	Helsinki	Oslo
XVI	1956	Melbourne	Cortina d'Ampezzo, Italy
XVII	1960	Rome	Squaw Valley
XVIII	1964	Tokyo	Innsbruck, Austria
XIX	1968	Mexico City	Grenoble, France
XX	1972	Munich	Sapporo, Japan
XXI	1976	Montreal	Innsbruck
XXII	1980	Moscow	Lake Placid
XXIII	1984	Los Angeles	Sarajevo, Yugoslavia
XXIV	1988	Seoul	Calgary
XXV	1992	Barcelona	Albertville, France

During the initial years, 1896 to 1911, the young Olympic Games struggled for their existence. They were, as Lucas (1980) described, years of "trial and tribulation" (p. 45). The games of 1896, though, were a remarkable success. Athens, adorned with Hellenic symbols, was transformed into "a magic spectacle" (*Les Jeux Olympiques*, 1896, p. 52). Highlighted by the victory of Spiridon Loues in the marathon, the games themselves closed in "a scene of indescribable excitement" ("The Olympic Games," 1896, p. 24). As Szymiczek (1976) noted, "Athens, in 1896, had given the most brilliant start to the history of the modern international Olympic Games" (p. 28).

The legacy of the Athens games, however, was not reaffirmed in either the Paris games of 1900 or the St. Louis games of 1904, both of which were universally recognized as sporting disasters. In both instances, the games were presented as appendages to a World's Fair. Even Coubertin

(1931) himself declared that the 1900 games were consigned "to a humiliating vassalage" (p. 59) in the Paris Exposition. As a result of the failures in Paris and St. Louis, interim games were held in Athens in 1906. Although, as Lucas (1973) stipulated, these "games probably saved the Olympics from a premature death" (p. 74), it fell to the British with their prodigious organizational skill and keen sense of ritual to provide stability and credibility to the Olympic Movement. "In one gigantic stride," wrote Henry (1976) of the 1908 London Olympics, "Baron de Coubertin's offspring had leaped the tremendous gap between the uncertainties of childhood and the robust all-conquering virility of manhood" (p. 70).

During the years 1912-1927, the Olympic Games grew in credibility and stature. More than 2,500 athletes representing 28 nations competed in the 1912 Stockholm games, and nearly 3,000 athletes from 44 countries assembled for the Paris games of 1924. The resumption of the games after World War I in war-torn Belgium attested to the resilience of the Olympic movement. The 1912 Stockholm Olympics also saw the introduction of the art and cultural competitions. Financial austerity inevitably precipitated the somewhat primitive conditions in Antwerp, but as Coubertin (1931) noted, "everything had to be created from scratch" (p. 157). The games of 1924, celebrated for the second time in Paris, were a vast improvement on both the Antwerp games and, more significantly, on the previous Paris games of 1900. "The difference between the Olympic Games of 1900 at Paris and the Olympic Games of this year," declared Amos Alonzo Stagg (1924), "was so great that it is impossible for me to describe" (p. 99). The first winter games were also held in 1924, in Chamonix, France.

The Olympic Games emerged as a significant international phenomenon between 1928-1945. The 1936 Berlin Olympics in particular attested to the ascendant appeal of international sport and, more profoundly, the political uses to which it could be put. Under the auspices of Goebbels, the German Olympics became a reflection of the chauvinist, racist, and militarist intentions of Germany's political leadership. Even though the 1936 "Nazi Olympics" (Mandell, 1971) may have been "an important episode in the establishment of an evil political regime" (Mandell, 1971, p. x), Germany in effect had shrewdly and successfully organized the games as a component of the Nazi propaganda machinery. In the process, Germany made considerable gains in terms of patriotic revitalization and international credibility. As Goodhue (1976) points out, "One cannot detach 1936 from the previous Olympic Games. It was not simply an aberration. The conditions that made 1936 possible were apparent in the development of the games from 1900 to 1932" (p. 40). Even by 1912 as Lucas (1980) observed, "the Olympic Games had ceased to be 'games' or an ideal place in which to 'play' " (p. 95). Olympic athletic prowess in both organization and performance increasingly became a measure of national worth, a source of national identity, and an opportunity for international prestige in the games of Amsterdam, Los Angeles, and Berlin.

The period 1945-59 has been aptly characterized by Lucas (1980) as "a prelude to gigantism" (p. 137). Certainly, none of the games in this era spawned the technological and financial enormity of subsequent Olympics, and each mollified the mass pageantry that typified the 1936 Berlin games. They were, according to Lucas (1973), "pleasurable" rather than "grandiose" affairs (p. 80). The games between 1945 and 1959 also foreshadowed an East-West political enmity that was to color them for years to come. After a 40-year absence, Russian athletes competed again in the 1952 Helsinki games. As Edwards (1981) wrote, "In 1952, the attention of the world shifted from the performances of individual athletes competing for world recognition to a Cold War drama being acted out in the international sports arena by two titans locked in ideological struggle" (p. 233). Political tensions were also expressed in the 1956 Melbourne games when a bloody manifestation of the Russian invasion of Hungary broke out in a water polo match between the two countries.

If the years, 1945-59 were "a prelude to gigantism," then all subsequent years constituted the "era of gigantism" itself. The trend began with the 1960 Rome Olympics, "a nearly uncontrollable sports festival" as Lucas (1973, p. 82) called it. A record 5,902 athletes from 84 countries competed in some of the most ornate, dramatic, and lavish facilities ever built for the games. "No Olympics in history had more sumptuous appointments" commented Kieran, Daley, and Jordan (1977, p. 323). The Rome games cost $400 million and television rights sold for $1.2 million. The 1964 Tokyo Olympics, the "Science Fiction Olympics," as the London *Times* ("Sour End," 1964, p. 6) called them, cost a staggering 700 million yen, or over $2 billion by American financial measurements. "A new city was being born just to accommodate the Olympic Games," observed Kieran et al. (1977, p. 363). Subsequent games were similarly used to generate civic renewal, particularly in Mexico City, Munich, and Montreal. The $500 million cost of staging the 1968 Mexico City games sparked several demonstrations, and 10 days before the opening ceremonies, a confrontation between demonstrators and the Mexican authorities resulted in 267 deaths and 1,200 injuries. In Montreal, massive expenditures resulted in a $1 billion debt, which Pierre Fortin (quoted in "Quebec Swallows," 1976) claimed at the time would cost "every Canadian $11, every Quebecer $100, and every Montrealer $267" (p. 23). In reaction to the escalating costs of staging the games, the 1984 Olympics were awarded to Los Angeles, and for the first time in modern Olympic history a host city was not held financially responsible for the games. The sales of the television rights for the 1984 "Corporate Olympics" for $225 million provided almost 45% of the $500 million budget for hosting the games.

Since 1960 the games have also become increasingly politicized. During the 1972 Munich games, a Palestinian terrorist group of the Black September invaded the Olympic village. As a result, 11 members of the Israeli Olympic team perished. The episode poignantly attested to the global significance that the games had attained; as one terrorist revealed,

We recognize that sport is the modern religion of the western world . . . so we decided to use the Olympics, the most sacred ceremony of this religion, to make the world pay attention to us. (quoted in Killanin, 1983, p. 70)

Political manifestations also erupted in subsequent Olympics. The African boycott of the 1976 Montreal games, the United States boycott of the 1980 Moscow games, and the Soviet-led boycott of the 1984 Los Angeles games illustrated that the Modern Olympics had, in the most recent era, entered the forum of international diplomacy.

Considered collectively, the Olympic games may rightly be viewed, as MacAloon (1981) concludes, as "the privileged expression" (p. x) and "*the* dramatic celebration of world-historical process" (p. 271). More than any other institution of our era, the Olympics reflect and express the geopolitical dimensions of the 20th century. Taken individually, they each constitute a unique cultural manifestation of their time, while at the same time maintaining a remarkable continuity of ritual and ideology and of code and purpose. Each Olympic celebration presents a worthy case study in its own right, and each stands as an identifiable episode in the history of the games themselves.

In the first reading in this section, le Renovateur, Pierre de Coubertin himself, exalts in the success of the 1896 Athens games. He concludes, "On the world at large the Olympic games have, of course, exerted no influence as yet; but I am profoundly convinced that they will do so." By 1932 they had clearly done so, and Al Stump describes the inauspicious preparations for one of the most cosmopolitan and widely acclaimed games of the pre-World War II era, the 1932 Los Angeles games. The success of the games in the face of a worldwide depression led Zimmerman (1976) to conclude that "the accomplishment must go down in the history of the movement as one of its finest hours" (p. 53).

However, whereas the 1932 games may have provided the Olympics with one of their finest hours, the 1936 Berlin games provided them with one of their most controversial. Consequently, in the third reading in this section, Allen Guttmann discusses the 1936 games, paying particular attention to the boycott debate that preceded the games themselves and that emerged in reaction to Hitler's antisemitic policies. Guttmann also focuses on the role of Avery Brundage, the President of the American Olympic Committee, in the boycott controversy, arguing in the end that the Berlin Games were an important step on Brundage's path to Olympic leadership.

The final two essays in this section focus on the two most recent Olympics, the 1980 Moscow Games and the 1984 Los Angeles Games. Although both games may well be best remembered for successive boycotts by the superpowers, the boycott issue is the subject of only one of these two readings, namely James Nafziger's commentary on the U.S. boycott of the 1980 Moscow games. In this essay, Nafziger presents the U.S. boycott as a reflection of foreign policy during the Carter administration, and argues that ultimately it was both ineffectual and imprudent, and possibly illegal. In the final reading, Howard Nixon concentrates on the financial foundations of the 1984 Los Angeles games rather than the reciprocal boycott carried out by the Soviet Union. For although the Soviet-led boycott may have received more attention and generated more debate than the capitalist organization of the games, the precedent-setting decision of the IOC to permit an organizing committee to operate as a private corporation led Associated Press correspondent Geoffrey Miller (1979) to declare that "if the Olympic Games are celebrated in the year 2000 the birth pangs of the 1984 Games at Los Angeles will be seen in retrospect as a turning point in Olympic history" (p. 135).

References

Coubertin, P. de. (1931). *Memories Olympiques*. Lausanne: Bureau International de Pedagogie Sportive.

Edwards, H. (1981). Crisis in the modern Olympic movement. In J. Segrave & D. Chu (Eds.), *Olympism* (pp. 227-241). Champaign, IL: Human Kinetics.

Goodhue, R.M. (1976). The development of Olympism, 1900-32: Technical success within a threatening political reality. In P. Graham & H. Ueberhorst (Eds.), *The modern Olympics* (pp. 27-39). Cornwall, NY: Leisure Press.

Henry, B. (1976). *An approved history of the Olympic Games*. New York: G.P. Putnam's Sons.

Kieran, J., Daley, A., & Jordan, P. (1977). *The story of the Olympic Games 776 B.C.-1976*. Philadelphia: J.B. Lippincott.

Killanin, Lord. (1983). *My Olympic years*. New York: William Morrow.

Les Jeux Olympiques, 776 av. J.C.-1896. (1896). Athens: Beck.

Lucas, J.A. (1973). The modern Olympic Games: Fanfare and philosophy, 1896-1972. *The Maryland Historian*, **4**, 71-87.

Lucas, J.A. (1980). *The modern Olympic games*. New York: A.S. Barnes.

MacAloon, J.J. (1981). *This great symbol: Pierre de Coubertin and the origins of the modern Olympic games*. Chicago: University of Chicago Press.

Mandell, R. (1971). *The Nazi Olympics*. New York: Macmillan.

Miller, G. (1979). *Behind the Olympic rings*. Lynn, MA: H.O. Zimman.

Quebec swallows an Olympic debt. (1976, August 23). *Business Week*, p. 23.

Richardson, R.B. (1896). The new Olympian games. *Scribner's Magazine*, **20**, 267-286.

Stagg, A.A. (1924). Impressions of the Olympic games of 1924. *Proceedings of the NCAA*, **9**, 99-112.

Szymiczek, O. (1976). Athens 1896. In Lord Killanin & J. Rodda (Eds.), *The Olympic games* (pp. 27-28). New York: MacMillan.

Sour end to "science fiction" Olympics. (1964, October 26). *The Times* [London], p. 6.

The Olympic games. (1896, April 16). *The Times* [London], p. 24.

Zimmerman, P. (1976). Los Angeles 1932. In Lord Killanin & J. Rodda (Eds.), *The Olympic games* (pp. 53-56). New York: MacMillan.

Suggested Reading

Henry, B. (1976). *An approved history of the Olympic Games.* New York: G.P. Putnam's Sons.

Johnson, W.O. (1972). *All that glitters is not gold: An irreverent look at the Olympic Games.* New York: G.P. Putnam's Sons.

Kieran, J., Daley, A., & Jordan, P. (1977). *The story of the Olympic Games: 776 B.C.-1977.* Philadelphia: J.B. Lippincott.

Mandell, R. (1971). *The Nazi Olympics.* New York: MacMillan.

Schaap, R. (1963). *An illustrated history of the Olympics.* New York: Alfred A. Kneef.

Ueberoth, P. (1985). *Made in America.* New York: William Morrow.

11
The Olympic Games of 1896

Pierre de Coubertin

The Olympic games that recently took place at Athens were modern in character, not alone because of their programs, which substituted bicycle for chariot races, and fencing for the brutalities of pugilism, but because in their origin and regulations they were international and universal and consequently adapted to the conditions in which athletics have developed at the present day. The ancient games had an exclusively Hellenic character; they were always held in the same place, and Greek blood was a necessary condition of admission to them. It is true that strangers were in time tolerated; but their presence at Olympia was rather a tribute paid to the superiority of Greek civilization than a right exercised in the name of racial equality. With the modern games it is quite otherwise. Their creation is the work of "barbarians." It is due to the delegates of the athletic associations of all countries assembled in congress at Paris in 1894. It was there agreed that every country should celebrate the Olympic games in turn. The first place belonged by right to Greece; it was accorded by unanimous vote; and in order to emphasize the permanence of the institution, its wide bearings, and its essentially cosmopolitan character, an

Originally published in *The Century Magazine*, LIII, 1 (November 1896), pp. 39-55. Reprinted by permission.

international committee was appointed, the members of which were to represent the various nations, European and American, with whom athletics are held in honor. The presidency of this committee falls to the country in which the next games are to be held. A Greek, M. Bikelas, has presided for the last 2 years. A Frenchman now presides and will continue to do so until 1900, since the next games are to take place at Paris during the Exposition. Where will those of 1904 take place? Perhaps at New York, perhaps at Berlin or at Stockholm. The question is soon to be decided.

It was in virtue of these resolutions passed during the Paris Congress that the recent festivals were organized. Their successful issue is largely owing to the active and energetic cooperation of the Greek crown prince Constantine. When they realized all that was expected of them, the Athenians lost courage. They felt that the city's resources were not equal to the demands that would be made upon them, nor would the government (M. Tricoupis being then prime minister) consent to increase facilities. M. Tricoupis did not believe in the success of the Games. He argued that the Athenians knew nothing about athletics; that they had neither the adequate grounds for the contests nor athletes of their own to bring into line; and that, moreover, the financial situation of Greece forbade her inviting the world to an event preparations for which would entail such large expenditures. There was reason in these objections; but on the one hand, the prime minister greatly exaggerated the importance of the expenditures, and on the other, it was not necessary that the government should bear the burden of them directly. Modern Athens, which recalls in so many ways the Athens of ancient days, has inherited from her the privilege of being beautified and enriched by her children. The public treasury was not always very well filled in those times any more than in the present, but wealthy citizens who had made fortunes at a distance liked to crown their commercial career by some act of liberality to the mother-country. They endowed the land with superb edifices of general utility—theaters, gymnasia, temples. The modern city is likewise full of monuments that she owes to such generosity. It was easy to obtain from private individuals what the state could not give. The Olympic games had burned with so bright a luster in the past of the Greeks that they could not but have their revival at heart. And furthermore, the moral benefits would compensate largely for all pecuniary sacrifice.

This the crown prince apprehended at once, and it decided him to lend his authority to the organizing of the first Olympic games. He appointed a commission with headquarters in his own palace; made M. Philemon, ex-mayor of Athens and a man of much zeal and enthusiasm, secretary-general; and appealed to the nation to subscribe the necessary funds. Subscriptions began to come in from Greece but particularly from London, Marseilles, and Constantinople, where there are wealthy and influential Greek colonies. The chief gift came from Alexandria. It was this gift which made it possible to restore the Stadion to its condition in the time of

Atticus Herodes. The intention had been from the first to hold the contest in this justly celebrated spot. No one, however, had dreamed that it might be possible to restore to their former splendor the marble seats that, it is said, could accommodate 40,000 persons. The great inclosure would have been utilized and provisional wooden seats placed on the grassy slopes that surround it. Thanks to the generosity of M. Averoff, Greece is now the richer by a monument unique of its kind, and its visitors have seen a spectacle that they can never forget.

Two years ago the Stadion resembled a deep gash, made by some fabled giant, in the side of the hill which rises abruptly by the Ilissus and opposite Lycabettus and the Acropolis, in a retired, picturesque quarter of Athens. All that was visible of it then were the two high earth embankments that faced each other on opposite sides of the long, narrow racecourse. They met at the end in an imposing hemicycle. Grass grew between the cobblestones. For centuries the spectators of ancient days had sat on the ground on these embankments. Then, one day, an army of workmen, taking possession of the Stadion, had covered it with stone and marble. This is the work that has now been repeated. The first covering served as a quarry during the Turkish domination; not a trace of it was left. With its innumerable rows of seats and the flights of steps that divide it into sections and lead to the upper tiers, the Stadion no longer has the look of being cut out of the hill. It is the hill that seems to have been placed there by the hand of man to support this enormous pile of masonry. One detail only is modern. One does not notice it at first. The dusty track is now a cinder path, prepared according to the latest rules of modern athletics by an expert brought over from London for the purpose. In the center a sort of esplanade has been erected for the gymnastic exhibitions. At the end, on each side of the turning, antiquity is represented by two large boundary stones forming two human figures and excavated while the foundations were being dug. These were the only finds; they add but little to archaeological data. Work on the Stadion is far from being completed, 18 months having been quite insufficient for the undertaking. Where marble could not be placed, painted wood was hastily made to do duty. That clever architect M. Metaxas cherishes the hope, however, of seeing all the antique decorations restored—statues, columns, bronze quadrigae, and, at the entrance, majestic propylaea.

When this shall be done, Athens will in truth possess the temple of athletic sports. Yet it is doubtful whether such a sanctuary be the one best suited to the worship of human vigor and beauty in these modern days. The Anglo-Saxons, to whom we owe the revival of athletics, frame their contests delightfully in grass and verdure. Nothing could differ more from the Athenian Stadion than Travers Island, the summer home of the New York Athletic Club, where the championship games are decided. In this green enclosure, where nature is left to have her way, the spectators sit under the trees on the sloping declivities, a few feet away from the Sound, which murmurs against the rocks. One finds something of the same idea at Paris and at San Francisco, under those Californian skies that so recall the skies of Greece, at the foot of those mountains that have the pure outlines and the iridescent reflections of Hymettus. If the ancient amphitheater was more grandiose and more solemn, the modern picture is more *intime* and pleasing. The music floating under the trees makes a softer accompaniment to the exercises; the spectators move about at friendly ease, whereas the ancients, packed together in rigid lines on their marble benches, sat broiling in the sun or chilled in the shade.

The Stadion is not the only enduring token that will remain to Athens of her inauguration of the new Olympiads: She has also a velodrome and a shooting stand. The former is in the plain of the modern Phalerum, along the railway that connects Athens with the Piraeus. It is copied after the model of that at Copenhagen, where the crown prince of Greece and his brothers had an opportunity of appreciating its advantages during a visit to the King of Denmark, their grandfather. The bicyclists, it is true, have complained that the track is not long enough and that the turnings are too abrupt; but when were bicyclists ever content? The tennis courts are in the center of the velodrome. The shooting stand makes a goodly appearance, with its manor-like medieval crenelations. The contestants are comfortably situated under monumental arches. Then there are large pavilions for the rowers, built of wood, but prettily decorated, with boat houses and dressing rooms.

While the Hellenic Committee thus labored over the scenic requirements, the international committee and the national committees were occupied in recruiting competitors. The matter was not as easy as one might think. Not only had indifference and distrust to be overcome, but the revival of the Olympic games had aroused a certain hostility. Although the Paris Congress had been careful to decree that every form of physical exercise practiced in the world should have its place on the program, the gymnasts took offense. They considered that they had not been given sufficient prominence. The greater part of the gymnastic associations of Germany, France, and Belgium are animated by a rigorously exclusive spirit; they are not inclined to tolerate the presence of those forms of athletics that they themselves do not practice; what they disdainfully designate as "English sports" have become, because of their popularity, especially odious to them. These associations were not satisfied with declining the invitation sent them to repair to Athens. The Belgian federation wrote to the other federations, suggesting a concerted stand against the work of the Paris Congress. These incidents confirmed the opinions of the pessimists who had been foretelling the failure of the fêtes, or their probable postponement. Athens is far away, the journey is expensive, and the Easter vacations are short. The contestants were not willing to undertake the voyage unless they could be sure that the occasion would be worth the effort. The different associations were not willing to send representatives unless they could be informed of the amount of interest which the contests would create. An unfortunate occurrence took place almost at the last moment. The German press, commenting on an article that had appeared in a Paris newspaper, declared that it was an exclusively Franco-Greek affair; that attempts were being made to shut out other nations; and furthermore, that the German associations had been intentionally kept aloof from the Paris Congress of 1894. The assertion was acknowledged to be incorrect, and was powerless to check the efforts of the German committee under Dr. Gebhardt. M. Kémény in Hungary, Major Balck in Sweden, General de Boutonski in Russia, Professor W.M. Sloane in the United States, Lord Ampthill in England, Dr. Jiri Guth in Bohemia, were, meantime, doing their best to awaken interest in the event and to reassure the doubting. They did not always succeed. Many people took a sarcastic view, and the newspapers indulged in much pleasantry on the subject of the Olympic games.

Easter Monday, April 6, the streets of Athens wore a look of extraordinary animation. All the public buildings were draped in bunting; multicolored streamers floated in the wind; green wreaths decked the house fronts. Everywhere were the two letters "O.A.," the Greek initials of the Olympic games, and the two dates, B.C. 776, A.D. 1896, indicating their ancient past and their present renascence. At 2:00 in the afternoon the crowd began to throng the Stadion and to take possession of the seats. It was a joyous and motley concourse. The skirts and braided jackets of the *palikars* contrasted with the somber and ugly European habiliments. The women used large paper fans to shield them from the sun, parasols, which would have obstructed the view, being prohibited. The king and the queen drove up a little before 3:00, followed by Princess Marie, their daughter, and her fiancé, Grand Duke George of Russia. They were received by the crown prince and his brothers; M. Delyannis, president of the Council of Ministers; and the members of the Hellenic Committee and the international committee. Flowers were presented to the queen and princess, and the cortège made its way into the hemicycle to the strains of the Greek national hymn and the cheers of the crowd. Within, the court ladies and functionaries, the diplomatic corps, and the deputies awaited the sovereigns, for whom two marble armchairs were in readiness. The crown prince, taking his stand in the arena, facing the king, then made a short speech, in which he touched upon the origin of the enterprise, and the obstacles surmounted in bringing it to fruition. Addressing the king, he asked him to proclaim the opening of the Olympic Games, and the king, rising, declared them opened. It was a thrilling moment. Fifteen hundred and two years before, the Emperor Theodosius had suppressed the Olympic Games, thinking, no doubt, that in abolishing this hated survival of paganism he was furthering the cause of progress; and here was a Christian monarch, amid the applause of an assemblage composed almost exclusively of Christians, announcing the formal annulment of the imperial decree; while a few feet away stood the archbishop of Athens and Père Didon, the celebrated Dominican preacher, who, in his Easter sermon in the Catholic cathedral the day before, had paid an eloquent tribute to pagan Greece. When the king had resumed his seat, the Olympic ode, written for the occasion by the Greek composer Samara, was sung by a chorus of 150 voices. Once before music had been associated with the revival of the Olympic games. The first session of the Paris Congress had been held June 16, 1894, in the great amphitheater of the Sorbonne, decorated by Puvis de Chavannes; and after the address of the president of the congress, Baron de Coubertin, the large audience had listened to that fragment of the music of antiquity, the hymn to Apollo, discovered in the ruins of Delphi. But this time the connection between art and athletics was more direct. The games began with the sounding of the last chords of the Olympic ode. That first day established the success of the games beyond a doubt. The ensuing days confirmed the fact in spite of the bad weather. The royal family was assiduous in its attendance. In the shooting contest the queen fired the first shot with a flower-wreathed rifle. The fencing matches were held in the marble rotunda of the Exposition Palace, given by the Messrs. Zappas and known as the Zappeion. Then the crowd made its way back to the Stadion for the footraces, weight putting, discus throwing, high and long jumps, pole vaulting, and gymnastic exhibitions. A Princeton student, Robert Garrett, scored highest in throwing the discus. His victory was unexpected. He had asked me the day before if I did not think that it would be ridiculous should he enter for an event for which he had trained so little! The stars and stripes seemed destined to carry off all the laurels. When they ran up the "victor's mast," the sailors of the *San Francisco*, who stood in a group at the top of the Stadion, waved their caps, and the members of the Boston Athletic Association below broke out frantically, "B. A. A.! rah! rah! rah!" These cries greatly amused the Greeks. They applauded the triumph of the Americans, between whom and themselves there is a warm feeling of good will.

The Greeks are novices in the matter of athletic sports and had not looked for much success for their own country. One event only seemed likely to be theirs from its very nature—the long-distance run from Marathon, a prize for which has been newly founded by M. Michel Bréal, a member of the French Institute, in commemoration of that soldier of antiquity who ran all the way to Athens to tell his fellow citizens of the happy issue of the battle. The distance from Marathon to Athens is 42 kilometers. The road is rough and stony. The Greeks had trained for this run for a year past. Even in the remote districts of Thessaly young peasants prepared to enter as contestants. In three cases it is said that the enthusiasm and the inexperience of these young fellows cost them their lives, so exaggerated were their preparatory efforts. As the great day approached, women offered up prayers and votive tapers in the churches, that the victor might be a Greek!

The wish was fulfilled. A young peasant named Loües, from the village of Marousi, was the winner in 2 hours and 55 minutes. He reached the goal fresh and in fine form. He was followed by two other Greeks. The excellent Australian sprinter Flack, and the Frenchman Lermusiaux, who had been in the lead the first 35 kilometers, had fallen out by the way. When Loües came into the Stadion, the crowd, which numbered

60,000 persons, rose to its feet like one man, swayed by extraordinary excitement. The King of Servia, who was present, will probably not forget the sight he saw that day. A flight of white pigeons was let loose, women waved fans and handkerchiefs, and some of the spectators who were nearest to Louës left their seats and tried to reach him and carry him in triumph. He would have been suffocated if the crown prince and Prince George had not bodily led him away. A lady who stood next to me unfastened her watch, a gold one set with pearls, and sent it to him; an innkeeper presented him with an order good for 365 free meals; and a wealthy citizen had to be dissuaded from signing a check for 10,000 francs to his credit. Louës himself, however, when he was told of this generous offer, refused it. The sense of honor, which is very strong in the Greek peasant, thus saved the nonprofessional spirit from a very great danger.

Needless to say that the various contests were held under amateur regulations. An exception was made for the fencing matches, because in several countries professors of military fencing hold the rank of officers. For them a special contest was arranged. To all other branches of the athletic sports only amateurs were admitted. It is impossible to conceive the Olympic games with money prizes. But these rules, which seem simple enough, are a good deal complicated in their practical application by the fact that definitions of what constitutes an amateur differ from one country to another, sometimes even from one club to another. Several definitions are current in England; the Italians and the Dutch admit one that appears too rigid at one point, too loose at another. How conciliate these divergent or contradictory utterances? The Paris Congress made an attempt in that direction, but its decisions are not accepted everywhere as law, nor is its definition of amateurship everywhere adopted as the best. The rules and regulations, properly so called, are not any more uniform. This and that are forbidden in one country, authorized in another. All that one can do, until there shall be an Olympic code formulated in accordance with the ideas and the usages of the majority of athletes, is to choose among the codes now existing. It was decided, therefore, that the footraces should be under the rules of the Union Française des Sports Athlétiques; jumping, putting the shot, and so forth, under those of the Amateur Athletic Association of England; the bicycle races under those of the International Cyclists' Association, and so forth. This had appeared to us the best way out of the difficulty; but we should have had many disputes if the judges (to whom had been given the Greek name of ephors) had not been headed by Prince George, who acted as final referee. His presence gave weight and authority to the decisions of the ephors, among whom there were, naturally, representatives of different countries. The prince took his duties seriously, and fulfilled them conscientiously. He was always on the track, personally supervising every detail, an easily recognizable figure, owing to his height and athletic build. It will be remembered that Prince George, while traveling in Japan with his cousin, the czarevitch (now Emperor Nicholas II), felled with his fist the ruffian who had tried to assassinate the latter. During the weight lifting in the Stadion, Prince George lifted with ease an enormous dumbbell and tossed it out of the way. The audience broke into applause, as if it would have liked to make him the victor in the event.

Every night while the games were in progress the streets of Athens were illuminated. There were torchlight processions, bands played the different national hymns, and the students of the university got up ovations under the windows of the foreign athletic crews and harangued them in the noble tongue of Demosthenes. Perhaps this tongue was somewhat abused. That Americans might not be compelled to understand French, nor Hungarians forced to speak German, the daily programs of the games, and even invitations to luncheon, were written in Greek. On receipt of these cards, covered with mysterious formulae, where even the date was not clear (the Greek calendar is 12 days behind ours), every man carried them to his hotel porter for elucidation.

Many banquets were given. The Mayor of Athens gave one at Cephissia, a little shaded village at the foot of Pentelicus. M. Bikelas, the retiring president of the international committee, gave another at Phalerum. The king himself entertained all the competitors, and the members of the committees, 300 guests in all, at luncheon in the ballroom of the palace. The outside of this edifice, which was built by King Otho, is heavy and graceless; but the center of the interior is occupied by a suite of large rooms with very high ceilings, opening one into another through colonnades. The decorations are simple and imposing. The tables were set in the largest of these rooms. At the table of honor sat the king, princes, and ministers, and here also were the members of the committees. The competitors were seated at the other tables according to their nationality. The king, at dessert, thanked and congratulated his guests, first in French, afterward in Greek. The Americans cried "Hurrah!"; the Germans, "Hoch!"; the Hungarians, "Eljen!"; the Greeks, "Zito!"; the French, "Vive le Roi!" After the repast the king and his sons chatted long and amicably with the athletes. It was a really charming scene, the republican simplicity of which was a matter of wonderment particularly to the Austrians and the Russians, little used as they are to the spectacle of monarchy thus meeting democracy on an equal footing.

Then there were nocturnal festivities on the Acropolis, where the Parthenon was illuminated with colored lights, and at the Piraeus, where the vessels were hung with Japanese lanterns. Unluckily, the weather changed, and the sea was so high on the day appointed for the boat races, which were to have taken place in the roadstead of Phalerum, that the project was abandoned. The distribution of prizes was likewise postponed for 24 hours. It came off with much solemnity, on the morning of April 15, in the Stadion. The sun shone again, and sparkled on the officers' uniforms. When the roll of the victors was called, it became evident, after all, that the international character of the institution was well guarded by the results of the contests. America had won nine prizes for athletic sports alone (flat races for 100 and 400 meters; 110-meter hurdle race; high jump; broad jump; pole vault; hop, step, and jump; putting the shot; throwing the discus), and two prizes for shooting (revolver, 25 and 30 meters); but France had the prizes for foil fencing and for four bicycle races; England scored highest in the one-handed weight lifting contest, and in single lawn tennis; Greece won the run from Marathon, two gymnastic contests (rings, climbing the smooth rope), three prizes for shooting (carbine, 200 and 300 meters; pistol, 25 meters), a prize for fencing with sabers, and a bicycle race; Germany won in wrestling, in gymnastics (parallel bars, fixed bar, horse leaping), and in double lawn tennis; Australia, the 800- and 1,500-meter footraces on the flat; Hungary, swimming matches of 100 and 1,200 meters; Austria, the 500-meter swimming match and the 12-hour bicycle race; Switzerland, a gymnastic prize; Denmark, the two-handed weight lifting contest.

The prizes were an olive branch from the very spot, at Olympia, where stood the ancient Altis, a diploma drawn by a Greek artist, and a silver medal chiseled by the celebrated French engraver Chaplain. On one side of the medal is the Acropolis, with the Parthenon and the Propylaea; on the other a colossal head of the Olympian Zeus, after the type created by Phidias. The head of the god is blurred, as if by distance and the lapse of centuries, while in the foreground, in clear relief, is the Victory which Zeus holds on his hand. It is a striking and original conception. After the distribution of the prizes, the athletes formed for the traditional procession around the Stadion. Louës, the victor of Marathon, came first, bearing the Greek flag; then the Americans, the Hungarians, the French, the Germans. The ceremony, moreover, was made more memorable by a charming incident. One of the contestants, Mr. Robertson, an Oxford student, recited an ode that he had composed, in ancient Greek and in the Pindaric mode, in honor of the games. Music had opened them, and Poetry was present at their close; and thus was the bond once more renewed which in the past united the Muses with feats of physical strength, the mind with the well-trained body. The king announced that the first Olympiad was at an end and left the Stadion, the band playing the Greek national hymn and the crowd cheering. A few days later Athens was emptied of its guests. Torn wreaths littered the public squares; the banners that had floated merrily in the streets disappeared; the sun and the wind held sole possession of the marble sidewalks of Stadion street.

It is interesting to ask oneself what are likely to be the results of the Olympic Games of 1896, as regards both Greece and the rest of the world. In the case of Greece, the games will be found to have had a double effect, one athletic, the other political. It is a well-known fact that the Greeks had lost completely, during their centuries of oppression, the taste for physical sports. There were good walkers among the mountaineers and good swimmers in the scattered villages along the coast. It was a matter of pride with the young *palikar* to wrestle and to dance well, but that was because bravery and a gallant bearing were admired by those about him. Greek dances are far from athletic, and the wrestling matches of peasants have none of the characteristics of true sports. The men of the towns had come to know no diversion beyond reading the newspapers, and violently discussing politics about the tables of the cafés. The Greek race, however, is free from the natural indolence of the Oriental, and it was manifest that the athletic habit would, if the opportunity offered, easily take root again among its men. Indeed, several gymnastic associations had been formed in recent years at Athens and Patras, and a rowing club at Piraeus, and the public was showing a growing interest in their feats. It was therefore a favorable moment to speak the words *Olympic games*. No sooner had it been made clear that Athens was to aid in the revival of the Olympiads than a perfect fever of muscular activity broke out all over the kingdom. And this was nothing to what followed the games. I have seen, in little villages far from the capital, small boys, scarcely out of long clothes, throwing big stones or jumping improvised hurdles, and two urchins never met in the streets of Athens without running races. Nothing could exceed the enthusiasm with which the victors in the contests were received on their return to their native towns by their fellow citizens. They were met by the mayor and municipal authorities and cheered by a crowd bearing branches of wild olive and laurel. In ancient times the victor entered the city through a breach made expressly in its walls. The Greek cities are no longer walled in, but one may say that athletics have made a breach in the heart of the nation. When one realizes the influence that the practice of physical exercises may have on the future of a country, and on the force of a whole race, one is tempted to wonder whether Greece is not likely to date a new era from their year 1896. It would be curious indeed if athletics were to become one of the factors in the Eastern question! Who can tell whether, by bringing a notable increase of vigor to the inhabitants of the country, it may not hasten the solution of this thorny problem? These are hypotheses, and circumstances make light of such calculations at long range. But a local and immediate consequence of the games may already be found in the internal politics of Greece. I have spoken of the active part taken by the crown prince and his brothers, Prince George and Prince Nicholas, in the labors of the organizing committee. It was the first time that the heir apparent had had an opportunity of thus coming into contact with his future subjects. They knew him to be patriotic and high-minded, but they did not know his other admirable and solid qualities. Prince Constantine inherits his fine blue eyes and fair coloring from his Danish ancestors, and his frank, open manner, his self-poise, and his mental lucidity come from the same source; but Greece has given him enthusiasm and ardor, and this happy combination of prudence and high spirit makes him especially adapted to govern the Hellenes. The authority, mingled with perfect liberality, with which he managed the committee, his exactitude in detail, and more particularly his quiet perseverance when those about him were inclined to hesitate and to lose courage, make it clear that his reign will be one of fruitful labor, which can only strengthen and enrich his country. The Greek people have now a better idea of the worth of their future sovereign: They have seen him at work and have gained respect for and confidence in him.

So much for Greece. On the world at large the Olympic Games have, of course, exerted no influence as yet; but I am profoundly convinced that they will do so. May I be permitted to say that this was my reason for founding them? Modern athletics need to be *unified* and *purified*. Those who have followed the renaissance of physical sports in this century know that discord reigns supreme from one end of them to the other. Every country has its own rules; it is not possible even to come to an agreement as to who is an amateur, and who is not. All over the world there is one perpetual dispute, which is further fed by innumerable weekly, and even daily, newspapers. In this deplorable state of things professionalism tends to grow apace. Men give up their whole existence to one particular sport, grow rich by practicing it, and thus deprive it of all nobility, and destroy the just equilibrium of man by making the muscles preponderate over the mind. It is my belief that no education, particularly in democratic times, can be good and complete without the aid of athletics; but athletics, in order to play their proper educational role, must be based on perfect disinterestedness and the sentiment of honor.

If we are to guard them against these threatening evils, we must put an end to the quarrels of amateurs, that they may be united among themselves, and willing to measure their skill in frequent international encounters. But what country is to impose its rules and its habits on the others? The Swedes will not yield to the Germans, nor the French to the English. Nothing better than the international Olympic Games could therefore be devised. Each country will take its turn in organizing them. When they come to meet every 4 years in these contests, further ennobled by the memories of the past, athletes all over the world will learn to know one another better, to make mutual concessions, and to seek no other reward in the competition than the honor of the victory. One may be filled with desire to see the colors of one's club or college triumph in a national meeting; but how much stronger is the feeling when the colors of one's country are at stake! I am well assured that the victors in the Stadion at Athens wished for no other recompense when they heard the people cheer the flag of their country in honor of their achievement.

It was with these thoughts in mind that I sought to revive the Olympic Games. I have succeeded after many efforts. Should the institution prosper—as I am persuaded, all civilized nations aiding, that it will—it may be a potent, if indirect, factor in securing universal peace. Wars break out because nations misunderstand each other. We shall not have peace until the prejudices that now separate the different races shall have been outlived. To attain this end, what better means than to bring the youth of all countries periodically together for amicable trials of muscular strength and agility? The Olympic Games, with the ancients, controlled athletics and promoted peace. It is not visionary to look to them for similar benefactions in the future.

12
The Games That Almost Weren't

Al J. Stump

March 1925. Baron Pierre de Coubertin, president of the Comité International Olympique, in a confidential letter from Paris to William May Garland, president of the California Olympiad committee: "In case of Holland failing to fulfill her engagements . . . in the IX Olympiad . . . would Los Angeles be willing or not to take up 1928 instead of 1932? An answer must be given immediately. Therefore we beg that you shall consult without delay upon receiving this letter with the mayor of Los Angeles and the organizing committee. . . . You can telegraph if you like. . . . *Yes* or *No.*"

The "Garland Group"—some three dozen industrialists, oil-field developers, tourism promoters, and assorted businessmen—discussed the matter. There was disagreement, but Garland's view prevailed, and within a week he sent a polite no-thanks reply: He sympathized with the plight of the Comité International, but America would not be rushed on such an important matter. Nineteen thirty-two it was to be.

Garland and his associates thought, of course, that they were playing it safe. California was booming as never before, its sunshine, moviemaking, beaches, and real estate already becoming the stuff of myth. A giant Coliseum, built with the Olympics in mind, had been completed

Originally published in *American Heritage*, 1982, **33**, 64-71. Reprinted by permission.

in 1923, and all other facilities were at least in the planning stage. Garland's prestigious group included the movie tycoon Louis B. Mayer, Mayor John Porter, and Los Angles *Times* publisher Harry "Sell 'em Sunshine" Chandler. "I'll give you a $10,000 donation tomorrow," said one aspiring merchant to the officials, "to be on that board." What could go wrong?

What went wrong was the Depression. During 3 years of struggle and chaos it looked as though America's first Olympics was headed for total disaster.

The stock market collapsed, and by 1930 unemployment in the Golden State reached 700,000, with close to 350,000 of the workless located in Los Angeles and adjacent Orange County. Soup kitchens handled lineups on the main streets of Broadway, Spring, and Figueroa, some of them only blocks from the looming Memorial Coliseum in Exposition Park. Mayor Porter ordered a drastic $5.3 million reduction in the city budget. Cutbacks of 30,000 Hollywood movie industry jobs and of aviation, oil, and mercantile payrolls increased the pinch. Things slipped further, and the area reached new highs in suicides (79 off one bridge alone), arson for profit, and seizure of property by the tax collector.

Publicly the Olympic backers showed no alarm. Billy Garland began a series of shuttle trips to Europe, signifying that interest in sport remained strong and that he was busy coordinating it. In November of 1929 Garland was in Rome to meet with Pope Pius XI and Italy's premier, Benito Mussolini. The Pope praised the amity furthered by the Games. As for Mussolini, Garland remarked to newsmen, "I told him he resembled Napoleon, and he seemed pleased." In Portugal roving ambassador Garland visited a puzzled state secretary who inquired, "Just where is your state?" Garland unfurled a map of California's 158,693 square miles, with his town identified. "That is a very long, expensive way from here," said the secretary, discouragingly. Returning home, perched on a Malacca cane and smoking British "Fortunate Hits" cigarettes, he was always optimistic in public, proclaiming a Europe bound to snap back. Garland promised coolly, "We'll welcome the races of man to our beautiful, hospitable southland as never before."

Garland wasn't so breezy in private. An office associate once related, "Billy would stand under an oil portrait of himself in a track suit, wearing his tortoiseshell glasses, with a starter's gun about to explode—titled *Our Champ*—and with tears in his eyes tell of the destruction he'd seen." The situation he described over brandy to his fellow executive committeemen was gloom from the British Isles to the Danube, the price of mass death and an estimated $45 billion wartime loss of production. "It's terrible," he said. "If it wasn't for 300,000 Americans over there, none of the better hotels could stay open." He honestly felt things would pick up, but at London's Claridge's Hotel he'd sat through a melancholy meeting with tiny Baron de Coubertin and his colleague Count de Baillet-Latour. "For your 1932 ambitions, it now does not look so certain," they warned, as if hinting that L.A. might have done better if it had grabbed the opportunity to stage the games in 1928. "Continental affairs are darkening. You should look to the giant South America and the Orient for support." Another ominous note was the fear expressed by foreign politicians of the reaction to sending 50 to 200 discus tossers and gymnasts halfway around the globe in an era of breadlines.

Closed sessions of Garland's blue-ribbon planning council were held at City Hall, where members winced at the news and sent their general secretary, Zack J. Farmer, to Berlin for the Olympic Congress in 1930. Farmer was received by President Paul von Hindenburg. Although Germany waded in debt, Hindenburg promised to earmark a sum assuring full participation at Los Angeles—more than 150 of his finest musclemen. Within months Adolf Hitler, climbing toward power, led a Reichstag attack against friendly competition and kicked out the appropriation. Now it looked as if the *Vaterland*, home of great wrestlers, weight lifters, and fencers, was lost—a loss that might set a trend toward more dropouts.

California old-timers compared the dismal winter of 1931 to the 1880s, when the crash in land values ruined many pioneers, and now protestors appeared in the state capital of Sacramento carrying signs: "Groceries Not Games!" and "Olympics Are Outrageous!" Two hundred armed officers guarded the state's borders, turning back the wandering, hungry "Okie-Arky army." Critics called California's governor James "Sunny Jim" Rolph an affable do-nothing. Pressured to end the frivolous sporting carnival to be, he said, "These games are an impossible venture. What do they want, riots?" But Rolph stopped short of asking for a cancellation, aware of the electoral weight carried by the big-league businessmen under Garland. Garland's policy was to avoid clashes. He only commented that a million-dollar state bond issue to bankroll the production had been OK'd by taxpayers in 1928, well before the crunch came, and, anyway, that what the area needed was a rousing, blues-chasing, big party showing how stout the public's spirit remained. The Games were slated to open on July 30. An order for 2 million tickets was issued, and work began on the most dramatic of Olympic torches, one that would flame 107 feet above stadium level. More was spent on a special peat-clay cycling track, a lagoon for rowing, a monstrous scoreboard, and 300 Teletype machines for the press.

In the history of what Baron de Coubertin devoutly spoke of as *religio athletae*, preliminary stages of the Olympics had often been controversial. Influential Athenians opposed the first revived Games in 1896, objecting to the cost. Between 1898 and 1900, the Union des Sports Athlétiques of France and Coubertin fought for "rights" to the Paris Games. Four years later Louisiana Purchase Exposition sponsors in St. Louis converted the Games into a shabby sideshow for their World's Fair, and in Stockholm in 1912 nationalistic squabbling marred the meet. Yet for wild charges and suspense, nothing had quite matched conditions in the self-styled paradise by the Santa Monica Mountains as 1931 ended. Among the popular California social reform crusades drawing mobs to tent meetings were "Technocracy" and "Plenty for All." One evening while the

Technocrats were busy blasting poverty and wasteful spending, a member cried, "They're big sports, all right! Bringing Germans and Japs to town! Down with their damned circus!" By moonlight a raiding party identified as Technocrats and Plentyites smashed windows of shops displaying Olympic pennants and streamers and burned many of them. Luckily for the promoters the uprising occurred beyond city limits and could be dismissed as trouble from outsiders unable to imagine the glory or the income due from visitors converging for the supershow.

With the opening ceremony just 6 months away, committeemen worked with nerves on edge, aware that a hex, or something worse, hung over them. A friendly Comité International inspection team, arriving to check the arena facilities, was expected to praise the new construction. But it stepped into a sizzling heat wave. With the temperature at 103°, the inspectors complained that athletes from cold climates would suffer dizziness, spasms, and nosebleeds. That made headlines. Across the world, coaches and trainers cabled the Comité's headquarters in Switzerland, swearing they wouldn't risk their stars. While wrestling with all that, the Los Angeles Organizing Committee (LAOC) had another visitor: Avery Brundage, the burly, often truculent president of the American Olympic Association. Brundage outlined Olympic protocol and declared that his association would make such appointments as the frock-coated greeters of VIPs at the Games and the stadium public address announcers. Billy Garland recoiled and snapped, "The hell you will, sir! This is entirely our affair." Brundage stormed off and took the issue to his predecessor as American Olympic boss, Army Chief of Staff Douglas MacArthur. One of the surviving members of the LAOC of 1932, 82-year-old Gwynn Wilson, recalls what happened next: "MacArthur showed up for 4 days, sizing us up, and then went away. We had trouble enough without losing local control and didn't budge an inch." What MacArthur recommended isn't known, but Brundage appealed to Coubertin and Count de Baillet-Latour, who finally settled the power battle by telling the LAOC, "Proceed as you wish. Our prayers are with you."

Freakish warm weather and a hostile Avery Brundage were two matters; the Congress of the United States was another. Government aid—fiscal, moral, or both—was needed to backstop expenses and give Uncle Sam's blessing to a shaky project. Congress offered nothing, however, not even after the LAOC formally invited President Herbert Hoover to preside at the opening ceremony. For 36 years it had been unbroken tradition that heads of state or royal consorts did the honors, and from King George I of Greece to Gustaf of Sweden to President Gaston Doumergue of France and beyond, no lapse in this matter of pomp and prestige had been known. Hoover's answer was, "I will be unable to attend because of the press of duties." With the Depression tormenting him, Hoover couldn't spare the time, but in refusing to appear he seemed to be censuring a carnival some claimed would cost $2 million. Hoover reportedly told friends, "It's a crazy thing. And it takes some gall to expect me to be part of it." Some newspapers saw the President's absence as an outright slap in the face.

On the international front there was a frightening silence. Less than 5 months before the Games were to begin, not one nation had said positively it would attend, and it appeared that California was moving toward a disaster. The Winter Olympic Games of '32 were held at Lake Placid, New York, with a turnout of only 17 countries (St. Moritz in 1928 had drawn 26 teams) and without big crowds. Meanwhile, Japanese troops had invaded Manchuria, creating the puppet state of Manchukuo. This aggression was widely condemned, but Japan blandly requested an Olympic entry blank for Manchukuo. The captured territory had no official credentials whatever, and, badly as the LAOC needed bodies, it was obliged to reject the crude bid. Furious Tokyo sportslords threatened to prevent their vaunted swimmers, pole vaulters, and horsemen from crossing the sea.

On March 1 Billy Garland and Zack Farmer, still outwardly buoyant and confident, were in San Francisco trying to drum up trade. The best they could do was unload a few packets of tickets to convention agencies and American Legion posts; they wrote off the Bay Area and caught a Southern Pacific express home. There they doggedly forged ahead, hiring ticket clerks, planning press accommodations, reserving a fleet of buses for team transport, and polishing up a second vast stadium, Pasadena's Rose Bowl, for what their publicity bulletins insisted would be droves of customers. Sticking to that belief wasn't easy with "Hoovervilles"—clusters of crate-wood shacks thrown up in arroyos and on hillsides—dotting the city's outskirts.

Heading into April crippling new setbacks left the LAOC staggering, and its members considered a step, unheard of in peacetime, of calling off the Games. The Comité International's track-and-field federation, cracking down on amateurs who took illegal payoffs, banned Paavo Nurmi, the fabled "Flying Finn" and defending Olympic 10,000-meter champion, along with Jules Ladoumegue of France, world-record holder in the mile run. Two of Los Angeles's top drawing cards were gone. When Garland asked Coubertin, "How could you do this to us?" the nobleman sternly reminded Billy that the Games were never canceled, "whatever may be the adverse circumstances."

In Amsterdam, Baron Schimmelpenninck van der Oye of the Comité dealt another blow: Smaller European states were not gaining political support for the trip. "I am desolated," said the baron. So was the LAOC's ticket department. Handsomely engraved tickets priced at a low $1 to 3 were a drug on the market. Less than 15,000 had been sold by early May and, for lack of action, the Coliseum sales force went on half-time shifts. The man on the street wasn't buying.

Since the autumn of 1931, when the risk to their reputations had become clear, many of the sponsors had lost enthusiasm; they favored admitting a mistake and cutting their losses. According to later disclosures, about half the sponsors wanted to quit. The showdown came at the Los Angeles Athletic Club, where Garland, his face pale, and *Times* publisher Harry Chandler attacked the "cold feeters." Tempers flared; a recess was called. While the defectors waited, Chandler phoned the technical expert Bill Henry in New York and asked him to hurry home. Henry, a persuasive, admired newspaperman, spoke feelingly of "keeping our sacred word," of not welshing as Americans, even if only a handful of guests showed up. Henry's words made the difference. The decision was to hang on. The hope, according to one critic, was that the patron saint of the Games—Zeus—would perform a miracle.

General Secretary Zack Farmer, a gutsy 40-year-old, was not one to depend upon saints. In 1930 he had presented the Olympic Congress in Berlin with a revolutionary plan to house all athletes and attendants in a common village. Traditionally the nations had lived apart, trained secretly, broken no bread together, and mingled only in competition. Farmer found this sad and asked for a "spiritual assembly" where brotherhood could flower through close daily association. To many of the Congress, sharing one space was collectivism; they met the plan with mockery and hostility. Farmer wrote in his memoirs, "Some were afraid . . . open racial clashes were predicted . . . the idea was shot full of danger, no doubt about that." But the secretary continued to push his "Dream Village," and suddenly in late spring, only 90 days before the opening gun, it met an encouraging response. The British, Danes, and Swedes said they'd compete, and explained why: A cost-cutting, unified camp would enable their California hosts to offer housing, meals, and local transport for $2 per person per day. The promoters had also guaranteed to bring them to America at charges they could afford. How was this possible? "First we found that a cooperative village could support a $2 fee," explained Zack Farmer. "Then we told the Transatlantic Steamship Conference that they were sailing with empty cabins in the Depression and made a deal." The deal provided a 20% fare reduction on off-season rates for all comers, matched by U.S. railroads in cross-country travel ($100 roundtrip, New York to the Coast). Total overhead for faraway countries would average $500 per man, far under the normal $2,000. Various federations had doubted that such a saving was possible but, shown the proof, changed their attitude. Japan, abruptly reversing itself after the Manchukuo incident, said it was coming and with a splash. It named no fewer than 203 athletes and, for good luck, threw in a paper kite-flying team of boys and girls. Argentina had failed to raise travel money, tried again, succeeded, and signed up 60 participants. Cuba hit on the shrewd method of loading its team's ship with sugar and tobacco and then auctioning the cargo at ports en route, thus subsidizing its boxers and runners. Still, half a dozen sign-ups with time running out amounted to little.

Then from Vienna came sensational news. Prince Ferdinand von und zu Liechtenstein declared, "We Austrians will hold the faith and go, even if I must pay the cost myself. Immortal Olympia must prevail!"

Challenged by the prince, European pride was stirred, and France and Italy entered a combined 196 contestants. In the Reichstag, Hitler's campaign against fraternizing came under attack, and a flickering chance remained that Germany would join. Good things were happening to the LAOC so quickly that hope revived and Billy Garland, the intrepid gambler, rushed construction of a 250-acre, decorative "village of the universe" that would house 2,000 on a mesa near the Coliseum. Economists bit their lips. The "village" boasted kitchens, lounges, barbershop, post office, Greek theater, saunas, wireless center—even valets. It cost $400,000.

Signs were changing, but Americans still were not backing their own champions. The fund-raising drive lagged everywhere—and the Los Angeles public remained as coldly uninterested as ever. Ticket manager J.F. Mackenzie looked out his Coliseum window at fewer buyers than you'd find at a small college football game. Mackenzie wondered if Avery Brundage might not be right in his latest speculation from Chicago: "I wonder if this will be the first of the series to play mostly to a crowd of newspapermen." (In Garland's later years—he died in 1948 at age 82—he spoke of haunted nights, of a nightmare of Vice-President Charles Curtis, named by Hoover as his stand-in, opening the festivities to 10,000 kids, some pensioners, and the LAOC's creditors.)

Something rather Zeus-like, however, was looking out for the party givers at zero hour. Governor Jim Rolph at last stopped complaining. In June the funding of America's team suddenly picked up, and within weeks most of the needed $350,000 was banked. President von Hindenberg circumvented Hitler and, on the $2-per-day, all-you-can-eat plan, named a 125-man German contingent. Mexico signed up 50 athletes. Finland 40. India and South Africa added 36. Along came the Australians, Swiss, Dutch, Spanish, Greeks, Canadians, Hungarians, Uruguayans, and New Zealanders. The Brazilian team, taking its clue from Cuba, stored 50,000 bags of coffee aboard a freighter and started north, peddling beans as it went. As the entry list reached 30 nations, with such world champions as hammer thrower Dr. Patrick O'Callaghan of Ireland, broad jumper Chuhei Nambu of Japan, and swimmer Clarence ("Buster") Crabbe of the United States to be on display, townspeople awoke and the first ticket queues formed. The lines grew daily, from dozens to hundreds to many hundreds. Idled clerks were returned to work and midway in the last-ditch month of July they were swamped by fans.

During the week of July 11 to 18, business exploded. Thirty-five thousand seats were sold in one 72-hour period. Between July 25 to 30, $310,000 came rolling in. "It was like a whirlwind, it happened so fast," remembers Arnold Eddy, a businessman who was an LAOC official in 1932.

Nowhere I know of have so many folks decided to turn out for something at the last minute. The great rush didn't come until we were right down to the wire, in the last 18 days. We couldn't understand what had happened to the town—even now I'm not sure—but Olympic fever caught on and we needed extra police to control the mobs. With everyone so broke, it was amazing to see them shoving money at us, fighting to get in. The fact is that we didn't sell out the Coliseum until just hours before the show began, which is about as close as you can shave it. But, by George, it was sold! And what a relief that was.

Interest had grown in the East, and special Olympics-bound trains rolled westward. Al Jolson ordered 200 seats for friends. Sensing a hit, movie stars—Douglas Fairbanks, Charlie Chaplin, Marlene Dietrich, John Gilbert, Clara Bow, Mary Pickford—volunteered to entertain the visitors; merchants, awake at last, strung the streets with 5,000 foreign flags. The Hollywood Bowl entered the act with a gala civic musical at giveaway prices, in recognition of hard times. Sweden and India, the first teams to arrive, were met with brass bands and overwhelmed with hospitality. In one of the cruelest years of the Depression, a whole city responded so fully that Count de Baillet-Latour, in the Comité seat of honor, shook his head at the sight of the largest arena on earth, packed to the brim. "Formidable, incredible," he said. Two days earlier, on July 28, American soldiers using tear gas had routed a "Bonus Army" of World War I vets marching in Washington. There were many casualties.

One hundred and five thousand people filled Memorial Coliseum on opening day, with another 15,000 turned away—by far the largest audience in Olympic history. Forty nations and 2,050 athletes, officials, and trainers paraded, and the Organizing Committee, sparing no expense, presented a white-robed chorus of 1,500 singing "Hymne Olympique," coveys of white doves, 300 musicians, and a 10-gun cannonade. The United States squad of 357 marched wearing berets (they'd swapped hats with the French to kick off the brotherhood theme). Attendance held up in record style for all 16 days of play, averaging 65,000 in the main plant alone, with close to 1 million watching the crosstown marathon. Among the emerging heroes and heroines were America's track sensation Mildred ("Babe") Didrikson; miler Luigi Beccali of Italy; Ireland's Pat O'Callaghan; and Argentina's Juan Zabala, marathoner. For the first time, an audience saw victors suitably and regally crowned: the victors' podium was invented by the LAOC and has been used at all subsequent Olympics.

Performances were brilliant, with an unprecedented 33 new Olympic records set and 16 world marks broken. Technically, artistically, soulfully, the "doomed" show surpassed any ever seen and to this day is considered a model of how the hallowed Greek holiday should be celebrated. The most notable success of all was Zack Farmer's village. Two thousand young athletes went happily arm-in-arm, conversing by sign language, and experiencing something new to most—the absence of class distinction and racial conflict. Twenty-three athletes of noble lineage—lords, counts, baronets, princes—slept and ate in the village alongside brick-layers, tradesmen, and farmers. The system worked so well that the LAOC was mentioned for the Nobel Peace Prize.

For Billy and his associates, it was a glittering triumph. Garland's sculp-tured image appears today on a Coliseum wall, a tribute to the boosters in straw hats—shaken and scared, tempted to surrender, but hanging on when all seemed lost. No doubt Los Angeles couldn't afford such a blowoff; no doubt it contrasted sorely with the common plight. But the Games had brought thrills and a needed *élan*; they were a significant and enduring social laboratory and forged a new sense of solidarity in an unde-fined boomtown. More than 900 reporters, who came from every conti-nent to cover the event, described the scenic and agricultural splendors of Los Angeles. The city's present mayor, Tom Bradley, ranks the Olym-piad as an important municipal turning point and led the movement to return the pageant for a second time to the United States and to his city. The campaign succeeded, and 52 years later, in 1984, Games XXIII were concentrated in the same sports park, the Coliseum. Garland's ghost may hover about. It was Garland who once asked England's young Lord David Burghley what he got out of taking part in the Games. Burghley, a 400-meter hurdler known as "is 'urdling 'ighness," replied, "I met all of the people here and all were equal. It's an experience I'll never for-get." Nor would it be forgotten by those who dug far down for the price of admission.

13
The Nazi Olympics

Allen Guttmann

At its 29th Session in Barcelona (April 1931) the International Olympic Committee (IOC) had been unable to select the venue for the 1936 games, but a subsequent mail ballot showed 43 votes for Berlin and only 16 for Barcelona (and 8 abstentions) (Mayer, 1966). Like the treaties of Locarno and Rappallo, which formalized the acceptance of the Weimar Republic within European political culture, the choice ratified the reintegration of Germany within international sports. When the IOC's decision was announced, on May 13, 1931, Heinrich Brüning was Chancellor of Germany and a centrist coalition ruled; when the games were actually held, the National Socialists were in power and Adolf Hitler was Chancellor. It was not what the IOC had expected.

The Nazis themselves were, despite frequent statements to the contrary by subsequent commentators, not enthusiastic about sports. Ideologically, they were far closer to the indigenous German tradition of *Turnen*, that is, to the gymnastics movement inspired by the early 19th-century prophet of nationalism, Friedrich Ludwig Jahn. Although Jahn himself had liberal as well as conservative tendencies, the more liberal of his followers went into exile after the failure of the Revolution of 1848. (Many of the *Turner* emigrated to Chicago, where they created a flourishing gymnastics movement by the time of Brundage's childhood arrival

Originally published in *The Games must go on: Avery Brundage and the Olympic Movement*, 1984, New York: Columbia University Press. Reprinted by permission.

there.) The *Turner* who remained in Germany became increasingly conservative, nationalistic, and romantic. They were loyal to Kaiser Wilhelm,
to German *Kultur*, which they wished to spread both within Europe and
overseas, and to an intuitive, irrationalist *Weltanschauung*. It was, therefore, inevitable that Die Deutsche Turnerschaft was hostile to the development of modern sports with their internationalism, their quantification,
their obsession with records. Since the Olympic Games were from the
very start internationalist, since the motto *"altius, citius, fortius"* embodied
the progressive and competitive aspects of modern sports that Die
Deutsche Turnerschaft had resisted, it was no wonder that the organization was, as we have seen, initially hostile to the games and never more
than half-heartedly committed to them.[1]

The Nazis adhered to a *Weltanschauung* even more romantic than that
of rival nationalist movements and were at first contemptuously dis-
missive of modern sports ("What Jews praise is poison for us"; Bruno
Malitz, quoted in Bernett, 1982, p. 219). Hitler made an exception for boxing, which he saw as a display of physical courage and as a metaphor
for the *Existenzkampf*, but his relationship to other sports was minimal.
As one historian remarked, "Sports were quite alien to Hitler's inner self"
(Otto Dietrich, quoted in Krüger, 1972, p. 36). Consequently, informed
observers had every reason to wonder about the new regime and its attitude vis-à-vis the Olympic Games planned for Berlin.

Among the most worried were, quite naturally, the president and the
secretary of the organizing committee, Theodore Lewald and Carl Diem.
Lewald, son of a Berlin lawyer and civil servant, had been a member of
the IOC since 1924 and served also as president of the national Olympic
committee (and as chairman of the Deutscher Reichsausschuss für
Leibesübungen, the closest German equivalent to the AAU). Although
Lewald typified the best in the austere Prussian tradition of public service, he had reason to be anxious about his personal safety as well as
about the future of the Olympic movement; his father had converted from
Judaism to Christianity and the Nazi journal *Völkischer Beobachter* had begun to cry out for his dismissal.[2] The secretary of the organizing committee, Carl Diem, was a self-made man whose father, like Avery Brundage's,
had deserted the family. Young Diem had made his own way, initially
as a sports journalist. He discovered that he had organizational as well
as reportorial talent and, by the age of 30, he was captain of the German
team that competed at the Stockholm Olympics in 1912. Despite his lack
of formal education, he eventually developed into a remarkable scholar,
still known for his comprehensive world history of sports (published in
1960) and for a large number of monographs on sport history. In 1920,
with support from Lewald and the Deutscher Reichsausschuss für
Leibesübungen, he founded the Deutsche Hochschule für Leibesübungen, a university dedicated to the scientific study of sports. Although
Diem was enough the child of his times to have been an ardent nationalist
in the 1920s, he was definitely a proponent of modern sports rather than

of *Turnen*, and he was not bigoted about the achievements of other nations. He was an admirer of American sports, which he felt to be better organized than German sports. In 1930 he published *Sport in Amerika*, a glowing account of the playgrounds, athletic clubs, YMCAs, and—especially—collegiate gymnasia, field houses, tracks, and pools that he and Lewald visited during a 5-week tour of the United States in 1929.[3]

Because Diem became an intimate friend of Avery Brundage and a key figure in the stormy controversy over American participation in the 1936 Olympics, it is necessary to say a word more about the American tour of 1929. Diem and Lewald arrived in Chicago by train on May 19 and were met at the station by Brundage, who invited them to tea with various notables from Chicago's large German-American community. Brundage and Diem had a further chance to become acquainted the next day at a dinner at the Hotel Atlantic. They got on extremely well, and Diem was subsequently touched that Brundage gladly traveled the 900 miles to New York in order to preside at the farewell banquet held on June 9 at the posh Astor Hotel (Diem, 1929, 1931).

The Nazi seizure of power jeopardized Diem's position within German sports. Because the faculty of the Deutsche Hochschule für Leibesübungen included several Jews and Diem's wife, Liselott, was of partially Jewish ancestry, Diem was denounced by the Nazis as a "weisser Jude" (white Jew) (Diem, 1976). Given the endangered position of both the president and the secretary of the organizing committee and the shrill hostility of the Nazis to sports in general and the Olympics in particular, no one was very optimistic about the 1936 games. On March 16, 1933, one day after the *New York Times* began to question the appropriateness of Berlin as the Olympic site, Lewald was received by Hitler at the Reichskanzlei. To Lewald's astonishment and relief, Hitler did not order an immediate end to the preparations. This was not because he had suddenly changed his mind about modern sports and Olympic ideals but because propaganda minister Josef Goebbels, who was at the audience in the Reichskanzlei, had realized that the games were a splendid opportunity to demonstrate German organizational talent and physical prowess. Lewald was forced to resign from his post with the Deutscher Reichsausschuss für Leibesübungen, but Baillet-Latour personally intervened with Hitler in order to stipulate that Lewald continue to serve as president of the organizing committee. Diem lost his post at the Deutsche Hochschule für Leibesübungen but was allowed to continue as secretary of the organizing group. In April, Lewald was optimistic (or dishonest) enough to write to Brundage that "there will not be the slightest discrimination made in the Berlin Games because of religion or race and furthermore . . . every participant has the fullest assurance of a kind, hearty, and courteous reception" (Lewald to Brundage, 1933). On October 5, Hitler toured the site of the games, inspected the progress in construction, and became positively lyrical about the prospects. He promised the startled committee the full financial support of his regime, a sum later set at

20,000,000 Reichsmarks. "Lewald and Diem were unable to believe their ears" (Krüger, 1972, pp. 12, 63).

Hitler's willingness to act as host allayed one set of anxieties and aroused another. The IOC was not at all certain that the Nazis were ready to abandon their Fascist principles in order to stage the games by Olympic rules, which clearly forbid racial or religious discrimination. General Charles Sherrill, one of the three American members of the IOC, wrote to the American Jewish Congress and reassured them, "Rest assured that I will stoutly maintain the American principle that all citizens are equal under all laws" (Krüger, 1972, p. 49). As Sherrill and 28 other members of the IOC assembled in Vienna on June 7, 1933, the discrepancy between Nazi doctrine and Olympic rulebook was a central issue. Baillet-Latour, reelected president at this session by a nearly unanimous vote, joined Sherrill and William May Garland as the two Americans questioned Lewald and Karl Ritter von Halt about Jewish participation. The crux of the matter was not the acceptance of Jewish athletes on foreign teams but rather the right of *German* Jews to try out for their national team. Lewald and von Halt were able to secure a written guarantee from the Reichsinnenministerium that German Jews did indeed have this right: "All the laws regulating the Olympic Games shall be observed. As a principle German Jews shall not be excluded from German Teams at the Games of the XIth Olympiad" (International Olympic Committee, 1933, p. 9). Sherrill was surprised at his own unexpected success. He told AAU official Frederick W. Rubien all about it on June 11. It had been the hardest fight he had ever been through. The Germans had yielded slowly and initially offered merely to publish the Olympic rules, but Sherrill had pushed them until they telephoned Berlin and came through with a formal written statement of acceptance for Jewish athletes within the German team. He informed Rubien that he had had to persuade his British colleague on the Executive Board, Lord Aberdare, that the IOC was indeed within its rights to demand that the makeup of the German team conform to rule. The victory, thought Sherrill, was complete (Sherrill to Rubien, 1933).

It was not. The reliability of Nazi guarantees, written or oral, was called into question by the discrimination against Jewish athletes, who were allowed to use public sports facilities but who were expelled from the private sports clubs which were the center of German athletics. Since Brundage had followed Douglas MacArthur as president of the American Olympic Association, Bernard S. Deutsch of the American Jewish Congress addressed an open letter to him to alert him to this violation of the spirit if not the letter of the guarantees offered by the Reichsministerium (Deutsch to Brundage, 1933; *New York Times*, 1933). Brundage had already written Kirby on May 31, 1933, that the "very foundation of the modern Olympic revival will be undermined if individual countries are allowed to restrict participation by reason of class, creed or race" (Brundage to Kirby, 1933), but he seems not to have answered Deutsch's letter because it was his principle to reply to all private communications but not to public statements. It was Kirby who pressed the issue. In his 40 years as an advocate of amateur sports, he was an unusually eloquent defender of the principle of equality. To a fellow member of the American Olympic Committee, he wrote, "I am and have been always very serious in my conclusion that sport is the only true democracy. . . . " It doesn't matter "whether you are rich as Croesus or as poor as Job's turkey" (Kirby to Gilbert, 1933). To Kirby, religious discrimination was even worse than economic disadvantage. For the convention of the American Olympic Committee on November 22, he prepared a resolution which threatened a boycott unless German Jews were allowed in fact as well as theory to "train, prepare for and participate in the Olympic Games of 1936" (Kirby, 1933). Brundage expressed reservations about the forthright tone of the resolution and Kirby defended his stand with characteristic vigor: "Undoubtedly it is generally wiser to 'let sleeping dogs lie,' but unfortunately these dogs are not sleeping, they are growling and snarling and snipping and all but biting." Kirby admired and had affection for Lewald and Diem, but "the democracy of sport . . . is bigger than Lewald or Diem or Brundage or Rubien—and certainly than Kirby" (Kirby to Brundage, 1933). The AOA passed a somewhat milder version of Kirby's resolution.

Even as the AOA deliberated, Reichssportführer Hans von Tschammer und Osten issued a statement that Jews were not barred from sports clubs by any official *governmental* decree,[4] but Brundage was not reassured by the sophistical distinction. He wrote to Baillet-Latour, "The German authorities have displayed a singular lack of astuteness in all of their publicity. On this subject, every news dispatch that has come from Germany seems to indicate that the Hitlerites do not intend to live up to the pledges given to the IOC at Vienna" (Brundage to Baillet-Latour, 1933). Brundage kept his worries private because he did not want to cause unnecessary difficulties for his friends Lewald and Diem and von Halt. Kirby, however, refused to ignore the frequent newspaper reports of discrimination against Jewish athletes. He was among the Madison Square Garden speakers at an anti-Nazi rally held by the American Jewish Committee on March 6, 1934.

When the IOC convened in Athens on May 15, 1934, Britain's Lord Aberdare, who had earlier been ready to accept German assurances, now expressed concern about reports from Germany and asked his German colleagues "if the pledge given in Vienna last year had been given practical application and if it really was possible for Jews to go into training with the object of participating in the Olympic Games" (International Olympic Committee, 1934, p. 8). Garland asked the same question and Lewald and von Halt declared officially:

It goes without saying that the Pledges given by Germany in Vienna in 1933 to admit to the German Olympic team German Sportsmen of Non-Aryan origin, provided they have the necessary capability, will be strictly observed and facilities for preparation will be given to all sportsmen. (International Olympic Committee, 1934, p. 8)

For that purpose, the Deutscher Leichtathletik-Verband (German Track and Field Association) had invited Jewish sports organizations to submit the names of potential Olympic team members.

The IOC was satisfied. The American Olympic Association was not. When it met on June 14, it postponed acceptance of the official German invitation to the games until after an on-the-spot investigation by President Brundage. His American colleagues may have expected a dispassionate appraisal of the situation, but the German consulate in Chicago reported on September 3 to its embassy in Washington that Brundage's mission was to "find in Germany . . . what he lacked in America" (Teichler, 1982, p. 25). The consulate assumed that Brundage's mind was already made up—in Germany's favor.

Brundage wrote Diem that he and Elizabeth meant to sail on the S.S. New York of the Hamburg-American Line on July 25 and indicated his desire to talk with Sportführer von Tschammer und Osten as well as with leaders of Jewish sports organizations (Brundage to Diem, 1934). The primary purpose of the trip to Europe, however, was not the investigation of Nazi discrimination but attendance at the IAAF congress in Stockholm in late August. The Brundages arrived at the German port of Cuxhaven on August 3 and went on to Scandinavia, where they spent most of the month. They traveled as far north as Norway's North Cape, where Elizabeth was so seriously ill that Avery "for a time . . . despaired of her life" (Brundage to Garland, 1934). She recovered somewhat while they were in Stockholm for the conference, but she may not have accompanied her husband on his first trip to the Soviet Union, where he was impressed by the effort to modernize physical education as well as factory production.

When the IAAF meetings began with festivities at Edström's villa, Vestoräas, about 60 miles from Stockholm, Brundage and Diem began to discuss the German problem. During lunch at Stockholm's Grand Hotel, Brundage met with Diem, von Halt, Lewald, and Justus W. Meyerhof, a Jewish member of the Berliner Sport-Club. Diem made notes on the discussion:

> We showed Brundage documents indicating that the Jews are able to participate freely in sports and to train for the Olympic team. Meyerhof told us that he had offered to resign from the Berliner Sport-Club but that the resignation had not been accepted. I was seldom as proud of my club as at that moment. Brundage was visibly impressed. He plans to speak with leaders of Jewish sports when he visits Berlin. (Diem, 1934, p. 51)

That evening, August 29, the Brundages dined with Diem, von Halt, and Sigfrid and Ruth Edström at the elegant Gyldenen Freden. Over coffee

and cognac, after the ladies had retired, Edström and Brundage offered
Diem *Bruderschaft*, which moved Diem immensely (Diem, 1934, p. 52).
Before seeing Diem again in Berlin, the Brundages went south. Post-
cards from "A" and "E" to Elizabeth's niece, Jean Harper, tell of perfect
September weather in Venice (Brundage & Brundage to Harper, 1934).
While touring Italy and Yugoslavia, Brundage had ample time to ponder
Edström's thoughts on the Jewish problem, that is, that

> As regards the persecution of the Jews in Germany I am not at all
> in favor of said action, but I fully understand that an alteration had
> to take place. As it was in Germany, a great part of the German nation
> was led by the Jews and not by the Germans themselves. Even in
> the U.S.A. the day may come when you will have to stop the activi-
> ties of the Jews. They are intelligent and unscrupulous. Many of my
> friends are Jews so you must not think that I am against them, but
> they must be kept within certain limits. (Edström to Brundage, 1933)

The on-the-spot investigation of German conditions did not begin until September 13, the day after the Brundages' arrival in Koenigsberg in
East Prussia. Because Brundage did not speak German well, he was forced
to rely on interpreters. It was an additional drawback that he was never
allowed to talk alone with representatives of the Jewish sports clubs. He
met Reichssportführer von Tschammer und Osten and "liked him very
much" and listened carefully when he was told that there was no discrimination and that Jewish athletes were quite likely to make the team
(Brundage to von Halt, 1934). This was also the message communicated
by Brundage's oldest German friend, Karl Ritter von Halt. Brundage's
report to the American Olympic Association was strongly in favor of accepting the invitation. To the press he announced, "I was given positive
assurance in writing by Tschammer [und] Osten, Germany's official Olympic representative [an error], that there will be no discrimination against
Jews. You can't ask more than that and I think the guarantee will be fulfilled" (*New York Post*, 1934). Brundage's doubts about the Reichssportführer's sincerity were stifled by the intensity of his faith in the importance
of the games. Further assurances came in the form of a letter sent by
Rudolf Hess to Baillet-Latour, in which Hess informed the IOC president
that the law of August 16, 1934, which forbade all contact between Nazis
and Jews, did not apply to sports (Bohlen, 1979).
The eighteen-member American Olympic Committee met in New York
on September 26, one day after Brundage's return from Europe, and
resolved unanimously (even the skeptical Kirby was now convinced) that
"in the light of the report of President Brundage and the attitude and
assurances of the German Olympic Committee and the representatives
of the German Government . . . , we accept the invitation of the German
Olympic Committee" (Rubien to Diem, 1934).[5] Any hopes that this decision might terminate the controversy quickly evaporated. The *New York
Times* for September 27 was full of bad news (from Brundage's perspective): Samuel Untermyer of the Anti-Defamation League, listing instances

of Nazi persecution of Jewish athletes, called for a boycott of the games; Representative Emmanuel Celler of New York charged that Brundage had "prejudged the situation before he sailed from America. The Reich Sports Commissars have snared and deluded him" (*New York Times*, 1934). The AAU held its annual convention December 7-9 and voted to postpone acceptance of the German invitation—a clear sign that Untermyer and Celler were not the only holdouts. For Brundage, who was accustomed to a more subservient AAU, the vote was tantamount to a declaration of no confidence. Passions flamed; the lines hardened.

By mid-1935 an intensive boycott campaign was in full swing. Brundage's position had always been that sports and politics should be strictly separate: "The AOC must not be involved in political, racial, religious or sociological controversies" (Brundage to Kirby, 1934). (By "sociological," of course, he meant "social.") All that could be asked of the Nazi regime, from his perspective, was that it accept Olympic rules and allow German Jews to try out for the German team, and the highest German officials had promised that this would indeed be the case. What was good enough for him was also good enough for Pierre de Coubertin, whom the German organizing committee assiduously courted. Although the founder was scrupulous about not attending either the sessions of the IOC or the games themselves, he did agree, after a visit to Lausanne by Diem and Lewald, to record a radio message that the organizers were able to use, on August 4, 1935, as the first of a broadcast series publicizing the Berlin games (Teichler, 1982).

Brundage explained his view of the matter in a 16-page pamphlet, "Fair Play for American Athletes," published by the AOC. He asked if the American athlete was to be made "a martyr to a cause not his own" and he repeated his arguments about the separation of sports from politics and religion. American athletes should not become needlessly involved in "the present Jew-Nazi altercation." The entire problem, in his eyes, was that opponents of the Nazi regime were not satisfied with Olympic rules; they really wanted a boycott to undermine Nazism; they meant to use the games as a political weapon.

Brundage was not wholly inaccurate. It was inevitable that the boycott movement attracted anti-Nazis of all sorts, including those totally uninterested in sports. The Communist Party was active in all anti-Nazi campaigns (until the Molotov-von Ribbentrop Pact of 1939), and American Jews were naturally eager to express their opposition to Hitler by whatever means were available. But, in Brundage's mind, *all* of the pro-boycott camp had enlisted for political reasons and "all of the real sport leaders in the United States are unanimously in favor of participation in the Olympic Games which are above all considerations of politics, race, color or creed" (Brundage to Brailas, 1936). Criticism of his position he casually dismissed as "obviously written by a Jew or someone who has succumbed to the Jewish propaganda" (Brundage to Halbach, 1936). Writing to IOC president Baillet-Latour, he referred to the "Jewish proposal to boycott the Games," as if only Jews had reason to oppose Nazism (Brundage to Baillet-Latour, 1935).

Brundage's relations with Charles Ornstein, a Jewish member of the AOC, deteriorated into petty hostility and his friendship with Judge Jeremiah T. Mahoney, Brundage's successor as AAU president, turned into enmity. Guido von Mengden, press secretary for the Reichsbund für Leibesübungen, denounced Mahoney as a "powerful Jewish financier" (quoted in Bernett, 1976, p. 47). Brundage, somewhat better informed about ethnicity in America, characterized the Roman Catholic judge's opposition to the games as politically motivated. Mahoney had mayoral ambitions in New York and New York was notoriously "over-populated" with Jewish voters. Therefore, Mahoney must have been insincere. Brundage refused to acknowledge that Roman Catholics had excellent reasons to fear Hitler, who had made no secret of his neo-paganism or of his hatred for the church he had been born into. The Catholic journal *Commonweal* was for a boycott (as was the Protestant publication *Christian Century*); in July of 1935 the Catholic War Veterans appealed to the AOC to nullify its agreement with the Germans (Gottlieb, 1972). The boycott movement included a number of politically prominent Catholics such as James Curley and David I. Walsh of Massachusetts and Fiorello LaGuardia and Al Smith of New York; and a Gallup Poll taken in March of 1935 showed 43% of the entire population in favor of a boycott, but Brundage continued obstinately to see a conspiracy of Jews and Communists. This was not the *result* of anti-Semitism, which seems not to have been a part of Brundage's makeup prior to the fight over the boycott, but rather the *cause* of it.[6] On this question, Kirby wrote Brundage one of the harshest letters Brundage ever received: "I take it that the fundamental difference between you and me is that you are a Jew hater and Jew baiter and I am neither" (Kirby to Brundage, 1936b). It was the battle over the acceptance or rejection of the invitation to Berlin that turned Brundage—for a period of several years—into an anti-Semite. Having been assured by men he knew and trusted that the German government accepted the Olympic rules, believing as he did that the games were the most important international institution of the century, a force for peace and reconciliation among peoples, he simply failed to understand that there were men of good will who did not agree with him. He was unable to imagine motives that were other than biased by ethnic identity or political radicalism. Once he had made up his own mind, he attributed to opponents the most despicable of motives and an almost satanic insincerity.

As a result, his statements became nearly hysterical. Writing as president of the AOC and addressing the "sport-loving public of the United States," he announced that "there will be teams representing the United States in the 1936 Games" and he lashed out at the opposition:

The bitter feelings engendered, the attempted coercion and intimidation by fair means or foul, the vicious and insidious propaganda which are being used in this campaign largely by individuals who have never learned the lessons of amateur sport and thus do not hesitate to use methods contrary to all codes of sportsmanship, are an indication of what may be expected if religious, racial, class or political issues are allowed to intrude in the council halls of sport where they have no place. . . . Many of the individuals and organizations active in the present campaign to boycott the Olympics have Communistic antecedents. Radicals and Communists must keep their hands off American sport. (Brundage, 1935)

Mahoney's chief contribution to the "vicious and insidious propaganda" was a pamphlet entitled "Germany Has Violated the Olympic Code" (1935). Writing in the form of an open letter to Lewald, Mahoney cited specific cases—the expulsion of Jews from sports clubs and from public facilities, the ban on competition between Jews and other Germans, the exclusion of world-class high jumper Gretel Bergmann from the Olympic team. Every allegation has been verified by subsequent scholarship.

Mahoney had the facts, Brundage had the votes. Mahoney and Ornstein offered a boycott motion at the annual meetings of the Metropolitan Association of the AAU, October 8, 1935, and the motion was tabled, 77-32 (*New York American*, 1935). On December 6, the national organization met, also in New York, which Brundage thought disadvantageous for his side of the quarrel. He had earlier written to Garland, "You can't imagine what the situation is in New York City, where because of the fact that 30 or 40% of the population is Jewish, the newspapers are half given up to the German situation" (Brundage to Garland, 1935). In London, Carl Diem wrote anxiously in his diary, "Today, the American Olympic Committee is meeting in New York to decide the question of its participation in the Olympic Games" (Diem, 1935).

Diem and Brundage had reason to worry, for the vote was close, but the motion to investigate further failed by 58 1/4 to 55 3/4 and the AAU formally accepted the invitation to participate in the winter games at Garmisch-Partenkirchen and the summer games in Berlin. It was one of the bitterest struggles of Brundage's career and one which he never forgot. Decades later, he still referred to "the viciousness of the contest to prevent a United States team from participating" and to the "great victory for Olympic principles" ("Opening Address," 1969, p. 41). And, decades later, he was still referred to as "an avowed admirer of Hitler" (Ballinger, 1981, p. 32).

While Brundage was winning his victory in the United States, his opponents had carried the battle elsewhere. The third American member of the IOC (in addition to Sherrill and Garland) was Ernest Lee Jahncke. Former Assistant Secretary of the Navy under President Herbert Hoover, Jahncke was clearly not a man tarred by Brundage's somewhat wild brush.

No more than Jeremiah Mahoney was he a Jew or a Communist. On November 27, the *New York Times* printed his appeal to Baillet-Latour:

> [The] plain and undeniable fact is that the Nazis have consistently and persistently violated their pledges. Of this they have been convicted out of their own mouths and by the testimony of impartial and experienced American and English newspaper correspondents. . . . It is plainly your duty to hold the Nazi sports authorities accountable for the violation of their pledges. . . . I do not doubt that you have received all sorts of assurances from the Nazi sports authorities. Ever since they gave us their pledges in June, 1933, they have been lavish with their promises. The difficulty is that they have been stingy with their performance of them.
>
> However much you would like us to believe that the Germans have kept their pledges, the fact is that the Nazi sports authorities have dissolved Catholic sports clubs and have denied Germany's Jewish athletes adequate opportunity to condition themselves for competition in the Olympic elimination contests and this, of course, is equivalent to excluding them as a group from the German team. . . .
>
> Does it surprise you that under these conditions few non-Aryan athletes have been able to attain Olympic form? Or that under these conditions the Reichssportführer is willing to assure you that such athletes who hold "sufficient records" will be admitted to the elimination contests?
>
> No one pretends that the Games should be taken away from Germany merely because Jews are not admitted to Nazi sport clubs. The point, my dear Count, is that by excluding them from those clubs the Nazis have . . . excluded them from the use of training facilities and opportunities for competition. . . .
>
> Let me urge upon you that you place your great talents and influence in the service of the spirit of fair play and chivalry instead of the service of brutality, force and power. Let me beseech you to seize your opportunity to take your rightful place in the history of the Olympics alongside of de Coubertin instead of Hitler. (*New York Times*, 1935)

Baillet-Latour, who had previously informed Brundage that he was ready to come to the United States in order to combat personally the Jewish campaign to prevent American participation in the games, found Jahncke's letter discourteous and answered him in anger. Baillet-Latour informed Jahncke that the president's duty was to execute the decisions of the committee (Baillet-Latour to Brundage, 1935a, 1935b; Baillet-Latour to Jahncke, 1935).[7] The Count saw Jahncke as a traitor who was for inexplicably spiteful reasons unable to accept the personal assurances of honorable men like Diem, Lewald, von Halt, Brundage, and, of course, Baillet-Latour himself. He asked Jahncke to resign from the IOC and, when Jahncke refused, arranged for him to be expelled.

Meanwhile, all was not well in the United States either, despite the favorable vote of the AAU. It was not easy to raise money for any purpose in a depression. The bitterness of the fight over participation had soured many potential contributors, especially among the normally philanthropic Jewish population. Three months before the team was supposed to depart, Kirby, Treasurer of the AOA, wrote dolefully, "We are in a hell of a hole financially" (Kirby to Brundage, 1936a). Until the last minute, it was uncertain whether or not the entire team would be able to make the journey to Berlin. It was a sign of the times, and of the mood, that the official report of the AOC listed contributions as small as ten cents.

Protest took other forms than the withholding of customary contributions. Mahoney, Ornstein, and others who favored a boycott staged alternative games, the rather pretentiously named "World Labour Athletic Carnival," August 15-16, 1936, at Randall's Island, New York (Holmes, 1971). Although Dietrich Wortmann of the AAU's Foreign Relations Committee complained about the use of the AAU's name in connection with this meet, AAU secretary Daniel J. Ferris defended the right of the opposition to go ahead with official sanction (Ferris to Brundage, 1936). That Wortmann stooped to such petty harassment indicates the intensity of passions aroused by the boycott fight. Ferris wrote Brundage on the matter but seems not to have received a reply. Radical groups, meanwhile, planned a much more elaborate workers' "Olimpiada" in Barcelona, but the outbreak of the Spanish Civil War in July of 1936 interrupted the event just as the athletes had begun to arrive.[8] And the drama in Berlin was so spectacular that its rivals have been almost completely forgotten.

Difficulties dogged Brundage's heels even on shipboard, but they were of a nonpolitical nature. Eleanor Holm Jarrett was a veteran swimmer who had already competed in two Olympics. As a 15-year-old she had tied for fifth place in the 100-meter backstroke at Amsterdam and she had won the event with a world record at Los Angeles in 1932. Now a married woman of 22, she asked for and was denied permission to join the passengers in first-class accommodations (at her own expense). She showed no inclination to abide by the strict rules governing behavior while aboard the S.S. Manhattan. According to her roommate, she went to a party and returned to their cabin at 6:00 a.m., intoxicated. Although placed on probation, Jarett was allegedly found drunk by the chaperone of the women's team. That Jarrett smoked, gambled, and missed meals added to the officials' horror ("statements by May Lou Petty," 1936). The AOC decided to withdraw her from competition and Brundage refused to alter the decision even after he was handed a petition signed by 220 coaches and athletes. Because Eleanor Holm Jarrett was a very beautiful woman as well as a great athlete, the press reacted gleefully ("Eleanor Bares Olympic Story") and newspapers published cheesecake photographs of the "water nymph" (see *Chicago American,* 1936; *Chicago Daily News,* 1936; *Chicago Sunday Times,* 1936; *Chicago Tribune,* 1936). Brundage has appeared, ever since, in the guise of a killjoy.[9]

Brundage had other, more important worries. Counting on the repeated guarantees of his German friends and carried along by his own belief in Olympism, he had risked his moral authority on behalf of the games. If the Nazis failed to keep their promises, what then? In countless letters and speeches, he later claimed that the Nazis *did* keep their word, that they followed the Olympic rules, that German Jews who qualified athletically for the competitions were indeed allowed to compete. It is certainly true that the Nazis invited two "half-Jews" (i.e., athletes of mixed religious background) to participate. Helene Mayer, who had won a gold medal in fencing in 1928, was brought back to Germany from Los Angeles, where she had lived for a number of years (she had won three national championships in the United States). Rudi Ball was invited to play on the ice hockey team. Because Nazi law did not yet define *Mischlinge* as Jews, Mayer and Ball were, technically, *not* examples of good faith. More important, Jewish athletes of Olympic calibre *were* barred from the games. Gretel Bergmann had highjumped 1.60 meters that summer, 4 centimeters better than her "Aryan" rival, Elfriede Kaun, but Bergmann was kept from the Olympic team on the pretext that she was not a member of an officially recognized sports club. This was an anticipation of catch-22 because her club, Stuttgarter Schild, was barred from membership in the official Fachamt für Leichtathletik (Special Office for Track and Field) presided over by none other than Brundage's close friend, IOC member Karl Ritter von Halt. Other Jews who might have won places on the team were intimidated or lacked facilities to train and failed to achieve their potential. Even before the games began, Lewald confessed to an American consul, George Messersmith, that he had lied to the American Olympic Committee (Krüger, 1972, pp. 154-155).

One must give Baillet-Latour some credit for doing his best to hold the Nazis to their word. Although he had written Brundage that he was not personally fond of Jews (Baillet-Latour to Brundage, 1933), he did attempt to force the Nazis to admit qualified Jews to the team and he, on at least two occasions, forced a change in Hitler's policies. When Baillet-Latour heard, shortly before the beginning of the winter games, that the streets and roads of Garmisch-Partenkirchen were placarded with anti-Semitic signs, he demanded that the placards be removed—and they were (Poplimont, 1956). At the summer games, Baillet-Latour intervened dramatically in a frequently misreported and misunderstood incident.

In legend, the incident concerned Jesse Owens. It is alleged that Hitler refused to offer Owens his hand after the first of his four track and field victories. In actuality, Hitler never had a chance to refuse to congratulate Owens. As Karl Ritter von Halt related the episode in 1955, Hans von Tschammer und Osten brought the first victors, who happened to be Germans and Finns, to Hitler's box, where the Führer congratulated them. Baillet-Latour was furious at this form of favoritism and complained the next day to von Halt and was accompanied by him to call upon Hitler, whom the Belgian then scolded for this infraction of Olympic protocol. Hitler excused himself and subsequently greeted German victors in private (*Bulletin du C.I.O.*). In Brundage's trenchant sports imagery, "Hitler backed water fast" (*Bulletin du C.I.O.*, 1953, p. 14).

Were the games a propaganda triumph for the Nazis? The question is not easily answered. Predictably, Brundage was sure that they were not: "It is true that the Hitler regime made every effort to use for its own purposes this great festival of the youth of the world, but it was arranged and controlled entirely and exclusively by non-Nazis for the benefit of non-Nazis" ("The Olympic Story," p. 18). In his official report to the AOC, Brundage asserted that the games had been a contribution to "international peace and harmony" ("Report of the President," 1937, p. 27). A great deal more needs to be said. Hitler had told Diem and Lewald that he wanted to impress the world with the magnificence of the games, and the world was impressed. The facilities, especially the Olympic stadium itself, were monumental and the pageantry, which can still be vicariously experienced in Leni Riefenstahl's documentary *Olympia*, was truly extraordinary. Among Diem's inspired innovations was an enormous iron bell upon which was inscribed, *Ich rufe die Jugend der Welt* (I call the youth of the world). It was also Diem's inspiration that a torch be lit by the rays of the sun at the altar of Zeus in Olympia and carried by a relay of thousands of runners to the stadium in Berlin, where it was used to ignite the Olympic flame. (The idea came from a passage in Plutarch's *Life of Numa Pompilius*, where the flame is ignited at the altar of Athena, not Zeus [Leiper, 1976].)

The enthusiasm of the mostly German crowd was enormous as it greeted the world's athletes. The 383 members of the American team, the men in white trousers and blue coats, the women in white skirts and blue jackets, were led into the stadium by AOC President Brundage. They were welcomed by the crowd, as were the other foreign teams. The various athletic events were contested with a minimum of controversy and the athletic achievements were stellar. The organizing committee arranged a splendid series of social, cultural, and artistic events for the public and, with the help of the German government, entertained the IOC royally. There was, for instance, a huge dinner party for 2,000 at the famed Pfaueninsel ("Peacock Island") and a reception at the opening of a new museum containing the spectacularly beautiful Hellenistic altar from the Temple of Zeus at Pergamon (Brundage to Schöbel, 1963; Dodd & Dodd, 1941, pp. 339-344). The most impressive of Diem's many artistic contributions was *Olympische Jugend*, a Festspiel with dances choreographed by Mary Wigman to music composed by Carl Orff and Werner Egk; the performers included a chorus of a thousand, 60 male dancers, and 80 female dancers. Small wonder that thousands of ordinary tourists left with a sense of aesthetic fulfillment, a conviction of German efficiency, and a vague impression that National Socialism was not the horror that they had imagined it to be on the basis of newspaper or newsreel reports. The swastika was very much in evidence, but Hitler's role had been minimized. Baillet-Latour told Hitler bluntly that the host was limited to a single sentence that Baillet-Latour had typed up for him to speak. Intentionally or not, Hitler's response was comic: "Count, I'll take the trouble to learn it by heart" (Mayer, 1966, p. 142).

The strongest evidence for Brundage's assertion that the games were not a propaganda triumph is the fact that Jesse Owens was unquestionably the star of the games. Setting a world record of 10.3 seconds for 100 meters and an Olympic record of 20.7 seconds for 200 meters, he went on to jump an astonishing 8.06 meters and to help set still another world record in the 400-meter relay. One of the most respected of British journals noted that "The German spectators, like all others, have fallen completely under the spell of the American Negro Jesse Owens, who is . . . the hero of these games" ("Olympic Games," 1936, p. 230). When the Nazi periodical *Der Angriff* sneered at the Negro athletes as America's *schwarze Hilfstruppe* (black auxiliaries), the editors were immediately rebuked by the propaganda ministry, which had specifically ordered that the black athletes not be insulted (Teichler, 1976). In 1937, the press was directed to portray Owens favorably. The popular picture-and-text series sponsored by the German cigarette firm Reemtsma featured no fewer than seven glossy paste-in photographs of Owens, including one of him lying on the grass chatting shoulder-to-shoulder with the German jumper Luz Long, whose generous advice helped Owens to his world-record long jump (*Die Olympischen Spiele 1936,* 1936). Owens was described in the text as the *Wunderathlet* of the games and the most popular of all the track and field athletes (*Die Olympischen Spiele 1936,* 1936). He also appears in Leni Riefenstahl's film as if he were a real Olympian, a divinity, the god of sports. Gerard de Houville's review of the film was aptly entitled "Les Dieux du stade"; Owens, he wrote, was "beau comme une statue de bronze animée" (*Revue de Deux Mondes,* 1938, p. 935). In the film the camera focuses on Owens as it focused on no other athlete, not even Glen Morris, the American winner of the decathlon. Propaganda minister Goebbels, whose office secretly financed the film, demanded that Riefenstahl cut the footage devoted to Owens, but she bravely refused, relying on Hitler's favor to protect her from Goebbels' ire (Bernett, 1973). Ironically, neither Owens nor any other black champion was pictured in the Atlanta *Constitution,* the most liberal of Southern newspapers.

It was also ironical that the American coaches Lawson Robertson and Dean Cromwell violated "customary standards of sportsmanship . . . and the feelings of individuals" by cutting Marty Glickman and Sam Stoller, the only Jews on the American track team, from the 400-meter relay, which consisted of Owens, Ralph Metcalf, Frank Wykoff, and Foy Draper. The reason for the coaches' substitution was probably the tendency to favor

216   Guttmann

athletes from one's own university rather than anti-Semitism. Draper was a student and Cromwell his coach at the University of Southern California (Johnson, 1972; Mandell, 1971).

To the degree that Owens made a mockery of the Nazi myth of "Nordic" superiority, the games were not a propaganda coup, but the overall impression of the games must have added to Hitler's prestige. Pierre de Coubertin himself, in an interview published by the Parisian paper *Le Journal*, remarked that the games had been organized with "Hitlerian strength and discipline" (quoted by Teichler, 1982, pp. 35-36).

Propaganda coup or not, the games were unquestionably an important step on Avery Brundage's path to Olympic leadership. On the first day of the 35th Session, July 30, the wrath of the IOC against dissenter Jahncke was expressed in its vote to expel him: 49-0. Garland abstained, but he expressed his disapproval of his American colleague. (Charles Sherrill, the third American member, had died suddenly on June 25.) Jahncke was gone and the IOC now consisted of like-minded men in agreement with one another, at least in regard to the correctness of their decision to keep the games in Garmisch-Partenkirchen and Berlin. Who had a better right to represent the IOC in the United States than the man who had fought like a lion to frustrate the boycott and bring the American team to Berlin? Brundage was elected unanimously and the official notes specifically record that his election was "en remplacement de M. Lee Jahncke" ("Procès-verbale," 1936, p. 2).

Notes

1. On the Deutsche Turnerschaft's hostility to modern sports, see Bernett (1982, pp. 15-42).

2. On Lewald and his relationship with the Nazis, see Krüger (1975).

3. For Diem the best source is his posthumous autobiography, *Ein Leben für den Sport* (1976); his apologia for his role during the Hitlerzeit appeared, edited by L. Pfeiffer, as *Der Deutsche Sport in der Zeit des Nationalsozialismus* (Diem, 1980).

4. Henri Baillet-Latour to Brundage, December 1, 1933 transmitting an English translation of an order dated November 21, 1933 (Avery Brundage Collection, Box 42). On the Reichssportführer, see Steinhofer (1973).

5. Rubien was secretary of the AOC.

6. For the opposite view of the matter, see Krüger (1978).

7. Brundage told Baillet-Latour that the reply to Jahncke was "straight from the shoulder" (Brundage to Baillet-Latour, 1936).

8. On the "Olimpiada" see Steinberg (1980) and Kidd (1980).

9. For a retrospective view see Welch (1980).

References

Baillet-Latour, H. to Brundage, A. (1933, December 1). Avery Brundage Collection, Urbana, IL, Box 42.

Baillet-Latour, H. to Brundage, A. (1935a, October 10). Avery Brundage Collection, Urbana, IL, Box 42.

Baillet-Latour, H., to Brundage, A. (1935b, December 10). Avery Brundage Collection, Urbana, IL, Box 42.

Baillet-Latour, H. to Jahncke, E.L. (1935, December 13). Avery Brundage Collection, Urbana, IL, Box 42.

Ballinger, L. (1981). *In your face: Sports for love and money.* Chicago: Vanguard.

Bernett, H. (1973). *Untersuchungen zur Zeitgeschichte des Sports* [Investigations into the contemporary history of sport]. Schorndorf: Karl Hofmann.

Bernett, H. (1976). *Guido von Mengden.* Berlin: Bartels & Wernitz.

Bernett, H. (1982). *Der Sport im Kreuzfeuer der Kritik* [Sport in the crossfire of criticism]. Schorndorf: Karl Hoffman.

Bohlen, F. (1979). *Die XI Olympischen Spiele Berlin 1936* [The 11th Olympic Games Berlin 1936]. Cologne: Pahl-Rugenstein.

Brundage, A. (1935, October 26). Avery Brundage Collection, Urbana, IL, Box 243.

Brundage, A. to Baillet-Latour, H. (1933, December 28). Avery Brundage Collection, Urbana, IL, Box 42.

Brundage, A. to Baillet-Latour, H. (1935, September 24). Avery Brundage Collection, Urbana, IL, Box 42.

Brundage, A. to Baillet-Latour, H. (1936, January 6). Avery Brundage Collection, Urbana, IL, Box 42.

Brundage, A. to Brailas, E. (1934, January 14). Avery Brundage Collection, Urbana, IL, Box 153.

Brundage, A. to Diem, C. (1934, July 13). Avery Brundage Collection, Urbana, IL, Box 22.

Brundage, A. to Halbach, B. (1936, March 17). Avery Brundage Collection, Urbana, IL, Box 153.

Brundage, A. to Kirby, G.T. (1933, May 31). Avery Brundage Collection, Urbana, IL, Box 28.

Brundage, A. to Kirby, G.T. (1934, March 3). Avery Brundage Collection, Urbana, IL, Box 28.

Brundage, A. to Garland, W.M. (1934, October 5). Avery Brundage Collection, Urbana, IL, Box 56.

Brundage, A. to Schöbel, H. (1963, January 7). Avery Brundage Collection, Urbana, IL, Box 62.

Brundage, A. to Halt, K.R. von. (1934, October 22). Avery Brundage Collection, Urbana, IL, Box 57.

Brundage, A., & Brundage, E. to Harper, J. (1934, September 9). Avery Brundage Collection, Urbana, IL, Box 240.

Bulletin du C.I.O. (1953, January 15). p. 14.

Bulletin du C.I.O. (1955, August 15). pp. 34-35.

Chicago American. (1936, July 25). Avery Brundage Collection, Urbana, IL, Box 235.

Chicago Daily News. (1936, July 25). Avery Brundage Collection, Urbana, IL, Box 235.

Chicago Sunday Times. (1936, July 26). Avery Brundage Collection, Urbana, IL, Box 235.

Chicago Tribune. (1936, July 28). Avery Brundage Collection, Urbana, IL, Box 235.

Deutsch, B.S. to Brundage, A. (1933, October 8). Avery Brundage Collection, Urbana, IL, Box 153.

Diem, C. (1929). *Amerikareise 1929* [American voyage 1929]. Cologne: Carl-Diem-Institute.

Diem, C. (1931). *Sport in Amerika* [Sport in America]. Berlin: Weidmannsche Buchhandlung.

Diem, C. (1934). *Reise nach Schweden 1934* [A voyage to Sweden 1934]. Cologne: Carl-Diem-Institute.

Diem, C. (1935, December 7). [Diary]. Cologne: Carl-Diem-Institute.

Diem, C. (1976). *Ein Leben für den Sport* [A life for sport]. Ratingen: A. Henn.

Diem, C. (1980). *Der deutsche Sport in der Zeit des Nationalsozialismus* [German sport in the era of National Socialism]. (L. Pfeiffer, Ed.). Cologne: Carl-Diem-Institute.

Dodd, W.E., Jr., & Dodd, M. (Eds.). (1941). *Ambassador Dodd's diary, 1933-1938.* New York: Harcourt, Brace.

Edstrøm, S. to Brundage, A. (1933, December 4). Avery Brundage Collection, Urbana, IL, Box 42.

Ferris, D.J. to Brundage, A. (1936, June 5). Avery Brundage Collection, Urbana, IL, Box 23.

Gottlieb, M. (1972). The American Controversy over the Olympic Games. *American Jewish Historical Quarterly*, **61**, 181-213.

Holmes, J. (1971). *Olympiad 1936*. New York: Ballantine Books.

International Olympic Committee. (1933). *Bulletin de C.I.O.*, **8**, 9.

International Olympic Committee. (1934). *Bulletin du C.I.O.*, **9**, 8.

Johnson, W.O. (1972). *All that glitters is not gold*. New York: Putnam's.

Kidd, B. (1980). The popular front and the 1936 Olympics. *Canadian Journal of the History of Sport and Physical Education*, **11**, 1-18.

Kirby, G.T. (1933). *Resolution for the convention of the American Olympic Committee on November 22, 1933*. Avery Brundage Collection, Urbana, IL, Box 28.

Kirby, G.T. to Brundage, A. (1933, November 2). Avery Brundage Collection, Urbana, IL, Box 29.

Kirby, G.T. to Brundage, A. (1936a, March 17). Avery Brundage Collection, Urbana, IL, Box 29.

Kirby, G.T. to Brundage, A. (1936b, May 27). Avery Brundage Collection, Urbana, IL, Box 29.

Kirby, G.T. to Gilbert, A.C. (1933, December 14). Avery Brundage Collection, Urbana, IL, Box 26.

Krüger, A. (1972). *Die Olympischen Spiele 1936 and die Weltmeinung* [The 1936 Olympic Games and world opinion]. Berlin: Bartels & Wernitz.

Krüger, A. (1975). *Theodor Lewald*. Berlin: Bartels & Wernitz.

Krüger, A. (1978). Fair play for American athletes: A study in Anti-Semitism. *Canadian Journal of the History of Sport and Physical Education*, **9**, 36-49.

Leiper, J. (1976). *The International Olympic Committee: The pursuit of Olympism 1894-1970*. Unpublished doctoral dissertation, University of Alberta, Edmonton.

Lewald, T. to Brundage, A. (1933, April 29). Avery Brundage Collection, Urbana, IL, Box 33.

Mandell, R. (1966). *The Nazi Olympics*. New York: MacMillan.

Mayer, O. (1966). *A travers les anneaux olympiques* [Through the Olympic rings]. Geneva: Cailler.

New York American. (1935, October 9).

New York Post. (1934, September 26).

New York Times. (1933, October 9). Avery Brundage Collection, Urbana, IL, Box 153.

New York Times. (1934, September 27).

New York Times. (1935, November 27).

Olympic Games. (1936, August 7). *Spectator,* p. 230.

The Olympic story. (Chapter 8, p. 18). Avery Brundage Collection, Urbana IL, Box 330-331.

Die Olympischen Spiele 1936 [The 1936 Olympic Games]. (1936). Altona-Bahrenfeld: Reemtsma.

Opening address to the 55th session of the IOC, Munich, May 23, 1959. (1969). In *Speeches of Avery Brundage.* Lausanne: Comité International Olympique.

Popliment, A. (1956, October 15). Berlin 1936. *Bulletin du C.I.O.,* pp. 46-47.

Proces-verbale de la 35ième session du Comité International Olympique [Minutes of the 35th Session of the International Olympic Committee]. Berlin, July 30-31 and August 15, 1936, p. 2. Lausanne: International Olympic Committee.

Report of the President. (1937). *Games of the XIth Olympiad.* New York: U.S. Olympic Association.

Revue de deux mondes. (1938, August 15). 8th series, p. 935.

Rubien, F.W. to Diem, C. (1934, October 8). Avery Brundage Collection, Urbana, IL, Box 35.

Sherrill, C. to Rubien, F.W. (1933, June 11). Avery Brundage Collection, Urbana, IL, Box 35.

Statements by May Lou Petty and Ada Taylor Sackett. (1936). Avery Brunage Collection, Urbana, IL, Box 235.

Steinberg, D.A. (1980). Workers' sport and united front, 1934-36. *Arena Review,* **4,** 1-6.

Steinhofer, D. (1973). *Hans von Tschammer und Osten.* Berlin: Bartels & Wernitz.

Teichler, H.J. (1976). Berlin 1936—Ein Sieg der NS—Propaganda? [Berlin 1936—A victory for National Socialist propaganda?]. *Stadion,* **2,** 285.

Teichler, H.J. (1982). Coubertin und das Dritte Reich [Coubertin and the Third Reich]. *Sportwissenschaft,* **12,** 25-40.

Welch, P. (1980). Where are they now? *The Olympian,* **7,** 15.

14
Diplomatic Fun and the Games: A Commentary on the United States Boycott of the 1980 Summer Olympics

James A.R. Nafziger

President Carter was depicted in one political cartoon as a good old country boy fishing from a bridge into the troubled waters of the Middle East. Although he apparently had not caught anything, a huge Russian bear beneath the bridge was busily scooping up fish with its paws.

Originally published in the *Willamette Law Review*, 1980, 17, 67-81. Reprinted by permission.

This allegory of Soviet-United States relations needs little revision to take account of President Carter's windmill tilting against the 1980 Summer Olympic Games. His "call" for a boycott of the Games[1] was ineffective, costly, unjust, and unwise, and it may have been illegal. This recent experience provides an excellent case study of the relationships between "domestic" and "international" issues, private and public sectors, and law and policy in the conduct of foreign affairs. The boycott experience also reflects the content and style of foreign policy during the Carter administration, the extent of its commitment to the rule of law, and the capacity of the United States to implement its policy.

Boycotts are common in the international sports arena (Cheffers, 1979; Espy, 1979; *Library of Congress Information Bulletin*, 1980; McIntosh, 1978; Meynaud, 1966; Nafziger & Strenk, 1978). In 1956 six nations withdrew from the Olympics to protest two international political events: Egypt, Iraq, and the People's Republic of China withdrew to protest the Suez invasion, whereas Spain, Holland, and Switzerland withdrew to protest the Soviet invasion of Hungary. The Soviet Union has boycotted Chilean teams since the fall of the Allende government. Several African teams, mostly under governmental direction, boycotted the 1976 Olympics to protest the participation of the New Zealand team, which had earlier allowed one of its teams to meet South African athletes in rugby, a non-Olympic sport. Czechoslovakia, Hungary, Russia, Mexico, and India have refused to allow their teams to meet in Davis Cup tennis competition against teams from South Africa. Further, boycotts were directed against teams, even integrated ones, from Rhodesia before it became Zimbabwe.

To paraphrase the famous statement of von Clausewitz: Athletic competition, like war, represents an extension of politics by other means. The father of the modern Olympic Games, Baron Pierre de Coubertin, envisaged international athletic exchange as the free trade of the future that no nation would regulate to its political advantage (Coubertin, 1908). Considering the course of 20th-century history, it is remarkable that this aspiration has prevailed. Nevertheless, the Games are political. This politicization is a healthy outlet for international tension, except when politics interfere with the function of the Games. Two recent examples of interference are the African boycott of the 1976 Games in Montreal and the Canadian government's refusal to permit the Taiwanese team to participate in those Games as the recognized representative of China. (On the African boycott, see Nafziger & Strenk, 1979, pp 269-271, 284-285; on the China recognition issue, see Nafziger & Strenk, 1979, at 265-266, 281-283). Consequently, bad precedent confronted the organizers of the Moscow Olympics.

Against this historical and political background, it is not surprising that political conflicts threatened the Moscow Games well before the invasion of Afghanistan. As early as 1976, United States Senator Bill Bradley, former Olympic and New York Knicks basketball player, wrote a prophetic scenario in which "the President of the United States would call a boycott of the 1980 Olympic games just two weeks before they were to begin in Moscow, citing national security and difficulty with the Soviet Union as the reasons" (quoted in Spiegel, 1980, p. 8, col. 4). By September 1979, several months before the invasion, the 1980 Games were "troubled" by a serious threat of Olympic boycotts in response to international political conflicts (*Saturday Review*, 1979, p. 12). One such threat was that the United States would boycott the 1980 Games to protest Soviet treatment of political dissidents (Williams, 1979).

Particularly relevant were these words, spoken 3 years before the 1980 Games by Lord Killanin, the president and chief spokesman of the International Olympic Committee: "I am watching Moscow very, very closely. But so much can depend on the relationships of the major powers at the time. The first Carter impact has been of going away from detente. That can create the atmosphere in which the Games [will] have to take place" (quoted in *Olympic Review*, 1977, p. 538). Lord Killanin's crystal ball proved to be clear. He added that the United States-Soviet rivalry worried him in another respect: "There is no doubt at all that Moscow is anxious to run the Games extremely well and there is no doubt afterwards that the United States will want to show that they can do them better" (quoted in *Olympic Review*, 1977, p. 538).

Thus, the Soviet invasion of Afghanistan may be seen, in the Middle East cliché, as "the straw that broke the camel's back" and not as the sole cause of the President's call for a boycott of the 1980 Olympic Games.

The Call for a Boycott as an Example of Foreign Policy

One need not question President Carter's good faith. He does not seem to have sought an unreasonable confrontation with the Soviets after they invaded Afghanistan nor did he use that invasion simply as a pretext for doing what was inevitable. Instead, the President's action is characteristic of the good intention but questionable and quixotic judgment often underlying his foreign policy. Specifically, six points emerge from the boycott experience that relate directly to that judgment.

First, the delicate balance between détente and containment had become impaired by early 1980. President Carter's preference for a jerry-built foreign policy platform of highly selective initiatives premised on human rights collapsed because of unsound construction. Worst of all, it may have given human rights a bad name with many Americans. Instead of a solid diplomatic, economic, and military platform for pursuing peace and resisting Soviet expansionism, the Carter administration hastily built a human rights platform with ersatz materials. Therefore, it is easy to understand how the Russian bear—certainly not the friendly "Misha" that served as a mascot of the 1980 Games—thought it could scoop up some more fish beneath the bridge.

Second, once the bear was on the prowl, the invasion of Afghanistan may have been one of those frustrating instances where the United States could take no effective action short of shooting the bear. Preferably, the bear should be kept away from the fish by long-range strategy and not by after-the-fact punishment such as the Olympic boycott. If the United States fails to keep the bear away from the fish, its options are severely limited: It cannot be the world's policeman, although it is in a good position to effectively prevent Soviet expansionism in some parts of the world. Afghanistan, however, does not seem to be one of them.

Third, recent instances of United States intervention, such as in the Dominican Republic (Nanda, 1966) and Cambodia ("Symposium on United States," 1971), were similar in a number of important respects to the Soviet involvement in Afghanistan. As a result, the United States may not have had clean hands with which to respond to the Soviet invasion.

Fourth, President Carter exaggerated the utility of this boycott as a political sanction and thereby grossly misjudged the balance between its benefits and costs. This is largely because in President Carter's judgment the Afghan crisis was "the greatest threat to peace since the Second World War" (Department of State Bulletin, 1980b, p. 33). Moreover, the President assumed that the boycott and other unilateral sanctions[2] would somehow soften the Soviets.

Vice President Mondale and Secretary of State Vance similarly took extreme positions. In explaining the United States position before the International Olympic Committee, Secretary of State Vance claimed that "to hold the Olympics in any nation that is warring on another is to lend the Olympic mantle to that nation's actions" (Department of State Bulletin, 1980b, p. 50). Vice President Mondale went further: "History holds its breath," he said, "for what is at stake is no less than the future security of the civilized world" (quoted in Moore, 1980, pp. 30, 32). Polite observers may well respond to that comment by holding their breaths, too.

Fifth, in failing to respect the international rule of law that is offended by the boycott, President Carter neglected a creditable defense to the domestic political pressures in favor of the boycott.

Last, and most importantly, President Carter may have discounted the genuine power of people whose liberties are endangered. He should have acknowledged the capacity of poorly equipped partisans, even under communist domination, to wage aggressive and effective insurgency. At the "Circus in Moscow," the Afghan team entered no shooting events, only events in hand-to-hand combat (boxing and wrestling) (Kahn, 1980). The focus of the United States response to the Afghan invasion should have been more on the Afghans instead of the Soviets. By offering military assistance to the Pakistani regime of General Zia-ul-Haq, President Carter's response was an indirect, rather than a direct, means for better equipping the Afghan resistance.[3] Fortunately, General Zia scoffed at the amount of the aid and the United States was relieved of a welter of further entanglements.[4]

On the Merits of the Boycott

The compelled boycott of the 1980 Olympic Games failed to accomplish world-order objectives even though the Games did not enjoy full participation. The lack of clarity and purpose in Carter's boycott contributed to the policy's ineffectiveness.[5] Assuming that the object of the boycott was to nudge the Soviets out of Afghanistan and to deter them from further expansionism, rather than to stop the Games, the boycott was a futile gesture. The Soviets are still encamped in Afghanistan and remain undeterred from further expansionism by the sanctions imposed by the Carter administration. The boycott failed for several reasons.

First, athletic boycotts seldom succeed and are typically counterproductive. One observer has written that a "boycott, as a tool for bringing about political change, has been effective only in the case of small and relatively defenseless countries" (Cheffers, 1979, pp. 512, 513). For example, boycotts directed against South Africa have had almost no impact on apartheid. In fact, the Supreme Council for Sport in Africa, which was largely responsible for the African boycott of the 1976 games, later repudiated its withdrawal. The Council concluded that the cause of Black Africa would have been better served by the participation of the African teams (see the remarks of Brendan O'Reilly, quoted in *Olympic Review*, 1980a, p. 113).

Boycotts tend to have the unintended effect of hardening the positions of targeted countries. Those countries do not want to be viewed as yielding to foreign pressures. This is particularly characteristic of the Soviet Union and other totalitarian states. For example, despite the threat and imposition of boycotts by several countries in support of Russian dissidents, the Soviet government further restricted dissident citizens (Willis, 1980). In this year of Jesse Owens's death, it is poignant to recall not only that he opposed the boycott of the 1980 Games, but that his successes in the 1936 Berlin Olympics (Holmes, 1971) were among the few contemporary affronts to Naziism. Conversely, a United States boycott of the Berlin Games would have been ineffective.

Second, since détente began to unravel, the Kremlin has been insensitive to Western, or even Third World, criticism. Third, boycotts discourage exactly what should be encouraged: the use of the arena of sports rather than battlefields to flex national muscles. Last, the boycott is not apt to deter Soviet expansionism since they are not scheduled to host the Olympics in the near future. Thus, the boycott does not provide an ongoing deterrent, at least to the Soviet Union.

The Boycott Was Costly

Besides being ineffective, the boycott was costly to this country. The United States wasted political energy and valuable political clout by insisting that its allies endorse the boycott against their better judgment.

In addition, United States allies were confused about what the United States expected to accomplish with a joint boycott. A political cartoon portrayed Coach Carter at the chalkboard, talking his players through a complicated play called "Allied Master Plan for USSR, Iran, Olympics, etc." His players, each bearing the name of one of the United States allies, were all equipped for different sports. A British cricket player highlighted the players' confusion: "Now that I know *who* we're playing, I should like to know exactly *what* we're playing." It is one thing for the United States to boycott the Olympics, but another to force the issue onto the playing field of the Western alliance. Indeed, even if the boycott had been wise, withdrawal of the United States team *alone* would have spoiled the Games. Instead, Allied leaders were pressed to explain the significance of the boycott to their nationals without appearing to be servile to those "pushy Yankees." National perceptions that the countries which participated in the boycott were subservient will also be costly, even though the world scorned the Soviet invasion.

The Boycott Was Unjust and Unwise

Traditionally, the United States government has avoided directly supporting Olympic athletics in recognition of the private nature of the Games and the more or less amateur status of their participants. For the Carter administration to interfere with athletes' individual civil rights and to manipulate amateur athletics for political gains is unfair. It seems ironic for an administration that premised its foreign policy on human rights to coerce United States athletes to boycott the Olympics. Further, athletes from countries which competed in Moscow also suffered unjustly from the effects of the 1980 Olympic boycott (Eldridge, 1980a, 1980b).

Finally, the boycott was unwise. To be sure, hosting the Games was a triumph for the Soviet Union, as the President emphasized. Just as important, however, they were a partial triumph for all those who favor a liberalization of Russia by opening it up to what has been described as "the biggest cultural invasion of them all" (Williams, 1979, pp. 12, 15). Had the United States not boycotted the Olympics, television would have amplified that invasion. Thus, NBC could have accomplished much in the United States national interest by intelligent, on-the-scene commentary. Additionally, the more moderate members of the Soviet regime appear to have been the chief sponsors of the invitation by Moscow to host the Games (Williams, 1979). The United States has now discouraged their efforts to liberalize Soviet totalitarianism. The principle of boycotts as a form of official protest is subject to great abuse, for it may jeopardize the future of the Olympic Movement.

The Legality of the Boycott

The legality of the boycott is questionable under international and domestic law. Internationally, the boycott may have violated the Olympic

Charter and Helsinki Accords. Domestically, the action may have violated the Amateur Sports Act of 1978.

International Law

The "supreme authority" of Olympic competition is the International Olympic Committee (IOC). This committee is governed by the Olympic Charter.[6] The IOC "is a body corporate by international law having juridical status and perpetual succession" (IOC, 1984, Rule 11). Although the IOC is a nongovernmental organization, under customary international law its rules regulate Olympic competition in the same manner as the rules of the International Committee of the Red Cross regulate humanitarian activity in time of war and other emergency.[7]

The Olympic Charter mandates that "[e]very person or organization that plays any part whatsoever in the Olympic movement shall accept the supreme authority of the IOC and shall be bound by its Rules and submit to its jurisdiction" (IOC, 1984, Rule 4). Although neither the IOC nor the Charter can command sovereign obedience, the rules of the Charter have been generally accepted as international custom, particularly by the European states. For example, a 1977 Belgian court decision, echoing the view of the French courts, the Council of Europe and the High Court of Justice of the European Communities, ruled that the international rules of sport supersede national policies and laws to the contrary (Bondoux, 1978; Garrigues, 1979). Also, at its 1978 meeting, the Second Conference of European Sports Ministers adopted an antinationalist resolution that explicitly confirmed the authority of the Olympic Charter.[8] Jurists have established the Rules of the Olympic Charter at the highest legal order of authority (Silance, 1977).

Under the Fundamental Principles of the Olympic Charter, the United States government, as an "organization [playing a] part in the Olympic movement" (IOC, 1984, Rule 4), must respect the "aims of the Olympic movement." These aims are as follows:

- To promote the development of those physical and moral qualities which are the basis of sport
- To educate young people through sport in a spirit of better understanding between each other and of friendship, thereby helping to build a better and more peaceful world
- To spread the Olympic principles throughout the world, thereby creating international goodwill
- To bring together the athletes of the world in the great four-yearly sport festival, the Olympic Games (IOC, 1984, Rule 1)

The Olympic boycott would seem to have offended at least the last three of these aims. Even the most basic goals of the first aim have been violated by the United States government to the extent that its call for a boycott inhibited amateur athletics. The boycott violated more than just the principles of Olympic competition. Rule 3 of the Charter provides: "No discrimination [in the Olympic Games] is allowed against any country or person on grounds of race, religion or politics." It is arguable that the President's call for a boycott also may have offended Rule 9, which states, "The Games are contests between individuals and not between countries." Similarly, Soviet manipulation of the Games for propaganda may violate that provision.

Rule 24 obligates National Olympic Committees (NOCs) to be autonomous, to resist all political pressures, and to enforce the Rules and Bylaws of the IOC. Further, the rule provides that "NOCs shall be the sole authorities responsible for the representation of their respective countries at the Olympic Games. . . ." Bylaw V(7) defines the term "representation" to cover the decision to participate. Violations of the rules, such as yielding to political pressures, expose NOCs to penalties (IOC, 1984, Rule 25). Thus, President Carter violated the emerging custom of international athletic competition by refusing to accept the full authority of either the IOC or the United States Olympic Committee (USOC); by placing the USOC in an unconscionably awkward position; and by threatening legal action against the latter in the event of its noncompliance with the boycott.

Moreover, the President's boycott policy may have violated the Helsinki Accords (*Department of State Bulletin*, 1975; *International Legal Materials*, 1975), which define East-West relations. In those Accords, signed by the Soviet Union, the United States, Canada, and all European countries except Albania, the signatories pledged that: "In order to expand existing links and co-operation in the field of sport, the participating State will encourage contacts and exchanges of this kind, including sports meetings and competitions of all sorts, on the *basis of the established international rules, regulations and practice*" (*Department of State Bulletin*, 1975, p. 341; *International Legal Materials*, 1975, p. 1315; emphasis added). These rules are not simply technical "rules of the game," such as the distance between goal posts, but the organizational rules of the Olympics and other established competitions.[9]

Domestic Law

The boycott may have also violated domestic law. The Amateur Sports Act of 1978 vests *exclusive* jurisdiction in the United States Olympic Committee in "all matters pertaining to the participation of the United States in the Olympic Games and in the Pan American Games, including the representation in such games" (Public Law No. 95-606, 1978). Arguably, under the Act the President has no authority to interfere in such arrangements. President Carter's heavy hand on the United States Olympic Committee,[10] however, amounted to such interference. Not only the President (*Weekly Compilation of Presidential Documents*, 1980c), but his Attorney General and White House Counsel (Moore, 1980, at pp. 30, 31) clearly indicated that they intended to seek legal sanctions if the United States Olympic Committee or individual athletes refused to comply with the boycott. This lack of jurisdiction under the Amateur Sports Act is probably why the White House elevated the issue to the national security level. Short of a declaration of war, the President could justify legal sanctions only by resorting to the provisions of the Export Administration Act of 1979 (Public Law No. 96-72, 93 Stat. 503, 1979) or the International Emergency Economic Powers Act (Public Law No. 95-223, 91 Stat. 1626, 1977). Both acts require an underlying economic transaction, and the latter requires presidential findings of an "unusual and extraordinary threat with respect to which a national emergency has been declared" (Public Law No. 95-223, 202b, 1977). The application of these laws to the boycott is questionable. Except for this authority, however, sanctions against athletes or athletic organizations refusing to comply with the boycott (*Los Angeles Times*, 1980a) would violate the Amateur Sports Act, as well as the constitutional protections of the freedom to travel and due process (Neier, 1980; Nowak, Rotunda, & Young, 1978).

The Alternatives

The many problems of the Olympic Movement[11] can be resolved. To avoid political excesses American athletes proposed the following plan for their participation in Moscow (*Oregon Statesman*, 1980). They would not appear in opening and closing ceremonies or attend the awards ceremonies to accept any medals. They would arrive in Moscow just before they compete and leave immediately afterward, remaining in the Olympic Village or training facilities during their time on Soviet soil. Further, they would not sightsee or engage in any tourist activities. In addition to these proposals by United States athletes the IOC responded in two ways. It amended its rules to provide for greater flexibility in the selection of flags and emblems for use in the Games.[12] Also, the IOC allowed NOCs to decide whether to participate in Olympic ceremonies.[13]

Sir Roger Bannister, the great British runner, called the Olympics "one of the great leavening forces for good in the 20th century" (quoted in Atkin, 1980, p. 18, col. 4). Whether that is so, it is well to recall language from the *Final Report of the President's Commission on Olympic Sports* (United States President's Commission, 1977). It "deplores the actions of governments which deny an athlete the right to take part in international competition," "calls upon world sports leaders to take whatever steps are necessary to eliminate the misuse of the Games," and notes "with deep regret the declining ability of the nations of the world to separate sport from politics" (United States President's Commission, 1977, p. 1). Though that report was submitted to the White House in January 1977, just 3 1/2 years before the boycott, it was apparently forgotten.

Notes

1. To be sure, the United States Olympic Committee (USOC), not the President, made the formal decision against participation by United

States nationals in the 1980 Games. See Defrantz v. United States Olympic Committee, 492 F. Supp. 1181 (D.D.C. 1980), where the District Court of the District of Columbia upheld the statutory and constitutional rights of the USOC not to enter a United States team.

2. It is very difficult to identify exactly what sanctions the Carter administration unilaterally imposed against the Soviet Union. A review of the *Weekly Compilation of Presidential Documents* from January through July 1980 reveals both indirect and direct measures. Indirect measures included the recall of the United States ambassador to Moscow, a request to the Congress for a suspension of SALT II deliberations, delays in opening or allowing the opening of consulates of the United States and the Soviet Union, revival of selective service registration, a call for increased defense appropriations, accelerated development of rapid deployment forces and of the MX and cruise missile systems, a withdrawal of trade preferences for Afghanistan, and offers of military assistance to Yugoslavia and several Middle Eastern states. Direct measures included curtailment of federal licensing of a range of high technology and strategic items for export to the Soviet Union; an embargo on phosphate and grain shipments there; a ban on fishing by Soviet nationals within the 200-mile zone off United States coasts; and a curtailment of cultural, scientific, and other exchange programs between the two countries.

A State Department representative listed the following additional measures:

> An increase of funds for the Voice of America and Radio Free Europe, the reduction of our personnel at the Embassy in Kabul, the proscription on the issuance of visas for Soviet personnel to come to the United States, the suspension of negotiations on a general trade agreement with the Russians, laying groundwork for the United Nations General Assembly resolution denouncing the Soviet invasion, and demanding that the Soviets withdraw their troops . . . , increasing efforts to get our allies and other countries to restrict credit to the Soviet Union, and discouraging the Asian Development Bank and other international loan agencies from extending any more grants or loans to Afghanistan. (Shaplen, 1980b, pp. 44, 66)

On March 28, 1980, under the Export Administration Act of 1979, Public Law No. 96-72, 93 Statute 503 (1979), President Carter directed the Secretary of Commerce to enforce the Olympic boycott by taking the following measures:

1. To deny all pending validated license applications for goods and technology to be used in support of or in connection with the summer Olympic games in Moscow;

2. To revoke all outstanding export licenses for Olympic-related exports that have not already been shipped;

3. To impose validated license controls on all exports not now requiring validated licenses to be used in support of or in association with the summer Olympic games in Moscow. No such licenses shall be granted;

4. To prohibit other transactions and payments associated with all Olympic-related sports. Among other transactions, the order will bar NBC from making any further payments or exports under its contracts relating to the United States television rights for the Olympic games. (*Weekly Compilation of Presidential Documents* 561 [1980b])

3. On the importance of providing direct assistance to the Afghan rebels, see, for example, Herati (1980).

4. An informative study of the Iran crisis attributes the Pakistani decision to that country's concern "about the effect that American aid would have not only on Russia but also on India" (Shaplen, 1980a, pp. 43, 49). For a glimpse into the Pandora's box of problems presented by the overture to Pakistan, see Shaplen (1980b), pp. 44, 53-56.

5. The President premised the boycott on the presumed danger to the United States athletes and spectators (*Department of the State Bulletin*, 1980a, Special-B), and, on another occasion, in the deterrence of future aggression and to send the Soviets a "signal of world outrage" (*Department of the State Bulletin*, 1980b, p. 51). The Secretary of State, however, viewed the boycott as retribution for the Soviet violation of the Olympic principle against contemporaneous involvement by a sovereign host in open warfare (*Department of the State Bulletin*, 1980b, p. 50).

The following dialogue took place at a presidential news conference February 13, 1980:

Q. You have said that the Soviets have to be made to pay a price for invading Afghanistan, and your counsel has said that our boycott of the Olympics is not intended to be punitive. How do you explain the seeming difference between these two positions?

A. We have no desire to use the Olympics to punish, except the Soviets attach a major degree of importance to the holding of the Olympics in the Soviet Union. In their own propaganda material, they claim that the willingness of the International Olympic Committee to let the games be held in Moscow is an endorsement of the foreign policy and the peace-loving nature of the Soviet Union.

To me it's unconscionable for any nation to send athletes to the capital of a nation under the aegis of the Olympics when that nation—that host nation—is actively involved in the invasion and subjugation of innocent people. And, so, for that reason, I don't believe that we are obligated to send our athletes to Moscow.

And I would like to repeat, if the Soviet Union does not withdraw its troops from Afghanistan by the 20th of this month, then neither I nor the American people nor the Congress will support the sending of an Olympic team to Moscow this summer. (*Department of the State Bulletin*, 1980b, Special-D)

6. Rule 23 of the Charter provides that "the IOC is the final authority on all questions concerning the Olympic games and the Olympic movement." Rule 4 refers to the "supreme authority of the IOC."

7. See, for example, Lador-Lederer (1963). The rules and bylaws of the Olympic Charter appear to have been accepted as legal authority in Defrantz v. United States Olympic Committee, 492 F. Supp. 1181 (D.D.C. 1980).

8. Resolution adopted by the Second Conference of European Ministers Responsible for Sport, London, April 4-7, 1978, reprinted in *Olympic Review*, June 1978, p. 391. For further background, see Howell (1978), p. 290.

9. The qualifying adjective *international* in a code or agreement such as the Helsinki Accords is properly construed to refer to the relations among nations at the more or less governmental level.

10. President Carter on occasion seems to have assumed that he had the power, with or without a decision by the USOC, to order the boycott (see Note 1). For example, the President warned athletes on March 21, prior to the decision of the USOC, as follows: "I can't say at this moment what other nations will not go to the Summer Olympics in Moscow. Ours will not go. I say that not with equivocation; the decision has been made" (*Weekly Compilation of Presidential Documents* 518 [1980a]).

11. See, for example, "The President of the IOC Meets the Problem of Olympism," *Olympic Review*, September 1977, p. 495. The major problems are the scope and size of the Games, the nationalistic elements in the Olympic Movement, issues of recognition, the general relationship between politics and sports, the role of sports in promoting human rights, professionalism in the "amateur" arena, and the doping of athletes. See also Jones (1980) and Nafziger (1971, 1975).
   On a recent hearing on the question of sports and apartheid in South Africa, see *U.N. Monthly Chronicle*, May 1980, p. 14. On the decision of the IOC to recognize the government of Beijing, see

Olympic Review, April-May 1979, p. 221. On the problem of doping, see Howald (1978). On the response of the Olympic Movement to this problem, see de Mérode (1979).

12. An amendment to Rule 24 providing that "the flag and the emblem used by NOC at the Olympic Games shall be submitted to and approved by the IOC Executive Board," IOC, *Modifications to the Olympic Charter Adopted by the 82nd Session of the IOC at Lake Placid 2*, has been interpreted as a means for each NOC "to use, during the Olympic ceremonies, the flag and anthem of its choice and thus assist athletes" (*Olympic Review,* May 1980, p. 230).

13. The IOC sympathetically considered special requests from the NOCs with respect to such boycott-related problems as the use of flags and anthems in Olympic ceremonies, financing, and transportation (*Olympic Review,* May 1980, p. 227). Several teams did not participate in ceremonies, and others participated by using Olympic rather than national flags (see Kahn, "The Sporting Scene— Circus in Moscow," *New Yorker,* August 18, 1980, pp. 58, 59, 80; and *Los Angeles Times,* July 21, 1980, Section 3, p. 1, col. 1).

References

Atkin, R. (1980, February 12). Olympic voices for reform. *Christian Science Monitor,* p. 18, col. 4.

Bondoux, B.R. (1978, August-September). Law and sport. *Olympic Review,* pp. 494-502.

Cheffers, J. (1979, September). The foolishness of boycott and exclusion in the Olympic movement. *Olympic Review,* pp. 512-513.

Coubertin, P. de. (1908). *Une campagne de vingt-et-un ans, 1887-1908* [A 21-year-old campaign, 1887-1908]. Paris: Librarie de l'Education Physique.

Defrantz v. United States Olympic Committee, 492 F. Supp. 1181 (D.D.C. 1980).

de Mérode, A. (1979, January). Doping tests at the Olympic Games in 1976. *Olympic Review,* p. 10.

Department of State Bulletin. (1975). [Secretary Kissinger's news conference of February 25]. Vol. 72, p. 323.

Department of State Bulletin. (1975). [Conference on security and cooperation in Europe. Final act]. Vol. 73, p. 322-350.

Department of State Bulletin. (1980a, January). [President J. Carter premised the boycott on the presumed dangers to U.S. athletes and spectators]. Special B.

Department of State Bulletin. (1980b, March). [Secretary Vance remarks: U.S. favors transfer of Summer Olympics]. Vol. 80, p. 50.

Eldridge, L. (1980a, May 27). Olympics: Big "losers" even before flame is lit." *Christian Science Monitor,* p. 1, col. 1.

Eldridge, L. (1980b, July 17). Moscow Olympics: What they are . . . what they might have been." *Christian Science Monitor,* p. 12, col. 1.

Espy, R. (1979). *The politics of the Olympic Games.* Berkeley: University of California Press.

Garrigues, C. (1979, June). The impact of community law on physical and sports activities. *Olympic Review,* pp. 345-346.

Herati, H. (1980, July 23). An Afghan refugee's message to Americans. *Christian Science Monitor* p. 23, col. 1.

Holmes, J. (1971). *Olympiad 1936: Blaze of glory for Hitler's Reich.*

Howald, H. (1978, May). Medical and pharmacological means of influencing performance in top competition sport. *Olympic Review,* pp. 297-302.

Howell, D. (1978, May). Governmental responsibilities in sport. *Olympic Review,* pp. 290-292.

International Legal Materials. (1975).

International Olympic Committee. (1982). *Modifications to the Olympic Charter adopted by the 82nd session of the IOC at Lake Placid 2.* Lausanne: Author.

Jones, C. (1980, May 22). Will Olympic rings be broken? *Christian Science Monitor,* p. 12.

Kahn, E.J., Jr. (1980, August 18). The sporting scene—Circus in Moscow. *New Yorker,* pp. 58-59, 80.

Lador-Lederer, J. (1963). *International non-governmental organizations.* Leyden: A.W. Sythoff.

Library of Congress Information Bulletin. (1980, May 30). [Annotated list of books on the Olympic Games. Appendix I]. p. 185.

Los Angeles Times. (1980a, April 11). [no title]. p. 1, col. 3.

Los Angeles Times. (1980b, July 21). [no title]. Section 3, p. 1, col. 1.

McIntosh, P.C. (1978, July). Politics and sport: A background paper. *Olympic Review,* pp. 427-430.

Meynaud, J. (1966). *Sport et politique* [Sport and politics].

Moore, K. (1980, April 21). The decision: No go on Moscow. *Sports Illustrated,* pp. 30-31.

Nafziger, J.A.R. (1971). The regulation of transnational sports competition: Down from Mount Olympus. 5 *Vanderbilt Journal of Transnational Law,* 180-212.

Nafziger, J.A.R. (1975). Legal aspects of a United States foreign sports policy. *8 Vanderbilt Journal of Transnational Law*, 837-855.

Nafziger, J.A.R., & Strenk, A. (1979). The political uses and abuses of sports. *10 Connecticut Law Review*, 259-289.

Nanda, V. (1966). The United States' action in the Dominican crisis: Impact on world order. *43 Den. Law Journal*, 439-479.

Neier, A. (1980, May 3). Right to travel. *Nation*, p. 516-517.

Nowak, J., Rotunda, R., & Young, J. (1978). *Handbook on constitutional law.* St. Paul, MN: West.

International Olympic Committee. (1984). *Olympic charter.* Lausanne: Comité International Olympique.

Olympic Review. (1977, September). [no title]. p. 583.

Olympic Review. (1979, April-May). [no title]. p. 221.

Olympic Review. (1980a, March). [no title]. pp. 113-115.

Olympic Review. (1980b, May). [no title]. pp. 227, 230.

Oregon Statesman. (1980, April 3). Section D, p. 4, col. 5.

The president of the IOC meets the problems of Olympism. (1979, September). *Olympic Review*, pp. 12-16.

Public Law No. 95-223. (1977).

Public Law No. 95-606. (1978).

Public Law No. 96-72. (1979).

Saturday Review. (1979, September 1). [no title].

Shaplen, R. (1980a, June 2). Eye of the storm—I. *New Yorker*, pp. 43-89.

Shaplen, R. (1980b, June 16). Eye of the storm—III. *New Yorker*, pp. 44-95.

Silance, L. (1977, October). Interaction of the rules in sports law and the laws and treaties made by public authorities. *Olympic Review*, pp. 619-628.

Spiegel, R.H. (1980, February 5). Fixed Greek Olympics? *Wisconsin State Journal*, p. 8, col. 4.

Symposium on United States military action in Cambodia. (1971). *65 American Journal of International Law*, 1-83.

United States President's Commission. (1977). *The final report of the President's Commission on Olympic sports, 1975-1977.*

Weekly Compilation of Presidential Documents. (1980a). [President J. Carter's remarks to representatives of U.S. team]. Vol. 16-12, pp. 517-521.

Weekly Compilation of Presidential Documents. (1980b). [White House statements on prohibition of U.S. transactions to the Olympic Games]. Vol. 16-13, pp. 560-561.

Weekly Compilation of Presidential Documents. (1980c). [President J. Carter's remarks to American Society of Newspaper Editors' annual convention]. Vol. 16-15, pp. 631-637.

Williams, R.M. (1979, September 1). Moscow '80: Playing for political points. *Saturday Review,* pp. 12-16.

Willis, D.K. (1980, May 1). Arrests, trials, searches: Soviets prepare for Olympics. *Christian Science Monitor,* p. 3, col. 3.

15

The Background, Nature, and Implications of the Organization of the "Capitalist Olympics"

Howard L. Nixon II

The 1984 Los Angeles Summer Olympic Games were heralded as the "first no-frills, debt-free, back-to-basics Games in modern history" (Kennedy, 1982, p. 84). Organizers saw them as a revival of the spirit and themes of Olympism advanced by Baron de Coubertin at the turn of the century (see, e.g., Ueberroth comments in Kennedy, 1982, p. 86). At the same time boosters and partisan observers hailed them as "an effective worldwide advertisement for capitalism" (e.g., Eason, 1984). Peter V. Ueberroth, President of the Los Angeles Olympic Organizing Committee (LAOOC), was showered with accolades for his managerial innovations and business acumen as manager of the nearly flawlessly administered Los Angeles Games (see, e.g., Axthelm, 1984b; Kennedy, 1982). As he promised, the 1984 Summer Games were the most financially successful modern Olympics.

As the "Capitalist" or "Free Enterprise" Games, run for the first time by a private corporation rather than a city, the 1984 Los Angeles Olympic Games were a source of controversy and criticism as well as applause. They were organized only after a power struggle involving the city of Los Angeles, the International Olympic Committee (IOC), and the United States Olympic Committee (USOC) (Miller, 1979). Their free enterprise format was seen by critics as a source of excessive profiteering and a "betrayal of sacred (Olympic) traditions" (Simonov, 1984). A boycott by the Soviet Union and 18 other countries occurred (Reich, 1984). Taxpayers, who were not supposed to assume any financial responsibility for the Games, ultimately assumed an estimated $100 million of security costs (Kirshenbaum, 1984). The unexpected size of the surplus was calculated at $250 million or more by some estimates (Peters, 1984) and was 10 to 25 times more than pre-Olympic predictions. The surplus was a source of controversy because Olympic dignitaries at the Games, visiting nations, LAOOC staff members and volunteers, and local communities had been asked to make sacrifices for the sake of austerity and the financial solvency of the Games (Creamer, 1984).

Before the Los Angeles Games, Ueberroth said that the LAOOC's management approach, which relied on sports and business people, would be copied in the future (Kennedy, 1982). After the Soviet boycott announcement, he rejected the notion that the Los Angeles Olympics would be the last ones and instead referred to them as pivotal. In fact, despite controversy and criticism about economics and politics, the LAOOC produced an Olympics that was a popular and financial success. Prior Olympic obituaries seemed premature. Indeed, according to *Sports Illustrated* writer William Oscar Johnson (1984b), the Los Angeles Olympics had injected "new enthusiasm" into an Olympic movement that had become "listless" after Moscow announced its boycott.

With the uncertainties of world economics and politics, pressures to reform the Olympics, and indications that the new IOC President, Juan Samaranch, was considering significant reforms ("Olympic Movement," 1984) even as he continued to espouse cherished ideals of Olympism (Samaranch, 1984), the future of the Olympics is difficult to predict. Nevertheless, the major organizational aspects of the Los Angeles Games can be identified and connected to major trends and events in recent Olympic history. We can then consider the implications of the organization of the 1984 Summer Olympics for future Olympics and Olympic reform. The purpose of the remainder of this chapter is to present and discuss a theoretical framework meant to link key organizational features of the Los Angeles Games—including especially their reliance on television—to a historical context. Possible implications for the future concerning the spirit of Olympism and the popular appeal of the Games will also be discussed. These possible implications of current patterns of Olympic organization will be considered in relation to a dilemma of reform they might pose for Olympic officials and future Olympic hosts.

A Theoretical Framework

In his analysis of the dominant character of modern sport, Sewart (1981) focused on American football and the extent to which it had become rationalized by corporate capitalism and transformed into a spectacle that degraded or trivialized the integrity or inherent value of sport. His conception of modern sport as a commodity to be marketed, packaged, and sold for profit as an entertainment spectacle suggests its connection to television. Altheide and Snow (1978) have analyzed the relationship between television and modern professional sports and have argued that the commercial-profit orientation of television networks often is at odds with the integrity of the sports they cover.

The application of the insights of Sewart and of Altheide and Snow to the Olympics makes it possible to understand important aspects and implications of the organization of the 1984 Los Angeles Olympics. A theoretical framework incorporating their general insights and placing them in the Olympic context will serve as the basis in this chapter for understanding the nature and implications of the Capitalist Games. Figure 1 portrays the main elements of this theoretical framework.

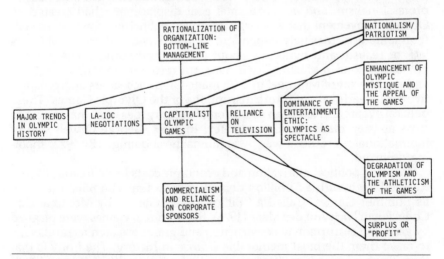

Figure 1   A theoretical framework for analyzing the nature and implications of the organization of the 1984 capitalist Olympic Games of Los Angeles.

Historical Background

During the 20th century, the Olympic Games and Movement have sub-verted the original ideals and goals of Olympism concerning amateurism, the preeminence of the individual athlete, sportsmanship, and international understanding that were promoted by Baron de Coubertin (Espy, 1979). The growth of the Olympic Movement, which has included the IOC, national committees, and international sport federations, also has created commercial pressures tied to the escalating costs of producing Olympic Games. In addition, since Los Angeles staged its anachronistic Depression-era Olympic extravaganza in 1932 to showcase itself as well as sport, Olympic Games have become competitions between hosts (Goodhue, 1980). This invidious competition added to the political manipulation of the Games and fueled an escalation of costs and deficits.

The expansion of the Olympic Movement and growth of the Games have created organizational pressures that have diverted attention from the athlete, whose interests were at the heart of Coubertin's Olympism, to the survival and viability of the organizations (Espy, 1979). In combination with nationalism, commercialism, and the related burst of professionalism that have occurred with the rise of professional sports in America since the 1950s, the displacement of classic goals in the Olympic Movement has represented a fundamental subversion of the Olympic Creed.

By the 1970s, the subversive forces of nationalism, commercialism, professionalism, and organizational goal displacement had created an Olympic Movement that was large, complex, politicized, commercialized, fragmented, increasingly dependent on television, and criticized for its lack of realism and hypocrisy about politics and money. The political demonstrations in Mexico City in 1968, the terrorism in Munich in 1972, and the boycott of Montreal in 1976 made Olympic leaders and prospective hosts fearful about future disruptions of the Olympic Games. These political events also led to an escalation of security measures that increased costs as they made the Games safer. In 1959, George Orwell said of international sport that it was "war minus the shooting." By 1972, shooting occurred.

Domestic political motivation and economic costs in 1976 caused Montreal to be left with a $1 billion debt after spending $1.4 billion to stage its Summer Games. Called a "Billion-Dollar Game" by Montreal City Councilman Nick Auf der Maur (1976), the Montreal Games were plagued by graft and corruption in construction and grandiose architectural plans to make them the most memorable Games in history. The irony is that they were planned as "modest and non-political" (Wright, 1978). Although the burden for Canadian taxpayers has been enormous, large profits were earned by banks, entrepreneurs, developers, construction companies, and advertising agencies (Wright, 1978). This fact shows the evolution of the Olympics into a public burden and a private bonanza.

It also indicates why Denver voters rejected the responsibility of financing the 1976 Winter Games after their city had been chosen to host and why other cities with dreams of hosting an Olympics had become fearful of the financial costs.

Negotiations Between Los Angeles and the IOC

In 1978, when a delegation representing Los Angeles led by Mayor Tom Bradley bid for the right to host the 1984 Summer Olympics, the concerns of possible political disruption and especially escalating financial liability were prominent elements in the background of negotiations with the IOC. Having failed twice before in its bids to host the 1976 and 1980 Summer Games, the Los Angeles delegation approached the 1978 negotiations with a truculent attitude and began making demands that in some cases would constitute a breach of the Olympic Charter if granted (Mahon, 1984; Miller, 1979; Overend, 1979). Despite facing a defiant challenge that offended or angered many of its members the IOC accepted the Los Angeles bid and capitulated on a number of major demands because Los Angeles was the only formal candidate to host the 1984 Summer Games. The IOC was reluctant to further damage the prestige of the American Olympic movement after the Denver defection and two prior rejections of Los Angeles bids.

The major concession by the IOC was to allow Los Angeles to breach Rule 4 of the Olympic Charter, which entrusted the honor *and financial responsibility* of hosting an Olympic Games to a city and stated that the Games were to be organized "to the satisfaction and in accordance with the requirements of the International Olympic Committee" (Miller, 1979, p. 141). With a sharp memory of Montreal's debt and the majority of its taxpayers unwilling to host an Olympics that might produce a deficit, the city council of Los Angeles refused to sign a contract with the IOC that obligated the city and USOC to joint financial responsibility for the Games. Indeed, a 1978 city charter amendment declared that "the city shall not, directly or indirectly, appropriate or disburse city funds for the purpose of promoting the 1984 Olympic Games" (Kennedy, 1982, p. 90).

After seven difficult months of negotiations, a USOC plan to award the Games to Los Angeles and absolve the city from financial responsibility was accepted by the IOC. After being awarded the Games, Los Angeles was allowed to turn them over to an independent organizing committee, which accepted joint financial responsibility with the USOC. This arrangement led Geoffrey Miller to observe that "it was a sad fact of a changing world that only one city came along to ask for the Games of 1984 and then was not ready to accept the responsibility of financing them." He also pointed out that acceptance of the USOC plan by the

IOC was "a case of breaking the rule first and changing it afterwards" (Miller, 1979, p. 147-148). Even the reluctant acceptance of such "deviance" could be seen both as a reflection of an erosion of IOC power and as an indication of its pragmatism.

IOC pragmatism is noteworthy because it frequently is seen as rigid and unwilling to change. In fact, in this situation with the 1984 Olympics and many other situations prior to it, the IOC was willing to make concessions to practical economic and political pressures to permit the Games to go on even as its leadership continued to pronounce the principles of Coubertin's Olympism and decry economic and political intrusions into the Olympic arena.

The LAOOC and the Capitalist Games

Acceptance of the USOC plan for financing and running the 1984 Summer Games meant that the Los Angeles Olympic Organizing Committee was allowed to operate as a private corporation. In operating this way, the LAOOC was a departure from all prior organizing committees in modern Olympic history.

The nationwide 2-month search for a person to run the LAOOC concentrated on finding someone who would be able to organize and stage a "Spartan Olympics" that was modest, inexpensive, and entirely privately financed. The man chosen for the job of President of the LAOOC was Peter V. Ueberroth. He was a successful business entrepreneur who was a self-made millionaire and a proponent of free enterprise. He also had credentials as a genuine sportsman. He promised a much less expensive and even profitable Olympics that would recapture the spirit of Olympism put forth by Baron de Coubertin at the beginning of the century.

In fact, Ueberroth proved to be an excellent manager who combined his roles as organizer, promoter, financier, and diplomat-politician in a manner characteristic of textbook models of the modern sport manager (see, e.g., Goodhue, 1980). Indeed, his managerial performance, the huge profit—called a surplus by the nonprofit LAOOC—his leadership generated, and the popularity of the Games with the American public and press earned Ueberroth the honor of being chosen *Time* magazine's "Man of the Year" for 1984 as well as the Major League Baseball Commissioner.

The Los Angeles Olympics radically reversed the pattern of escalating expenditures and debts for Olympic hosts. The LAOOC budget was $513 million, which was approximately 6% of the estimated $9 billion budget for the 1980 Moscow Games (Kennedy, 1982). Its main funding sources were the worldwide sale of television broadcast rights, commercial sponsorship fees, ticket revenues, and the sale of Olympic coins. The single biggest source of revenue was $225 million from the ABC television network, which was a substantial increase over the $87 million that NBC had agreed to pay Moscow before the American boycott. In funding its Olympics in this way, the LAOOC departed from the pattern established in 1948 of relying primarily on government subsidies, Olympic lotteries, and donations to fund the Games ("A Sports Fan's Guide," 1983).

In addition to the right it earned to organize and run its Olympics as a private (nonprofit) corporation and the $225 million contract with ABC, the LAOOC and Los Angeles Games set records with the 180 hours of television coverage and the participation of 7,800 athletes from 140 nations. The People's Republic of China sent a team for the first time in 50 years. A record 15 new events were introduced, with 11 for women (Kennedy, 1982; Kirshenbaum, 1984; Pauly, 1984). The unprecedented surplus, which was to be used largely to benefit USOC and amateur sports in Southern California and throughout the rest of the U.S., led to headlines such as "L.A. Olympics Are A Gold Mine For U.S." (Peters, 1984). Of course, because the size of the surplus was unexpected and generated complaints of deception and exploitation, it also led to other headlines such as "The Olympic Surplus: Who Gets the Gold?" ("The Olympic Surplus," 1984) and "A Surplus of Ill Will" (Creamer, 1984).

In breaking up the Los Angeles Olympics into smaller, dispersed competitions to take advantage of existing facilities or venues and save new construction costs, Peter Ueberroth was seen as an "inadvertent Olympic reformer"—returning the Games to a smaller scale—as well as a conscious innovator (Kirshenbaum, 1984). In view of the organizational reforms and innovations and the financial outcome that reflect his management, it is easy to understand why the Los Angeles Games have been seen as Ueberroth's "personal triumph" (Kirshenbaum, 1984). However, no organization as large as the LAOOC or an event of the magnitude of the L.A. Summer Olympics can accurately be viewed as the product of one man. The negotiations between Los Angeles and the IOC created pressures for rationalizing organization and management, private commercial investment, and a reliance on television. These administrative, commercial, and entertainment factors were more fundamental and powerful elements in the organization and success of the 1984 Summer Olympics than the personality and actions of one man, even one so talented and influential as Peter Ueberroth.

Ueberroth and the LAOOC were compelled to seek the capitalist path of organization for their Olympics because the city of Los Angeles and state of California and their citizens had made clear their opposition to government subsidies. Faced with such financial constraints, the LAOOC planned a Spartan Olympics with a modest budget and few frills, and its administrative decisions were guided largely by "bottom-line" financial pressures (Edwards, 1984; Kirshenbaum, 1984).

According to Edwards (1984), the predominant influence of bottom-line questions such as "How much will it cost?" and "How much will it produce?" made the 1984 Los Angeles Olympics "the most commercialized . . . in history" (p. iii). In his view, everything that could have been sold was sold to generate revenue or secure facilities and services.

Despite its free enterprise format and complaints about rampant pro-fiteering, the Los Angeles Olympics could be seen as less commercial-ized than the 1980 Lake Placid Winter Olympics. The Los Angeles Games were less commercialized in the sense that the number of commercial sponsors and their use of their Olympic support for their own commer-cial purposes were substantially reduced in Los Angeles. With an aver-sion to the "crass commercialism" and "bad economics" of Lake Placid with its 381 sponsors and deficit, Ueberroth restricted the number of spon-sors to a maximum of 35, required each to pay a minimum of $4 million, and tried to capitalize as much as possible on contributions from them such as in-kind services (Eason, 1984; Mahon, 1984). In effect, then, by reducing crass commercialism Ueberroth created a small exclusive club of large corporate sponsors and reduced the opportunities for smaller busi-nesses to take part in or identify officially with the Olympic tradition.

Though arguments might exist about the amount or style of commer-cialization of the Los Angeles Olympics, there is no question that they were the corporate capitalist Olympics. Mayor Tom Bradley said about the role of business in the Los Angeles Games that "private sector con-tributions have made the Olympics possible. We are greatly in debt to the corporate citizens of this country who have stepped forward to finance the games" (quoted in Eason, 1984, p. 53). Thus in 1984, the Olympics had become reliant on the Big Business influence that former IOC Presi-dent Avery Brundage had lamented in 1960 as an "obvious danger to Olympic ideals" (Espy, 1979, p. 73). In 1984, this influence was applauded by organizers of the Games.

Critics (e.g., "Guardian Viewpoint," 1984) have contended that cor-porate sponsors (and American chauvinism) were the big winners of the Los Angeles Summer Olympics. However, questions have been raised about the public relations and monetary return for Olympic investors. Advertisers and sponsors themselves have insisted that their main in-terest was to be the "good corporate citizens" that Mayor Bradley called them, that is, to provide private support of the Olympics when govern-ment support disappeared (Dentzer, 1984b). Despite such public motives, though, doubts exist about whether corporations will support future Olympics to the same extent as they did in 1984, especially if the Games are not on their own soil and sponsorship is as costly as the LAOOC made it (Dentzer, 1984b).

The Influence of Television

Although big business in general played a crucial role in the financial suc-cess of the Capitalist Games, television—as a corporate commercial enterprise and as an entertainment medium—added to its own status as the predominant influence over the Games. Olympic observer John Lucas

(1984) noted that the IOC had received a half billion dollars from world television corporations since 1964 and was moving in the direction of becoming a "prisoner of the networks" (p. 29). The steep escalation of payments to Olympic hosts in recent years already has been noted, and this escalating pattern did not end with Los Angeles. To fill in the picture presented earlier, television broadcast rights for the Lake Placid Winter Games in 1980 cost ABC $15.5 million; the 1980 Moscow Games involved a commitment from NBC of $87 million; broadcast rights for the 1984 Winter Games at Sarajevo cost ABC $91.5 million; rights for the Los Angeles Games cost ABC $225 million; the Calgary Winter Games in 1988 will cost ABC $309 million; and the cost of television rights for Seoul's Summer Games in 1988 are expected to push the spiral further upward, perhaps as high as $750 million to $1 billion (Kirshenbaum, 1984; "Olympic TV Gold," 1984).

Revenue from the sale of television broadcast rights clearly was the key ingredient in the formula for financial success of the 1984 Los Angeles Olympics. However, the expectation by future Olympic organizers and IOC leaders of a continuation of the recent pattern of steeply escalating television payments could place the Olympic movement on a precarious financial footing and make it a very vulnerable prisoner of the networks.

A recent report from the BBDO ad agency indicated that the three major American networks had steadily increased their sport coverage since 1979, while the audience for these programs was declining. Furthermore, television executives were beginning to wonder whether investment in an Olympic Games was worth the financial risks, and they were casting some doubt on whether they would be willing to pay the $750 million to $1 billion that backers of the Seoul Olympics would like to receive (Pauly, 1984).

With an estimated $3 billion Korean investment in the Seoul games likely (Sanoff, 1984), negotiations with the television networks have obviously become very important to the financial success of the Games and the Olympic movement in general. However, the influence of television over the Games is not restricted to financial aspects. Television also exerts control over the character of the Olympics as an event. The pervasive presence and imprint of television in the Olympic arena have made the Olympics an entertainment spectacle, which has stimulated patriotic feelings of viewers for profit and degraded the integrity of Olympism and the athleticism of the Games. At the same time, the television coverage enhances the mystique of the Games that has made them so popular with athletes and fans.

In their analysis of ABC-TV coverage of the Montreal Olympiad, McCollum and McCollum (1980) contended that the aim of this coverage was not to report details of each sporting event but to promote their own programming and cover the events peripheral to the sport activities. Television networks use their programs—including major events such as the Olympics—to draw viewers to commercial messages (Altheide & Snow,

1978). As businesses, television networks earn profits by selling advertising time to other businesses. The amount they can charge their commercial sponsors corresponds to the size of their audience. For example, because ABC had a very large audience for its coverage of the Los Angeles Games, it was able to charge up to $260,000 for some prime time 30-second spots, during which it also promoted its own new shows for the 1984 fall season (Pauly, 1984). Obviously, then, television networks profit most by attracting the largest possible audiences to their programs and ads. Thus, in a sense, programs are "commercials for commercials" (Altheide & Snow, 1978). This orientation, driven by a profit motive, typically leads television networks to be concerned more about ratings than the integrity or quality of what they show.

If the television networks were concerned about promoting the spirit of Olympism, they would pay little attention to the national affiliations and rivalries of the teams and athletes, ignore the unofficial "medal standings" of nations, and ignore the nationalistic displays of flags and anthems during ceremonies for medal winners and to open and close the Games. However, the public tends to see the Olympics as a competition between nations ("Newsweek Poll," 1984). Spectators and athletes have voiced their displeasure about IOC experiments in denationalization at recent Olympic Games (Espy, 1979, p. 196).

In this context, television networks are inclined to emphasize patriotic or chauvinistic themes. For the 1984 Los Angeles Games, ABC officials cautiously advanced the "More U.S. Medals/Higher Ratings Theory" after news of the Soviet boycott threatened to reduce popular interest in the Games (Taaffe, 1984). This theory was that the absence of the Soviet bloc would enhance the success of American athletes in Los Angeles and thereby stimulate a large American television audience.

In fact, ABC's broadcasts were criticized at first by IOC officials for being too pro-American. This criticism was muted when it was learned that American telecasts were tailored for U.S. viewers, while foreign viewers saw different coverage (Sanoff, 1984). However, the deliberate manipulation of coverage for different audiences, which helped produce the large audience that ABC needed, reflected the underlying motivation of ABC to fire patriotic feelings to serve its own ends at the expense of Olympic ideals.

By playing to the chauvinistic feelings of viewers, television coverage merely added to the deeply entrenched tradition of nationalism that has been part of the modern Olympic Games since their inception. In doing so, television helped maintain the Olympics' popular appeal. This fact points out an interesting irony of the Olympic Games: Factors and events that seem to subvert the ideals of Olympism may contribute to the popular appeal of the Games and help perpetuate their mystique as an unparalleled international spectacle. The fact that Baron de Coubertin did not include such a spectacle in his vision of Olympism or the Games seems to have had little bearing on the evolving reality of the Olympic Games or their appeal.

Sports Illustrated writer Frank Deford (1984) captured the essence of what television does with the Olympics when he said, "The problem is that the Olympics are unlike all other sporting events. ABC (or whatever network happens to be involved) doesn't end up covering the Games in the journalistic sense, but edits them to make the best variety show" (p. 20). Thus rather than celebrating sport and the Games in the spirit of Olympism that was invoked by Peter Ueberroth and that recalled the memory of Baron de Coubertin (Kennedy, 1984, p. 86), television coverage has tended to present the Olympics in a way that has exploited the rhetoric of Olympism and has been intended primarily to serve the commercial interests of the network.

Implications for Change

The 1984 Capitalist Olympic Games of Los Angeles were a departure from Olympic tradition and the Olympic Charter. Their architect and manager, Peter Ueberroth, said they would be copied in the future. However, other hosts aspiring to copy the LAOOC model will unlikely be able to generate the resources or IOC backing to run their own Capitalist Games with the same degree of financial or popular success and independence as the Los Angeles Games (Dentzer, 1984b). Furthermore, future bidders from the socialist world will not want to follow the lead of the LAOOC. Nevertheless, the organization of the Los Angeles Olympics by the LAOOC raised important issues and provided important lessons for Olympic planners.

Though they showed the distinctive imprint of one man, Peter Ueberroth, the 1984 Los Angeles Olympic Games relied more on rational business practices, commercial sponsorship, and television revenue and coverage. These prominent organizational features of the Los Angeles Games reflected the unconscious or conscious decision by Olympic organizers and IOC officials to sacrifice Olympism and the preeminent concern for the athlete for the more practical benefits of financial support, organizational viability, and the perpetuation of the popular appeal of the Olympic Games. From economic and administrative perspectives, this approach is quite rational. However, a consequence for Olympic officials of accepting this "goal displacement" and "degradation of Olympism" is that their idealistic rhetoric of Olympism is made to seem more unrealistic or hypocritical.

Criticisms of the anachronistic or precarious nature of the Olympic Games and of unrealistic or hypocritical pronouncements by Olympic officials have made current IOC leaders much more openly receptive to significant reforms than past leaders (see, e.g., Samaranch Interview, 1984). Proposed reforms have included the introduction of open competition that is scaled down and divided among a number of different sites or is situated at a permanent site (see, e.g., Dentzer, 1984a; Edwards, 1981,

1984; Espy, 1979; Lucas, 1984). Another reform would be the construction of a year-round Olympic Center at a permanent site for the Games, which would be a business and profit-making operation for recreational, nonprofessional, and world professional sporting events (Lucas, 1984). Another proposal is the establishment of political forums at Olympic Games to allow the open expression of political views that are inevitably a part of the Olympics (Edwards, 1981). Many of these suggested reforms are meant to bring the formal organization of the Olympic Movement and IOC more in line with the prevailing political and economic realities of international sport and to make the Games more modest, manageable, and affordable.

What may not be readily apparent about these reform proposals is that the implementation of many of them could achieve their desired political, economic, or administrative ends at the expense of a reduction in the intensity and appeal of the Olympics for both athletes and the sport public (Axthelm, 1984a). The appeal of the Games is based mainly on their mystique of being "the Olympics" (Kirshenbaum, 1984). This Olympic mystique stems from the powerful symbolic cultural significance of the Games as a grandiose entertainment spectacle and ceremonious festival (see MacAloon, 1982). Olympic track and field coach Brooks Johnson asserted, "We've gotten hung up on the wrong concept. The Olympics isn't an athletic show, it's a nationalistic extravaganza. Think about it, the most expensive tickets are for the opening and closing ceremonies, not for sports events" (quoted in Johnson, 1984a). In terms of the spirit of Olympism, he was correct, of course. However, if the Olympics were merely an athletic show, they would not have their mystique.

The symbolic significance of the Games rests on the juxtaposition of national anthems and flags with transnational Olympic symbols such as the Olympic flame, rings, anthem, flag, and pageantry (MacAloon, 1982). They are a "symbolic refuge" (Nixon, 1984, chapters 6, 7) that provides both vicarious thrills and temporary escape from everyday pressures for their audience.

A dilemma of reform for Olympic officials is that the Olympic mystique seems to be fueled by lofty Olympic rhetoric about universal participation, pure amateurism, sportsmanship, and international understanding and peace *and* by the contradictory realities of nationalism and commercial promotion. Nationalism is glorified as patriotism by television commentators and politicians, and corporate commercial promotion glorifies the Olympics as a spectacle.

The hold of the Olympic mystique has enabled the modern Games to survive political, economic, and administrative pressures and problems. However, they are less likely to survive in their current form as a major international spectacle if Olympic officials allow too many concessions to reality in rhetoric or in practice. The problem for Olympic officials is that an uncertain connection links the Olympic mystique to the rhetoric of Olympism and the realities of nationalism, commercialism, professionalism, bureaucracy, and entertainment. The continuing challenge for Olympic officials committed to the current stature, size, and cultural significance of the Olympics is to espouse ideals and make practical organizational reforms that preserve the Olympic mystique.

References

Altheide, D.L., & Snow, R.P. (1978). Sports vs. the mass media. *Urban Life, 7,* 189-204.

Auf der Maur, N. (1976). *The billion-dollar game.* Toronto: Lorimer.

Axthelm, P. (1984a, May 21). Should the Games go on? *Newsweek,* pp. 22-24.

Axthelm, P. (1984b, July 30). A manager from Olympus. *Newsweek,* p. 40.

Creamer, R. (1984, November 26). A surplus of ill will. *Sports Illustrated,* p. 21.

Deford, F. (1984, August 20). Olympic scorecard. *Sports Ilustrated,* pp. 15-20.

Dentzer, S. (1984a, July 30). Money and hypocrisy. *Newsweek,* pp. 68-69.

Dentzer, S. (1984b, August 20). What price prestige? *Newsweek,* pp. 28-29.

Eason, H. (1984, March). The unstated message of the 1984 Olympics. *Nation's Business,* p. 53.

Edwards, H. (1981). Crisis in the modern Olympic movement. In J. Segrave & D. Chu (Eds.), *Olympism* (pp. 227-241). Champaign, IL: Human Kinetics.

Edwards, H. (1984). The free enterprise Olympics. *Journal of Sport and Social Issues, 8,* i-iv.

Espy, R. (1979). *The politics of the Olympic games.* Berkeley: University of California Press.

Goodhue, R.M. (1980, October). "Real world politics" and the conduct of sport, the Olympic example: Implications for sports managers. *Arena Review, 4,* 28-37.

Guardian viewpoint: The Olympics' real winners. (1984, August 22). *Guardian,* p. 22.

Johnson, W.O. (1984a, May 21). Is there life after Los Angeles? *Sports Illustrated,* pp. 32-36.

Johnson, W.O. (1984b, December 24). A rich harvest from a sea of trouble. *Sports Illustrated,* pp. 60-84.

Kennedy, R. (1982, November 22). Miser with a Midas touch. *Sports Illustrated*, pp. 82-98.

Kirshenbaum, J. (1984, July 18). The 1984 Olympics. *Sports Illustrated*, pp. 14-18.

Lucas, J. (1984, January). The survival of the Olympic idea. *Journal of Physical Education, Recreation, and Dance*, pp. 29, 32.

MacAloon, J.J. (1982). Double visions: Olympic Games and American culture. *The Kenyon Review*, **4**, 98-112.

Mahon, G. (1984, March 12). Is this any way to run an Olympics? *Barron's*, pp. 6-7, 39.

McCollum, R.H., & McCollum, D.F. (1980). Analysis of ABC-TV coverage of the 21st Olympiad Games, Montreal. *Journal of Sport and Social Issues*, **4**, 25-33.

Miller, G. (1979). *Behind the Olympic rings*. Lynn, MA: Zimman.

Newsweek poll. (1984, May 21). *Newsweek*, p. 24.

Nixon, H.L., II. (1984). *Sport and the American dream*. West Point: Leisure Press.

Olympic movement has grown "stronger" despite boycotts. (1984, August 20). [Interview with H.E. Samaranch]. *U.S. News & World Report*, p. 27.

The Olympic surplus: Who gets the gold? (1984, November 26). *Newsweek*, p. 48.

Olympic TV gold. (1984, February). *USA Today*. (Source: American Broadcasting Company).

Orwell, G. (1959, October 4). Quoted by *New York Times*.

Overend, B. (1979, September). The duel for the '84 Olympics. *Runner's World*, pp. 85-87.

Pauly, D. (1984, August 20). ABC's Olympian payoff. *Newsweek*, pp. 30-31.

Peters, K. (1984, December 20). L.A. Olympics are a gold mine for U.S. *Burlington Free Press*.

Reich, K. (1984, May 21). Doleful days for the Games. *Sports Illustrated*, pp. 16-22.

Samaranch, H.E. (1984, September). Speech to IOC. *Olympic Review*, pp. 597-600.

Sanoff, A.P. (1984, August 20). Los Angeles puts fresh shine on Olympic gold. *U.S. News & World Report*, pp. 25-26.

Sewart, J.J. (1981, September). The rationalization of modern sport: The case of professional football. *Arena Review*, **5**, 45-53.

Simonov, V. (1984, February). The capitalist Olympics. *World Press Review*, p. 52.

A sports fan's guide to the 1984 Olympics. (1983, May 9). [Interview with Peter Ueberroth]. *U.S. News & World Report*, pp. 125-126.

Taaffe, W. (1984, May 21). Shrewd planning should keep ABC in the money. *Sports Illustrated*, p. 21.

Wright, G. (1978). The political economy of the Montreal Olympic Games. *Journal of Sport and Social Issues, 2*, 13-18.

Individuals and Events

Taken both individually and collectively, the 20 celebrations of the modern summer and winter Olympic Games constitute a remarkable historical record. But no less significant are the numerous performances of individual athletes whose successes and failures comprise Olympic history. In fact, their stories may become the most indelibly etched in memory and may most poignantly touch emotions and passions. No doubt the 1984 Los Angeles Olympics will take their place in Olympic history as the first games to be run by a private corporation and the first games to be compromised by a Soviet-led boycott. No doubt they will also be remembered for the return of the mainland Chinese to the Olympic "family." But as monumental as these episodes may be in terms of the economic and political development of the Olympic Movement, and indicative as they may be of the status of international relations, the individual performances of Carl Lewis and Daley Thompson, of Mary Lou Retton and Ecaterina Szabo, of Zola Budd and Mary Decker were no less appealing, dramatic, or profoundly evocative. Nor are these various performances trivial or inconsequential. Rather, they are deeply symbolic. For as anthropologists and social scientists have long realized, individual athletic performances encapsulate the hopes, dreams, experiences, and prejudices of individuals, social groups, and nations. The history of the games may, in the end, be rightly viewed as the stories of individual athletes whose successes have increasingly attracted the attention of a worldwide audience, and whose performances have increasingly provided spectators with a vehicle upon which they can project their expectations and anxieties. As MacAloon (1981) writes,

> From a small public novelty of Belle Epoque, an athletic competition wrapped in a prepotent historical conceit and adorned with verdant social claims, the Games had been transformed in four decades into a crucible of symbolic force into which the world poured its energies, and a stage upon which it played out its hopes and its terrors, every four years. (p. 4)

The symbolic power of individual performances was evident in the Olympics from the very beginning. When the diminutive Greek shepherd, Spiridon Loues, won the 1896 Athens marathon race amid cries of "Elleen! Elleen!," he unleashed the passions of a watching nation. The official report of the 1896 Games describing the scene read:

> The atmosphere resounded on every side with unending cries of victory. Women waved handkerchiefs, the men their hats; little Greek flags, carefully concealed until now, were unfurled; quite beside themselves, the people demanded that the band play the national hymn. (Les Jeux Olympiques, 1896, p. 84)

So great was the symbolic power of Loues's victory that he was showered with gifts, honored by royalty, and acclaimed as a national hero. James Connolly (1908) was even inspired to pen a romantic 19th-century novelette based on the epic tale of Loues's feat. The scene, of course, has been repeated numerous times. In effect, Loues set the stage, and countless other athletes have served to personify the aspirations of a nation. How many Americans did not bask in the reflected glory of a Mark Spitz, or a Joan Benoit, or a Scott Hamilton? How many English did not similarly beam with pride as a result of the exploits of a Torvill and Dean, an Eric Liddell, or a Mary Peters?

Such symbolically rich events are not restricted to gold medal performances or framed solely within a nationalistic context. When the Italian marathoner, Pietro Dorando, staggered across the finish line in the 1908 London marathon only to be disqualified for having been given assistance by a sympathetic official, the appeal of his performance transcended national barriers. In fact, Queen Alexandra of England awarded Dorando a special medal for his heroic effort. Similarly, when a lone African marathoner entered the Munich stadium hours after the Games had officially been closed, or when Gabriela Andersen-Schiess tortuously weaved her way to the conclusion of the 1984 Los Angeles marathon, their courage and resolution transcended racial and gender considerations. In effect, of course, any athlete or team, in any sport, during any Olympiad, embodies the potential to publically display and reaffirm both individual and collective beliefs about moral character, cultural values, and national identity.

As Loy (1981) has argued, extraordinary Olympic athletic performances provide spectators with "identity voyages" through which individuals achieve vicarious identification with relevant role models. Loy maintains that "spectators through the process of identification with the outstanding performances of 'generalized others' can experience a degree of 'vicarious success' which serves to enhance their own 'self-esteem' and sense of 'moral worth' " (p. 277). Focusing on the attributes of moral character, Loy shows how numerous Olympic performances provide public displays of courage, gameness, integrity, gallantry, and composure. Athletes can also embody alternative attributes, and in so doing the Olympic arena provides a setting for the interplay of diverse and often divergent cultural images and values.

Nor are symbolically relevant performances ultimately restricted solely to athletic achievements. As MacAloon (1981) has shown, the history of the Olympic games constitute a forceful combination of the elements of spectacle, festival, drama, games, and ritual. Numerous other individual actions provide spectators with equally apposite "identity voyages," as in the case of the victory stand demonstration by Tommy Smith and John Carlos during the 1968 Mexico City games. The symbolism of their action was well described by Smith himself, who in a taped interview with Howard Cosell stated,

> I wore a black right-hand glove and Carlos wore the left-hand glove of the same pair. My raised right hand stood for the power in black America. Carlos' raised left hand stood for the unity of black America. Together they formed an arch of unity and power. The black scarf around my neck stood for black pride. The black socks with no shoes stood for black poverty in racist America. The totality of our effort was the regaining of black dignity. (quoted in Edwards, 1969, p. 104)

The stories of the athletes themselves constitute the focus of the three readings in this section. In the first two essays, Glenn Begly and E.M. Swift focus on two of the most memorable events in recent Olympic history. In the first of these, Begly relives the now infamous U.S.-U.S.S.R. men's basketball final at the 1972 Munich games. In the second reading, E.M. Swift recounts the story of the U.S. men's ice hockey successes at the 1980 Lake Placid Olympics. On both occasions, the rivalry between the U.S. and the U.S.S.R. took on larger-than-life proportions. Although the final outcome differed in each instance, both indicate how athletic performances serve to operate as political metaphor and as powerful forms of political ritual.

In the final reading, John MacAloon presents a thought-provoking analysis of the power and appeal of the Olympic games in which he acutely demonstrates how individual athletic performances evoke deep cultural themes. Arguing that "in the Olympics, we appropriate living persons and turn them into abstract members of social groups and ideal representations of that which we wish ourselves as a people to be," Mac-Aloon shows that through the process of vicarious sport involvement, individuals address fundamental questions about self and national identity.

References

Connolly, J.B. (1908). An Olympic victor. *Scribner's Magazine*, **44**, 18-31, 205-217, 357-370.

Edwards, H. (1969). *The revolt of the black athlete*. New York: Free Press.

Les Jeux Olympiques. (1896). Athens: Beck.

Loy, J. (1981). An emerging theory of sport spectatorship: Implications for the Olympic Games. In J. Segrave & D. Chu (Eds.), *Olympism* (pp. 262-294). Champaign, IL: Human Kinetics.

MacAloon, J.J. (1981). *This great symbol: Pierre de Coubertin and the origins of the modern Olympic Games*. Chicago: University of Chicago Press.

Suggested Reading

Guttmann, A. (1984). *The games must go on: Avery Brundage and the Olympic movement*. New York: Columbia University Press.

MacAloon, J.J. (1984). Olympic games and the theory of spectacle in modern societies. In J.J. MacAloon (Ed.), *Rite, drama, festival, spectacle* (pp. 241-275). Philadelphia: ISHI.

MacAloon, J.J. (Ed.). (in press). *The 1984 Olympic Games: Anthropological perspectives*. Chicago: University of Chicago Press.

Metheny, E. (1972). Symbolic forms of movement: The Olympic Games. In M.M. Hart (Ed.), *Sport in the socio-cultural process* (pp. 269-276). Dubuque, IA: William C. Brown.

Metheny, E. (1972). Symbolic forms of movement: The feminine image in sport. In M.M. Hart (Ed.), *Sport in the socio-cultural process* (pp. 277-290). Dubuque, IA: William C. Brown.

The speeches of President Avery Brundage, 1952-1968. Lausanne: International Olympic Committee.

16

A Matter of Time: The U.S.A.-U.S.S.R. Basketball Game at the 1972 Munich Olympics

Glenn Begly

For the United States, the nadir of the 1972 Olympic Games in Munich was unquestionably the basketball game in which the Americans confronted the Soviet Union for the gold medal. The result of that game, according to official Olympic records, was 51-50 in favor of the team from the Soviet Union. But the final 3 seconds, or 1 second, or 6 seconds—depending on the source consulted—provoked the most heated dispute of the entire 1972 Games. Moreover, this single event symbolized two principal issues of the 1972 Munich Olympics: the political implication of the games for nations of the Eastern and Western blocs and a dramatic depreciation in American athletic performance in Olympic competition.

Taken in its largest sense, the United States-Soviet Union basketball game was representative of the pervasiveness of Cold War politics in the modern Olympics. As Espy (1981) observes, with the entrance of the Soviet Union into the Olympics in 1952, the political conflict between East and West permeated the athletic arena and intensified over the three Olympic Games prior to Munich. As prominent leaders of Eastern and Western blocs, the Soviet Union and the United States attached particular significance to athletic confrontations with their respective rival ideologies. Athletic relationships between the two superpowers since the end of World War II reflected the general tone of international relations between the United States and Soviet Union: sometimes antagonistic, sometimes more genial, but always rivals. Whatever the ongoing rhetoric about the inherent value of sport and its disassociation from the political sphere, the United States and the Soviet Union overtly used international sport to proselytize their respective societies (Kanin, 1978). Undoubtedly, the increasing prominence of the Olympics in the international media lent the air of a Cold War drama to those events in which competitors from East and West competed directly against one another.

The American efforts at Munich were typified by disarray and confusion. Apart from controversies over biased officiating, the American experience at Munich was one of poor preparation, lack of organization, and disasterous management. The bitter fruits of these labors were major upsets of American performers in wrestling, boxing, and shooting. Especially painful for the United States team were the blunders in swimming and track and field, which had long been strongholds of American Olympic teams. Chief among these errors were the disqualification of ace swimmer Rich Demont over the inadvertent use of a cold remedy and the incredible failure of two of America's brightest track and field stars to appear for their qualifying heat because of confusion on the part of their coach about the starting time. To the American press and public these disasters represented a rising, almost insidious conspiracy against the United States team (Kirschenbaum, 1972b). So, with American athletic prestige at the lowest point, the basketball game with the Soviets took on a heightened importance.

Reaction to the Defeat

In the United States, reaction to the defeat was a mixture of shock, disbelief, and indignation. "No Olympic defeat was as frustrating or humiliating," declared *Time* ("Dampening the Olympic Torch," 1972, p. 58). The game was variously referred to as "the bitterest pill to swallow" (Grimsley, 1972, p. B-3), "the Great Gold Robbery" ("Soviets Upset," 1972, p. 3-1), and the greatest three second violation in the history of the sport" (Markus, 1972, p. 1). The *Denver Post* declared that this single contest

turned ill fortune into disaster for the shell-shocked Americans in these Olympic Games . . . It was the crowning blow in an incredible series of accidents and reversals that have turned these international contests into a harrowing nightmare for the powerful team that has dominated the Olympics for years. ("Soviets Stun," 1972, p. 43)

With funereal finality, Grimsley (1972) proclaimed that "America's heretofore unblemished red, white, and blue basketball face is now a tear-stained red. Period" (p. B-3).

Although the game is now Olympic history, the defeat of the U.S. basketball team has never been accepted in American quarters. Even after 14 years, a number of questions remain: (a) Was the American press accurate in its attribution of responsibility for the loss? (b) Was there any evidence of unfair officiating, as claimed by many American journalists? and (c) Did the loss precipitate any changes in United States Olympic Committee policy on basketball?

Basketball: America's National Sport in the Olympics

In order to fully comprehend the reaction of the American press to the defeat, a number of cogent facts relevant to U.S. competition in Olympic basketball must be reviewed. First and foremost, the United States had thoroughly dominated basketball since the introduction of the sport to the Games in 1936. Not only had the American squad won every gold medal, but a team from the United States had never suffered a single loss in that 36-year span. Nearly every *New York Times* (September 1-11, 1972) article on the 1972 team made some mention of the long winning streak. *The Final Report of the President's Commission on Olympic Sports 1975-1977* observed that "more than anywhere else, the game has effective 'national sport' status" (1977, p. 35). Obviously, a great deal of national pride was at stake in the basketball competition, intensified by a championship contest with a team representing America's most prominent political and ideological rival.

> To be sure, a number of knowledgeable individuals advised caution in prediction of an easy U.S. victory: There was concern about sports Americans usually dominate. Fears were again being raised that the U.S. basketball team, tall but young, might finally lose a game. (Kirschenbaum, 1972a, p. 35)

Henry Iba, coach of the American team, warned that the Russians were not to be taken lightly. John Bach, assistant to Iba, said, "I warned them [United States Olympic Committee] in 1960, 1964, and 1968 that we would have to take our best players in order to continue winning."[1] The general feeling, however, was that a U.S. gold medal was inevitable. Despite the warning statement, *Sports Illustrated* predicted an American gold, and

Time, after the preliminary rounds of the basketball competition, observed that the "U.S. team seemed likely to leave Munich unbeaten" ("Olympic Games," 1972, p. 27). The American players had little doubt that they could beat the Soviets. Doug Collins, whose crucial play was to set the stage for the controversial climax of the game, declared that "Iba will see. So will the Russians and all them others. We'll win it all. Talent always prevails" (Kirkpatrick, 1972, p. 31).

Thus the scenario for "a chaotic finish unparalleled in the sport of basketball" was complete (Amdur, 1972, p. V-1). The United States not only expected to win but, in light of the previous disappointments of the Games, desperately needed to win to recover a portion of its lost pride.

The Game: Chaos and Controversy

Even though the game was started at the late hour of 11:45 p.m. Munich time, in order to appease American television interests, the arena was nevertheless filled well beyond its official capacity. The partisans of each team were clearly evident by their banners, vocal support for their favorites, and dress, which was representative of national colors. The crowd waited impatiently through a preliminary game, then flooded the arena with cheers as the two squads took the floor for the deciding contest.[2]

From the opening tap, the Russians used an effective pattern offense and a rugged defense to control the game. Twice, once in the first half and once in the second, the Soviets held 10-point leads. Rough play was the order of the day; one player from each team was ejected for fighting, and Jim Brewer of the American five was knocked unconscious and had to leave the game. With only minutes to play, the Russians led by 6 points, and it appeared as if the United States team was in serious danger of losing for the first time in nearly 4 decades. Suddenly, behind a strong offensive surge, the Americans cut the Soviet lead to a single point. With the clock showing less than 30 seconds, the Russians carefully protected their slim margin. Then, when the Soviet stall was on the verge of success, Doug Collins of the United States tipped away an errant pass, recovered the ball, and raced for what appeared to be a certain winning goal. However, before he could shoot, Collins was fouled by a Russian defender and crashed heavily to the floor. He was awarded two foul shots. The clock showed 3 seconds.

Collins, although dazed, made both free throws to put the United States ahead for the first time, 50-49. Immediately after the second shot, the Soviets passed the ball inbounds. After 2 seconds, Renate Righetto, the Brazilian referee, halted the contest, indicating an official time-out. One second remained. The Soviet attempt to score when the ball was again put into play was far off the mark. The horn sounded; the jubilant Americans had apparently won the gold.

From behind the scorer's table, Dr. R.W. Jones, president of the International Federation of Amateur Basketball (FIBA), addressed the timer and indicated that 3 seconds remained. The officials restored order, and the Americans reluctantly resumed their position on the floor. The Russians put the ball into play once more, but this time a long inbounds pass was successful, and Alexander Belov scored at the buzzer to give victory to the Soviets.

The ensuing scene was one of utter pandemonium. The floor was crowded with the delirious Russians and their joyful supporters, while Henry Iba and the United States assistant coaches protested heatedly to the officials. A number of the shocked and angry American players wept openly. The American delegation quickly announced that it would file an official protest with the Jury of Appeals. That protest, submitted immediately after the game, contended that "The U.S.A. is protesting the extra three seconds granted because the game according to FIBA rules was over" (Mols, 1972, p. 6).

The reaction of the American press reflected two basic themes, one erroneous and one in accord with the position actually taken by the United States team. The first reaction was characterized by indignation and anger against the Soviets. "Our Russian brothers browbeat the Brazilian referee. . . . They used Russian terror mathematics to stretch one second to a useful six" (Povich, 1972, p. D-1). No evidence shows that the Russians in any way intimidated the official or used coercion to influence the amount of time remaining in the game. Rather, the Soviets merely took advantage of the opportunity provided by the intervention of Dr. Jones. Further, the protest filed by the United States makes no mention of foul play by the Russians. Herb Mols, the manager of the American team, even complimented the Soviets for their play "for 39 minutes and 57 seconds" (Mols, 1972, p. 14).

The more accurate American accounts focused on the events subsequent to the filing of the protest. The main thrust of this reaction was criticism of Dr. Jones for his interference in the game. Jones was castigated as a "dictator" ("Soviets Upset," 1972, p. V-1) and "the man the Americans blamed for the defeat" ("Soviets Stun," 1972, p. 27). The American protest maintained that Jones, in fact, had no right to tamper with either the officials at the table or the referees. However, the contention of the American press that Jones had been responsible for awarding an illegal time-out to the Soviets was totally incorrect. A delay in the game occurred after the inbounds pass following Collins' second foul shot, and the Russian team was able to regroup at that time. The delay was in response to an official time-out ordered by the Brazilian referee because of "members of the Soviet team near the controlling table" (Mols, 1972, p. 5).

The question remains: Was the United States justified in its protest? Clearly, the section of the document that objected to awarding a time-out after the first Soviet inbounds pass encroaches on a matter that was subject solely to the judgment of the officials. As noted above, the Brazilian official indicated that an official time-out was taken because of crowding around the scorer's table. This decision was well within his domain as the first referee.

The actions of Dr. Jones, however, are another matter. After the conclusion of the game, the Brazilian referee, Renato Righetto, refused to sign the score sheet. The other official, a Bulgarian, signed and left the arena quickly. Righetto claimed that he was protesting the addition of the extra 3 seconds. In a sworn statement, he said that the return of the clock to 3 seconds was "irregular" and continued,

> I consider what happened [the additional time] as completely illegal and an infraction to the rules of a basketball game. We [the officials] were unconsciously involved. Mr. Iba and I were doing the same protest. (Mols, 1972, p. 17)

Righetto's testimony was corroborated by that of Hans-J. Tenschert, the official scorekeeper for the game. Tenschert was present at the announcement of the resolution of the protest by the Jury of Appeals. The American team manager and press, upon receiving the news that the protest had been rejected, vented their collective wrath on Ferenc Hepp, the Jury's representative, for the actions of the board. In the midst of this tempest, Tenschert indicated that he, as official spokesman for the individuals assigned to the scorer's table, had a statement that might shed some light on the controversy.

> It has been said that the referee came to the table showing one second. This is true. No one at the table actually said there were three seconds to be played. The signal did not come from the table. . . . The ball [had] been in play two seconds. . . . Mr. Bigot [the timer] did not override the three second signal from Jones, and the referee had no choice but to accept it. (Mols, 1972, p. 18)

The addition of the 3 seconds, then, was completely illegal, according to both FIBA rules and the principal officials. Jones was extremely reluctant to discuss the matter; he even denied giving the signal for 3 more seconds of play, despite the testimony of Tenschert that he approached the table. Lacking concrete evidence, one can only speculate on his motives. Curiously, in a letter dated September 23, 1972, he conceded that "with a real American team, the Russians can be beaten by 20 points," but added, "The time when even a second rate American team could win the gold medal is passed!" (Mols, 1972, p. 16). Did his evaluation of the 1972 American team as "second rate" indicate a resentment against the success of the United States in Olympic basketball? Only Dr. Jones can answer this question.

In the mind of the American press, the result of the appeal was a foregone conclusion. Although the official split of the vote was not released, newspapers indicated a 3 to 2 margin in favor of the Russians. Allegedly, the jurors from Poland, Cuba, and Czechoslovakia favored the Soviets, whereas the jurors from Puerto Rico and Italy were sympathetic to the

American case. Newspaper accounts claimed that the decision was "marked with political overtones" (*San Francisco Chronicle*, 1972, C-1, 27). *The Houston Post* said that the United States was "legislated out of a comeback" by "an apparent ignoring of the rules by a five-man board designed to absolve the protest" ("U.S. Cagers," 1972, D-1). Again, no firm evidence exists to prove that the vote occurred along ideological lines. Moreover, an article in the *Detroit News* offered the interesting possibility that the Soviet victory had the potential to create an international incident (Middlemas, 1972, D-1).

The defeat of the American basketball team prompted a number of changes in the United States Olympic basketball program. First, the size of the United States Olympic Basketball Committee (USOBC) was reduced from 49 members to 10. In its more swollen version, the committee was frequently frustrated by the fact that the Amateur Athletic Union (AAU) controlled 25 of the 49 votes. Thus the AAU maintained effective veto power over any unapproved procedures. The AAU also helped to perpetuate an unwieldy method of player selection based on quotas from the AAU, NCAA, NJCAA, and military factions. Under the revised system, the Committee became obliged only to select the best players available for the squad, regardless of their affiliation. Another change involved training procedures. In the years up to and including the Munich Olympics, the preparation for the Games occurred mainly at various military institutions. The players abhorred this system. John Bach, assistant to Iba and long-time member of the USOBC, indicated that the adverse reaction of the players to the training conditions severely affected the team's ability to prepare for the competition ahead.[1] Finally, the USOBC selected a new coach, Dean Smith of the University of North Carolina, for the 1976 Olympics. Iba had already retired, but the selection of Smith represented a change in coaching philosophy. Whereas the teams of the Iba era emphasized careful, deliberate offensive play and a conservative defense, the 1976 team was notable for a pressing, offensive style of play. This mode of play was vastly more suited to the background of the players than that advocated by Iba.

In the final analysis, the bitterness and disappointment that resulted from the defeat of the United States basketball team in Munich can never be erased. Simply put, the Soviets are the official winners of the gold medal for basketball in the 1972 Olympic Games, and no amount of evidence that the American team was treated unjustly can alter that result. If anything, the loss prompted significant positive changes in the American Olympic basketball program. The 1976 team, using new methods of training and player selection, went to Montreal aiming not only to regain the gold medal, but to obtain revenge for the 1972 loss as well. The Montreal Games did see the return of the U.S. to supremacy in Olympic basketball because the United States men's team defeated Yugoslavia for the gold medal. Ironically, however, the long-awaited rematch with the Russians never occurred because the Soviet team was defeated in the semifinal round of play.

Notes

1. Interview with John Bach, 1972 Olympic assistant men's basketball coach. The Pennsylvania State University, November 8, 1976.
2. Author's observation of the U.S.-U.S.S.R. gold medal basketball game. Munich, West Germany, September 8, 1972.

References

Amdur, N. (1972, September 10). Soviet quintet wins, 51-50, ending U.S. supremacy. *The New York Times*, Sec. V, pp. 1, 3.

Basketball appeal denied. (1972, September 11). *San Francisco Chronicle*, Sec. C, pp. 1, 27.

Dampening the Olympic torch. (1972, September 25). *Time*, pp. 58-60.

Espy, R. (1981). *The politics of the Olympic Games*. Berkeley: University of California Press.

The Final Report of the President's Commission on Olympic Sports 1975-1977. (1977). Washington, DC: U.S. Government Printing Office.

Grimsley, W. (1972, September 12). Talk of the times. *Kansas City Star*, p. B-3.

Kanin, D. (1978). Superpower sport and cold war detente. In B. Lowe, D. Kanin, & A. Strenk (Eds.), *Sport and international relations* (pp. 249-263). Champaign, IL: Stipes.

Kirkpatrick, C. (1972, July 3). Babes who are going a-gunning. *Sports Illustrated*, pp. 30-31.

Kirschenbaum, J. (1972a, August 28). Buzz before the curtain. *Sports Illustrated*, pp. 30-37.

Kirschenbaum, J. (1972b, September 18). A sanctuary violated. *Sports Illustrated*, pp. 20-27.

Markus, R. (1972, September 10). Cagers lose by 1—protest. *Chicago Tribune*, p. 4-1.

Middlemas, L. (1972, September 1). We wuz robbed. *Detroit News*, p. D-1.

Mols, H. (1972). *Three seconds—to be or not to be. A report of the USA vs USSR basketball game at the 1972 Munich Olympics*. Unpublished manuscript prepared for the U.S. Olympic Basketball Committee.

Olympic games. (1972, September 7). *Time*, pp. 37-39.

Povich, S. (1972, September 11). Olympic ideal big loser at Munich. *Washington Post*, p. D-1.

Soviets stun U.S. basketball team. (1972, September 10). *Denver Post*, pp. 27, 43.

Soviets upset cagers, 51-50. (1972, September 11). *Los Angeles Times*, Sec. V, p. 1.

U.S. cagers upset. (1972, September 11). *Houston Post*, p. D-1.

17

A Reminder of What We Can Be

E.M. Swift

The impact was the thing. One morning they were 19 fuzzy-cheeked college kids and a tall guy with a beard, and the next . . . WE BEAT THE RUSSIANS! In Babbitt, Minnesota, hometown of forward Buzzie Schneider, guys went into their backyards and began firing shotguns toward the heavens. Kaboom! Kaboom! WE BEAT THE RUSSIANS! In Santa Monica a photographer heard the outcome of the game and went into his local grocery store, a mom-and-pop operation run by an elderly immigrant couple. "Guess what?" he said. "Our boys beat the Russians." The old grocer looked at him. "No kidding?" Then he started to cry. "*No kidding?*"

In Winthrop, Massachusetts, 70 people gathered outside the home of Mike Eruzione, who had scored the winning goal and croaked out the national anthem. Not *God Bless America*, which is what the players were singing in Lake Placid. *The Star-Spangled Banner.*

One man was listening to the game in his car, driving through a thunderstorm, with the U.S. clinging to a 4-3 lead. He kept pounding his hands on the steering wheel in excitement. Finally he pulled off the highway and listened as the countdown started . . . 5 . . . 4 . . . 3 . . . 2 . . . 1 . . . WE BEAT THE RUSSIANS! He started to honk his horn. He yelled inside his car. It felt absolutely wonderful. He got out and started to scream in the rain. There were 10 other cars pulled off to the side of the road,

10 other drivers yelling their fool heads off in the rain. They made a huddle, and then they hollered together—WE BEAT THE RUSSIANS! Perfect strangers dancing beside the highway with 18-wheelers zooming by and spraying them with grime.

We. The U.S. Olympic hockey team wasn't a bunch of weird, freaky commando types. They were our boys. Clean-cut kids from small towns, well groomed and good-looking, who loved their folks and liked to drink a little beer. Our boys. Young men molded by a coach who wasn't afraid to preach the values of the good old Protestant work ethic, while ever prepared to stuff a hockey stick down an offending opponent's throat. And don't think that didn't matter, given the political climate at the time—the hostages, Afghanistan, the pending Olympic boycott of the Moscow Games.

But there was more to the story than the moment of victory.

The members of the 1980 U.S. Olympic hockey team weren't named Sportsmen of the Year because of the 60 minutes they played one Friday afternoon in February. The game with the Soviet Union meant nothing to the players politically. Even its impact was largely lost on them until much later, confined as they were to the Olympic Village in Lake Placid, listening to one dinky local radio station and reading no newspapers. ''If people want to think that performance was for our country, that's fine,'' says Mark Pavelich, the small, quiet forward who set up Eruzione's winning goal. ''But the truth of the matter is, it was just a hockey game. There was enough to worry about without worrying about Afghanistan or winning it for the pride and glory of the United States. We wanted to win it for ourselves.''

Not ourselves as in I, me, mine. Ourselves the team. Individually, they were fine, dedicated sportsmen. Some will have excellent pro hockey careers. Others will bust. But collectively, they were a transcendant lot. For 7 months they pushed each other on and pulled each other along, from rung to rung, until for 2 weeks in February they—a bunch of unheralded amateurs—became the best hockey team in the world. The best *team.* The whole was greater than the sum of its parts by a mile. And they were not just a team, they were innovative and exuberant and absolutely unafraid to succeed. They were a perfect reflection of how Americans wanted to perceive themselves. By gum, it's still in us! It was certainly still in *them.*

So for reminding us of some things and for briefly brightening the days of 220 million people, we doff our caps to them, *in toto.*

Leadership, of course, was the key. These guys didn't descend on their skates from a mountaintop preaching teamwork and brotherhood. Are you kidding? They were all stars, *la crème de la crème.* Many had egos yay big and heads the size of pumpkins. Fifteen of the 20 had been drafted by NHL clubs and considered the Games a stepping-stone to the big time. They could showcase their individual talents, prove they could handle a grueling schedule, and, thank-you-bub, where do I sign? Herb Brooks, the coach, made it the most painful stepping-stone of their lives.

"He treated us all the same," says every last member of the team. "Rotten."

Karl Malden, the actor who plays Brooks in the forthcoming ABC-TV movie on the team, *Miracle on Ice*, which will be aired in March, has never met Brooks, but he has studied him on videotape, especially his eyes. "I'd hate to meet him in a dark alley," Malden says. "I think he's a little on the neurotic side. Maybe more than a little. Any moment you think he's going to jump out of his skin."

That's one man's opinion. Malden, that hard-boiled scowler who has no pity in his heart for anyone leaving home without American Express traveler's checks, was brought to tears not once but twice by the sight of goaltender Jim Craig asking, "Where's my father?" after the team had beaten Finland to win the gold medal, first on television, then months later on videotape. Truly, this team plucked many different heartstrings.

Brooks was as sentimental as a stone throughout. After the victory over Finland, he shook hands with two or three people behind the bench then disappeared into the dressing room. Says Malden, "He could have smiled just once, during the game with Norway, or Romania. But he didn't. Then after working 7 months for something, the moment he gets it he walks away from it. You tell me, is that a normal man?"

All right. No. But Malden is wrong about one thing. If you were to meet Brooks in a dark alley, you wouldn't be frightened. He would barely notice you. His mind would be a million miles away. You'd wonder where. He's a driven perfectionist. His wife, Patty, an attractive, bubbly woman, recalls seeing their daughter, Kelly, crawling around and straightening rugs when she was 10 months old. Patty groaned, "Oh, my God, I've got another one!" Brooks is also a brilliant motivator and, like all great coaches, an innovator. He motivates largely through fear. Schneider, who also played under Brooks for 3 years at the University of Minnesota, says, "He pats you on the back but always lets you know he has the knife in the other hand."

Significantly, the pat is on the back, the knife is front and center. Brooks isn't one to sneak around confrontation. "I gave our guys every opportunity to call me an honest son of a bitch," he says now. "Hockey players are going to call you a son of a bitch at times anyway, in emotion. But they could call me an honest one because everything was up front."

They do, and it requires very little emotion. But most—if not all—of the players realize that if Brooks had been any different, they couldn't possibly have accomplished what they did. "It was a lonely year for me," says Brooks. "Very lonely. But it was by design. I never was close to my university players because they were so young. But this team had everything I wanted to be close to, everything I admired: the talent, the psychological makeup, the personality. But I had to stay away. If I couldn't know all, I didn't want to know one, because there wasn't going to be any favoritism."

Players like Phil Verchota, who played for Brooks for 4 years at Minnesota and then all of last year, have still never heard so much as a "Nice day today, eh, Phil?" out of Brooks. "Say hi, and you'll get hi back," Verchota says. "Not even that sometimes." The man scared the daylights out of them. Gave them the willies. He wasn't human. But he could coach, and they never questioned that for a second.

Which isn't to say they never questioned his methods. (His obsession, of course, was a given.) One of the devices Brooks used to select his final team was a psychological test of more than 300 questions that he had specially prepared. He was looking for a certain type of player, and the test was designed to show how certain people would react under stress. He thought he'd try it. There would be 68 players at the August tryout camp in Colorado Springs, and he had to cut them down to 26 in a matter of days. He would leave no stone unturned.

One player—an eventual Olympic hero—said, "Herb, I'm not taking this. I don't believe in that stuff."

"Why's that?" Brooks asked.

"Oh, it's a lot of bull, psychology."

"Well, wait a minute. Here's what it might show. It's not as important as what goes on out on the ice, but it's something we can use. I don't want to miss anything."

"I don't want to take it," the player said.

Brooks nodded. "OK. Fine. You just took it. You told me everything I wanted to know." He was steaming.

"How'd I do?"

"You flunked."

The next day the player took the test.

What kind of competitor was Brooks looking for? Big strong kids who could *skate through a wall*? Guys who could *fly*? Who could *pay the price*? Who could make the puck *tap dance*? Good Lord, spare us. Brooks wanted young, educated kids who were willing to break down stereotypes, were willing to throw old wives' tales about conditioning and tactics out the window. He wanted open-minded people who could skate. "The ignorant people, the self-centered people, the people who don't want to expand their thoughts, they're not going to be the real good athletes," Brooks says. "They're not going to be able to keep that particular moment, that game, that season in the proper perspective. I believe it. Understand this world around you."

When Brooks talks about "ignorant, self-centered people who don't want to expand their thoughts," he's describing 90% of the National Hockey League. For better or worse, most of the players trying out for the Olympic team were hoping to jump from there to the pros. So they wanted to show the NHL scouts that they could do it the NHL way— ugh, me fight, me chop, me muck. That doesn't work in international hockey, and Brooks would have none of it. The players had to learn a new style of play in 7 months. In simplest terms, they had to learn what any touch football player knows by the fifth grade—that crisscross patterns and laterals are more effective than the plunge. They had to learn not to retaliate, which is almost un-American.

All that was easy, because weaving, passing, holding onto the puck is simply a more enjoyable way to play the game. Smashing that stereotype was a cinch. But conditioning? There is no mind in the world that is open enough to enjoy the tortures of Herbies.

Herbies are a relatively common form of windsprint that all hockey players do, but only the Olympians call them by that name. End line to blue line and back, to red line and back, to far blue line and back, all the way down and back. Rest. Two or three sets of Herbies at the end of practice is about as much punishment as most coaches are willing to dish out. The day before a game, it's a rare coach indeed who'll submit his players to even one Herbie, and by the time you reach the NHL, your Herbie days are pretty much over. Hey, we're in the bigs now. We play ourselves into shape.

Bull. In the 1979 Challenge Cup the Soviets skated rings around the NHL All-Stars late in the games. The Russians can do Herbies till the cows come home. They skate as hard in the last shift of a game as they do in the first, and it has nothing to do with emotion or adrenaline. They have always been the best-conditioned hockey players in the world.

Peter Stastny, the Czechoslovakian Olympic star who defected last summer to the NHL's Quebec Nordiques, says the one thing that most shocked the international hockey community about the performance of the young Americans (average age: 22) was their conditioning. The Soviets had always been at one level, with everybody else at a level below. Suddenly here are a bunch of *Americans,* for heaven's sake, whom the Russians are huffing and puffing to keep up with in the third period. Who *are* those guys? In the seven games played in the Olympics, the U.S. team was outscored nine goals to six in the first period, but outscored its opponents 16-3 in the third. What got into them? Steroids?

Herbies.

"It's a selling job," says Brooks. "When you want to push people who are living a good life in an affluent society, you have to do a selling job." The sales pitch went like this: Skate or you're off the team. You're gone. No pro contract. No big money. Gone.

In his own words, Brooks was "smart enough to know I was dumb." How do you get a hockey player in shape the way the Russians were in shape? Nobody knew, not in the hockey world. So Brooks went to coaches of track and swimming—areas in which American athletes have been trained to compete successfully on the international level—and found out about anaerobics, flexibility exercises, underloading, overloading, pulse rates, the works. Then he transferred this information to his players, who, because they were educated, because they were open-minded, were willing to listen. Willing to give it a try. Sure, we'll run up and down that hill to the Holiday Inn after practices. Sure, we'll do another Herbie.

Twenty-five minutes of sprints today without pucks? Sure, we'll do it. And for 6 months they hated Brooks' guts.

There was a moment of truth for this team. A moment when they became one. It was back in September of 1979 when they were playing a game in Norway. It ended in a 4-4 tie, and Brooks, to say the least, was dissatisfied. "We're going to skate some time today," he told them afterward. Then he sent them back onto the ice.

Forward Dave Silk recalls it this way: "There were 30 or 40 people still in the stands. First they thought we were putting on a skating exhibition, and they cheered. After a while they realized the coach was mad at us for not playing hard, and they booed. Then they got bored and left. Then the workers got bored, and they turned off the lights."

Doing Herbies in the dark . . . it's terrifying. But they did them. Schneider happened to have been thrown out of the game, and he had already changed into his street clothes. He was watching in horror as his teammates went up and back, up and back. Again and again and again. But instead of feeling reprieved, he felt guilty. "Should I get my skates on, Patty?" he asked Assistant Coach Craig Patrick. "Cool it, Buzz," Patrick replied.

It ended at last, and Brooks had the players coast slowly around the rink so that the lactic acid could work itself out of their muscles. And that was when forward Mark Johnson broke his stick over the boards. Mark Johnson, who made the team go. Mark Johnson, who was its hardest worker, its smartest player. Mark Johnson, whom Brooks never, *ever* had to yell at. And you know what Brooks said—*screamed*—after skating those kids within an inch of their lives? "If I ever see a kid hit a stick on the boards again, I'll skate you till you *die!*" They believed him. And they would have died, just to spite him. Says Silk, "I can remember times when I was so mad at him I tried to skate so hard I'd collapse, so I could say to him, '*See what you did?*'" But they weren't an all-star team anymore. They were together in this, all for one. And Brooks was the enemy. And don't think he didn't know it. It was a lonely year by design, all right.

"He knew exactly where to quit," says John Harrington, a forward whose place on the team was never secure. "He'd push you right to the limit where you were ready to say, 'I've had it, I'm throwing it in'and then he'd back off."

For Brooks, the trick was knowing where that limit was for every player. They may have been a team, but they were still 20 different personalities. The first time Brooks saw Silk skate at the Colorado Springs training camp, he took him aside and said, "I don't know if you *can't* skate or you *won't* skate, but I intend to find out." Silk had been an All-America at Boston University and had the reputation of playing his best in the biggest games. Brooks wanted him on the Olympic team, but he knew that Silk needed more speed. So he promised to ride him, to embarrass him, to rant and rave at him all season long. And even *then*, Brooks implied, he'd probably be too slow. For 3 months Brooks gave Silk not one single word of encouragement. *Silk, you're too damn slow!* Then one day in practice the team was warming up, skating around the rink, when Silk heard, "Keep at it, your skating's getting better." He looked around and saw Brooks. "He never even looked at me," Silk says. "He kind of whispered it on the way by. It made me feel so good I wanted to skate around and holler."

When Brooks was at Minnesota, he had an unofficial rule against facial hair. He would have liked a clean-shaven Olympic team, too. Trouble was, Ken Morrow, the team's steadiest defenseman, a gentle giant who minded his own business, happened to have a beard already. He'd had one in college, and he rather liked it. And the New York Islanders rather liked Morrow. So rather than risk pushing Morrow too far, rather than risk having the little matter of a beard be the straw that sent Morrow to the big money 6 months ahead of his teammates, Brooks came up with a rule custom-made to keep Morrow around. Anyone who had had a beard before training camp could keep it. It was new growth that was a no-no.

Brooks treated Johnson differently, too. Johnson is a competitor, one of those rare players who find the puck on their stick all night long. He is absolutely dedicated to hockey and was dedicated to the team—a leader by example. Yet, until September, Johnson had no idea where he stood. No one did—Brooks had an ax over everyone's head. But Brooks took Johnson aside shortly after the Skate Till You Die episode and told him, "You're the guy who's going to make or break us. When you're really playing, our whole team gets better."

"It was a real shocker," Johnson recalls. "I was just worried about making the club, and he throws a curve like that at you. What can you say? You take a big gulp and swallow it down."

Craig knew he was the man who would be in goal. He had played brilliantly in the 1979 World Cup championship tournament for Brooks, and by waiting a year to turn professional, he had been all but assured of being the starting goalie for the Olympics. But while the personalities of the rest of the team fit together like a jigsaw puzzle, Craig's cockiness and penchant for yapping kept him apart. He wore on people. For Christmas his teammates gave him a giant jawbreaker, hoping to shut him up. But what the heck, he was the *goalie*, and goalies are kind of ding-y anyway, right? But the psyche of a team is a fragile thing, and when Brooks saw he had a goaltender who wasn't going to fit in, he made sure that he wasn't going to start messing things up. So he told Craig to keep his trap shut about whose fault the goals were, shoulder the blame himself, and buy the beer after the game. Don't muddy the waters. It was funny; Craig and Brooks struck up a friendship during the year. They were voluntary outcasts who worked, played, and thought very much as one.

There was a player on the team who had Brooks' ear—the captain, Eruzione. Brooks had wanted him to be captain practically from the start. He was a leader; he was sensitive; he was a catalyst. But the captain had to be elected by the team. So Brooks campaigned. He confided in Eruzione in front of the other players, assigned him responsibilities, showed him respect. He was even prepared to miscount the ballots, but he didn't have to. The players liked Mike, too. But even Eruzione wasn't spared Brooks' menacing knife. With three games remaining in their exhibition schedule and the first Olympic game less than 2 weeks away, Brooks called Eruzione aside and told him he wasn't playing well. *Uh-huh*. Mike, you're a great captain and a great guy, but you've got to start pulling your oar. *Uh-huh*. Or else I'll have to tell the press you've hurt your back and are coming to Lake Placid as an assistant coach. *SAY WHAT*?

He was going to cut his own captain? After 57 games he was going to say, "Come along and be my assistant—you aren't good enough!" Well, the hell with you. And Eruzione went out and scored five goals in those last three games. Not only that, when word got out that the coach was prepared to cut the *captain*—holy cow, I'd better work my little behind off. And Brooks did the same thing to Craig, telling him it was too bad, but obviously he had worked him too hard, played him in too many games, and now the goalie was fighting the puck and the only thing to do was to get Steve Janaszak, his backup, ready. . . . *SAY WHAT*? You're not giving my job away *now*, not *now*, not after 6 months of this crud. . . . But you're fighting the puck, Jimmy. . . . I'll fight you, you cur. . . . I'll show you who's ready and who's not.

So they went to Lake Placid united as ever against their coach. *They would show him!* Twenty players, the ones who had survived all the cuts, still hungry to prove themselves. Six who had traveled with the team all year were dropped just before Lake Placid. The last forward to go was a young man named Ralph Cox. Brooks himself had been the last forward cut from the gold medal-winning 1960 U.S. hockey team, and the one time all year that his callous front came down was when he cut Cox. "He was such a gentleman that I cried on it," says Brooks. "I had a little flashback of myself at the time. And you know what he told me? True story. He said, 'That's all right, coach, I understand. You guys are going to win the gold medal.' *Ralph Cox* said that. And when we won it, that's who I thought of. Ralph Cox."

At the time, though, Brooks was thinking, "What have you been smoking, Coxy?" The U.S. team was seeded No. 7 in the eight-team field and had the toughest draw in the tournament, facing Sweden and Czechoslovakia—the second and third seeds—in the first two games. Further, in the final exhibition game, the Soviets—almost exactly the same team that had whipped the NHL All-Stars a year earlier—had routed the U.S. 10-3. Welcome to the big time, Yanks. The Americans were hoping for a bronze.

They hoped to get two points in those first two games, one win or two ties. If they didn't, they could pack it in, because there'd be no chance for a medal. The scouting report on Sweden said that technically the Swedes were as good as any team in the world at skating, passing, and shooting, but in tough games their spirit could be broken. But you couldn't let them get a lead on you. Stay close.

In the first period the young, nervous U.S. team stayed close. The Swedes led 1-0, and they had outshot the Americans 16-7, but Craig had kept the U.S. hopes alive with outstanding work in goal. And the Americans had some chances of their own—both Rob McClanahan and Eric Strobel missed breakaways in the first 4 minutes. So now it was behind them, those first-period jitters.

But in the dressing room Brooks was furious. *Insane*. McClanahan had suffered a severe charley horse—McClanahan, who played on the first line with Johnson, who was left wing on the power play, who could *fly*—and one of the trainers told him to get his equipment off and put ice on the bruise, that's all for tonight. A *trainer*, for heaven's sake. And McClanahan *did* it. He was sitting in there in his underwear, an ice pack on his thigh, and the door flew open and there came Brooks, and *was he mad!* "You gutless son of a bitch! Nobody's going belly-up now!"

"Instead of coming in and yelling at us as a team, he picked on Robbie," Johnson recalls. "It was the craziest locker room I've ever been in. He's swearing. Everyone else is swearing. Robbie's swearing and crying. Then Robbie follows him out into the hall and is screaming at him, 'I'll show you!' And in a minute here's the door flying open again and Herbie's coming back yelling, 'It's about time you grew up, you baby. . . .'"

At that point Johnson yelled at Eruzione to get Brooks out of there. Can you beat that? *The star player was yelling at the captain to get the coach out of the locker room.* Finally, Jack O'Callahan, a defenseman who wasn't dressed for the game because of an injury, grabbed Brooks from behind; Brooks and McClanahan were jawbone to jawbone and O'Callahan was afraid they'd start swinging. Meanwhile, the rest of the team was sitting there thinking, "We're one period into the Olympics, down one lousy goal, and the coach loses his marbles."

But had he? McClanahan put his stuff back on, and the U.S. team went onto the ice, outshot the Swedes in the second period, and tied the game 1-1. McClanahan couldn't even sit down between shifts; his leg was too sore to bend. He'd stand there at the end of the bench, as far away from Brooks as he could get, then hop out when it came time to play. *I'll show you!* And he finished the tournament with five goals, tying Johnson and Schneider for tops on the team. Sweden scored early in the third period to take a 2-1 lead, but in the final minute the U.S. pulled Craig from the net and Bill Baker boomed home the tying goal off a centering pass from Mark Pavelich with 27 seconds left. The U.S. had pulled out one of the two points it needed and, what's more, everybody got to know each other a little better. "It was mayhem in here," Schneider said afterward. "But that's what's going to win it for us, emotion and talent put together."

Said Brooks, "Maybe I've been a little too nice to some of these guys." Honestly.

The fanfare didn't really start to build until after the U.S. beat Czechoslovakia 7-3 two nights later. That was the game in which, with little time remaining and the game well in hand, Johnson was injured by a dirty check (no pun) and on TV the nation heard the wrath of Herb Brooks firsthand. His proposal to wed a Koho hockey stick with a certain Czechoslovakian gullet provoked 500 irate letters, but it also piqued the curiosity of the nonhockey-minded public. Hey, this guy's all right! And those players. They're so *young*. Let's keep an eye on these guys—but what's icing?

Norway . . . Romania . . . West Germany, down they went, each game a struggle in the early going, pulled out in the third period when those nameless kids who looked about 15 simply blew the opposition away. And afterward the players would line up at center ice and smile those great big wonderful smiles, many of which actually displayed teeth, and *salute the fans*. They'd hoist their sticks to the fans on one side of the rink; then they'd turn around and hoist them to the other side. It was a terrific routine.

One of the reasons they still *were* nameless was that Brooks had forbidden them to attend the postgame press conferences, enraging both the U.S. Olympic Committee brass and the players' agents. The players themselves were none too keen on the idea, either, though they understood the reasoning. This team wasn't built around stars, and the press conferences were set up to handle only three players. You couldn't have three players getting all the publicity and not believing they were the stars. So no players attended them. Only Brooks. Then when the press accused Brooks of hogging the limelight, *he* refused to attend anymore and sent Craig Patrick in his place. Now everyone was mad at *him*. But without the pressure of the spotlight, the team stayed just as loosey-goosey as a colt on a romp. Hey, this was *fun*! But the Russians were coming.

The day before the U.S.-Soviet game, Brooks held a meeting after practice and told his players that the Russians were ripe; they were lethargic changing lines, their passes had lost their crispness. All season long he had told them that Boris Mikhailov, 13 years the Soviet captain, looked like Stan Laurel. You can't skate against Stan Laurel? The players would roll their eyes: *Here goes Herbie*. . . . But now, 24 hours before the game, they could see it. The Russians *were* ripe. The timing was right. Forget that 10-3 pre-Olympic defeat. That was a lifetime ago. It was, too.

"The Russians were ready to cut their own throats," says Brooks. "But we had to get to the point to be ready to pick up the knife and hand it to them. So the morning of the game I called the team together and told them, 'It's *meant to be*. This is your moment and it's going to happen.' It's kind of corny and I could see them thinking, 'Here goes Herb again. . . .' But I *believed* it."

The idea was to stay close. "It was in the backs of our minds that we might win," recalls Schneider, "but nobody would say it. They'd think you were off your rocker." Craig made some big saves early, but the Russians scored first. Five minutes later Schneider tied it on a 50-foot shot from the left boards. The Soviets took the lead again, but with one second left in the first period Johnson scored to make it 2-2. That was a big goal. When the Russians came out for the second period, Vladislav Tretiak no longer was in goal; he'd been yanked. Vladimir Myshkin was in the nets, the same Myshkin who had shut out the NHL All-Stars in the '79

Challenge Cup. The Soviets got the only goal of the second period and outshot the Americans 12-2.

Brooks told his players to divide the third period into four 5-minute segments. They didn't have to tie the game in the first segment, or even the second. There was lots of time. Stay with them. Make them skate. The first 5 minutes of the third period were scoreless. Then at 8:39 Mark Johnson tied the game 3-3 on a power play. Bedlam. Go, clock, go! "I remember thinking we might actually have a chance to tie," says Pavelich. But the U.S. team had barely had a chance to think of that improbability when Eruzione scored what Harrington calls "one of the great slop goals of all time." The puck was behind the Soviet net, and Harrington and a Soviet defenseman were battling for it. Somehow the puck squirted along the boards to Pavelich, who hammered at it and was promptly smashed face-first into the glass. He never saw the end result. The puck caromed off the boards and slid into the slot, directly to Eruzione, whom Pavelich hadn't seen. Eruzione snapped a wrist shot past Myshkin. There were exactly 10 minutes to go. U.S. 4, U.S.S.R. 3.

That's how it ended. No one remembers much about those final 10 minutes except that they took forever. No one breathed. The shifts were insanely short because, by the players' admission, no one wanted to be on the ice when the Great Red Bear awoke and there was hell to pay. Craig, who had been tying up the puck at every opportunity during the tournament, slowing down the play, now wouldn't touch it. *I don't want it, man, you take it!* He was afraid, and rightly so, that if his teammates lined up for a face-off in their own zone and had time to think about the absurdity of leading the Russians, had time to peer up at the clock and brood about the time remaining, their knees would turn to goo.

But they never panicked. Shoot, this was a ball compared with doing Herbies in the dark. Indeed, if anyone panicked it was the Russians, who started to throw in the puck and chase it—NHL hockey, by gosh—who misfired shots and who, at the end, never pulled their goalie, never gave it that last desperate try that the U.S. had made work against Sweden.

And then it was over. The horn sounded and there was that unforgettable scene of triumph, the rolling and hugging and flinging of sticks. The flags. My God, what a sight. There was the shaking of hands, the staggered, reluctant exit from the ice. But it wasn't until the U.S. players were back in the locker room that the enormity of what they had done hit them. "It was absolutely quiet," recalls Janaszak. "Some guys were crying a little. You got the impression that the game wasn't over, because no one is ever up a goal on the Russians when a game is over. No one believed it."

It was then that somebody started a chorus of *God Bless America*, 20 sweaty guys in hockey uniforms chanting, ". . . from the mountains, to the valleys, na-na-na-na-na, na-na-na. . . !" Nobody knew the words. And where was Brooks? Holed up in the men's room, afraid to come out and ruin their celebration. "I almost started to cry," he says. "It was probably the most emotional moment I'd ever seen. Finally I snuck out into the hall, and the state troopers were all standing there crying. Now where do you go?"

Of course, the tournament wasn't over yet. If the U.S. had lost to the Finns on Sunday, it would have finished in *fourth place*. No medal. Brooks came into the locker room Saturday, took one look at guys signing sticks and pictures, and began throwing things around and telling them, "You aren't good enough for all this attention! You're too damn young! You don't have the talent!" So the eyes rolled and the lips buttoned—but they listened, because what he was saying was obvious to all of them by now. They had come too far to blow it. And on Sunday they won the gold medal by beating an excellent Finnish team 4-2, but they needed three goals in the third period to do it. Really, they weren't even worried. They *knew* they would do it, because if you can outscore the Russians in the third period, two goals to none, you can sure as heck outscore the Finns. They believed absolutely in themselves. And Verchota, McClanahan, and Johnson went out and scored—bing, bing, bing.

They counted down the seconds, slapping their sticks on the boards, screaming to each other, to the refs, to the crowd. Again pandemonium, slightly less frenzied than 2 days before, the handshakes and the gradual retreat from the scene of their triumph. And then a bit of irony. The cameras captured the goalie, Craig, searching the crowd for his father. It brought tears; it made him a hero in the eyes of the country. But, in truth, he was searching for someone to share this moment with. Like Brooks, he was separate, apart from this team. He had no close friendships, and now he needed one.

The final, uplifting moment they gave us was at the gold medal ceremony, when Eruzione called his teammates up on the platform with him. After that they marched around the rink as if they owned the place, singing and carrying on. They were definitely not cooling it; they were happy young men. And they *did* own the place. They owned the whole country for a while. It just made you want to pick up your television set and take it to bed with you. It really made you feel good.

It is over now. Unlike other clubs, Olympic teams self-destruct into 20 different directions and careers afterward—at least in this country. There is never a next year for them. They write their story once.

18

Double Visions: Olympic Games and American Culture

John J. MacAloon

In one way or another, at one time or another, to one degree or another, nearly everyone cares about the Olympics. In scarcely 90 years the Games have grown from a *fin-de-siècle* curiosity into an international culture performance of global proportion. Participants in an Olympic Games—athletes, officials, dignitaries, press, technicians, support personnel; and artists, performers, scientists, and world youth campers attending ancillary events—now number in the tens of thousands and are drawn from as many as 140 nations. Two or three million persons, many journeying from afar, watch the events live, and the broadcast audience is staggering. According to reasonable estimates, 1.5 billion people—approximately one out of every three persons then alive on the earth—watched or listened to part of the proceedings at Montreal in 1976, as 2.0 billion did at Los Angeles. Adding a "guesstimate" of the newspaper

Originally published in *The Kenyon Review*, 1982, 4, 98–112. Copyright 1982 by Kenyon College. Reprinted with permission of the author and *The Kenyon Review*.

audience and of those interested in the Games but prevented by political censure, boycott, or lack of technical facilities from following them, the figure rises toward half the world's population.

The faces of entire cities have been permanently altered by the Games, and their impact on regional and national economies is considerable. Throughout their modern history, the Olympics have variously rejuvenated or destabilized political regimes. The first Games, in Athens in 1896, helped topple two consecutive Greek governments (see MacAloon, 1981, pp. 179-190, 256-261). In 1980, an American president convinced much of his nation that, short of sending a bomb or an army, the most serious political step that could be taken against the Soviet Union was not sending an athletic team to their Games. In 1984, the Soviet leadership risked severe dissension within the Warsaw Pact alliance in order to reciprocate.

Not a few individuals have had their lives taken or saved, their pockets lined or emptied, their happiness insured or stolen from them by the Olympics. For many, many more, the routines of daily life grind to a halt for 2 weeks every 4 years. Weddings are postponed, crops go untended, work is interrupted, and the Olympics crowd most other topics out of conversation. In short, the Games are an institution without parallel in nature and scope in the 20th century. Insofar as there exists, in the Hegelian-Marxian phrase, a "world-historical process," the Olympics have emerged as its privileged expression and celebration.

I mean to say more about how and why so many around the world care so much about the Olympics. But at the risk of sounding like Lewis Carroll's Mad Hatter, I must first assert just the opposite: that against this backdrop, what is striking about the Games is that these same multitudes so readily put them out of mind and concern. Every amateur athlete lives with the question "Who cares about the Olympics anyway?" and these very words were incongruously uttered to me by a high White House official at the height of the feverish Moscow debate in 1980. As for the general American public, the Olympics typically disappear from conversation, newspapers, and public debate within weeks of their closing. In the short term, Los Angeles clearly represents a departure from this usual pattern, for example, in the carryover into presidential electoral politics. ("The Republicans talk about the Olympics, we talk about compassion": so began Mario Cuomo's campaign stump speech.) (see MacAloon, in press). But, in the long run, it is doubtful that the experience of 1984 will much alter that curious American paradox: Nearly everyone cares about the Olympic Games, and hardly anyone cares about them at all. This is a puzzle worth lingering over. As anthropologists know, such paradoxes inevitably signal the presence of deep cultural themes and ambivalences. Nor is it a simple matter of something faulty in American receiving wires, for as Gregory Bateson elegantly demonstrated, it is in the nature of play-forms to precipitate such paradoxes (1972, pp. 177-200).

The Olympics are primarily, though not exclusively, athletic games. They focus on human bodies: bodies dashing, soaring, lifting, tumbling, balancing, gliding, plunging, laughing, grimacing, weeping; bodies exploring and extending the limits—in the words of the Olympic motto—of swiftness, height, and strength. The body is the central fact and means of each of our experiences. A body is something humans everywhere possess. Thus it serves as the central source of metaphors and symbols by which we configure the rest of our psychological, social, and cultural worlds, as innumerable philosophers and social scientists, hard-nosed and soft-hearted ones alike, have pointed out. We are, as we say, a "social body," creating and transmitting a "body of feelings, ideas, and opinions."

Because, even among cultural relativists, no one disputes that humans everywhere possess more or less the same bodies, some have been led to proclaim that disciplines like sport that are composed out of bodily movements offer universal means of communication, universal "languages." The French playwright Jean Giraudoux, after watching the 1924 Paris Olympics, was moved to remark that sport "is the Esperanto of the races" (1928, p. 88). At its broadest level, this assertion is incorrect, as Olympic history itself repeatedly demonstrates. To mention but one example, the finest long-distance runners in the world are the Tarahumara, or Rarámuri, Indians who live in and around the Barranca del Cobre in Chihuahua, Mexico. Rarámuri means "the people who run on foot." In the greatest of their races, Rarámuri men may cover up to 200 miles, running continuously through difficult terrain (and kicking a ball besides). Rarámuri women (propelling a hoop by sticks) have been known to cover 90 miles nonstop and young children 30 or 40 (Kennedy, 1969). Measurement of their exercise physiology suggests the need for an upward revision of estimated human potential, and this in a culture that is by Western standards malnourished (Balke, 1965; Nabakov, 1981). Yet to the great frustration of the Mexican government, every effort to prepare Rarámuri for the Olympics has failed. Away from their canyons, their comrades, and the bracing ministrations of their sorcerers, put on circular tracks or city streets by trainers with stopwatches and asked to compete with total strangers, the "people who run" don't run very well.

Olympic sport is not a language everyone can speak. In semiotic terms, sport is universal on the level of the code, the "phonemic" level, the body. But it is not universal on the "morphemic" or semantic levels, the particular cultural organizations represented by each sport. Though they have folk roots, nearly every Olympic sport issues from large-scale civilizations, primarily those of Europe and America. And even within this tier of social types, there is a certain Babel of tongues. The average American can make just about as much out of judo, team handball, or biathlon as the average Sri Lankan can out of basketball, or the average Kenyan out of gymnastics, ice hockey, or synchronized swimming.

Still, the potential of the body as a code for composing and construing

282   MacAloon

meaning is vast indeed. It has served as a sort of riverbed into which
Olympic-style sport has flowed wherever modern social and political institutions have had an impact. Although not a universal language, Olympic sport is a world language with many dialects, rather in the way that
mathematics and music, Christianity and Buddhism, capitalism and
socialism are "world languages." One third of the world's populations
find something quite meaningful in some regions of Olympic sport and
so assemble around it in the attempt to speak, however haltingly, to one
another.

As for the United States, no nation devotes more of its resources of
money, time, and attention to sport, here under the particular aspects
of school, professional, Olympic, and increasingly adult participatory
sport. We take this set of institutions thoroughly for granted, though it
is barely a century old. In that dram of historical time, sport has colonized
our leisure and industry, our family relations and gender identities, our
media, school architecture and urban planning, our popular art and everyday speech, our national folklore, ritual, and mythology. This fascination, this madness for sport cross-cuts racial, ethnic, religious, political,
class, age group, and lately—thanks to the women's movement—sex
boundaries. Contemplating all this, some have been led to proclaim that
sport is our national church or, phrased more carefully, a central cult in
the American civil religion (Novak, 1976). Perhaps national theater is a
more apt expression, but whatever we choose to call it, it is clear that
should our fanciful colleague the Martian ethnographer ever arrive to observe us, an account of our passion for sport will appear not long after
the chapters on money and sex in his report.

Yet for all of this national preoccupation, most competitive amateur athletes and not a few professionals feel marginal and isolated in the greater
scheme of things. This perception has more to do with certain kinds of
experience than with long hours of training in set-aside spots. It strikes
most acutely at those who are having their most important experiences
in sport. Even today, when every closet has a pair of Nikes or Adidas
and a sportscaster has made it to the presidency in part for endorsing
a quarterback's bill, athletes learn to speak of certain things only among
themselves, if they speak of them at all. It begins with the little leaguer
whose parents fawn on his every play and tell him that his character and
values ride on the issue, then anxiously wring their hands should he suggest that the game is the most important thing in his life. It ends with
the Olympic hero or heroine, expropriated by a nation hungry for heroes,
then cast aside and forgotten.

This is no simple matter of winners and losers. The greatest single feat
in recent Olympic history was performed by a lanky black man from
Brooklyn who, in 1968, broke the world long jump record by 2 feet. When
he saw his distance flashed on the board, he took a single step, his legs
buckled beneath him, and he crumbled to the ground sobbing, "No, no!"
As others pulled him up to celebrate, he is said to have sensed that he
had shattered not just a world record but the delicate mainspring of his

own life. He had leaped quite literally out of his world, and in the subsequent years, as he wandered like a ghost from arena to arena, even
the most parasitical sportswriters avoided him.

Nor is it a simple matter of America's well-known inability to remember Promethean feats by members of her oppressed minorities. The small
handful of Olympic heroes—typically very white, very male, with very
Yankee names—who make good money for a time in the movies or selling cereal on television, eventually feel the lash of what can only be called
revenge, wielded by journalists in the name of the greater culture. No
one should have been surprised at the sudden appearance in the spring
of 1980 of interviews portraying Bruce Jenner, the all-American boy on
the Wheaties box, as an ignorant and jingoistic fool whose life was a bad
joke. One had only to look at the editorial and sports pages of the major
American newspapers that, in their enthusiasm for the Moscow boycott,
seized an occasion to display with impunity their secret malice toward
the same Olympic athletes they would have otherwise been bending over
backwards to celebrate. Through explicit commentary and editorial selection of informants, Olympic athletes were collectively portrayed as naïve,
selfish, petulant, inarticulate children. And this just as the nation was
turning a hockey game into an international political victory, an editorial
cartoonist was substituting the players in that game for the marines in
the famous statue of Iwo Jima, and President Carter was all but knight-
ing them all for doing what he couldn't, delivering a blow of some sort,
any sort, to Soviet national pride. Among the athletic notables of 1984,
in the different context of a feast of patriotism and national self-
importance, Carl Lewis, Mary Decker, Rick Carey, and Bill Johnson have,
for different reasons, already felt the sting. The anthropologist aware of
this cultural pattern would not wish to predict the future fates of others
currently riding high in the popular and commercial imagination, like
Mary Lou Retton, Greg Louganis, or Steve Lundquist.[1]

Athletes as a group are not paragons of insight and virtue or of ignorance and vice. Indeed, 20 years of research in sport psychology and sociology have shown that they are not paragons of anything but are, save
for their physical prowess, distressingly like any other congruent subset
of Americans. The point is rather that we project onto them a polarized
set of stereotypes, noble and admirable on one side, infantile and loutish
on the other. These stereotypes absorb and echo deep themes in our
culture.

All great athletes, as was once said of great mountain climbers, are artists
in the cultivation of grand emotions, not in the verbal expression of them.
This same thing can be said of ballet dancers and symphony conductors,
yet we have no stereotypic epithets like "dumb leotard" or "neander-
thal baton-waver" to parallel the "dumb jock." This revealing bit of symbolism reflects and evokes the deep-seated dualism of our culture, the
separation of the mind or soul from the body that it "inhabits" or, as
we also say, in which it is "imprisoned," awaiting one or another form
of release. "Oh, that this too, too solid flesh would melt." We conceive

the body to be the opponent of our higher mental and moral faculties, the avenue of our lower natures, or uncultured natures. And, of course, we know which bodily part is lowest, most imperious, and mindless: precisely the one supported by the article of clothing we've seized upon to symbolize the presumed brutishness of athletes. (We've been slow to develop a parallel insult for women athletes, so rather incongruously, though not insignificantly, we've been referring to them as "dumb jocks," too.)

Our cultural understanding of the emotions is equally dualistic and ambivalent, not surprisingly since, from our metaphysics to our sciences to our everyday speech, we code them primarily as bodily processes in contrast to mind. As Marcel Proust once remarked, "We feel in one world, we think, we give names in another. Between the two we can establish a correspondence, but we cannot overcome the interval." Olympic athletes catch Americans up into preoccupation with bodies and with emotions. We cultivate and celebrate this, but the more we are captivated, the more thoroughly we must turn away, lest something in our cultural system breaks down.

The Games are also games. Whether we pride ourselves on it or not, we are a fiercely pragmatic people given, as certain economists like to say, to maximizing our individual interests. American games, and particularly Olympic Games, lie at the center of a nexus of contending interests. Yet, for all that, they remain games, in which persons devote themselves thoroughly to what has been called "the conquest of the useless." Despite the fantastic (some would say "obscene") profits from Los Angeles and the growing number of Olympic-eligible athletes, agents, and entrepreneurs making a living in sport, the Games are still much more a playing with images of money, status, and power than they are a rational means of acquiring these. As Dostoevsky wrote about his own gambling obsession, "Though God knows I need it, I swear that it is not for the money that I play," so we know about our Olympic obsession. The Games offer us a brief release from our world of getting and spending, but in order to keep the utilitarian aspect of our cultural self-image intact, we defensively insist in our newspapers and conversation that the Olympics "are all commerce and politics anyway." If this were so, then surely we would include them categorically among the most serious of things, but we cannot bring ourselves to do this either. We recoil in the opposite direction and insist that they are, after all, "mere games," "mere entertainment."

Here is more revealing language. Not only do we devote extraordinary resources to games per se, we have appropriated "game" as a root metaphor for describing everything we think most serious in life: "the political game," "the game of love," "business gamesmanship," "the academic game." We refer to everyday social interaction as "games people play," and we know that those masters of ultimate action, our Pentagon generals, spend a good deal of their time playing "war games." Even our theologians, at least a little *outré* band of them, have gotten into what one of them calls "the game game," by insisting that Einstein was wrong, that God does play dice with the universe, and that salvation ought to be a "joyous game" (Miller, 1973). Yet, simultaneously and to an extent perhaps unknown in other cultures, we speak deridingly of "mere games," of "just playing around": "Are you being straight with me or just playing games?" "Is this real or just a game?" In highly dramatic fashion, the Olympics ignite and fuel this deep cultural problematic.

I have spoken thus far only of the athletic games of the Olympics, but clearly much more than sport is involved in their attraction of so much attention. The quality of competition may be equally good in world championships, but even the soccer World Cup does not draw as the Olympics do. Neither, in the United States, does the Super Bowl or the World Series, and many who care nothing for sport and would never tune in to such events watch the Olympics.

Olympic sport events are encased in a set of rituals surrounded by a huge festival and take on the magnitude of a spectacle. Game, rite, festival, and spectacle are genres of performance, analogous to literary genres, and are bound together into a complex performance system in the Olympics (MacAloon, 1984). Each of these genres casts a net, or as musicians and admen prefer to say, provides a hook, to draw into the system diverse groups of persons. If I could show an Olympic film, I could demonstrate this experimentally. Some would have their attentions seized by the first images of monumental vistas and massing crowds of spectators and journalists—by the spectacle; some by the street scenes of joy and mirth, by the clowns, sidewalk musicians, and public drinking—by the festival; some by the Opening Ceremonies—the ritual; some by the first sport contests seen—by the games. However one is first hooked, one is then subject to being reeled into the other genres that compose the thing. Because I can't show a film, let me give just two examples of Americans recruited by spectacle into ritual and game.

A young woman who worked for the International Olympic Committee in Switzerland told me:

> I just came to work here because I needed a job. All I knew about the Olympics was that they were "the greatest spectacle in sport," as Jim McKay the TV guy says. . . . When Munich came along, I decided to go over, though I didn't feel terribly excited or anything. I was sitting in the Opening Ceremony and I couldn't believe it. When the torchbearer came into the stadium and the crowd roared, I suddenly began to cry. I remember thinking, "So this is what it's all about!" I don't think I'll ever forget that moment as long as I live.

A businessman from New York City happened to sit next to me in the Montreal stadium. He said he didn't follow sports much and knew nothing about track and field but that he and his wife happened to be passing through on vacation. "We're just tourists," he said, "thought we shouldn't miss this so we could tell our friends back in the city we were here." As the afternoon wore on he began to barrage me with questions about track, the competitors, and the Olympics. When two Americans came in first and second in the 400-meter hurdles, he was ecstatic and during their victory ceremony, visibly moved. His vacation plans were shortly forgotten and his 1-day stay turned into a week. I saw him twice again, once arguing about communism with some French students in the plaza outside the stadium and again at the Closing Ceremonies, which he said "were like being in church" and "choked me up when they took down the [Olympic] flag."

Others who come for sport find themselves drawn in the opposite direction, into ritual and festival, and this includes athletes themselves. The New Zealand champion Peter Snell's experience is fairly typical. At his first Games, he watched the Opening Ceremonies from the stands, having decided only at the last moment to go at all. Four years later, he would have been "extremely reluctant" to miss any of the rites (Snell, 1971, p. 26).

Olympic rituals, like all rites, are sets of evocative symbols organized processually in space and time. Olympic rituals take body symbolism, join it with symbols of determined social categories, and meld the whole into expressions of Olympic ideology that the rituals are designed to render emotionally veridical. In these ritual, sociological, and ideological aspects lie more clues about the Olympic paradox. Let me first give a normative interpretation of the rites, one congruent with the intentions and understandings of Olympic authorities.

Olympic rituals are organized around the classic schema of rites of passage well known to anthropologists (Gennep, 1960; Turner, 1967). The Opening Ceremonies, including the lighting of the sacred flame at ancient Olympia and its relay to the "New Olympia," are rites of separation from "ordinary life" initiating the period of public liminality. In the Opening Ceremonies, the juxtaposition of national symbols and the symbols of the transnational, Olympic, "human" community is stressed. The athletes and officials process into the stadium in national groups marked by distinctive flags, anthems, emblems, and costumes. In the second stage of the rite, the Olympic flag is carried into the stadium and is lifted above all the national flags, the Olympic anthem is played, and the Olympic flame arrives to consecrate the festival. Then the president of the International Olympic Committee invites the chief of state of the host nation to pronounce the formula opening the Games. In each of these ways, the symbols of the Olympic community are positioned hierarchically above those of the nation-states, but without contravening them. The third phase of the rite consists of a visually alluring pageant of music and dance that shifts the mood from the excited expectation and high solemnity of the first phases to the joy that is prescribed to be the dominant mood of the festival.

In the Victory Ceremonies, a third level of identity is brought to the fore, that of the individual iconically symbolized by the athlete's body. In the Victory Ceremonies, the results of the games are confirmed and consecrated. The individual's unique achievement is first honored with the symbolic rewards of the Olympic community, the medals and olive branch cut from the grove of Zeus at Archaia Olympia, presented by a member of the IOC. Then the nations of the victors are honored by the raising of the national flags and the playing of the champion's anthem; and the nations, through their master symbols, honor the victors, presented in their new double identities as native sons and daughters and as initiated representatives of a wider human community.

The Closing Ceremonies are rites of reaggregation with ordinary life. Here the role of the national symbols is altogether reduced. Only the anthems of Greece and of the present and subsequent host nations are heard. The flags and name placards of each country are separated from the athletes and carried into the stadium in alphabetical series by anonymous young women from the host country. Since 1956, the athletes process in an unruly band, not formally segmented by nationality, dress, event, or degree of success. This is offered as a ritual expression of the bonds of friendship and mutual respect transcending barriers of language, ethnicity, class, and ideology that the athletes are said to have achieved during the festival. At the same time, it is a symbolic expression of the "humankindness" believed to be necessary to all men and women, a final display and emotional proof that patriotism and individual achievement are not incompatible with true internationalism but are indispensable to it. After the Olympic flame is extinguished and the flag solemnly carried from the stadium, the barriers between athletes, spectators, and officials are broken down and thousands may remain exulting together on the field far into the night.

I have called this the "normative" exegesis because it shakes out of official Olympic documents and is broadly confirmed by observation and the testimonies of many athletes and spectators. Much of the mass attention given to the Olympics is laid at the door of these alluring, consistent, and powerful rites, the closest we have been able to come to true world rituals. (Not the least of the failures of the United Nations has been its inability to generate evocative ceremonials.)

But there are other sorts of Olympic ritual experiences in which dissonant exegeses join, conflict, or do both with the normative ones just given. In them lie further clues to the other side of the Olympic puzzle. Take the social categories dramatized in these rites. All of us are individuals, citizens of the nation-state, and at some level at least, bearers of a notion of generic "human-beingness." But Olympic symbology constructs and portrays these identities as abstractions—as it must to draw together so many very different peoples—and much gets left out of formal representation along the way.

There is no place, for example, for representing those subnational group identities of race, ethnicity, or ideology that are, for many, the core of their beings. It is precisely in the name of these that most ritual protests in the Olympics come. The most famous such episode in recent years was the protest of the black American champions Tommie Smith and John Carlos on the victory stand in Mexico City. They carried into the rite a number of symbols to express solidarity with black America and to performatively describe its condition: African beads, buttons reading "Olympic Project for Human Rights" placed over the U.S.A. logo on their uniforms, shoeless feet to represent poverty, and most importantly, black-gloved hands that they raised in defiant clenched fists while bowing their heads in a gesture of bondage at the moment when the American flag went up and "The Star-Spangled Banner" was played. Whatever one cares to think of its politics, this was an act of symbolic genius. They did not destroy the rite, but hot-wired it to their own purposes. Once the anthem has begun, it cannot be stopped, and for 50-odd seconds the audience was imprisoned, forced to read the anthem's message and theirs simultaneously: "Oh, say can you see" . . . 'No, we refuse to look'; "What so proudly we hailed" . . . 'We do not hail racist America and refuse to accept her hailing of us for we know what we will be returning to' . . . and so on. In short, they refused to accept the ritual construction of a national identity and solidarity they found deceitful.

Many examples of the principled intrusion of subnational group identities into the Games could be given, but instead I will pass on to the experience of another American on the Mexico City victory stand, as described to me in an interview. It reflects a generic *opposition* between games and rites, a different kind of struggle over national identity, and a private protest against the replacement of real individuality by the stereotypic construction of the hero.

Dick Fosbury, an Oregonian scarcely known on the American scene and unheard of elsewhere, astounded Olympic audiences not only by winning the high jump, but by doing so with a style never seen before. Instead of frontally rolling over the bar, he flew over it backwards in what is now known as the "Fosbury flop." This had been thought physically impossible and was such an outrage to the aesthetic canons of the sport that Europeans took it as an archetypal expression of the American character: achievement through innovation whatever the cost to dignity and decorum.

After telling me at length about what he felt while jumping—his sense of absolute risk and absolute control, of engagement and distance, and the certain though unspeakable knowledge that he would prevail—Fosbury described his victory ceremony:

> You know I was really high at the time . . . I got really emotional when they started playing the anthem. . . . I didn't cry, but I could have. . . . I started thinking about the people in Oregon . . . some people from my hometown, some people at college, some of my best friends. . . . I could feel the ties and what other people had done just to get me there. . . . This thing really began to kind of overwhelm me . . . a surge, a real shot of just different kinds of emotions, surging in waves through my body.

It was really funny. . . . Before I ever went down there, I felt that we were going as individuals. We happened to be from the United States and we were wearing their uniforms, but it was an individual competition. . . . I wasn't jumping against the Russians, or the Germans, or the Swedes, or whoever, I was jumping against each individual competitor and so I didn't feel an identity with the United States that much. But it was, just when they started playing the national anthem, you know you hear it through different ears then. It was a different tune. It brought an emotional identity that I never felt before. I felt identification with the people back home, but at the same time it brought through patriotic feeling, you know. It . . . you really felt welcome.

Suddenly Fosbury's voice changed and he abruptly changed the subject. When he returned to it some moments later, it was to say startlingly different things.

[While I was jumping] it was an internal and inward concentration, and when I was in the ceremony it was external. . . . Everything comes from the outside, from *them*. You know, I didn't need the victory ceremony at all. No, I didn't need it. I just wanted to be out there jumping. As far as the awards ceremony, that's part of the institution of the Games. It's the ceremonial type deal and I'm not into ceremonies that much.

At that time in my life, I was . . . trying to break away from authority, and that's part of ceremonies in general, that there's an authority. . . . I don't like to be treated as though I'm on a pedestal. I just don't have that strong a personality or a desire to be singled out. And that's what the ceremony does. . . . I don't want to be a model. I don't want to be a hero. . . . In the ceremony, it seems like you're a vessel, like you're the symbol or the hero. You know, you're something other than you.

To "mere bodies," "mere emotions," and "mere games," we must now add "mere symbols" and "mere rituals," for Fosbury was expressing not just personal but widely held American views. We live, as many have argued, in a deritualized society, or rather, one that prefers its ritual experience in bits and pieces. We understand not only ritual authority but the authority of social relations generally as threats to our individual intentions and wills. Our embeddedness in social groups and their claims upon us are things we much prefer to forget, ignore, or even protest. And, to an extent unknown in many other cultures, we contrast symbols and substance, symbols and reality. We speak of "mere words," "mere rhetoric," "mere images," and "mere heroes," though like any human group, we cannot live without such "symbolic vessels."

In the Olympics, we appropriate living persons and turn them into abstract members of social groups and ideal representations of that which we wish ourselves as a people to be. Later they recoil when they feel what has been done to them, and later we recoil too. Perhaps because they are "just athletes," perhaps because we sense that what has been done to them can be done in less pleasant ways to us too, perhaps because we become aware of the conflicting things they and we are asked to represent. Fosbury felt this last experience acutely:

> Being a college student at that time, I was against everything the government was doing as far as Viet Nam and as far as resisting any kind of protest the people were doing legitimately. So I was really against the United States government and so I really was kind of antipatriotic. And then I go to the Olympic Games and they play the anthem and I get this overwhelming feeling and it was pretty confusing. I couldn't believe it was happening. I guess it didn't make any sense to me. Maybe I did feel proud to be an American and proud to be from Oregon and proud to be representing my friends and different people from my hometown, but at the same time I didn't respect the government.

The Olympics drew Smith and Carlos and Fosbury into a deep questioning of the relationship between local, regional, racial, and political solidarities and national patriotism; and between patriotism and nationalism. Years later, these three are still laboring to understand, and there are many like them. Indeed, the Olympics lead multitudes of us, every 4 years, to ask the same sorts of questions. They are not simple ones, but because we have not found ourselves on victory stands, we more readily put them out of our minds when the Games are over.

I have focused my remarks on the United States, but I want to end with the world, where I began. Just as we find core cultural themes and anxieties reflected and refracted in the performances of our Olympic athletes, so do the Japanese, East Germans, Kenyans, Brazilians, and the rest. However, no country watches only its own athletes. We construct and test images of our rivals and of the exotic strangers with whom we are increasingly conscious of sharing a world. If athletics are the peoples' art, then the Olympics are the peoples' ethnography and diplomacy. In this feast of interpretation, this international Rorschach test, we measure who we think we are by who we think the others are and are measured by them in turn.

The topic of Olympic international politics is usually raised in its "epic" forms—the 1936 Berlin Games; the Rhodesian and South African expulsions; the Munich massacre; the 1976 African-, 1980 American-, and 1984 Soviet-led boycotts—but its "lyric" forms are just as significant.

My concluding tale is of the 1976 women's gymnastics and of the three performers who composed its main plot. None of them were American, but Americans followed the event with exceeding interest and constructed their own story line about it, which I summarize from the (largely male) media commentary. Nadia Commeneci won, but Americans made her their heroine of the Games because of what she represented, and represented in contrast to Ludmilla Turischeva who was cast as the heavy, on multiple levels of gender, sexuality, athletic style, nationality, and ideology.

Nadia was a prepubescent girl, at once asexual and cute. Her style was described as "pixie-ish," natural, agile, and exuberant. Her personal politics were unknown, but as a girl she was presumed to be a political innocent, and as a Romanian, a political captive of the Soviets. (Americans typically and foolishly code all adult athletes from Eastern Europe, especially male athletes, as committed members of the "Soviet bloc.")

Ludmilla was the perfect opposite, the perfect symbolic opponent in the American construction of the tale. She was a mature woman of disturbing sexual attractiveness, married, what's more, to Valery Borzov who had beaten us at our own game, the sprints; a marriage that conjured up vague fears of a Soviet superrace. Ludmilla's style, it was said again and again, was that of the classical ballerina (ballet not only joining the low and the high, but eminently Russian). She was described as cultured, strong, and polished, and her personality found to be stern and serious. (To my knowledge no American commentator allowed him- or herself to notice that Ludmilla alone among the women gymnasts fought back tears on the victory stand.) She was not only a Russian and therefore Nadia's "captor" but, even more threatening to many Americans, she was a political woman, a full member of the Soviet Communist Party and promoted by it as the model of Soviet womanhood.

Good dramas always have a liminal, mediating figure, and to Americans, Olga Korbut played the role in this one. Four years earlier, she had been the innocent pixie, but now she was neither girl nor woman, "struggling through puberty," as it was said, "washed out and washed up," an awkward and styleless "rag doll" whose personality had "gone flat." She was a Russian, but with a small r, neither political nor innocent of politics, because of the capital the Soviets had made out of her. In the early stages of the competition, Americans in Montreal ridiculed her and cheered when she failed. But by the end, when it was apparent that Nadia had foiled Ludmilla at every turn, Olga became a tragic figure who drew American pity and kind applause.[2]

This is but one example of a very general process, the construction of texts out of Olympic events to tell ourselves stories about our rivals.[3] In this case, we used cultural conventions of sex to explore our notions about the Soviet Union and our relationships with "her." On the one side, Americans sought, and seek, to discover the human face of state socialism, for if the Soviets are humans like ourselves, then some accommodation might yet be reached. On the other side, Americans wished, and wish, that Soviet strengths turn against them, that their captives revolt, and that their women all turn out to be "Nadias" and "Olgas" and not "Ludmillas."

These are relatively subtle messages; we were cruder about it when "Soviet bloc" athletes, like the East German women swimmers in 1976, competed directly with and dominated our own. In this case, we fell all over ourselves proclaiming them to be machines, robots, drugged automatons, and—anyway—unfeminine. More than poor losing is involved here. We needed, and need, "Soviet bloc" athletes to be these things because machines can be unplugged and drug supplies cut off, and because alternative (and truer) explanations were more frightening. Acknowledging the educational and organizational superiority of their sport system brings the anxious suspicion that they are superior in other domains as well. By 1984, American Olympic sport was more centralized, rich, bureaucratically organized, and imitative of certain East European techniques and procedures. This has made it difficult for popular commentators to maintain the "us/them" contrast associated with the preferred American cultural understanding that "ours" win through force of individual character, "theirs" through an impersonal "system." Though these structural changes were politically driven, we cannot bring ourselves to take at face value what every state-socialist country proclaims as a simple matter of fact: that sport is not just a metaphor for, an occasional symbolic vehicle of politics, but rather that sport *is* politics. Olympic sports are entrancing to be sure. We too devote ourselves to them. But they are, after all, "mere games," "mere symbols," whereas politics is serious business. Or is it? One has to wonder, for we, as much or more than any other people known, speak constantly of "mere politics," "mere political rhetoric," "mere politicians playing political games." And they are beginning to speak this way, too. "Politics in this country," worried Gary Hart in withdrawing his candidacy for president, "is on the verge of becoming another form of athletic competition or sporting match."

Of all our cultural contradictions and confusions, this is surely the most dangerous. The Olympic Games will never solve it for us; indeed, they solve nothing for us. But they force us to take dramatic if brief consciousness of it every 4 years, just as they force us to ask ourselves whether there really is such a thing as America and such a thing as humankind. The Games condense these ultimate questions into neat little dramas of action and character about which we feel compelled, millions of us, to tell stories. But then again, these are "just stories," aren't they?

Notes

1. On American heroes and antiheroes from the 1984 Games, see Bonham (in press), Chalip and Chalip (in press), and MacAloon (1987).

2. Olympic stories are transformational and episodic; one Games provide a sequel to a story created in a previous Games. In 1980, Americans were absent, the Soviets "robbed" Nadia of the all-around

medal, and her coach Bela Karolyi defected. In 1984, the Soviets were absent, Nadia was a celebrated guest, Karolyi's American pupil Retton won the all-around and the Romanians the team title (see Bonham, in press).

3. My approach here follows Clifford Geertz, who has argued that ludic and ritual performances contain stories that people "tell themselves about themselves." As the present example shows, however, peoples also tell stories about themselves by telling stories about other peoples (see Geertz, 1973).

References

Balke, B. (1965). Anthropological and physiological observations on Tarahumara endurance runners. *American Journal of Physical Anthropology*, **23**, 293-301.

Bateson, G. (1972). A theory of play and fantasy. In *Steps to an ecology of mind* (pp. 177-200). New York: Ballantine Books.

Bonham, J. (in press). Gymnastic body, somatic discourse, and aesthetic-change. In J.J. MacAloon (Ed.), *The 1984 Los Angeles Olympic Games: Sociocultural perspectives*.

Chalip, P., & Chalip, L. (in press). The Olympic athlete as hero. In J.J. MacAloon (Ed.), *The 1984 Los Angeles Olympic Games: Sociocultural perspectives*.

Geertz, C. (1973). Deep play: Notes on the Balinese Cockfight. In *The interpretation of cultures*. New York: Basic Books.

Gennep, A. van (1960). *The rites of passage*. Chicago: University of Chicago Press.

Giraudoux, J. (1928). *Maximes sur le sport* [Maxims on sport]. Paris: Grasset.

Kennedy, J.G. (1969). La carrera de bola Tarahumara y su significacion [The Tarahumara kickball race and its meaning]. *America Indigena*, **29**, 17-42.

MacAloon, J.J. (1981). *This great symbol: Pierre de Coubertin and the origin of the modern Olympic Games*. Chicago: University of Chicago Press.

MacAloon, J.J. (1984). Olympic games and the theory of spectacle in modern societies. In J.J. MacAloon (Ed.), *Rite, drama, festival, spectacle* (pp. 241-280). Philadelphia: ISHI.

MacAloon, J.J. (1987). An observer's view of sport sociology. *Sociology of Sport Journal*, **4**(2), 103-115.

MacAloon, J.J. (in press). The political economy of the Los Angeles Games. In J.J. MacAloon (Ed.), *The 1984 Los Angeles Olympic Games: Sociocultural perspectives*.

Miller, D. (1973). *Gods and games.* New York: Harper Torchbooks.

Nabakov, P. (1981). *Indian running.* Santa Barbara, CA: Capra.

Novak, M. (1976). *The joy of sports.* New York: Basic Books.

Snell, P. (1971). Experiences in connection with the Olympics. *Proceedings of the International Olympic Academy,* **10**, 26.

Turner, V.W. (1967). *The forest of symbols.* Ithaca, NY: Cornell University Press.

Issues and Problems

The Olympic movement has been beset with problems since its inception in 1894. In the early years, the IOC's deliberations generally amounted to discussions on the development of an autonomous and stable program, the definition of amateurism, the participation of women, and the selection and protection of Olympic emblems, symbols, and protocol. Within a few decades, the IOC also became enmeshed in a variety of problems that arose as a result of the phenomenal growth of sport and the cultural, economic, and spectatorial magnitude of the games themselves. The Olympics of today reflect the striking dimensions of modern life, and of a sporting world that has undergone revolutionary changes since Coubertin first disclosed his philosophy of Olympism. The IOC's allegiance to its founding principles and practices in the face of a changed world has inevitably drawn the Olympic Movement into the midst of numerous debates and controversies. Of the many issues and problems currently confronting the Olympic Movement, among the most persistent are amateurism, politics, nationalism, commercialism, the participation of women, and the use of drugs.

The question of who should be able to compete in the Olympic Games has been a subject of debate since the 1894 International Congress. To this day it remains one of the most controversial components of the Olympic Movement. Coubertin himself was adamantly opposed to professionalism in sport, arguing rather for "the true theory of amateurism, which declares the uselessness of the professional and desires his disappearance" (1900, p. 809). Although the 1896 and 1900 games included fencing events for professionals, by 1911 the IOC had adopted a resolution that sanctioned professionals and restricted participation to amateurs. In 1925 the IOC resolved that an athlete taking part in the games must not be a professional in any sport, must not have been reinstated as an amateur after knowingly becoming a professional, and must not have received compensation for lost salaries. Furthermore, athletes were required to declare their amateur qualifications by signing an Olympic oath. During subsequent years, the IOC maintained its defense of the amateur code, particularly under the auspices of Avery Brundage, who "preached amateurism like an apostle of a religion and skirmished like a knight of King Arthur defending the Holy Grail" (Miller, 1979, p. 56). However, the uncompromising ways of Brundage gave way to the liberalism of Killanin, and in an attempt to eradicate some of the hypocrisies surrounding the Olympic stance on amateurism, the IOC passed an amendment to the amateur code in 1974. Described by Lucas (1977) as "easily the most liberal piece of legislation ever passed by the International Olympic Committee in its 82 years of existence" (p. 8), the new rule permitted reimbursement for loss of salary, lifted restrictions on the length of time an athlete could spend on training and competing, and permitted IFs, NOCs, governments, and private organizations to assist aspiring Olympians. Since 1974 other innovations have been introduced, including the establishment of trust funds and the introduction of age criteria to determine eligibility. In June, 1985, the IOC ratified a proposal that will permit professional ice hockey, tennis, and soccer players under the age of 23 to compete in the 1988 Olympics.

Like the issue of eligibility, politics has also been a feature of the Olympic Movement from the very beginning. Although Coubertin proclaimed Olympism to be beyond ideology and politics, he organized the Olympics on the basis of the nation-state, and in so doing he created a contradiction that has worked itself out over the last 90 years. As guilty as Coubertin was of manipulating political forces to launch the Olympic Movement, others have been equally guilty in order to sustain it. Consequently, despite acclaimations of political purity, the IOC has behaved in a political manner on numerous occasions. In the case of the recent China issue, the discontinuity between ideal and reality was cogently expressed by New York State Supreme Judge Norman Harvey, who commented,

> The IOC disavows and deplores any actions by anyone that might tend to utilize the games for political purposes. However, the IOC failed to show the same degree of courage when it considered the two Chinas issue. In order to encourage participation of athletes from the People's Republic of China, it bargained away the rights of the athletes from Taiwan. It made the political decision that there is no Republic of China and that the athletes who swear allegiance to the

Republic of China would be placed in a category different from that of all other athletes participating in the games. (quoted in Smith, 1980, p. 55)

Outside forces have also exploited the games for political purposes. Boycotts, demonstrations, protests and walkouts have been a common feature of the games throughout the 20th century. However, at no time was the politicalization of the movement made more evident, particularly to an American public, than during the 1980 U.S.-led boycott of the Moscow games over the Soviet invasion of Afghanistan. The *New York Times* declared, "Taking politics out of the Moscow games is about as feasible as taking alcohol out of vodka" ("The Games Nations Play," 1980, p. A18). The reciprocal Soviet-backed boycott of the 1984 games further indicated that the apolitical sanctity of the Olympic Movement is an ideal that has become badly eroded.

The disjunction between ideal and reality has also expressed itself in the excessive displays of nationalism that have become a marked feature of the games. Although Coubertin believed that "the Olympiads have been reestablished for the rare and solemn glorification of the individual athlete" (quoted in Henry, 1976, p. 8), the increased growth and success of the games have caused the needs of the individual athlete to be subjugated to the dictates of the nation-state. In recent years, no country has better utilized sport for national recognition than East Germany, which has, in the words of reporter William Johnson (1972), created an "environment like a Brave New World breeding factory" (p. 37). Furthermore, the publication of medal tables, unofficial point-scoring systems, the use of national anthems, flags, and parades, and the nationally structured prize ceremonials have all served to undermine Coubertin's ideal of "internationalism." Consequently, although IOC presidents may have declared that the Olympic movement is strictly nonpolitical, and although Rule No. 9 in the *Olympic Charter* states that "The Games are contests between individuals and teams and not between countries" (1984, p. 8), clearly both politics and nationalism are an inherent feature of the games, deeply embedded in the infrastructure of the Olympic movement itself.

Commercialism is another issue which demonstrates the disjunction between ideal and reality. Although the *Olympic Charter* (1984) states that "The Olympic Games are not for profit . . . neither individuals, organizations or nations shall be permitted to profit from them . . . commercially" (p. 68), the reality is that the games have become a commercial bonanza for athletic and business interests alike. Top track and field athletes and skiers make as much as $500,000 a year, and heroism in sport has been parlayed into a sales gimmick that serves to glorify the free enterprise system. The financial success of the games, spearheaded by the sales of television rights, has not only undermined the noncommercial stance of the Olympic Movement but has also undermined the credibility of the IOC's eligibility regulations. The irony is well captured in Nixon's article on the 1984 capitalist Olympics in this volume, in which he notes "factors and events that seem to subvert the ideals of Olympism may contribute to the popular appeal of the Games and help perpetuate their mystique as an unparalleled international spectacle" (p. 246). But the commercialization of the summer Games hardly matches the rush for "white gold" that has transformed the winter Olympics into a commercial extravaganza. The winter Olympics have long been the lifeblood of equipment manufacturers and the tourist industry. In 1968 the French government committed $135 million to the Grenoble Games, and fierce business competition ensued prior to the 1964 Sapporo Games. For, as *Le Monde* ("A Marquet to be Conquered," 1972) recognized, "What is at stake is the conquest of the biggest winter sports market in the world, namely Japan. The sale of no less than 16 million pairs of skis is up for grabs, with all that goes with it" (p. 4).

Unlike the problems of eligibility, politics, nationalism, and commercialism, the issue of women's participation in the Olympics does not, in general, arise in the form of a discrepancy between ideals and reality. It arises more in the form of a century-long struggle against negative social attitudes and institutionalized discrimination. The main obstacles to women's participation in the early games arose both from the accepted custom that women were not suited physically or socially to competitive sport and from Coubertin's Victorian philosophy about women. As a result, no women officially competed in the 1896 Athens Games. Even by the 1920 Antwerp Games women still only competed in three sports: tennis, swimming, and ice skating. The following years were dominated by a power struggle that developed within the International Amateur Athletic Federation over the IOC's refusal to include women's athletics in the Antwerp games. Women's athletics were finally included in the 1928 Amsterdam Games. The struggle for control of women's athletics also had the side effect of launching the highly successful women's Olympics, which were first held in Paris in 1922 and subsequently in Gothenburg (1926), Prague (1930) and London (1934). Since World War II the women's Olympic program has been expanded, and numerous Olympians have emerged to capture the hearts and imagination of a worldwide audience, from Wilma Rudolf in the 1960s to Mary Lou Retton in the 1980s. In 1968 Janice Lee Romary of San Mateo, California became the first woman to carry the flag in the opening ceremonies. In 1977, *The Final Report of the President's Commission on Olympic Sports* recommended the establishment of programs and policies to facilitate the growth of women's sport and to eliminate discriminatory practices. Despite considerable progress, the battle for equality continues, often in the face of powerful cultural traditions, which in many contemporary societies still restrict women's participation in sport.

The final issue treated in this section is the use of drugs in sport, which according to past IOC President, Lord Killanin (1983), "is more insidious than even the greatest commercial and political exploitation" (p. 155). Although the finger has typically been pointed at the East Europeans, particularly the East Germans, for raising biological research to the level of a state institution, in recent years the use of drugs in sport has been tightly woven into the entire panoply of international sport, including American sport. Evidence of drug use in the Olympics emerged in the 1950s, when broken ampules and syringes were found in the changing rooms of speed skaters at the 1952 Oslo Winter Games. During the 1960 Rome Olympics, Danish cyclist Knud Jensen died after taking amphetamines and nicotine acid, and in response, the IOC established its Medical Commission a year later. Routine examinations of athletes began during the 1968 Grenoble and Mexico City games, and by 1976 the Commission had drawn up a list of forbidden substances that were classified into five groups: psychomotor stimulants, sympathomimetic amines, central nervous system stimulants, narcotic analgesics, and anabolic steroids. Since the Commission began its vigil, numerous athletes have been disqualified, struck from the record, or had their medals taken away. More recently, eight members of the U.S. weight lifting team failed precompetition drug tests at the 1983 Pan American Games in Caracas, Venezuela. Despite the increased efforts of the IOC Medical Commission and numerous other national and international medical associations, the situation prevails. "It's like a nuclear arms race," the *New York Times* ("New Drugs, New Problems," 1983) recently reported, "Every time you catch up with one thing, they just invent a new one" (p. C8). Particular concern is currently being voiced over the new and largely untested growth hormones.

These issues variously form the subject of the five essays in this section. In the first reading, Andrew Strenk presents a critical analysis of the eligibility code, arguing that the IOC's stance is both hypocritical and unrealistic, and that the Games should be open to all. Jean Leiper presents a broad historical overview of the controversial issues of politics and nationalism in the Olympics. Leiper also appraises the value of several recommendations that have more recently been advocated as a means to alleviate the politicalization of the games. In the third reading, Richard Gruneau and Hart Cantelon analyze the issue of commercialism, arguing ultimately that the 1984 Olympics represents less of a departure from traditional practices than "a more fully developed expression of the incorporation of sporting practice into the ever-expanding marketplace of international capitalism." They also argue that the Los Angeles Games represent a classic metaphor for the economic crisis of the 1980s and the laissez-faire policies adopted by some western governments, including the U.S. under the presidency of Ronald Reagan.

In order to examine the issue of women's participation in the Olympic movement, Betty Spears uses four women to symbolically represent three distinct eras in the history of the Olympics. These women are Tryphosa during the ancient Greek era, Melpomene during the late 19th century, and both Nadia Comenici and Joan Benoit during the current era. Spears also evaluates the IOC's current position on women's sport. In the final reading, Marjorie Shuer documents the use of the most controversial drug on the IOC's list of prohibited drugs, namely anabolic steroids. Few drugs have received as much attention recently as steroids, particularly in the U.S., for as Johnson (1985) recently noted,

> It is a spreading wildfire that is touching athletics at every level of sport. From NFL stars to iron-pumpers in small town gyms, from high school bench warmers to college All-Americans, thousands of American athletes, both male and female are routinely ingesting or injecting anabolic steroids to increase their strength or improve their all-around sense of athletic and personal self-worth. (p. 40)

References

Coubertin, P. de. (1900). The meeting of the Olympic Games. *North American Review, **170**, 802-812.

The Final Report of the President's Commission on Olympic Sports, 1975-1977. (1977). Washington, DC: U.S. Government Printing Office.

The games nations play. (1980, January 8). *New York Times,* p. A18.

Henry, B. (1976). *An approved history of the Olympic Games.* New York: G.P. Putnam's Sons.

Johnson, W.O. (1972). *All that glitters is not gold: An irreverent look at the Olympic Games.* New York: Putnam's Sons.

Johnson, W.O. (1985). Steroids: A problem of huge dimensions. *Sports Illustrated,* **62**, 38-49.

Killanin, Lord. (1983). *My Olympic Years.* New York: William Morrow.

Lucas, J.A. (1977). Olympic Games crisis—Reform and reaffirmation. *Journal of Health, Physical Education and Recreation,* **77**, 6-10.

A marquet to be conquered. (1972, January 30). *Le Monde,* p. 4.

Miller, G. (1979). *Behind the Olympic rings.* Lynn, MA: H.O. Zimman.

New drugs, new problems. (1983, November 14). *New York Times,* p. C8.

Olympic Charter. (1984). Lausanne: The Committee.

Smith, R. (1980, February 10). Affairs of State. *New York Times,* p. 55.

Suggested Reading

Auf der Maur, N. (1976). *The billion-dollar game: Jean Drapeau and the 1976 Olympics.* Toronto, Ontario: James Lorimer.

Brohm, J.M. (1978). *Sport: A prison of measured time.* London: Inks Links.

Espy, R. (1981). *The politics of the Olympic Games.* Berkeley: University of California Press.

Glader, E. (1978). *Amateurism and athletics.* Cornwall, NY: Leisure Press.

Graham, P., & Ueberhorst, H. (Eds.). (1976). *The modern Olympics.* Cornwall, NY: Leisure Press.

Journal of Sport and Social Issues. (1978). 2(1).

Kanin, D. (1981). *A political history of the Olympic Games.* Boulder, CO: Westview Press.

Simri, U. (1979). *Women at the Olympic Games.* (Monograph Series, No. 7). Netanya, Israel: Wingate Institute for Physical Education and Sport.

19

Amateurism: The Myth and the Reality

Andrew Strenk

By 1986, the situation of the amateur athlete, with the exception of the American collegiate and high school sport scene, had reached a point that could best be described as "The amateur is dead, long live the amateur." On the one hand, a series of decisions by international sport organizations and leaders over the course of the previous 20 years had opened the door significantly to greater participation in international sport events by more of the world's athletes. On the other hand, the concept of amateurism still exerted a strong and lingering influence on the sport community.

In 1971, the International Olympic Committee (IOC) decided to eliminate the term "amateur" from Article 26 of the IOC Charter, and henceforth defined status in terms of eligibility. One year later, in 1972 at the 59th Session of the IOC in Moscow, the IOC approved of the "broken time" concept—financial reimbursement of athletes for the time lost away from a job during attendance at athletic training camps. By 1981, IOC President Juan Antonio Samaranch had completed the shift in emphasis away from defining an amateur by concentrating on defining a professional. By the time that the IOC Congress ended in Baden Baden in 1981, clearly conscience, not income or conduct, would determine status. An amateur was one who determined that he or she was one (Scherer, 1981).

The IOC's decisions in 1971-1972 shifted the burden for defining eligibility to the international sport federations. The individual federations chose a variety of ways to define eligibility but almost universally moved away from the classic concept of the amateur. In so doing, they followed in the footsteps of many national sport federations, which had previously moved away from the classic English definition of amateur. The Eastern European nations had fashioned their own definitions of the "state amateur" in the late 1940s. Many Third World nations had adopted similarly liberal interpretations of the term amateur in the 1960s and 1970s.

In the United States, this shift in attitudes became evident in the early 1980s. In 1981, several top distance runners formed the Association of Road Racing Athletes (ARRA). The ARRA developed a circuit of road races, with Nike openly sponsoring the series and openly awarding prize money. Jordache offered above-the-table prize money at a marathon in Atlantic City in 1981. The Athletics Congress (TAC), the national governing body for track and field in the U.S., adopted the concept of trust funds in 1982, allowing athletes to place their earnings in a fund, and withdraw funds for living expenses as needed. In 1982, TAC approved the payment of prize money in conjunction with the USA/Mobil Grand Prix. The TAC movement into the arena of officially sanctioned prize money brought the international federation for track and field, the International Amateur Athletic Federation (IAAF), along. In 1985, the Mobil Grand Prix went international and became the IAAF/Mobil Grand Prix, with a total of $542,000 in prize money at stake. The IAAF increased the amount to $763,000 for 1986. Winners were not considered to be professionals (Almond, 1981, 1982).

Many of these changes went unobserved by the general public, but the 1984 Olympic Games brought the consequences of these actions to the attention of a larger audience. The result was often confusion. At the 1984 Winter Olympic Games, conflict over the eligibility of various professional athletes was evident in the sports of ice hockey and alpine skiing. In ice hockey, professionals were defined as those athletes who had played in more than 10 games in the National Hockey League. Players on other professional leagues (International League) or on European professional teams were not considered professionals, and were therefore eligible to compete in the Olympic Games. Still, Canadian attorney Alan Eagleston questioned the 1980 status of American players Ken Morrow and Mike Eruzione. The United States challenged, in turn, the status of three 1984 Canadian players who had signed NFL contracts (D. Anderson, 1984). Two double Olympic alpine skiing champions at Lake Placid in 1980, Ingemar Stenmark of Sweden and Hanni Wetzel of Luxembourg, were declared ineligible to compete in 1984 at the Winter Olympic Games in Sarajevo, despite their eligibility for the World Cup and world championships. Other skiers, including most of the top European skiers and the

Americans Phil and Steve Mahre, were earning high five-figure incomes but remained eligible by continuing to filter their monies through federation trust funds (Lochner, 1984).

In tennis, professionals were deemed to be those players who were older than 20, regardless of whether they had ever won prize money. Players who were 20 or younger, regardless of their earnings, were classified as nonprofessionals as far as eligibility for the Olympic Games was concerned. Therefore, Mats Wilander, Jimmy Arias, Andrea Jaeger, and Kathy Rinaldi—all part of the sports "junior riche"—became eligible.

In track and field, Americans Renaldo Nehemiah, the world record holder in the 110-meter hurdles, and Willie Gault, ranked seventh on the all-time list of 110-meter hurdles competitors, were prohibited from competing in the Olympic Games because they had signed contracts to play in the National Football League. Brian Oldfield, the world's best shot-putter, who as a professional athlete had earned less than several dozen amateurs, was also banned. Yet athletes such as Sebastian Coe, Steve Ovett, Edwin Moses, Mary Decker, Carl Lewis, Alberto Salazar, and others earned hundreds of thousands of dollars apiece in 1984 and still retained their eligibility and competed in the Olympic Games in Los Angeles. *Runner's World* reported Lewis's 1984 earnings to be well over $780,000, with Moses earning more than $600,000 (Cart & Harvey, 1984).

In soccer, the Fédération International de Football Association (FIFA) decided in 1959 that players who participated in the 1958 World Cup could not play in the Olympic Games. In 1978, FIFA refined its Olympic eligibility statute to preclude players from European and South American world championship teams. One result was that Canada, playing a team of professionals, eliminated Mexico, which played with nonprofessionals, from the 1984 Olympic soccer tournament. Yet in 1980, Mexico had been disqualified from the Olympic soccer competition because it had played professionals. In 1984, Canada adopted a position that even players in the North American Soccer League were eligible, as long as they had not signed a personal publicity contract (Jones, 1984). The decision by Canada and other nations to play professionals led American soccer officials to alter the official American stance. In March, 1984, the United States Soccer Federation (USSF) fired coach Manfred Schellscheidt, who had selected and trained an all-amateur team, and replaced him with Alkis Panagoulias, who favored using professionals. Thirteen amateurs were replaced by 13 professionals. Four amateurs were retained for the Olympic Games (Ripton, 1985).

In boxing, the U.S. Amateur Boxing Federation (USABF) decided that for 1984, boxers could be supported by sponsors and remain eligible as long as the athlete did not obligate himself to sign a professional contract with the sponsor (Shuster, 1984).

Thus tremendous inroads had been made in opening the Olympic Games to qualified athletes, but the concept of "amateur" had added five victims—Stenmark, Wetzel, Nehemiah, Gault, and Oldfield—to a long list of athletes who had run afoul of this term in the 20th century. While increasingly appearing to be a curious anachronism, nonetheless, amateurism remains a central concept in American ideas about sport. *Webster's New World Dictionary* defines amateur as "a person who engages in some art, science, sport, etc. for the pleasure of it rather than for money; a nonprofessional; specifically, an athlete who is variously forbidden by rule to profit from his athletic activity" (Webster, 1982, p. 42).

The Concept

The IOC's infamous Rule 26, long a standard in the world of sports, defined an amateur in 1960 as "one who participates and always has participated solely for pleasure and for the physical, mental or social benefits he derives therefrom, and to whom participation in sport is nothing more than recreation without material gain of any kind, direct or indirect" (Thayer, 1960, p. 74). Additional clauses noted that athletes who were subsidized by governments, educational institutions, or businesses could not be amateurs, nor could those individuals who received military or civil service posts in return for athletic service. Participation in training camps for more than 2 weeks a year, acceptance of athletic scholarships, or employment as a teacher of sport or physical education or as a coach constituted professionalism as much as the acceptance of money in return for competition, as did profiting commercially from one's athletic fame in the media, press, movies, or theater. Neglect of one's vocation or career for sport, the signature of a professional contract, the use of one's name or picture in advertising, or participation in a competition with professionals also "professionalized" an individual (Thayer, 1960, p. 74).

As a concept, amateurism involves much more than simply a measure of income. The term embraces ideas of fair play, good sportsmanship, honesty, adherence to the technical rules of the sport, a lack of commercialization, a certain ambivalence in relation to victory or defeat, and the acceptance of a code of moral behavior. In short, purity of intent and conduct are of paramount importance in order to be considered an amateur. Avery Brundage (IOC, 1968), IOC President from 1952-1972, remarked,

> Amateur sport is a delicate and fragile thing. Its values are intangible. They come from the delight of physical expression, the broadened outlook, the deepened experience, the self-satisfaction and joy of accomplishment to the participant. It is an enlargement of life but it must be pure and honest, or it is nothing at all. (p. 68)

Brundage was clearly one of the more eloquent defenders of the term in a long line of educators and sport leaders extending back to 1866 (Stump, 1957), when the term made its first appearance in the sport community. As defined over the next 120 years, an amateur is an ethical being. A certain moral conduct is expected from those upon whom the term has been conferred. To identify individuals as amateurs is to reach an ethical judgment about their moral character. If an individual conducts himself, or herself, in a prescribed manner, then the sport community judges that person to be an amateur.

Conversely, should an individual fail to conform to the expected patterns of moral behavior, he or she is judged not to be an amateur and is suspended. While the legal definition, for purposes of eligibility, has shifted markedly over the last 20 years in the sport community, the moral definition has not. The result is the continuing confusion that plagues the sport world in 1986.

"There is a fundamental difference between professional and amateur sports that goes beyond the technical distinction of whether the athlete makes money from his sport," noted Peter Gent (1978), a veteran with 5 years experience as a receiver for the Dallas Cowboys in the National Football League, and author of *North Dallas Forty* and *The Franchise*.

> Professional athletes are first and foremost show business, dealing with illusion and entertainment. The first responsibility of the players is to the audience, not themselves. By committing himself to amateur ideals, the athlete develops socially desirable skills and attitudes. Audience satisfaction is not supposed to be a factor in amateur athletics.

Gent argued that "when success is measured by the individual athlete's personal growth, the value of the experience can be incalculable, teaching traits like discipline, physical coordination, cooperation, self-sacrifice, a sense of community and dedication." Gent's definition of amateurism is in the classic tradition of the concept. "Amateur sports, by emphasizing the thrill of performance, have the potential to build character, enhance self-esteem, and create a nation of healthy, capable, confident, well-adjusted citizens" (p. 7).

The comments of two such different individuals as Avery Brundage and Peter Gent reflect the ethical dimension of the concept of amateurism. Ethical judgments are passed with a definite purpose—usually to develop what observers perceive as a stronger moral character in relation to the existing moral code of a society. Ethical judgments contain an emotive quality. The purpose is to motivate individuals to undertake an action, to continue an action, or to refrain from that action.

In the world of criminal behavior, societies enforce their ethical judgments through capital punishment, imprisonment, fines, and/or rehabilitation. If theft is prohibited, but thieves are sanctioned, the initial purpose inherent in the laws has been undermined. If, in addition, a society continues to give lip service to a belief that is ignored in practice, then hypocrisy often becomes rampant. In the world of sports, the concept of amateurism repeatedly produced numerous cases of greed, dishonesty, cheating, fraud, hypocrisy, exploitation, violations of civil and human rights, suspicion, and manipulation. As a result, the goals of fair play, good sportsmanship, honesty, and cooperation often were lost. In short, efforts to promote amateurism as a philosophy of sport more often encouraged exactly the practices that officials sought to condemn. The monopoly position of sporting bodies encouraged abuses, both intentional and unintentional.

Open-minded observers had long noted the contrast between the ideal and reality. Few voiced it openly until French journalist Andre Chassaignon, an editor for *Mirror des Sports*, challenged IOC President Avery Brundage over the issue in 1959 (Johnson, July 24, 1972, p. 34). In the following years, it became increasingly evident that if amateurs still existed, they were not to be found at the Olympic Games, world championships, world cups, or other international sporting events. In the socialist countries of Eastern Europe, the state subsidized every elite athlete, converting them in practice into *state professionals*, although the term *state amateur* was the designated terminology. In Africa, Asia, and much of Western Europe, governments also supported athletes financially and materially. In the Federal Republic of Germany, a private, nongovernmental foundation, *Sporthilfe*, assumed the same role. In Canada, *Sport Canada* supported athletes. In the U.S.A., outstanding athletes received university scholarships worth tens of thousands of dollars. Commercial sporting goods firms, such as Adidas, Puma, Nike, and others engaged athletes as marketing consultants and added large, under-the-table bonuses and subsidies. The result was that Olympic competitors remained amateurs on paper, but in practice, they were professionals.

An analysis of the forces that fueled this commercialization of sport is beyond the scope of this essay, but they included more widespread competition, more costly equipment and technology, greater political pressures to win, and a variety of other factors that drove the cost of athletic competition skyward.

A review of a variety of the more noted amateurism cases is useful in studying the concept of amateurism, its application, and its consequences. A researcher is hard pressed to find a well-known Olympic champion who was an amateur. Almost every famous American Olympic athlete failed to meet some aspect of the amateur concept and at some time in his or her career lost their amateur standing. The same fate befell athletes from other nations, although to a lesser degree over time.

The Identification of Class

First and foremost, the concept of amateurism was one of class distinction. Gentlemen were amateurs in Great Britain, where the ideals of amateurism first took hold in the mid-19th century. Amateur statutes, written for ostensibly sporting reasons, served to keep the aristocracy's often more robust and physically stronger lower-class rivals off the playing fields and tracks. Manual and menial workers were specifically excluded. Extensive involvement in sporting activities without pay or any visible means of outside financial support gave the impression of substantial financial means, which in turn was considered to enhance one's honor (Veblen, 1979). Play without pay was a mark of status and affluence.

As a result of this philosophy, John B. Kelly, an American rowing champion, was disqualified from the prestigious Henley Regatta in 1920. As a bricklayer, he worked with his hands and thus violated the existing amateur regulations of his day (Arlott, 1973). A similar situation arose in 1936, when the Australian eight-oared shell was disqualified at the Olympic Games because one of the team members was a policeman. In the equestrian sports, amateur status was contingent upon being an officer. Noncommissioned officers were certainly not gentlemen. Therefore, by definition, they were professionals. In 1948, Gehnaell Persson of Sweden was promoted to the rank of officer for the London Olympic Games, thereby becoming an amateur. He won a gold medal, and after the conclusion of the Games, was quietly demoted back to his old rank. When international equestrian federation officials discovered what had happened, Persson was ruled to be a professional and lost his gold medal (Kluge, 1981). In 1932, Bink Hedburg and Rich Daubenspeck, two of the best water polo players in the U.S., were selected for the Olympic water polo team. When it was discovered that they both worked as lifeguards at the Venice Plunge, they were declared to be ineligible and were removed from the Olympic team (Wildman interview, 1984). For sport officials, these cases were very clear-cut—amateurs did not stoop to menial occupations that demeaned the status of a gentleman.

Financial Incentives

While many athletes lost their amateur status due to unfortunate socioeconomic career choices, even more lost their status because they accepted monetary rewards—conduct that was seen as unbecoming of gentlemen. The history of the early years of the Amateur Athletic Union, which came into being in the U.S. in 1880, is replete with numerous and frequent cases of bribery and excessive expense money.

Jim Thorpe.   Large numbers of American athletes lost their amateur standing either as a result of jurisdictional disputes or the promotional efforts of meet organizers. The Jim Thorpe case, however, was the most publicized of its day.

A double Olympic champion in 1912 in Stockholm, Thorpe became one of the first of a long line of Olympic heroes who was disqualified as a professional. The reversal of the IOC's decision some 70 years later did not fully compensate for the decision in 1913 to strip him of his two Olympic gold medals. Thorpe lost his medals because he had played semiprofessional baseball, a non-Olympic sport, for Rocky Mount and Fayetteville, North Carolina, in 1909 and 1910. His salary ranged from $60 to $100 a month. Unlike most of his collegiate fellow teammates, Thorpe had made an honest but unfortunate decision in choosing to play under his own name. The facts that he had never accepted money as a track athlete, that he turned down offers to turn professional, and that he had played baseball long before the Olympic Games appeared as a possibility for him did not sway the minds of either the AAU officials who reported his transgression or the minds of the IOC officials who suspended him. Thorpe's Indian background and lack of familiarity with aristocratic rules were not considered to be mitigating factors. Thorpe had signed a form whereby he had declared that he had never transgressed any amateur rules. His conduct, it was deemed, was unbecoming of a gentleman—he had accepted money for competing in a sport, and then had failed to report the action ("Athlete Thorpe Still Under Fire," 1913; "The Thorpe Case," 1913). His honesty in admitting his decision cost him his medals; other athletes who chose to say nothing retained their status.

Paavo Nurmi.   Another Olympic great who suffered a similar fate was the Finnish Olympic champion Paavo Nurmi, the most successful runner ever in the history of the Olympic Games. Winner of six Olympic gold medals in 1920, 1924, and 1928, and holder of 11 world records in distance running events, Nurmi was "deamateurized" in 1932 by the IAAF and barred from the 1932 Olympic Games in Los Angeles. Nurmi's expense accounts had long been the subject of controversy. Nurmi had accepted the liberal bonuses of meet promoters in the USA and Europe. Promoters, aware of the drawing power of Nurmi's name and the effect of his appearance on their financial statements, competed to offer Nurmi extra money. A series of meets in Germany in 1931 cost Nurmi his status; he was accused of accepting excessive expense money. The amateur code demanded that athletes never ask for money, which Nurmi had done. If money was offered, gentlemen were expected to reject the offers. Nurmi had not. Therefore, he was banned from further competition ("Nurmi's Entry," 1932). Nurmi was not alone in his fate in 1932. Jules Ladoumegue of France, who had broken Nurmi's world record in the 1,500 run, was also banned from the Games for accepting excessive expense money from meet promoters.

Gunder Haegg.   The expense money issue plagued the sport world for many years, despite IOC President Avery Brundage's declaration that "it has been said that Olympic rules handicap those who are not wealthy. This is not true. In fifty years, I have never known one boy too poor to participate in the Olympic Games; in fact, it can be established that 90% of all Olympic medals are won by poor boys" (IOC, 1968, p. 62). What Brundage did not mention was that most of these medalists were sooner or later ruled to be ineligible for accepting money or gifts.

In 1946, the Swedish world record holders and long distance running stars, Gunder Haegg and Arne Andersson, were declared professionals by the Swedish track and field federation. They had accepted some $10,000 in excessive expenses. In addition, seven other track and field athletes were banned from further competition, and another 30 eventually were cleared for insufficient evidence in what was one of the largest scandals to that point in time. Haegg delivered an opinion that many sport experts had argued since the days of Nurmi; namely, that amateur statutes actually hindered the establishment of new world records. Said Haegg, "It would be better if there was no hocus pocus about this professionalism. It is not easy for a poor boy who is a good athlete to refuse to accept large sums of money when they are offered him for just a few minutes of running" ("Haegg Labels Code," 1946, p. 21). Haegg's world record in the mile lasted until Roger Bannister broke it in 1954, and Haegg's 5,000-meter mark lasted until Emil Zatopek broke it in 1954. Veljo Heino, the Finnish world record holder in the 10,000-meter run, fared better than the Swedish runner. He only temporarily lost his amateur status because of expense account violations in 1946 ("Andersson, Haegg Rules Off," 1946).

Wes Santee.   In the 1950s, many Europeans became more relaxed about the interpretation of the amateur codes, but the Americans became much more conscious. Track stars Wes Santee, Parry O'Brien, Jesse Mashburn, and Sim Iness were temporarily suspended from competition for expense fund violations in 1954. O'Brien and Iness were both Olympic champions; Mal Whitfield, one of the stars of the 1948 and 1952 U.S. Olympic teams and a three-time Olympic champion, was eventually cleared of any "unamateurlike conduct," but his name was nonetheless removed from the list of Sullivan Award nominees for the year.

In 1956, the Wes Santee case erupted to refocus attention on expense accounts. Santee, a U.S. Marine and the world's fastest miler, was permanently suspended from competition for again accepting more expense money than allowed by the very stringent amateur codes. An investigation revealed that Santee had received more than $10,000 for running the mile in various meets during 1955. He received $600 at the Millrose Games in New York, $400 at the Fresno Relays in California, $350 at the Los Angeles Coliseum Relays and $400 at the Modesto Relays, in addition to his air transportation costs. At lesser meets, he received $250. A local Los Angeles meet promoter arranged for Wes and his wife to stay at the posh Beverly Hills Hotel during the meet and provided a free rental car and meals at the best local restaurants. The Coliseum Relays sponsor, the Southern California Committee for the Olympic Games, sent Santee an invitation for the 1955 meet along with a fancy wooden place setting. The mayor of Los Angeles personally sent a diploma requesting Santee's participation. Helms Bakeries in Los Angeles sent Santee fruitcakes for Christmas.

All of these violations of the gentleman's code were bad enough in the eyes of officials, but what finally ended Santee's career was the fact that he bargained for more. The Los Angeles promoter offered Santee $800 above and beyond expense money, but Santee asked for an additional $200, because one of the runners entered in the mile had fouled him in an earlier race. In 1956, the Amateur Athletic Union, which administered track and field, allowed $12 per day for living expenses and $3 a day for other expenses. Santee remarked, "If I had to do it over, I would follow the same pattern which others in my field have followed for twenty-five years. I don't feel like I'm a criminal for accepting more money than the rules permit" ("Santee Prepares," 1955, p. 36).

Appearance Fees

The expense money issue did not disappear, despite the best efforts of Avery Brundage, the AAU, and various officials. In 1970, Olympic 400-meter champion Lee Evans, former pole vault world record holder John Pennel, and former decathlon world record holder Russ Hodge were suspended from amateur competition by the AAU for accepting excessive expense money. Eventually reinstated, they suffered from a newspaper interview with meet promoter Hermann Hoffmann, who mentioned that he had paid them $1,000 apiece to ensure their participation (Underwood, 1967). One American competitor who was not named later confided

> Almost every meet here is dirty, if you want to call it that. I get paid at about 70% of the meets in the U.S. indoors and outdoors. I don't ask for anything, but if I'm offered, I accept. If it's $100, I take it. If it's $500, I take it. But I don't ask. (Underwood, 1969, p. 17)

Horst Ruediger Schloeske, a top West German runner of the era, noted, "If an athlete can get money, he should take it. And almost all of the Europeans do. Our top distance runner, Harold Norpoth, is very expert at making expenses." He continued, "He was supposed to be at a couple of meets but didn't show up. That's how they are; if the money isn't right, they don't compete" (Putnam, 1970, p. 48).

Over the years as the time, effort, and expenses increased and performance levels improved, the Western European and North American amateur sport community developed an underground economy to keep athletes competing, while the rules of amateurism ostensibly were preserved. Performance bonuses, special clinics and personal appearances, money laundering through track clubs, double contracting, double and even triple dipping on expenses, multiple airline tickets, and secret contracts with sport equipment and shoe companies funneled increasing sums of money to amateur athletes in Western nations. The creativity involved was at times quite good. One athlete sang songs at a track (Cart & Harvey, May 20, 1984a).

Meet promoters, long anxious to ensure the participation of key athletes, paid appearance money to ensure that an athlete entered a competition. Additional funds ensured that the athlete would not run, jump, or throw at another meet on the same day. Performance bonuses for stadium, meet, national, and world records sweetened the offers. American athletes competing on the European summer circuit might enter meets in Berlin, Cologne, Stuttgart, Mainz, Zurich, Lausanne, Nice, Athens, Milan, Rome, London, Helsinki, Oslo, Stockholm, and Brussels. For each meet, an athlete received an air transportation ticket from his hometown to the meet and back home again. The athlete crossed the Atlantic only twice; he or she would cash in the other tickets and keep the money (Reid, 1979).

By 1976, the prices commanded by athletes for performance fees were reaching $20,000 for a top athlete capable of setting a world record. At the Weltklasse in Zurich in 1976, the meet promoter later reported that every athlete received at least 2,000 francs just to start; total fees reached well over 300,000 francs, or $75,000 (Hartmann, 1976). The amateur situation contributed greatly to the collapse of the first professional track association because athletes could make more money as amateurs than as professionals. "We are naive to think that our athletes aren't already professionals. Our top athletes are making $800-$1,000 a weekend on the indoor circuit," noted Bob Newland, a track promoter and manager of the 1976 U.S. Olympic track team (Florence, January 31, 1978, p. 6).

In 1979, many top track and field stars chose not to compete in the USOC-sponsored National Sports Festival, the Soviet Spartaciade, and other events where the price was not right (Rosenthal, 1979). Olympic team member Steve Smith, a pole vaulter, noted that in 2 years as a professional, he made $61,000, an amount that he termed "chicken feed" in comparison to what the amateurs were earning (Florence, January 31, 1978). In 1981, the French sport newspaper L'Equipe reported that Olympic champion Sebastian Coe's price to compete in Paris was $14,000, while the Daily Mail reported that his price for a meet in Brussels was $18,400. Coe's income for the year 1981 was reported to be over $300,000 ("Morning Briefing," July 15, 1981).

Dwight Stones.   During his 6-year reign as the world's best high jumper, Dwight Stones, a two-time Olympic medalist, estimated that he earned $200,000 (Reid, 1979). At Philadelphia in 1976, Stones earned an extra $500 from a promoter at the last minute by threatening to stop jumping and not break the world record. "I told his little cohort boy that was kind of acting as a liaison . . . I will not even have the bar raised unless he guarantees me $500 for breaking it" ("Stones," May 22, 1979). Stone's strategy was to break the record as often as possible, but in the smallest possible increments. "You had to slice the baloney thin, because you got a bonus each time you broke the record. So why mess up and break it by more than you should?" (Reid, 1979, p. 22).

To the writers of the amateur rules, such conduct was ungentlemanly and unsportsmanlike. Performance shaving was as horrible as accepting money. Stones retorted, "I guess that's what these guys who wrote the rules had in mind—that money corrupts the sport." He continued, "But I don't believe that entirely. If you're bringing people into an arena, you deserve more than just air fare, room and board" (Reid, 1979, p. 22).

Stones nonetheless ran afoul of the amateur regulations, and was suspended from competition in 1978 along with Olympians and American record holders Jane Frederick, Kate Schmidt, and Francie Larrieu. The four competed in the "Superstars" television series. Stones refused to turn his winner's share of $33,400 over to the AAU, and instead gave it to the Desert Oasis Track Club. The AAU rules in 1978 permitted track clubs to accept such funds, but Stones was the only member of the DOTC. Frederick, at the time the leading performer in the world in the pentathlon, won $17,600 and gave it to the Pacific Coast Club, a team only slightly larger than Stones's "team." The AAU delivered an ultimatum—turn over the money or lose amateur status. Frederick noted, "I must professionalize myself and give the money to the AAU. In other words, there's no such thing as an amateur anymore" (Lichtenstein, 1979, p. 39).

The absurdity of amateur regulations paralleled the dishonesty and hypocrisy of athletes as well as the venality and exploitation of officials. In the early 1960s, Olympic champions Harold and Olga Connolly were asked to appear on a television show in Los Angeles. The AAU threatened to remove their amateur status because they would receive $300. When the Connollys answered that they would appear for free, the AAU officials in Los Angeles demanded $300 nevertheless (Assembly Interim Committee, 1965).

While Stones and Frederick were being prosecuted, Frank Shorter, the 1972 marathon Olympic champion and 1976 runner-up, was helping to produce commercials for Hilton Hotels. Shorter was paid for his time, but Hilton also made a $25,000 donation to the AAU while engaging Shorter as a marketing representative ("AAU Gets $25,000," 1979; Good, 1979). Shorter was willing to share the money he earned. Stones was not. That difference became the dividing line between professional and amateur.

Guy Drut.   Often the difference between amateur and professional was the difference between honesty and dishonesty. Believing that a new era of openness was dawning, Guy Drut of France, the 1976 Olympic champion in 110-meter hurdles, admitted to taking under-the-table payments after his victory. The result was the end of his amateur career ("It's a Week of Retirements," 1976). Yet cash payments were rampant in Montreal. Bob Newland remembered, "In Montreal I saw a contract with the terms spelled out. They offered $5,000 if their shoe was worn in the qualifying . . . $5,000 if you wore it in the quarterfinals and $10,000 if you wore it in the finals and won a gold medal" (Florence, January 31, 1978, p. 1).

The Great Shoe Contract War

The expense money issue dated back to the days of Paavo Nurmi, but the shoe contract money dated to 1960 and Olympic 100-meter champion Armin Hary of West Germany. Puma, a West German sport shoe manufacturer, had begun to pay soccer players to switch from rival brand Adidas to Puma. At Rome, Puma representatives convinced Hary to switch to Puma; financial inducements insured brand loyalty. Over the next several years, as more athletes defected to Puma, Adidas found it necessary to respond by instituting monetary payments, too. The result was a full-scale bidding war at the 1968 Olympic Games in Mexico City, where almost every athlete who was a finalist was on the payroll of at least one of the shoe companies. The IOC initially threatened suspensions, but as the dimensions of the ungentlemanly activity became apparent, it became clear that in some events no athletes would be left to award medals to because so many had accepted some money from one of the companies. One American athlete admitted that he had gone from company to company until he received his top price, which was $10,000 (Underwood, 1969). Another American Olympic champion switched from Adidas to Puma just before he won his gold medal and received $6,000 for his last-minute change. He spent the money on a new automobile. He also promised to wear Puma for the rest of his career. He commented, "Why shouldn't I? I never got anything before. Why should I sit around like a hermit when everyone else is making money out of these people. If I can give them publicity, they ought to pay me for it" (Underwood, 1969, p. 20).

In Mexico, a third American athlete negotiated back and forth between Puma and Adidas to see which firm would fly his wife to the Games. Because both firms agreed, Puma finally won by agreeing to fly the wife to Mexico City and then fly both the athlete and his wife to Acapulco after the Games. Other runners were less bold—two Australian athletes accepted $1,000 apiece and then stayed in their rooms for most of the duration of the Games, afraid that they would be caught and asked to explain where they had inherited so much cash. The scandal began to unravel when another American athlete accepted $500 from Adidas, became scared, and notified American officials that he had found $500 in a new pair of shoes. An investigation later determined that only five medalists in track and field did not receive some type of payment. A strict enforcement of Rule 26 of the IOC Charter would have sent the American track and field team home with no medals (Underwood, 1969).

Horst Dassler, chief executive officer of Adidas, commented, "When we could see people, very important medal prospects, who used to wear Adidas, now in the brand name Puma, it was hard to sit back and let this happen. So the bargaining began—you pay the same, we'll stay with Adidas" (Underwood, 1969, p. 21). Perhaps the most telling statement was made by one of the athletes involved. "World class athletes would not be world class athletes without taking money. They would never be able to afford the proper training and diet" (Underwood, 1969, p. 17).

The Endorsement Problem

Karl Schranz.   Officials in track and field were not the only ones searching for a true amateur. Officials in the sport of alpine skiing were similarly preoccupied in the 1960s and 1970s. Hank Kashiwa and Rick Chaffee, two top-ranked American skiers, suffered the penalty for openly signing contracts with ski equipment manufacturers rather than accepting under-the-table cash payments. Both were banned from the 1972 American

Olympic team (Johnson, 1970). The IOC stepped in at Sapporo to disqualify the World Cup champion, Austrian Karl Schranz, for professionalism. Schranz suffered the penalty, not because he was the only skier earning unauthorized money, but because he was earning more and was more open about the fact.

Bob Lange, president of one of the major ski manufacturing firms, said in 1970, "The basic prize for a fairly good male skier on a boot is $2,250, plus prize money. There is a base of about $750 for first place, $500 for second place, $300 for third. Some—like Schranz—cost a lot more." Aware of his value, Schranz, like Nurmi, Haegg, Santee and other outstanding athletes, adjusted his terms to the market. "I remember I offered Karl $5,000 in Waterville Valley last year (1969)," said Lange. "He said, 'I like your product and I'd like to but. . . . ' I offered him a hair more than $5,000, but, no, he went back to his old company again for a lot more" (Johnson, 1970, p. 15). Lange noted that his company alone was spending $250,000 in 1970 on athletes. President Avery Brundage would have preferred that the IOC disqualify the entire Austrian and French ski teams, but in the end only Schranz, the most prominent and highest-earning skier, was declared ineligible for the Winter Olympic Games.

The actual acceptance of money was not essential in the determination of status. If an athlete signed a professional contract prior to an Olympic Games and was careless enough to admit it, he or she could lose eligibility. That particular fate befell two West German ice skaters in 1964 at the Winter Olympic Games. Marika Kilius and Hans Juergen Baeumler, silver medalists in ice skating in Innsbruck, lost their medals when word leaked out that they had signed a contract with a professional ice show prior to the Games (Kluge, 1981).

Babe Didrikson.   In the ideal world of gentleman amateurs as envisioned by the self-appointed leaders of the 20th-century sport community, gaining any material advantage through sport was as dangerous and morally reprehensible as actually accepting cash. Material advantage ranged from expensive gifts to allowing one's picture to be used in advertising, or attempting to use one's name in order to gain fame through the written press, radio, or television. Quite a fair number of athletes became entangled in this regulation of amateurism. One of the more famous cases was that of Babe Didrikson, one of the darlings of the 1932 Olympic Games in Los Angeles. Didrikson was the winner of two gold medals and one silver and the holder of several world records and was proclaimed by some journalists as the world's greatest woman athlete. Didrikson was declared a professional and banned from further track and field competition following the 1932 Games. She ostensibly allowed her photograph to be used in conjunction with an automobile advertisement. She argued that she had not endorsed the action nor profited financially from it, but Avery Brundage, a major AAU official at the time, suspended her ("Babe Didrikson," 1933; Johnson & Williamson, 1975). Didrikson's case was somewhat undermined by the fact that she rather suddenly came into the possession of an $835 new red Dodge coupe. Her $69 monthly stenographer's salary did not appear to cover the monthly $90 car payments.

In 1947, Brundage focused his attention on another woman and another automobile—this time a yellow convertible. The city of Ottawa presented Barbara Ann Scott, an ice skater who had won the world championship in 1947, with an automobile. Brundage threatened to remove the skater's Olympic eligibility unless she returned the car. Eventually she did, went on to compete in the 1948 Winter Olympic Games, won the gold medal, and came home to Canada to accept another car. She retired before she could be suspended (Martin, 1948).

Bill Toomey.   Toomey survived the great shoe scandal in Mexico City in 1968 with his eligibility intact. However, when he did a series of radio commercials for Nutrament, a health food supplement produced by the Drackett Company where he was employed, he lost his amateur standing. The Olympic gold medal winner and world record holder commented, "The AAU calls me Joe Commercial, but I don't feel like that because I really do something for Drackett. When I was hired, I told them I didn't want a job where I was just a trophy, because that's strictly a no-future thing." Toomey continued, "I actually used Nutrament when I was at the University of Colorado and I studied journalism. I studied to do what I'm doing now, so I feel pretty legit" (Reed, 1971, p. 43).

In 1956, Cliff Blair, a record holder in the hammer throw, lost his position on the American Olympic team by writing newspaper articles on life in the Olympic Village for the *Boston Globe*. Blair maintained that he was not being compensated for his work, but the American Olympic officials decided that he nonetheless had attempted to use his fame to advance his career—a professional activity. Buster Crabbe, the only American male to win a gold medal in swimming at the 1932 Olympic Games, chose to accept an offer to work in the movie industry and thereby compromised his amateur standing.

Ski Advertising.   In 1968, Avery Brundage banned six top skiers for posing after a competition with their brand name skis for photographs. Brundage's effort to disqualify the alpine ski medalists at the 1968 Winter Olympic Games because they accepted free equipment from manufacturers failed, but as a defender of the amateur code, his intention was correct. Triple gold medalist John Claude Killy of France, ostensibly a poor customs official, appeared in Paris in a new orange Porsche sports car following his triumphs at Grenoble—an addition to his fleet of another Porsche, two Alfa Romeos, and two Puegeots. Killy allegedly sold a photograph of himself with his medals and gave an exclusive interview to *Paris Match*. Killy refused to confess, and he retained his standing, although he continued to be a target for officials who were convinced that he was acting in a most unamateurlike fashion (Brown, 1968).

Killy narrowly escaped in 1968, but in 1971, Brundage struck at 10 alpine skiers from a number of different countries who were, according to the IOC, using their sport reputations to promote themselves. The 10 Europeans had worked as ski coaches at a ski clinic camp at Mammoth Mountain, California, so Brundage suspended them. Athletes who coached were making themselves professionals. At the same time, Brundage cited 50 additional skiers who, he charged, were no longer amateurs because they allowed their pictures to be used for advertising purposes. Such a wide-reaching ban aroused the international ski federation, FIS, to opposition in time to prevent a wholesale eviction of the sport's elite from international competition ("Amateurs on the Skids," 1971; Boegel, 1979; Bonaventure, 1972).

Lee Calhoun.   One of the many cases that involved what sport officials considered a criminal-like action was that of Lee Calhoun, the 1956 Olympic champion in 110-meter hurdles. He was suspended for appearing on the NBC program, "Bride and Groom," and accepting wedding presents from the show. He and his wife received gifts valued at $2,500 plus tickets for a round-trip flight to Paris and spending money for the vacation. His mere appearance on the show was sufficient to disqualify him from further competition according to the amateur statute Section 1d of Rule VII of the AAU Code. His acceptance of the gifts simply made the violation more serious. Calhoun managed to regain his amateur standing by turning down the gifts and trip and profusely apologizing to numerous AAU officials (Thayer, 1960).

A similar case involved 1956 Olympic sprint champion Bobby Morrow. Invited on a television program to demonstrate the use of the newly introduced starting blocks, he almost was suspended for appearing even though no honorarium was involved.

Other Issues Affecting the Amateur Concept

Johnny Weismuller.   The list of American sport stars who were suspended, banned, or evicted from competitive sports is a lengthy one, and includes Johnny Weismuller. Weismuller, a five-time gold medalist at two Olympic Games in 1924 and 1928, and a tremendously popular sport hero, fell victim to the infamous *contamination rule*. This concept revolved around what is best termed unauthorized contact with professionals. An amateur who competed in a competition against a professional, even if he or she received no money, became "contaminated," and ineligible for further competition. The event in question did not need to be a competition— working out with a professional or appearing in an exhibition or demonstration with, prior to, or following a professional was sufficient to besmirch an individual's amateur standing. Weismuller, along with American Olympic gold medalists Martha Norelius, Pete Desjardins, and Helen Meany—all of whom were multiple gold medalists—appeared in a water show in Miami after the 1928 Olympic Games. The AAU promptly interceded and banned the four athletes from further swimming competition (International Swimming Hall of Fame Yearbook, 1971).

Charlie Paddock.   The pitfalls for the gentleman athlete were many and varied, and many concerned conduct rather than monetary or material gain, contamination, or the capitalization upon athletic fame. Paddock managed to violate all these rules in the course of his long career. The Olympic 100-meter dash champion in 1920, and the first runner to carry the title of "world's fastest human," he was barred from competition for the first time in 1923 when he competed in a non-AAU-sanctioned meet in Paris. The sanctioning process ostensibly worked to protect the athlete from the manipulation and exploitation of promoters, but in saving the individual from one evil, the process delivered him into the manipulation and exploitation of officials. Competition in unsanctioned meets was corruption of the worse sort, according to the statutes. This guilt by association was long a standard part of the amateur code. In 1973, a good part of the American swimming elite lost their eligibility when the international swimming federation banned them for visiting the People's Republic of China and competing in a series of demonstrations in a non-member country.

Paddock's career was colored by an unending series of conflicts with sport officials. In 1928, and again in 1932, Paddock was banned, reinstated, and banned again because of his work in the motion picture industry. Paddock responded by producing affidavits showing that he had received no remuneration for his film activities. In addition to American efforts to bar him from competition, the British also attempted to have him removed from competition because of certain critical statements about the British that he had made during the course of radio interviews. In essence, Paddock was not acting like a gentleman; therefore, he could not be an amateur ("Paddock Undecided," 1932).

Eleanor Holm.   The status of amateur extended into the area of personal conduct. The consumption of alcoholic beverages or drugs, the refusal to obey an official, or any conduct that officials decided was unbecoming of an amateur, could and often did, cost an athlete his or her eligibility. One such case was the incident that cost Eleanor Holm a gold medal in the 1936 Berlin Olympic Games.

The Olympic champion in 1932 in Los Angeles in the 100-meter backstroke, Holm qualified for the U.S. Olympic team. She had not lost a race in 7 years. Along with her teammates, she sailed from New York on the *S.S. Manhattan*. Following curfew violations for failing to go to bed early enough and reports that she had consumed alcohol in public, Avery Brundage banned her from participation in the Olympic Games. When the film actress agreed to write for an American news agency during the Games, the international swimming federation (FINA) banned her from all further aquatics competitions (Archdeacon, 1983; "Brundage Expels," 1936; "Eleanor Holm Jarrett Dropped," 1936).

The public consumption of alcoholic beverages and the violation of curfew regulations have cost many other amateur athletes their eligibility or resulted in suspensions ranging from a few months to several years. In 1946, the American swimming champion Joyce McCrae of the Crystal Plunge team, holder of six national records, reportedly drank a glass of beer at a tavern at Jacksonville, Indiana just prior to the national championships at Shakamak State Park, Indiana. She was suspended from the meet for conduct unbecoming of an amateur. As recently as 1979, the AAU suspended 18 members of the American national swim team. Thirteen swimmers, including the top American woman swimmer of the period, Tracy Caulkins, were suspended for 3 months for missing curfew at the U.S.A.-U.S.S.R. dual meet at Austin, Texas in April, 1978. Five additional swimmers were suspended for 1 to 2 years each for recreational drug abuse (Bell, 1979).

Jessie Owens. The question of what conduct was appropriate for an amateur remained a controversial issue for many decades. In essence, unamateurlike conduct usually meant challenging an official. Freedom of speech was not a civil right granted to most athletes; outspokenness usually resulted in being banned. In 1920 at the Paris Olympic Games, Dan Ahearn, a triple jumper, was suspended from the team for refusing to sleep in a bed that was too short. A threatened boycott of the Games by his teammates forced his reinstatement.

In 1968, Wade Bell ran the 800 meters in the Olympic Games in Mexico City in an unofficial uniform because his assigned uniform did not fit; he was suspended from the team. More prominent suspensions were leveled against 200-meter gold medalist Tommie Smith and bronze medalist John Carlos for failing to follow appropriate decorum on the awards podium. Four years later, similar penalties were leveled against Olympic 400-meter champion Vince Matthews and runner-up Wayne Collett in Munich for a similar offense.

Among the most noted of these conduct victims was Jesse Owens, winner of four gold medals at the 1936 Olympic Games in Berlin, Germany. His world record in the long jump stood for 2 1/2 decades, but his amateur status lasted only a few months beyond the Berlin Games. Following the Games, the AAU organized a tour of Europe for the track and field team. Owens competed in Germany, and then, rather than continuing on to Scandinavia, he asked to be allowed to return home. Permission was refused, whereupon he left the team and returned home anyway. The AAU, which had heavily promoted his appearances, promptly suspended him from further competition. "They thought of me as their performing monkey, a running machine that never broke down and that would do some good p.r. work for America while mainly doing a lot more good for the old AAU," remarked Owens (Owens & Niemark, 1971, p. 162). Having arrived in Europe with only $7.40 in his pocket and one suit of clothes, Owens borrowed funds from his coach to return home, where his wife and child awaited his return and needed his support. He notified the AAU of his decision via telegram. Forced out of amateur ranks, he later officially turned professional ("AAU Suspends Owens," 1936; "Owens to Wait," 1936).

Dawn Fraser. One final case illustrates the dimensions of the amateur conduct concept. Dawn Fraser was a world record holder in swimming from Australia, and remains the only swimmer to ever win the same event in three consecutive Olympic Games. The first woman to break the minute barrier in the 100-meter freestyle, she became entangled in an attempt to steal an Olympic flag from the Imperial Palace grounds in Tokyo, Japan in 1964, following the conclusion of the Games.

The Amateur Swimming Association of Australia subsequently banned Fraser in March, 1965 from competitive swimming for 10 years. Three other Australian swimmers received suspensions of 3 to 4 years for marching in the Tokyo Opening Ceremonies against orders. Fraser might well have won the 100-meter freestyle in Mexico City in 1968, but it is impossible to speculate because she had been banned from the swimming community (Fraser & Gordon, 1965).

Conclusion

A study of the history of sport competition in this century reveals that the Olympic Games have seldom involved all the world's best athletes, for many of the best athletes were not allowed to compete because of various violations of the amateur code. Among those who did successfully compete, many more lost their amateur standing for transgressions committed prior to or during the Olympic Games. The amateur rules often were counterproductive. Those athletes who were honest suffered the most, and the punishment meted out to them insured that other athletes remained silent, lied, or deceived officials in order to retain their eligibility. As a code of conduct and as a philosophical concept, amateurism was a failure. Rather than promoting virtue, good sportsmanship, and honesty, the amateur code encouraged hypocrisy, dishonesty, and corruption.

A detailed accounting of the payments to athletes in Eastern European nations—the state athletes—has not been covered in this essay; it is sufficient to note that IOC President Samaranch in 1986 has declared these athletes to be state professionals, a point that has been argued by knowledgeable observers since 1945 (Brokhin, 1977; Knecht, 1971, 1978; Rastvovov, 1955; Schwartz, 1959; Toth, 1975).

Too much time and too many resources have been wasted on the meaningless dialogue about, and the search for, the true amateur. The Olympic movement faces far greater problems in the areas of drug abuse, commercialization, and politicization. Hopefully, the day is no longer far off when athletes, regardless of their occupation or career, income level, or birthright will be able to compete in the Olympic Games, and the Games will truly be a place for the world's greatest athletes to measure themselves against worthy opponents.

References

AAU gets $25,000 to let Shorter do TV commercial. (1979, April 17). *Los Angeles Times*, Part III, p. 4.

AAU suspends Owens. He refused to go on tour. (1936, August 18). *New York Times*, Part I, p. 1.

Almond, E. (1982, June 9). Long run for Bill Rodgers: He's been chasing dollars, failing to win marathons. *Los Angeles Times*, Part III, p. 13.

Almond, E. (1981, November 6). Why Rodgers chose not to run: The price wasn't right. *Los Angeles Times*, Part III, p. 1.

Although there is no prize money in track, sometimes it pays to run. (1982, February 22). *Los Angeles Times*, Part III, p. 1.

Amateurs on the skids? (1971, January 11). *Newsweek*, pp. 55-56.

Amateurs outdated, Mahre says. (1984, February 1). *New York Times*.

Amdur, N. (1984, February 11). More pressure to liberalize amateur code likely. *New York Times*.

Andersson, Haegg rules off as pros. (1946, March 18). *New York Times*, p. 18.

Anderson, D. (1984, January 30). Let's face it: Olympic stars aren't amateurs. *Los Angeles Herrald Examiner*, p. D6.

Anderson, J. (1984, May 19). Olympic amateur ideal exceptions are outrageous. *Los Angeles Daily News*, p. 3.

Archdeacon, T. (1983, May 17). "Champaign Girl" still full of fizz. *Miami News*, p. 1A.

Arlott, J. (1973). Edwardian sports. In R. Lukas (Ed.), *From Metternich to the Beatles*. New York: Mentor.

Assembly Interim Committee on Governmental Efficiency and Economy. (1965). *Hearing on amateur athletes and amateur athletic competition, December 20-21, 1965*. Sacramento: California Assembly.

Athlete Thorpe still under fire. (1913, January 26). *New York Times*, Part IV, p. 1.

Babe Didrikson visitor here. (1933, January 5). *New York Times*, p. 25.

Bell, W. (1979, January). Eighteen swimmers suspended by AAU. *Swimming World*, **20**(1), p. 59.

Boegel, H. (1979, February 9). Millionen-Spiel im Schnee [Million-dollar games in the snow]. *Die Zeit*, p. 22.

Bonaventre, P. (1972, February 14). Amateurism, pros and cons. *Newsweek*, p. 59.

Brokhin, Y. (1977). *The big red machine*. New York: Random House.

Brundage expels Mrs. Jarrett anew. (1936, August 9). *New York Times*, p. 5.

Butterfield, R. (1948, June 14). Avery Brundage. *Life*, pp. 115-126.

Brown, S. (1968, March 18). Tale of two idols. *Sports Illustrated*, pp. 23-25.

Brundage backs down. (1971, August 2). *Newsweek*, p. 84.

Cart, J., & Harvey, R. (1984, April 22). Appearance fees—It's all how they look. *Los Angeles Times*, Part II, p. 1.

Cart, J., & Harvey, R. (1984, April 22). It's not the sport of kings, but it may pay as well. Track and field, once mainly a trophy dash, now hands off checks as if they were batons. *Los Angeles Times*, Part III, p. 3.

Cart, J., & Harvey, R. (1984a, May 20). How athletes weave their way through the rules to the bank. *Los Angeles Times*, Part III, p. 17.

Cart, J., & Harvey, R. (1984b, May 20). Westerners to run for more money in the Olympics. Eastern bloc pullout means more athletes will find cash in their shoes after the games. *Los Angeles Times*, Part III, p. 1.

Chataway, C. (1960, August 15). Let's end this hypocrisy now. *Sports Illustrated*, p. 83.

Denlinger, K. (1980, February 9-10). The IOC's approach to the final hurdle. *International Herald Tribune*.

Diester, G. (1976, November 12). Eiskalt wie Profis: Die illegalen Zahlungen zwingen Vereine und Verband, den Amateurstatus der Spieler noch einmal zu überdenken [Ice-cold pros: The illegal payments force associations and clubs to reconsider the amateur status of athletes]. *Die Zeit*.

Dreyfuss, J. (1984, May 20). The Olympics as a Pro-Am tourney. Gold medalist says amateurism is an outdated concept. *Los Angeles Times*, Part IV, p. 1.

Eleanor Holm Jarrett dropped from Olympic Team for breaking training. (1936, July 24). *New York Times*, p. 21.

Final Report of the President's Commission on Olympic Sports, 1975-1977 (2 vols.). (1977). Washington, DC: Government Printing Office.

Florence, M. (1978, January 31). Winter gypsies. *Los Angeles Times*, Part II, p. 1.

Florence, M. (1978, June 30). AAU suspends Stones, 3 women over TV money. *Los Angeles Times*, Part III, p. 1.

$4,000 each to players. Moscow report of payment to players. (1945, December 19). *New York Times*.

Fraser, D., & Gordon, H. (1965). *Below the surface. Confessions of an Olympic champion*. New York: William Morrow.

Garrison, L. (1969, March 7). Furor in France. Government backs Killy as affair is viewed as a threat to national honor. *New York Times*.

Gent, P. (1978, November 26). Some hard thoughts on games people play. *Los Angeles Times*, Part II, p. 7.

Good, P. (1979, July). The selling of our Olympic teams. *Sport*, p. 30-36.

Graf von Krockow, C. (1972). *Sport und Industriegesellschaft* [Sport and the industrial community]. Munich: Piper.

Haegg labels code as bar to records. (1945, March 25). *New York Times*, p. 21.

Hartmann, R. (1976, October 8). Tingeln durch Europa [Dancing through Europe]. *Die Zeit*, p. 21.

Harvey, R. (1984, August 17). American track athletes seek spending-style gold in Europe. *Los Angeles Times*, Part III, p. 1.

Hero in the dock. (1968, March 15). *Time*, pp. 56-57.

Holbreich, C. (1984, January 26). Amateurs can take it to the bank. *USA Today*.

How to see Europe on $20,000 a year. (1975, October 4). *Los Angeles Times*, Part III, p. 1.

International Olympic Committee (Ed.). (1968). *The speeches of President Avery Brundage*. Lausanne: IOC.

IOC board: Pros under 23 OK in three sports for '88. (1985, March 1). *Los Angeles Times*, Part III, p. 1.

IOC changes viewpoint on professionals. (1984, February 5). *Los Angeles Times*, Part III, p. 10.

International swimming hall of fame yearbook, 1971. (1971). Fort Lauderdale: ISHOF.

It's a week of retirements: Guy Drut's the latest to go. (1976, October 3). *Los Angeles Times*, Part III, p. 2.

Johnson, W.O. (1970, March 9). The name is the name of the game. *Sports Illustrated*, pp. 13-17.

Johnson, W.O. (1972, January 17). The big man lowers his Olympic boom. *Sports Illustrated*, pp. 18-19.

Johnson, W.O. (1972, July 24). Defender of the faith. *Sports Illustrated*, pp. 32-43.

Johnson, W.O., & Williamson, N. (1975, October 13). Babe. *Sports Illustrated*, pp. 48-54.

Jones, G. (1984, January 25). Olympic soccer eligibility—the bomb waiting to go off. *Los Angeles Times*, Part II, p. 1.

Kaiser, U. (1975, February 14). Geld für die Amateure [Gold for amateurs]. *Die Zeit*.

Kluge, V. (Ed.). (1981). *Die Olympische Spiele von 1896 bis 1980* [The Olympic Games from 1896 to 1980]. Berlin: Sportverlag.

Knecht, W. (1971). *Amateur 72*. Mainz: Von Hase und Koeller.

Knecht, W. (1978). *Das Medaillenkollektiv* [The medal collective]. West Berlin: Holzapfel.

Lawren, W. (1984, January). Fanning the professional flames. *Western's World*, pp. 44-48, 72.

Lichtenstein, G. (1979). Talent times five. *Quest*, 3(6), 35-39.

Lochner, R. (1984, February 6). A medal could bring some golden figures. *Los Angeles Times*, Part III, p. 1.

Louis Scott cleared. (1913, January 9). *New York Times*, p. 10.

Maher, C. (1978, July 21). Stones sues over his suspension, claims AAU is a monopoly, illegally keeps him from competing. *Los Angeles Times*, Part III, p. 1.

Marshall, J. (1980, March 3). Hi, do you remember me? *Sports Illustrated*, pp. 48-51.

Martin, P. (1948, June 12). Bogeyman of sport. *Saturday Evening Post*, pp. 28, 142ff.

McCallum, J. (1982, October 25). The regilding of a legend. *Sports Illustrated*, pp. 48-65.

Money is in Europe, so are the track stars. (1975, July 19). *Los Angeles Times*, Part III, p. 1.

Moran, S. (1979, December 26). John Smith poised for a dream 400. Reinstated by AAU, quarter miler hopes for a chance at Olympics. *Los Angeles Times*, Part III, p. 8.

Morning briefing. (1981, July 15). *Los Angeles Times*, Part III, p. 4.

Murray, J. (1978, September 7). Off with his head! *Los Angeles Times*, Part III, p. 1.

Newhan, R. (1977, February 2). An 8.8 100 ultimate goal of team McTear. *Los Angeles Times*, Part III, p. 1.

Nurmi's entry for Olympics rejected by unanimous decision after hearing. (1932, July 29). *New York Times*, p. 19.

Oates, R. (1983, April 6). Avery Brundage believed that purity was for others. *Los Angeles Times*, Part III, p. 1.

Official predicts lifetime amateur ban for Stones. (1978, July 14). *Los Angeles Times*, Part III, p. 3.

Oldfield eligible for Olympics after reinstatement by AAU. (1979, December 1). *Los Angeles Times*, Part III, p. 4.

Owens to wait until he returns home before making decision on pro offers. (1936, August 17). *New York Times*, p. 23.

Owens, J., & Niemark, P. (1971). *Blackthink*. New York: Pocket Books.

Paddock undecided on next move. (1932, January 20). *New York Times*, p. 25.

Putnam, P. (1970, July 27). Victory over Germany but a loss to the AAU. *Sports Illustrated*, p. 48.

Range, P.R. (1979, August). Going for the gold. *Playboy*, pp. 106-179.

Rastvorov, Y. (1955, June 6). Red amateurs are pros. *Life*, pp. 93-106.

Reed, W. (1971, April 12). The ineligible married man. *Sports Illustrated*, pp. 42-48.

Reich, K. (1983, January 19). Thorpe's victory. Olympic medals returned to his family 70 years after they were taken away. *Los Angeles Times*, Part III, p. 1.

Reid, R. (1979, April 2). This Stones left no stone unturned. *Sports Illustrated*, pp. 22-23.

Ripton, R. (1985, October 3). From disappointment to determination. Bruin soccer star got boot at Olympics. *Los Angeles Times*, Sec. W, p. 12.

Rosenthal, B. (1979, July 29). When money didn't show, neither did the athletes. *Long Beach Independent Press Telegram*, pp. 51, 59.

Santee prepares to appeal his suspension by the AAU. (1955, November 1). *New York Times*, p. 36.

Santee, W. (1956, November 19). People, places and payoffs. *Life*, pp. 99-110.

Scherer, K.A. (1981, February 24). Die Samaranch Formel: Amateur ist, wer sich dafür hält [The Samaranch formula: An amateur is whoever considers himself to be one]. *Deutscher Sportbund Informationsblatt*, p. 8.

Schollander, D., & Savage, D. (1971). *Deep water*. New York: Crown.

Schwartz, H. (1959, January 27). No time for also-rans. *New York Times*, p. 37.

Scott, J. (1971). *The athletic revolution*. New York: Free Press.

Shamateurism. (1972, February 7). *Time*, p. 72.

Shaplen, R. (1960, July 23). Amateurism. *The New Yorker*, pp. 28-71.

Shorter, F., & Bloom, M. (1984). *Olympic gold. A runner's life and times*. Boston: Houghton Mifflin.

Shuster, R. (1984, February 8). Amateurism: Every sport has its idea. *USA Today*.

Smith, R. (1980, January 15). Dwight Stones turns amateur. *International Herald Tribune*, p. 9.

Stones cleared by the AAU for reinstatement. (1979, November 29). *Los Angeles Times*, Part III, p. 1.

Stones: I broke record for cash. (1979, May 22). *Los Angeles Times*, Part III, p. 5.

Stones still on suspension as judge denies injunction. (1978, August 18). *Los Angeles Times*, Part III, p. 4.

Stump, A. (1957, October). Puritan of the Simon Pures. *Coronet*, pp. 117-120.

Thayer, C. (1960, August 15). A question of the soul. *Sports Illustrated*, pp. 72-83.

The Thorpe case shifts to New York. (1913, January 27). *New York Times*, p. 1.

Toth, R. (1975, October 20). Soviet "amateurs" get early start. *Los Angeles Times*, Part III, p. 1.

Underwood, J. (1969, March 14). No goody two shoes. *Sports Illustrated*, pp. 14-23.

Veblen, T. (1979). *The theory of the leisure class*. Harmondsworth: Penguin.

Webster's New World Dictionary of the American Language (2nd college ed.). (1982). New York: Simon and Schuster.

Wildman, H. (1984, July 17). Interview. (Wildman was a member of the 1932 and 1936 U.S.A. Olympic water polo teams)

20
Politics and Nationalism in the Olympic Games

Jean M. Leiper

The political difficulties facing the 1980 and 1984 summer Olympic Games were the culmination of more than 80 years of the growth, development, and acceptance of sport as an important human endeavor. The widespread involvement of youth in sport experiences was one of the basic purposes for the founding of the modern Olympic Games, and the present situation proves the success of that intent. Only enterprises that contain broad common interests can be politically manipulated at the level that affected these later Olympics. The phenomenal growth of interest in sport, particularly since World War II, has played a role in encouraging the recent debacles.

That the true base for political intervention in the Olympic Games is the rampant sport nationalism that the Games have fostered ever since their modern origins in 1896 is a common charge. However, sporting nationalism was well underway by that period, and if the Olympic Games had not appeared on the scene other contests certainly would have provided ever-increasing opportunities for nationalistic aggrandizement through sport. Even the ancient Greek Olympic Games had nationalistic overtones because one of their characteristics was the intensity of city-state rivalries. In fact, Solon, the archon of Athens in the early 6th century B.C., legislated a reward of 500 drachmas for every Athenian who won at the Olympic Games in an effort to increase Athens' image (Harris, 1964). Many people contend that nationalism in sport spawns politics in sport.

The boycotts of the Moscow and Los Angeles Olympic Games are the most damaging of all the political actions that have affected the Olympics over the years. The loss of the strong United States athletes in 1980 and the Russian and East German athletes in 1984 casts some suspicion on the value of the medals won by the remaining athletes. The other boycotting nations would probably not have been noticed by their absence, and the results would then not have been so skewed. This was the situation in other Olympic boycotts that occurred in 1956 and 1976. The insertion of nonsport politics into the Olympic world is not new—Berlin, 1936 and the Munich Massacre of 1972 are examples—but neither of these events were allowed to interfere with the normal Olympic presentations.

The escalation of the effect of nationalism and politics on the Olympic Games was surprisingly slow, although inevitable. The fact that the Games were reestablished after the hiatus of both World Wars is proof of the resilience of international sport and of the determination of the International Olympic Committee (IOC) to see their sporting festival survive. Also, the media must receive much credit, or rather, the nonexistent technology of the earlier years should, for it allowed a much greater obscurity to all types of events. Possibly, the main culprit in the Olympic disaster is satellite television! The increase in politicization of sport and of the Olympic Games parallels the spread of television technology.

The exploitation of athletic achievements by governments is another major contributing factor to international sport politics. When governments began to subsidize athletes heavily, only the most naive could have hoped that sport would not become a tool of international political one-up-manship.

The IOC must also bear responsibility for the present state of affairs. Some of the structures and patterns established in the early years have encouraged political use of the Games. The IOC has continually seen the Olympic Games as a sporting event with a philosophy that placed the Olympics above such mundane preoccupations as politics. This ideal just might have succeeded if the IOC's main concern had been active participation in worldwide education in the precepts of that ideal. Unfortunately, the IOC abdicated that responsibility to the National Olympic Committees (NOCs) and did little to insist that it was fulfilled. Even so, it is hard to believe that such a program could have prevailed against political needs as assessed by world leaders.

Obviously, these factors contributing to the political downfall of the Olympic Games are an incomplete list. Such developments as commercialism, size of the Games, and professionalism have also played roles in bringing about the present state of affairs. The factors are interdependent, and actions to resist contamination by one aspect often enhanced the damage caused by another.

Before specific incidents in the nationalistic and political history of the Olympic Games are examined, three major dichotomies must be identified:

- nationalism versus politics
- politics and sport versus politics and the Olympic Games
- sport-related politics versus non-sport-related politics

Nationalism Versus Politics

An important difference exists between nationalism and politics with reference to sport. Nationalism might well be explained as the attitude that the total reputation of a country can be enhanced through sport success because the citizens' pride is heightened and the world's respect is promoted. Politics, in contrast, is the magnification of a nation's international power and influence particularly in nonsport activities by the manipulation of the sporting event.

Any time a contest takes place between athletes of different countries nationalism *must* be a factor in the competition; politics need not be.

The use of the international achievements of citizens to enhance prestige both at home and abroad is not limited to sport, as a look at the fields of business, culture, and science will prove. But nationalism in this context is not politics. Supporters of the "sport and politics don't mix" position might be able to accept nationalism as a natural attitude while protesting political interference.

The seeds of today's political problems were sown during the founding years of the modern Olympic Games through an acceptance of a nationalistic base. The Congress of the Sorbonne (IOC, 1894) (the group that in 1894 agreed to the institution of the modern Olympic Games), when identifying the principles under which the Games would operate, opened the door to government participation by stating that "support of governments" (IOC, 1894) would be necessary for the Games to succeed. They also required that countries hold eliminations for the selection of the competitors they sent to the Games. This clearly identified that all participants were to be national representatives.

Nationalistic clashes appeared early in Olympic history. The Germans claimed that they had not been invited to the Sorbonne Congress and that Coubertin had insulted them, and therefore, they would not send athletes to Athens in 1896 (Henry, 1948). Some German participants did attend but it appeared they were club athletes, not nationally selected representatives. Because most of the competitors (including the Americans) represented clubs and not countries, however, acceptance was not a difficulty, regardless of the Congress of the Sorbonne's dictate about national eliminations. Even members of the IOC have come under criticism because of their nationality. In 1914, a British member resigned because the German members were not ousted when the war began (Mayer, 1960). In 1908 at London, the USA complained about biased British Judges (Killanin & Rodda, 1976). Similar charges have been made in almost every Olympics since, particularly when athletes from unfriendly nations face each other, but the damage they have done is negligible. A surge of nationalism is always engendered in the host nation every time the Games are held, but rarely does it reach levels occasioning international criticism.

Coubertin's efforts to create an IOC free from any type of influence was based on the methods of membership selection. He rejected representatives of nations or sports as the basis for sitting on the IOC. He reasoned that choosing a man because of his dedication to sport and to the Olympic Games would avoid manipulation by any type of group with special interests. He stressed that the representation involved was reverse, *from* the IOC *to* the countries and sport groups. Possibly, the Olympic movement reached a position of prestige because of this lack of interest-group representation. Many of the IOC members appear to have considered the good of the Games before any other concerns. This situation changed after World War II when members who depended on their governments for their positions and finances were included in the governing group. Also, the burgeoning of all international sport increased the power of the International Federations (IF) and more and more IOC members were closely connected to various IFs. In recent years, power blocs have developed in the IOC as members with common backgrounds have grouped together in voting. Some examples are the socialist bloc, the black or African bloc, and the Spanish bloc. Dealing with these groups has become a major concern of any city bidding to host the Games. Today, few IOC members are free of all these nationalistic influences.

One recent problem with international sport that is often laid at the door of nationalism is the use of dangerous drugs by athletes. Actually, the subject is not as new as many think—drug problems were present in the 1908 Olympic Games (Killanin & Rodda, 1976). Whether then or now, the motivation is as much for personal glory as it is for national pride. The road to the Olympics or world championships is not undertaken by the athlete in order to increase his or her nation's prestige but for personal challenge and ego. He or she competes for self, and often is surprised to find, on arriving at the victory podium, how moved he or she is when the flag is raised and the anthem is played. Certainly, the provision of drugs to athletes by coaches appears to be on the increase, but it is too great a generalization to suggest that the reason is a completely nationalistic one.

In spite of the above statement, a country's athlete support systems obviously are directed toward national image. In these days when top performance requires full-time training and medical and technological expertise of a highly sophisticated nature, government participation is almost mandatory. When funding involves government dollars, the results must contribute to government interests—in this case a positive international sport reputation. The accumulation of Olympic medals by a nations' athletes supposedly tells the world that the nation is vigorous, energetic, physically strong, and supportive of sporting values. In a sense, the athlete speaks for his nation in actions, and only rarely in words. Because sport can communicate so easily across language, cultural, and political boundaries, its voice is becoming more powerful. Sport is more easily understood by all social classes than are political, economic, or religious issues. The skill of high jumping is the same whether the athlete is Moslem, Christian, or atheist, and whether his country is democratic or totalitarian.

The communication abilities of sport leads to a discussion of "representative" sport, which is the vehicle of nationalism and has grown rapidly in the 20th century. The "we're number 1" syndrome is at the heart of the problem. In spite of earlier suggestions that nationalism in sport is here to stay, it is disturbing to accept that the winning athlete is judged not only to represent his or her country in the contest, but also to *be* representative of his or her country. Once the athlete reaches a position of international acclaim all his or her beliefs, values, and behaviors become a focus for media investigation. If the athlete shows great dignity, sense of humor, dedication, and respect for opponents, we attribute those characteristics to his or her country. The whining or bragging athlete creates feelings of distaste for his or her nation as well as for him- or herself. Obviously, none of these persons are representative of the citizens of their nations—or rather, all of these traits exist in individuals of the nations, but the nations as a whole cannot be identified as having only one set of characteristics. Just as the athletes' sporting prowess is not shared by their countrymen, neither are their attitudes and personalities. This fact is one deficiency of representative sport, be it parochial or international.

An intriguing aspect of representative sport nationalism is that we equate winners but not losers as exemplifying our country. If winning provides us with pride that the world now sees us as strong, talented, courageous, and dedicated, is it equally accepted that losing means we are weak, timid, superficial, and that our political and economic system is wrong? Obviously not. But, we can't have it both ways. If winning presents so positive an image that we let it carry our attributes on its shoulders, then we must agree that we're inadequate as a people when "we" lose. Surely our security as nation groups is not so fragile as that.

One of the most interesting aspects of nationalism in the Olympic Games is how often it is criticized, particularly by those who rarely experience winning (the story rapidly changes at the acquisition of Olympic gold). The founder of the modern Olympic Games, Pierre de Coubertin, consciously incorporated into the Olympic ceremonies some of the traditions that we now identify as being so nationalistic as to encourage various types of political intervention into the world of Olympic sport. The parade of athletes by nations in the Opening ceremonies and raising the flag and playing the national anthem of the winners in the victory ceremonies are examples. Avery Brundage (past IOC President) was one of the most determined adherents of eliminating flag-raising and national anthems. At least three times he proposed doing away with these manifestations of nationalism, but each time his motion was rejected by vote of the IOC General Assembly (Leiper, 1976). Walter Umminger has explained why the chances are now slight of such action ever being approved by the IOC. Since World War II, IOC membership has been extended to citizens of many emerging nations. Umminger claims that these new countries are struggling for recognition as independent nations and that the symbols of such achievement are a national flag, a seat at the United Nations, a national airline, and Olympic gold (Umminger, 1963). Obviously, these recent IOC members would not vote for the elimination of flags and anthems—suppose their athletes won gold and no one knew from where they came? This sentiment also applies to any suggestions of removing the march past by nations at the Opening ceremonies.

Another testimony to rampant nationalism in the Olympic Games is the medals table, which the IOC vehemently criticizes. Until 1914 (IOC, 1921) there were official IOC tabulations, but at the Lausanne Congress of that year such a compilation was realized to be contrary to the IOC's own insistence that the Olympic Games were contests between individuals and not nations and was hardly conducive to the international peace and goodwill intent of Olympism. At that time and afterward the IOC has repudiated the validity or relevance of medal tables. Their continued existence is due to both media and NOC dedication to determining an overall "winner" of the Olympic Games. Over the years these groups have used several different methods of identifying the most powerful nations, including point values allocated to placements (and even these have been constructed in a fashion to benefit the interests of their own countries) and total medal counts.

In some respects the national bias that is intensified by the Olympic Games can have a positive effect. Many nations of the world have internal conflicts between one area or segment of society and others. Canada is a perfect example, with French Canadian Quebec differing from the rest of the country in both cultural atmosphere and political aims. But when Olympic Games time comes around, there is a tremendous sense of unity supporting the Olympic athlete, regardless of area of origin. The appreciation of western Canada for a Gaetan Boucher or Sylvie Bernier from Quebec is matched by the east's acclaim of the west coast rowers and Alberta's synchronized swimmers. Nationalism and representative sport can be positive factors when they provide a sense of unity where division often exists.

The question remains, How can nationalism be kept in healthy perspective? Legislation will not do it, either by nations or by the IOC. As is true for so many of the world's other problems, only education of the people will change attitudes and prejudices. The IOC hands the issue of Olympic education to each NOC and leaves it at that. Few NOCs establish programs that provide a wide exposure to all facets of the Olympic movement, particularly that of Olympic philosophy. They are more likely to encourage jingoistic attitudes than to broaden skill appreciation, attitudes of sportsmanship, and respect for opponents regardless of national origins. Eliminating nationalism in the Olympic Games or any other international sporting event is impossible; changing its face might be achieved.

Surely all of these signals of nationalism are relatively innocuous compared to the damage inflicted by politics on both the athletes and the Olympic Games festival. The degree to which the athlete is employed as an instrument of nationalism (a criticism often laid) is probably equalled by the athletes' use of the international sporting scene for his personal ambition. But when governmental political intervention uses the athlete as a pawn for international power politics that have nothing to do with the sporting world, it is time to be concerned.

The most surprising aspect of the 1980 Olympic Games fiasco is that it was 85 years before politics caused such a major interference with the festival, if we ignore the complete cessation of Olympic competition in 1916, 1940, and 1944. Considering the nationalistic base of the modern Olympic Games, the IOC has been fortunate that major political interventions have not ruined the Games long before now.

Any student of the Olympic movement is aware that the most dependable factor in the history of IOC decision-making is inconsistency. Powerful countries receive different treatment from that given to politically insignificant ones. Political interference is deplored when the IOC is being manipulated but approved when it is doing the manipulating. Definitions are altered according to expediency rather than principle. But then, what major business or government in the world does not act similarly?

Politics in the IOC

In spite of recurring protestations of political purity and disassociation from political involvement, the IOC has rarely known a period of freedom from political problems. In the last 2 decades, the storms created by political interests have been well documented by the media, and most sides of the issues have been exposed to public scrutiny. The IOC has protested against these manipulations, but has usually found itself on the horns of a dilemma—no action that it would take would satisfy everyone. Every time, the main consideration of the IOC was to preserve the existence of the Olympic Games in the face of all difficulties. The IOC appears to be convinced that if even once more the Games are cancelled or postponed it will be their end.

True politics became an issue after both World Wars with the problem of inviting the losing side to the Games of 1920 and 1948. Because both the greater number of nations and the most powerful ones in the Olympic movement had been the victors, the losers' turning up on the "friendly fields of contest" such a short time after the end of hostilities was sure to cause tensions. For the 1920 Games, the problem was solved in two ways. First, only those countries represented on the IOC were allowed to compete (IOC, 1919). Because no one had any information about the previous members from the "Central Powers," those countries were not listed as eligible. Second, the Games organizing committee, being in control of transmitting the invitations, had the final word (Coubertin, 1931). After World War II the same ploys would not work because of changes in the Olympic rules, so a new logical excuse was devised. The IOC decided that because only countries with NOCs could compete, the countries occupied by the Allied forces (Germany, Italy, and Japan) did not fit this category; the occupied countries had no internal governments and therefore no legal institutions such as NOCs (IOC, 1946).

IOC recognition of NOCs must exist before a country can send competitors to the Games. Political factors have often influenced achievement of this recognition. In the early 1920s, both Morocco and the Philippines wanted to enter the Games under their own emblems and flags, but because they were not self-governing they had to compete as part of their governing nations' teams. These potential conflicts were resolved when the governing powers (France and the U.S.) agreed that Morocco and the Philippines could display their own flags (IOC, 1921).

The case of Ireland was not so easily decided. In 1920, Ireland requested participation under the British flag but as a separate group (IOC, 1920). Because of internal political problems in Ireland a decision was postponed. Even after Ireland's acceptance, apparently in 1922 when an Irish IOC member was named, difficulties over the name of the NOC continued until 1951 (IOC, 1951).

The first major political uproar surrounding the Games concerned the 1936 Olympics, which were to be held in Berlin. When Hitler came to power, the Games had already been allocated to Berlin. Very soon sport groups around the world feared the effect of Nazi policies on Games participants and protested the political use to which the Germans were putting the Games. Although the IOC was accused of ignoring the problem, its members were very concerned. Led by President Baillet-Latour, the IOC repeatedly demanded German assurances that Olympic regulations would be followed. This situation may well have been the beginning of the IOC's long-standing position that if Olympic protocol is observed, then the internal politics of the country must be of no concern to the IOC. To judge the German national political environment would have been to open the IOC door to political involvement, and that door might really have been the lid to Pandora's box. In retrospect, the IOC's ambition to keep politics separate from the Olympic movement was doomed to failure, but in 1934 the German promises convinced the IOC that this could be done. Even so, Baillet-Latour had four confrontations with Hitler, and more than once threatened withdrawal of the Games from Germany if political manipulation did not cease (Popliment, 1956). In each case Hitler backed down, and overt Nazi propaganda and political intervention ended. In one face-off, Baillet-Latour (Brundage, 1948) stated the feeling of many Olympic purists of the time when he arrogantly exclaimed to Hitler:

The Olympic Games are not held in Berlin, Los Angeles or in Amsterdam. When the 5-circled Olympic flag is raised over the Stadium it becomes sacred Olympic territory and theoretically, and for all practical purposes, the Games are held in ancient Olympia. There, I am the master. (p. 21)

The entry of the U.S.S.R. into the Olympic Circle in the late 1940s presaged the rampant growth of nationalistic emphasis in the Olympic Movement. At the same time, a less noticeable controversy existed that eventually exploded in the Munich Massacre of 1972. In 1948 Israel attempted to enter athletes in the Games. One IOC member contended (IOC, 1948) that no action was necessary because "Palestine is no longer a state and Israel has no Olympic Committee" (p. 2). The Egyptian member suggested (IOC, 1948) that the treatment would be different depending upon which group had asked for entry.

If it was Palestine which has the great majority of the population, he would advise an affirmative answer. If it was Israel his advice is negative. This country, geographically as we know it, is in no condition to enter the games. (p. 2)

In 1951 two sport committees from Israel—one Palestinian in membership, and the other Israeli—asked for recognition. They were told to get together so that "all athletes of the country without distinctions of race, religion, or opinion would be admitted into the organization" (IOC, 1951, p. 12). They must have conformed to the IOC's demand, because in 1952 Israel was recognized (IOC [Oslo], 1952). Palestine, having no country or NOC, could not be considered according to the IOC rules.

All these difficulties were of short duration and might even be classed as minor compared to the dilemmas posed by the requests for recognition by the two Germanies, the two Chinas, and the two Koreas. The German question developed first and, with the support of the British occupying forces, West Germany was accorded recognition in 1951 (IOC, 1951). When East Germany asked for the same treatment some members resisted, feeling that one country would therefore have twice the number of competitors of other nations (IOC, 1951). A series of meetings of the IOC executive with the two Germanies' representatives failed to reach accord, so only West Germans competed in 1952 (IOC [Helsinki], 1952). By 1956 some agreements were finally made, and a united team of East and West German athletes participated using a common flag, uniform, and emblem (IOC, 1956). President Avery Brundage (IOC, 1956) was very pleased and stated, "we have obtained in the field of sport what politicians have failed to achieve so far" (p. 30). By 1968, the joint team concept was no longer acceptable to either Germany, and when the IOC recognized a separate East German NOC, the two split (IOC, 1968).

The two Chinas problem began in 1952 and was not finally solved until 1980. In the meantime, a good many controversial incidents occurred, not the least of which was the Canadian government's refusal to allow Taiwanese athletes into Canada for the 1976 Games under their official Olympic name of "Republic of China." Mainland China had been recognized in 1954 but had withdrawn in 1958 over the issue of Taiwan remaining in the Olympic Movement (Berlioux, 1976). The Eastern Bloc nations, however, led by the U.S.S.R. (still friendly with China at the time) insisted that the Taiwan NOC must change its name so that in the future mainland China might again be recognized by the IOC. The name "Chinese Olympic Committee" for Taiwan was not acceptable to mainland China (IOC, 1959). After arguing the issue from 1959 to 1968, the IOC finally designated Taiwan as the "Republic of China," its name in the United Nations (IOC, 1968). By 1976, Taiwan had been turned out of the United Nations and mainland China was in. This action may have encouraged Canada to forbid Taiwanese athletes entry for the Montreal Games under the Republic of China label, even though Prime Minister Trudeau, in 1970, had promised that all Olympic rules and protocol would be followed if Montreal was granted the Games. The reason for the government's action would seem to have been appeasement of the mainland Chinese to assure the sale of wheat to that country. The IOC could do nothing except remove the Games from Montreal (a rather drastic step when international athletes had already begun arriving in Montreal), so it capitulated and Taiwan did not compete, refusing to change either its name or flag on the spot. The struggle between the two Chinese factions about the names of their NOCs continued with both sides maintaining their right to the title "China." Finally, Taiwan was forced to yield as the world began to accept the mainland as the voice of the Chinese people. Taiwan became the "Chinese Taipei Olympic Committee" in order to retain its recognition by the IOC. The mainland group was designated the "Chinese Olympic Committee," sending its first Olympic team to Lake Placid in 1980.

An investigation of the Olympic Charter shows that the "Congress of the Sorbonne" comment made earlier (about government support for the Olympic Games) was never written into the Olympic rules and regulations except for the requirement that athletes represent their country through their NOC. Neither were any protestations made about political involvement. As early as 1923, however, Edstrom of Sweden (IOC, 1923), a future IOC President, insisted that "the IOC must avoid all interference in the political sphere" (p. 27). The feeling at that time was apprehension about the IOC interfering with national politics, not that its own organization and program would be interfered with by outside agencies. Not until 1949 did the word "politics" appear in the Fundamental Principles of the Olympic rules, and then it was part of a new "no discrimination" clause. Rising nationalism was recognized in .1955 with the admonition that "the Games are contests between individuals and not between nations" (IOC, 1955, p. 6). In the same year, the rules (IOC, 1955) setting out the duties and responsibilities of NOCs included a statement that "NOC's must be completely independent and autonomous and entirely removed from political, religious or commercial influence" (p. 12). Probably, these statements were a result of the entry of the U.S.S.R. into the Olympics, the cold war moving into the sport arena, and the growing awareness of the German and Chinese problems.

In 1962, a statement clarifying the IOC's meaning of "country" and "nation" began with "Since the Olympic Movement is non-political" (IOC, 1962, p. 6). They obviously took for granted that its position was well known, although this was the initial such statement printed in the Charter. Further refutation of any IOC political connections was made in 1966 when a clause about recognition of an NOC stated, "Recognition of an Olympic Committee does not imply political recognition as this is outside the competence of the International Olympic Committee" (IOC, 1966, p. 12).

Despite such insistence against politics in the Olympic rules, infractions have become more and more common. NATO membership caused trouble in 1968. The city of Grenoble almost had the Olympic Winter Games moved to another location because of France's refusal to give visas to the East Germans. As a member of NATO, France did not recognize East Germany as an independent country. The solution this time appeared to be to bring the East Germans in under one combined German team, although it had not been planned that way by either Germany. Certainly the East German athletes attended (Killanin & Rodda, 1976), so they must have been granted visas in this fashion.

Today, great danger seems to exist that the Olympic Games will soon expire soon. The political manipulation of the Olympics by governments has accelerated to a point where the IOC is almost incapable of defending the festival, and the Games will join their ancient antecedent. The trend that has reached the boiling point is the direct use of the Olympic Games by governments to force some nation to change its international political position. From an isolated incident of the "tempest in a teapot" genre to worldwide manipulation by governments in 85 years, the IOC has come of political age.

Politics and Sport
Versus Politics and the Olympic Games

Although the high visibility of the Olympic Games has made them more vulnerable to political manipulation, the problem affects all international sport. Other sport events such as the 1979 World Women's Basketball Championships have suffered from boycotts for political reasons, but the low profile of the media coverage has resulted in little general awareness of either the action or the reason behind it. The entire world of international sport is being hurt by political intervention, not just the Olympics. Even a casual look at the patterns of scoring in judged events (such as gymnastics and figure skating) in any international contest provides clear evidence of national bias. Refereeing is subject to the same weakness, whether in the Olympics or in any other competition. The Olympics are simply a more conspicuous theater and a more useful stage on which to mount a political position. The IOC cannot expect to be left in peace when the whole world of international sport is increasingly riddled with political maneuvering. The IOC position of "We are concerned with sport, not politics" may be an objective, but it certainly is not a statement of fact because sport itself is closely bound up with politics.

This attitude of the IOC is another reason why politics are more noticeable when the Olympics are involved. The IOC's insistence on the political purity of the Games heightens awareness when political interference occurs. When other world class contests are affected, the situation is likely to be treated as an annoying incident, not a major catastrophe. But the Olympics, with its nonpolitical propaganda, draws much more attention and criticism when politics infiltrate the bastion. If the Olympic Games cease to exist, however, other events can be expected to take on greater prestige to fill the gap and will therefore inherit the same problems.

Sport-Related Politics
Versus Non-Sport-Related Politics

The use of sport for political reasons can be divided into two realms— that of sport-related results or non-sport-related results. Coubertin's motives for desiring the reestablishment of the Olympic games were basically nonsport related. They were to heighten the vigor of French youth through sport participation and to build their loyalty and pride in France through international competition. Most of the political incidents in the Olympic Games have been caused by using sport to obtain power that could be applied to national or international situations in which the focus was unrelated to sport. In the early years of the Olympic Games, these occurrences created only minor disturbances because they were instigated within the sport world, with the exception of Hitler's efforts in Berlin in 1936. Since World War II, the confrontations have been increasingly fomented by political groups who have no direct connection with the daily operation of sport. This permits the manipulation to be more visible and obvious.

For many observers, the distinction between sport-related and non-sport-related politics is artificial. The "life is politics" line of thinking would prohibit such a separation. This aspect of the problem appears to be one of the most obvious examples of the IOC and like-minded persons not living in the present. When even one major nation insists that sport is an integral tool in the struggle of the proletariat against the bourgeoisie and proceeds to put such beliefs into practice, it is very difficult for any others not to go the same route to greater or lesser degrees.

Some Western athletes, who criticized the boycott of the Moscow Olympics on the basis of the Afghanistan invasion, were sympathetic to the black boycott of 1976 and to the exclusion of South Africa from Olympic competition. They theorized that the Moscow boycott had nothing to do with sport, but the black boycott was an attempt to attain equality of sport opportunity for black people in South Africa. In other words, for some politics for sport-related ends is justifiable, but politics for nonsport reasons is unacceptable.

The suggestions most often offered to limit the political use of the Olympic Games appear to be cosmetic alterations, and the basic problems cannot be eliminated. As long as the Olympic Games or any other international events attract the attention of the world, they will be used by modern governments for propaganda purposes. This tendency will increase rather than decrease. The syndrome must be faced and lived with. But, for argument's sake, let us look at some of the most common suggestions made to alleviate political problems in the Olympic Games.

Build a permanent site for the Olympic Games. This idea has been propounded by various persons for many years. The Moscow disaster placed it front and center, with Greece being the favored site. Unless enclosed facilities are to be built, the Greek summer heat is too oppressive for top performances in many sports. The alternative is spring or autumn Games, a possibility if seasonal training is no longer a concern of the world's athletes. Another factor must be considered, however. In the years prior to 1974, many athletes and governments might well have objected to holding the Games in a country with Greece's record on human rights. Government changes are to be expected, and faith can be placed in few for future political "purity." Switzerland, a neutral country, would seem to have the best record for stability, as well as being the country most acceptable to most nations as a permanent home.

Another question would be the source of financing. Annual contributions from all nations in the Olympic movement is the proposed solution. But this type of system is the supposed source of the United Nations financing and many nations have reneged on that commitment.

Spread the Games' locations over several cities of the host nation. This proposal might alleviate some of the problems of facilities and accommodation, but it would also diminish the impact of the Olympic celebration. More local citizens might attend some one sport event, but those persons who wished to see many sports would find it almost impossible.

The problem of international conflicts causing political manipulations would not be solved because the IOC would still have to choose the host nation. The Moscow and Los Angeles boycotts would not have been avoided by holding the Games in 10 or 15 cities of the host nation instead of three or four.

Reduce the size of the Games. This action could well solve the political interference difficulties because the Games would lose their great prestige and become less important as an international theater. However, only two methods for reducing the Games appear to be feasible: Eliminate some sports or reduce the number of entries. The IOC has struggled with this issue for many years. The attempt to prevent the growth of the Games is the reason sports such as volleyball, synchronized swimming, and archery have not been included until recently. More pressure appears to exist to expand the Games than to reduce them.

The suggestion that the Games' size be controlled by being more selective about entries is equally weak. Already, in team sports, pre-Olympic eliminations prevent all but the top eight (depending on the sport) from competing. In individual events, one of the strongest elements of the Olympics is that each country is allowed one entry regardless of skill standards. Surely this freedom must encourage small nations in sport. Restricting entries to only the few of the world's best would narrow the competition to the big powers as in present world championships in most sports. One of the unique features of the Olympics would disappear.

The elimination of some sports might discourage interest in the Olympic Games and therefore avoid political interventions, but allowing only the best athletes to compete would have an opposite effect.

The problem of politics affecting the operation of international sport in general, and the Olympic Games in particular, appears to be with us as a permanent difficulty. As Swampo Sie (1978) observed, "Perhaps it is time for proponents of a pure Olympic movement to begin making provision for the realities of politics in sports" (p. 295). The question for the future remains, How?

References

Berlioux, M. (1976). The history of the International Olympic Committee. In Lord Killanin & J. Rodda (Eds.), *The Olympic Games: 80 years of people, events, and records* (p. 19). Don Mills, Ontario: Collier-Macmillan Canada.

Brundage, A. (1948). Why the Olympic Games? *Report of the United States Olympic Committee.* New York: USOC.

Coubertin, P. de. (1931). *Memoires Olympique.* Aix-en-Provence: Paul Robaud.

Harris, H.A. (1964). *Greek athletes and athletics.* London: Hutchinson.

Henry, B. (1948). *An approved history of the Olympic Games.* New York: Putnam's Sons.

International Olympic Committee. (1894). *Bulletin of the International Olympic Committee for the Olympic Games,* 1, 4.

International Olympic Committee. (1919, April 5). *Minutes of the General Assembly: Lausanne, 1919.* Lausanne: The Committee.

International Olympic Committee. (1920, August 17). *Minutes of the General Assembly: Antwerp, 1920.* Lausanne: The Committee.

International Olympic Committee. (1921, June 5 and 6). *Minutes of the General Assembly: Lausanne, 1921.* Lausanne: The Committee.

International Olympic Committee. (1923). *Minutes of the General Assembly: Rome, 1923.* Lausanne: The Committee.

International Olympic Committee. (1946). *Minutes of the General Assembly: Lausanne, 1946.* Lausanne: The Committee.

International Olympic Committee. (1948). *Minutes of the General Assembly: London, 1948.* Lausanne: The Committee.

International Olympic Committee. (1951). *Minutes of the General Assembly: Vienna, 1951.* Lausanne: The Committee.

International Olympic Committee. (1952a). *Minutes of the General Assembly: Helsinki, 1952.* Lausanne: The Committee.

International Olympic Committee. (1952b). *Minutes of the General Assembly: Oslo, 1952.* Lausanne: The Committee.

International Olympic Committee. (1955). *Olympic rules and regulations.* Lausanne: The Committee.

International Olympic Committee. (1956). *Minutes of the General Assembly: Cortina D'Ampezzo, 1956.* Lausanne: The Committee.

International Olympic Committee. (1959). *Minutes of the General Assembly: Munich, 1959.* Lausanne: The Committee.

International Olympic Committee. (1962). *Olympic rules and regulations.* Lausanne: The Committee.

International Olympic Committee. (1966). *Olympic rules and regulations.* Lausanne: The Committee.

International Olympic Committee. (1968). *Minutes of the General Assembly: Mexico City, 1968.* Lausanne: The Committee.

Killanin, Lord, & Rodda, J. (Eds.). (1976). *The Olympic Games: 80 years of people, events and records.* Don Mills, Ontario: Collier-Macmillan.

Leiper, J. (1976). *The International Olympic Committee and the pursuit of Olympism 1894-1970.* Unpublished doctoral dissertation, University of Alberta, Edmonton.

Mayer, O. (1960). *A travers les anneaux Olympiques*. Geneva: Pierre Cailler.

Popliment, A.G. (1956). Berlin 1936. *Bulletin of the IOC*, **55**, 47.

Sie, S. (1978). Sport and politics: The case of the Asian Games and the GANEFO. In B. Lowe, D. Kanin, & A. Strenk (Eds.), *Sport and international relations*. Champaign, IL: Stipes.

Umminger, W. (1963). *Supermen, heroes and gods*. New York: McGraw-Hill.

21
Capitalism, Commercialism, and the Olympics

Richard Gruneau
Hart Cantelon

To the names of Jim Thorpe, Bob Mathias and Rafer Johnson, add the name Plymouth Voyageur . . . Some athletes run fast. Some run far. Some throw a heavy object over great distances. A rare few have the surpassing versatility to succeed at several disciplines. Plymouth Voyageur has that versatility. (Chrysler advertisement in the special pre-Olympic edition of *Life* magazine)

The American Broadcasting Company featured nearly 180 hours of coverage of the 1984 Los Angeles Olympics. In Canada, the English and French channels of the Canadian Broadcasting Corporation presented approximately 200 hours of Olympic coverage. During that time and in the months leading up to the Games, American and Canadian consumers were bombarded with advertising by "official" Olympic sponsors and other companies hoping to link their products with the Games. Examples include such stalwart corporate entitites as IBM, Canon, Levi's,

Motorola, and a whole host of representatives from the food and beverage industry. The Los Angeles Olympics not only gave us an official Olympic soft drink (Coca-Cola), but also an official Olympic fast food company (McDonald's), an official Olympic convenience store (Southland/7-Eleven), and an official Olympic "snack food" (Snickers/Mars).

Clearly Snickers bars, Coke, Big Macs, and Slurpees do not have a great deal to do with high-performance sport. But this fact is not a relevant consideration in the highly commercialized sport world of the 1980s. What is important for the sponsoring companies is only that their products become associated in the public mind with the Olympics. The rationale for this is straightforward. Effective advertising is predicated upon establishing a set of deeply rooted symbolic connections with a target audience. At one level these connections might advertise the corporation itself. Through the Olympics, a business can toughen its corporate image while simultaneously portraying itself as a caring corporation doing good public work. At another level, the connections are meant to create a positive image of the product a corporation actually produces. For example, an Olympic sponsor might try to build upon the idea that sport today symbolizes and helps to define youth and that the exciting features of youth culture can be expressed in commodity consumption. If products like Coke, McDonald's hamburgers, Snickers bars, Canon cameras, or Levi's clothes can be defined as fashionably sporty, they become highly desirable commodities. The strength of such connections between high-profile sports and market-segmented advertising of various types explains the ease with which the Los Angeles Olympic Organizing Committee (LAOOC) was able to attract corporate sponsors, each willing to pay a minimum of $4 million for the exclusive right to market their products under the Olympic logo.

Many people object to such obvious commercialism. They believe the essence of the Olympic spirit is the practice of sport for its own sake and that the modern Games have distorted this principle. For these people the Los Angeles Olympics have come to symbolize new heights in the corruption of sport. The politics of the modern Games is one thing, these critics argue, and Los Angeles had plenty of that with the Soviet and East European boycott and the unbridled nationalism of American fans and television commentators. But the real problem is that any remaining vestiges of Olympic ideals seemed to vanish as a result of these "Corporate Games." What replaced these ideals, the argument runs, is simply the lure of the big buck. American sprinter Carl Lewis's option to not try for a world record in order to save himself for the four gold medal effort meant millions in endorsements. Canadian boxer Willie de Wit stayed outside the Olympic village and had his manager talk frankly of the economic importance of an Olympic triumph. The seamless interweaving of live television coverage and commercial breaks allowed Bob Beaman to act as a spokesman for a beer company while wishing Carl Lewis luck in the attempt to break the world long jump record. All of these things, critics argue, were symbolic statements in an Olympics where the race for sponsorship and endorsements, both by athletes and Olympic organizers, assumed greater importance than the eventual race for the finish line.

In our view, an Olympics so dominated by commercial interests is upsetting. However, we think it necessary to be far more precise than most critics usually are about why this is worth worrying about. Criticism of commercialism in the Olympics needs to be based upon analysis, not idealism or wishful thinking. We should recognize the extent to which the modern Olympic ideal of friendly international competition, pursued modestly and for its own sake, was compromised right from its inception at the end of the last century. We also need to examine the social forces and contradictory tendencies associated with the direction the Olympic movement appears to have taken. We might even consider the radical notion that the Olympic promise can never be realized in societies that equate personal worth with position in the marketplace and that transform all objects of human production into commodities that can be exchanged for profit.

In this chapter we argue that the Los Angeles Games represent only a partial departure from practices established in earlier Olympics. They are not some kind of fall from Olympic grace so much as a more fully developed expression of the incorporation of sporting practice into the ever-expanding marketplace of international capitalism.

The Games also became a clear metaphor for the economic crisis of the 1980s and the laissez-faire solutions adopted by some western governments. For example, among the many messages provided by the Los Angeles Games, one can readily identify the dubious claims of Thatcherism and Reaganomics: Reduce the fiscal responsibilities of the state in the area of social services, open the gates to private capital, and everybody will benefit. Yet, mixed with this message is a much deeper statement about the idealized moral economy of capitalism: Profitability is the ultimate factor in determining the value of human endeavor, and the marketplace is the fairest judge of human capacity.

The clarity of these symbolic messages in the organizational style of the Los Angeles Olympics tells us something more general about the social development of sport in this century. In Los Angeles the march of capital into sport was less mediated than ever before by the romantic nonutilitarian values that have always been associated with the Olympic movement. In actuality what has occurred is nothing less than the maturation of a new social definition of sporting practice that can be understood in political and economic terms. Emerging forms of social class and political expression throughout the 20th century have played a key role in shaping dominant conceptions of what sport ought to be. In the face of these emerging forms, older competing definitions of the meaning of sport have receded to a residual position in western cultures (see Cunningham, 1980; Gruneau, 1983).

Amateurism, Commercialism, and the Contradictions of the Olympics

What does it really mean to say that a particular social definition of sport is actually a form of class and political expression? What forms of class and political expression have characterized the Olympic movement? What forces in modern societies have exerted pressures on dominant class practices in the Olympics, and how has this been changing? In order to answer these questions we must consider the ideological foundations of the modern Olympic movement as it developed at the end of the 19th century.

The values of amateurism have always been at the core of the Olympic movement. Historians have told us that the social definition of sport as a purely amateur endeavor was essentially a creation of the "proper" Victorian middle class. Within the culture of this class a clearly defined sense of what constituted "manly" character was linked to a whole set of values seen to be associated with gentlemanly conduct and civilized social behavior. These values were expressed in a social definition of sporting practice that emphasized the moral primacy of fair play over the pursuit of victory, the preference for versatility over specialization, and the standards of personal restraint, selflessness, and modesty over self-centeredness and excesses in emotion (see Bailey, 1978; Gruneau, 1983; Mangan, 1981). The amateur code led to an almost puritanical conception of sport—a conception that went beyond mere games and encompassed a whole way of life. The strength of the amateur code was more than just a reflection of these seemingly innocent cultural values. Rather, it was a unique expression of patriarchal sentiment joined to class power. The men of the public school and university world, the clerks and upwardly mobile bankers and merchants, became the prominent figures in the formation of sport organizations by virtue of their influence and authority in their families and in the society at large. Their notions of what sport ought to be became the dominant view in the late 19th century.

The process of winning credibility for a particular social definition of sport was accomplished only by actively rejecting and downgrading other rival conceptions. The echoes of popular recreations from the past continued to provide a more festive and hedonistic alternative to the sober discipline and standards of gentlemanly propriety characteristic of the developing culture of amateurism in the late 19th century. But these popular traditions were being greatly undermined by the new demands of work-discipline in industrial life, and they were flatly rejected by well-established members of the bourgeoisie. In what seemed to be an increasingly Protestant era, sheer pleasure in games was simply an unacceptable goal, especially for the working classes. Their responsibilities, after all, lay in industrial production, not in leisure, and their forms of recreation were heavily regulated by the dominant class (see Bailey, 1978; Cunningham, 1980).

So neither the idle play of aristocrats nor the festive games of the men and women of earlier folk cultures were defined as sport by Victorian middle-class males. Class and patriarchal distinction were important to their views, but more significant was the manner in which the amateur code effected a unique compromise between social ascription and the advancing utilitarian sentiments of the industrial age. Indeed, amateur sport became established as a prominent feature of a utilitarian Victorian culture precisely because it transformed apparently useless game-contests into something useful. However, the uses of sport had to be limited to moral training and personal development rather than economic gain. The receipt of economic rewards for athletic proficiency was not only perceived to be ungentlemanly, it was vaguely threatening as well. Accepting money was seen as a threat because equating sporting skill with economic reward challenged the Victorian bases of social ascription and symbolized dangerous ways of thinking about equality in society at large. The idea that social rewards should be based *solely* on merit and not upon the fact of one's social origin or position in society was a radical concept.

For many members of the late 19th century upper and middle classes, such radical democratic ideas were simply unthinkable. Some historians have argued that this view led them to be wary of open competition in sport, whereas the lower classes might view victory in the contest as proof of equality (see Dunning & Sheard, 1978; Gruneau, 1983). Because professionalism opened up opportunities for athletic excellence to the working class, it was viewed with suspicion and hostility. Yet this hostility was legitimated through a host of ideological arguments. Most notably, professionalism was seen to debase play by emphasizing spectacle over participation and the outcomes of contests rather than the so-called higher morality of sportsmanship. Amateurism, on the other hand, was portrayed as the most refined and the most civilized form of sporting practice.

The Baron de Coubertin, the self-appointed founder of the modern Olympics, was greatly influenced by these class-biased sentiments. He believed the Olympic movement should dramatize virtues of modesty and discretion in the pursuit of a good contest and that the Games should occur as a cultural event in accordance with what he took to be the classical artistic traditions of ancient Greece. However, nothing was inherently classical about Coubertin's conception of sport. His view of sport and its virtues owed far more to *Tom Brown's Schooldays* (Hughes, 1968) and the ideology of English public school athletics than to the ancient Games.

Indeed, as Bruce Kidd has aptly noted, Coubertin did not revive the Olympics of classical antiquity. Rather, "he *appropriated* and *recast* the symbols of the ancient Games for his own purposes" (Kidd, 1984, p. 71).

De Coubertin's romanticism often obscures what these purposes really were, but one can find clues in the strange set of contradictory tendencies that always surrounded his own view of the Games and that became deeply embedded in the Olympic Movement. Coubertin wrote, for example, of the role the Games might play in peace and international understanding while harboring a nationalistic commitment to upgrade the physical fitness of French youth. He wrote that the Games ought to be "for everyone, with no discrimination on account of birth, caste, wealth, situation or occupation," and he was fond of referring to sports as a "democracy of ability" (Tomlinson, 1984, p. 97). But he opposed the entry of women into Olympic competition, and he was firmly committed to the class-restrictive notion of "pure amateurism."

Not everyone found it quite so easy to live with these contradictions. For example, many athletes who accepted the notion that sport ought to be a true democracy of ability saw an obvious tie between equality, athletic success, and social honor. Equal opportunity was a condition of open competition that led to the best performances by those with the most ability. Yet, the amateur code demanded that sport should be a subordinate area of life where the development of athletic ability could only be pursued by gentlemen on a casual and part-time basis. The difficulties of reconciling this contradiction virtually guaranteed a great deal of ambiguity about the exact nature and limits of amateurism.

Tensions associated with such ambiguities were fueled by a growing recognition of the obvious biases manifest in the amateur code. Under the amateur code sport clearly was only a true democracy of ability for male members of the dominant class. Barriers to women's involvement were readily evident, and, in some of the more extreme early forms of the code, merely being an artisan, tradesman, or laborer was enough to disqualify anyone from having an amateur status. But generally the code discriminated in a more subtle way. Few of the laboring masses in late 19th- and early 20th-century capitalism had the time, opportunity, or social resources to develop high skill levels in sport unless some remuneration was involved. For these people life was governed by the time clock and the factory whistle, not the playing field (see Cunningham, 1980; Gruneau, 1983; Thompson, 1967).

Even among those with time and resources who were committed to amateurism in the abstract, considerable debate existed about what degree of actual behavior the code would allow. The fact that one could achieve both enjoyment and social honor through sporting success provided such incentive to refine skills and strive for victory that the primacy of other elements in the sporting experience was often threatened. The popular Olympic motto, "faster, higher, stronger," did little to suggest any opposition to this tendency (see Lucas, 1977).

Broad changes in the social organization of work throughout the 19th century contributed greatly to this tendency. As farmers and artisans were forced off the land and became wage earners in the cities, they created a market for products and services that had hitherto been provided in a noncommodified form through the family and community. For example, clothing that had once been either made in the home or bartered for became mass produced and could be purchased with a portion of one's wages. A similar process was occurring with respect to entertainment. Traditional home and community-centered forms of entertainment, along with many new forms of recreational expression, were transformed into commodities for purchase (see Braverman, 1974; Thompson, 1983; Walvin, 1978).

Political economists refer to this process of converting entertainment into commodities as the creation of capitalism's "universal market." The logic of capitalist production tends to transform all areas of human experience into relationships governed by economic exchange. This process is important because, amateurism notwithstanding, sporting competition was clearly drawn into the universal market during the latter half of the 19th century.

What was the main basis for this change? One can answer this question by indicating how the incorporation of various forms of traditional work into wage labor and industrial routine created a separation between work time, which was owned by an employer, and leisure time, which was ones own. However, the choices available during leisure time were shaped by the degree to which the new forms of industrial work had destroyed traditional forms of family and community life and their accompanying spaces, times, and opportunities for amusement. As a result, time spent away from work gradually became dependent upon the marketplace as a source of personal gratification. This situation gave considerable impetus to the commodification of all forms of entertainment and popular recreation. For example, sport facilities were provided by entrepreneurs for a fee, admission was charged for watching sporting events, and new markets developed for sporting equipment (see Goldman, 1984). Because the industrial division of labor defined most forms of wage work as masculine and domestic work as feminine, primarily males used a portion of their wage packets to partake in the emerging commodified forms of sporting entertainment. For most women, leisure time meant something entirely different.

The transformation was part of an emerging world that the guardians of the Olympic credo wanted to resist. In the face of increasingly secular and market-oriented tendencies all around them they continued to assert a view of the world that, for all its idealistic overtones, was steeped in patriarchal biases and class prejudice. But ideals alone are not enough to realize practical objectives in a political or cultural project. People are forced to work with available social materials, and this usually involves important compromises and pragmatic decisions. We are often told about the noble goals of the Olympic movement, but we seldom hear about the less noble, more practical considerations.

The most pragmatic of these considerations has always been the question of money. Ironically, in order to achieve the higher ideals proposed for the Games, the founders of the Olympics were forced into relationships of convenience with purely entrepreneurial interests. This fact does not imply that the affluent and aristocratic members of the early Olympic committees were necessarily hostile to capitalism. They were clearly not, especially when capitalism could be tailored to suit their interests. Rather, for the IOC members something about capitalism seemed greatly incompatible with the possibility of preserving the noncommercial ideals of the Games.

This point should be clarified. No matter what the intentions of the founders of the modern Olympics, the actual possibilities open to them were limited by the nature of the economic system as a whole and the network of social institutions associated with it. In a capitalist economy any large-scale sporting activity will involve at least some commercialization. Facilities have to be built, services provided, land bought and sold, and the whole thing requires financing. The economic realities associated with holding the Games were evident right from the start.[2]

The Olympic Games:
From Trade Fair Sideshow
to International Spectacle

Alliances between International Olympic Committees and local entrepreneurial interests in the host nations of the earliest Games are readily apparent. The 1900 Games were held in conjunction with the Paris Universal Exhibition, and the 1904 Games were incorporated into the St. Louis World Fair (see Kanin, 1981). In the latter city the sporting events occurred in the midst of areas reserved for displays of weaving machines, tractors, threshers, and other examples of industrial and agricultural equipment. Baron de Coubertin and his associates were so upset by this crass trade fair atmosphere that they arranged a special off-year Olympics to be held in Athens in 1906.

Despite such apparent setbacks, the relationship of convenience between business and the Olympics continued. The London Games of 1908 were linked to the Anglo-French exhibition, and the British, who had just signed a trade agreement with the Russians, put pressure on Finland to march behind the Russian flag in the opening ceremonies (see Whannel, 1983). One can see by this example how even in 1908 the Olympics were drawn into the economic struggles of modern nation states. In the Stockholm Games of 1912 competitors could no longer enter as individuals but only as part of a national team. This change was affected largely for convenience but it has had a significant long-term effect (see Kanin, 1981).

By the time of the Los Angeles Olympics of 1932, state and civic officials in western nations were aware that the Games had considerable utility for promoting national prestige, civic pride, tourism, urban development, and commercial growth. Los Angeles had sought the Games in order to demonstrate to both the eastern American financial establishment and the rest of the world that Southern California was a thriving commercial and cultural center. Colored by a proximity to the romance and glamour of Hollywood, the 1932 Los Angeles Olympics symbolized many of the positive features of the "American Dream." Yet, large numbers of people were critical of the expenditure of public funds on sport during a time of national economic crisis and depression. Nonetheless, more than 700 news reporters gathered in Los Angeles (at that time, the most ever assembled for any sporting event), and stories from the Games were sent around the world on transoceanic cable. As it turned out, the Games proved to be extremely popular and even turned a modest profit (see Espy, 1979; Kanin, 1981).

The successful 1932 Los Angeles Olympics were an effective symbol for a powerful young nation flexing its international muscle in the markets and cultures of the world. Four years later, Adolph Hitler hoped to utilize the Games in a far more obvious and spectacular way to symbolize Germany's return to power under National Socialism. The infamous 1936 "Nazi Olympics" fell well short of meeting Hitler's dream of demonstrating Aryan superiority to the world and were marked by international controversy (see Kanin, 1981; Mandell, 1971). Yet they introduced a new scale and level of cost to the Olympic movement.

The Berlin Games also demonstrated the extent to which the economic and political stakes associated with the Olympics had risen throughout the first 40 years of this century. As the imperial powers jostled for position in an international capitalist system, this struggle became symbolically dramatized with the performances of individual athletes and national teams. The intensity of this drama contributed to the success and popularity of the Olympic movement (see Espy, 1979). By the end of World War II, and with the addition of competitors from the Soviet Union for the first time since 1912, the stage was set for the Olympics to become an international spectacle of unprecedented visibility and importance.

The postwar Olympics proved to be a news reporter's dream. Not only did the Games combine pageantry and excitement with powerful romantic images of universalism and the human quest for excellence, but they had political overtones that helped guarantee a large and interested audience for Olympic coverage. In the case of privately owned forms of media, this meant a vast pool of potential consumers ready to be tapped by commercial sponsors. Thus an extremely close relationship began to develop in the postwar era between television and the Olympics. Television net-works in the mid-1950s had little more than a passing involvement with the Helsinki Games, but the American networks became impressed with the public response to nationwide broadcasts of events from the Squaw Valley Winter Olympics in 1960. Later that summer, the Rome Olympics were broadcast throughout the industrialized world. The implications of this for the commercialization of Olympic sport were highly significant. Public interest in the Games could now be given a monetary value mea-sured in terms of potential advertising rates, and sporting stars could be-come highly visible international sales representatives for the sporting goods industry (see Seifart, 1984; Whannel, 1984).

The Italians did not participate in the 1948 London Games, but they won the World Cup Soccer Championship in 1950 and were anxious to further dramatize their return to the world stage following their defeat in World War II. The Olympics were an ideal vehicle for touting the suc-cesses of the Italian postwar recovery and for establishing even stronger trade contacts with North America. As a result the Italians spent lavishly on the Games by widening the roads for the games traffic and develop-ing several public works projects as well as the constructing of athletic facilities (see "Olympic Rome," 1960). Japan also used the Games in 1964 to announce its ascendency in postwar international trade, and they went the Italians one better in the scale of Olympic construction. Elaborate ath-letic facilities, expressways, and rail lines were all built in order to bolster tourism and local commerce and impress potential trade partners.[3] The 1968 Mexico City Games were equally extravagant and strained Mexico's financial resources despite a state orchestrated "national sports effort" designed to raise funds. Criticisms of spending priorities that put money in the hands of bankers, developers, contractors, and owners of tourist facilities, at the expense of projects that might have alleviated massive poverty in Mexico, were simply brushed aside[4] (cf. Brohm, 1978).

Throughout the late 1950s, IOC President Avery Brundage had sought to reduce the size and cost of the Games. He was particularly critical of the more than $60 million budget projected for the Rome Games (a bud-get that seems paltry by today's standards). The key point here is that Brundage's concerns had little effect. By the 1960s the IOC had effectively lost control of the economic scale of the Olympics.[5] For one thing, the Soviet Union was ardently championing the sporting interests of Third World countries as a part of its international sport policy, and this meant strong pressures to add teams and events rather than reduce them (see Bazunov, 1973). More significantly, holding the Games and performing well in them had become such powerful symbols of national character and economic stature that an almost built-in tendency existed for an ex-panding Olympic spectacle. Finally, the Olympics of the 1960s were close-ly intertwined with a powerful international bloc of financial, travel, retail, and media interests whose potential profits were tied to the increasing size and visibility of the Games (see Espy, 1979).

Los Angeles 1984:
Economic Crisis and the Olympics

The 1970s witnessed the ever-escalating fusion of state and private interests in the Olympics. The 1964 Winter Games in Innsbruck, Austria, cost more than $100 million, but the 1972 Winter Olympics in Sapporo, Japan cost nearly 7 times that much (see Espy, 1979; Snyder & Spreitzer, 1983). Along the same lines, the 1972 Summer Olympics in Munich cost an incredible $750 million (see Gilbert, 1973), but in Montreal 4 years later costs soared to $1 1/2 billion. Reported estimates of the cost of the 1980 Games in Moscow vary considerably but range between $2 and 9 billion.[6]

Sales of public bonds, direct state investment, and donations from local entrepreneurs cannot adequately cover such staggering sums. As a result, Olympic organizing committees were virtually forced into marketing the Olympics themselves as a commodity. Sales of television rights have been a major and expanding source of revenue since 1960, as has sponsorship by various corporate bodies (Miller, 1979). The Rome Olympics had 46 private sponsors that made goods and services available to the Games (see "Olympic Rome," 1960). In 1976, Montreal associated itself with 168 "official" products (including the ubiquitous Coca-Cola, which paid $1.3 million for rights, and provided all the Coke athletes could drink for the duration of the Olympics). Moscow showed its proclivity for state capitalism by endorsing 200 Olympic products, and the 1980 Winter Olympics at Lake Placid found 381 buyers for the Olympic logo.[7]

Yet all this money was not enough. For example, the 381 corporate sponsors at Lake Placid only generated $9 million in revenue, far short of what was required. Montreal also failed to raise sufficient corporate revenues and desperately tried to create additional revenue with all manner of state-sponsored sales schemes from lotteries to Olympic coins. All these fundraising schemes were failures. Due to financial mismanagement, corruption, and the scale of Montreal mayor Jean Drapeau's grand ambitions, the 1976 Games left a $1 billion deficit—a deficit for which Montreal taxpayers are still paying (Auf de Maur, 1976).

In the wake of the Montreal experience, hosting the Games no longer looked quite so attractive. The international bloc of commercial interests that profited so well from the Olympics had not been paying the majority of the costs, and potential hosts of the Games appeared to believe the Olympics may have reached a point of diminishing returns. Thus only two cities were in the running for the 1984 Summer Games, Los Angeles and Tehran (then still under the rule of the Shah). Tehran eventually withdrew and Los Angeles became the only applicant.

But the late 1970s were not a time to justify massive amounts of public spending. Throughout California a stubborn resistance to tax increases signified the broader assault on public spending that was developing throughout western capitalist countries. California, the state that first elected Ronald Reagan to public office, had widespread support for his laissez-faire views on modern economics. In a city-wide referendum only 34% of the citizens of Los Angeles said they would support the Olympics if it cost them any money. The city then amended its charter so that Los Angeles taxpayers would not be liable for an Olympic deficit.

Rule 4 of the IOC charter (IOC, 1983) insists that host cities be liable for costs incurred during an Olympic Games, and the IOC was extremely upset about the amendment of Los Angeles city bylaws. Yet with no other applications for the 1984 Games some kind of compromise had to be arranged. The compromise allowed the United States Olympic Committee and a private nonprofit corporation to share joint responsibility for financing the Olympics. These two groups in turn contracted to guarantee zero financial liability for the city of Los Angeles. So even though the Olympics were "officially" awarded to the city, a private company came to actually run the show. The private corporation created the Los Angeles Olympic Organizing Committee (LAOOC) and demanded that it be given complete control over all Olympic planning—another condition reluctantly agreed to by the IOC (see Miller, 1979).

The LAOOC immediately set out to design what Chairman Peter Ueberroth referred to as "a private Olympics without government subsidies" (Callaghan, 1983, p. 73). It established a $500 million budget and designed a corporate sponsorship plan that was nothing short of brilliant in its simplicity. The LAOOC restricted the number of corporate sponsors to 30 but jacked the price up to a minimum of $4 million, plus provision of corporate services where possible. A third requirement was that sponsoring companies demonstrate "a commitment of some sort to sporting youth" (Callaghan, 1983, p. 75).[8]

Thus began one of the most unique and publically visible business deals in the history of corporate capitalism. Atlantic Richfield Co. helped to refurbish the Los Angeles Coliseum, Southland Corporation (7-Eleven convenience stores) built the Olympic velodrome, IBM supplied computer equipment, AT&T (and Motorola) set up the communications, General Motors provided the cars, Levi's provided "official" clothing, and McDonald's built the Olympic pool. Not surprisingly, most of these and other sponsors also made plans to invest large amounts of money advertising on ABC's Olympic broadcasts in an attempt to make the Games the central element of their 1984 marketing strategies. For example, Coca-Cola not only gave the LAOOC $12.6 million in order to be designated the official Olympic soft drink, but also is estimated to have spent more than $30 million to advertise on Olympic telecasts. Anheuser Busch planned to spend an extra $30 million peddling beer during the Games, and Levi Strauss and Co. planned to spend more than $40 million in order to use the Olympics as a vehicle to extend "brand awareness" outside the company's traditional image as manufacturers of denim jeans and shirts (see Yovovich, 1983).

These are just a few examples of the advertising strategies used by the 30 official Olympic sponsors. In fact, actually many more companies were formally involved with the Olympics because the LAOOC also licensed 43 independent companies to sell a wide variety of merchandise embossed with the Olympic logo. Furthermore, similar sponsorship arrangements were made between various corporations and the different National Olympic Committees. However, the most important point to make about all of this is that the selling of the Olympics in Los Angeles went on without apology. Indeed, following in the wake of the obvious Olympic successes, many previous critics of the Games actually came to admire the Los Angeles approach. The Olympics were held without increasing tax burdens, hotel and retail businesses in Los Angeles and in the sports industry seemed to benefit, and the Games earned an estimated surplus in excess of $215 million, much of which was earmarked for the U.S. Olympic committee and various youth sport groups (see Ajemian, 1985).[9] Peter Ueberroth appeared to anticipate these successes throughout the year leading up to the Games. He argued that the Los Angeles approach would be the economic savior of the Olympics because it was not interested in staging an expensive spectacle to enhance a national image. As a private company rather than a nation, Ueberroth was fond of saying, "We have no statement to make. We are celebrating sport" (Callaghan, 1983, p.78).

But what *kind* of sport did the LAOOC celebrate? How true is Peter Ueberroth's argument that the Los Angeles Olympics had no statement to make? A highly specialized and commercially-oriented elite sport is being supported here, not a form of recreational sport for the broadest possible number of participants. Furthermore, the statement made by having the names of the great corporations plastered over Olympic facilities and littered throughout Olympic advertising is an obvious one: Such sponsorship signifies the omnipresence of corporate capital in our lives, even to the extent of dominating our games (see Inglis, 1977). This capital is in no way innocent of politics or national sentiment, as the Los Angeles Games clearly showed. American capitalism held the Los Angeles Olympics, and the Games took on the character of a hymn to American initiative, skill, showmanship, and entrepreneurial ability.[10]

All of this commercialism at the L.A. Olympics is further evidence of the extent to which sport in modern capitalist societies has been drawn into capitalism's universal market. People still enjoy sports for all the old reasons—for the drama and excitement, the aesthetics of the well-played shot, the mastery, and the courageous performances. But the major forums for creating and celebrating these qualities have changed in ways that often subvert the very qualities that make sport so appealing. In sports we want to see the expression of human personal powers in a way that momentarily transcends the dominant categories that govern our everyday lives. Carl Lewis's cautious passing in the long jump was so disturbing because it juxtaposed the possibility of the ultimate realization of Lewis's physical powers with the kind of rational calculation that one might expect from an investment counselor.

The paradox, however, is that at the highest levels the investment counselors and the marketing executives have now become necessary for staging big-time athletic contests. Certainly at the community level sport might retain ties to a popular aesthetics that go beyond purely economic considerations. No matter how commodified or commercially oriented, one will always witness acts of drama, courage, and power that speak to a human yearning for utopian possibilities. But such moments are likely to live in increasing and perilous conflict with the forces sustaining the very structures that constitute modern sports as social possibilities (see Gruneau, 1983). Indeed, if the lines of what constituted sport as a cultural product were once blurred by an indissoluble connection with folk cultures and class prejudice, they are now blended fully into the class and consumer-oriented logic of postwar international capitalism. Throughout this century sport has become progressively more commodified to the point where, at its highest levels, it is now a simple division of the entertainment and light consumer goods industries.

However, the continuing incorporation of sport into capitalism's universal market in this century has not gone unopposed. Considerable resistance can be found both from the lingering antiprofessional traditions of amateurism and the popular resistance against the use of public revenues to build elaborate facilities and to offset Olympic deficits. Yet the result of this latter resistance was to clear the way for the "McLympics" (as many commentators called them) and another stage in the commodification of international sport. Government policies throughout the majority of the capitalist countries have done little to oppose this development. Instead, they have readily incorporated high degrees of commercialism into their programs. National Olympic Associations and individual sporting associations have also made major financial arrangements with corporate sponsors in order to ensure adequate funding (see Cantelon, 1984; Kidd, 1981). The result has been a coalescence of business, voluntary, and state interests in the pursuit of international sporting success. However much the interests of these various groups may diverge, economic and political necessity has forced compromises and has subtly reinforced a particular view of what sport is and ought to be in our society.

Concluding Comments

We have argued that out of the contested Olympic terrain comprised of struggles between men and women, different social classes, nation states, and other interest groups, a new dominant social definition of sport has slowly been consolidated. The definition is built on the emergent elements of late 19th-century patriarchy and commercial sport and is now sealed through the broad social and political/economic changes of the 20th century in the newly won legitimacy of a fully commodified Olympic movement. Within this context sporting practice is widely understood (ideally) as a completely open, achievement-based activity, conducted for the purposes of sporting careers and economic reward. Also included is the notion that enjoyment in sport is tied to skill acquisition, that specialization is the basis for excellence, and that economic reward of some type or another is justified and necessary in order to achieve at the highest levels.

We want to emphasize that none of this could have occurred without fundamental changes in the economic organization and the class structure of the capitalist societies of the 20th century and especially in the postwar era. As a result of these changes the dominant culture of the modern middle classes is a long way from that of the Victorian gentlemen. Now we have a culture that combines a commitment to scientific rationality with the pursuit of the good life through mass consumerism. At the state level this culture is technical, bureaucratic, and corporate. At the popular cultural level it is individualistic and commodity-oriented. The culture also has expanded the utilitarian justification in sport from the moral and the personal to the economic and the professional.

The Los Angeles Olympics represented and embodied all of these changes in an uncompromising and unprecedented way. But they were also something more. At a time when right-wing governments in western capitalist nations were waging a full-scale assault on the concept of the welfare state, the successful commercialism of the Los Angeles Olympics signified the apparent triumph of capitalist enterprise over welfare state planning and public expenditure.[11]

In many respects this apparent triumph was a false one. Government involvement with sport, and especially Olympic sport, in the era of the postwar welfare state, has rarely had anything to do with public welfare. Rather, it has been more tied to Keynesian strategies of economic stimulation, national image marketing, and capital accumulation.

Of course, a state might put public money in sport to a different use. For example, a different orientation might argue that public money is better spent on small decentralized facilities and the enhancement of programs and opportunities at the municipal level and in conjunction with community groups and local authorities. The problem, however, is that such an approach does not meet the needs nor fit readily into the culture of the bloc of shared interests that have become associated with international high-performance sport. These interests and this culture are better served by massive centralized facilities, a star-centered training and publicity system, and a complex infrastructure of sport scientists, coaches, technical personnel, and bureaucrats.

After the $1 billion deficit of Montreal it became evident to many people that the use of public funds for projects created largely for political image mongering or pure capital accumulation should be more closely monitored. In this sense one can truly understand the fears of Los Angeles taxpayers when approached with the prospect of hosting the Olympics in their city. Most people tend not to benefit directly from the Olympics except in some sort of passive spectatorial way. For this reason legitimate grounds will always exist for debate whether the good feeling that comes from international sporting success or from hosting international sporting contests is worth the expenditure. Certainly, had Montreal's $1 billion deficit been allocated to other areas, the effects could have been stunning. How much low-rent housing could have been provided? How many years of subsidized public recreation or community sport would Quebec citizens have had? To what extent would money spent on day care or on inexpensive mass transit have opened up opportunities for sporting participation for women, the handicapped, or the chronically unemployed? Instead, the Games that were held primarily benefited local and international commercial interests, middle-class sport associations and bureaucracies, and the sport professions.

When the citizens of Los Angeles adopted the principle that the people who benefit most from the Olympics should also pay for it, they took one more step toward the full scale demystification of Olympic sport and the dominance of a new social definition of sport's meaning and legitimate features.

The long-term results of these changes are difficult to predict. In North America a growing concern is that residues of the ideology of amateurism are obscuring recognition of the fact that many international athletes are quasi-professionals or state employees with rights to representation, due process, compensation for injury, and so on (see Kidd & Eberts, 1982). Athletes have even talked of forming trade unions, and some parents are wondering why child athletes are not governed by laws similar to those that regulate child performers in the theater (see Cantelon, 1981). The march of capital into sport has generated its own contradictions.

Undoubtedly, modern sport will eventually get these problems sorted out through basic liberal reforms and new legal and organizational structures. But what we find most troubling is the probability that the shared bloc of vested interests involved with modern Olympism has increasingly been able to impose its definition of sport upon all of us. Commodified and highly commercialized sport, with its star system and instrumental character, is presented as natural and inevitable. Furthermore, sport is presented not as something qualitatively different from recreational or community sport, but as something representing that sport pushed to its logical extension. As this occurs, and we see evidence of it everywhere, the Olympics become something, ironically, that stand in the way of increasing opportunities for sport as an economically nonproductive activity.

All of this strikes us as something that demands a new kind of resistence in sport. By "new resistence" we do not mean a revolt against the apparent "corruption" of some idealized Olympic spirit, or an attempt to reassert an amateurism that was always loaded with class prejudice and patriarchal bias. Nor are we referring to a California-style revolt against the use of any public expenditures in sport whatsoever. Rather, we are suggesting a struggle to assert a counterdefinition of amateur sport as a noncommodified set of social practices open to everyone, and to ensure that this definition is adequately supported in the funding programs of the welfare state. People objecting to the messages embodied in the Los Angeles Olympics have a clearly defined political agenda, one that aligns them with all those groups in western capitalist societies opposed to a philosophy that finds virtue in the commodification of everything.

Notes

1. A shorter and slightly different version of this paper was originally published by R. Gruneau in Tomlinson and Whannel (1984). The version that appears here stems from discussions held during research on the Queen's University Centre for Sport and Leisure Studies television project. The authors wish to acknowledge the support of the Social Sciences and Humanities Research Council that made these discussions possible.

2. Auf du Maur (1976) notes, for example, that the Athens Games in 1896 had projected expenses of approximately 200 drachmas but ended up costing more than a million.

3. The aggressiveness of Japanese industrialists did not escape the attention of the Japanese Olympic Committee. As reported in *Business Week* ("Yen for the Games," 1964) the JOC noted how "Japanese businessmen . . . view the Olympics as a chance in a lifetime to show their wares to the international set."

4. To cite just one of many examples, the 1968 Olympic Village was built by Mexican banking interests. It was leased to the Olympic Committee and later converted into middle-income condominiums, which were sold to well-heeled citizens. Furthermore, an area of lush landscape and truck farms was destroyed by digging a ditch to house the rowing events (see "Mexico City's Olympic Feats," 1968).

5. Brundage lamented that the Olympics had become "a huge business enterprise instead of another sports event" (Brundage Papers, Circular 487, University of Illinois). In another reference he bemoaned "the materialism of our times which tends to reduce the Games to a commercial carnival" (Brundage Papers, Circular 57).

6. See, for example, Callaghan (1983) and Snyder and Spreitzer (1978).

7. See Callaghan (1983, p. 72) and Farber (1983).
8. See Ajemian (1985); Callaghan (1983); and Farber (1983).
9. It would be incorrect, however, to believe that the Los Angeles Games did not cost American taxpayers money. While official data are hard to get it has been estimated that the cost of security and policing alone ranged between $50 and $100 million.
10. This was no more evident than in the remarkable enthusiasm that surrounded the medal winning performances of American athletes and in the attitude of Peter Ueberroth himself. After being named "Man of the Year" by *Time* January 7 (1985, p. 25) he commented, "People weren't afraid to stand up and cheer for the country . . . and the rest of the world saw how caring America can be." Future scholars may well see the Los Angeles Olympics as a cultural event that dramatically signified the final assuagement of the feelings of impotence and confusion following the Vietnam experience and the Iranian hostage-taking.
11. Witness Peter Ueberroth's statement that "In the U.S. . . . there's a spirit of can-do, can-work, can-accomplish—you can do things without being on the Government dole" (*Time*, January 7, 1985, p. 25).

References

Ajemian, R. (1985, January 7). Master of the Games. *Time*, pp. 20-25.

Auf de Maur, N. (1976). *The billion-dollar game: Jean Drapeau and the 1976 Olympics.* Toronto: J. Lorimer and Co.

Bailey, P. (1978). *Leisure and class in Victorian England: Rational recreation and the contest for control 1830-1885.* London: Routledge and Kegan Paul.

Bazunov, B. (1973). Stages of integration. *Sport in the USSR*, 2, 18-19.

Braverman, H. (1974). *Labour and monopoly capital.* New York: Monthly Review Press.

Brohm, J.-M. (1978). The Olympics and capitalist accumulation. *Sport: A Prison of Measured Time.* London: Pluto Press.

Brundage, A. *Avery Brundage collection.* University of Illinois, Urbana.

Callaghan, T. (1983, October 17). Eve of a new Olympics. *Time*, pp. 72-81.

Cantelon, H. (1981). High performance sport and the child athlete: Learning to labour. In A. Ingham & E. Broom (Eds.), *Career patterns and career contingencies in sport* (pp. 258-286). Vancouver: University of British Columbia Press.

Cantelon, H. (1984). The Canadian absence from the XXIInd Olympiad: Some plausible explanations. In M. Ilmarien (Ed.), *Sport and international understanding* (pp. 145-151). Berlin: Springer-Verlag.

Cunningham, H. (1980). *Leisure in the Industrial Revolution, 1780-1880.* New York: St. Martin's Press.

Dunning, E., & Sheard, K. (1978). *Barbarians, gentlemen and players: A sociological study of the development of rugby football.* Oxford: M. Robertson.

Espy, R. (1979). *The politics of the Olympic Games.* Berkeley: University of California Press.

Farber, M. (1983, August 19). No free lunch at McLympics. *Vancouver Sun,* p. 9.

Gilbert, D. (1973, February 10). Munich's giant hangover. *Edmonton Journal,* p. 8.

Goldman, R. (1984, Winter). We make weekends: Leisure and the commodity form. *Social Text,* **8,** 84-103.

Gruneau, R. (1983). *Class, sports and social development.* Amherst: University of Massachusetts Press.

Hughes, T. (1968). *Tom Brown's schooldays.* New York: Airmont.

Inglis, F. (1977). *The name of the game.* London: Heinemann.

International Olympic Committee. (1983). *Olympic charter.* Lausanne: Comité International Olympique.

Kanin, D.B. (1981). *A political history of the Olympic Games.* Boulder: Westview Press.

Kidd, B. (1981). Sport and the Canadian state. In V. Crafts (Ed.), *Proceedings of the National Association for Physical Education in Higher Education* (pp. 239-250). Champaign, IL: Human Kinetics.

Kidd, B. (1984). The myth of the ancient Games. In A. Tomlinson & G. Whannel (Eds.), *Five ring circus: Money, power and politics at the Olympic Games* (pp. 71-83). London: Pluto Press.

Kidd, B., & Eberts, M. (1982). *Athletes' rights in Canada.* Toronto: Ministry of Tourism and Recreation.

Lucas, J. (1977). Early Olympic antagonists: Pierre de Coubertin versus James E. Sullivan. *Stadion,* 3(2), 258-272.

Mandell, R.D. (1971). *The Nazi Olympics.* New York: Macmillan.

Mangan, J.A. (1981). *Athleticism in the Victorian and Edwardian public school: The emergence and consolidation of an educational ideology.* Cambridge: Cambridge University Press.

Mexico City's Olympic feats. (1968, March). *Fortune,* pp. 149+.

Miller, G. (1979). *Behind the Olympic rings.* Lynn, MA: Zimman.

Olympic Rome. (1960, July 16). *Economist*, pp. 289-290.

Seifart, H. (1984). Sport and economy: The commercialization of sport by the media. *International Review of Sport Sociology*, **9**, 305-315.

Snyder, E.E., & Spreitzer, E.A. (1983). *Social aspects of sport* (2nd ed.). Englewood Cliffs, NJ: Prentice-Hall.

Thompson, E.P. (1967, December). Time, work-discipline and industrial capitalism. *Past and Present*, pp. 56-97.

Thompson, G. (1983). The presentation and consumption of leisure: Blackpool as a "site" of pleasure. In A. Tomlinson (Ed.), *Leisure and popular culture forms* (pp. 116-148). Brighton: Chelsea School of Human Movement, Brighton Polytechnic.

Time. (1985, January 7). [no title]. **125**(1).

Tomlinson, A. (1984). De Coubertin and the modern Olympics. In A. Tomlinson & G. Whannel (Eds.), *Five ring circus: Money, power and politics at the Olympic Games* (pp. 84-97). London: Pluto Press.

Walvin, J. (1978). *Leisure and society 1830-1950*. London: Longman.

Whannel, G. (1983). *Blowing the whistle*. London: Pluto Press.

Whannel, G. (1984). The television spectacular. In A. Tomlinson & G. Whannel (Eds.), *Five ring circus: Money, power and politics at the Olympic Games* (pp. 30-43). London: Pluto Press.

Yen for the games: Japan has spent heavily to prepare for next month's Olympics. (1964, September 26). *Business Week*, pp. 40-41.

Yovovich, B.G. (1983, February 7). The 1984 Olympics: A run for the money. *Advertising Age*, pp. M9-10.

22
Tryphosa, Melpomene, Nadia, and Joan: The IOC and Women's Sport

Betty Spears

The issue of women in the Olympic movement is symbolized by both ancient and modern female athletes—Tryphosa, Melpomene, Nadia, and Joan—each of whom represents women's sport in a period important in the history of the Olympic Games. In defiance of feminine *arete* (i.e., desirable womanly qualities), which determined women's role in ancient Greek society, Tryphosa won races in several ancient athletic festivals, but not at Olympia. Although Coubertin did not want women in the modern Games, the Greek woman runner, Melpomene, is said to have challenged late 19th-century concepts of womanhood by unofficially competing in the marathon in 1896. In contrast to Tryphosa's and Melpomene's little noted athletic performances, the world watched and marveled at the athletic excellence of Nadia Comaneci in 1976 and Joan Benoit in 1984. In this chapter, I will examine briefly the cultural perspective of women and women's sport in ancient Greece, the late 19th century, and today's Games. I will suggest the relationship of ancient and modern sportswomen to the IOC's position on women's sport.

An Ancient Greek Sportswoman

In planning for the revival of the Olympic Games, Pierre de Coubertin deliberately combined both ancient and modern sport concepts, correctly surmising that a replication of ancient athletic festivals would not be successful in the modern world. For example, the Olympic movement is a modern concept devised by Coubertin to promote the idealized international sport that he envisioned. Rather than choosing a permanent site for the modern festivals, Coubertin proposed holding the Games in different cities throughout the world. He omitted ancient events such as the pankration and added modern sports such as shooting, fencing, tennis, and cycling. Coubertin also retained the celebration of virile, male sport and attempted to continue the ancient tradition of excluding women from the Olympic Games, a custom consistent with woman's role in ancient Greek culture.

Throughout Greek history feminine arete or desirable womanly qualities were beauty and "chastity, modesty, obedience, and inconspicuous behavior" (North, 1966, p. 1). Homer's Andromache, the classic example of feminine arete, was a good wife and skilled in the household arts. Of all the well-known characters in the *Iliad* and the *Odyssey*, only Nausicaa engaged in games and sport-like activities. In the 6th century B.C., Solon, the Athenian lawgiver, endorsed the arete from Homer's time as the preferred behavior for women. Only in Sparta did women exercise and compete in athletics, and then only to produce sound babies, preferably male. As the Greek empire expanded during the Hellenistic period, the center for philosophy and culture remained in Athens, where the ancient teachings of Solon reaffirmed the traditional female arete. Although some girls attended school in the newer, distant Greek cities and sometimes became artists, musicians, physicians, and writers, little evidence shows that feminine arete changed substantially during the 1,200-year period of the ancient athletic festivals.

With women striving for attributes such as modesty and inconspicuous behavior, the evidence for women's sport during this period is not surprisingly rather scant. Homer describes Nausicaa playing an informal ball game, Pausanias recounts the Herean Games, Plutarch reports the Olympic victory of Cynisca's horses, and several authors refer to Sparta's female athletes. However, these authors did not focus on women in sport and certainly could not be considered sportswriters. Created over centuries by wandering bards, Homer's poetry is an account of early Greek daily life and values. Pausanias' *Description of Greece*, the major source of information about the Herean Games, was written at least 800 years after the period he described. In contrast to these infrequent and casual references to women's sport, accounts of men's sport and athletics abound in ancient Greek literature. Homer vividly describes events from chariot racing to boxing. Pausanias furnishes a detailed account of the Olympic Games, and Herodotus, Thucydides, and other Greek authors refer to the Olympic Games and athletic festivals such as the Pythian, Isthmian, and Nemean Games.

Archaeological evidence of women's sport-like activities in ancient Greece does exist. Statuettes, epigrams, and vase paintings suggest that women drove chariots, swam, engaged in informal ball games, and juggled balls. Statuettes of female runners from the Archaic period and later inscriptions and bronzes are further proof of women's sport. Vase paintings depicting women juggling balls and swimming are considered authentic sources of daily life activities. But for each vase depicting women in sport-like activities, about 20 show men in athletic activities in palaestra scenes. Whereas the names of five women whose horses won races appear on surviving victory lists from Olympia, hundreds of men's names are recorded. Certainly, in ancient Greece the importance of men's sport and athletics with their vital role in honoring gods and the lack of importance of women's sport cannot be denied.

This relationship between men's and women's sport is reflected in Coubertin's planning for the modern Olympic Games. What Coubertin could not have known was that by the 1st century A.D., girls *did* compete in ancient athletic festivals, although not at Olympia. Tryphosa's victories were not known until 1909, well after the first modern Olympiad. Even though the fragments bearing the information about Tryphosa had been discovered in 1894, they were not pieced together until 1909.

Not only Tryphosa, but also her sisters, Hedea and Dionysia, were female victors. The inscription reveals that Hermesianax, perhaps an early example of a devoted father of athletic girls, dedicated a statue to Apollo in honor of his three daughters who won events at three major festivals and two local festivals. The girls competed in and won single-course races, chariot races, and races in armor. Tryphosa was honored for winning the single-course race at the Pythian Games and the Isthmian Games. Hedea won the race in armor at the Isthmian Games and the single-course race at Nemea and at the Sicyonian Games, and Dionysia was the victor of the single-course race at the Asclepian Games. One other inscription of a girl victor exists bearing the information that Nicegora won a race, but the site of the race is not known, and the date of the race has not been established.

How might Coubertin have changed his plans for the modern Olympic Games had he known about these athletic girls? Might he have considered Tryphosa a forerunner of the few emerging sportswomen of the 1890s and a rationale for including women in the modern Games? Possibly, but probably not. Typical of the majority of people in the late 19th century, Coubertin did not approve of women's sport. Throughout his writings, he expressed his views against women in sport. He did not think well of women perspiring in public, assuming positions he deemed ungainly, and appearing in public riding horses, skiing, or playing soccer. His views are summarized in a 1912 essay (Leigh, 1974), "Women in the Olympic Games," in which he defined the Olympic Games as "the solemn and periodic exaltation of male athleticism with internationalism as a base, loyalty as a means, art for its setting, and female applause as reward" (p. 76). Indeed, more than 1,700 years after Tryphosa won races in ancient Greece, little appeared to have changed in the cultural perspective of women and women's sport.

A 19th-Century Sportswoman

Just as the desirable qualities of women in ancient Greece were characterized by feminine arete—chastity, modesty, obedience, and inconspicuous behavior—19th-century womanhood was defined by similar characteristics—piety, purity, domesticity, and submissiveness. These ideals represented the role Coubertin thought appropriate for women: admiring, approving, and applauding the male athlete, but not being an athlete. Nineteenth-century fashion for women with long, heavy skirts and pinched waists helped mold women into inactive roles. By the end of the century, however, when the Olympic Games were being revived, social and technological factors had created a climate in which society, albeit perhaps grudgingly, had begun to accept some modest sport-like pastimes for women. Croquet, introduced in the mid-19th century, could be played by women despite their long, multilayered skirts. Later, the bicycle brought not only enjoyment and freedom to many women, but also a change in fashion. Bicycle enthusiasts abandoned their corsets, donned bifurcated skirts well above the ankles, and enjoyed a new freedom from restrictive clothing. By 1887 a sufficient number of women played tennis in the United States to warrant a national championship. In addition to providing quiet pastimes and gentle competition, sport and exercise became an accepted means of improving women's health, especially in the women's colleges. By the 1890s women rowed, fenced, played basketball, golfed, and played many other sports.

Although Coubertin's plans for the modern Games ignored the growing number of sportswomen and excluded them from the beginning, one source (Foldes, 1964) suggests that women sought to compete. Melpomene, the Greek woman runner, was reported to have applied for entry. After training secretly for 3 weeks, she sought permission to take part in the 1896 marathon. The officials refused her application, but Melpomene unofficially ran the distance of 40 km from Marathon to Athens in 4 1/2 hours, about 1 1/2 hours slower than the winner. According to the story, the Greek newspaper *Akropolis* applauded Melpomene and reported that the Olympic Committee had been discourteous in not allowing the Greek woman to run.

Beginning in 1900 women officially received gold medals in an occasional Olympic event. Gradually more women entered Olympic competition. The turning points for women occurred in 1910 when the international swimming federation requested events for women in the 1912 Games and in 1926 when the international athletic federation agreed to recommend a program of five events for women in the 1928 Games. The International Olympic Committee (IOC) slowly and grudgingly accepted women in a few sports. In sharp contrast to this position, Coubertin and the IOC supported and promoted men's sport during the early Olympiads. Disappointed in the carnival atmosphere of the 1900 and 1904 Games, Coubertin instituted an "interim" festival in 1906 to encourage serious international competition in Olympic sports. At that time international sport lacked consistent rules, trained officials, and governing bodies. Coubertin encouraged the improvement of these facets of men's international sport which, in turn, helped establish the Olympic Games as an important international sport event. In comparison with men's sport, the IOC neither fostered nor assisted the expansion of women's sport. By 1948 women competed in five sports in the summer Games in contrast to 18 for men. In that year 385 women represented 9.4% of the Olympic athletes and competed in 12.7% of the total Olympic events (Simri, 1977).

The Modern Sportswoman

In recent Olympiads the situation has improved. The women's summer program in 1976 included 13 sports and approximately 25% of the events. The 1,274 women athletes represented 17% of the Olympic athletes. Due to international tensions, both the 1980 and 1984 summer Games lacked full participation. Eighty-one national teams competed in Moscow and 141 at Los Angeles. By this time the women's program had more than tripled since 1948. Volleyball was added to the women's program in 1964, archery in 1972, and rowing, basketball, and team handball in 1976. In 1980, women's field hockey became the 14th Olympic sport. With the addition of cycling and synchronized swimming and the separation of shooting events for men and women, the women's 1984 program listed 15 sports with two more, equestrian and yachting, open to women. Of the approximately 220 events in 24 sports held at Los Angeles, women competed in 62 events in 15 sports. They also entered equestrian and yachting events. Perhaps the marathon caused the greatest excitement over new events for women in 1984. The women's program did not include boxing, judo, modern pentathlon, soccer, water polo, weight lifting, or wrestling.

The increase in women's Olympic sport reflects a small but significant change in the cultural perspective of women and women's sport. As late as 1970, clinical psychologists agreed with the long-held views of feminine arete and 19th-century womanhood, characterizing healthy adult females as dependent, emotional, intuitive, and passive. However, a recent synthesis of current literature reveals that many of today's women are now seen as rational, competent, autonomous, assertive, independent and self-fulfilled (Sherblom, 1980).

These attributes are more compatible with sport than ancient feminine arete and 19th-century womanhood, and perhaps have contributed to the current revolution in women's sport evident all around us. Women jockeys no longer bring raised eyebrows. Nancy Lopez and Martina Navratilova are reported on major telecasts as a matter of course. Although women's professional sport has grown at a surprising rate, the surge in women's school and college sport is phenomenal. In the United States' high schools, women's basketball increased more than 300% in just 8 years, and almost 400,000 more women competed in track and field in 1978-79 than in 1971 ("National Federation," 1979). Another indicator of women's greater involvement in sports was the rapid development of the Association of Intercollegiate Athletics for Women, which grew from 280 members in 1971, its first year, to more than 850 member institutions in 8 years. In 1981 the National Collegiate Athletic Association assumed control of intercollegiate sports for women. By 1984 the association offered championships for women in 15 sports. In the United States, collegiate programs proved to be an important factor in developing world-class women athletes in Olympic sports.

These examples and data represent women's sport in the United States, but similar changes have also taken place in other countries, especially those of Eastern and Western Europe. The modern sportswoman is epitomized by a Romanian woman, Nadia Comaneci, who achieved the first perfect score in Olympic gymnastics, and Joan Benoit, who won the first women's Olympic marathon. Born of working parents in 1961 in Onesti, Romania, Comaneci first competed in gymnastics at the age of 7 and soon adopted a childhood routine of daily school work followed by 3 or 4 hours of gymnastic practice. By 1975 she had earned gold medals in international competition. During the 1976 Olympic Games, Comaneci startled the world by receiving not only the first "10," or perfect score in gymnastics, but six additional "10s." Returning home after the Olympic Games, Comaneci became the youngest recipient of the Romanian title Hero of Socialist Labor. She continued to compete, winning a gold medal for her balance beam performance in 1980 at Moscow.

In contrast to the youthful Comaneci, Benoit won her first Olympic gold medal at the age of 27. Brought up in Cape Elizabeth, Maine with sports-minded brothers, Benoit skied and played high school sports. She did not run seriously until she began a conditioning program following a broken leg in a ski accident. She began to concentrate on running as a student at Bowdoin College. In her last year, 1979, she won the women's Boston marathon. After graduating from college, she coached cross-country track for a time, but gave that up to train. She broke the 1983 women's Boston marathon time with her time of 2:22.43 and won the first women's Olympic marathon in 1984.

Although both women were born at a time when women were seen as dependent, emotional, intuitive, and passive, they have become Olympic gold medalists and international sport stars, representing today's women. In many countries, especially in Europe and North America, young girls train in sport and achieve athletic excellence. Whereas Melpomene alone challenged the Olympic executives in 1896, in 1976 Comaneci was one of more than 1,200 Olympic women athletes from basketball and volleyball players to runners and rowers who demonstrated the potential of women's sport in the Olympic Games. In Los Angeles, the success of Benoit and other women athletes was an integral part of the Games. Athletes, spectators, and the media celebrated women's athletic excellence without regard to gender.

The IOC and Women's Sport

Although the phenomenal growth of the women's program in the Olympic Games is possible only because of changes made by the IOC, this body has not yet fully admitted women to the Olympic movement. The IOC is to be commended for the increased program for women. It is also encouraging that sports for women must be played widely in at least 35 countries and three continents rather than in the 50 countries and three continents required for men (IOC, 1984).

However, the Olympic Charter continues to treat women as if they are a questionable part of the Olympic Games. The latest *Olympic Charter* (1984) retains the Olympic discrimination clause that reads, "No discrimination in them [the Olympic Games] is allowed against any country or person on grounds of race, religion or politics" (p. 6). By omitting the word "sex" in the discrimination clause, the IOC implies that discrimination against women is acceptable. If the word "sex" were added to the principle on discrimination, then Rule 28 could be eliminated. This rule states that "Women are allowed to compete according to the rules of the IFs concerned and after the approval of the IOC" (p. 18). A careful reading of the rules regarding the eligibility code, age limit, medical code, and the sports program make Rule 28 unnecessary.

Another regulation states that "Competitors in sports restricted to women must comply with the prescribed tests for femininity" (p. 19). Many women athletes find this test a form of unnecessary harassment and discrimination, and some persons have suggested that if women are subjected to a femininity test, then men should submit to a test for masculinity.

The language used by the IOC is another deterrent to the full acceptance of women in the Olympic movement. The IOC is responsible for the Games being "ever more worthy of the high ideals which inspired their revival by Baron Pierre de Coubertin and his associates" (IOC, 1984, p. 9). Because Coubertin's "high ideals" did not include women and because women have had to struggle to become a part of the Games and the Olympic movement, that statement implies that women are unimportant in the modern Olympics. The charter should be modified to interpret these ideals for today's world. Just as Coubertin arranged the revival of the Olympic Games for the late 19th century, the IOC should plan for the 21st century, encouraging both men and women to strive for human excellence through sport.

Throughout the world women have had little access to decision-making bodies in sport. This situation also pertains to international sport organizations and to the IOC. Until recently the IOC had no women members, but now a few are women in a body of 88. The IOC should use its influence to involve more women in sport governing bodies, including national federations and National Olympic Committees.

Conclusion

This chapter has examined ancient and modern women athletes in order to provide some insights into the IOC's position on women's sport. Tryphosa portrays a woman athlete who defied ancient feminine arete and raced in athletic festivals. Melpomene, the Greek woman who allegedly ran in the 1896 marathon, represents the battle of women to become part of the Olympic Games. Comaneci and Benoit typify today's female athletes who are making significant contributions to international sport and the Olympic Games.

The future of women in the modern Olympic Games and the Olympic movement is controlled by the IOC. To meet the present and future needs of women athletes throughout the world, the IOC must modify the *Olympic Charter* to clearly recognize women as members of the Olympic movement, athletes in the Olympic Games, and equal with men as human beings. The modifications suggested in this chapter are consistent with the aims of the Olympic movement stated in Fundamental Principle 1:

> To educate young people through sport in a spirit of better understanding between each other and of friendship, thereby helping to build a better and more peaceful world. (IOC, 1984, p. 6)

These changes would clearly establish the IOC's position on women's sport. The IOC would then recognize women as human beings who are unwilling to return either to ancient feminine arete or 19th-century womanhood ideals but who are eager to be an integral part of the modern Olympic Games.

References

Foldes, E. (1964). Women at the Olympics. *Report of the Fourth International Olympic Academy* (pp. 105-114). Olympia, Greece: The International Olympic Academy.

International Olympic Committee. (1984). *Olympic charter.* Lausanne: Comité International Olympique.

Leigh, M. (1974). *The evolution of women's participation in the summer Olympic Games, 1900-1948.* Unpublished doctoral dissertation, The Ohio State University, Columbus.

National Federation of State High School Associations. (1979, December 30). *New York Times,* Sec. V, p. 7.

North, H. (1966). *Sophrosyne.* Ithaca, NY: Cornell University Press.

Sherblom, P. (1980). *Four variables affecting role strain in women.* Unpublished manuscript, University of Massachusetts, Amherst.

Simri, U. (1977). *A historical analysis of the role of women in the modern Olympic Games.* Netanya, Israel: The Wingate Institute for Physical Education and Sport.

23
Steroids

Marjorie Shuer

Steroids, in this case, is short for *anabolic steroids*—synthetic derivatives of the male hormone testosterone that emphasize the hormone's muscle-building effects (that's what the word *anabolic* means) and deemphasize its masculinizing, or androgenic, effects. Testosterone controls the development of the male reproductive organs and secondary sex characteristics: hairy chests and chins, baldness patterns, deep voices.

It also helps the body retain nitrogen, which is essential for synthesizing proteins and building muscles. This fact has captured the imagination of more than one athlete.

No one seems to know exactly when steroids were first used in sport. *Science* magazine marshalled some evidence in 1972 that Soviet men and women athletes were taking a male hormone to improve their performances as early as 1954. In the same article John D. Zeigler, a physician and former coach of the U.S. weight lifting team, said he started giving steroids to team members in 1959 but gave it up when he found that placebos worked just as well.

That puts Dr. Zeigler right in line with most of the rest of his medical colleagues. Almost as quickly as athletes heard about steroids, they heard about how steroids really didn't work.

No matter. In the summer of 1973 a Senate committee met to investigate drug use in American athletics. The information that came out at

Originally published in *Women's Sport and Fitness*, April 1982, pp. 19-23, 58. Reprinted by permission.

those hearings established at least a 10-year pattern of steroid use in American bodybuilding, weight lifting, football and track and field events like the discus, the hammer throw, and the shot put.

Harold Connolly, who won a gold medal for the United States in the hammer throw in the 1956 Olympics, testified that he first became aware of steroids in Rome at the 1960 Games. Rumors that the Russians were using some substance to increase their strength abounded. By 1964, according to Connolly, the secret was out and U.S. athletes were scrambling to even the odds.

"Just prior to the 1964 Olympic Games in Tokyo," he said, "all around me more and more athletes were using steroids . . . and one began to feel that he was placing himself at a disadvantage if he didn't get on the sports medicine bandwagon."

The epidemic showed no signs of slowing. "I knew any number of athletes on the 1968 team who had so much scar tissue and so many puncture holes in their backsides that it was difficult to find a fresh spot to give them a new shot."

This sort of attitude, and the rumors and facts of steroid use, were not lost on the international sports organizations.

"The banning of anabolic steroids was considered necessary as early as 1967," says Dr. Arnold Beckett, longtime member of the International Olympic Committee Medical Commission, "but this class of compounds was not included in the list of doping agents banned for the 1968 and 1972 Olympic Games because suitable tests to determine the presence of all the drugs of this class had not been developed."

Scientists caught up to steroid users at about the same time the Senate did. Two methods of detecting steroid use were perfected in 1973 and put into effect, experimentally, early the next year. (Official testing would not occur until 1976.)

In the early '70s the story of steroid use was, by and large, a story about men. The athletes that talked and were talked about in Washington, DC, in 1973, and the athletes most researchers expected to nab with their tests, were men.

Not that women were totally ignored. Connolly warned the senators that more and more women were beefing up with steroids. But no woman athlete stood up and confessed to pill popping or syringes in the ladies' locker rooms, and the focus remained on the men. Then came the swimming meet in Belgrade.

Deena Deardurff, talking about the mood of her team after the East German victories in 1973, described feelings similar to those Harold Connolly identified in the male track and field world a decade earlier.

We wondered if our country would start, since everyone else was doing it. Were we going to have to turn to drugs in the long run to stay on the same level as everyone else?

I wanted to win more than anything else in the world, but I didn't want to look like the East Germans. I didn't want to go to that extent. I wanted to do the best with what I had.

Anabolic steroids can be swallowed (their most popular form) or injected, and they differ in name and chemical detail. But all anabolic steroids available today have androgenic as well as anabolic effects on the man or woman who takes them. So far, scientists have been unable to totally isolate the masculinizing from the muscle-building effects of testosterone derivatives.

Men normally produce 5 to 10 milligrams of testosterone a day. Adding to that total with steroids does not necessarily make a man more manly. In fact, on the androgenic side, steroids are linked to lower natural testosterone levels and a decrease in sperm production. A steroid user may become infertile unless he stops using the drug.

The androgenic effects in women are just as serious and much more visible. Women naturally have about 0.1 milligram of testosterone in their bodies, about 1/2 to 1% the amount in men. Even a low dose of anabolic steroids can cause outward signs of masculinization in a woman— whiskers, baldness, deepening of the voice, and clitoral enlargement— and these effects may be irreversible. In addition, steroids frequently cause acne in women users.

The Physician's Desk Reference also lists menstrual irregularities as a side effect of steroids. Like reproductive disturbances in men, though, these have so far been found to be reversible as long as steroid use is discontinued.

Physicians are concerned about as yet unknown long-term side effects of anabolic steroids in both men and women. And they are particularly uneasy about young women taking a male hormone.

"When we've had 20 years of follow-up on the doping of female athletes with anabolic steroids, their use may be regarded as not merely unethical, but criminal," suggests Dr. Clayton Thomas, vice-president of medical affairs for Tampax and a consultant on human reproduction for the Harvard School of Health.

If you take little Mary Jane and some other girls and you put half of them on anabolic steroids when they are young, I have no idea what it is going to do to their offspring. But I have enough inclination regarding the long-term effects of such drugs to know that it could be quite disastrous.

A few long-term risks of steroid taking are known. Studies show that steroids disrupt liver structure and function and can cause liver cancers as well as other liver ailments. Steroids can also cause changes in the body's metabolism of carbohydrates and fats, which can accelerate arteriosclerosis and lead to heart disease or high blood pressure.

There are orthopedic risks as well. Tendons aren't affected by steroids, so if a muscle grows and the tendon does not, the tendon may become inflamed and rupture. Steroid-enlarged muscles may also cause increased stress on the skeleton and may produce degenerative joint diseases. And, in young boys and girls, steroids affect bone development and can permanently stunt growth.

With this multitude of dangerous side effects, anabolic steroids are hardly considered wonder drugs and have very limited use in standard medical practice. They are used to replenish testosterone in patients who lack it, according to Dr. Ralph Cheung, endocrinology fellow at Stanford University. In addition, they are occasionally used in the treatment of anemia and end-stage kidney disorders.

Overall, however, "they have a very restricted medical usefulness, and their use requires close supervision by a doctor," says Professor V. Winn of St. Mary's Hospital Medical School of London. "There is no justification for the use of anabolic steroids by healthy subjects."

Doctors and researchers seem to agree on the negative effects of anabolic steroids. But whether or not steroids increase strength and improve athletic skills is a murkier issue. According to a 1980 speech by Allan J. Ryan, a doctor and the editor of *The Physician and Sportsmedicine*, 25 studies have dealt seriously with the question. Many of them did find a gain in bulk and weight, but nearly as many ascribed this to water retention. Twelve of the studies concluded that anabolic steroids increase strength; 13 concluded that they don't.

Such contradictory results are only part of the problem. Steroid experiments vary greatly in design and method, and that variation allows criticisms from all sides. Athletes who believe in steroids grumble that the research doesn't reflect the way steroids are really used. Dosages are low, they say, and other factors like training regimens and diet aren't taken into proper account. A lineup of doctors disagrees: The real problem with the studies is that they don't meet scientific criteria—they aren't double blind, or they have skewed samples, or they draw unwarranted conclusions.

Ryan's summary finds that the best of the research done so far, by anyone's standards, proves anabolic steroids ineffective in strengthening muscles: "There is a substantial body of evidence that will stand very close scrutiny to indicate that anabolic steroids will not contribute significantly to gains in lean muscle bulk or muscle strength in healthy young adult males."

Note that final qualifier. In this country no studies, good or bad, have ever been done on the effect of anabolic steroids on healthy women. And it is unlikely that such tests will ever be done here. Dosing females with male hormone doesn't fit the guidelines for human subject research in the United States.

Common sense leads one to believe that male hormones would have a greater effect, androgenically and anabolically, in women than in men.

Dr. Irving Dardik, chairman of the U.S. Olympic Committee Sports Medicine Council, offers one theory:

> If you give a woman anabolic steroids during that period when growth hormones are utilized in the process of muscular development, there could be a masculinization of the muscle that would ordinarily be there, and this would perhaps be beneficial in terms of athletic performances.

Some researchers think that looking for a direct connection between steroids and increased muscle strength in either men or women is to miss the real performance-boosting qualities of the drug. Dr. Raymond Brooks, who developed part of the tests used to detect steroids in the body, told *The Physician and Sportsmedicine* that he thought it could be the androgenic, not the anabolic, effects of steroids that accounted for the performance gains that many athletes swear follow steroid use.

"I think the androgenic action makes the athlete more aggressive, more competitive, so the athlete trains harder, for a longer time perhaps. Any increase in performance is a result of harder training."

Theories aside, for men and particularly for women, the dangers of anabolic steroids are scientifically proven; the benefits are not. Yet many athletes and many coaches seem to believe precisely the opposite.

The 10 victories that went to the East German women at the World Swimming Championships in Belgrade are 10 solid gold reasons why athletes take steroids. Many are convinced on the basis of such performances that steroids work; many more feel that as long as the competition has them, they must have them too. And many who are unconvinced personally are persuaded by a coach or a colleague who is a true believer.

Patty Van Wolverhare-Hayes, gold medalist in the hurdles at the 1971 Pan American Games and a member of the 1964 and 1968 Olympic squads, describes the kind of pressure exerted on women athletes to take steroids.

"Some girls were forced into it, of course; some were young and easily intimidated; some trusted and believed they wouldn't do well unless they took steroids." Still, Wolvehare-Hayes says that a "very few women—a handful that I know of" use steroids in this country.

Denise Cornell, a member of the Naturite Track Club and the track and field team at California State University at Northridge from 1977 to 1979, can speak from personal experience. Her coach in those years was Chuck DeBus, the controversial mastermind of the Naturites—a team that has won 8 out of 10 national championships under his leadership. Cornell relates how DeBus first approached her concerning steroids.

> He brought it up even before the season started. He was blunt with me. He said, "I have Winstrol [the brand name of one anabolic steroid]. Do you want some?" He pressured everyone and pushed them on everybody. He did it in subtle ways by saying, "You really

need this protein synthesizer to have with your Naturite vitamins and all the protein you're eating in order to train harder. Do you want to be faster? Do you want to be stronger? Do you want to do heavier workouts so you will be better? You're going to get beaten if you don't take these."

A teammate of Cornell's, Lisa Kinimaka, echoes her story.

He was so damn obvious. He told about six of us that he wanted to talk to us privately after practice. He told me that he thought I should consider taking steroids, and this bull story that it was going to make me feel better, work harder, and that a person with my physique would be incredible with them. He told me to think about it for a week.

After that time I told him I didn't think it was such a good idea. He told me that I was living in the past and that I would never be as good competitively as I was before because I was older and the competition was getting tougher and it's harder to improve when one is older.

At one point I told him I was taking steroids when I actually wasn't. It made him feel better to think that I was taking them because he believed in them so much.

Cornell and Kinimaka saw some good and some bad effects of anabolic steroids in their teammates who took them. When Kinimaka returned from the long Christmas vacation during the 1977-78 season, she found that "there were some girls who had put on 25 pounds and were running just incredible sprints. They were just kicking ass and I couldn't believe it."

"Some of the girls were able to take on heavier workloads and recover quicker than before, but there were also people injured from overtraining," Cornell adds. "The steroids would add too much weight too soon and the connective tissue, it seemed, wasn't ready for the increase. There was incredible water retention and people's faces would get 'mooned out.'"

One of DeBus's runners will admit to taking the drugs. Kathy Scatena, a middle-distance runner who grew up in Bakersfield, California, took steroids during the 1976-77 season.

I only took steroids for a very short time—2 months—so I really don't have the side effects. No menstrual problems, no facial hair, no acne. I did get bulkier and I gained a little weight. I could do more in workouts, and the only side effect really was that little injuries started coming up—I had trouble with my arches. I could feel it a lot more because I was working out a lot more.

The main thing people have to understand is that you have a coach who is a really good talker, and he knows his stuff. I grew up in a small town. I didn't know questions to ask, and I'm not a person to doubt my coach's word—DeBus is about the best coach you'd ever come across as far as workouts and training. If he's going to tell me something is good, I'm not going to say, "You're full of shit."

Scatena says that DeBus told her not to talk to her teammates about the steroids. If she did, he would deny encouraging her to take them.

In fact, DeBus does deny the stories of Scatena, Kinimaka, and Cornell. "There was absolutely no steroid use at Northridge," he says. "I abhor the use of steroids; I'm totally against it. If they want to test my athletes any time, they can."

How many women in American sports are taking steroids? It's been said that asking a women if she takes steroids is like asking a man if he wears panty hose—it's questioning her sexuality. But asking a man if he takes steroids is like asking him if he takes vitamins.

Jane Frederick, seven-time U.S. pentathlon champion and a member of the 1972 and 1976 Olympic teams, says:

If you talk about men's track and field, you can easily put the steroid use up to the 75 to 80% range in the United States. This includes athletes who have tried steroids or who use them consistently in training. But with women it's hard to tell because it is such a tight-lipped issue.

It appears that in America women really do use anabolic steroids less than men do. Observers guess anywhere from 10 to 50% in track and field. But other sports are implicated as well. Bodybuilding and weight lifting, for instance, and perhaps cycling and speed skating—although use of steroids in the latter two is considered rare.

In whatever numbers, women athletes are getting and using steroids here. Some deny that it goes on; many more just don't want to talk about it. Maren Seidler, 11 times U.S. champion in the shot put and a member of four consecutive Olympic teams, explains why:

So much of what you read is just people pointing fingers at other people and explaining away their successes. Still, I'd be naive to think that steroid use doesn't go on. It so permeates the sport that you can't give it much consideration because it'll make you go crazy.

Women athletes contemplating steroid use in the U.S. at least have a choice. In the Eastern bloc, steroids and other drugs appear to be tightly woven into the fabric of sport.

GDR track star Renate Neufeld, a member of the 400-meter relay team, defected in 1978. She brought along samples of tablets she was taking at her coach's insistence. They were analyzed at the West German Sports

Institute in Cologne and found to be similar to Dianabol, a popular steroid in the West.

Neufeld became an East German champion in the spring of 1976. Her coach, Gunther Klann, gave her the tablets shortly after that, telling her they were vitamins. He reminded her of her obligation to East Germany and told her that she could talk to the sports-club doctor if she had reservations about the pills. (Consulting an outside physician was against the rules.)

She was supposed to take the tablets for 2 to 3 weeks, then stop for 10 days, then repeat the cycle. In a short time Neufeld noticed effects that she recognized from a Western television broadcast on steroids.

> It didn't only manifest itself in my muscles, but the effects there were so strong that I limped from pain when just walking normally. Both legs quickly increased in diameter and the club masseuse expressed her opinion that I was probably taking hormone tablets like the others. I obtained a light growth of hair on my upper lip, and like the other girls I didn't menstruate anymore.

In April 1977 Neufeld made the East German Olympic team. She was becoming increasingly leery of taking the "vitamin" tablets and concerned about her ability to conceive and have children. She began to take the tablets randomly and finally stopped altogether. And when Klann asked her if she was taking them, she told him the truth.

Retribution followed swiftly. Neufeld was prevented from competing in the Junior European Cup meet in Prague; her "salary," a stipend based on her victories and other accomplishments, was cut and she was warned she could lose her elite position as an athlete entirely. But Neufeld was determined not to take the tablets.

Soon afterward she was pulled out of bed at 6 a.m. by plainclothes state security police and interrogated. At the same time her fiancé, Bulgarian journalist Pentscho Spassov, was also interrogated. Both were released, but Neufeld was forbidden to see Spassov again. As soon as possible, they fled the country.

A year later another defector from East Germany, Renate Vogel, finally confirmed the steroid rumors that accompanied the GDR swimming victories in Belgrade. She had been the 1971 East German champion in the 100- and 200-meter breaststroke; she topped her career with golds in both at the world championships in 1973 and, later that year, set a world record.

Vogel remembers a blue pill, dubbed the "muscle pill," that she took in gradually reduced dosages, a schedule that is common for steroids.

> The blue pills started after the 1972 Olympics in Munich. We had 10 pills per day to take, vitamins, pills against the flu, etc., so when extras were added they didn't stick out.

> In the 1973 season we began to get injections also. We were given two injections per week when we were in training camp. No one was

sure which shots were the steroids because we were also pumped full of Vitamins B, C and D.

In the beginning I really didn't think anything of it. You know, when you are around other athletes like yourself, you don't notice the difference in body size. There were very few people on the team who thought about it or really cared. They were of the opinion that the main thing was to swim quickly, and it didn't matter how.

I started to notice the effect of the steroids when my clothes didn't fit anymore. This was in the beginning of 1973. In retrospect I can see I had really broad shoulders. I went from a size 40 to 44 or larger (size ten to 14 plus in the United States). My period hardly ever came.

Testing athletes for drugs, and disqualifying them if the tests come up positive, began officially at the Mexico City Olympics in 1968. A sample of athletes, including some of the winners and a randomly chosen group of finalists, submitted to a battery of tests designed to expose users of a number of banned drugs.

Steroid testing, a complex, two-part procedure, began officially at the 1976 Games in Innsbruck and Montreal. "The criteria for determining whether steroids are present in athletes are very stringent, much more stringent than the standards for hospital patients," Raymond Brooks told one interviewer.

Not only must we say that an illegal substance has been used, we have to positively identify the substance. The first procedure we use, radioimmunoassay, screens out all but 10 to 20% of the urine samples. The second procedure, gas chromatography-mass spectrometry, is expensive and time-consuming, but we need it to positively identify the substance.

No steroid positives came up at the Winter Games in Innsbruck. But that summer in Montreal, anabolic-steroid testing detected eight users—seven male weight lifters (two from the United States) and one female discus thrower—Danuta Rosani of Poland. Three weight lifting medals, two golds and one silver, had to be returned to the Olympic committee.

The list of women who have been found to have anabolic steroids in their urine at international competitions reads like a Who's Who in the world of track and field. It includes East German Ilona Slupianek, the world's foremost shot-putter, who was disqualified in 1977. In 1978, after the European Championships in Prague, Nadyezhda Tkachenko, a Soviet pentathlete, had to give up her gold medal and face disqualification.

In 1979 three of the world's best middle-distance runners were caught: Bulgarian Totka Petrova and Rumanians Natalia Marasescu and Illeana Silai. Petrova was first in the world in the 800 and 1,500 meters in 1979, and she won both the European and World Cups in the 1,500. Marasescu set a new world record in the mile in January of 1979 and was ranked second in the 1,500. Silai was third in the world in the 1,500 that year.

Steroid testing can't catch all guilty athletes. Some slip by because of the way test samples are chosen. And there are ways to beat the testing system itself.

If an athlete's timing is right, she can stop taking steroids before a competition where she may be tested, and her urine will show no trace of the drug. The trick, of course, is in the timing, and it's a difficult trick to pull off.

"There is no standard timetable," says Dr. Dan Hanley, former U.S. representative of the IOC Medical Commission.

Anabolic steroids are fat-soluble. If they are taken into the body in large doses like athletes are taking today—100 milligrams per day every day—the body can't possibly excrete them, so they are stored in the fat and excreted very slowly over a period of time. Two months? Six months? How much did you take? How much is built up? There is no precise way to tell when all the steroid is excreted except by continual testing.

And there are other ways to cheat on anabolic-steroid tests. Athletes have been known to catheterize themselves with "clean" urine just before going in for the test, for instance. Others have taped bladders full of urine between their legs.

When steroid tests are successful and a user is exposed, the rules call for the athlete to be banned for life from international competition. In practice, however, there have been no lifetime bans. Instead, after a period of disqualification (the minimum ban now is 18 months, but it has been as little as 6 months or a year), an appeal can be filed. So far every appeal has been successful.

Very few of the women who have been disqualified have disappeared from international competition. On the contrary, many have gone on to spectacular personal bests. Ilona Slupianek, for instance, was disqualified for about a year. She returned to competition and won the European Championships in 1978. In 1980 she won a gold medal in the Moscow Olympics and was named "Woman Athlete of the Year" by a panel of 22 international experts. At that time she held 8 of the top-10 throws of all time.

Nadyezhda Tkachenko was back in action 18 months after her 1978 disqualification. She took a gold in Moscow with a high-point score of 5,083—the first woman pentathlete to surpass the 5,000-point mark.

The reinstatement of the track and field women who were caught with positive steroid tests in 1979 is particularly interesting. There were seven in all from the U.S.S.R., Bulgaria, and Rumania. The 18-month suspension rule was in effect, and all it took was simple arithmetic to realize that none of the seven would be eligible for the 1980 Moscow Games.

As the athletes' governments tried to find a way to reinstate them in time for the Olympics, the governing body for international track and field, the International Amateur Athletic Federation (IAAF), was tackling another problem: professionalism. Specifically, a number of U.S. athletes were reinstated by the IAAF after they backed away from earlier decisions to cross the line between amateur and pro. Because the IAAF let the Americans off that hook, some thought it would be forced to let the Eastern Europeans off the steroids hook as well. In fact, two of the seven did not seek reinstatement; the others were allowed to compete on July 1, 1980, just in time for the Moscow Games.

The erosion of the lifetime ban angers many athletes. "It really upsets me," says Canadian pentathlete Diane Konihowski, winner of two Pan American Games gold medals and a victor in the British Commonwealth Games.

In September of 1978 Tkachenko was banned—initially for life—and a year and a half later she's reinstated. She ends up breaking a world record and winning the gold medal at the Olympics. I don't agree with that, because in that year and a half she had lots of time to really put the 'roids into herself.

I don't do any of that, and it bugs me knowing the amount of time that I have to put in, and the amount of hard work. To go into a competition *au naturel* and to compete against someone who is chemically prepared is not fair.

Nineteen eighty was a very puzzling year as far as drug testing was concerned. There were no positives for women in track and field or any other sport at the Olympic Games.

Dr. Arnold Beckett of the IOC Medical Commission suggests that the reason was a relatively new method devised to beat the system. "Many athletes stopped the use of anabolics several months before the Games and shifted to testosterone, which isn't among the prohibited drugs."

In unofficial, experimental testing, Dr. Beckett took portions of the urine samples from Lake Placid and Moscow and tested the samples for exogenous testosterone, that is, testosterone added to the body's natural production. He found that 8% of the athletes at the Winter Games had used testosterone. At Moscow the results were significantly higher: Six to 15% of the male athletes and between 12 and 20% of the women, including 16 gold-medal winners, were positive.

Beckett says the system for detecting added testosterone is nearly perfected, and he expects the hormone to be on the list of banned substances "before 1984."

Last year, though, it seemed that not all athletes had perfected the art of switching from anabolic steroids to natural testosterone in time for doping control at various competitions. The tests caught four women athletes. Austrian runner Karoline Kafer and Soviet shot-putter Nunu

Abashidze were nabbed at the indoor European Championships at Grenoble, France. Australian shot-put star Gael Mulhall and Swedish sprinter Linda Haglund were also disqualified in 1981 because of positive steroid tests.

The steroid ban is about as enforceable as the 55-mile-per-hour speed limit. The tests can be finessed, and the punishments meted out to the guilty are hardly a deterrent to steroid use.

But the organizations that govern international sports are trying to hold the line—closing loopholes in the testing process, working to keep up with those who are trying to beat the system. They talk about stepping up steroid testing, if time and money would allow, to include year-round spot checks of athletes. They talk about tightening the penalties for offenders, if politics would allow. And they talk about education—getting the word out about what steroids can and can't do.

But the fact is, the official word about steroids has been out among athletes for years. And despite the fact that it is more negative than positive, many athletes prefer to believe their peers and their eyes, which tell them that the benefits of steroids *can* outweigh the risks—especially if the competition has them.

In the end, the use of anabolic steroids among athletes will probably only stop when the next performance-boosting "miracle" comes along. And researchers are working on it.

A member of the IOC Medical Commission warns that neither the Eastern bloc nor the Western bloc is above making winning robots out of their athletes. One U.S. scientist, a researcher in neurophysiology, describes a possible Brave New World in sports: "If you are trying to develop superfolk, I can tell you for a fact that the way to do it is through substances in the brain. There are many proteins there that can absolutely turn someone into a raging superstar if tapped appropriately." This particular researcher has already succeeded in producing an excess of natural testosterone and related compounds in animals—all by implanting and stimulating electrodes in their brains.

The reason to create "superfolk," of course, is to win. And that is at the heart of the matter.

Back in 1973, Harold Connolly explained the problem succinctly: "The overwhelming majority of international track and field athletes I know would take anything and do anything short of killing themselves to improve their athletic performance." Unfortunately, his explanation still holds true today.

The Future of the Games

In a very real sense, the Olympic Games were born of one man's dream. They were born of an idealistic and romantic conception of sport whose philosophic genesis can be traced back to the athletic ideal of ancient Hellenism. Baron de Coubertin revered the ancient Greek triumvirate of mind, body, and spirit. He became an equally ardent admirer of the late 19th-century Anglo-American amateur sport movement, and was profoundly influenced by the role played by sport in the English public school system. Consequently, in keeping with the values of a Victorian culture that viewed sport as a moral and social rather than an economic and political endeavor, Coubertin formulated his doctrine of Olympism, which reified the athlete into what Lucas (1976) has aptly described as ''a kind of Greek reincarnation, a modernday medieval knight, a slightly modified aristocratic English gentleman-athlete'' (p. 35). But although sport was to contribute to the enoblement of the individual, it was also to enhance universal peace. Writing in 1908, Coubertin declared,

> The revival of the Olympic Games on a basis conforming to the conditions of modern life would bring together every four years the representatives of the nations of the world, and we can well believe

that these courteous and peaceful contests would constitute the highest of international activities. (pp. 91-92)

However, although the Games may have begun as a forum for the youth of the world to unite in peaceful competition through educational amateur sport, they have increasingly become a vehicle for the achievement of ulterior goals. "How much longer," asks the *New York Times* ("The Dying Flame," 1976), "will it take a youthful generation of athletes the world over to recognize how crassly they are being exploited by persons and organizations paying allegiance to less than noble goals?" (p. 22). Coubertin never intended the Games to be symbolic ideological battles between nations. Nor were they intended to be a theater for individuals, groups, and countries to make political statements. The Olympics were not founded for the benefit of corporate business or as a proving ground for medical technology. They were not established so that athletes could make their fortunes. Nor was their main function to provide television entertainment for millions. Yet they have become all these things, and in so doing Coubertin's 19th-century invention has become a 20th-century reality of a very different sort.

In the early years, the Games were generally reflective of their cultural heritage. They were largely amateur, noncommercial, and for the most part devoid of political and national excesses. But though they may have been born in privilege, their absorption into popular culture has ensured their remarkable success. Buffeted by sweeping technological, economic, political, and demographic changes, the Games of today are professional, commercial, nationalistic, political, and endowed with rich cultural significance. Their transformation has been swift and radical and from the very beginning the Games have attracted both supporters and critics. "No more Olympic Games" declared the *Literary Digest* ("Are the Olympic Games Worthwhile?" 1924, p. 48). In the same year *The Living Age* ("Olympic Discords," 1924) wrote, "There is nothing so effectual as sport in making the mass of people in one country respect the people of another" (p. 343).

In recent years, the voices of criticism have become particularly pronounced, largely in response to the perceived discrepancy between the IOC's espoused ideals and the reality of the Games. The Olympic Games are not "an intrinsically bad institution," writes Johnson (1972):

It is their mythology which makes them seem such a force for cynicism and hypocrisy. It is the attempt to clothe the Games in grand ideals they could never realize which makes them so fallible, so undermined and so corrupted by man's meanest motives. (p. 292)

Athletes, coaches, reporters, historians, and educators alike have criticized the games as an example of humankind's worst proclivities toward deceit and self-deception (see Czula, 1975). In one of the most virulent assaults on the Games, the *Economist* recently proclaimed,

If you accept the gloomy idea that mankind is inherently belligerent, there may be a case for staging quadrennial homeopathic war— substitutes, ritual periods during which the commentators whip up popular frenzy and everybody's glands get a healthy flushing out without any actual recourse to high explosives, poison-gas or nuclear weapons. But this was not the original Coubertin objective. The whole business of huge state apparatuses, each dedicated to piling up the number of 'golds' recorded opposite one nation's name is nauseatingly unolympic. ("Games People Play," 1976, p. 12)

Even a more conservative commentator like historian John Lucas (1973) has argued that "increasing chauvinism and commercialism have defaced the Olympics and taken away some of the idealism that Coubertin built into the games" (p. 71).

Given the severity of the problems facing the Olympic Movement, suggestions concerning the future of the games have been numerous, ranging from calls for abolition to proposals for reform. Calls for abolition have emerged most commonly from the political left, particularly in Europe. In 1972, for example, the École Emancipée initiated an Anti-Olympic Campaign on the grounds that the Olympics represented an extension of industrial capitalism. Three years later a draft appeal for the establishment of an Anti-Olympic Committee was published (Brohm, 1978) condemning the games as "a vast commercial circus" (p. 172) and "a godsend for the bourgeoisies and bureaucracies of the world" (p. 171). The Olympics have also been censured in North America. Prior to the 1976 Montreal Games, Canadian commentator McMurty (1973) wrote, "I suggest, then, that we take the ball, the ball we've now got as the next Olympic promoters and fire it into the air. And as it sits up there like a torch for all the world to see, let the voices grow from us that we've had enough" (p. 60). On the eve of the 1980 Moscow Olympics, American commentator Axthelm (1980) noted, "the Olympics have simply grown too big, too political, too artificial. Avery Brundage was wrong. The Games need not go on" (p. 63).

Proposals for reform, on the other hand, have aimed at preserving the games and the international force for goodwill that they represent. Although reform proposals have been a feature of the aftermath of every one of the 20 games held to date, the enormous pressures under which recent games have operated have caused the proponents of reform to increasingly adopt platforms that are comprehensive and in some cases radical. Writing in the wake of the 1972 Munich games, for example, Lucas (1973) argued that "only drastic means can arrest the present collision course of the Olympic movement" (p. 84). As a result Lucas presented 12 reform proposals that included the establishment of a permanent Olympic site in Switzerland, increased selection of Olympic athletes onto the IOC, the creation of five roving ambassadors, the elimination of the racial discrimination clause from the Olympic principles, the termination of national anthems and flag raising during the victory ceremonial, and participation in the opening ceremonies parade by sport and event rather than by nation (p. 84). In a similar plea for drastic modifications, ex-Olympian Bill Bradley (1976) proposed that the games should be open to everyone, that team sports should be eliminated, that every athlete should get a participants medal, that the Olympics should be permanently situated in Greece, and that the games should be more participant oriented. To date none of these proposals have been fully instituted by the IOC.

Several more recent proposals have aimed specifically at depoliticizing the games. Edwards (1981), for example, has advocated the establishment of an officially mandated political forum as part of the foundations of his "Third Olympic Era." Espy (1981) has suggested a complete overhaul of the Olympic superstructure whereby association and identification are based on regional rather than nation-state representation. But one of the most enduring and at least publicly popular proposals has centered on the idea of a permanent site for the games; the idea being to defuse the political, racial, and ideological conflicts that are rekindled each time the choice of the site for the games arises.

The idea of a permanent home for the games is, of course, not new. As long ago as 1896 after the phenomenal success of the Athens games, King George of Greece alluded to the possibility of Greece becoming the "stable and permanent site" of the games (Coubertin, 1908, p. 127). The idea gained widespread support on the eve of both the 1980 and 1984 games. Among those who have advocated a permanent home for the games are former U.S. President Jimmy Carter, former U.S. Secretary of State Henry Kissinger, Australian Prime Minister Malcolm Fraser, and Greek Prime Minister Constantine Caramanlis. Caramanlis, in fact, has formally proposed that Olympia be accepted as the permanent home of the summer games, offering to turn the area into a neutral zone under the jurisdiction of the IOC. Other suggestions have included establishing several permanent sites, one in each continent, or one in the west and one in the east. The Boston Globe ("Depoliticizing the Olympics," 1980) even proposed denationalized games that "move from nation to nation, with a previously designated alternative site which could be activated on a delayed basis under emergency conditions" (p. 10).

Although both abolitionists and reformers have tended to garner most of the publicity, some people maintain that the games be retained exactly as they are—political, commercial, and volatile, but an accurate reflection of the contemporary international sociopolitical milieu. Which of these three positions will gain ascendency during the latter years of the 20th century remains a moot point. Each, however, is represented in the readings in this section.

In the first essay, David Rose presents an abolitionist perspective, arguing ultimately that the games should be discontinued because "they pay obsequious respect to human dignity and to an honest yearning for the survival of the planet." Espy, on the other hand, views the games as a window into the very "soul of man." Although Espy considers various reforms, including the idea of a permanent site and the feasibility of opening the games to all competitors, he sees neither as offering a satisfactory solution to the problems confronting the games. He concludes that the games remain a perfect reflection of the structural and organizational patterns of life in the 20th century, and their appeal is grounded in the competitive nature of humankind.

In the next two essays, ex-Olympian Sir Roger Bannister and historian John Lucas present reformist points of view, arguing that the ideals of Olympism and the games are worthy of preservation. Bannister advocates a reduction in the size of the games, the elimination of team sports, the establishment of a permanent site, and the defusion of the nationalistic Olympic displays. In his decalogue of Olympic reform Lucas also calls for the establishment of a permanent "Olympic Games Center," the enlargement of the summer games, the institution of an equable fee for participating nations, the curtailment of displays of nationalism, the broadening of the IOC's membership, and the expansion of the International Olympic Academy concept.

In the final essay, Allen Guttmann presents a sociopsychological interpretation of the games. While not denying the important role of economics in the 20th-century transformation of the games, Guttmann views the psychological process of identification whereby spectators emotionally identify with the athletes they observe as being most responsible for the abuses that have perverted the Olympic ideals. Most conspicuously evident in the chauvinist fervor that accompanies the games, Guttmann concludes that whether the Games approach or disappoint our ideals, the best rationale for their continuation is that they ultimately "provide us with a dramatic indication of who we are."

References

Are the Olympic games worth while? (1924, August 2). *Literary Digest*, p. 48.

Axthelm, P. (1980, January 21). Boycott the Olympics. *Newsweek*, p. 63.

Bradley, B. (1976, July 21). Five ways to reform the Olympics. *New York Times*, p. 33.

Brohm, J.M. (1978). *Sport: A prison of measured time*. London: Inks Links.

Coubertin, P. de. (1908). *Une campaign de vingt-et-un-ans: 1887-1908*. Paris: Librarie de L'Education Physique.

Czula, R. (1975). Pierre de Coubertin and modern Olympism. *Quest, 24*, 10-18.

Depoliticizing the Olympics. (1980, February 1). *The Boston Globe*, p. 10.

Edwards, H. (1981). Crisis in the Modern Olympic movement. In J. Segrave & D. Chu (Eds.), *Olympism* (pp. 227-241). Champaign, IL: Human Kinetics.

Espy, R. (1981). *The politics of the Olympic Games.* Berkeley: University of California Press.

Games people play. (1976, July 24). *The Economist*, pp. 12-13.

The dying flame. (1976, August 2). *New York Times*, p. 22.

Johnson, W.O. (1972). *All that glitters is not gold: An irreverent look at the Olympic Games.* New York: Putnam.

Lucas, J.A. (1973). The modern Olympic games: Fanfare and philosophy: 1896-1972. *The Maryland Historian*, 4, 71-89.

Lucas, J.A. (1976). The influence of Anglo-American sport on Pierre de Coubertin—Modern Olympic Games founder. In P.J. Graham & H. Ueberhorst (Eds.), *The modern Olympics* (pp. 17-26). Cornwall, NY: Leisure Press.

McMurty, J. (1973, January). A case for killing the Olympics. *Maclean's*, pp. 34, 57-58, 60.

Olympic discords. (1924, August 23). *The Living Age*, p. 343.

Suggested Reading

Hoberman, J.M. (1986). *The Olympic crisis: From its origin to the Moscow Games.* New Rochelle, NY: Caratzas.

Killanin, Lord. (1983). *My Olympic years.* New York: William Morrow.

Lucas, J.A. (1980). *The modern Olympic Games.* New York: A.S. Barnes.

Miller, G. (1979). *Behind the Olympic rings.* Lynn, MA: H.O. Zimman.

Segrave, J., & Chu, D. (Eds.). (1981). *Olympism.* Champaign, IL: Human Kinetics.

Tomlinson, A., & Whannel, G. (Eds.). (1984). *Five ring circus: Money, power and politics at the Olympic Games.* London: Pluto Press.

24

Should the Olympic Games Be Abolished?

David A. Rose

The 1984 Olympic Games in Los Angeles marked the third consecutive Summer Olympics in which athletes from a substantial number of the member-nations did not participate. These Games also marked the fifth consecutive Summer Olympics in which political issues intruded on the athletes' and fans' desire to concentrate on the events. Once again, the question of "amateurism" was debated and more barriers fell to the point where amateurs competing in some Olympic sports are now among the most highly paid athletes in the world.

In spite of these troubles, L.A. has been billed as the Games that saved the Olympics ("Man of the Year," 1985). L.A. not only did not stick taxpayers with a postcelebration financial "hangover," L.A. turned a profit. No violence took place at the Games, and everybody attending live seemed to have a good time. Of course, hundreds of millions more watched the Games on television. The Olympic heritage seems saved.

With the general feeling toward the Olympics much improved and candidates lining up to host the Games into the foreseeable future, the time is right to seriously ask, Should the Olympic Games be abolished?

Method of Inquiry

The question of abolishing the Olympics can be broken down into four criticisms (cf. Goodhart & Chataway, 1968; Johnson, 1972; McMurty, 1973): The Games are too big, too commercial, too professional, and too political. In this chapter, recent developments in the Olympics will be examined to determine if these criticisms are accurate. Suggested reforms will also be explored to ascertain if they negate the criticisms, and thereby the appropriateness, of abolishing the Games. If the criticisms stand, it may be concluded that the Games should be abolished.

Should the Olympics Be Abolished Because They Are Too Big?

The size of the Olympic Games has increased dramatically over the past 35 years, as others in this book (e.g., Gruneau & Cantelon [chapter 21]; Nixon [chapter 15]) note. Gruneau and Cantelon also note that this growth has not always been welcomed by leaders of the Olympic movement.

Given the aristocratic heritage of the Games, we first examine the idea that the Games are too big because they are *less* socially exclusive. In this regard much of the growth appears to be consistent with the spirit of the Games. More nations are members now; more nations' people have the free time and money to develop sport interests and skills; the legitimacy of women in sport is now recognized; and the legitimacy of diverse ethnic sporting interests is now recognized. In this regard, the Olympics are likely only to get bigger.

Conversely, exclusivity seems inconsistent with the spirit of the Games. Because the world is no longer ruled by feudal aristocrats, a sporting gathering of each country's sociopolitical elites would presumably not help make the world better and more peaceful. Nor would the events likely manifest the best performances or competitions.

A central concern in thinking the Games are getting too big are the problems typically associated with large size: inefficiency, waste, and fraud. Two factors must be noted in this regard. First, very little is known about the organization and conduct of the Olympic movement, the International Olympic Committee (IOC), and the National Olympic Committees (NOCs) (cf. Annotated Bibliography, 1984; Segrave & Chu, 1981). This lack of information suggests that rather than being too large, the Games are still relatively inconspicuous. Indeed, a study of U.S. Olympic programs (Zornow, 1977) found most problems stemmed from lack of size: Either the organizations were too small or, when compared to other events of more local interest, the Games took second place.

What makes the Olympics appear so big is the collective and singular impact they can have on a region. The 1984 Games in L.A. are a good example. Their sheer size forced people to alter their lives to accommodate the event. Transportation and housing were special concerns for L.A. Prior to the Games, the crush of incoming guests was widely expected to gridlock the whole city. One particularly heavy period of competition came to be labelled "Black Friday" because it carried the highest probability of stopping the city's traffic. Housing was also expected to be a problem because owners of hotels, motels, and private residences were expected to exploit the shortage of rooms for the 2-week period of the Games.

As history revealed, however, preevent hysteria "worked" (cf. Reich, in press). Normal traffic patterns were altered after extensive planning and negotiation, special bus transportation was provided to and from venues, competitive sites were geographically dispersed, relatively few visitors came to L.A. for the games, and their numbers were offset by an exodus of many locals.

Rather than suggesting the Games are a manageable event, however, L.A.'s inadvertant success here points to a new form of exclusivity. More specifically, the Summer Games have become so large that in their present format, only a few cities, regions, and nations of the world can handle them. But in handling them, they are made virtually a local event, attracting not an international but a local audience. Television improves this exclusivity only marginally.

The size of the Games compels television to present the events in circus-like fashion, a pseudo "Wide World of Sports" in real time instead of tape-delayed. In addition to disrupting the natural "seasonal" (in both the sporting and meteorologic sense) rhythms of each sport, this concentration of events makes it impossible for spectators to appreciate more than a handful of sports, teams, or individual stories for a relatively instantaneous amount of time. Enjoyment of the drama of sport is minimized, except for the occasional spontaneous moment (e.g., the 1980 U.S. Olympic hockey team) outbreak.

How can the size of the Games be reduced to human scale without inhibiting their spread? Staging the Games at different sites, staggering competition throughout the year, and staging competition in a more classical tournament format would all minimize the collective and/or singular impact of the Games.

The likelihood of implementing any or all of these ideas is not great. In addition to the Olympic tenet of awarding the Games to a "single entity" and location, a number of factors reinforce large size: power accruing to sport leaders, consistency between corporate organizations' budgets and business goals and Olympic involvement, and consistency between local and national political goals and present arrangement. In this respect the size question is partially a symptom of the other three structural issues.

Should the Olympic Games Be Abolished Because They Are Too Professional?

The Games, it is said, should be abolished because they have been "corrupted" and are now "hypocritical." The Olympics were at one time thought to be the ultimate in amateur competition. For years, the IOC's official stance was to prohibit professional athletes from participating in the Games (cf. Strenk, chapter 19 in this volume). This question of eligibility revolved around the challenge of defining "amateur" and "professional." During the 1970s, existing definitions became problematic to sport leaders in the capitalist West. Although athletes from communist-governed countries were financially supported, they were not professional by definition. "Professional" was defined in a circular and/or capitalist way: Professional athletes were athletes who played professional sports or made their living from sports.

The conflict inherent in this ambiguity was well known in the U.S. but had worked to its advantage as athletes from college sport programs played an increasingly important role on U.S. Olympic teams. In this system, sustaining high-level performance after college usually meant being independently wealthy or so dedicated to sport as to abandon normal endeavors. When communist countries took this system one step further, by supporting noncollege, postcollege, and "minor" sport athletes, the capitalist West, including the U.S., found itself at a disadvantage. The President's Commission on Olympic Sports (PCOS) (Zornow, 1977) advocated an expected response: Professionalize American programs. Under pressure from the U.S. and other capitalist countries, the IOC changed its rules. Thus while the Games remain nominally amateur, for all practical purposes the barrier has been dropped.

Concomitantly, the concept of the "elite" athlete has largely displaced the concept of the amateur while incorporating the tenets of professionalism without stepping over the abyss of the dreaded label (cf. Glencross, 1980). The term also covers the different kinds of Olympians now possible in the capitalist West. Three types are especially notable: (a) professionals making substantial amounts of money either directly from competing or from product endorsements related directly or indirectly to their success in the most popular sports (e.g., Bruce Jenner, Carl Lewis, Mary Lou Retton, and almost any downhill skier), (b) corporate/government professionals, that is, individuals whose athletic efforts are supported by corporate entities but whose sport interests prevent them from joining Category A (e.g., U.S. women's volleyball team), and (c) the old amateurs, the wealthy and/or sportingly asocial, whose sports are basically subcultural (e.g., any archer, any kayaker) or whose persona and/or personality prevent them from marketing themselves into Category B (e.g., Tommy Smith, any female rower).

But as the above suggests, what on the surface appears to be a major advance removing hypocrisy actually exposes a conceptual and organizational morass. In effect, the *only* thing that has changed is the acceptance of financial support for a few more athletes. This change is formalized in Canadian sports, with the distinction between "Sport Canada," the elite and now-supported athletes, and "Fitness Canada," everybody below the elite few (cf. Hoffman, 1982). The inclusion of professionals, however, appears more arbitrary than systematic and more a byproduct of the history of governing bodies than of guidelines intended to maintain Olympism. Thus, for example, track and ski pros are in, and soccer and basketball pros are out, if they play for the "wrong" team.

Given the confusion, not surprisingly, voices calling for more amateurism compete with those advocating more professionalism. Neither is very persuasive. As professional sport, the Olympics become nothing more than a stop on the pro tour, albeit an infrequent one. But replacing a desire to make money with a passion for sport does not clearly alter matters: A passion for sport and for peace are not necessarily correlated. A passion for sport may be associated with passion for war or for conspicuous consumption.

In order to sort out these matters, it is necessary to ask a more fundamental question, What are the Olympics? That is, what is the social nature of the Olympic Games; what is the social purpose, or the social function, of the Olympics? Without an answer to this question, there is no way to say *when* the Olympics are professional sport or when they are "too" professional.

Answers to these questions have been provided by Rose (1980, 1985). The Olympics are an example of "semiprofessional sport." Semiprofessional sport is sport in which teams represent the quality of the sponsoring organizations. In the case of the Olympics, the organizations are nations. The key concept here is "representative." As it applies to the Olympics, this concept raises two issues.

The first of these issues is the "representativeness" of the sports of the Olympics. On the face of it, one might assume that Olympic sports were somehow representative of the sporting interests of the earth's population. The main problem is that this standard does not incorporate popular participation. For example, the PCOS (Zornow, 1977) study of Olympic programs in the U.S. revealed that few Olympic sports had much popular support, either participant or spectator. Some, such as luge, had so little support that one would be hard pressed to distinguish between elite and other levels of skill. If these findings from the U.S. can be generalized, no sport likely qualifies as an Olympic sport unless the weakest criteria are applied (cf. Edwards, 1981). Thus unless one believes that "elite" (in the sense of social elite) sports are the vehicle for promoting peace, the current Olympic program is inconsistent with its purpose.

The second issue is the representativeness of the participants. Borrowing from the debate in U.S. college sport on this topic, the phrase here is "citizen-athlete." What has previously been thought of as an attempt to define amateurism in this context may be seen as an attempt to define the boundaries between "semi-pro," "acceptably pro," and "unacceptably pro" Olympians.

As semi-pro sport, Olympic teams are composed of citizen-athletes, individuals who are citizens first and athletes second. These people are contributing members of their nation whose life chances are consistent with their contribution and who have an interest and ability in sport. As acceptably professional sport, Olympic teams are composed of individuals who are athletes first and citizens second: people whose life chances are contingent on sport, and who contribute to society through work opportunities that sport brings them. As unacceptably pro sport, teams are composed of people who are athletes first and citizens not at all: people who are not contributing members of their society, but whose life chances are consistent with or better than other members solely because of their athletic ability.

In other words, the Games are *too* professional if Olympians are athletes first and citizens not at all. The criteria here are both national and international, economic and moral. For example, U.S. athletes can now routinely make millions of dollars in a few years of sport performance. The social acceptability of this windfall depends on a variety of issues, including the source(s) of the revenue, the distribution of the revenue within the sport structure, the reasons society does not spend its resources in an alternative way, and the impact of the fortune on the individual's life, both during the sport career and after. Nor is the issue here just one of making fabulous salaries from sport; the issue encompasses more fundamental needs as well. Does anyone know how many starving people could be saved by the diet of one elite athlete?

The Games are not likely to be conducted as semi-pro or acceptably pro sport in the forseeable future. People in the U.S., for example, are able to view pro franchises as "their" team merely because the franchise is located in "their" city. Likewise, adoring alumni cheer college sport teams whose members have the most tenuous academic credentials. Given the trend in the Olympics over the last 20 years, political elites seem more concerned with having medal winners than a healthy populace. In other words, the commercial and political stakes of winning that are the root of the shift toward unacceptably professional sport have inverted the Olympic ideal: It is the winning, not the taking part. Change the context and you can change the rules. To find out if the context is likely to change, we will examine the other reasons for abolishing the Games.

Should the Olympic Games Be Abolished Because They Are Too Commercial?

Financially, the Olympics have grown to an impressive size. What is more important in this regard is that time and energy invested in the Games seem motivated less by good will than by a desire to make money. More specifically, the Games seem to be another example of the general public footing the bill while a few politicians and wealthy elites reap impressive financial gains (cf. Brohm, 1981; McMurty, 1973). With respect to the Games themselves, prior to L.A. little restraint was put on the financial demands of either the IOC or the various sports federations. Host locales were expected to spare no expense, including toward the IOC itself. When combined with abuse and inefficiency by the hosts, disaster naturally followed, as the Montreal Games demonstrated.

Leery of financing such sport works, voters in Colorado opposed hosting the Winter Games. Voters in Los Angeles forced the Summer Games to "go private" for the first time: The L.A. Olympics were conducted by a nonprofit organization, the Los Angeles Olympic Organizing Committee (LAOOC). Local laws were enacted to prohibit public monies from being spent on the Games.

This arrangement forced the LAOOC to exercise cost controls in expenditures and aggressively market the Games to generate revenues (cf. Reich, in press). Administrative costs were minimized by shrewd use of a small paid staff and extensive use of volunteers. Facilities' costs were kept low by making extensive use of existing facilities and by enlisting corporations to build new ones. The LAOOC was equally successful with marketing. Television rights to the Games were sold for a new record amount after the LAOOC had bargained down the IOC's share of television income. "Official" sponsor status sold to large corporations and new attendance records brought in additional millions. The spectacular profit, "surplus" as it was officially labelled by the LAOOC, realized in this venture has led many to believe that L.A.'s operation is a prototype for the future.

In spite of L.A.'s apparent success, ample room exists for skepticism, regarding elimination of abuse and the extent to which this system can be generalized for future Olympics.

In L.A. the abuse was more subtle than in previous Games. First, in spite of the claim of being "privately funded," reason exists to doubt the extent to which private sources voluntarily funded the Games. The U.S. tax code being what it is, money, equipment, facilities, and time "donated" by corporations and private individuals will ultimately be paid for by John Q. Public. Costs for security were, of course, billed to the public. Any lodging, meals, tickets, and the like that went directly or indirectly into Olympic coffers *but* were treated as a business expense for tax purposes will also ultimately be paid out of public money. While not an abuse of the public's finances, the seemingly unending parade of "official whatever's of the 1984 Olympics" was certainly an assault on the public's sensibility, such as it is.

Also, the *way* in which this money was spent is also subtly abusive. The real precedent of the L.A. Games was its role as the first Games to finance future Olympic and sport programs of the host region and country. Whereas all participants in a sport event typically share in the receipts, the LAOOC voted not to share even part of its surplus with teams from other countries. This left more money for the needy sport programs of southern California and the USOC. Once those were taken care of and surplus money was still left, the LAOOC changed its charter so that money could be spent on the arts in southern California. While marginally legal, this decision constituted a clear betrayal of its public trust and an

unprecedented variation on the theme of keeping elites happy using public funds. Another betrayal so blatant that state law had to be changed
in order to make it legal was the $800,000 in bonuses awarded to the
LAOOC's top two executives.

L.A.'s "success" will probably not be duplicated. One advantage L.A.'s
promoters had, particularly compared to Munich and Montreal, was their
ability to use existing facilities. As both a cost-conscious and status-
confident Games, L.A.'s promoters did not need to build many new
facilities and did not need to build ornate facilities that would impress
the world. Another advantage was the ability to deal with American
television and American multinational corporations during a time of rising patriotism and economic optimism. A third advantage was the
LAOOC's status as a private organization, by which it avoided public
scrutiny of its financial condition and thereby sustained its image as a
"strapped" operation. Finally, the L.A. Games also benefited from unique
local conditions that boosted attendance:

- A subcultural worship of the body and things sporting
- A heterogeneous ethnic population interested in both the different
  sports and participating teams
- A fad-conscious population prone to following the latest trend, which
  the Games became as the 2-week Olympiad progressed

If one makes the safe assumption that the Games will not be transacted
strictly through donations at any time in the foreseeable future, the question remains: What is "acceptable" commercialization of the Olympics?
The key issue in any commercial transaction is "fairness" in the market
sense of the term; that is, fair amounts and distribution of revenues, costs,
and surplus or loss. The problem is, as a singular event, the Olympics
appear not to have a "market." The solution, then, is to create a market,
or market-like conditions. The abuses of recent Olympics suggest how
to do this.

Stated simply, "fairness" means "lack of distortion" of the local
economy. Donations to the Games then become adjustments from fair
value: down for costs, up for revenues. The key principle here is: Hosting the Games should be done by a region that can show a base of support, including facilities, for the activities it desires to host. This principle
challenges the economic wisdom of many current practices by Olympic
promoters.

The above principle challenges the ideas of awarding the Games to an
economically disadvantaged region and then making demands regarding facilities and of awarding the Games to a single location. Ongoing
support for an activity implies an existing infrastructure capable of
handling the Games, a ready means of determining market value for capital and labor, use of equipment whose life will extend beyond the Games,
and personnel who understand how to administer the competition. In

its present mode of operation, the Olympics take on a certain irreversibility that invites abuse. If decentralized, the Olympics could be shifted easily to other candidates, the "first and second runners-up," should a problem arise.

This principle also challenges the way that the television rights for the Games are sold. The present system of awarding rights to one group for the entire Games fails to link rights fees with the actual activities broadcast, so the "fairness" of the total price cannot be determined. To determine a fair price, divide sports into at least the following three categories: those having a market value as a regular event in a country, those having value as a special event, and those having value as part of a pool of other such sports. In the U.S., for example, basketball falls into the first category; gymnastics, the second; canoeing, the third. Television programmers would be free to bid for sports in any of the categories. Fees for Olympic events would be commensurate with fees paid nationally for the same activities.

This principle also challenges the way that corporate sponsorship is awarded. At present, being an "official whatever of the Olympics" means nothing more than "you paid your money, you get the title" for your advertising campaign. The honor, however, should depend not so much on the size of one's coffers and a meld with Olympic audience demographics as on civic-mindedness and corporate good behavior. Thus, polluters, money launderers, and international arms merchants need not apply. Money donated by the honored corporations would be a publicly announced percentage of their profits (not their ad budgets), matched by a similar percentage of employee wages and salaries.

Live attendance would be the main source of income for the hosts of the events. Television income would be used to support the movement as a whole, and would be split between the NOC of the country, the IOC, and to all NOCs participating in that sport. Distribution of all income would be established ahead of the Games. Should a surplus arise, it would be set into reserve, pooled, and distributed nationally and internationally for development programs and research promoting health in the general population.

These measures, too, are unlikely to be implemented. In a time when the leading capitalist nation and the leading communist nation are struggling with severe economic problems, when the world is flirting with economic depression and is unable to develop an economic order in which every individual has a reasonably equal chance at living out a full life, why expect the Olympics to be economically efficient, to be anything more than conspicuous consumption? Exposed as a movement without a following, the Olympic movement has been forced to sell itself in order to survive. Selling isn't necessarily bad—if the movement and the Games are a worthy cause. Are they? For an answer to the question, we turn to the last reason to abolish the Games.

Should the Olympic Games Be Abolished Because They Are Too Political?

The IOC and the individual NOCs were originally intended to be non-governmental bodies whose members were "above" political concerns. Similarly, as the ancient Olympics were a respite from political affairs of the day, the modern Olympics were to be likewise. Instead, thinking that politics and Olympic sport are inextricably linked has become almost conventional (Goodhue, 1976; Goodhart & Chataway, 1968; Kanin, 1981; Lowe, Kanin, & Strenk, 1978; Lapchick, 1978). Within the Games, politics is seen in the selection and actions of the host nation, in the participation of national teams, and in the playing of national anthems and raising of national flags during victory ceremonies. Increasing politicization has occurred from the competition for prestige among the nations, particularly between the core countries of the capitalist world and communist-governed countries (cf. Espy, 1979; Kanin, 1978; Riordan, 1974).

The IOC has attempted to be diplomatic here. It has tried to internationalize the Olympic movement by spreading the privilege of hosting the Games to different regions of the world and has adhered resolutely to the stand that "the Games must go on" (cf. Guttmann, 1984). Nevertheless, some people contend that diplomacy is not enough. They argue that the Games are being destroyed by politics; that to return to the ideal of pure sport, reforms must be introduced. These include reforms such as eliminating national teams and the playing of national anthems, locating the games at a permanent and politically neutral site, or prohibiting the superpowers or any political troublespot from hosting the Games. What is missing in all of these suggestions, however, is a logic that explains how "pure" sport helps promote peace and how it avoids being merely an illusion of peace or titillating entertainment. The significant question then is: Can the Games be depoliticized? Can politics be kept out of the Games? If so, how? If not, what kinds of politics should the Olympic movement practice?

As noted earlier, the Olympic Games are an example of a form of sport called semiprofessional sport; that is, sport in which teams represent sponsoring organizations (Rose, 1980, 1985). Because the organizations represented by Olympic teams are nations, the Games are by definition political. They are in effect *both* sport *and* politics. Indeed, precisely this link has propelled the Games to the prominence they have attained. But contrary to the notion that the link is inimical to peace, the link is necessary if peace through sport is to be accomplished. Peace is, after all, a political objective and outcome.

In semiprofessional sport, however, a tension exists between community and rivalry (cf. Kyrolainen & Varis, 1981). The predominance of rivalry in recent years has created an awareness of the political nature of the Olympics. The rivalry of the Olympics parallels the rivalry of both intra- and international politics, as the old political order passes out of existence and a new one is formed. In effect, it is not that the Games are more political; it is that the world they represent is more divided. For example, the Jesse Owens myth of equality of opportunity for blacks in the U.S. was no less a political statement than was the black fist salute of 1968 that shattered it. Similarly, for many years after World War II, selecting a neutral site might have been possible when the U.S. ruled the world: an OlympicsLand in southern California, perhaps. Today, rivals to U.S. power make such a decision extremely unlikely.

While political points can be made through sports, political action depends on decisions outside the Games. This idea can be understood most readily by comparing the events following the 1936 Games with those following the 1980 and 1984 Games. In all three cases, the success of the host's teams was a wellspring of patriotism, albeit in the latter two cases only through suspension of disbelief in the equality of the competition. But so far only the 1936 Games have been followed by acts that led to a world war (cf. Clumpner, 1978; Hazan, 1982; Mandel, 1971, 1978).

Thus, as a quasi-independent arena, the sports world need not merely reflect the state of the "real" world. The sports world can be used to promote a better world by linking participation in the Olympics and the honor of hosting the Olympics with positive behavior in the real world. This linkage would attempt to institutionalize a political process in which advances by nations are honored and recognized while antisocial behavior is repudiated and participation in the Games forbidden (cf. Partington, 1982). For example, nations making advances in reducing illiteracy, infant mortality, crime, or in improving nutrition, conservation, or employment would be given the honor of competing to host one or more sports. If such a procedure had been in place, the debate would have explored the wisdom of awarding the Games to a region where concerns about human rights violations exist (Moscow) or where the local economy's heavy dependence on military contracts gives substantial impetus to the arms race and international conflicts (L.A.).

Likewise, Olympic member-nations would debate whether or not to extend invitations to teams from nations at war, thought to be contributing to the likelihood of war, or violating fundamental human rights. In other words, institutionalize the process, implicit in boycotts, by which *national* teams are held accountable for their *nation's* actions. At the same time, change the basis of individual participation so that athletes (e.g., Sydney Maree) may repudiate the conduct of their nation without having to pledge allegiance to another country.

Finally, if the Olympics were truly an international celebration of peace through sport, they would be more like current national and religious festivals, such as the Fourth of July or Christmas, and less like a television extravaganza. The Olympics would stop the world; they would establish a time and forum in which to assess the state of the world and applaud advances and rebuke failures. The Games would celebrate all forms of culture, not just the physical culture of sport; they would educate people of one culture about other cultures.

But the Olympics will not likely become an international celebration of peace. With armaments the major growth industry of the world, with the continuing failure of the two superpowers to control the nuclear arms race, with the democratic process breaking down, with armed struggle the growing way to settle differences, and with revolution the only way to increase one's life-chances, the political problems of the Olympic Games are insignificant by comparison. Only the socially elite or emotionally crippled can delude themselves by contemplating how to reform the Games without linking such thoughts to reforming the world. Abolish the Games, not because they are *too* political, but because they pay obsequious respect to human dignity and to an honest yearning for the survival of the planet.

References

Annotated bibliography. (1984). *Sociology of Sport Journal*, **1**, 1.

Brohm, J. (1981). Theses toward a political sociology of sport. In M. Hart & S. Birrell (Eds.), *Sport in the sociocultural process* (3rd ed., pp. 107-113). Dubuque, IA: Wm. C. Brown.

Clumpner, R.A. (1978). Federal involvement in sport to promote American interest or foreign policy objectives: 1950-1973. In B. Lowe, D.B. Kanin, & A. Strenk (Eds.), *Sport and international relations* (pp. 400-452). Champaign, IL: Stipes.

Edwards, H. (1981). Crisis in the Olympic movement. In J. Segrave & D. Chu (Eds.), *Olympism*. Champaign, IL: Human Kinetics.

Espy, R. (1979). *The politics of the Olympic Games*. Berkeley, CA: University of California Press.

Glencross, D.J. (Ed.). (1980). Sport and elite athlete—A sports sciences review. *Proceedings of the 50th AN-ZAAS Congress*.

Goodhart, P., & Chataway, C. (1968). *War without weapons: The rise of mass sport in the twentieth century and its effect on men and nations*. London: Allen.

Goodhue, R.M. (1976). The development of Olympism, 1900-1932: Technical success within a threatening political reality. In P. Graham & H. Ueberhorst (Eds.), *The modern Olympics* (pp. 27-39). Cornwall, NY: Leisure Press.

Guttmann, A. (1984). *The Games must go on: Avery Brundage and the Olympic movement*. New York: Columbia University Press.

Hazan, B. (1982). *Olympic sports and propoganda games: Moscow, 1980*. New Brunswick, NJ: Transaction.

Hoffman, H. (1982). Survival in the Canadian sports system. In J.T. Partington, T. Orlick, & J.H. Salmela (Eds.), *Sport in perspective* (pp. 6-11). Ottawa: Coaching Association of Canada.

Holmes, J. (1971). *Olympiad 1936: Blaze of glory for Hitler's Reich*. New York: Ballantine.

Johnson, W.O. (1972). *All that glitters is not gold: An irreverant look at the Olympic Games*. New York: Putnam.

Kanin, D.B. (1978). Superpower power sport in Cold War and "detente." In B. Lowe, D.B. Kanin, & A. Strenk (Eds.), *Sport and international relations* (pp. 249-262). Champaign, IL: Stipes.

Kanin, D.B. (1981). *A political history of the Olympic Games*. Boulder, CO: Westview Press.

Kyrolainen, H., & Varis, T. (1981). Approaches to the study of sports in international relations. *Current Research on Peace and Violence*, 4(1), 55-88.

Lapchick, R.E. (1978). A political history of the modern Olympic Games. *Journal of Sport and Social Issues*, 2(1), 1-12.

Lowe, B., Kanin, D.B., & Strenk, A. (Eds.). (1978). *Sport and international relations*. Champaign, IL: Stipes.

Man of the year. (1985, January 7). *Time*, pp. 20-40.

Mandel, R. (1971). *The Nazi Olympics*. New York: Macmillan.

Mandel, R. (1978). Sportsmanship and Nazi Olympism. In B. Lowe, D.B. Kanin, & A. Strenk (Eds.), *Sport and international relations* (pp. 135-152). Champaign, IL: Stipes.

McMurty, J. (1973, January). A case for killing the Olympics. *MacLean's*, pp. 34, 57-58, 60.

Partington, J.T. (1982). Humanizing the sport system: An Olympic proposal. In J.T. Partington, T. Orlick, & J.H. Salmela (Eds.), *Sport in perspective* (pp. 17-19). Ottawa: Coaching Association of Canada.

Reich, K. (in press). *Secrets of the Organizing Committee*.

Riordan, J. (1974). Soviet sport and Soviet foreign policy. *Soviet Studies*, 26, 322-343.

Rose, D. (1980). *Physical culture. A critique of the American sociological study of sport*. Unpublished doctoral dissertation, University of Massachusetts, Amherst.

Rose, D. (1985). Theoretical and practical confusion about the Olympics. In G. Redmond (Ed.), *Sport and politics* (pp. 185-191). Champaign, IL: Human Kinetics.

Segrave, J.O., & Chu, D.B. (Eds.). (1981). *Olympism*. Champaign, IL: Human Kinetics.

Zornow, G. (1977). *Report of the President's Commission on Olympic sports, 1975-1977*. Washington, DC: U.S. Government Printing Office.

25
The Olympic Games: Mirror of the World

Richard Espy

The modern Olympic Games are a mirror through which the world views itself, and with narcissistic pleasure it relishes the vision. How else can one explain the indomitable popularity of a spectacle that is forever rife with conflict? The Games are an expression of the world as it is, as it is structured, as it operates. In essence, they are a celebration of mankind, however fallible.

The nature of this celebration is one of competition, the same competition that exists in the world at large. The Games are not just a competition of individuals, but more a competition of nations, to see which is the best and which will prevail. From the outset the modern Olympic Games were structured so that each athlete was subordinated to the state as its contestant. Athletes were not judged as individuals, they were identified as representatives of their states. Athletes were not competing against one another, nations were, and had this not been the case the Olympic Games would not exist today because they would have died from lack of interest.

Olympic officials would have one believe that somehow the conflicts and the politics that result from this nation-versus-nation structure are

407

intrusions and have no relationship to the Games themselves. Olympic officials claim their Games are solely competitions among individuals, and it is the individuals that are important and for which the Games exist. Such ideals serve better as excuses for the existence of the Games than for the reality of the Games. The reality is that the conflicts and the politics are not intrusions but are inherent in the Games.

The world can be viewed as a system of organizations that are constantly evolving into higher or other forms. In this sense, a nation-state is but another organization having basically the same characteristics as other organizations, though its purpose may be different. The IOC and other international sport organizations comprise a set of organizations with specific purposes and goals. All organizations reflect a collective consciousness of specific combinations of individuals. Each organization has certain facets to its personality that are utilized for the achievement of its goals, just as an individual uses his personal characteristics to meet his purposes. In this sense, organizations are individual units on the world scene. When an organization structures itself in terms of other organizational entities (e.g., international sport in terms of nation-states), the facets of other organizations (the nation-state) become a part of the first organization (international sport). Because politics are a facet of nation-states, politics become a part of international sport. The only way to divorce politics from international sport is to alter the organizational structure of sport.

Politics, then, are inherent in the Olympic system, and the international sport organizations and the Olympic Games are variant arenas of world politics. The political issues that the Olympic system has confronted underscore this concept. The majority of these issues has involved the question of recognition. At the end of World War II, Germany and Japan were not recognized nor were they allowed to participate in the Games until such time as the occupation authorities gave their consent. In the case of Germany, the issue then became no longer a question of the recognition of Germany per se, but of East or West Germany. The estrangement that erupted between the occupation authorities became an important part of the United States-Soviet, East-West conflict and carried over into the question of German recognition. That same estrangement was exhibited in the later questions of Soviet and Chinese recognition. In the latter case, the issue was similar to that of Germany.

As time went on and relations eased between the East and the West, the question of German recognition became less of an issue. By 1968, it was resolved to the satisfaction of both sides. Conversely, the problem of Chinese recognition remained because of the deepening Sino-Soviet dispute and the Chinese cultural revolution of the late 1960s. Even by the 1970s the issue had not been resolved, and considerable trouble ensued at both the 1976 Summer Games and 1980 Winter Games as a result of the changing world politics and the emergence of the People's Republic of China (PRC) onto the world political scene. The question was finally put to rest at the 1984 Games, where both Chinas (the PRC and

Taiwan) competed under a mutually agreeable format, also a product of changing world political conditions and all participants' recognition of these conditions.

On other fronts the question of Olympic recognition mirrored that in the world at large, this time concerning South Africa and Rhodesia, what is now Zimbabwe. In both cases the issues reflected the African political situation and the protest against white-ruled, racist regimes. The African dissent was in part supported by other Third World areas and by the Soviet bloc countries. The Third World support represented anticolonial nationalistic sentiment; the Soviet bloc support manifested the continuing East-West conflict and the drive for solidarity with the underdeveloped, nonaligned areas. The increasing success of a boycott threat of the Olympic Games over the issue of South Africa and Rhodesia throughout the period 1956-1984 demonstrated the rise of the Third World as an alternative power source. Area Games were another source of political confrontation, dramatizing regional controversies that had spillover effects into the Olympic Games and the world at large. The Games of the New Emerging Forces (GANEFO) episode of 1963 and the Asian Games of 1974 are good cases in point.

Within the ranks of the Olympic system, increasing controversy occurred between the respective organizations that was basically the product of nationalism and commercialism. Nationalism elicited demands by national committees for expanded participation in the Olympic system. Commercialism had its major effect on the international sport federations and their increasing difficulty, under the influence of financial inducements, in conducting their sports in an amateur context. Here the sport federations were increasingly at odds with the IOC. For all three organizational groups—the IOC, the national committees, and the international federations—the role of television in the Olympic Games had become a bone of contention, especially as the Olympic and international sporting system expanded throughout the world. This expansion caused a corresponding escalation of expenditures necessary for staging sporting contests and maintaining and perpetuating the sport organizations. Earlier sources of revenue, primarily private donations, no longer were adequate to meet the expanded tasks of the sport organizations. The sale of television rights for enormous sums was seen as a panacea for this revenue deficit. The problem was determining the distribution of the revenue. The distribution problem, combined with increasing division among the three organizations, produced a struggle for control within the Olympic system. The problem also subjected that system to external control as financial considerations became paramount, for in order to maintain financial solvency, the organizations developed a dependency on outside commercial and television interests.

These political and economic interests represented a vast organizational nexus evolving throughout the world. Following World War II, a nucleus of nation-states in Europe, Asia, and the American continents formed the bulwark of the prewar state system. This nucleus, primarily composed of the Soviet Union, Europe, and North America (and peripherally including South America) took the lead in establishing the predominant postwar relationships. The relationships among the nation-states in the nucleus created the conditions for the East-West estrangement that continues to dominate the world political scene. That estrangement in turn helped to forge regional integration movements—political, economic, and military—that formed organizational structures beyond the nation-state and beyond a purely national perspective.

The nucleus sought to consolidate its position once again and to establish a system of relations among states, bilateral or multilateral, which included both regional and world organizations such as the United Nations. The colonial areas, imbued with nationalistic fervor, sought to break away from their colonial status and to establish their own separate nation-states. By the mid-1960s this process was nearly complete, expanding the nation-state system around the world and in turn propelling nationalism to its zenith. At the same time, the nationalism that had spawned the separation movements from the colonial powers brought the new states together, forming a nonaligned force against the East and West power blocs. This unification was expressed by declarations of nonalignment or by establishment of regional arrangements (e.g., the OAU, LAFTA) for mutual political and economic protection from more powerful states. As nationalism began to reach its zenith, the catalytic effect of environmental conditions (economic, military, and political) caused nationalism itself to evolve worldwide into a higher form, producing a more international or integrated organizational framework.

A further organizational evolution occurred, that of the transnational organization. These organizations had existed for some time, but following World War II their increase was phenomenal. As the economies in the nucleus states prospered, technology grew by leaps and bounds. The necessity for the protective umbrella of the nation-state became less important, in some cases a hindrance, as the sense of security became more controlled. The primary transnational operator was the multinational business firm, but other transnational actors increased in number and importance (e.g., sport organizations) as the nation-state system expanded, spreading nationalism worldwide and creating conditions conducive to the orientation of the individual beyond his own state boundaries.

These organizational forces and trends were apparent in the Olympic system. The East-West conflict was most strongly exhibited in the question of German recognition and in the competition between the Soviet Union and the United States. As an indicator of the evolving and expanding nation-state system, the German question became less of an issue over time, as other issues reflecting changing world relationships (such as the issue of South African and Rhodesian participation) took its place. Similarly, as the United States and the Soviet Union consolidated their respective positions worldwide, and as other power blocs arose, the tension between the United States and the Soviet Union in the world and at the Games eased. By the mid-1970s, as economic and political conditions in the United States and throughout the world destabilized, primarily the result of the end to American involvement in Vietnam and sharply escalating prices for oil, relations between the United States and the Soviet Union once again became strained. This situation was reflected in the Olympics in back-to-back boycotts in 1980 and 1984, first by the United States, then by the Soviet Union.

The Olympic system and international sport further reflected growing internationalism. As the nation-state system expanded, so did the Olympic movement and international sport, each growing in interest and prestige. In 1975 the IOC, having reached an international stature comparable to other international organizations and having encountered more and more problems commensurate with that stature, decided to register with the United Nations as a recognized international organization having legal status ("Lausanne, 9th-11th February," 1974, p. 92).

The Olympic system is unique in that not only does it qualify as an international organization by virtue of its national identification, it also qualifies as a transnational organization in that it comprises a set of private organizations. The growth in prestige and interest acquired in its capacity as an international organization applies equally in its role as transnational actor. The corollary growth of commercial and media influence in the Olympics and sport further indicates their own increasing impact on the world at large, illustrating the mutualism existing between transnational actors on the world scene today.

The Olympics has provided a forum for international competition and confrontation and also has been an actor in that process. The IOC and the other sport organizations have sought to carry out their tasks within the amateur sport system, but in the context of the nation-state system. At the same time, they have been forced to respond to external stimuli in order to maintain control over the amateur sport system.

The original emphasis of the Olympic Games was supposed to be on the athlete, but the structure of the Games and the sport organizations caused the emphasis, for reasons of efficiency, to be on the organizations. The division of labor was made easier but at the expense of the importance of the athlete. This diminishing of the athletes' importance was illustrated time and again, most poignantly during the boycott threats and the successive boycotts of the 1976, 1980, and 1984 Games.

Olympic officials could have dealt with the problem in an organizational context had they simply recognized that politics within this organizational framework was an integral part of sport. Although some Olympic leaders have recognized this, none has been successful in minimizing the politics because none has been willing to act on the Olympic ideal and deal with the athletes as individuals. Instead, Olympic leaders have continued to work only with organizations.

Several incidents underscore this. Following World War II, with the arrival of Soviet forces in Eastern Europe, many athletes fled as exiles to the United States and elsewhere in the West. These athletes sought to participate in the 1952 and 1956 Games, but an IOC rule prohibited an athlete from participating in the Games for one country if he had previously participated for another country. Similarly, an athlete could not participate if he were not a citizen of that country and had not received the necessary affiliation with its sport organizations. The exiles sought special dispensation or a change in the rules. They wanted to participate as athletes, as individuals, behind the Olympic flag, or in whatever way was possible. The IOC refused. It submitted the question to the Council of Europe, which conversely agreed with the exiles (Mayer, 1960, pp. 212-220), but the IOC would not tolerate anything contrary to its rules or to the established organizational pattern and persisted in its refusal. Clearly, the organization mattered more than the athlete.

At the 1976 Games the boycott left many athletes unable to participate. After so much training and effort in preparation the disappointment was great, but most resigned themselves to their fate. A few did not. One such athlete was James Gilkes of Guyana. Spurred on by earlier declarations of the IOC that any athlete who wanted to participate could do so under the Olympic banner—a ploy to sabotage the boycott—Gilkes decided to do just that and applied to the IOC. After much deliberation the IOC turned him down, reaffirming the Olympic rules ("IOC Rejects Gilkes' Pleas," 1976).

The IOC's inability to live up to its ideal is symptomatic of a worldwide situation. The issue is more a misrepresentation of the individual in an organizational context than a question of the individual versus the organization. An individual may be a member of an organization, but if he has no input into that organization he is likely to be misrepresented. The sport organizations are not organizations of athletes, which they purport to be, but rather bureaucratic administrative structures. The administrative apparatus is in each case the real organization.

When Filbert Bayi of Tanzania was refused the opportunity to compete against John Walker of New Zealand before the 1976 Games, Bayi did not make the decision (Kornheiser, 1976), his sport organization did. Bayi had absolutely no say in the matter, although he was the one to do the running. The situation is a common one. The Olympics are only an isolated example, but also a representative one.

World society is a complex of organizations. The organizations are set up with specific purposes and goals. The achievement of these goals is paramount. In order to achieve the stated goals, the organization must be maintained. Through time the latter consideration becomes paramount, and the former goal becomes the expedient justification for the existence of the organization. Therefore, the primary goal of the organization is organizational health—the maintenance of the organization at any cost. In order to achieve this maintenance, an organization sets up specific routines and standard patterns of behavior through standard operating procedures. Through these procedures an organization can control its internal and surrounding environments by coordinating and categorizing the issues and problems it faces into set patterns of operation and routine. An organization attempts to avoid uncertainty because uncertainty—the lack of standard behavior—creates chaos, and chaos disrupts organizational patterns, then the organizational structure, and finally the organization itself.

The organization is a co-optive device; it must be in order to sustain its existence. It must have adherents; it must grow; but the growth is defined in terms of size rather than quality. Quality, unlike size, is not readily measured. Size can be measured and used as an index of organizational health and existence. Thus growth is defined in terms of such indicators as budget, manpower, and territory. The main problem for any organization lies in the conflict between its organizational patterns of behavior and its stated purpose for existence; that is, in the maintenance of the organization as opposed to its stated ideal (Allison, 1971).

In this light, the Olympic system can be analyzed in terms of its past performance as a determinant of its future potential. For the IOC and all the amateur sport organizations, their own maintenance has been paramount, utilizing the ideals of their organizations as excuses for their existence. The IOC and the sport organizations have standardized their behaviors and procedures in order to control their environments. They have set up structures of organization and procedure in terms of nation-states in order to control the athletic world. The sport organizations have been symbols of nation-states—the dominant organizational units on the world scene—and as such have been able to maintain their existence through the process of identification. Their growth along with the nation-state, and hence the identification factor, has facilitated the opportunity to co-opt all the amateur sport organizations into the Olympic movement as the only legitimate sport movement. The Olympic movement has been forced to define its health in terms of the growth and size of its organizations rather than in terms of its ideals. The ideals have been made secondary but have been used as the primary justification for its existence.

The international system has been changing, however, and the Olympic organizations have found it increasingly difficult to categorize the environment into standard procedure. When the attempt has failed, as in the 1976, 1980, and 1984 boycotts, the credibility of the organizations has been lowered. Increasingly, in the latter years of the period 1944 to 1984, as the Olympic system has retrenched its routine the central questions of Olympic ideals and the rights of the individual athletes have become burning issues. The Olympic system has been viewed increasingly as archaic and inadequate for the performance of international sport because it has not been perpetuating but has been hampering that performance and because the individual has not been sufficiently considered.

The latest example of this inadequacy concerns the planning for the 1988 Summer Games, slated for Seoul, South Korea. Following the great financial success of the 1984 Summer Games in Los Angeles, where a $150 million-plus surplus was realized (Hayes, 1984), Olympic planners were looking ahead to the 1988 Games, hoping to achieve the same financial success. Based on past performance, Olympic leaders were anticipating vast television revenues to further fill their organizations' coffers. American television rights for the 1984 Summer Games had been sold for $225 million and the same rights for the 1988 Winter Games had been sold for $309 million. Projections for the American rights, which form the bulk of the revenue of world television rights as well as the bulk of Olympic organizational revenue, to the Seoul Games were from $750 million to $1 billion (Reich, 1984a).

A hitch occurred, however. The 13-hour time differential between Seoul and New York was such that finals events, which generally take place in the evening, would take place in the middle of the night or early morning New York time—definitely not prime time when the advertising dollar is greatest. American television networks indicated to Olympic leaders that they would be unwilling to pay such vast sums as were being anticipated unless finals events were rescheduled for the very early morning hours Seoul time, so they could be viewed in the evening—prime time—in New York (Reich, 1984a).

At first, Olympic leaders, frightened at any loss of anticipated revenue, indicated their willingness to go along with the change. Athletes, however, were not so obliging and indicated as much. Olympic leaders, already faced with the very real possibility of another Soviet bloc boycott of the Games, decided to risk a loss of revenue and hold the finals events as scheduled. Their reasoning, however, was not the product of sympathy or solidarity for the athletes, but rather was the result of fear for the independence of their organizations. They feared that if they became too dependent financially on television, television would eventually dictate to them how to run their Games and their organizations (Reich, 1984b).

Although this fear is indeed well founded, and an issue that will not go away in the foreseeable future, consideration for the individual athlete once again took a back seat to consideration of the organization, in spite of the fact that according to Olympic leaders the Olympics exist for the athletes. The ideal is again shown to be the excuse for but not the reality of the organization.

This situation will doubtfully change in the future. The Olympic Games are simply too popular to provide any incentive for Olympic leaders to substantially change their Games, their organizations, or their manner of conducting Olympic affairs. An occurrence at the 1980 Moscow Games illustrates this point.

The United States-led boycott of the Games, in response to the Soviet invasion of Afghanistan in December of 1979, had created the situation at the Games where 62 countries who had originally planned to attend did not. Nevertheless, several key U.S. allies in Western Europe did attend, in spite of their own denunciations of the Soviet action. As a means of voicing their own displeasure with the Soviets and a way to show some solidarity with the United States, the national committee leaders from these attending Western European countries had asked and had received permission from the IOC for special dispensation to not participate in the opening ceremonies, nor to have their countries' flags raised and anthems played at victory ceremonies. Very possibly the IOC approved the change more as an expedient maneuver to quell anti-Soviet sentiment in the Olympic movement and to mollify contentious factions than anything else.

These ceremonial changes were interpreted as a step toward denationalizing the Games, a step long advocated by many critics, as a means of depoliticizing the Games. The change did not have its intended effect, and in fact was roundly criticized and disliked by participants and spectators alike (Reich, 1980). The change remained a temporary measure and was not continued at the 1984 Games in Los Angeles, in spite of a reciprocal boycott of those Games led by the Soviet Union.

What this incident illustrates is the dilemma of the Olympic Games. The Games are popular because of their organizational structure—the identification with the nation-state system—and yet that organizational structure is the very reason the Games are so plagued with conflict. But were the Games' organizational structure altered in order to alleviate the conflict, as has been advocated by countless analysts, the popularity, indeed the *raison d'être* of the Games would cease. The Games would then most probably die with a whimper, as their forebears did more than 1,000 years ago.

Under such circumstances Olympic leaders would be foolish to make any substantive changes in their Games or their organizational structure unless they wish to ring the Games' death knell. Given Olympic leaders' past history for following the expedient path, this writer does not expect to see for the foreseeable future either substantive changes in the Games themselves or in the organizational structure.

This highly probable eventuality, nevertheless, begs the question of what can be done to quell some of the conflict that has so disrupted the Games in recent Olympiads and has so disheartened fan and participant alike. Because the Olympic Games are essentially a mirror of world society, the conflict that occurs at them is but a reflection of the same outside the arena of the Games. The question, then, is not really of control over the conflicts per se, but rather their manifestations at the Games. In recent Olympiads the manifestations primarily have taken the form of boycotts, and little reason exists to believe, given each boycott's relative nonsuccess, that this form of political expression, this political weapon, may be used at future Games.

This view is based upon the premise that each boycott did not accomplish its purpose, and in fact turned out to be counterproductive. The question is, did the boycotters learn this lesson? In the case of the African countries, the answer is a probable yes.

At least, the African countries learned, if the United States and the Soviet Union did not, that when it comes to the Olympic Games, participation is everything and nonparticipation is a soon-forgotten memory. In 1976, once the African countries participating in the boycott had left

the Olympic encampment and the Games had begun, the world forgot
or simply stopped caring about why the Africans were not there. What
mattered and what made the headlines were the Games and the participants who were there. That same phenomenon occurred in 1980 and
1984, only the players changed.

The reason the African countries learned what might be called "the
Olympic lesson," is that they had ample opportunity to repeat their 1976
boycott in 1980 and 1984. Not only were they cajoled to join the respective boycotts of the United States and the Soviet Union in 1980 and 1984,
but the circumstances prompting their 1976 boycott were themselves
repeated, or ones very similar, in 1980 and 1984. Yet, the African countries did not boycott again; they participated.

Obviously, by participating in 1980 and 1984 the African countries were
able to achieve considerable political capital with their respective hosts—
the Soviet Union and the United States. But, in fact, the decision to participate in the Games had been made long before either boycott had been
announced. The Supreme Council for Sport in Africa (SCSA) in 1979,
in response to a South African rugby tour of Britain, decided that in the
future the African response to offending countries that dared to engage
in sport contacts with apartheid South Africa would be undertaken on
a bilateral basis, involving numerous forms of contact and not just sport
(Hennessey, 1979; "Supreme in Moderation," 1979). No African boycott
would take place in 1980, and the implication for future Olympics was
clear: The Africans would attend.

Whether the United States and the Soviet Union have learned the same
lesson as the African countries remains to be seen. Clearly, neither
achieved what had been intended by their boycotts. The Soviet Union
did not leave Afghanistan, and remains there still, and the United States
was not embarrassed or damaged in any way by the Soviets and most
of their allies being absent from Los Angeles. In fact, the Los Angeles
Games were perhaps the most successful of all time: More countries participated than ever before, and they were the most profitable, ending well
in the black.

From these examples, then, the message seems quite clear regarding
the efficacy of boycotting the Olympic Games. Only time will tell if the
message is getting through.

If the message isn't getting through, and Olympic leaders are concerned
about the long-term effects of repeated boycotts of the Games, they might
institute at least two changes that might go far in preventing future boycotts, or at least certain kinds, and eliminating some of the conflict at the
Games. Although Olympic leaders will probably not seek any substantive organizational changes lest they wish to risk their Games, they could
institute one change with little ill effect. That change would be to move
the Games to a neutral site. For many years now Greece has been peti-
tioning the IOC to move the Games permanently to Greece, and just as
often the IOC has shown near-complete disinterest in the idea. Only after

the 1980 Games did the IOC appear to, for once, take the petition seriously, but as had happened repeatedly in the past, the matter died quietly.

A permanent neutral site would seem to be the solution to such imbroglios as occurred in 1980 and 1984, but it would have no impact over those such as occurred in 1976, for at the 1976 Games the boycott issue did not concern the site itself as it did in 1980 and 1984. For such conflicts as occurred in 1976, the IOC can only hope the "Olympic lesson" has been learned well.

A permanent neutral site would help the IOC and the Olympic sport organizations from becoming too dependent on television and other commercial interests because the Games would require much less expense to stage, thus necessitating less need for ever greater revenue sources with each succeeding Games.

Of course, finding a country that all can agree is neutral might pose a problem. As it stands, Greece cannot be deemed neutral, not while it remains part of NATO and American troops are stationed there. Switzerland is at least nominally neutral, and as it currently houses the headquarters of the IOC, some logic exists in making this country the permanent site of the Games. But as long as the IOC continues to receive numerous bids for its Games from cities throughout the world, there is little likelihood, much less support, for a permanent neutral site. The fact is, the Games are too popular for any one country or site to hold a monopoly on them.

The other change the IOC might undertake in hopes of lessening some of the conflict surrounding the Games would be to open the competition at the Games to all competitors regardless of profession. An obvious relaxation of the rules has occurred in recent years such that the distinction between what constitutes a professional—one who is paid to compete—and what constitutes an amateur—one who receives no monetary remuneration to compete—has blurred. Yet, the distinction still exists and becomes the subject of political conflict when the competition involves athletes from the East and West bloc countries.

Both sides cry foul when it serves their purposes (when their competitors win), citing violations of the amateur rules by the other side. Opening the competition to all regardless of profession would eliminate at least the opportunity to use the amateur rule as political fodder. It would not eliminate comparisons between the relative strengths of the competitors, and thus the relative strengths of the respective countries, but then to try and eliminate this would be to eliminate the very essence of the Olympic Games, and ultimately the Games themselves.

In the final analysis, the Olympic Games are in every one of us. They mirror the soul of mankind, for we, if nothing else, are competitive animals, as are all animals ultimately. The Games are unique from other sporting contests and from other avenues of interaction in that they are structured uniquely to correspond to the major patterns of organizational interaction of mankind on Earth in the 20th century. But this structure would mean nothing without the presence of a competitive soul, and this soul ultimately drives the Games and will ensure for the foreseeable future their continued existence.

References

Allison, G.T. (1971). *Essence of devision: Explaining the Cuban missile crisis.* Boston: Little, Brown.

Hayes, T.C. (1985, May 23). Olympic group reports a $150 million surplus. *New York Times*, Sec. VI, p. 8.

Hennessey, J. (1979, December 19). African sports leaders call for break with Britain. *The Times*, p. 1.

IOC rejects Gilkes' pleas to compete on his own. (1976, July 23). *Los Angeles Times*, Sec. III, p. 9.

Kornheiser, T. (1976, May 23). Africa threat casts a cloud on Montreal Olympics. *New York Times*, Sec. V, p. 8.

Lausanne, 9th-11th February 1974, Meeting of the Executive Board. (1974, March-April). *Olympic Review* (No. 76-77), p. 92.

Mayer, O. (1960). *A travers les anneaux Olympiques.* Geneva: Pierre Cailler.

Reich, K. (1980, July 28). Olympians cool to neutral flag, song. *Los Angeles Times*, Sec. I, p. 13.

Reich, K. (1984a, September 26). T.V. may dictate Olympic finals at 9 AM, Korea time. *Los Angeles Times*, Sec. III, p. 12.

Reich, K. (1984b, November 27). Olympic events won't be changed to suit T.V., officials decide. *Los Angeles Times*, Sec. III, p. 6.

Supreme in moderation. (1979, December 24). *The Times*, p. 8.

26
The Olympic Games: Past, Present, and Future

Sir Roger Bannister

The Olympic ideals have developed separately from the Games themselves and are not entirely dependent on them. Thus, we must distinguish between the Olympic Games on the one hand and the Olympic ideals, Olympism, and the Olympic Movement that promotes these ideals on the other.

The Olympic ideals are embodied in the 1979 Olympic Charter, which states that the Games promote

> the development of those finest physical and moral qualities that come from contests on the friendly fields of amateur sport. They bring together the youth of the world in a great quadrennial sports festival, thereby creating international respect and good will and helping to construct a better and more peaceful world. (p. 108)

Originally published in *Olympism* (pp. 140-147) edited by Jeffrey Segrave and Donald Chu, 1981, Champaign, IL: Human Kinetics. Reprinted by permission.

Not surprisingly, such startling claims provoke skepticism in the harsh modern world of materialism and conflict.

We must also concern ourselves a little with the ancient Olympics because the modern Olympic Movement has a number of practical rules and regulations that it is reluctant to change, in part, because these hark back to some of the rules that surrounded the ancient Olympics and were designed to protect them from external and political interference. The ancient Olympics were the greatest festival of the ancient world. As many as 40,000 spectators attended, having passage to and from the Games at Olympia in the neutral state of Elis. The Games were tightly controlled by judges, who resisted changes in the small program. The levels of skill were very high and coaching also reached a high standard. Finer points of technique were critically admired. Specialization was so great that it was actually 200 years before one person won all three classic athletic events. The ancient Games also had unpleasant, brutal, and violent aspects. Can you imagine a four-horse chariot race in which out of 41 chariots, only one chariot finished? Can you imagine the brutality of boxing, which sometimes led to the death of the competitors?

But underneath this, the Games had a religious basis, and cultural contests took place outside the Games but alongside them. Unattractive features, like a fairground, also surrounded the Games. One observer mentioned the gamblers, touts, and pimps that abounded. But the judges who controlled the Games, in their wisdom, succeeded in establishing an international event, and these Games survived for almost 1,000 years in a world of squabbling, warring city-states—a world not so different from our own. The modern Olympic Movement, by comparison, has survived with difficulty a mere 80 years.

What was the secret of the continuing competition of the ancient Olympics, and why did they last so long? The Greeks and the Romans delighted in fierce competition. They were elitist, and in the antielitist mood of much of our contemporary world, this is perhaps difficult to understand. Many people, particularly the Spartans, also regarded the Games as a training for combat. The Spartans eventually carried physical training to excess and introduced a kind of barracks life, almost from the age of 7. For a time, they held control of success in the Games, but others who showed more skill than harshness in training were eventually more successful than the Spartans.

The Greeks of the ancient Games tried to tackle a number of problems, many of which are still problematic today. It is perhaps surprising to learn that one problem that the Greeks did *not* seem to worry about was amateurism. Certainly, the victor only received a laurel leaf, but athletes were capable of earning large sums of money by competing in other games. There seemed to be no problem about receiving financial reward; sums have been calculated up to the equivalent of $40,000 for success in regional games. These regional games were very frequent, taking place in different parts of the ancient world. The holding of many small games is not without its parallel today.

Why, then, did the Games fail? One reason was the acceptance of Christianity and the fact that these Games were essentially a pagan festival. The second factor was the increasing size and cost, not only of the Games themselves but also of the satellite games that mushroomed, some of which were artfully labeled by their promoters as "Olympic." A final departure from tradition occurred when the Emperor Nero traduced the Games by devising a 10-horse chariot race. Of course, his chariot won amid antics that helped to lead up to his assassination a year later. Herod bought the presidency of the Games, which had previously been kept independent, by a large bribe. A general feeling was well summarized in Juvenal's famous rebuke to the plebs: "Once you elected generals, heads-of-state, commanders of legions, now you only care for bread and the Games."

The modern revival was the single-handed creation of the inspired Frenchman Pierre de Coubertin, who borrowed from the British public school sporting ethos and grafted this onto the Greek ideas brought into focus by the exploration of Olympia in the 1880s. Until then, the site had been a malarial swamp, the ruins of the ancient Olympic stadium destroyed by vandals and earthquakes. But Coubertin, who has been dealt with unfairly by a number of modern analysts, created a set of principles, and his brilliant idea remains, in my view, one of the great leavening forces for good in the 20th century.

These ideas inevitably had to be modified because they were appropriate to his day and the state of the world at that time. But the fact that they had to be modified did not mean that they did not have merit then and some merit in analysis as we look at them today. The four principles of modern Olympism as paraphrased by Leiper (1976) are first, that physical health leads to better moral character; second, the athlete should be an amateur to benefit fully from the sports experience; third, international cooperation through sport increases international goodwill; fourth, sports and aesthetics should be linked through the cultural world of arts and letters. These ideas lay behind the renewal of the Games and the development of the modern Olympics.

A number of problems had arisen in the ancient Olympics that were very similar to the problems that we have today, for example, specialization in the modern Olympics. In the ancient Olympics, a great wrestler named Milo carried a 4-year-old bull's carcass on his shoulders round the stadium and then ate the flesh. That event provoked Galen's remark about an act of "surpassing witlessness." To me, Milo's act conjures up the problem of the "anabolic man"; a problem to which I shall return later.

Another problem with which the Greeks wrestled, and with which we are still wrestling today, is the extent to which the Olympic Games benefit either the individual or society. To what extent is the glorification of the athlete, at the expense of spiritual and mental development, actually unhealthy (in other words, in direct contravention of Coubertin's ideal)? Certainly, Pindar, the Greek poet, overworked the words *fame, toil, endurance,* and *wisdom.* But it is also true that in having not only stadia for the elite but also gymnasia for ordinary citizens, the Greeks made it clear that it is possible for society to benefit from two interlinked levels of sport; that is, the example of seeing supreme performances by great athletes inspires many others to take part in sport and physical recreation. The idea that a rigid dichotomy exists between the two is misleading.

Let us now consider what have been the particulary outstanding achievements of the modern Olympics. I think the most extraordinary has been the surge of record breaking over the last 50 years, the series of extraordinary performances and many remarkable champions. No record is secure from being broken. The general public needs a sharp reminder, as it watches on television, the kind of superhuman effort that is required by athletes to reach the point where they become selected for the Games, let alone to detach themselves from all the good athletes who are there and achieve some remarkable feats. These feats reflect not only the athletes' physical capacity but something of their personality, too, which is able to transcend the mere performance. In the field of running, we think of Nurmi or Zatopeck as Olympic athletes who come into this category. Those who write about the Games have an enormous responsibility in interpreting these exceptional achievements. They must rise above chauvinism and write about this kind of person in a way which reflects the achievement as one, not for an individual, not for a country, but for humankind as a whole.

It is possible to speak cheerfully about the quest for excellence, the international cooperation, and the inventive genius of exploiting techniques to advance records which the Games have represented. But, of course, harmful and unpleasant things have come to light through the course of the modern Olympics. It is good that medicine should be harnessed to produce better performances; for instance, to enable marathon runners to recover from the 26-mile races without damage to their heart or circulation. But medicine is sometimes misused, and there is a Pandora's box from which knowledge flows that is by no means good. I have been particularly concerned with the way in which some athletes will pay seemingly any price for athletic success. Anabolic steroids have become so misused that this is now a major threat to top-level sport. These steroids involve a distortion of the human frame with health risks that no doctor would think acceptable and have turned many of the 250-pound heavyweights of the 1950s to the super heavyweights of the 1970s. I have had some experience with this problem through the British Sports Council and with the attempts to introduce complex methods of testing to try to catch those who are involved in this form of cheating. Some dozen athletes in the world have been disqualified as a result of these tests. But the problem remains that we must have an attitude of continuing vigilance in sport to try to eliminate this form of drug abuse. It is not merely anabolic steroids. We suspect that drugs are used in some countries to delay puberty and preserve the "elfin" type of physique in young girls needed for success in Olympic gymnastics. The price of eternal vigilance in sport, in relation to abuses of this kind, has become very high and is going to become even higher.

The problem of amateurism has also bedeviled the modern Olympics and has become increasingly complex. Twenty years ago it was possible to be a student or have a job and still train for an hour a day and achieve athletic success, even Olympic success. But the pattern has completely changed. As the level of performance has escalated, it has become necessary to give a larger part of the day to training. Athletes must now train many hours each day to have any chance of success. I do not begrudge athletes the financial support that they need and I welcome the revision of amateur rules, so that almost any broken-time financial compensation the national governing bodies approve is accepted as reasonable. This applies in the Western democracies as well as in the socialist Eastern states. I do not quarrel with broken-time payment because it is much fairer than the system at the turn of the century whereby the participation in sport was practically, and almost by rule, restricted to middle and upper classes, while artisans and others were excluded from taking part. But, of course, the capacity to pay for this kind of financial support depends on the economic wealth of the country and the importance that it attaches to sporting success and prestige. At present, promising third world athletes who want to take part in sport full-time might as well whistle into the wind, unless they are able through other skills and abilities to earn themselves a training abroad or enter into the teaching profession.

Financial compensation is a step toward the goal of equality of opportunity and represents a reduction in the double dealing into which athletes have unwillingly been drawn. But I think it is very important that some kind of code of moderation should be hammered out. I find my blood freezing at the thought of athletics becoming one frenetic, big-money deal as corrupting for the players as it is for the onlookers. There is one other word of warning about the increasing amount of time being spent in training. I have noticed, certainly as far as runners are concerned, that beyond a certain point spent in training, performance sometimes worsens. Too great a degree of self-involvement with the intricacies of training can, as it were, distract the more balanced part of the athlete's mind that to me is still the critical part of great athletic achievement.

Perhaps more worrying than the problem of amateurism in the Olympics is the Games' sheer size. At the time of the Munich Olympics, Schumacher, an Anglicized West German, was writing his book, *Small Is Beautiful* (1974). Those were then the biggest Games. They had a mere 14,000 competitors and 20,000 newsmen, and they cost $600 million. The Montreal stadium is still neither paid for nor completed.

The Games inevitably grow for several reasons. First, they have become a chance for wealthy countries to show off their skills and power, to have the biggest Games ever. Second, sportspeople themselves want the inclusion of their sport on the rather arbitrary list of the 22 sports included in the Olympic Games because it elevates their sport to the world's sporting peerage and gives them kudos and growth potential. By the same token, the exclusion of an established sport gives rise to howls of anguish and a rear-guard action that has so far thwarted any significant pruning of events.

What is the basic objection to size? If, as it claims, the Olympic Movement is worldwide, then the holding of Games should not be the sole prerogative of half a dozen countries because of the enormity of the expense. The citizens of Detroit, after their leaders' original bid for the Olympics, turned down their city for consideration, preferring to see their taxes used in other ways. It was this that opened the way for Moscow's bid. And, of course, for all major powers East and West, sport has become very clearly part of political ideology. The triumphs, the health, and the apparent happiness of their sportspeople reflect the success of their particular philosophy and way of life. This is an attitude which particularly applies to East Germany, where every modern device of training and selection has been used to produce a remarkable number of champions out of proportion to the small size of this country. Another great consequence of the increasing size of the Olympics and perhaps the most serious of all has been the danger of the use of the Games by any protest groups, or even terrorists, wishing to capture the world audience of perhaps 1 billion viewers through the television and the media. This may be a peaceful demonstration, as when Tommy Smith and John Carlos clenched their fists on the victory rostrum in Mexico; or it can be violent and terrible, as when the Arab terrorists killed Israeli athletes at Munich.

It may seem paradoxical that despite all these problems, I believe international sport in general, and the Olympic Games in particular, remain one of the great causes in the world that are capable of engaging the most serious determination of our young people and harnessing much of that explosive energy and idealism that is latent in human beings. The Olympic Movement can still, I believe, make a modest but very genuine contribution to peace. When we think of peace, it must mean more than the armed truce of the present day in which every side bristles with arms, and the mind is numbed to the reality of words like *megadeaths* and *final solutions* to problems, problems about the Middle East, about oil, about Europe. The dangers of the situation are fueled by ignorance, suspicion, and fear. I believe that the Olympics have been a force for good in the past. The world needs areas of neutrality in sport and the arts where exchanges and detente can still occur despite the tragedies and chicanery of conventional politics.

I accept the average athletes' dedication to their sporting ambitions and lack of wider political concern or sophistication; it could hardly be otherwise. But the fact that so many sportspeople do come together in a generally friendly competition is a very important achievement. Of course, no one can any longer pretend that politics are not involved in sport. The question is, what principles should govern their interaction? By accepting the fact of political involvement, we are more likely to be able to understand the problems involved and to persuade those responsible to change the Games, making them more likely to survive. The kind of changes that I would support, which would make the future of the Olympics more probable, are the following: The first is reducing them in size by returning to the sports in which individuals test their strength, skill, and speed against each other. Team sports that can engender ill feeling would be eliminated, and in any case, many of these sports already have their own world championships.

Second, I would support moving the Olympics to a permanent single site or preferably multiple neutral sites. Of countries so far mooted, I would prefer Switzerland, already the home of so many international organizations because of its great political stability. Perhaps one center might eventually be founded on each continent on a rotating basis. This would also have the merit of sustaining interest in each venue and spreading specialists' sports facilities across the world.

Third, I would support a defusing of the nationalistic Olympic displays. The parades, the flag ceremonies, the national anthem playing could be curtailed. The emphasis should be on patriotism, not nationalism.

And finally I want to suggest, as Leiper (1980) has proposed, that in connection with the Olympic Games and the Olympic Movement, the whole may be greater than the sum of its parts. In the words of the poet Robert Browning, "A man's reach must exceed his grasp or what's a heaven for?" We must not give up an ideal because it has not been attained. Given a move towards the changes that I have suggested, the Olympic Games should remain one of the great hopes of the world. It is in the deepest interests of the future of the world for them to continue.

References

International Olympic Committee. (1979). *Olympic charter*. Lausanne, Switzerland: Author.

Leiper, J.M. (1976). *The International Olympic Committee and the pursuit of Olympism*. Unpublished doctoral dissertation, University of Alberta, Edmonton.

Leiper, J.M. (1980). *The Olympic ideal: Is it valid today as a philosophical basis of the Olympic Games*. International Council for Sport and Physical Recreation.

Schumacher, E.F. (1976). *Small is beautiful*. London: Abachus.

27

A Decalogue of Olympic Games Reform

John A. Lucas

The need for reform in the Olympic Movement, as in any humanly created institution, is a pressing necessity. But to change the Olympic Games to a sport spectacle devoid of any symbolism is to kill it rather than cure it. The special quality of the games, distinctly different from scores of athletic world championships, is immediately noticeable for most Olympic Games participants. And yet, among scholars of the Olympic Movement, an unmistakable malaise pervades its future. The universality of the play instinct, humankind's passion for competing in and watching games, plus the special attraction of the Olympic Games combine to make the immediate demise of the games unlikely. But all human institutions are inherently imperfect, and if loving care and sensible revisions are not at work, the Olympic Movement and the Olympic Games will die prematurely. When the Olympic Games function close to their inherent capacities (it has

Originally published in *Olympism* (pp. 148-153) edited by Jeffrey Segrave and Donald Chu, 1981, Champaign, IL: Human Kinetics. Reprinted by permission.

happened), they approach the epitome of what sport philosopher Francis Keenan called "competitive cooperation" (Keenan, 1975).

Konrad Lorenz postulated the ultimate importance of aggression in animal and human behavior for their survival and vigor. Anthropologist Richard Leakey, in his 1977 book *Origins*, emphasized that humankind's age-old "quality of cooperation" is the basic characteristic of humanity and the key to its extraordinary progress in the last thousand generations (Leakey, 1977, p. 256). Both forces—aggression and cooperation—work at close to their ultimate level in the minds and bodies of some Olympic athletes. There is no mass collection of special people absorbed in quite so unique a struggle as that of 8,000 Olympic athletes. It is an experiment that should be allowed to continue. Humanity's eternal enemies of suspicion, greed, and materialism, however, threaten the quality of the Olympic Games and that institution's efforts to harness aggression and cooperation in some kind of universal symbiosis. There are thousands of young men and women in every country whose athletic aspirations toward excellence represent a global imperative. The Olympic Games need to remain a viable means by which such individual and collective goals may be partially attained.

I believe in the Olympic Idea and the Olympic Games. I believe in them so strongly that after 25 years of athletic competition, attendance at the Games, and library research, I must call for carefully orchestrated reform. Each of the Olympic Committee presidents—Coubertin, Baillet-Latour, Sigfrid Edstrom, Mr. Brundage, and Lord Killanin—has pointed out the need for change. So have responsible journalists, since 1896, pointed out needed changes in the IOC and Games' structure. They should be listened to, unlike the army of nincompoops who, over the decades, have served up a nondirected, inflammatory mishmash of "incidents" that have taken place at the 19 Olympic Games. This kind of mindless Olympic tattle-tale, always unaccompanied by rational alternatives, proving only that mortal human beings are imperfect, serves no healing purpose. I know of no one close to the Olympic Games Movement who does not believe changes are necessary. The Olympic dialectic—the power potential of human aggression and cooperation—is humankind's dialectic. A grand synthesis of human pugnacity and human love is a "categorical imperative." One laboratory for such a synthesis is the Olympic Games.

I subscribe to only a few of the following suggestions for Olympic reform. My own "Decalogue" of ideas follows later in this chapter. Olympic Games criticism, much of it fatuous, without pretense at sensible solutions, continues to grow. From around the world, suggestions for change in the IOC and Olympic Games structure may be divided into eight areas:

1. Simplify and reduce the size of the Games. Some possibilities are to reduce the number of events, especially team sports; to reduce entries by insisting on much higher standards; to eliminate the policy of at least one automatic entry from each nation.

2. Enlarge the scope of the Games by lengthening the traditional 15-day period; have multiple Olympic Games sites; increase the number of sports.

3. Have an "open" Olympic Games with all champions eligible for competition.

4. Reduce excessive nationalism by radical alteration of one or more actions dealing with Opening Ceremony parade, uniforms, national anthems, national flags, medal presentation, Olympic Village lifestyle, and an increased emphasis on the "One World" approach of the Closing Ceremonies.

5. Reduce or eliminate what a number of critics perceive as heavy religiosity, neo-pagan ritualism, excessive symbolism, pageantry, even mysticism about many Olympic Games' ceremonies, especially the Opening Ceremonies.

6. Reform the International Olympic Committee with a one nation-one vote democratization; include younger ex-athletes as members; vote in qualified women; subsidize qualified but poor members of the IOC; continue the liberalization of the IOC rules and regulations.

7. Disband the Olympic Games. Ever since 1908, there have been persistent voices claiming that the Games do more harm than good. The latest cries have been for separate world championships in each sport rather than an unwieldy multiple Olympic Games.

8. Create a single, permanent site for the Games.

It is not an absolute certainty that the Olympic Games will continue through the remainder of the 20th century and into the next. The escalation of world hunger, nationalistic zeal, inflation, political and social unrest, make the possibility of future games more tenuous. This universal disorientation, of course, has affected the Olympic Games, resulting in staggering costs, bureaucratic gigantism, growing political overtones, and even violence. Yet I feel that the demise of these international games would be a significant loss to young athletes on every continent. A survey questionnaire of Olympic competitors found overwhelming support for their individual experiences at the Olympic Games—regardless of whether they were gold medal winners or summarily eliminated in the first rounds of competition. Everyone is asked his or her opinion of the Olympic Games except the 45,000 athletes who, since 1924 in Paris, have participated in them. These athletes are infinitely more reliable witnesses than journalists, officials, commentators, spectators, and historians. And yet it is an almost uncontested fact that the Olympic Games are running a high fever; a return to a homeostatic state is imperative. The following "Decalogue" of Olympic Games reform suggestions—a compromise between runaway utopianism and a call for their abolition—is a synthesis of old ideas plus several concepts of my own. I take full responsibility for the whole package. The suggestions do not include comments on the Winter Games, which I think should rotate every 4 years between a site in Asia, Europe, and North America.

Sport is not an ideology or a religion. Value and purpose, only attainable through struggle, are part of the Olympic Games, and individual participants in the Games may come away with virtue and self-knowledge. But lately, the Olympic Games for almost everyone concerned, have become a "rat race." The IOC's consideration and implementation of some or all 10 of these proposals should allow the modern Olympic Games to emerge into the 21st century in a better organizational position to fulfill their visionary but attainable mission of offering the best in athletic competition amidst an environment of fair play.

1. A permanent "Olympic Games Center" should be built in either (a) central Switzerland, (b) western Scandinavia, or (c) Athens, Greece.
2. The summer Olympic Games should be enlarged to include more sports, more competitors, and should be conducted over a 20- to 25-day period rather than the restrictive 15 days.
3. This "Olympic Center" would be, in every sense, a business and profit-making operation. It would be open 365 days a year, every year (except during the Olympic Games) for recreational, non-professional, and world championship professional sporting events.
4. The "Olympic Center" would be staffed by 1,000 service and professional persons—all permanent, well-paid specialists. Some of these personnel would include sport physicians, sport medicine specialists, sport administrators, coaches, trainers, and technicians. The International Olympic Committee headquarters, which would include the library and archival records of the Olympic Movement, would be located at the "Center."
5. The "Olympic Center" would be ready in the year 1996—the 100th birthday of the modern Olympic Games.
6. The $5 billion needed to build and maintain the "Olympic Center" would come from (a) fees from the several million visitors a year who would use the facilities for a hundred different recreational activities; (b) ticket sales from the several million fans enjoying regional, national, and international nonprofessional and professional athletic competitions in several scores of different sporting events; (c) worldwide private and public donations; (d) loans from international banks; and (e) television monies and ticket sales income from the quadrennial summer Olympic Games.
7. Admission to and participation in these summer Olympic Games should be based on an entry fee of 1/400,000th of a member-nation's Gross National Product (GNP) or based on a country's per capita GNP multiplied by the total number of athletes and officials sent to the Games. Using the first formula, a nation with a trillion-dollar GNP would pay a million-dollar entry fee; poorer countries would pay much less. Under the second formula, a wealthy country with a per capita GNP of $6,000 sending a 200-person delegation would pay a fee of $1,200,000. Smaller countries and poorer countries, of

course, would have significantly less to pay. Tiny nations and some third world countries would be assessed less than $10,000.

8. Excessive displays of nationalism must be reduced during Olympic Games award ceremonies. Ultranationalism and pride in one's country are not the same thing. The former is debilitating intellectually and personally dehumanizing. Pride in one's country, on the other hand, is to be encouraged in every sphere. The national anthems of four nations, for example, do not need to be listened to 100 times during the Olympic Games; this has occurred in recent Games. The purpose of the Olympic Idea (Olympism) is not advanced one bit by this nearly endless repetition. Raising national flags and playing national anthems should be abolished during the Olympic Games ceremonies. A single medal award period should be set aside at the end of each day; loudspeakers, scoreboards, and world television could inform the world of the champion's name and his or her country. Medals should be awarded to all winners on any given day while the "Olympic Hymn" is playing. Smaller nations, so very animated at an Olympic victory, would not be robbed of a single glory, as 1 to 2 billion people would be instantaneously informed of the athlete's name and national origin. All other Olympic Games ceremonies and protocol should remain as they have been.

9. The International Olympic Committee needs to broaden its social sensitivity in several ways: (a) Highly qualified women should be selected for membership; (b) highly qualified sport leaders without large independent incomes or financial support from their NOC should, nevertheless, be encouraged by the IOC to accept membership in that organization with the understanding that the IOC shall subsidize the travel and housing expenses during the period of Olympic Games' business and during the persons' tenure on the committee.

10. The International Olympic Academy (IOA) concept should be expanded to eventually include an academy in every one of the more than 147 member-nations of the IOC. The tenets of the Olympic Movement, the fair play philosophy of "Olympism," cannot be spread widely nor rapidly enough through the quadrennial Olympic Games or the annual summer school of sport philosophy at Olympia, Greece (IOA). Every country in the world that is a member of the IOC should seek assistance from its National Olympic Committee to start an Olympic Academy at home. (See chap. 14, "The Need for Reform in a New Olympic Era," Lucas, 1980.)

In March of 1831, amidst critical reform efforts to correct ancient voting inequities in the English parliament, Thomas Babington, Lord Macaulay was heard to say, "Reform, that you may preserve." This is exactly how I feel about the Olympic Games and IOC reforms. These two institutions have so much good and so much potential for greater good that they need to be preserved. But only certain reform measures enacted in an evolutionary manner during the 1980s will save the Olympic Movement from both self-destruction and the ugly forces from outside the Olympic circle. The Olympic Idea is a unique concept. Born in the 19th century, it grew unevenly during the 20th century. Those nurturing the idea deserve great credit, for despite many errors in judgment, the concept has spread worldwide. During the 1970s, encouraging changes occurred in the rules of the Olympic Movement. The next era must see larger modifications in its entire structure lest inflation, narrow national politics, violence, and the continuation of a universal misinformation about the Olympic mission kill an international institution now full grown. For every fistfight at the Olympic Games, there have been a thousand moments of elation. As Hal Willard said in *The Washington Post:*

> Somewhere, perspective and proportion elope with sweet reason. In my mind, and I think in the minds of most sports fans, the petty cheating of a fencer shrivels into insignificance beside the prolonged and unanimous international sharing of triumph with Bruce Jenner in his decathlon victory. (Willard, 1976, p. A19)

It becomes increasingly true that "the way up the mountain," that is, solutions to the innumerable problems challenging and perplexing humankind, are rooted in an expanded body of scientific data that finds its beneficial way to the masses. But it is not enough to sustain the human animal, for as the American historian Samuel Eliot Morison said in his book, *The Great Explorers,* "The tree of knowledge bears no fruit unless it is rooted in love" (Morison, 1978, p. 274). The world of sport, including Olympic Games sport, combines exhilarating competition with the divine spark of compassion, and can become increasingly one avenue of individual and collective self-fulfillment.

References

Keenan, F. (1975, September). Justice and sport. *Journal of the Philosophy of Sport,* **2,** 121-122.

Leakey, R.E., & Lewin, R. (1977). *Origins.* New York: E.P. Dutton.

Lucas, J. (1980). *The modern Olympic Games.* New York: A.S. Barnes.

Morison, S.E. (1978). *The great explorers—The European discovery of America.* New York: Oxford University Press.

Willard, H. (1976, August 11). The Olympics—A triumph of the spirit. *The Washington Post,* p. A19.

28

The Modern Olympics: A Sociopsychological Interpretation

Allen Guttmann

When the ancient Greeks gathered together at Olympia to celebrate the quadrennial athletic festival in honor of Zeus, father of the gods, they represented not only the cities of the mainland but also Greek colonies scattered from one end of the Mediterranean to the other. Their presence at Olympia symbolized the unity of Hellenic civilization. When modern athletes assemble at whatever site the International Olympic Committee (IOC) has chosen to host the Olympics, they are sometimes said to represent the dream of international reconciliation and good will. No doubt they do. But they also embody the differences that have always prevented the realization of that dream. As the contributors to this present volume of essays have shown, no serious student can analyze the modern Olympics without discussing—at the very least—differences in gender, religion, race, ideology, and nationality. If there is a consensus, more or less, that sexism, religious fanaticism, racism, ideological dogmatism, and nationalism are among the major roadblocks on the way to Olympia, then much less agreement exists on the interactions of these factors. Certainly, no widely accepted explanatory model for the transformation of Coubertin's *fin-de-siècle* intentions exists today.

Some feminists blame patriarchy, and certainly Pierre de Coubertin shared Victorian notions about proper sex roles. If Coubertin had had his way, women would never have been allowed to compete in the modern games. Patriarchy, however, is too limited a concept to explain Olympic history fully. Realizing this, many feminists describe themselves as Marxists (or Marxist-feminists). If we consider European as well as American scholarship, Marxism emerges clearly as the most common approach to sport history, and capitalism is the most frequently named villain. While not denying the important role of economics in sport history as in other areas, I align myself with the non-Marxists and propose a somewhat different model, one derived in part from Max Weber's conviction that economic analysis is a necessary but not sufficient mode of historical interpretation. Specifically, I propose to focus first upon psychological considerations and only then to indicate some of their political and economic consequences.

The Process of Identification

It may seem willfully perverse to assert that the psychological process of identification is a fundamental factor in an explanatory model for the transformation of the modern Olympics, but identification is indeed such a factor. Directly or indirectly, identification is responsible for most of the abuses that have disfigured recent Olympiads and disillusioned many who have shared Coubertin's dream.

For reasons not very well understood even by the psychologists who have investigated the phenomenon, sport spectators identify emotionally with the athletes they observe. There seems to be an irresistible tendency to become partisan, to cheer for this team and jeer at that one, to become empathetically involved with one or another of the contestants. In most cases, the spectator's identification is derived from some sociological category, physical aspect, or personality trait that he or she shares (or would like to share) with the athlete. In other words, spectators feel themselves somehow represented by athletes with whom they share locale, educational institution, gender, religion, race, ideology, or nationality. The list of possible grounds for identification is limitless. Doubtless, men and women named Lewis or Decker feel personally enhanced when their namesakes win a race. (A very sober historian was recently pleased to discover a Hungarian swimmer named Guttmann at the 1896 Olympics.)

Because men and women named Lewis or Decker seldom congregate in numbers large enough for any significant collective behavior, such a nominal identification is presumably harmless. When athletes represent cities and schools, identification begins to have serious social consequences. Unquestionably, hundreds of thousands of people are ready to rush madly through the streets of any modern city in order to celebrate a victory won by "their" young men and women, most of whom were born almost anywhere except in the city they now represent. The physical damage done by this kind of urban identification is usually small—a few broken windows and overturned automobiles, a looted store or two, some skinned knuckles and battered chins, and a great deal of trash. When the athletes represent educational institutions, the physical damage is usually less and the ethical damage greater. The drive to enhance "school spirit" by scoring touchdowns or goals pervert educational ideals when coaches recruit illiterate students and pay them to defeat their equally analphabetic rivals.

These identifications by locale and educational institution have had little effect on the modern Olympics. (Students with athletic scholarships were technically ineligible for the games, but none was ever barred for this reason.) Gender-based identification has, however, had some influence on the Olympics, and identifications based on religion, race, ideology, and nationality have all been—and will continue to be—of major importance.

Specific Identification Bases

Gender

Because men and women rarely meet in direct athletic competition, the possibilities of direct gender-based rivalries are limited. However, a recent tic compares the achievements of today's champion female runners and swimmers with those of the male contestants at earlier Olympics. The hysterical gender-based partisanship generated by the infamous Bobby Riggs-Billie Jean King tennis match is a sign of what must be expected if men and women move from indirect to direct competition. Even without such competition, most feminists want women fully represented at the games. One reason is the possibility that female spectators respond more intensely to female athletes and male spectators to males. It is also possible that male and female spectators respond more intensely to athletes of the *opposite* sex, in which case another well-known factor—not identification—is at work.

Religion

Religion is a more important distorting factor than is generally recognized. Adolf Hitler's obsessive hatred of Jews, which was racist as well as religious, jeopardized the 1936 Olympics and threatened to make a farce of

Olympic ideals. Islamic hostility was responsible for the exclusion of Israeli athletes from the Mediterranean and the Asian games, both of which were sponsored by the IOC. The only instance of outright terrorism ever to mar an Olympic celebration came because Palestinian terrorists perceived Israeli athletes as the symbolic embodiment of Zionist oppression. Fortunately, the religious commitment of Olympic athletes is not organizationally relevant (as, for instance, gender and nationality are). Indeed, the athletes' religion is usually unreported. The damage done to Olympism by this particular form of identification has been sporadic.

Race

Race provides another possibility for identification. Because racial identity is generally obvious, racism has been a far greater problem than religious fanaticism. The long and complicated controversies over South Africa make sense only when one realizes what it meant to white South Africans to imagine black athletes in "their" Springbok uniform. It was a form of representation and a possibility for identification which was anathema for most white South Africans. The first of the major boycotts, that by black African nations in 1976, came as a result of South African racism. (The IOC refused to bar New Zealand from the games after New Zealand's non-Olympic rugby players met a South African team.) Because the African boycotters acted from a sense of racial solidarity, one must say that race—if not racism—prompted them as well. That racism has, on the whole, been less disruptive at the Olympics than in local, regional, and national sports can be explained by the greater force at the international level of ideological and nationalistic identifications. Few Americans are so racist that they would prefer to see Edwin Moses lose to a Russian runner.

Ideology

The distortions of ideological identification have plagued the Olympics intermittently since 1936, when Hitler attempted to subvert the games to the glorification of "Aryan" athletes, but ideology has become an inseparable element since the Russian team arrived at Helsinki in 1952. The presence of *their* ideology inevitably created a greater self-awareness of *ours*. Since then, no victory by an American team is relished like one over the athletes of the Soviet bloc. The hysteria that followed the 1980 Lake Placid hockey win is a good example. Conversely, no loss is harder to bear than one inflicted by the Russians or Cubans. The bitterness that attended the controversial basketball final of 1972 is an instance. Ideological differences made it impossible for years to field teams representing both East and West Germany and both Communist and Nationalist China. Although athletes from opposite sides of the Iron Curtain often achieve an approximation of Olympic good will, journalists and specta- tors continue to be fanatically partisan. (ABC's effort to be impartial re- sulted in the filming of biographical sketches of Soviet athletes, but ideology frustrated the good-will effort when the Russians boycotted the 1984 games.) Because the Soviet bloc takes its ideological commitment more seriously (or at least more self-consciously) than most Americans or Europeans do, the obsession with victory over "capitalist" athletes is intense. When victory is achieved, Marxist scholars herald it in academic publications as a sign of ideological superiority, as a harbinger of global triumph, as History's *nihil obstat*.

Nationalism

Of all forms of identification, nationalism requires the most extended analysis on the part of those who wish to understand the modern Olym- pics. By and large, it is the most intense form of identification, especially when it combines with religion, race, or ideology. When a burly member of the African Methodist Episcopal Zionist Church squares off in the ring against a "godless Communist" East German boxer, it is a rare spectator who sits quietly and admires pugilistic finesse. If we borrow a term from the physical sciences, we can say that psychological identification is most intense when the various vectors of identification are parallel, but we can best gauge their individual magnitudes when they go in opposite direc- tions. On the whole, the force of nationalism seems to overwhelm every contrary identification. All but the most racially bigoted Englishmen now cheer for "their" blacks in competition with white foreigners. How Ameri- cans and Russians who are believers in Islam feel about American and Russian Jews in competition with athletes from Islamic nations like Algeria or Indonesia is an unanswered question. (One reason that it *is* un- answered may be that scholars are reluctant to ask it.)

The IOC has always been ambivalent, if not confused, about national- ism. Coubertin, despite the psychic wound inflicted upon him by France's humiliating defeat in the Franco-Prussian War, did his best to persuade German sport organizations to participate in 1896. He was personally patriotic, but he meant the Olympic Games to be international. He arranged, moreover, for the invitations to the first Olympics to be sent to sport organizations and to individuals—not to governments. In at least one instance, individuals from different countries were allowed to com- pete on the same team—an Englishman and a German won the first Olym- pic title in doubles tennis. The Olympic Charter proclaims that the games are contests between individuals and not between nations, and the IOC deplores attempts to count medals and calculate the overall winner of the games. On the other hand, the IOC encourages nations to form National Olympic Committees (NOC) and to organize teams. The NOCs are responsible for certifying the eligibility of the individual athletes. Recognition of the NOCs by the IOC is contingent upon the existence of national sport federations affiliated with the international sport federations for Olympic disciplines. In short, nationalism has far more organizational support than internationalism. Avery Brundage was fond of arguing that the teams sent by the NOCs really represent geographical areas and not political entities, but no Olympic official has ever seriously suggested that large nations be divided and small nations combined so that all teams are drawn from geographical areas of roughly equal population.

Less extreme organizational reforms have also been rejected. One repeated suggestion is that the Olympics be given a permanent site so that the politics of the host nation would no longer be an incitement to boycott and could no longer frustrate the Olympic Charter (as Canada did when Ottawa refused to accept the team from the Republic of China). Any permanent site, however, would have at least two disadvantages. In the first place, other cities would have to renounce hosting the games (and other nationals would have to forego some of the associated frenzy). In the second place, the IOC would have to surrender one of its most important functions, namely, choosing the sites of the summer and winter games. (Because wining and dining and otherwise wooing the IOC is part of every city's candidacy for host, surrendering this function would be a real sacrifice on the part of IOC members enamored of the good life.)

Some who share Coubertin's romantic philhellenism have been ready to disregard these two disadvantages and to suggest Greece as the permanent home of the Olympics. This suggestion is problematic for at least two reasons. First, Greece is very much involved in international politics. Its government was recently fascist, and democracy is not guaranteed to survive in the land of its invention. The present government is officially pro-Western and a partner in the NATO alliance, but it is also strongly anti-American. Although the Greek people may not share the anti-Americanism of their government, they are certainly hostile to the Turks. The crisis over the divided island of Cyprus is only the most recent in a long history of bitter animosity. Second, apart from political considerations, Greece is geographically and ecologically unsuitable. No adequate facilities exist for winter sports. Quite aside from its notoriously unsafe airport, Athens is one of the world's most overcrowded and polluted cities. Presumably, no one wants to return the games to Olympia, a small, isolated, archeologically precious site that would be overwhelmed physically and debased symbolically by the building of a modern sport complex and the invasion of hundreds of thousands of spectators.

Switzerland would be a better choice. Determinedly neutral in world politics, it already provides a home for the IOC, the Red Cross, and numerous other international organizations. The arguments against Switzerland are those against any permanent site: the loss of successive "moments in the sun" enjoyed by the present hosts and the loss of an important part of the IOC's raison d'être. Perhaps one should add that the choice of Switzerland would reinforce the sense that the Olympics are a part of the *European* heritage. Asians and Africans with no hope

ever of hosting the Olympics might find it hard to feel that the games
are indeed the world's.

Despite constant statements deploring the excesses of nationalism, the
IOC has not been able to act on a purely symbolic level either. Although
Avery Brundage and his supporters sought repeatedly to remove national
anthems and national flags from the victory ceremony and to replace them
with an Olympic trumpet fanfare and the five-ringed Olympic flag, their
efforts were invariably frustrated by a combination of nationalism and
ideology. IOC members from the Soviet bloc and from the Third World
repeatedly vetoed even these minimal efforts to reduce nationalism at
the games. It is one thing to sing the "Internationale" and to condemn
the chauvinism of the United States and its allies; it is something else
again to forego the nationalistic and ideological thrill of seeing one's own
red flag and hearing one's own anthem. When some of the European
teams competing in Moscow in 1980 *did* of their own accord surrender
the symbols of nationalism in order to protest against the Soviet Union's
invasion of Afghanistan, the spectators were disappointed. Apparently,
to feel themselves represented simply as men and women was too difficult for them. They needed the ethnocentric (and xenophobic?) excitement of the Union Jack and the *tricoleur*. For similar reasons, nothing has
come of the mild suggestion that the athletes be housed in the Olympic
Village and march in the Opening Ceremony by sport discipline rather
than by nations. Japanese swimmers may prefer to eat with and to march
with Dutch swimmers rather than with Japanese equestrians, but no one
has offered them this choice.

In short, very little inclination exists to mitigate the excesses of nationalism other than to declare that it is not good sportsmanship for spectators to be hysterically partisan. We should not exaggerate the power of
national identification. It *was* possible for Germans at the Berlin Olympics of 1936 to be impressed by Jesse Owens, whom they called the
Wunderathlet of the games. It *was* possible for Americans to be enchanted
by Olga Korbut and Nadia Comenici. Nonetheless, these are infrequent
cases, the happy exceptions to the dismal rule. The trend seems to be
toward more intensely nationalistic partisanship. The future does not look
bright.

Commercialism

Coubertin fought hard against nationalism, racism, and religious fanaticism (and for sexism), but he was less aware of the distortions of commercialization because the Olympic Games were originally too
unimportant for commercialization to be much of a threat. The years before World War I were an era of nascent corporate capitalism, but none
of the corporations that had begun to dominate the European and American markets looked to Athens for an entrepreneurial coup. A wealthy
Greek businessman from Alexandria donated money to restore the ancient

stadium of Herodes Atticus, but no placards advertised his generosity. By the time Avery Brundage became president of the IOC in 1952, the dangers of commercialization were becoming obvious.

The modern Olympics are now part of the universal market of advanced capitalism. They cost hundreds of millions and even billions of dollars to stage. Whether the spectacle is produced in Moscow or Zagreb or Lake Placid or Los Angeles, it is financed in part by the sale of television rights paid for mostly by corporate sponsors eager to hawk their products in commercial "spots" that continually interrupt coverage of the games (at least wherever commercial television is the rule). As Avery Brundage predicted when the IOC first began to contemplate the sale of television rights, the entire Olympic movement has become a hostage to the networks, dependent on the golden flow of cash from American, European, and Japanese television. The Soviet Union invested its material resources and its prestige in the 1980 games to the point where it was determined to produce an extravaganza even after NBC withdrew its financial support, but another host capable of the same obdurate disregard of economics is difficult to imagine.

How does the psychological process of identification relate to the commercialization of the Olympics? Although clearly identifications on the basis of gender, religion, race, ideology, and nationality have all played havoc with Olympic ideals, it is less obvious that the psychological phenomenon is causally related to commercialization. However, as advertisers have realized, psychological identification is an important aspect of modern commerce. The use of prominent athletes to endorse products is a relatively minor matter. Far more significant is the role of sports in attracting television viewers. If the athletes were not seen as representatives, if it were not for the tremendous force of national and other identifications, the vast majority of spectators would lose interest in the games, turn off their sets, and never see the advertisements. The proof of this can be seen when, immediately after each quadrennial Olympics, the spectators *do* lose interest in most of the sports that make up the Olympic program. Americans become involved in following professional team sports ("my city!") or semiprofessional intercollegiate sports ("my school!"). Others turn to professional soccer ("my club!"). Except for the Olympics, when the team represents the nation and can add a medal to the count, who watches volleyball or luge or dressage? Idealistically, one might respond that *some* people really do care about "minor" sports like track and field. *Some* people really do respond enthusiastically to athletic achievement on the basis of no other identification than that of common humanity. They marvel at the dive and not the diver. But such cosmopolitans seem to be relatively few. They are certainly too few to provide the huge audience necessary for the commercialization of the Olympics.

What we have, then, outside of the Soviet bloc, is a capitalistically organized market forever on the lookout for investment opportunities. Entrepreneurs were actually rather slow to realize the appeals of televised sports, and the sums once offered for grandiose spectacles like the Olympics now seem laughably small, for example, $600,000 for the rights to the 1964 games in Tokyo. But the doubts have vanished and the networks have moved in. For the $225 million it invested in Los Angeles, ABC garnered approximately $650 million from its sponsors, enough to encourage ABC to offer $309 million for the 1988 winter games in Calgary.

The games have become a part of the universal market of modern capitalism, but we must insist that capitalism is not responsible for the sports-mad public that exists in the Soviet Union and other avowedly anticapitalistic countries. The distortions of Olympism by nationalism and other identifications are at least as pervasive there as in the United States and Europe. The designation of official Olympic junk foods and the fragmentation of the games by advertisements can be blamed on capitalism, but the orgy of nationalism that accompanied the games in Moscow and Los Angeles cannot.

The Athlete

The similarity of responses East and West can also be seen when one examines the process of psychological identification as it shapes the behavior of athletes. For the athlete, the role of representative, of person with whom others identify, is both opportunity and burden. The lure of fame and fortune exists; so does the weight of responsibility. Although not all sport events involve spectators and the concomitant process of identification-representation, most do. The Little Leaguer cannot let his or her parents down. The high school star must win or suffer a humiliating loss of status. The intercollegiate athlete is expected, not quite literally, to do or die for the alma mater. The psychological burden upon the Olympic athlete is even greater. Success can make him or her world-famous; failure, often defined as receiving the silver medal, can make him or her the butt of sarcastic journalism and popular vilification. Although some athletes are doubtless driven by other psychological forces and would want desperately to be the best in the world even if no one were aware of their achievement, all Olympians realize that the eyes not just of Texas but of the world are upon them. This is, indeed, a recurrent theme in their autobiographies. That they are not paralyzed by stage fright can be attributed to their almost miraculous powers of concentration. That they are driven to attempt the superhuman is cause for some concern.

While I have at various times defended the notion that sports can be a realm of relative freedom in which we compete against each other and ourselves simply for the pleasure of the contest, I trust I have also shown awareness of the fact that this competition can become destructively intense. The Olympics are an arena where the burden of representation can drive an athlete to nearly suicidal behavior. Specifically, the pressure to achieve drives athletes to train for years, to treat their bodies as instruments, and to take drugs that can injure or kill.

442   Guttmann

World class performance in most sports now requires years of scientifically planned preparation. Athletes now train with an intensity unknown
in the balmy days of Victorian amateurism. Olympic athletes have
described workouts that felt like self-inflicted torture (and that have provided Neo-Marxist critics with evidence to decry the alleged inhumanity
of all sport). Motivated by the dream of Olympic victory, or simply by
the fear of disgraceful defeat, men and women force themselves through
hours of daily effort that would be disallowed by factory legislation if any
modern corporation attempted to exact it from its employees. Although
some athletes experience a mystic sense of unity in which they and their
physical selves seem one with the universe, the more common experience seems to be one of struggle to extend the limits of what is physio-
logically possible. The body then becomes an instrument. Unfortunately,
the body is an instrument that can be damaged. Instead of a sense of
"flow" or a "peak experience," the athlete is grimly conscious of a torn
Achilles tendon. It is a rare Olympic autobiography that does not record
injuries and periods of incapacitation. At the Olympic level, the physical
educator's happy notion that sports are good for you has become
questionable. That Olympic gymnasts doomed to a later life of aches and
pains say that it was worth it proves the fascination of representative sport
for those who are the representatives.

The IOC has long since abandoned its efforts to limit the duration of
training, and it has never tried to legislate the intensity of workouts, but
the IOC is still determined, probably quixotically, to regulate the use of
drugs. One must write "regulate" instead of "abolish" because harmless drugs are accepted and harmful ones seem to proliferate beyond the
ability of the IOC to control them. No sport organization opposes the use
of aspirin; none seems able to eliminate the use of anabolic steroids. The
quest for higher and higher levels of achievement, without which fame
and fortune are unlikely, tempts athletes to use amphetamines, anabolic
steroids, and other drugs that can cripple or kill. Educational programs
are clearly inadequate to warn about the dangers of drugs. *Why* do athletes persist when the risks are obvious? Their response, when questioned
anonymously, is to say that "everyone" does it and those who don't no
longer have a chance to win, but this response only raises another question. *Why* do they feel the need to win at any cost? Obviously the answer
is a complex one and economic rewards cannot be discounted even for
"amateur" athletes, but one motive for the Olympians is certainly the
constant awareness that they wear the uniforms of their homelands and
that millions of their countrymen expect them to extend themselves to
the point of exhaustion and collapse in the effort to run faster, throw further, lift more, and punch harder than their rivals. Where pecuniary
motives are present, they are usually secondary in the sense that fame
is the prerequisite for fortune. Material rewards are for those who *successfully* represent the ambitions of those who identify with them.

The athletes of the Soviet bloc and the "Third World" experience essentially the same pressure as athletes from the West. In fact, the sense

that they represent a nation and an ideology is probably even greater. Certainly the intensity of preparation is no less than in the West. Injuries are probably as common in the Soviet bloc as in the West, despite the superiority of their sports medicine. At present, no way exists to estimate whether harmful drugs are more common among the Olympians from the United States and Europe or from the Soviet bloc; no reason exists to assume that the Russians, the East Germans, and the other representatives of Marxism-Leninism resort less frequently to drugs than do the athletes of the United States and its allies. The instrumentalization of the body in the pursuit of Olympic glory is a thoroughly international phenomenon. To think of it simply as the result of capitalism, as many French and German Neo-Marxists do, is foolish. The demise of capitalism would not mean the end of representational sports.

Conclusion

Ideally, at this point, an essay that purports to conclude a volume of essays on the Olympic Games ought to call for the continuation, for the reform, or for the abolition of the games. The Olympic Games are not what Pierre de Coubertin intended them to be. They will never be simply an occasion for athletes to compete in friendly rivalry, for spectators to admire extraordinary physical performances, and for everyone involved to feel himself or herself a part of the family of man. But the Olympic Games are not the opposite, either. They are not simply occasions for sexism, racism, religious fanaticism, ideological display, nationalism, commercialism and the instrumentalization of the body. Every 4 years, as the Olympics more nearly approach or more tragically disappoint our ideals, they provide us with a dramatic indication of who we are. Perhaps that is the best argument for their continuation.